# STATICS

HARI KISHAN

ATLANTIC
PUBLISHERS & DISTRIBUTORS (P) LTD

ATLANTIC
PUBLISHERS & DISTRIBUTORS (P) LTD

7/22, Ansari Road, Darya Ganj, New Delhi
Tel.: +91-11-4077 5252, 2327 3880
E-mail: orders@atlanticbooks.com
Web: www.atlanticbooks.com



**Published by Atlantic Publishers & Distributors (P) Ltd 2024**





Printed & bound in India by Atlantic Print Services

# Preface

Statics is a fundamental subject in the field of engineering and physics that deals with the study of the behaviour of rigid bodies at rest or in uniform motion under the action of external forces. The principles of statics are essential for the design and analysis of structures, machines, and systems in engineering and science. This book is a comprehensive guide to the subject of Statics, with a focus on three essential topics—Common Catenary, Centre of Gravity, and Virtual Work. These topics are crucial in understanding the principles of statics, and their applications are widespread in various fields of science and engineering.

The book contains a rich collection of solved examples, illustrative examples, and exercises to help the reader master the concepts of the subject. The solved examples provide a step-by-step explanation of the solution process, while the illustrative examples provide a broader perspective on the application of the concepts. The exercises range from simple to challenging, and they are designed to test the reader's understanding and problem-solving skills.

The first chapter of the book introduces the concept of Common Catenary, which is the curve formed by a flexible, uniform cable or chain suspended between two points. The chapter discusses the derivation of the catenary equations, the determination of its properties, and its practical applications in science and engineering. The second chapter of the book focuses on the Centre of Gravity, which is the point at which the weight of an object can be considered to act. The chapter covers the concept of the centroid, the determination of the center of gravity of simple and composite bodies, and its applications in the analysis of structures and machines. The third chapter of the book deals with Virtual Work, which is a powerful tool used to determine the equilibrium conditions of a system. The chapter explains the concept of virtual displacement, the principle of virtual work, and its applications in solving problems involving systems in equilibrium.

The book is intended for students of science and engineering, as well as professionals in these fields who require a comprehensive understanding of the principles of statics. The book can also serve as a valuable reference for researchers and academics in the field of mechanics. It is hoped that the book will provide readers with a solid foundation in the subject of Statics and help them develop their problem-solving skills.

**Hari Kishan**

# Preface

# Contents

# Detailed Contents

Chapter 1

# Common Catenary

## 1. Definitions

**(i) Perfectly Flexible String:** A string which offers no resistance to bending at any point is called a perfectly flexible string. In such a case, the resultant action across any normal section of the string (called its tension) is along the tangent to the string. A normal section of the string can be supposed to be so small that the string, in general, can be treated as a curved line, so that we shall be able to speak of its tangent. Note that a chain whose links are very small and perfectly smooth may be treated as a flexible string.

**(ii) Catenary:** When a thin, heavy inextensible string hangs freely, under the action of gravity, between two points which are not in the same vertical line, then the curve in which it hangs is called a catenary.

If the weight per unit length of the string is constant, then the catenary is called a common catenary or uniform catenary.

*Note*: Here in this chapter, the catenary which we shall deal with will be a common catenary. So, by the word catenary, we shall mean common catenary throughout this chapter.

## 2. Intrinsic Equation of Common Catenary

Let a uniform string $ACB$ be suspended freely from the points $A$ and $B$ which are not in the same vertical line. $C$ is the lowest point of the common catenary. It is obvious that the tangent to the curve at $I$ is horizontal. Let $P$ be any point on the portion $AB$ of the string. Let $s$ be the distance of $P$ from $C$ measured along the arc length of the string. If $w$ is the weight per unit length (or line density) of the string, then the weight of portion $CP$ of the string will be $ws$ acting vertically downwards through the C.G. of the arc $CP$.

Let us consider the equilibrium of the portion $CP$ of the string. We find that the portion $CP$ of the string is in equilibrium under the action of the following forces:

(i) Tension $T_0$ at the lowest point $C$ acting horizontally.

(ii) Tension $T$ at the point $P$ acting along the tangent at $P$ making an angle $\psi$ with the horizontal line.

(iii) The weight $ws$ of the arc $CP$ of the string acting vertically in the downward direction through its centre of gravity $G$.

Since these forces are not parallel, therefore all these forces must meet in a point, say $R$.

Resolving these forces horizontally and vertically, we get,

$$T \cos \psi = T_0 \quad ...(1)$$

$$T \sin \psi = ws \quad ...(2)$$

Dividing (2) by (1), we get

$$\tan \psi = ws/T_0 \quad ...(3)$$

For the sake of convenience, let the tension $T_0$ at the lowest point $C$ of the centenary be $T_0$ taken as equal to the weight of length $c$ of the string, so that

$$T_0 = wc \quad ...(4)$$

Then, from (3) and (4), we get

$\tan \psi = ws/wc \quad \Rightarrow \tan \psi = s/c$

$$\Rightarrow s = c \tan \psi \quad ...(5)$$

Equation (4) is called the intrinsic equation of the catenary. Here, the quantity $c$ is called the parameter of the catenary.

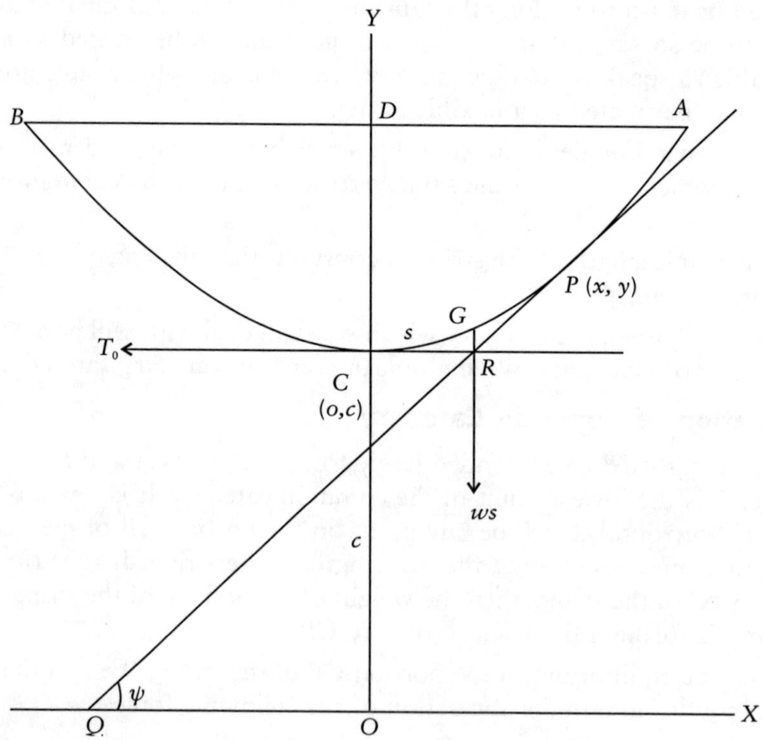


**Remarks**

(i) From equation (1),

$$T \cos \psi = T_0$$

This shows that the horizontal component of the tension at any point is constant. Therefore, we conclude that

"the horizontal component of the tension at any point of the common catenary is the same and is equal to $T_0$ the tension at the lowest point $C$ of the common catenary."

(ii) From equation (2),

$$T \sin \psi = ws$$

This shows that the vertical component of the tension at any point of the catenary is equal to the weight of the string from the lowest point $C$ to that point.

Also, $T \sin \psi \propto s$ | $\because$ $w$ is constant

Therefore, we conclude that

"The vertical component of the tension at any point $P$ of the common catenary is directly proportional to the arc length of string between the lowest point $C$ and that point $P$ and is equal to the weight of the arc length $CP$ of the string."

## 3. Cartesian Equation of Common Catenary

Refer to the figure of § 2. Let $O$ be a point vertically below $C$ such that $OC = c$. Take this point $O$ as origin and the horizontal and the vertical lines through $O$ as the axes of $X$ and $Y$ respectively. Referred to these axes, let the coordinates of the point $P$ be $(x, y)$.

The intrinsic equation of the catenary is

$$s = c \tan \psi \qquad \text{|Refer (5) of § 2} \qquad ...(1)$$

From differential calculus, we know that

$$\tan \psi = dy/dx \qquad \text{| slope of the tangent at } P \qquad ...(2)$$

From (1) and (2), we get

$$s = c\, dy/dx \qquad ...(3)$$

Differentiating both sides of (3) with respect to $(x)$, we get

$$ds/dx = c\, dy^2/dx^2 \qquad ...(4)$$

Also, from differential calculus, we know that

$$\frac{ds}{dx} = \sqrt{1 + \left(\frac{dy}{dx}\right)^2} \qquad ...(5)$$

$\therefore$ From (4) and (5), we get

$$\sqrt{1 + \left(\frac{dy}{dx}\right)^2} = c\frac{d^2y}{dx^2} \qquad ...(6)$$

Put $dy/dx = z$ ...(7)

so that $d^2y/dx^2 = dz/dx$ ...(8)

Substituting these in (6), we get

$$\sqrt{1+z^2} = c\frac{dz}{dx}$$

Separating the variables, we get

$$dx = c\frac{dz}{\sqrt{1+z^2}}$$

Integration yields,

$$x = c \sin h^{-1} (z) + A_1$$

where $A_1$ is an arbitrary constant of integration.

$$\Rightarrow x = c \sin h^{-1} (dy/dx) + A_1 \quad ...(9)$$

At the lowest point C of the catenary,

$x = 0$, $dy/dx = 0$ [since the tangent at C is parallel to the X-axis]

Substituting these values in (9), we get

$$0 = c \sin h^{-1} (0) + A_1$$

$$\Rightarrow 0 = 0 + A_1$$

$$A_1 = 0 \qquad \therefore \text{ (9) gives}$$

$$x = c \sin h^{-1} (dy/dx)$$

$$\Rightarrow (dy/dx) = \sin h\, (x/c) \qquad \Rightarrow dy = \sin h\, (x/c)\, dx$$

Integration yields,

$$y = c \cos h\, (x/c) + A_2 \quad ...(10)$$

where $A_2$ is an arbitrary constant of integration.

Referred to the assumed axes, the coordinates of C are $(0, c)$.

Therefore, at C,

$$x = 0 \text{ and } y = c$$

Substituting these values in (10), we get

$$c = c \cos h\, (0/c) + A_2$$

$$\Rightarrow c = c \cos h\, (0) + A_2 \qquad \Rightarrow c = c + A_2$$

$$\Rightarrow A_2 = 0 \qquad \therefore \text{ (10) gives}$$

$$y = c \cos h\, (x/c) \quad ...(11)$$

Equation (11) is called the cartesian equation of the catenary.

*Note*: Since $\cos h\, (x/c)$ is an even function of $x$, therefore, the curve is symmetrical about the Y-axis, i.e., the vertical line though the lowest point C of the catenary.

## 4. Some Important Definitions

(i) *Vertex*: The lowest point C of the common catenary is called the vertex of the common catenary.

(ii) *Directrix*: The horizontal line at a depth $c$ below the vertex C of the common catenary is called the directrix of the common catenary. In figure of § 2, $OX$ (the X-axis) is the directrix.

(iii) *Axis*: The vertical line $OC$ passing through the lowest point $C$ of the common catenary is called the axis of the catenary.

(iv) *Span*: If the points $A$ and $B$ from which the string in suspended are in the same horizontal line, then the distance $AB$ between the points $A$ and $B$ is called the span of the catenary. So, if $A$ be the point $(x, y)$, then span = $2x$

(v) *Sag*: The distance of the lowest point $C$ (vertex) from the horizontal line $AB$ is called the sag of the catenary. In figure of § 2, $CD$ is the sag, where $D$ is the mid-point of $AB$. So, if the ordinate of the point $A$ is $y$, then

$$\text{Sag} = CD$$
$$= OD - OC = y - c$$

(vi) *Parameter*: The quantity $c$ occurring in the cartesian equation $y = c \cos h\ (x/c)$ or the intrinsic equation $s = c \tan \psi$ of the common catenary is called the parameter of the catenary. Note that two centenaries are said to be equal if they have equal parameters.

## 5. Some Important Relations for the Common Catenary

**(i) Relation between $s$ and $x$**

The intrinsic equation of common catenary is

$$s = c \tan \psi$$
$$\Rightarrow \quad s = c\, dy/dx \mid \because dy/dx = \tan \psi$$
$$\Rightarrow \quad dy/dx = s/c \qquad ...(1)$$

Again, the cartesian equation of common catenary is

$$y = c \cos h\ (x/c) \qquad ...(2)$$

Differentiating (2) with respect to $x$, we get,

$$dy/dx = c \sin h\ (x/c).1/c$$
$$\Rightarrow dy/dx = \sin h\ (x/c) \qquad ...(3)$$

From (1) and (2), we get

$$s/c = \sin h\ (x/c)$$
$$\Rightarrow s = c \sin h\ (x/c) \qquad ...(4)$$

Equation (4) gives the relation between $s$ and $x$.

**(ii) Relation between $s$ and $y$**

We have,

$$y = c \cos h\ (x/c) \qquad ...(1)$$
$$s = c \sin h\ (x/c) \qquad ...(2)$$

Squaring and subtracting, we get

$$y^2 - s^2 = c^2 \{\cos h^2\ (x/c) - \sin h^2\ (x/c)\}$$
$$\Rightarrow \quad y^2 - s^2 = c^2$$
$$\Rightarrow \quad y^2 = s^2 + c^2 \qquad ...(3)$$

Equation (3) gives the relation between $s$ and $y$.

**(iii) Relation between $y$ and $\psi$**

We have,

$$y^2 = s^2 + c^2 \qquad ...(1)$$

$$s = c \tan \psi \qquad ...(2)$$

From (1) and (2), we get

$$y^2 = c^2 \tan^2 \psi + c^2 \quad \Rightarrow \quad y^2 = c^2 (\tan^2 \psi + 1)$$

$$\Rightarrow y^2 = c^2 \sec^2 \psi$$

$$\Rightarrow y = c \sec \psi \qquad ...(3)$$

Equation (3) gives the relation between $y$ and $\psi$.

**(iv) Relation between $x$ and $\psi$**

The intrinsic equation of the common catenary is

$$s = c \tan \psi \qquad ...(1)$$

Differentiating (1) with respect to $\psi$, we get,

$$ds/d\psi = c \sec^2 \psi \quad \Rightarrow \quad (ds/dx)(dx/d\psi) = c \sec^2 \psi$$

$$\Rightarrow dx/d\psi = c \sec^2 \psi \, (dx/ds)$$

$$\Rightarrow dx/d\psi = c \sec^2 \psi \cos \psi \mid \because dx/ds = \cos \psi$$

$$\Rightarrow dx/d\psi = c \sec \psi \quad \Rightarrow \quad dx = c \sec \psi \, d\psi$$

Integration yields

$$x = c \log (\sec \psi + \tan \psi) + A_3 \qquad ...(2)$$

where $A_3$ is an arbitrary constant of integration.

At the lowest point $C$, $x = 0$, $\psi = 0$

[since the tangent at point $C$ is parallel to the $x$-axis]

Substituting these values in (2), we get

$$0 = c \log (\sec 0 + \tan 0) + A_3 \quad \Rightarrow \quad 0 = c \log (1 + 0) + A_3$$

$$\Rightarrow 0 = c \log 1 + A_3 \quad \Rightarrow \quad 0 = c\,(0) + A_3$$

$$\Rightarrow A_3 = 0 \quad \therefore \text{(2) gives}$$

$$x = c \log (\sec \psi + \tan \psi) \qquad ...(3)$$

Equation (3) gives the relation between $x$ and $\psi$.

**(v) Relation between $x$, $y$ and $s$**

From § 5 (iv), we have,

$$x = c \log (\sec \psi + \tan \psi) \qquad ...(1)$$

Also, we have

$$s = c \tan \psi \qquad ...(2)$$

$$y = c \sec \psi \qquad ...(3)$$

(1), (2) and (3) give

$$x = c \log (y/c + s/c)$$

$$\Rightarrow x = c \log (y+s/c) \qquad ...(4)$$

Equation (4) gives the relation between $x$, $y$ and $s$.

**(vi) Relation between the tension $T$ and ordinate $y$**

From equation (1) of § 2, we have

$$T \cos \psi = T_0$$

$$T = T_0 \sec \psi \qquad ...(1)$$

Also, we have

$$y = c \sec \psi \qquad \text{| Refer § 5 (iii)} \qquad ...(2)$$

(1) and (2) give

$$T = T_0\, y/c$$

$$T = wc\,(y/c) \qquad |\because T_0 = wc$$

$$T = wy \qquad ...(3)$$

Equation (3) gives that relation between $T$ and $y$.

*Note*: we have,

$$T = wy$$

$\Rightarrow$ $T \propto y$ | $\because$ $w$ is constant

This shows that the tension at any point of the catenary varies as its height above the directrix.

**(vii) Relation between radius of curvature $\rho$ and ordinate $y$**

We have

$$s = c \tan \psi \qquad \text{| Refer § 2 (v)} \qquad ...(1)$$

$$\therefore\ \rho = ds/d\psi = c \sec^2 \psi \qquad ...(2)$$

Also, we have

$$y = c \sec \psi \qquad \text{|Refer § 5 (iii)} \qquad ...(3)$$

(2) and (3) give

$$\rho = c\,(y^2/c^2)$$

$$\Rightarrow\ \rho = y^2/c \qquad ...(4)$$

Equation (4) gives the relation between $\rho$ and $y$.

## 6. Geometrical Properties of Common Catenary

Let $ACB$ be a common catenary as shown in the figure. Let $OX$ and $OY$ be the axes of $X$ and $Y$ respectively. Let $P(x, y)$ be any point on it. Let $C$ be the lowest point of the common catenary. Let $T_0$ and $T$ be the tensions in the string at $C$ and $P$ respectively. Let the arcual distance $CP = s$. Let $w$ be the weight per unit length of the string. Then, the weight of the length $CP$ of the string is $ws$. Draw $PM$ perpendicular to $OX$ and $PG$ the normal at $P$ meeting $OX$ in $M$ and $G$ respectively. Draw $MN$, perpendicular from $M$ to $QP$. Then, we can find two geometrical properties of the catenary.

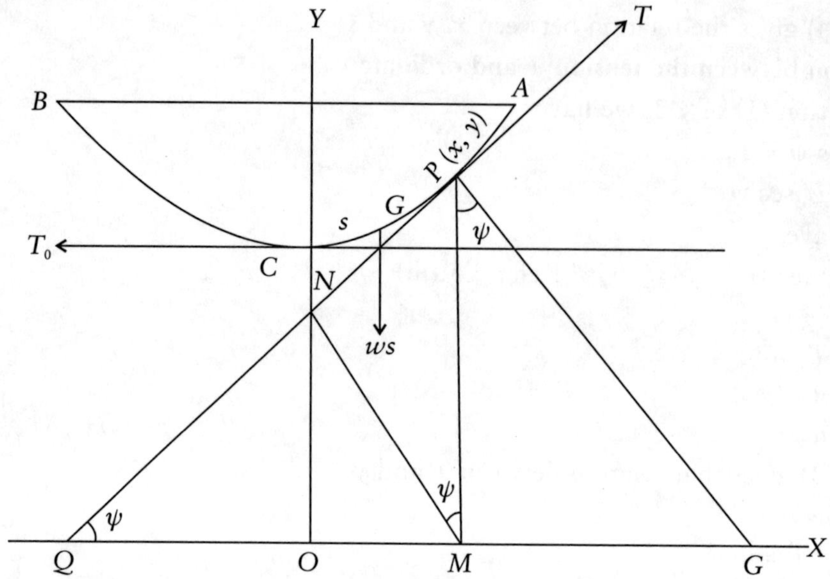


**Property 1.** The radius of curvature at any point of the common catenary is equal to the length of the normal intercepted between the curve and the directrix.

**Proof:** From figure, we have

$$\cos\psi = PM/PG \quad \Rightarrow \quad \cos\psi = y/PG$$

$$\Rightarrow PG = y\sec\psi \quad \Rightarrow \quad PG = c\sec\psi\sec\psi \;\mid\; \because y = \sec\psi$$

$$\Rightarrow PG = c\sec^2\psi \qquad \text{...(1)}$$

Also, we have

$$s = c\tan\psi \quad \Rightarrow \quad ds/d\psi = c\sec^2\psi$$

$$\Rightarrow \rho = c\sec^2\psi \qquad \text{...(2)}$$

From (1) and (2), we get

$$\rho = PG$$

**Property 2.** Distance of any point $P$ from the foot of the perpendicular from $M$ to the tangent at $P$ is equal to the arc length $CP$.

**Proof:** From figure, we have

$PN$ = Distance of $P$ from the foot of the perpendicular $N$ from $M$ to the tangent at $P$.

$$= PM\sin\angle NMP \quad \Rightarrow = y\sin\psi$$

$$= c\sec\psi\sin\psi \; \because y = c\sec\psi$$

$$= c\tan\psi \quad \Rightarrow = s \;\mid\because s = c\tan\psi$$

## 7. Two Important Deductions from Relation between Tension and Ordinate

We know that the relation between tension $T$ and ordinate $y$ is

$$T = wy$$

From this relation, we conclude that the tension at any point of a common catenary is equal to the weight of that portion of the catenary which hangs vertically from that point to the $X$-axis known as the directrix of the common catenary.

**Deduction 1:** If a long chain is thrown over two smooth pegs with two free ends of the chain just touching the directrix of the catenary, then it will be in equilibrium. Conversely, if the chain hanging over two smooth pegs is in equilibrium, then the free ends must lie on the directrix of the common catenary.

**Proof:** We know that the relation between tension $T$ and ordinate $y$ is

$$T = wy$$

This relation shows that the tension at any point of the catenary is proportional to the height of the point above the directrix of the catenary. Hence, if a string is thrown over two smooth pegs, not lying in the same vertical line, such that the portion of the string in between the pegs form a common catenary and the two free ends of the string hanging vertically touch the directrix of the catenary, then the string will be in equilibrium.

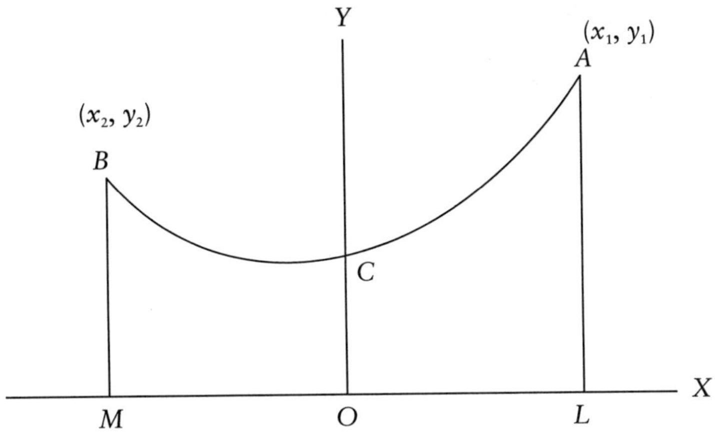


**Conversely**, if such a string is in equilibrium, then the two free ends will touch the directrix.

**Proof:** Let a string $LACBM$ be thrown over two smooth pegs $A(x_1, y_1)$ and $B(x_2, y_2)$ as shown in the figure. Let $w$ be the weight per unit length of the string. Since the two pegs $A$ and $B$ are smooth, therefore, the tensions in two portions of it on either sides of the peg will be equal and opposite.

Hence, from the figure, we have

Tension at $A$ = weight of the hanging portion $AC$ of the string

$$\Rightarrow \quad wy_1 = w.\,AL$$

$$\Rightarrow \quad y_1 = AL$$

Therefore, the free end $L$ lies on the directrix of the common catenary $ACB$.

*Note*: The tension in the string remains unaltered when it is passing round a smooth peg. Therefore,

Tension at $A$ = Tension in the hanging portion $AL$ of the string.

= Weight of the hanging portion $AL$ of the string

Similarly,

Tension at $B$ = Weight of the hanging portion $BM$ of the string

$$\Rightarrow \quad wy_2 = w.\,BM \qquad \Rightarrow \qquad y_2 = BM$$

Therefore, the free end $M$ lies on the directrix of the common catenary $ACB$.

*Note*: The tension in the string remains unaltered when it is passing round a smooth peg. Therefore,

Tension at $B$ = Tension in the hanging portion $BM$ of the string

= weight of the hanging portion $BM$ of the string.

**Deduction 2.** When a uniform inextensible string hangs freely under gravity passing over two smooth pegs not lying in the same vertical line, then the difference of the tensions at two points varies as the difference of their heights.

**Proof:** We know that

$$T = wy$$

Let $A$ $(x_1, y_1)$ and $B$ $(x_2, y_2)$ be the two smooth pegs not lying in the same vertical line. Let $T_1$ and $T_2$ be the tensions in the string at these points respectively.

Then, we have

$$T_1 = w\,y_1 \mid \text{at } A \qquad \Rightarrow \qquad T_2 = w\,y_2 \mid \text{at } B$$

$$\therefore \quad T_1 - T_2 = w\,(y_1 - y_2) \qquad \Rightarrow \qquad T_1 - T_2 \;\alpha\; (y_1 - y_2) \mid \because w \text{ is constant}$$

This shows that the difference of the tensions at the two points varies as the difference of their heights.

## ILLUSTRATIVE EXAMPLES

**Example 1:** A uniform hair of length $\ell$ is to be suspended from two points $A$ and $B$ in the same horizontal line so that either terminal tension is $n$ times that at the lowest point. Show that the span $AB$ must be

$$\frac{1}{\sqrt{n^2-1}}\log\left[n+\sqrt{n^2-1}\right]$$

**Sol.**

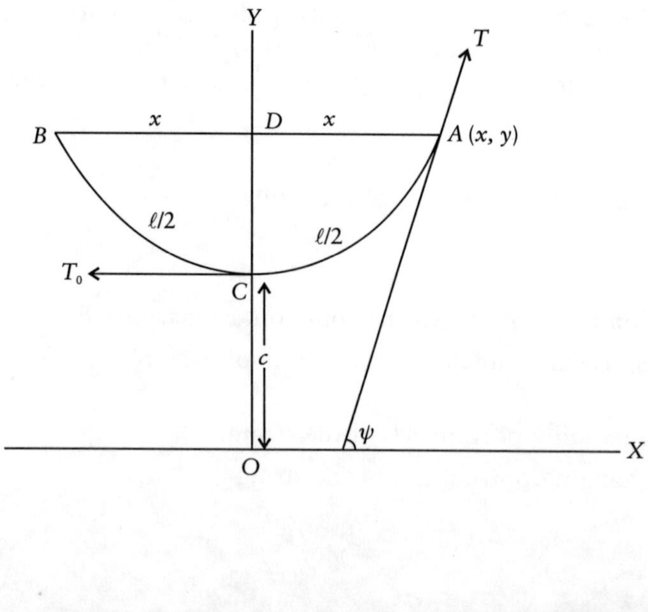

Length of the chain $ACB = \ell$

$\therefore$ Length of the arc $CA = \ell/2$, where $C$ is the lowest point of the chain. The directrix of the catenary $ACB$ is the horizontal line $OX$ at a depth $c$ below the lowest point $C$. $OY$ is the Y-axis through $C$.

Let the coordinates of the point $A$ be $(x, y)$.

Let $T$ be the terminal tension at $A$ making an angle $\psi$ with the horizontal line $OX$.

According to the problem,

Tension at $A = n$ Tension at the lowest point $C$

$\Rightarrow T = n\,T_0 \quad \Rightarrow \quad wy = n\,(wc)$

$\Rightarrow y = nc \quad \Rightarrow \quad c \sec \psi = nc \qquad |\because y = c \sec \psi$

$\Rightarrow \sec \psi = n \quad \Rightarrow \quad \sec^2 \psi = n^2$

$\Rightarrow 1 + \tan^2 \psi = n^2 \quad \Rightarrow \quad \tan^2 \psi = n^2 - 1$

$$\Rightarrow \tan \psi = \sqrt{n^2 - 1} \qquad ...(1)$$

We have,

$$s = c \tan \psi$$

At the point $A$,

$$\frac{\ell}{2} = c\sqrt{n^2 - 1} \quad \Rightarrow \quad c = \frac{\ell}{2\sqrt{n^2 - 1}} \qquad ...(2)$$

Now, span $AB$

$$= 2\,x = 2\,c \log(\sec \psi + \tan \psi)$$

$$= 2\frac{\ell}{2\sqrt{n^2 - 1}}\left(n + \sqrt{n^2 - 1}\right) \qquad | \text{ From (1) and (2)}$$

$$= \frac{\ell}{\sqrt{n^2 - 1}} \log\left(n + \sqrt{n^2 - 1}\right)$$

**Example 2:** A uniform chain of length $\ell$ which can just bear a tension of $n$ times its weight, is suspended between two points at the same level. Show that the least possible sag in the middle is

$$\ell\left(n - \sqrt{n^2 - \frac{1}{4}}\right)$$

**Sol.** Let $ACB$ be the catenary formed by the uniform chain of length $\ell$ suspended between two points $A$ and $B$ in the same horizontal line with its middle point $C$ as its lowest point.

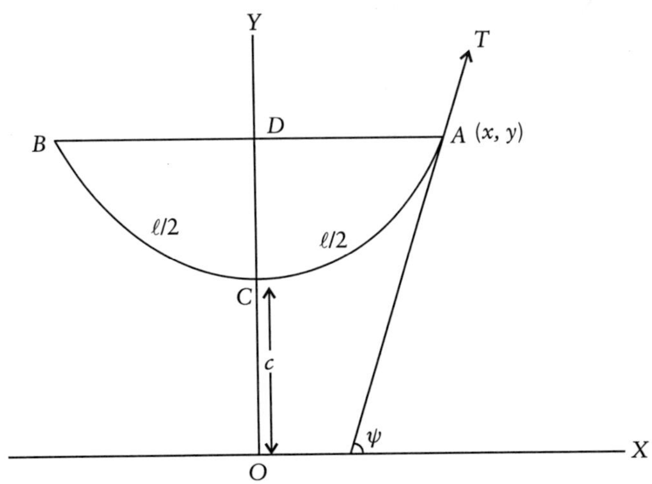

The directrix of the catenary $ACB$ is the horizontal line $OX$ at a depth $c$ below the lowest point $C$. $OY$ is the $Y$-axis through $C$.

Sag will the least when the terminal tension is maximum.

Also, maximum tension

$= n$ weight of the chain $= n\ell w$, where $w$ is the weight per unit length of the chain ...(1)

Let the coordinates of the point $A$ be $(x, y)$.

Let $T$ be the terminal tension at $A$ making an angle $\psi$ with the horizontal line $OX$.

According to the problem,

Tension at $A = n\ell w$

$\Rightarrow \; wy = n\ell w \qquad \Rightarrow \; y = n\ell$ ...(2)

We have,

$$y^2 = s^2 + c^2$$

At the point $A$,

$$n^2 \ell^2 = (\ell/2)^2 + c^2$$

$\Rightarrow \; n^2 \ell^2 = \ell^2/4 + c^2 \qquad \Rightarrow \qquad c^2 = (n^2 - 1/4)\, \ell^2$

$\Rightarrow \; c = \sqrt{n^2 - \frac{1}{n}}\,\ell$ ...(3)

$\therefore$ Least possible sag

$= y - c \qquad \Rightarrow \qquad = n\,\ell - \sqrt{n^2 - \frac{1}{4}}\,\ell$ |From (2) and (3)

$$= \ell\left(n - \sqrt{n^2 - \frac{1}{4}}\right)$$

**Example 3:** The extremities of a heavy string of length $2\ell$ and weight $2\ell w$ are attached to two small rings which can slide on a fixed horizontal wire. Each of these rings is acted upon by a horizontal force equal to $\ell w$. Show that the distance apart of the rings is $2\ell \log(1 + \sqrt{2})$.

**Sol.**

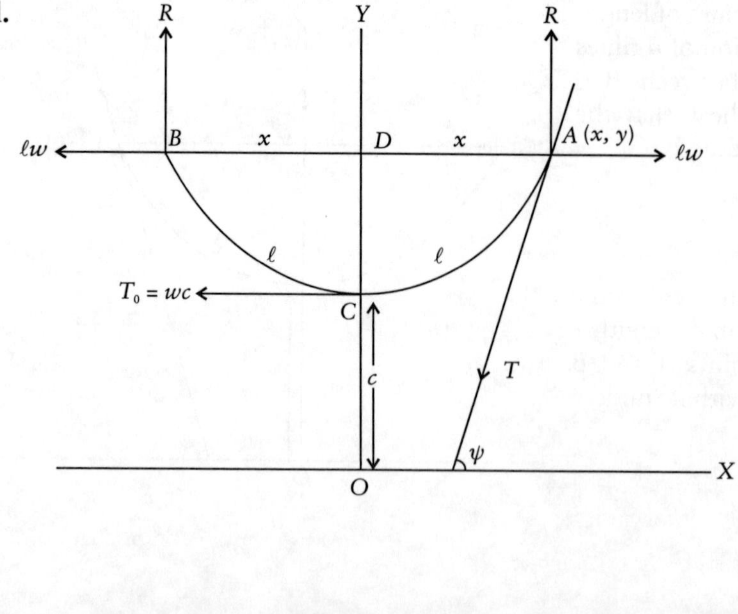

$ACB$ is a heavy string of length $2\ell$ and weight $2\ell w$. $A$ and $B$ are the rings which can slide on a fixed horizontal wire $AB$. Let $R$ be the normal reaction of the fixed horizontal wire on each ring. $C$ is the lowest point of the string $ACB$.

The directrix of the catenary $ACB$ is the horizontal line $OX$ at a depth $c$ below the lowest point $C$. $OY$ is the $Y$-axis through $C$.

Let the coordinates of the point $A$ be $(x, y)$. Let $T$ be the tension of the string at $A$ making an angle $\psi$ with the horizontal line $OX$.

By Symmetry,

$$\text{arc } CA = \ell$$

Let us consider the equilibrium of the ring at $A$. Forces acting on it are:

(i) horizontal force $\ell w$ at $A$

(ii) normal reaction $R$

(iii) tension $T$ of the string acting along the tangent at $A$.

Resolving horizontally, we get

$$T \cos \psi = \ell w \qquad \Rightarrow T_0 = \ell w \qquad | \because T \cos \psi = T_0$$

$$\Rightarrow \quad wc = \ell w \qquad | \because T_0 = wc \quad \Rightarrow c = \ell \qquad \text{...(1)}$$

Also, we have,

$$s = c \tan \psi$$

At the end $A$,

$$\ell = \ell \tan \psi$$

$$\Rightarrow \quad \tan \psi = 1$$

$$\Rightarrow \quad \psi = \pi/4 \qquad \text{...(2)}$$

$\therefore$ Distance apart of the rings

$$= \text{span} \quad \Rightarrow \quad = AB$$

$$= 2x \quad \Rightarrow \quad = 2c \log (\sec \psi + \tan \psi)$$

$$= 2\ \ell \log (\sec \pi/4 + \tan \pi/4) \qquad | \text{ From (1) and (2)}$$

$$= 2\ell \log (\sqrt{2} + 1)$$

**Example 4:** A given 2s of a uniform chain is hung between two points $A$ and $B$ at the same level and the tension has not to exceed the weight of $a$ length $b$ of the chain. Show that the greatest span is

$$\sqrt{b^2 - s^2} \log\left(\frac{b+s}{b-s}\right)$$

**Sol.**

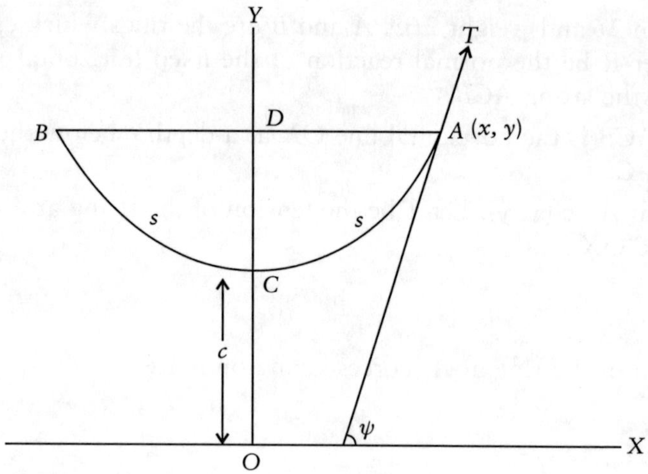


Let $ACB$ be the catenary formed by the uniform chain of length 2s suspended from two points $A$ and $B$ at the same level with its middle point $C$ as the lowest point. Let $c$ be the parameter of the catenary $ACB$ and $D$ be the middle point of the span $AB$.

The directrix of the catenary $ACB$ is the horizontal line $OX$ at a depth $c$ below the lowest point $C$. $OY$ is the $Y$-axis is through $C$.

Let the coordinates of the point $A$ be $(x, y)$. Let $T$ be the tension of the string at $A$ making an angle $\psi$ with the horizontal line $OX$. Then,

$$T = wy \qquad \text{...(1)}$$

It is clear that the span will be the greatest when the terminal tension, i.e., the tension at the points of suspension is the greatest.

Also, maximum tension = $wb$ | Given

where $w$ is the weight per unit length of the chain.

According to the problem,

Tension at $A = wb$

$$\Rightarrow \quad wy = wb \qquad \text{|From (1)}$$

$$\Rightarrow \quad y = b \qquad \text{...(2)}$$

We have,

$$y^2 = s^2 + c^2$$

At the end $A$, $b^2 = s^2 + c^2$ |From (2)

$$\Rightarrow \quad c = \sqrt{b^2 - s^2} \qquad \text{...(3)}$$

Also, $y = c \sec \psi$

At the end $A$,

$$b = c \sec \psi \qquad \Rightarrow \sec \psi = b/c \qquad \text{...(4)}$$

$$\therefore \quad \tan \psi = \sqrt{\sec^2 \psi - 1} = \sqrt{\frac{b^2}{c^2} - 1} = \frac{\sqrt{b^2 - c^2}}{c} \qquad \text{...(5)}$$

∴ Greatest span

$$= AB = 2x = 2c \log (\sec \psi + \tan \psi)$$

$$= 2\sqrt{b^2 - s^2} \log\left(\frac{b}{c} + \frac{\sqrt{b^2 - c^2}}{c}\right) \qquad = 2\sqrt{b^2 - s^2} \log\left(\frac{b + \sqrt{b^2 - c^2}}{c}\right)$$

$$= 2\sqrt{b^2 - s^2} \log\left(\frac{b + s}{\sqrt{b^2 - s^2}}\right) \qquad |\text{From (3)}$$

$$= 2\sqrt{b^2 - s^2} \log\left(\sqrt{\frac{b + s}{b - s}}\right) \qquad = 2\sqrt{b^2 - s^2} \cdot \frac{1}{2} \log\left(\frac{b + s}{b - s}\right) \qquad = \sqrt{b^2 - s^2} \log\left(\frac{b + s}{b - s}\right)$$

**Example 5:** A rope of length $2\ell$ metres is suspended between two points in the same level and the lowest point of the rope is $b$ metres below the points of suspension. Show that the horizontal component of the tension is

$\frac{w}{2b}(\ell^2 - b^2)$, $w$ being the weight of the rope per metre of its length.

**Sol.** $A$ and $B$ are the two points of suspension and $C$ is the lowest point of the catenary. The length of the rope $ACB$ is $2\ell$. Therefore, the length of the rope $CA = \ell$.

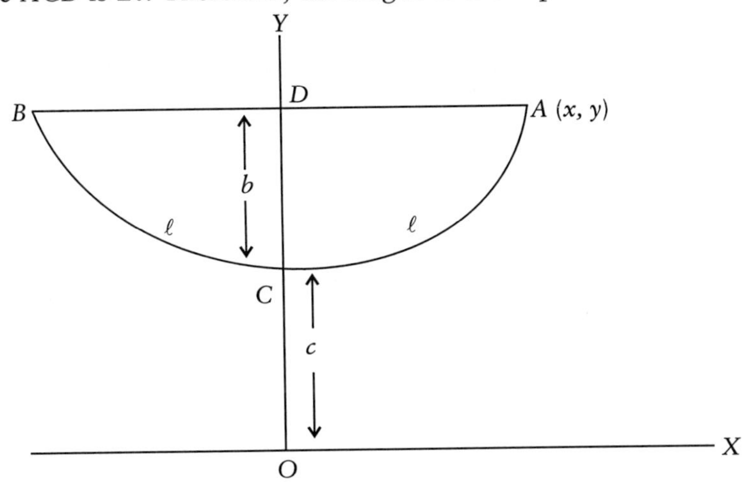


We have,

$$y^2 = s^2 + c^2$$

At the point $A$,

$$(b + c)^2 = \ell^2 + c^2 \quad \Rightarrow \quad b^2 + c^2 + 2bc = \ell^2 + c^2$$

$$\Rightarrow \quad b^2 + 2bc = \ell^2 \quad \Rightarrow \quad 2bc = \ell^2 - b^2$$

$$\Rightarrow \quad c = \frac{\ell^2 - b^2}{2b} \qquad \text{...(1)}$$

∴ The horizontal component of the tension

$$= T_0 \quad \Rightarrow = wc \quad \Rightarrow = w\left(\frac{\ell^2 - b^2}{2b}\right) \qquad |\text{From (1)}$$

**Example 6:** If a chain is suspended from two points $A$, $B$ on the same level, and depth of the middle point below $AB$ is $(\ell/n)$, where $2\ell$ is the length of the chain, show that the horizontal span $AB$ in equal to

$$\ell\ (n - 1/n) \log\left(\frac{n+1}{n-1}\right)$$

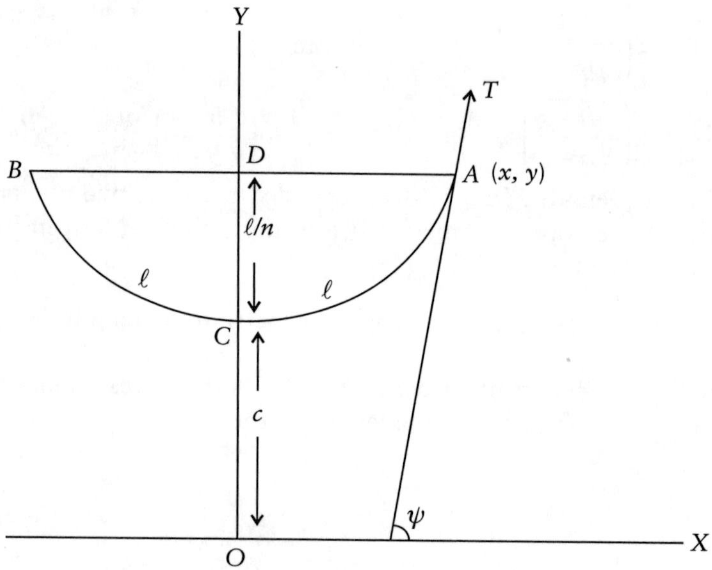


Let $ACB$ be the catenary formed by the chain of length $2\ell$ suspended from two points $A$ and $B$ on the same level with its middle point $C$ as the lowest point. Then,

length of the arc $AC = \ell$

Let $T$ be the tension of the chain at $A$ inclined at an angle $\psi$ with the horizontal. Let $OC = c$. Then, $c$ is the parameter of the catenary.

Also, $CD = \ell/n$ |Given

We have,

$$T = wy$$

At the point $A$,

$$T = w\ (\ell/n + c) \quad \text{...(1)}$$

Also,

$$y^2 = s^2 + c^2$$

At the point $A$,

$$(\ell/n + c)^2 = \ell^2 + c^2$$

$$\Rightarrow \frac{\ell^2}{n^2} + 2\frac{\ell}{n}c + c^2 = \ell^2 + c^2 \qquad \Rightarrow \frac{\ell^2}{n^2} + 2\frac{\ell}{n}c = \ell^2$$

$$\Rightarrow \ell/n^2 + 2c/n = \ell \qquad \Rightarrow 2\ell/n = \ell - \ell/n^2$$

$$\Rightarrow 2c = \ell n - \ell/n \qquad \Rightarrow 2c = \ell(n - 1/n)$$

$\Rightarrow \quad c = \ell/2\ (n - 1/n)$ ...(2)

From (1) and (2),

$$T = w\,[\ell/n + \ell/2\ (n - 1/n)]$$

$$= w\,\ell/2\ (n + 1/n) \quad ...(3)$$

Again,

$$T \text{ sing } \psi = ws$$

At the point $A$,

$$T \text{ sing } \psi = w\ell$$

$$\Rightarrow \sin\psi = w\ell/T$$

$$= w\ell \,/\, w\ell/2\ (n+1/n)$$

$$= 2n \,/\, n^2+1 \quad ...(4)$$

$$\therefore \tan\psi = 2n/n^2-1 \quad ...(5)$$

and, $\sec\psi = n^2+1 \,/\, n^2-1$ ...(6)

$\therefore$ Horizontal span $AB$

$$= 2x \quad \Rightarrow \quad = 2c \log(\sec\psi + \tan\psi)$$

$$= 2.\frac{\ell}{2}\left(n - \frac{1}{n}\right)\log\left(\frac{n^2+1}{n^2-1} + \frac{2n}{n^2-1}\right) \quad \Rightarrow \quad = \ell\left(n - \frac{1}{n}\right)\log\left(\frac{n^2+1+2n}{n^2-1}\right)$$

$$= \ell\left(n - \frac{1}{n}\right)\log\left\{\frac{(n+1)^2}{(n+1)(n-1)}\right\} \quad \Rightarrow \quad = \ell\left(n - \frac{1}{n}\right)\log\left(\frac{n+1}{n-1}\right)$$

**Example 7:** If the tangents at the points $P$ and $Q$ of a catenary are at right angles, prove that the tension at the middle point of the arc $PQ$ is equal to the weight of a length of the string that equal to half the arc $PQ$.

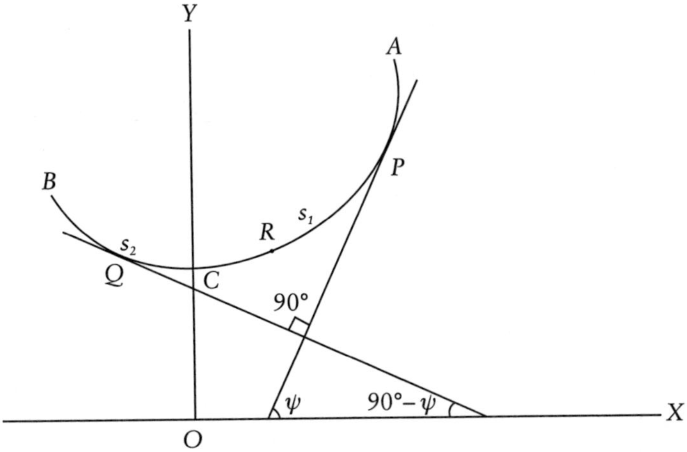


Let $R$ be the mid-point of the arc $PQ$. Let the ordinate of $R$ be $y$. Let arc $CP = s_1$ and arc $CQ = s_2$. Let the tangent at $P$ make an angle $\psi$ with the horizontal.

We have,

$s = c \tan \psi$

For the point $P$,

$s_1 = c \tan \psi$ ...(1)

For the point $Q$,

$s_2 = c \tan (90° - \psi)$

$\Rightarrow s_2 = c \cot \psi$ ...(2)

Also,

arc $CR$ = arc $CP$ – arc $RP$

$= s_1 - 1/2\ (s_1 + s_2)$ $\Rightarrow = 1/2\ (s_1 - s_2)$

$= 1/2\ (c \tan \psi - c \cot \psi)$ |From (1) and (2)

$= c/2\ (\tan \psi - \cot \psi)$ ...(3)

Again, we have

$y^2 = s^2 + c^2$

For the point $R$,

$$y^2 = \left\{\frac{c}{2}(\tan\psi - \cot\psi)\right\}^2 + c^2$$ |From (3)

$= c^2/4\ (\tan^2 \psi + \cot^2 \psi - 2 + 4)$ $= c^2/4\ (\tan \psi + \cot \psi)^2$

$y = c/2\ (\tan \psi + \cot \psi)$ $= c \tan \psi + c \cot \psi / 2$

$= s_1 + s_2 / 2$ |From (1) and (2)

$= 1/2$ (arc $PQ$) ...(4)

$\therefore$ Tension at $R$

$= wy$

$= w\ 1/2$ arc $PQ$ |From (4)

= weight of a length 1/2 (arc $PQ$) of the string.

**Example 8:** If $\bar{x}, \bar{y}$ be the coordinates of the centre of gravity of an arc of the catenary from the vertex to the point $P(x, y)$, show that

$$\bar{x} = x - c\tan\frac{\psi}{2}, \quad \bar{y} = \frac{1}{2}(y + x\cot\psi)$$

**Sol.** $$\bar{x} = \frac{\int \rho x ds}{\int \rho ds} \quad \Rightarrow \quad = \frac{\int_0^x x \frac{ds}{dx} dx}{\int_0^x \frac{ds}{dx} dx}$$

$$= \frac{\int_0^x \underset{\text{I}}{x} \underset{\text{II}}{\cosh\frac{x}{c}}}{\int_0^x \cosh\frac{x}{c}\, dx}$$

$\because s = \sinh\frac{x}{c}$

$\therefore \frac{ds}{dx} = \cosh\frac{x}{c}$

$$= \frac{\left[x\, c \sin h\frac{x}{c}\right]_0^x - c\int_0^x \sin h\frac{x}{c}\,dx}{\left[\sin h\frac{x}{c}\right]_0^x}$$

| On integrating the numerator by parts

$$= \frac{c\, x \sin h\left(\frac{x}{c}\right) - c^2\left[\cosh\left(\frac{x}{c}\right) - 1\right]}{c \sin h\left(\frac{x}{c}\right)} \quad \Rightarrow \quad = x - c\left[\frac{\cosh\left(\frac{x}{c}\right) - 1}{\sin h\left(\frac{x}{c}\right)}\right]$$

$$= x - c\left(\frac{\frac{y}{c} - 1}{\frac{s}{c}}\right)$$

$\because y = c \cos h\left(\frac{x}{c}\right)$

$s = c \sin h\left(\frac{x}{c}\right)$

$$= x - c\left(\frac{y - c}{s}\right)$$

$$= x - c\left(\frac{c \sec \psi - c}{c \tan \psi}\right)$$

$\because y = c \sec \psi,$

$s = c \tan \psi$

$$= x - c\left(\frac{\sec \psi - c}{\tan \psi}\right) \quad \Rightarrow \quad = x - c\left(\frac{1 - \cos \psi}{\sin \psi}\right)$$

$$= x - c\left(\frac{2 \sin^2 \frac{\psi}{2}}{2 \sin \frac{\psi}{2} \cos \frac{\psi}{2}}\right) \quad \Rightarrow \quad = x - c \tan \frac{\psi}{2}$$

Again, $\bar{y} = \dfrac{\int \rho y\, ds}{\int \rho\, ds} \quad \Rightarrow \quad = \dfrac{\int_0^x y \frac{ds}{dx}\,dx}{\int_0^x \frac{ds}{dx}\,dx}$

$$= \frac{\int_0^x c \cos h\frac{x}{c} . \cos h\frac{x}{c}\,dx}{\int_0^x \cos h\frac{x}{c}\,dx} \quad \Rightarrow \quad = \frac{\frac{c}{2}\int_0^x 2 \cos h^2 \frac{x}{c}\,dx}{\left(c \sin h\frac{x}{c}\right)_0^x}$$

$$= \frac{\frac{c}{2}\int_0^x \left(\cos h\frac{2x}{c} + 1\right) dx}{c \sin h\frac{x}{c}} \quad \Rightarrow \quad = \frac{\frac{1}{2}\left(\frac{c}{2}\sin h\frac{2x}{c} + x\right)_0^x}{\sin h\frac{x}{c}}$$

$$= \frac{\frac{1}{2}\left(c\sinh\frac{x}{c}\cosh\frac{x}{c}+x\right)}{\sinh\frac{\alpha}{c}} \Rightarrow = \frac{1}{2}\left(c\cosh\frac{x}{c}+\frac{x}{\sinh\frac{x}{c}}\right)$$

$$= \frac{1}{2}\left(y+\frac{x}{\left(\frac{s}{c}\right)}\right) \qquad \left|\because s = c\sinh\frac{x}{c},\quad y = c\cosh\frac{x}{c}\right.$$

$$= \frac{1}{2}\left(y+\frac{cx}{s}\right)$$

$$= \frac{1}{2}\left(y+\frac{cx}{c\tan\psi}\right) \qquad |\because s = c\tan\psi$$

$$= \frac{1}{2}(y+x\cot\psi)$$

**Example 9:** A kite is flown with 600 metres of string from the hand to the kite and a spring balance held in the hand shows a pull equal to the weight of 100 metres of the string inclined at 30° to the horizon. Find the vertical height of the kite above the hand.

**Sol.**

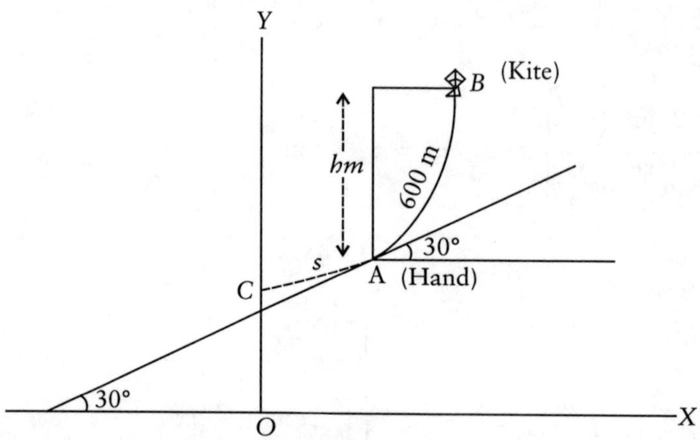


*A* is the hand. *B* is the kite. *AB* is the string of length 600 m. Let C be the lowest point of the catenary of which *AB* is a part. Let *w* be the weight per unit length of the string. Let the coordinates of the point *A* be $(x, y)$ referred to *OX* and *OY* as the axes. Let $OC = c$ (the parameter) and arc $CA = s$. According to the problem,

tension at $A$ = pull experienced by the hand at $A$

= weight of 100 m of the string

= $100\, w$ ...(1)

We have,

$$T = wy$$

At the point $A$,

$$\tau = w\, y_A \qquad ...(2)$$

From (1) and (2)

$$w\, y_A = 100 \text{ w}$$

$$y_A = 100 \text{ m} \qquad ...(3)$$

Also, we have,

$$s = c \tan \psi$$

At the point $A$,

$$s = c \tan 30° = c/\sqrt{3} \qquad ...(4)$$

Again, we have,

$$y^2 = s^2 + c^2$$

At the point $A$,

$$y_A^2 = s^2 + c^2$$

$$\Rightarrow \quad (100)^2 = c^2/3 + c^2$$

$$\Rightarrow \quad (100)^2 = 4c^2/3$$

$$\Rightarrow \quad c = 50\sqrt{3} \qquad ...(5)$$

Let $h$ be the vertical height of $B$ above $A$.

Then, from $y^2 = s^2 + c^2$, we get,

$$(y_A + h)^2 = (\text{arc } CB)^2 + c^2$$

$$\Rightarrow (100 + h)^2 = (s + 600)^2 + c^2$$

$$= (c/\sqrt{3} + 600)^2 + c^2$$

$$= (50 + 600)^2 + (50\sqrt{3})^2 \qquad |\text{From (5)}$$

$$= 650^2 + (50\sqrt{3})^2$$

$$= 422500 + 7500$$

$$= 430000$$

$$\Rightarrow 100 + h = 100\sqrt{43}$$

$$\Rightarrow h = 100(\sqrt{43} - 1)$$

$$\Rightarrow h = 555.7 \text{ metres nearly}$$

This is the required height.

**Example 10:** A heavy uniform string 90 inches long, hangs over two smooth pegs at different heights. The parts which hang vertically are of lengths 30 and 33 inches. Prove that the vertex of the catenary divides the whole length in the ratio 4 : 5. Also find the horizontal and vertical distances between the pegs. (Given that $\log \ell\ 2.5 = 0.9163$)

**Sol.**

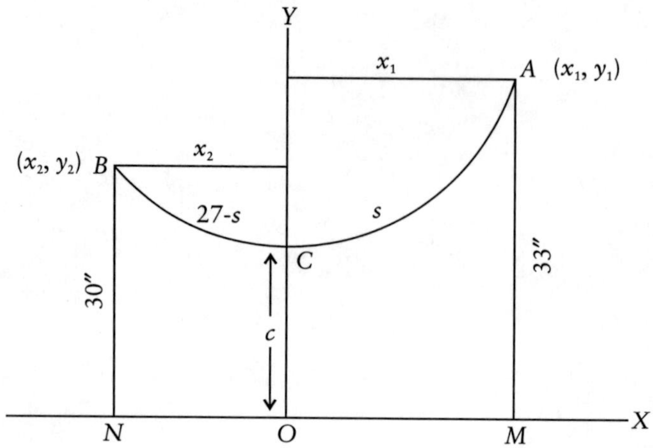


$A$ and $B$ are the two smooth pegs. $MACBN$ is the string 90 inches long hanging over $A$ and $B$. The portions $AM$ and $BN$ of the string hang vertically. The central portion $ACB$ of the string hangs in the form of a catenary whose lowest point is $C$. Let $OC = c$.

Then, $c$ is the parameter of the catenary.

According to the problem,

$$AM = 33 \text{ inches}$$

$$BN = 30 \text{ inches}$$

Let arc $CA = s$ inches

Then, arc $CB = 90 - (30 + 33 + s)$

$$= (27 - s) \text{ inches}$$

Referred to the axes $OX$ and $OY$, as shown in the figure, let the coordinates of the points $A$ and $B$ be $(x_1, y_1)$ and $(x_2, y_2)$ respectively.

Now, the tension at $A$ supports the weight of length $AM$ of the string. So, tension at $A$ = weight of the length $AM$ of the string

$$\Rightarrow \quad w\, y_1 = 33\, w$$

$$\Rightarrow \quad y_1 = 33 \text{ inches} \quad \text{...(1)}$$

Similarly, the tension $B$ supports the weight of length $BN$ of the string. So, tension at $B$ = weight of the length $BN$ of the string

$$\Rightarrow \quad w\, y_2 = 30\, w$$

$$\Rightarrow \quad y_2 = 30 \text{ inches} \quad \text{...(2)}$$

Hence, the points (ends of the string) will lie on the directrix of the catenary $ACB$.

We have,

$$y^2 = s^2 + c^2$$

At the point $A$,

$$33^2 = s^2 + c^2 \quad \text{...(3)}$$

At the point $B$,

$$30^2 = (27 - s)^2 + c^2 \quad ...(4)$$

Subtracting (4) from (3), we get

$$33^2 - 30^2 = s^2 - (27 - s)^2 \quad \Rightarrow (33 - 30)\,(33 + 30) = \{s - (27 - s)\}\,\{s + (27 - s)\}$$

$$\Rightarrow \quad 189 = (2\,s - 27)\,27 \quad \Rightarrow 7 = 2\,s - 27$$

$$\Rightarrow \quad 2\,s = 34$$

$$\Rightarrow \quad s = 17 \text{ inches} \quad ...(5)$$

**Length of the portion *CBN* of the string**

∴ Length of the portion $CAM$ of the string

$$= 27 - s + 30/s + 33$$

$$= 27 - 17 + 30\,/17 + 33 \quad \text{| From (5)}$$

$$= 40/50 = 4/5$$

Hence, the vertex $C$ of the catenary divides the whole length in the ratio 4 : 5.

Substituting the value of $s$ in Eq. (1), we get,

$$33^2 = 17^2 + c^2 \quad \Rightarrow c^2 = 33^2 - 17^2$$

$$= (33 - 17)\,(33 + 17) = 800$$

$$\Rightarrow \quad c = 20\,\sqrt{2} \text{ inches} \quad ...(6)$$

∴ The horizontal distance between the pegs

$$= x_1 + x_2$$

$$= c\left[\log\left(\frac{y_1 + s}{c}\right) + \log\left\{\frac{y_2 + (27 - s)}{c}\right\}\right]$$

$$= 20\sqrt{2}\left[\log\left(\frac{33+17}{20\sqrt{2}}\right) + \log\left\{\frac{30+(27-17)}{20\sqrt{2}}\right\}\right] \quad \text{| From (5), (6), (1) and (2)}$$

$$= 20\sqrt{2}\left(\log\frac{50}{20\sqrt{2}} + \log\frac{40}{20\sqrt{2}}\right) \quad \Rightarrow = 20\sqrt{2}\left(\log\frac{5}{2\sqrt{2}} + \log\sqrt{2}\right)$$

$$= 20\sqrt{2}\log\left(\frac{5}{2\sqrt{2}}.\sqrt{2}\right) \quad \Rightarrow = 20\sqrt{2}\log\frac{5}{2} \quad \Rightarrow = 20\sqrt{2}\log(2.5)$$

$$= 20 \times 1.414 \times 0.9163 \quad \Rightarrow = 25.91 \text{ inches}$$

Also, the vertical distance between the pegs

$$= y_1 - y_2 \quad \Rightarrow = 33 - 30 \quad \Rightarrow = 3 \text{ inches}$$

*Note*: Distance between the peg

$$= AB \quad \Rightarrow = \sqrt{(x_1 + x_2)^2 + (y_1 - y_2)^2}$$

$$= \sqrt{(25.91)^2 + (3)^2} \quad \Rightarrow \quad = \sqrt{(671.3281 + 9}$$

$$= \sqrt{680.3281} \quad \Rightarrow \quad = 26.08 \text{ inches}$$

**Example 11:** A heavy uniform string of length $\ell$ is suspended from a fixed point $A$ and its other end $B$ is pulled horizontally by a force equal to the weight of a length $a$ of the string. Show that the horizontal and vertical distances between $A$ and $B$ are

$$a \sinh^{-1}\left(\frac{\ell}{a}\right) \text{ and } \left(\sqrt{\ell^2 + a^2} - a\right) \text{ respectively.}$$

**Sol.**

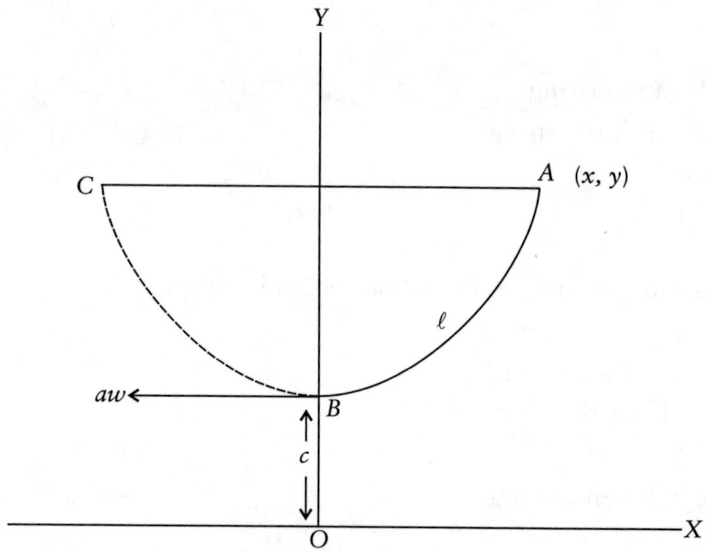


Let $AB$ be the heavy uniform string of length $\ell$ suspended from a fixed point $A$ and its other end $B$ pulled horizontally by a force equal to the weight of a length $a$ of the string, i.e., $wa$.

Since the tension at $B$ balances the horizontal force $wa$, therefore, the tension at $B$ must also be horizontal so that $B$ is the lowest point of the catenary of which $BA$ is a part.

$\therefore \quad T_0 = wc = wa$

$\Rightarrow \quad c = a$ ...(1)

Let us take the horizontal line $OX$ at a depth $c$ below $B$ as $X$-axis and $OY$, the vertical line through $B$, as $Y$-axis. Referred to these axes, let the coordinates of $A$ be $(x, y)$.

We have, $s = c \sin h\,(x/c)$

At the point $A$,

$\ell = a \sin h\,(\ell/a)$ |From (1)

$\Rightarrow x = a \sin h^{-1}\,(\ell/a)$ ...(2)

Also, we have $y^2 = s^2 + c^2$

At the point $A$, $y^2 = \ell^2 + a^2$

$\Rightarrow \quad y = \sqrt{\ell^2 + a^2}$ ...(3)

$\therefore$ Vertical distance between $A$ and $B$

$= y - c$

$\sqrt{\ell^2 + a^2} - a$ |From (1) and (2) ...(4)

Equations (2) and (4) respectively give the horizontal and vertical distances between $A$ and $B$.

**Example 12:** A uniform chain of length $2\ell$ is suspended by its ends which are on the same horizontal level. The distance apart $2a$ of the ends is such that the lowest point of the chain is at a distance $a$, vertically below the ends. Prove that if $c$ be the distance of the lowest point from the directrix of the catenary, then

$$\frac{2a^2}{\ell^2 - a^2} = \log\frac{\ell - a}{\ell + a} \qquad \text{and} \qquad \tanh\frac{a}{c} = \frac{2a\ell}{\ell^2 + a^2}$$

**Sol.**

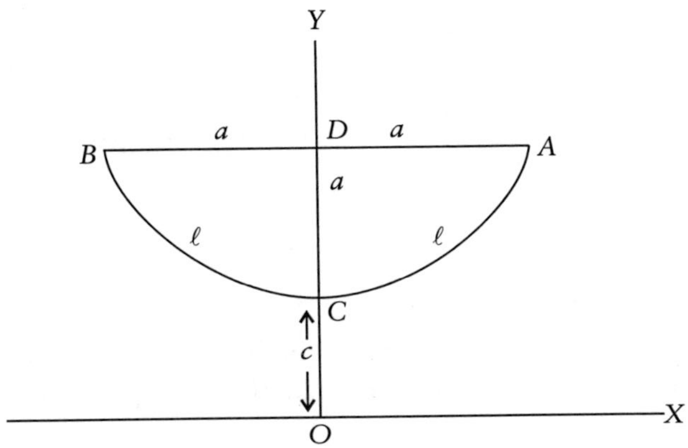


$A$ and $B$ are the ends of the chain of length $2\ell$ such that $AB = 2a$. $C$ is the lowest point of the catenary. $D$ is the middle point of $AB$.

$\therefore BD = DA = 1/2\ (BA) = 1/2\ (2a) = a$

Also, arc $CA$ = arc $CB = \ell$

$DC = a$

We have, $y^2 = s^2 + c^2$

At the end $A$, $(a + c)^2 = \ell^2 + c^2$

$\Rightarrow a^2 + c^2 + 2ac = \ell^2 + c^2 \qquad \Rightarrow a^2 + 2ac = \ell^2$

$\Rightarrow 2ac = \ell^2 - a^2 \qquad \Rightarrow c = \ell^2 - a^2/2a$ ...(1)

We have, $y = c \cosh (x/c)$

and $s = c \sinh (x/c)$

At the end $A$,

$c + a = c \cosh (a/c)$ ...(2)

and $\ell = c \sinh (a/c)$ ...(3)

Dividing (3) by (2), we get

$$\tanh\left(\frac{a}{c}\right) = \frac{\ell}{c + a}$$

$$= \frac{\ell}{\dfrac{\ell^2 - a^2}{2a} + a} \qquad \text{| From (1)}$$

$$= \frac{2a\ell}{\ell^2 + a^2} \qquad ...(4)$$

Again, we have $x = c \log (y+s/c)$

At the end $A$,

$$a = c\log\frac{(c+a)+\ell}{c} \qquad \Rightarrow = \frac{\ell^2-a^2}{2a}\log\frac{\frac{\ell^2-a^2}{2a}+a+\ell}{\frac{\ell^2-a^2}{2a}}$$

$$= \frac{\ell^2-a^2}{2a}\log\frac{\ell^2-a^2+2a^2+2a\ell}{\ell^2-a^2} \qquad \Rightarrow = \frac{\ell^2-a^2}{2a}\log\frac{\ell^2-a^2+2a\ell}{\ell^2-a^2}$$

$$= \frac{\ell^2-a^2}{2a}\log\frac{(\ell+a)^2}{(\ell-a)(\ell+a)} \qquad \Rightarrow = \frac{\ell^2-a^2}{2a}\log\frac{\ell+a}{\ell-a}$$

$$\Rightarrow \quad \frac{2a^2}{\ell^2-a^2} = \log\frac{\ell+a}{\ell-a} \qquad ...(5)$$

(5) and (4) give the required results.

**Example 13:** If α and β be the inclinations to the horizon of the tangents at the extremities of a portion of a common catenary and $\ell$ be the length of the portion, show that the height of one extremity above the other is

$$\frac{\ell\sin\left(\frac{\alpha+\beta}{2}\right)}{\cos\left(\frac{\alpha-\beta}{2}\right)},$$ the two extremities being on one side of the vertex.

**Sol.**

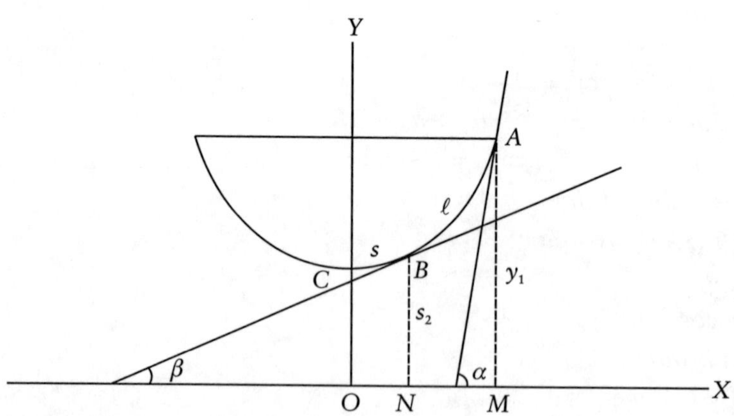


Let $AB$ the given portion of a common catenary. Let C be the vertex of the catenary. Let arc $CB = s$. Then, arc $CA = s + \ell$. Let $y_1$ and $y_2$ be the ordinates of the points $A$ and $B$ referred to the axes $OX$ and $OY$, as shown in the figure.

We have, $s = c \tan \psi$

At the point $A$, $s + \ell = c \tan \alpha$ ...(1)

At the point $B$,

$s = c \tan \beta$ ...(2)

Subtracting (2) from (1), we get

$\ell = c(\tan \alpha - \tan \beta)$ ...(3)

Also, we have, $y = c \sec \psi$

At the point $A$, $y_1 = c \sec \alpha$ ...(4)

At the point $B$,

$y_2 = c \sec \beta$ ...(5)

Subtracting (5) from (4), we get

$y_1 - y_2 = c(\sec \alpha - \sec \beta)$ ...(6)

Dividing (6) by (3), we get,

$$\frac{y_1 - y_2}{\ell} = \frac{\sec\alpha - \sec\beta}{\tan\alpha - \tan\beta} \quad \Rightarrow = \frac{\cos\beta - \cos\alpha}{\sin\alpha\cos\beta - \cos\alpha\sin\beta}$$

$$= \frac{2\sin\dfrac{\alpha+\beta}{2}\sin\dfrac{\alpha-\beta}{2}}{\sin(\alpha-\beta)} \quad \Rightarrow = \frac{2\sin\dfrac{\alpha+\beta}{2}\sin\dfrac{\alpha-\beta}{2}}{2\sin\dfrac{\alpha-\beta}{2}\cos\dfrac{\alpha-\beta}{2}}$$

$$= \frac{\sin\dfrac{\alpha+\beta}{2}}{\cos\dfrac{\alpha-\beta}{2}} \quad \Rightarrow y_1 - y_2 = \frac{\ell\sin\left(\dfrac{\alpha+\beta}{2}\right)}{\cos\left(\dfrac{\alpha-\beta}{2}\right)}$$

$y_1 - y_2$ gives the height of one extremity above the other.

*Note*: If the two extremities $A$ and $B$ of the portion $AB$ of the catenary lie on the opposite sides of the vertex $C$, then

$$\ell = s_1 + s_2 = c(\tan\alpha + \tan\beta)$$

$$\therefore \frac{y_1 - y_2}{\ell} = \frac{\cos\beta - \cos\alpha}{\sin(\alpha+\beta)} \quad \Rightarrow y_1 - y_2 = \frac{\ell\sin\left(\dfrac{\alpha-\beta}{2}\right)}{\cos\left(\dfrac{\alpha+\beta}{2}\right)}$$

**Example 14:** A box kite is flying at a height $h$ with a length $\ell$ of the wire paid out, and with the vertex of the catenary on the ground. Show that at the kite the inclination of wire to the ground is

$$2\tan^{-1}(h/\ell)$$

and that its tensions there and at the ground are

$$w = \ell^2 + h^2/2h \text{ and } w.\ \ell^2 - h^2/2h,$$

where $w$ is the weight per unit length of the wire.

**Sol.**

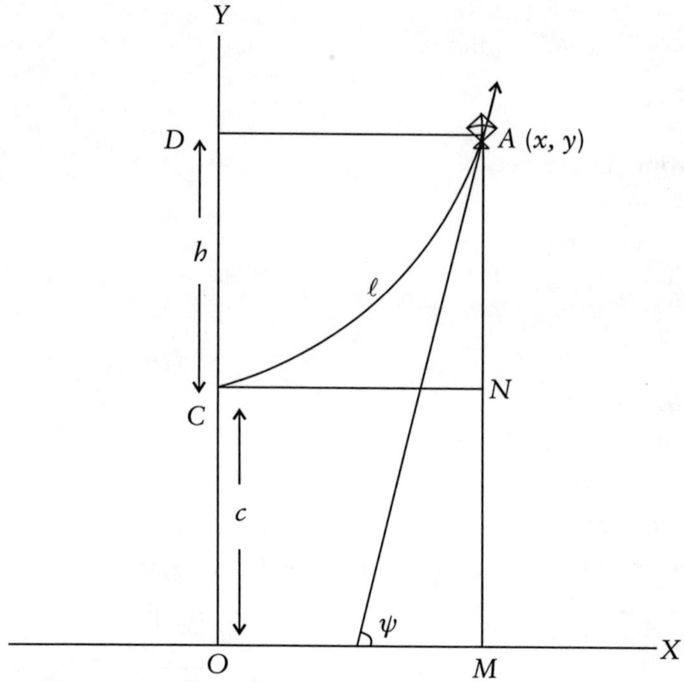


Let $A$ be the box kite and $C$ be the vertex of the catenary formed by the wire $AC$ of length $\ell$.

Let $CN$ be the horizontal ground which is parallel to the $X$-axis. Let $OC = c$. Then, $c$ is the parameter of the catenary. Referred to the axes $OX$ and $OY$, as shown in the figure, let the coordinates of $A$ be $(x, y)$. Let the tangent at $A$ make an angle $\psi$ with the horizontal.

We have, $y^2 = s^2 + c^2$

At the point $A$, $(c + h)^2 = \ell^2 + c^2$

$\Rightarrow c^2 + h^2 + 2ch = \ell^2 + c^2$ $\Rightarrow h^2 + 2ch = \ell^2$ $\Rightarrow 2ch = \ell^2 - h^2$

$\Rightarrow c = (\ell^2 - h^2 /2h$ ...(1)

We have, $s = c \tan \psi$

At the point $A$,

$\ell = \ell^2 - h^2 /2h \tan \psi$ |From (1)

$\Rightarrow \tan \psi = 2h\ell /\ell^2 - h^2$

$$\Rightarrow \tan \psi = \frac{2\left(\frac{h}{\ell}\right)}{1-\left(\frac{h}{\ell}\right)^2}$$

$= 2 \tan \theta /1 - \tan^2 \theta$ where $\tan \theta = h/\ell$

$= \tan 2\theta$

$\Rightarrow \psi = 2\,\theta$

$\Rightarrow \psi = 2 \tan^{-1} (h/\ell)$ ...(2)

We have,

$$T = wy$$

At the point $A$, $\tau = w\,(c + h)$

$$= w\left(\frac{\ell^2 + h^2}{2h} + h\right) \qquad \text{|From (1)}$$

$$= w\left(\frac{\ell^2 + h^2}{2h}\right) \qquad ...(3)$$

Also, tension at the ground

$$= T_0 \qquad \Rightarrow = wc$$

$$= w\,(\ell^2 - h^2 / 2h) \qquad \text{|From (1)}$$

**Example 15:** $A$ and $B$ are two points in the same horizontal line distant $2a$ apart. $AO$ and $OB$ are two equal heavy strings tied together at O and carrying a weight $W$ at O. If $\ell$ is the length of each string, $d$ the depth of O below $AB$, show that the parameter $c$ of the catenary in which either string hangs is given by

$$\ell^2 - d^2 = 2c^2 \{\cos h\,(a/c) - 1\}$$

and tension at $A$ or $B$ is

$$1/2d\,[\ell W + (\ell^2 + d^2)\,w]$$

where $w$ is the line density of the string.

**Sol.**

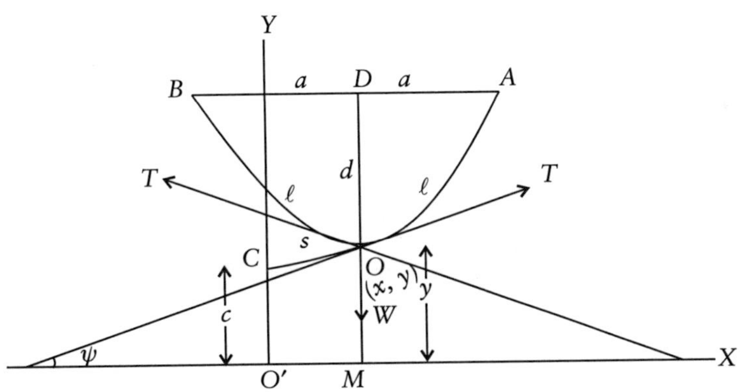


Due to symmetry, both the strings $AO$ and $BO$ will form equal catenaries intersecting at O. Let the catenary $AO$ be produced to C where C is the lowest point of the catenary. Let the tangent at O to either catenary make an angle ψ with the horizontal.

Let $T$ be the tension is either string at O. Thin, for equilibrium of the point O, on resolving vertically, we get

$$2\,T \sin \psi = w \qquad ...(1)$$

Referred to the coordinate axes $O'X$ and $O'Y$, let $y$ be the ordinate of the point O. Then, we have,

$$T = wy \qquad ...(2)$$

From (1) and (2), we get,

$$2\,wy \sin\psi = W \quad ...(3)$$

Let the arc length $CO = s$. Let $O'C = c$.

Then, $c$ is the parameter of the catenary $AC$.

We have, $s = c \tan\psi$

At the point O, $s = c \tan\psi$

$$= \frac{c\sin\psi}{\cos\psi} \quad \Rightarrow \quad = (c \sec\psi) \sin\psi$$

$$= y \sin\psi \qquad | \because y = c \sec\psi \quad ...(4)$$

From (3) and (4), we get, $2\,w\,s = W$

$$s = W/2w \quad ...(5)$$

We have, $y^2 = s^2 + c^2$

At the point O,

$$y^2 = s^2 + c^2 \quad ...(6)$$

At the point $A$,

$$(y + d)^2 = (s + \ell)^2 + c^2 \quad ...(7)$$

Subtracting (6) from (7), we get,

$$d^2 + 2yd = \ell^2 + 2s\ell$$

$$= \ell^2 - d^2 = 2\,(yd - s\ell) \quad ...(8)$$

We have, $y = c \cos h\,(x/c)$

At the point O,

$$y = c \cos h\,(x/c) \quad ...(9)$$

At the point $A$,

$$y + d = c \cos h\,(x{+}a\,/c) \quad ...(10)$$

Subtracting (9) from (10), we get,

$$d = c\,[\cos h\,(x{+}a\,/c) - \cos h\,(x/c)] \quad ...(11)$$

Again, we have, $s = c \sin h\,(x/c)$

At the point O,

$$s = c \sin h\,(x/c) \quad ...(12)$$

At the point $A$,

$$s + \ell = c \sin h\,(x{+}a\,/c) \quad ...(13)$$

Subtracting (12) from (13), we get,

$$\ell = c\,[\sin h\,(x{+}a\,/c) - \sin h\,(x/c)] \quad ...(14)$$

Substituting the values of $d$ and $\ell$ from (11) and (14) respectively in (8), we get,

$$\ell^2 - d^2 = 2c^2\,[\cos h\,(x/c)\,.\,\{(\cos h\,(x{+}a/c) - \cos h\,(x/c)\} - \sin h\,(x/c)\,\{\sin h\,(x{+}a/c) - \sin h\,(x/c)\}]$$

$$= 2c^2\,(\cos h\,(a/c) - 1] \quad ...(15)$$

$| \because \cos h\,A \cos h\,B - \sin h\,A \sin h\,B = \cos h\,(A - B);\ \cos h^2 A - \sin h^2 A = 1$

Again, tension at $A$ or $B$

$$= T_A = T_B = w\,(y + d)$$

$$= w\left(\frac{\ell^2 - d^2 + 2s\ell}{2d} + d\right) \qquad \text{|From (8)}$$

$$= w\left(\frac{\ell^2 + d^2 + 2s\ell}{2d}\right)$$

$$= \frac{1}{2d}\left[w(\ell^2 + d^2) + \ell W\right] \qquad \text{|From (5)}$$

**Example 16:** A heavy string hangs over two fixed small smooth pegs. The two ends of the string are free and the central portion hangs in a catenary. Show that the free ends of the string are on the directrix of the catenary. If the two pegs are on the same level and distance $2a$ apart, show that the equilibrium is impossible values the length of the string is equal to or greater than $2ae$.

**Sol.**

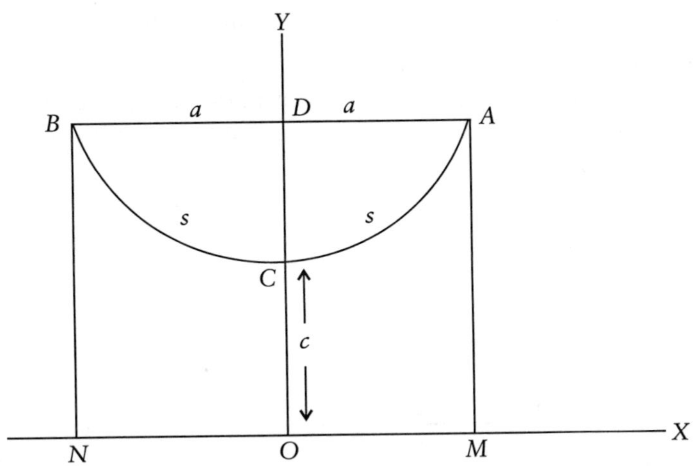


$A$ and $B$ are the two pegs such that $AB = 2a$. $MACBN$ is the string whose ends $M$ and $N$ are free and the central portion $ACB$ hangs in the form of a catenary. $NOX$ is the directrix of the catenary. C is the lowest point of the catenary. If $OC = c$, then $c$ is the parameter of the catenary.

Referred to the axes, as shown in the figure, let $y_1$ be the ordinate of $A$. Since the tension at $A$ supports the weight of hanging portion $AM$ of the string, therefore,

tension at $A$ = weight of hanging portion $AM$ of the string

$\Rightarrow wy_1 = w\,AM$, where $w$ is the weight per unit length of the string.

$\Rightarrow y_1 = AM$

Hence, the free end M of the string lies on the directrix of the catenary. Similarly, we can show that the free end $N$ lies on the directrix of the catenary.

Let arc length $CA = s$. Then, by symmetry, arc length $CB = s$.

Let $\ell$ be the length of the string. Then,

$$\ell = 2\,(y_1 + s)$$

$= 2\ (c \cos h\ \ a/c + c \sin h\ \ a/c)$ | $\because y = c \cos h\ \ x/c$; $s = c \sin h\ x/c$ and $x = a$ at $A$

$$= 2c\left[\frac{e^{a/c}+e^{-a/c}}{2}+\frac{e^{a/c}-e^{-a/c}}{2}\right]$$

$= 2\ ce^{a/c}$

Now, $\ell$ is minimum if $d\ell/dc = 0$ and $d^2\ell/dc^2$ is +ve

$d^2\ell/dc^2$ is +ve $\Rightarrow d\ell/dc = 0$

$$\Rightarrow \quad 2\left[e^{a/c} + ce^{a/c}\left(-\frac{a}{c^2}\right)\right] = 0 \qquad \Rightarrow 2e^{a/c}\left(1-\frac{a}{c}\right) = 0$$

$$\Rightarrow \quad 1 - a/c = 0 \qquad \Rightarrow a/c = 1 \qquad \Rightarrow \qquad c = a$$

$$\frac{d^2\ell}{dc^2} = 2\left[e^{a/c}\left(\frac{a}{c^2}\right) + e^{a/c}\left(-\frac{a}{c^2}\right)\left(1-\frac{a}{c}\right)\right] \quad \Rightarrow \quad = 2e^{a/c}\frac{a^2}{c^3}$$

At $c = a$,

$d^2\ell/dc^2 = 2e/a$ which is positive.

Hence, $\ell$ is minimum when $c = a$ and the required minimum value of $\ell$ is given by

$$\ell = 2a\ e^{a/a} = 2ae.$$

**Example 17:** A telegraph wire is made of a given material and such a length $\ell$ is stretched between two posts, distance $d$ apart and of the same height, as will produce the least possible tension at the posts. Show that

$$\ell = d/\lambda \sin h\ \lambda,$$

where $\lambda$ is given by the equation $\lambda \tan h\ \lambda = 1$.

**Sol.**

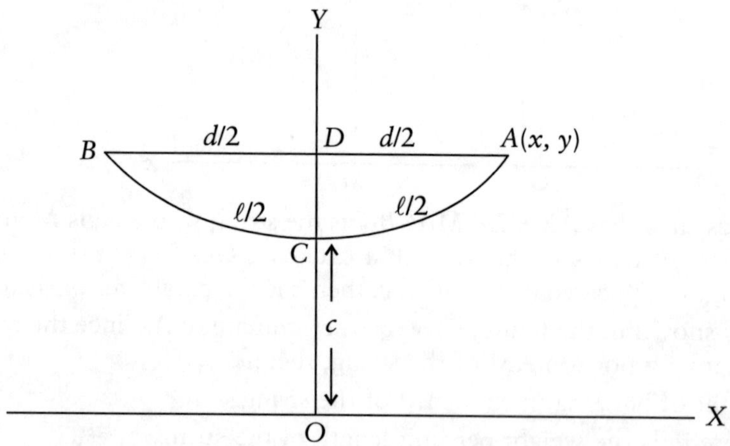


$A$ and $B$ are the two posts at the same height such that $AB = d$.

$D$ is the mid-point of $AB$.

$$\therefore AD = BD = d/2$$

Let $ACB$ be the catenary formed by the stretched telegraph wire $C$ is the lowest point of the catenary.

Arc $CA$ = Arc $CB$ = $\ell/2$.

Let $OC = c$, then $c$ is the parameter of the catenary.

Let $T$ be the tension at either post $A$ or $B$.

Then, $T = wy$

where $w$ is the weight per unit length of the wire and $(x, y)$ are the coordinates of the point $A$ referred to $OX$ and $OY$ as the coordinate axes, as shown in the figure.

$\Rightarrow \quad T = w\, c \cos h\, x/c \qquad |\because y = c \cos h\, x/c$

$\Rightarrow \quad T = w\, c \cos h\, (d/2c) \qquad |\because$ At $A$, $x = d/2$

If $T$ is minimum then $dT/dc = 0$ and $d^2T/dc^2$ is a positive quantity.

Now, $\quad dT/dc = 0$

$$\Rightarrow \quad w\left[\cos h\left(\frac{d}{2c}\right) + c \sin h\left(\frac{d}{2c}\right)\left(-\frac{d}{2c^2}\right)\right] = 0$$

$$\Rightarrow \quad \cos h\left(\frac{d}{2c}\right) - \frac{d}{2c}\sin h\left(\frac{d}{2c}\right) = 0 \qquad \Rightarrow \qquad \cos h\left(\frac{d}{2c}\right) = \frac{d}{2c}\sin h\left(\frac{d}{2c}\right)$$

$$\Rightarrow \quad \frac{d}{2c}\tan h\left(\frac{d}{2c}\right) = 1 \qquad \Rightarrow \qquad \lambda \tan h\lambda = 1 \text{ where } \lambda = \frac{d}{2c}$$

Again,
$$\frac{d^2T}{dc^2} = w\left[\sin h\left(\frac{d}{2c}\right)\left\{-\frac{d}{2c^2}\right\} + \frac{d}{2c^2}\sin h\left(\frac{d}{2c}\right) - \frac{d}{2c}\cos h\left(\frac{d}{2c}\right)\left\{-\frac{d}{2c^2}\right\}\right]$$

$$= \frac{wd^2}{4c^3}\cos h\left(\frac{d}{2c}\right)$$

which is a positive quantity for $c$ given by $dT/dc = 0$

Hence, $T$ is minimum when $\lambda \tan h\, \lambda = 1$,

where $\lambda = d/2c$.

We have, $\quad s = c \sin h\, (x/c)$

At the post $A$,

$$\frac{\ell}{2} = c \sin h\left(\frac{d}{2c}\right) \qquad \begin{vmatrix} \because \text{At } A, \\ s = \ell/2 \text{ and} \\ x = d/2 \end{vmatrix}$$

$$\Rightarrow \quad \ell = 2c \sin h\left(\frac{d}{2c}\right) \qquad \Rightarrow \; = d\frac{2c}{d}\sin h\left(\frac{d}{2c}\right)$$

$$= \frac{d}{\lambda}\sin h\lambda \qquad |\because \lambda = d/2c$$

**Example 18:** The end links of a uniform chain of length $\ell$ can slide on two smooth rods in the same vertical plane which are inclined in opposite directions at equal angles $\varphi$ to the vertical. Prone that the sag in the middle is $\ell/2 \tan \phi/2$

and also prove that the distance between the links is $\ell \cot \varphi \sin h^{-1} (\tan \varphi)$.

**Sol.**

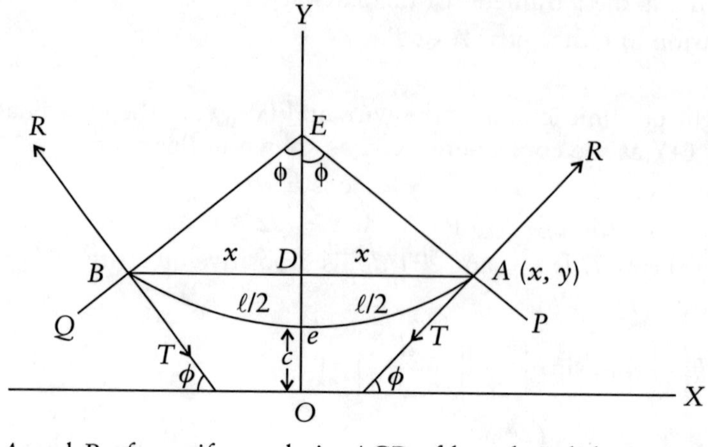


The end links $A$ and $B$ of a uniform chain $ACB$ of length $\ell$ slide on two smooth rods $EAP$ and $EBQ$ inclined at an angle $\psi$ to the vertical in the same vertical plane. The chain $ACB$ hangs in the form of a catenary with C as the vertex. So, due to symmetry,

arc $CA$ = arc $CB$ = $\ell/2$

The end link $A$ (or $B$) is in equilibrium under the action of the following two forces, namely:

(i) The normal reaction $R$ of the rod on the ring

and (ii) The tension $T$ in the chain at $A$ (or $B$).

So for the equilibrium of the ring $A$ (or $B$), these two forces most be equal and opposite.

By geometry, $\Psi = \varphi$

$\therefore$ For the point $A$ (or $B$), $\Psi = \varphi$

We have, $s = c \tan \Psi$

At the point $A$, $\ell/2 = c \tan \varphi$

$\Rightarrow \quad c = \ell/2 \cot \varphi$ ...(1)

$\therefore$ Sag in the middle $= y - c$

$= c \sec \varphi - c \quad \Rightarrow = c(\sec \varphi - 1) \quad \Rightarrow = \ell/2 \cot \varphi (\sec \varphi - 1)$

$$= \frac{\ell}{2}\frac{\cos\varphi}{\sin\varphi}\frac{1-\cos\varphi}{\cos\varphi} \quad \Rightarrow = \frac{\ell}{2}\frac{1-\cos\varphi}{\sin\varphi}$$

$$= \frac{\ell}{2}\frac{2\sin^2\frac{\varphi}{2}}{2\sin\frac{\varphi}{2}\cos\frac{\varphi}{2}} \quad \Rightarrow = \frac{\ell}{2}\tan\frac{\varphi}{2}$$

Also distance between the links $A$ and $B$ $= AB = 2x$

$= 2c \sin h^{-1}(s/c)$ | $\because s = c \sin h\,(s/c)$ <br> $\Rightarrow x = \sin h^{-1}\,(s/c)$

$$= 2\frac{\ell}{2}\cot\phi \sin h^{-1}\left(\frac{\frac{\ell}{2}}{\frac{\ell}{2}\cot\varphi}\right) \quad \Rightarrow \quad = \ell \cot\varphi \sin h^{-1} (\tan\varphi)$$

**Example 19:** A heavy chain of length $2\ell$ has one end tied at $A$ and the other end is attached to a small heavy ring which can slide on a rough horizontal rod which passes through $A$. If the weight of the ring be $n$ times the weight of the chain, show that the greatest possible distance from $A$ is

$\frac{2\ell}{\lambda}\log\left[\lambda + \sqrt{1+\lambda^2}\right]$, where $1/\lambda = \mu\,(2n + 1)$ and $\mu$ is the coefficient of function.

**Sol:**

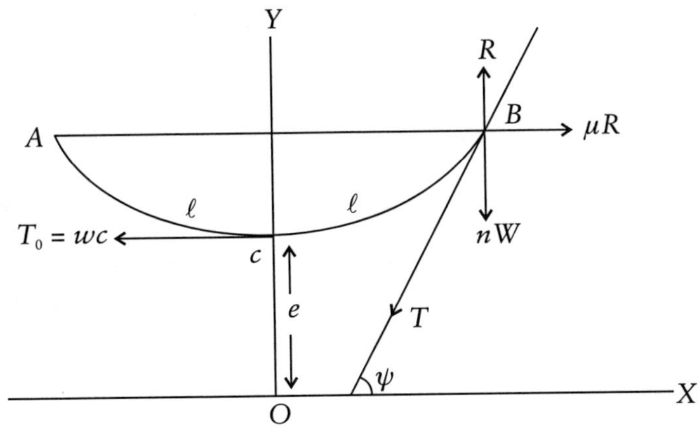


The distance $AB$ will be the greatest when the ring $B$ is in limiting equilibrium. In limiting equilibrium, the forces acting on the ring at $B$ are:

(i) The normal reaction $R$ of the rod on the ring.

(ii) Frictional force $\mu R$ acting along $AB$.

(iii) Weight $nw$ of the ring acting vertically downwards, where $w$ is the weight of the chain.

(iv) Tension $T$ at $B$ acting along the tangent at $B$ to the catenary.

Let the tangent at $B$ make an angle $\psi$ with $OX$. Then, resolving horizontally and vertically at $B$, we have

$$T\cos\psi = \mu R \qquad ...(1)$$

and $T$ sing $\psi = R - nw$

$\Rightarrow \quad T\sin\psi = R - 2\,n\ell w$ where $w$ is weight per unit length of the chain. ...(2)

Again, let us consider the equilibrium of the portion $CB$ of the chain whose arcual length is $\ell$. Then, we have,

$$T\cos\psi = T_0 = wc \qquad ...(3)$$

and $\quad T\sin\psi = w\ell$ ...(4)

From (1) and (3), we get,

$$\mu R = wc$$

$\Rightarrow \quad R = wc/\mu$ ...(5)

From (2),

$$R = T \sin \psi + 2\,n\,\ell w$$

$\Rightarrow \quad R = w\ell + 2\,n\,\ell w$ | From (4)

$\Rightarrow \quad wc/\mu = w\ell\,(2n + 1)$ | From (5)

$\Rightarrow \quad c = \mu\ell\,(2n + 1)$

$\Rightarrow \quad c = \ell/\lambda$ | $\because$ $1/\lambda = \mu\ (2\mu + 1)$ [Given] ...(6)

$\therefore$ Maximum span

$= AB \quad \Rightarrow = 2x \quad \Rightarrow = 2\,c\,\log\,(y+s\,/c)$

$$= 2c\log\frac{\sqrt{s^2+c^2}+s}{c} \qquad \Big|\because y^2 = s^2 + c^2$$

$$= 2\frac{\ell}{\lambda}\log\frac{\sqrt{\ell^2+\frac{\ell^2}{\lambda^2}}+\ell}{\frac{\ell}{\lambda}} \qquad \Big|\text{At B}$$

$$= 2\frac{\ell}{\lambda}\log\left[\sqrt{1+\lambda^2}+\lambda\right]$$

**Example 20:** If the end of a uniform inextensible string of length $\ell$, hanging freely under gravity, slide on a fixed rough horizontal rod whose coefficient of friction is $\mu$, show that at most they can rest at a distance.

$$\mu\ell\log\left[\frac{1+\sqrt{1+\mu^2}}{\mu}\right]$$

**Sol.**

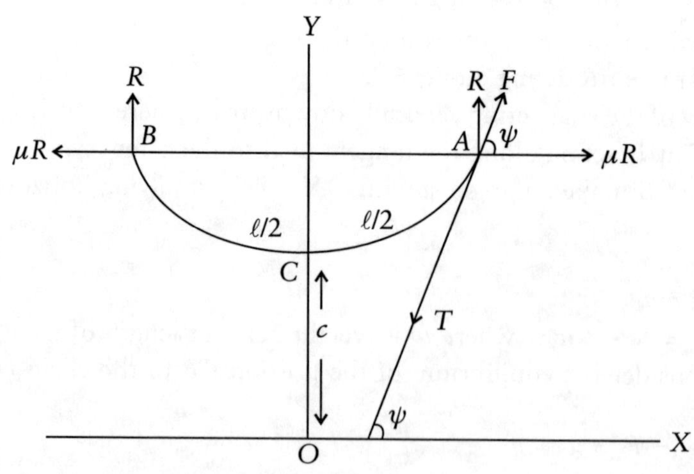


For maximum span, the end links $A$ and $B$ must be in limiting equilibrium. In limiting equilibrium, the forces acting on the end link $A$ are:

(i) The reaction $R$ of the rod on the end link $A$ perpendicular to the rod.

(ii) Force of friction $\mu R$ acting along $BA$.

(iii) Tension $T$ acting at $A$ along the tangent at $A$.

Let $F$ be the resultant of $R$ and $\mu R$. Then, for equilibrium, $T$ must be equal and opposite to $F$. Let the tangent at $A$ make an angle $\psi$ with the horizontal. Then,

$$\tan\psi = \frac{R}{\mu R} = \frac{1}{\mu} \quad ...(1)$$

$$\therefore \sec\psi = \sqrt{1+\tan^2\psi} \quad \Rightarrow \; = \sqrt{1+\frac{1}{\mu^2}} \quad |\text{From (1)}$$

$$= \frac{\sqrt{1+\mu^2}}{\mu} \quad ...(2)$$

$\therefore$ Maximum span $= AB$

$$= 2x \quad \Rightarrow \; = 2c\log(\sec\psi + \tan\psi)$$

$$= 2c\log\left(\frac{\sqrt{1+\mu^2}}{\mu} + \frac{1}{\mu}\right)$$

$$= 2c\log\frac{1+\sqrt{1+\mu^2}}{\mu} \quad ...(3)$$

Also, length of the string $\ell = 2s = 2c\tan\psi = 2c/\mu$ | From (1)

$$\Rightarrow \quad 2c = \mu\ell \quad ...(4)$$

From (3) and (4), maximum span $= \mu\ell\log\dfrac{1+\sqrt{1+\mu^2}}{\mu}$

**Example 21:** A length $\ell$ of a uniform chain has one end fixed at a height $h$ above a rough table, and rests in a vertical plane so that a portion of it lies in a straight line on the table. Prove that if the chain is on the point of slipping, the length on the table is

$$\ell + \mu h - \sqrt{[(\mu^2+1)h^2 + 2\mu\ell h]}, \text{ where } \mu \text{ is the coefficient of friction.}$$

**Sol.**

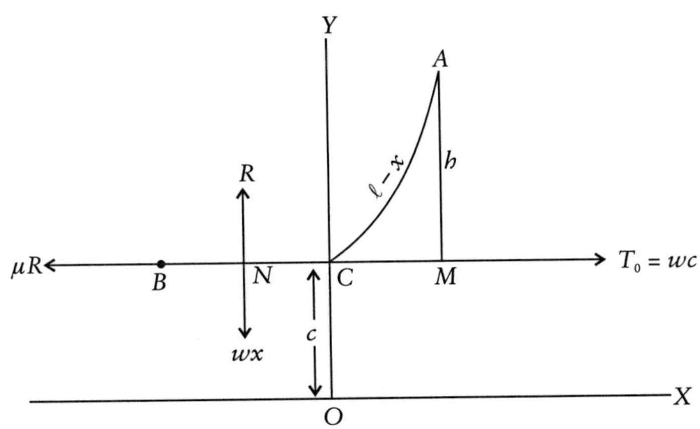

$ACB$ is the uniform chain of length $\ell$. The portion $BC = x$ (say) is on the table. The portion $CA = \ell - x$ is above the table and is hanging in the form of a catenary. C is the vertex of the catenary. $OC = c$ is the parameter of the catenary.

The portion $BC$ lying on the table is in equilibrium under the action of the following forces:

(i) The normal reaction $R$ acting vertically upwards at $N$, the middle point of $BC$.

(ii) The weight $wx$ of the portion $BC$ acting vertically downwards at $N$, where $w$ is the weight per unit length of the chain.

(iii) The tension $T_0 = wc$ acting horizontally at the lowest point $C$.

(iv) The frictional force $\mu R$ acting along $CB$.

Resolving these forces horizontally and vertically, we have

$$\mu R = T_0 = wc \qquad ...(1)$$

$$R = wx \qquad ...(2)$$

From (1) and (2), we get

$$c = \mu x \qquad ...(3)$$

We have, $y^2 = s^2 + c^2$

At the point $A$, $(c + h)^2 = (\ell - x) + c^2$

$\Rightarrow \quad c^2 + h^2 + 2ch = \ell^2 + x^2 - 2\ell x + c^2 \qquad \Rightarrow h^2 + 2ch = \ell^2 + x^2 - 2\ell x$

$\Rightarrow \quad h^2 + 2\,\mu xh = \ell^2 + x^2 - 2\ell x \qquad$ |From (3)

$\Rightarrow \quad x^2 - 2\,(\ell + \mu h)\,x + (\ell^2 - h^2) = 0$

$$\therefore \quad x = \frac{2(\ell+\mu h) \pm \sqrt{4(\ell+\mu h)^2 - 4(\ell^2 - h^2)}}{2} \qquad \Rightarrow x = (\ell + \mu h) - \sqrt{(\mu^2+1)h^2 + 2\mu\ell h}$$

discarding +ve sign before the radical as then $x > \ell$ which is not possible.

**Example 22:** One end of a uniform chain $ACB$ of length $\ell$ is attached to a fixed point $A$ at a height $h$ above a rough table. The portion $BC$ is straight and rests on the table in a vertical plane through $A$. If the end $C$ is free, prove that in the limiting equilibrium, the length $s$ of the hanging portion is given by the equation.

$$s^2 + 2\mu\, hs = h^2 + 2\mu\, h\ell$$

**Sol.**

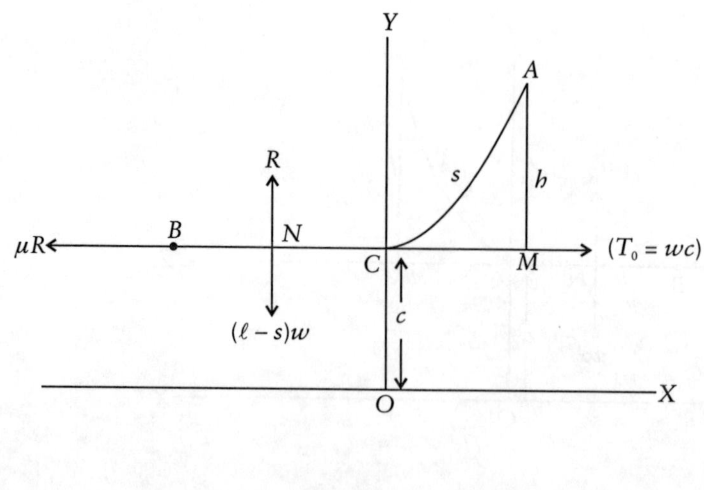

*ACB* is the uniform chain of length $\ell$. The portion $AC$ (= $s$) hangs in the form of a catenary. The portion $CB$ (= $\ell - s$) rests on the rough table. The portion $CB$ lying on the table is in equilibrium under the action of the following forces:

(i) The normal reaction $R$ acting vertically upwards at $N$, the middle point of $CB$.

(ii) The weight $(\ell - s)\, w$ of the portion $CB$ acting vertically downwards at $N$, where $w$ is the weight per unit length of the chain.

(iii) The tension $T_0 = wc$ acting horizontally at the lowest point C.

(iv) The force of friction $\mu R$ acting along $CB$.

Resolving these forces horizontally and vertically, we have,

$$\mu R = T_0 = wc \qquad ...(1)$$

$$R = (\ell - s)w \qquad ...(2)$$

From (1) and (2), we get, $\mu (\ell - s)w = wc$

$$\Rightarrow \quad c = \mu (\ell - s) \qquad ...(3)$$

We have, $y^2 = s^2 + c^2$

At the point $A$, $(c + h)^2 = c^2 + s^2$

$\Rightarrow \quad c^2 + h^2 + 2\,ch = c^2 + s^2 \qquad \Rightarrow h^2 + 2\,ch = s^2$

$\Rightarrow \quad h^2 + 2\mu\,(\ell - s)\,h^2 = s^2$ |From (3)

$\Rightarrow \quad h^2 + 2\mu\, h\, \ell = s^2 + 2\,\mu hs$

**Example 23:** A heavy chain of length $\ell$ rests with one end on a rough table and the other on a rough floor. It is stretched as far as possible so that the equilibrium is limiting. If $\mu$ be the coefficient of friction both for the table and the floor and $b$ the height of the table, show that the length on the floor is

$$\frac{\mu}{4}\left\{b + \frac{2\ell}{\mu} - \sqrt{b^2 + \frac{4b\ell}{\mu}}\right\} - \frac{b}{2\mu}, \text{provided that } \ell > b + \frac{b}{\mu}.$$

**Sol.**

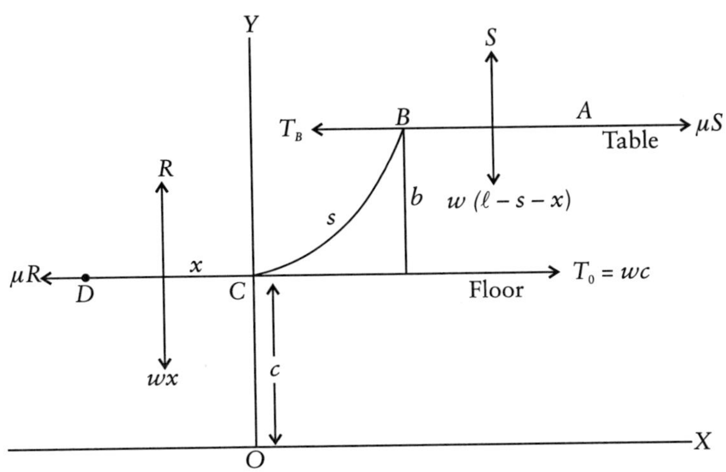


Let $ABCD$ be a heavy chain of length $\ell$. Let $CD$ (= $x$) be the portion of the chain lying on the floor. Let $BC$(= $s$) be the portion of the chain hanging in the form of a catenary. Let C be the vertex of the catenary. Let $OC = c$. Then, $c$ is the parameter of the catenary. Clearly, the remaining portion $AB$ ($= \ell - s - x$) will lie on the rough table.

According to the problem, the portions $CD$ and $AB$ of the string are in the limiting equilibrium. Therefore, the directions of the frictional forces $\mu R$ and $\mu S$ will be as shown in the figure. Let $w$ be the weight per unit length of the chain.

Consider the equilibrium of the portion $CD$ of the string lying on the floor. Resolving the forces vertically and horizontally, we get

$$R = wx \quad \text{...(1)}$$

$$\mu R = wc \quad \text{...(2)}$$

Substituting the value of $R$ from (1) in (2), we get,

$$\mu wx = wc$$

$$\Rightarrow \quad c = \mu x \quad \text{...(3)}$$

Let $T_B$ be the tension of the catenary $CB$ at $B$. Then,

$$T_B = wy$$

$$\Rightarrow \quad T_B = w(c + b) \qquad | \because \text{For the point } B,\ y = c + b \quad \text{...(4)}$$

Consider the equilibrium of the portion $AB$ of the string lying on the table. Resolving the forces vertically and horizontally, we get,

$$S = w(\ell - s - x) \quad \text{...(5)}$$

$$\mu S = T_B = w(c + b) \quad \text{...(6)}$$

Substituting the value of $S$ from (5) in (6), we get

$$\mu w(\ell - s - x) = w(c + b) \qquad \Rightarrow \mu(\ell - s - x) = c + b$$

$$\ell - s - x = c+b/\mu$$

$$s = \ell - x - c+b/\mu \quad \text{...(7)}$$

$$= \ell - x - \mu x+b/\mu \qquad |\text{From (3)}$$

$$= \ell - 2x - b/\mu$$

Clearly, $s > 0$

$$\therefore \quad \ell - 2x - b/\mu > 0 \quad \Rightarrow \quad \ell - b/\mu > 2x \quad \Rightarrow \quad \ell/2 - b/2\mu > x$$

$$\Rightarrow \quad x < \ell/2 - b/2\mu \quad \text{...(8)}$$

We have, $y^2 = s^2 + c^2$

For the point $B$, $(c + b)^2 = (\ell - x - c+b/\mu)^2 + c^2$

$$\Rightarrow \quad (\mu x + b)^2 = (\ell - x - \mu x+b/\mu)^2 + \mu^2x^2 \qquad |\text{From (3)}$$

$$\Rightarrow \quad \mu^2x^2 + b^2 + 2\mu bx = (\ell - x - x - b/\mu)^2 + \mu^2x^2$$

$$\Rightarrow \quad b^2 + 2\mu bx = (\ell - 2x - b/\mu)^2$$

$$= (\ell^2 + 4x^2 + b^2/\mu^2 - 4\ell x + 4bx/\mu - 2b\ell/\mu$$

$$\Rightarrow \quad 4x^2 - 2x(2\ell - 2b/\mu + b\mu) + \ell^2 + b^2/\mu^2 - 2b\ell/\mu - b^2 = 0$$

$$2(2\ell - 2b/\mu + b\mu) \pm$$

$$\Rightarrow \quad x = \frac{\sqrt{4\left(2\ell - \dfrac{2b}{\mu} + b\mu\right)^2 - 16\left(\ell^2 + \dfrac{b^2}{\mu^2} - \dfrac{2b\ell}{\mu} - b^2\right)}}{8}$$

$2(2\ell - 2b/\mu + b\mu) \pm$

$$= \frac{\sqrt{16\ell + 16\dfrac{b^2}{\mu^2} + 4b^2\mu^2 - 32\dfrac{b\ell}{\mu} - 16b^2 + 16b\ell\mu - 16\ell^2 - \dfrac{16b^2}{\mu} + \dfrac{32b\ell}{\mu} + 16b^2}}{8}$$

$$= \frac{2\left(2\ell - \dfrac{2b}{\mu} + b\mu\right) \pm 2\sqrt{b^2\mu^2 + 4b\ell\mu}}{8} \qquad \Rightarrow = \frac{2\ell - \dfrac{2b}{\mu} + b\mu \pm \sqrt{b^2\mu^2 + 4b\ell\mu}}{4}$$

$$= \frac{\ell}{2} - \frac{b}{2\mu} + \frac{b\mu}{4} \pm \sqrt{\frac{b^2\mu^2}{16} + \frac{b\ell\mu}{4}} \qquad \Rightarrow = \frac{\ell}{2} + \frac{b\mu}{4} \pm \sqrt{\frac{\mu^2}{16}\left(b^2 + \frac{4b\ell}{\mu}\right)} - \frac{b}{2\mu}$$

$$= \frac{\mu}{4}\left(\frac{2\ell}{\mu} + b\right) \pm \frac{\mu}{4}\sqrt{\left(b^2 + \frac{4b\ell}{\mu}\right)} - \frac{b}{2\mu} \qquad \Rightarrow = \frac{\mu}{4}\left[\frac{2\ell}{\mu} + b \pm \sqrt{b^2 + \frac{4b\ell}{\mu}}\right] - \frac{b}{2\mu}$$

$$= \frac{\mu}{4}\left[b + \frac{2\ell}{\mu} - \sqrt{b^2 + \frac{4b\ell}{\mu}}\right] - \frac{b}{2\mu} \qquad \text{...(9)}$$

Discarding –ve sign as otherwise $x$ will be greater than $\ell/2 - b/2\mu$ which is impossible as it contradicts (8).

Again, the hanging portion $s$ of the string must be greater than $b$.

Therefore, $s > b$

$$\Rightarrow \quad \ell - 2x - b/\mu > b \quad \Rightarrow \quad \ell > b + b/\mu + 2x \quad \Rightarrow \quad \ell > b + b/\mu$$

Aliter [For $\ell > b + b/\mu$]

$x > 0$

$$\Rightarrow \quad \frac{\mu}{4}\left[b + \frac{2\ell}{\mu} - \sqrt{b^2 + \frac{4b\ell}{\mu}}\right] - \frac{b}{2\mu} > 0 \quad \Rightarrow \quad \frac{\mu}{4}\left[b + \frac{2\ell}{\mu} - \sqrt{b^2 + \frac{4b\ell}{\mu}}\right] > \frac{b}{2\mu}$$

$$\Rightarrow \quad \frac{\mu}{2}\left[b + \frac{2\ell}{\mu} - \sqrt{b^2 + \frac{4b\ell}{\mu}}\right] > \frac{b}{\mu} \quad \Rightarrow \quad b + \frac{2\ell}{\mu} - \sqrt{b^2 + \frac{4b\ell}{\mu}} > \frac{2b}{\mu^2}$$

$$\Rightarrow \quad b + \frac{2\ell}{\mu} - \frac{2b}{\mu^2} > \sqrt{b^2 + \frac{4b\ell}{\mu}} \quad \Rightarrow \quad \left(b + \frac{2\ell}{\mu} - \frac{2b}{\mu^2}\right)^2 > b^2 + \frac{4b\ell}{\mu}$$

$$\Rightarrow \quad b + \frac{4\ell^2}{\mu^2} + \frac{4b^2}{\mu^4} + \frac{4b\ell}{\mu} - \frac{8b\ell}{\mu^3} - \frac{4b^2}{\mu^2} > b^2 + \frac{4b\ell}{\mu} \quad \Rightarrow \quad \frac{4\ell^2}{\mu^2} + \frac{4b^2}{\mu^4} - \frac{8b\ell}{\mu^3} - \frac{4b^2}{\mu^2} > 0$$

$$\Rightarrow \ell^2 + \frac{b^2}{\mu^2} - \frac{2b\ell}{\mu} - b^2 > 0 \Rightarrow \quad \ell^2 + \frac{b^2}{\mu^2} - \frac{2b\ell}{\mu} > b^2$$

$$\Rightarrow \left(\ell - \frac{b}{\mu}\right)^2 > b^2 \Rightarrow \quad \ell - \frac{b}{\mu} > b \quad \Rightarrow \quad \ell > b + \frac{b}{\mu}$$

**Example 24:** Show that the length of an endless chain which will hang over a circular pulley of radius $a$ so as to be in contact with two-thirds of the circumference of the pulley is

$$a\left[\frac{3}{\log\left(2+\sqrt{3}\right)} + \frac{4\pi}{3}\right]$$

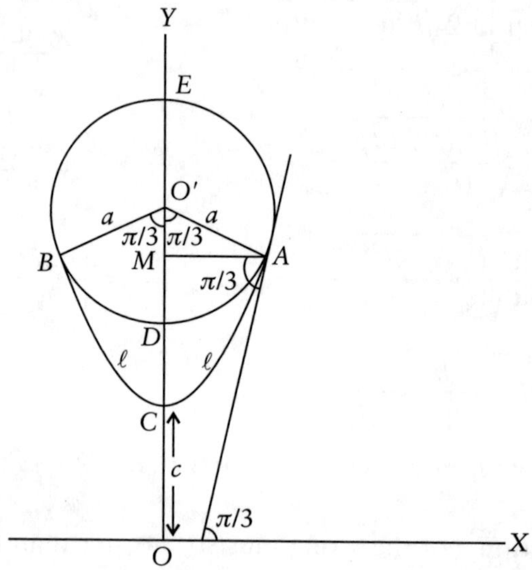


Let $AEBCA$ be an endless chain hanging over a circular pulley $AEBDA$ of centre O and radius $a$. Since the chain is in contact with two-thirds of the circumference of the pulley, therefore, length of portion $AEB$ of the chain $= 2/3\ (2\pi a)$

$= 4\pi a/3$ ...(1)

The remaining portion $ACB$ of the chain will hang in the form of a catenary with its vertex at the lowest point C. Its length is therefore twice the length of $AC$ (or $BC$).

$A$ and $B$ are the points where the chain separates from the pulley. Clearly, at these points the circle and the catenary will have common tangents.

Length of portion $ADB$ of the pulley = 1/3 of the circumference of the circle

∴ Angle subtended by it at the centre $O'$

$= 1/3\ (2\pi) = 2\pi/3$ ...(2)

By symmetry,

$\angle AO'M = \angle BO'M = 1/2\ (2\pi/3) = \pi/3$ ...(3)

By Geometry, the tangent at $A$ (or $B$) makes an angle $\pi/3$ with the horizontal.

Let $\ell$ be the length of arc $AC$ of the catenary. We have, $\quad \ell = c \tan \psi$

At the point $A$, $\ell = c \tan 60°$ $\Rightarrow$ $\ell = c\sqrt{3}$

$\Rightarrow$ $c = \ell/\sqrt{3}$ ...(4)

In right triangle $O'MA$, $\Rightarrow$ $AM = a \sin \pi/3$

$a\sqrt{3}/2$ ...(5)

We have, $x = c \log (\sec \psi + \tan \psi)$

At the point $A$,

$$\frac{a\sqrt{3}}{2} = \frac{\ell}{\sqrt{3}}\log\left(\sec\frac{\pi}{3} + \tan\frac{\pi}{3}\right) \Rightarrow \frac{a\sqrt{3}}{2} = \frac{\ell}{\sqrt{3}}\log(2+\sqrt{3})$$

$$\Rightarrow \quad \ell = \frac{3a}{2\log(2+\sqrt{3})} \qquad ...(6)$$

$\therefore$ Length of the endless chains $AEBCA$

= Length of the arc $AEB$ of the circle + length of the arc $ACB$ of the catenary

$= 4\pi a/3 + 2\ell$

$$= \frac{4\pi a}{3} + \frac{3a}{\log(2+\sqrt{3})} \qquad |\text{From (6)}$$

$$= a\left[\frac{4\pi}{3} + \frac{3}{\log(2+\sqrt{3})}\right]$$

**Example 25:** A uniform string of length $2b\beta$ is placed on a smooth circle of radius $b$ fixed in a vertical plane. The length of the string is greater than the circumference of the circle and portion of the string hangs in the form of a catenary below the circle. If $2(\pi - \alpha)\, b$ is the length of the string in contact with the circle, prove that $\sin^2 \alpha \sec \alpha = (\alpha - \beta - \pi) \cos h^{-1} (\sec \alpha)$

**Sol.**

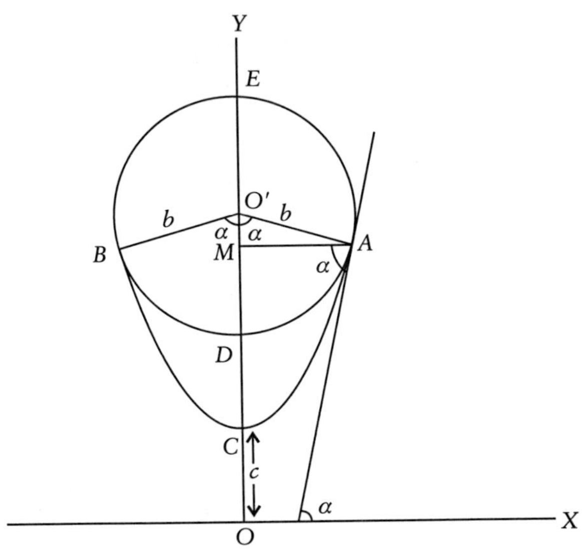

Let $AEBDA$ be a uniform string of length $2b\beta$ placed on a smooth circle $AEBDA$ of centre $O'$ and radius $b$. The portion $ACB$ of the string hangs in the form of a catenary below the circle with its vertex at the lowest point $C$.

Length of the string $AEB$ in contact with the circle $= 2(\pi - \alpha)b$

$\therefore$ Length of portion $ADB$ of the circle

$$= 2\pi b - 2(\pi - \alpha)b$$

$$= 2\alpha b \qquad \text{...(1)}$$

$\therefore$ Angle subtended by the portion $ADB$ of the circle at the centre

$$= \frac{2\alpha b}{b} \qquad \left|\because \text{Angle} = \frac{\text{Arc}}{\text{Radius}}\right.$$

$$= 2\alpha \qquad \text{...(2)}$$

By symmetry, $\angle AO'M = \angle BO'M = \alpha$

$A$ and $B$ are the points where the string separates from the circle. Clearly, at these points, the circle and the catenary will have common tangents.

By Geometry, the tangent at $A$ (or $B$) makes an angle $\alpha$ with the horizontal.

Length of arc $ACB$ of the string

$$= 2b\beta - 2(\pi - \alpha)b \qquad \Rightarrow = 2b(\alpha + \beta - \pi)$$

By symmetry

$$\text{Arc } CA = \text{Arc } CB = 1/2 \,.\, 2b(\alpha + \beta - \pi)$$

$$= b(\alpha + \beta - \pi) \qquad \text{...(3)}$$

We have, $s = c \tan \psi$

At the point $A$, $b(\alpha + \beta - \pi) = c \tan \alpha$

$$\Rightarrow \quad c = \frac{b(\alpha+\beta-\pi)}{\tan\alpha} \qquad \text{...(4)}$$

In right triangle $O'MA$,

$$AM = b \sin \alpha \qquad \text{...(5)}$$

We have, $s = c \sin h\,(x/c) = c \tan \psi$

$\Rightarrow \quad \sin h\,(x/c) = \tan \psi$

At the point $A$, $\sin h\,(b \sin \alpha/c) = \tan \psi$

$$\Rightarrow \quad \sin h\left\{\frac{b\sin\alpha\tan\alpha}{b(\alpha+\beta-\pi)}\right\} = \tan\alpha \qquad \text{|From (4)}$$

$$\Rightarrow \quad \sin h\left(\frac{\sin^2\alpha\sec\alpha}{\alpha+\beta-\pi}\right) = \tan\alpha$$

$$\Rightarrow \quad \sin^2\alpha \sec\alpha = (\alpha+\beta-\pi)\sin h^{-1}(\tan\alpha)$$

$$\Rightarrow \quad \sin^2\alpha\sec\alpha = (\alpha+\beta-\pi)\cos h^{-1}\sqrt{1+\tan^2\alpha} \qquad \left|\because \sin h^{-1}x = \cos h^{-1}\sqrt{1+x^2}\right.$$

$$\Rightarrow \quad \sin^2\alpha\sec\alpha = (\alpha+\beta-\pi)\cos h^{-1}(\sec\alpha)$$

**Example 26:** A uniform string of weight $w$ is suspended from two points at the same level and a weight $w'$ is attached to its lowest point. If $\alpha$ and $\beta$ are now the inclinations to the horizontal of tangents at the highest and the lowest points, prove that

$$\frac{\tan\alpha}{\tan\beta} = 1 + \frac{w}{w'}$$

**Sol:** The string initially hangs in the form of catenary $AC$, $B$, where $A$ and $B$ are the two points of suspension at the same level. When the weight $w'$ is attached to its lowest point $C_1$, then $C_1$ descends to $C_2$ vertically such that

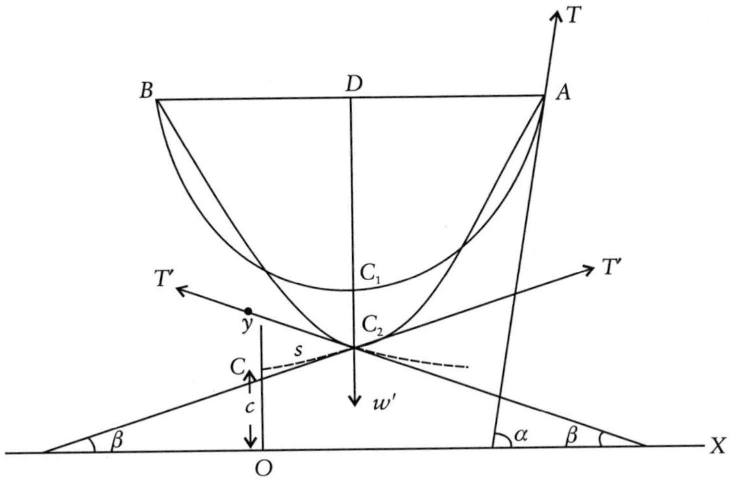


$AC_2 = BC_2 = \ell = AC_1 = BC_1$, where $2\ell$ is the length of the given string.

By symmetry, $A\ C_2$ and $B\ C_2$ are parts of equal catenaries. Let $C$ be the lowest point of the catenary of which $A\ C_2$ is a portion. Let arc $C\ C_2 = s$ and $w$ be the weight per unit length of the string.

$$\therefore\ w = (2\ell)\ w$$

$$\Rightarrow \quad w = \mathrm{w}/2\ell \qquad ...(1)$$

Let $T$, $T'$ be the tensions at $A$ and $C_2$ respectively. Let $OC = c$. Then, c is the parameter of the catenary.

We have, $\quad s = c \tan\psi$

At the point $A$,

$$s + \ell = c \tan\alpha \quad | \therefore \text{ tangent at } A \text{ makes an angle } \alpha \text{ with the horizontal.} \qquad ...(2)$$

At the point $C_2$,

$$s = c \tan\beta \quad | \therefore \text{ tangent at } C_2 \text{ makes an angle } \beta \text{ with the horizontal.} \qquad ...(3)$$

Dividing (1) by (2), we get

$$s{+}\ell/s = c \tan\alpha/c \tan\beta$$

$$\Rightarrow \quad 1{+}\ell/s = \tan\alpha/c_2 \tan\beta \qquad ...(4)$$

Now consider the equilibrium of the point $C_2$. Forces acting on $C_2$ are $T'$, $T'$ and $w'$ as shown in the figure.

Resolving vertically, we get

$$2T' \sin \beta = w' \quad ...(5)$$

But $T' = wy = wc \sec \beta$ ...(6)

From (5) and (6), we get,

$$2\, wc \sec \beta \sin \beta = w'$$

$\Rightarrow \quad 2\, wc \tan \beta = w' \quad \Rightarrow 2\, ws = w'$

$\Rightarrow \quad s = w'/2w$ ...(7)

From (4) and (7), we get,

$$\tan \alpha / \tan \beta = 1 + 2\ell w/w'$$

$\Rightarrow \quad \tan \alpha/\tan \beta = 1 + w/w'$ | From (1)

**Example 27:** A uniform chain of length $\ell$ and weight $W$, hangs between two fixed points at the same level, and weight $w'$ is attached at the middle point. If $k$ be the say in the middle, prove that the pull on either point of support is

$$\frac{k}{2\ell}w + \frac{\ell}{4k}w' + \frac{\ell}{8k}w$$

**Sol.**

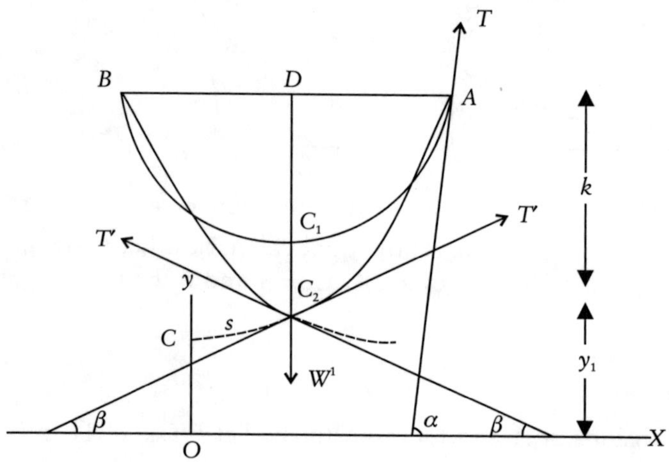


Let $w$ be the weight per unit length of the chain of length $\ell$. Then,

$$W = w\ell \quad ...(1)$$

The chain initially hangs in the form of catenary $A\,C_1\,B$, where $A$ and $B$ are the two points of suspension at the same level. When the weight $W'$ is attached to its lowest point $C_1$, then $C_1$ descends to $C_2$ vertically such that

$$A\,C_2 = B\,C_2 = \ell/2 = A\,C_1 = B\,C_1$$

By symmetry, $A\,C_2$ and $B\,C_2$ are parts of equal catenaries. Let $C$ be the lowest point of the catenary of which $A\,C_2$ is a part. Let arc $C\,C_2 = s$.

We have, $\quad s = c \tan \psi$

At the point $A$,

$$s + \ell/2 = c \tan \alpha \quad ...(2)$$

At the point $C_2$,

$$s = c \tan \beta \qquad ...(3)$$

Dividing (2) by (3), we get,

$$1 + \ell/2s = \tan \alpha/\tan \beta \qquad ...(4)$$

Now consider the equilibrium of the point $C_2$. Forces acting on $C_2$ and $T'$, $T'$ and $W'$ as shown in the figure. Resolving vertically, we get,

$$2\ T' \sin \beta = W' \qquad ...(5)$$

But $\quad T' = wy = wc \sec \beta \qquad ...(6)$

From (5) and (6), we get, $\quad 2\ wc \sec \beta \sin \beta = W'$

$\Rightarrow \quad 2\ wc \tan \beta = W' \qquad \Rightarrow 2\ ws = W'$

$\Rightarrow \quad s = W'/2w \qquad ...(7)$

From (4) and (7), we get,

$$\frac{\tan\alpha}{\tan\beta} = 1 + \frac{2\ell w}{2W'} \qquad \Rightarrow \qquad = 1 + \frac{\ell w}{W'}$$

$$= 1 + \frac{W}{W'} \qquad \text{|From (1)} \qquad ...(8)$$

From (4) and (8), we get,

$$1 + \frac{\ell}{2s} = 1 + \frac{W}{W'} \qquad \Rightarrow \qquad \frac{\ell}{2s} = \frac{W}{W'}$$

$$\Rightarrow \qquad s = \frac{\ell W'}{2W} \qquad ...(9)$$

Let $y_1$ be the ordinate of $C_2$. Then, ordinate of $A = y_1 + k$

We have, $\quad y^2 = s^2 + c^2$

For the point $C_2$,

$$y_1^2 = s^2 + c^2 \qquad ...(10)$$

For the point $A$,

$$(y_1 + k)^2 = (s + \ell/2)^2 + c^2 \qquad ...(11)$$

Subtracting (10) from (11), we get,

$$2k\ y_1 + k^2 = s\ell + \ell^2/4 \qquad \Rightarrow 2y_1 + k = s\ell/k + \ell^2/4k$$

$$\Rightarrow \qquad 2y_1 + 2k = s\ell/k + \ell^2/4k + k \qquad \Rightarrow y_1 + k = s\ell/2k + \ell^2/8k + k/2$$

$$= \ell/2k \cdot \ell W'/2W + \ell^2/8k + k/2 \qquad \text{|From (9)}$$

$$= \ell^2 W'/4kW + \ell^2/8k + k/2 \qquad ...(12)$$

$\therefore$ Tension at $A$ (or $B$) $\quad = w(y_1 + k)$

$$\frac{W}{\ell}\left(\frac{\ell^2 W'}{4kW} + \frac{\ell^2}{8k} + \frac{k}{2}\right) \qquad \text{|From (1) and (12)}$$

$$= \frac{\ell W'}{4k} + \frac{\ell W}{8k} + \frac{kW}{2\ell}$$

**Example 28:** A weight $W$ is suspended from a fixed point by a uniform string of length $\ell$ and weight $w$ per unit length. It is drawn aside by a horizontal force $P$. Show that in the position of equilibrium, the distance of $W$ from the vertical through the fixed point is

$$\frac{P}{w}\left[\sin h^{-1}\left(\frac{W+\ell W}{P}\right)-\sin h^{-1}\left(\frac{W}{P}\right)\right]$$

**Sol.**

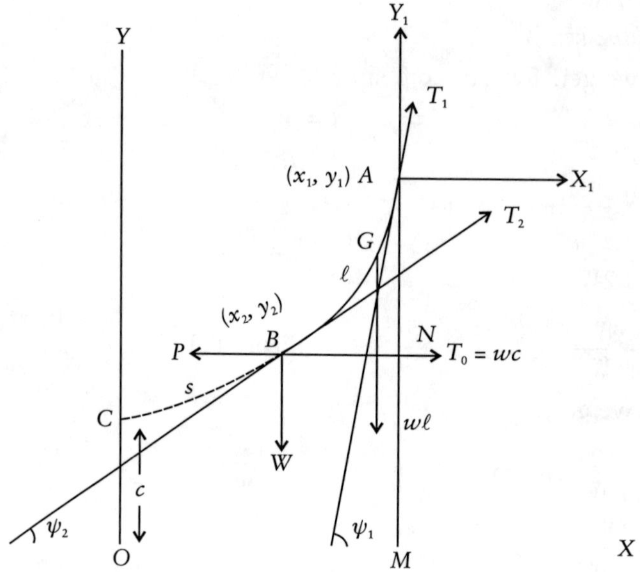


Let $AB$ be the given uniform string of length $\ell$ and weight $w$ per unit length suspended from a fixed point $A$ and a weight $W$ suspended from the end $B$. The weight $W$ is drawn aside by a horizontal force $P$ acting at $B$. Let $C$ be the lowest point of the catenary of which $AB$ is a part. Let $CB = s$ and $OC = c$. Then, $c$ is the parameter of the catenary $ABC$.

Let $T_1$ and $T_2$ be the tensions of the string at $A$ and $B$ making angles $\psi_1$ and $\psi_2$ with the horizontal respectively.

Consider the equilibrium of the point $B$. The forces acting on $B$ are $P$, $W$ and $T_2$. Clearly, the tension at $B$ must balance the resultant of $P$ and $W$. So,

$$\tan \psi_2 = W/P \quad \text{...(1)}$$

Let $X_1$ and $Y_1$ be the horizontal and vertical components of tension $T_1$ at $A$. Consider the equilibrium of the string $AB$. Resolving the forces acting on the string $AB$ horizontally and vertically, we get,

$$X_1 = P \quad \text{...(2)}$$

$$Y_1 = W + w\ell \quad \text{...(3)}$$

$$\therefore \tan \psi_1 = Y_1/X_1 = W+W\ell\ /P \quad \text{...(4)}$$

Let the coordinates of $A$ and $B$ be $(x_1, y_1)$ and $(x_2, y_2)$ respectively referred to the coordinate axes as shown in the figure.

We have,

$s = c \sin h\ (x/c) = c \tan \psi \qquad \Rightarrow \sin h\ (x/c) = \tan \psi$

At the point $A$, $\quad \sin h\ (x_1/c) = \tan \psi_1$

$\Rightarrow \quad \sin h\ (x_1/c) = W+\ell w/P$ |From (4)

$\Rightarrow \quad x_1 = c \sin h^{-1}(W+\ell w/P)$ ...(5)

At the point $B$, $\quad \sin h\ (x_2/c) = \tan \psi_2$

$\Rightarrow \quad \sin h\ (x_2/c) = W/P$ |From (1)

$\Rightarrow \quad x_2 = c \sin h^{-1}\ (W/P)$ ...(6)

We know that the horizontal component of tension at any point is constant and equal to $T_0 = wc$.

But the horizontal component of tension at $B$ is $P$.

$\therefore \quad wc = P$

$\Rightarrow \quad c = P/w$ ...(7)

$\therefore$ Distance of $W$ from the vertical through the fixed point $A$

$= BN \quad \Rightarrow \quad = x_1 - x_2$

$= c \sin h^{-1}\ (W+\ell w\ /P) - c \sin h^{-1}\ (W/P)$ |From (5) and (6)

$$= c\left[\sin h^{-1}\left(\frac{W+\ell w}{P}\right) - \sin h^{-1}\left(\frac{W}{P}\right)\right]$$

$$= \frac{P}{w}\left[\sin h^{-1}\left(\frac{W+\ell w}{P}\right) - \sin h^{-1}\left(\frac{W}{P}\right)\right]$$ | From (7)

**Example 29:** A ring of weight $wb$ is attached to the mid-point of a string of length $\ell$ and weight $w\ell$, which hangs symmetrically over two smooth pegs in the same horizontal line distance $2a$ apart, the ends of the string hanging vertically. Show that the parameter $c$ of the catenary is given by

$$b + \ell = e^{a/c}\left[b + \sqrt{4c^2 + b^2}\right]$$

**Sol.**

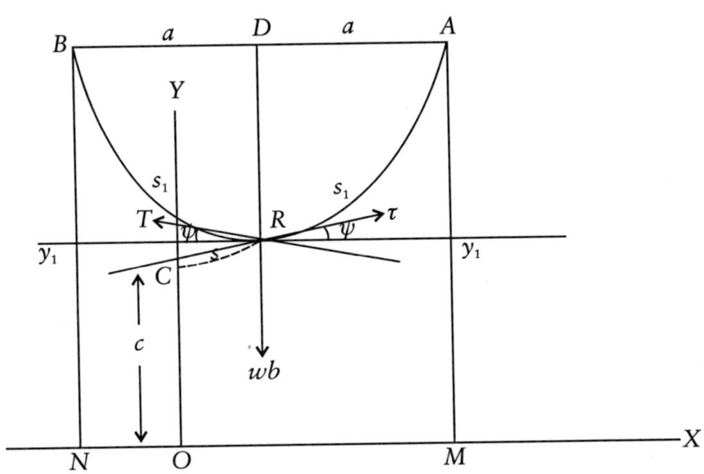

$A$ and $B$ are the two smooth pegs in the same horizontal line distant $2a$ apart. $R$ is the position of the ring. Let $C$ be the lowest point of the catenary of which $AR$ is a part.

Let arc $CR = s$ and arc $RA = s_1$. Referred to the axes, as shows in the figure, let the coordinates of the points $R$ and $A$ be $(x, y)$ and $(x_1, y_1)$ respectively.

Since the tension at $A$ supports the weight of length $AM$ of the string, therefore,

$$T_A = w \cdot AM$$
$$\Rightarrow \quad wy_1 = w \cdot AM$$
$$\Rightarrow \quad AM = y_1$$

Hence, the free end $M$ lies on the directrix $NM$.

Similarly, the free end N lies on the directrix $NM$.

Let us consider the equilibrium of $R$. Resolving the forces vertically, we get,

$$T \sin \psi + T \sin \psi = wb \quad \Rightarrow 2T \sin \psi = wb$$
$$\Rightarrow \quad 2wy \sin \psi = wb \qquad | \because T = wy$$
$$\Rightarrow \quad 2wc \sec \psi \sin \psi = wb \qquad | \because y = c \sec \psi$$
$$\Rightarrow \quad 2wc \tan \psi = wb$$
$$\Rightarrow \quad 2ws = wb \qquad | \because s = c \tan \psi$$
$$\Rightarrow \quad 2s = b$$
$$\Rightarrow \quad s = b/2 \qquad ...(1)$$

We have, $y^2 = s^2 + c^2$

At the point $R$,

$$y^2 = b^2/4 + c^2 \qquad |\text{From } (1)$$
$$\Rightarrow \quad y^2 = \frac{4c^2 + b^2}{4}$$
$$\Rightarrow \quad y = \frac{\sqrt{4c^2 + b^2}}{2} \qquad ...(2)$$

Again, we have, for the point $R$,

$$y = c \cos h \frac{x}{c} \qquad \Rightarrow s = c \sin h \frac{x}{c}$$

Adding, we get

$$y + s = c\left(\cos h \frac{x}{c} + \sin h \frac{x}{c}\right) \quad \Rightarrow = c\left(\frac{e^{x/c} + e^{-x/c}}{c} + \frac{e^{x/c} - e^{-x/c}}{c}\right) = c\, e^{x/c}$$

$$\Rightarrow \quad \frac{\sqrt{4c^2 + b^2}}{2} + \frac{b}{2} = ce^{x/c} \qquad |\text{From (1) and (2)}$$

$$\Rightarrow \quad \frac{1}{2}\left(b + \sqrt{4c^2 + b^2}\right) = ce^{x/c} \qquad ...(3)$$

Similarly, for the point $A$, we have

$$y_1 = c \cos h\,(x + a/c) \qquad \Rightarrow s + s_1 = c \sin h\,(x + a/c)$$

Adding, we get

$$s + s_1 + y_1 = c\left[\sin h\frac{x+a}{c} + \cos h\frac{x+a}{c}\right]$$

$$\Rightarrow \quad s + \frac{1}{2}\ell = c\, e^{x+a/c} \qquad \left|\because s_1 + y_1 = \frac{1}{2}\ell\right.$$

$$\Rightarrow \quad \frac{b+\ell}{2} = c\, e^{x+a/c} \qquad \text{| From (1)} \qquad \ldots(4)$$

Dividing (4) by (3), we get,

$$\frac{b+\ell}{b+\sqrt{4c^2+b^2}} = e^{a/c} \quad \Rightarrow b+\ell = e^{a/c}\left[b+\sqrt{4c^2+b^2}\right]$$

## EXERCISE 1(A)

1. It $T$ be the tension at any point $P$ of a catenary, and $T_0$ that at the lowest point $C$, prove that $T^2 - T_0^2 = W^2$, $W$ being the weight of the arc $CP$ of the catenary.
2. If the normal drawn at any point $P$ of a common catenary meets the directrix at $Q$, then show that $PQ = \rho$, where $\rho$ is the radius of curvature of the catenary at $P$.
3. Prove that for the catenary $y = c \cos h\, x/c$, the perpendicular dropped from the foot of the ordinate upon the tangent is of constant length.
4. Prove that if a uniform inextensible chain hangs freely under gravity, the difference of the tensions at two points varies as the difference of their heights above a horizontal line.
5. Show that the tangents at any two points $P$ and $Q$ of a common catenary intersect on the centre of gravity $G$ of the arc $PQ$.
6. A uniform chain of length 125 cm has its extremities fixed at two points in the same horizontal line. If the tension at each support is three times of that at the lowest point, then prove that the distance between the points is

$$\frac{125}{\sqrt{8}}\log\left(3+\sqrt{8}\right)$$

7. A uniform chain of length $\ell$, is suspended from two points $A$, $B$ in the same horizontal line. If the tension at A is twice that at the lowest point, show that the span $AB$ is

$$\frac{\ell}{\sqrt{3}}\log_e\left(2+\sqrt{3}\right)$$

8. The extremities $A$ and $B$ of a heavy uniform string of length $\ell$ are attached to two small rings which can slide on a smooth horizontal wire. Each of these rings is acted upon by a horizontal force $F = 1/2\, w\ell$, where $w$ is weight per unit length of the string. Prove that the span is $\ell \log(1 + \sqrt{2})$.
9. A heavy uniform chain is suspended from two fixed points $A$ and $B$ in the same horizontal line, and the tangent at $A$ makes an angle 45° with the horizontal. Prove that the depth of the lowest point of the chain below $AB$ is to the length of the chain as $(\sqrt{2} - 1) : 2$.

10. A chain is suspended in a vertical plane from two fixed points $A$ and $B$ which lie in a horizontal line 462 metres apart. If the tangent to the chain at $A$ is inclined a an angle $\tan^{-1} 3/4$ to the horizontal, find the length of the chain. (Given $\log \ell^2 = 0.693$)
[**Ans.** 500 metres]
11. A uniform chain has its ends fixed at $A$ and $B$ where $B$ is 20 feet above the level of $A$, and no part of the chain is below $A$. At $A$ the chain is inclined at $\sec^{-1}(5/3)$ to the horizontal and the tension there is equal to the weight of 100 feet of the chain. Prove that the length of the chain is 33 feet 11 inches to the nearest inch.
12. A heavy uniform chain $AB$ hangs freely under gravity with the end $A$ fixed and the other end $B$ attached by a light string $BC$ to a fixed point $C$ at the same level as $A$. The lengths of the string and chain are such that the ends of the chain at $A$ and $B$ makes angles of 60° and 30° with the horizontal. Prove that the ratio of these lengths is $(\sqrt{3} - 1) : 1$.
13. A string of length $\ell$ is attached to a fixed point $A$, and the other end $B$ is pulled with a force $wa$ inclined at an angle $\alpha$ to the horizontal, $w$ being the weight per unit length of the string. Show that the vertical distance of $A$ above $B$ is

$$\sqrt{\ell^2 + a^2 + 2a\ell \sin\alpha} - a$$

14. One extremity of a uniform string is attached to a fixed point and the string rests partly on a smooth inclined plane. Prove that the directrix of the catenary determined by the portion which is not in contact with the plane is the horizontal line drawn through the extremity which rests on the plane. If $\alpha$ is the inclination of the plane, $\beta$, the inclination of the tangent at the fixed extremity, and $\ell$ the whole length of the string, prove that the length of the portion in contact with the plane is

$$\frac{\ell \cos\beta}{\cos\alpha \cos(\beta - \alpha)}$$

15. A heavy uniform string is suspended from two points $A$ and $B$ in the same horizontal line, and to any point $P$ of the string a heavy particle is attached. Prove that the two portions of the string are parts of equal catenaries. If $\theta$ and $\phi$ be the angles of the tangents at $P$ made with the horizontal; $\alpha$, $\beta$ those made by the tangents at $A$ and $B$, show that

$$\frac{\tan\theta + \tan\varphi}{\tan\alpha + \tan\beta} \text{ is constant for all positions of } P.$$

16. An endless uniform chain is hung over two smooth pegs in the same horizontal line. Show that when it is in a position of equilibrium, the ratio of the distance between the vertices of the catenaries to half the length of the chain is the tangent of half the angle of inclination of the portions near the pegs.
17. A string of length $\ell$ hangs between two points (not lying in the same vertical line) and makes angles $\alpha$, $\beta$ with the vertical at the points of support. Show that if $K$ is the height of one point above the other, and the vertex of the catenary does not lie between them, then prove that

$$K\cos\left(\frac{\alpha-\beta}{2}\right)=\ell\cos\left(\frac{\alpha+\beta}{2}\right)$$

18. $A$ is the lowest point of a uniform thread hanging from two fixed points, $B$ and $C$. Let $a$, $b$ be the heights of $A$ and $B$ above the directrix of the catenary formed by the thread. Show that the length of the thread between $A$ and $B$ equals $\sqrt{b^2-a^2}$.

19. A uniform chain of length $2\ell$ and weight $2w$ is suspended from two points in the same horizontal line. A load $w$ is now suspended from the middle point of the chain and the depth of the point below the horizontal line is $h$. Show that the terminal tension is

$$\frac{w}{2}\cdot\frac{h^2+2\ell^2}{h\ell}$$

20. A heavy uniform string hangs over two smooth pegs in the same horizontal line. If the length of each portion which hangs freely is $n$ times the length between the pegs, prove that the whole length of the string is to the distance between the pegs as $k$ : log $k$, where

$$k=\sqrt{\frac{2n+1}{2n-1}}$$

21. If the length of a uniform chain suspended between points at the same level is adjusted so that the tension at the points of support is minimum for that particular span $2d$, show that the equation to determine $c$ is

$$\cot h\left(\frac{d}{c}\right)=\frac{d}{c}$$

22. A uniform heavy chain is fastened at its extremities to two rings of equal weights, which slide on smooth rods intersecting in a vertical plane and inclined at the same angle $\alpha$ to the vertical. Find the condition that the tension at the lowest point may be equal to half the weight of the chain and in that case, show that the vertical distance of the rings from the point of intersection of the rods is

$$\ell\cot\alpha\log(1+\sqrt{2})\qquad\text{where } 2\ell \text{ is the length of the chain.}$$

23. The end links of a uniform chain slide along a fixed rough horizontal rod. Prove that the ratio of the maximum span to the length of the chain is

$$\mu\log\frac{1+\sqrt{1+\mu^2}}{\mu},\ \text{where } \mu \text{ is the coefficient of friction.}$$

24. The end links of a uniform chain slide along a fixed rough horizontal rod. If the angle of friction be $\lambda$, prove that the ratio of the maximum span to the length of the chain is

$$\log\cot\frac{\lambda}{2}:\cot\lambda$$

25. An endless heavy chain of length $2\ell$ is passed over a smooth right circular cylinder, where axis is horizontal. $c$ is the length of the portion of the chain whose weight is equal to the tension at the lowest point and $2\alpha$ is the angle between the radius drawn to the points where the chain leaves the cylinder. Prove that

$$\frac{\ell}{c} = \tan\alpha + \frac{\pi - \alpha}{\sin\alpha}\log\tan\left(\frac{\pi}{4} + \frac{\alpha}{2}\right)$$

26. A uniform chain of length $\ell$ hangs between two points $A$ and $B$ which are at a horizontal distance '$a$' from one another with B at a vertical distance '$b$' above $A$. Prove that the parameter of the catenary is given by

$$2c\sin h\left(\frac{a}{2c}\right) = \sqrt{\ell^2 - b^2}$$

Prove also that if the tensions at $A$ and $B$ are $T_1$ and $T_2$ respectively, then

$T_1 + T_2 = W\sqrt{1 + \dfrac{4c^2}{\ell^2 - b^2}}$ and $T_2 - T_1 = Wb/\ell$, where $W$ is the weight of the chain.

27. A heavy string of uniform density and thickness is suspended from two given points in the same horizontal plane. A weight $(1/n)$th that of the string is attached to its lowest point. Show that if $\theta$ and $\varphi$ be the inclinations to the vertical of the tangents at the highest and lowest points of the string, then

$$\tan\varphi = (1 + n)\tan\theta$$

28. A uniform chain of length $\ell$ and weight $W$ hangs between two fixed points at the same level and a weight is suspended from its middle point so that the total sag in the middle is $h$. Show that if $P$ is the pull on either point of support, the weight suspended is

$$\frac{4h}{\ell}P - \left(\frac{1}{2} + \frac{2h^2}{\ell^2}\right)W$$

29. A uniform chain of length $2\ell$ and weight $W$ is suspended from two points $A$ and $B$ in the same horizontal line. A load $P$ is now suspended from the middle point $D$ of the chain and the depth of this point below $AB$ is found to be $h$. Show that each terminal tension is

$$\frac{1}{2h}\left[P\ell + \frac{(h^2 + \ell^2)W}{2\ell}\right]$$

30. A uniform inextensible string of length $\ell$ and weight $w\ell$, carries at one end $B$, a particle of weight $W$ which is placed on a smooth plane inclined at 30° to the horizontal. The other end of the string is attached to a point $A$, situated at a height $h$ above the horizontal through $B$ and in the vertical plane through the line of greatest slope through B. Prove that the particle will rest in equilibrium, with the tangent at $B$ to the catenary lying in the inclined plane of $\dfrac{W}{\omega} = \dfrac{(\ell - h)(\ell + h)}{\left(h - \frac{1}{2}\ell\right)}$

## 8. Tightly Stretched Strings and Approximations to a Catenary

**(i) Parameter $c$ of the catenary is large when the string is tight**

For a common catenary, we have

$$s = c\tan\phi$$

$\rho = ds/d\phi = c \sec^2 \phi$, where $\rho$ is the radius of curvature

At the lowest point C, $\phi = 0$

$\therefore \quad \rho = c$

This shows that $\rho$ increases with the parameter $c$, i.e., when $\rho$ is large, $c$ is large. But when the string is tight, sag is small and curvature of the curve is small. Hence $\rho$ is large. This means that $c$ is large when the string is tight. It shows that the curve is flat.

**(ii) The catenary approximates to a parabola when the string is tightly stretched**

Cartesian equation of the common catenary is

$$y = c \cos h\,(x/c)$$

$$= c\left[1 + \frac{1}{\lfloor 2}\left(\frac{x}{c}\right)^2 + \frac{1}{4}\left(\frac{x}{c}\right)^4 + \frac{1}{\lfloor 6}\left(\frac{x}{c}\right)^6 + \ldots.\right] \quad \ldots(1)$$

$$\because \cos hx = 1 + \frac{x^2}{\lfloor 2} + \frac{x^4}{\lfloor 4} + \frac{x^6}{\lfloor 6} + \ldots.$$

In case of a tightly stretched string, $c$ is large. Therefore, $x/c$ is small. Hence, neglecting the powers of $x/c$ higher than two, Eq. (1) reduces to

$$y = c\left[1 + \frac{1}{\lfloor 2}\left(\frac{x}{c}\right)^2\right] \quad \Rightarrow \quad y = c + \frac{x^2}{2c} \quad \Rightarrow \quad x^2 = 2c\,(y - c)$$

which is a parabola whose latus rectum is $2c$ and the vertex is $(0, c)$, the lowest point of the catenary. Hence, the catenary approximates to a parabola.

**(iii) Form of string near the vertex of the catenary**

At the vertex of the catenary, $x = 0$. So, near the vertex of the catenary, $x$ is small and therefore $x/c$ is small. Hence, as above in (ii), we get,

$$x^2 = 2c\,(y - c)$$

which is again a parabola.

**(iv) Form of string at points far away from the vertex**

At the points far away from the vertex, $x$ is very large. Therefore, $e^{-x/c}$ is very small. Hence,

$$y = c \cos h\left(\frac{x}{c}\right) \quad \Rightarrow \quad = \frac{c}{2}\left[e^{x/c} + e^{-x/c}\right]$$

$$= \frac{c}{2} e^{x/c} \qquad \text{| neglecting } e^{-x/c}\text{, being very small}$$

which is an exponential curve. Hence, the catenary approximates to an exponential curve at the points far away from the vertex.

## ILLUSTRATIVE EXAMPLES

**Example 1:** (a) A uniform chain is hung up from two points at the same level distance $2a$ apart. If $z$ is the sag at the middle, show that $z = c\,(\cos h\; a/c - 1)$. If $z$ be small compared to a,show that $2cz = a^2$ nearly.

(b) A telegraph will is supported by two poles distance 120 metres apart. If the sag be one metre and the weight of the wire be 100 gm per metre, show that the horizontal pull on each pole is 180 kg nearly.

**Sol.** (a)

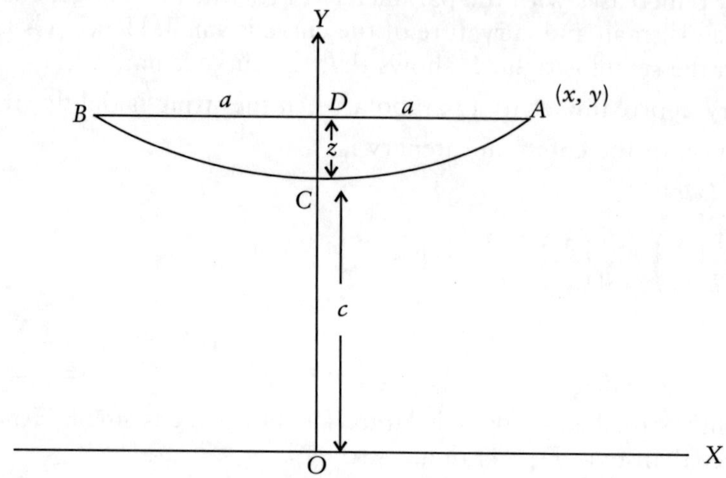


Let $ACB$ be the uniform chain hung up from two points $A$ and $B$ at the same level distant $2a$ apart. Let $D$ be the mid-point of $AB$. Then,

$AD = BD = a$

Sag $= DC = z$ | Given

Let $C$ be the lowest point of the catenary.

Let $OC = c$. Then $c$ is the parameter of the catenary.

Referred to $OX$, $OY$ as axes, as shown in the figure, the cartesian equation of catenary is

$$y = c \cos h\,(x/c) \qquad \text{...(1)}$$

Now, $z = OC \Rightarrow = OD - OC$

$= y - c \Rightarrow = c \cos h\,(a/c) - c$

$= c\,[\cos h\,(a/c) - 1]$

$$= c\left[1 + \frac{1}{\sqrt{2}}\left(\frac{a}{c}\right)^2 + \frac{1}{\sqrt{4}}\left(\frac{a}{c}\right)^4 + \ldots - 1\right]$$

$$= \frac{a^2}{2c} + \frac{a^4}{24c^3} + \ldots.$$

Since $z$ is small compared to $a$, therefore $c$ is very large.

$\therefore z = \dfrac{a^2}{2c}$ nearly | neglecting powers of $(a/c)$ higher than two

$\Rightarrow \quad 2cz = a^2$ nearly

(b) Here,

$z = 1$ m $\Rightarrow a = 60$ m $\Rightarrow = w = 1/10$ kg

Since $z$ is very small as compared to $a$, therefore,

$$2\,cz = a^2$$

$$\Rightarrow \quad c = \frac{a^2}{2z}$$

$= 60 \times 60/2 \times 1$ $\Rightarrow = 1800$ m

$\therefore$ Horizontal pull on each pole

$= T_0$ $\Rightarrow = wc$

$= 1/10 \times 1800$ $\Rightarrow = 180$ kg nearly

**Example 2:** A string of length $\ell$ and weight $W$ is tightly stretched between two poles of equal height. Find the approximate tension at the lowest point of the string.

**Sol.**

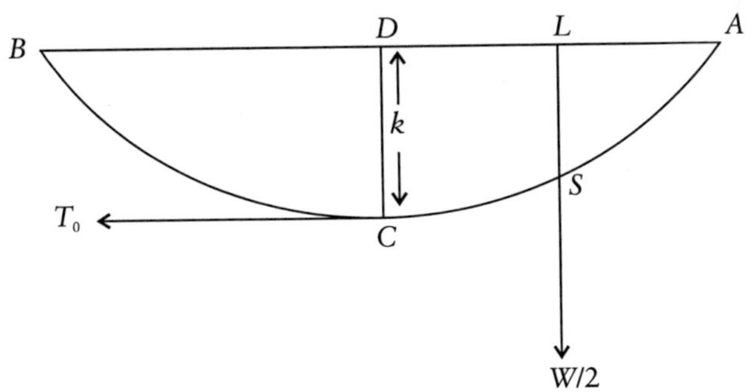


Let $ACB$ be a string of length $\ell$ and weight $W$, tightly stretched between two poles $A$ and $B$ of equal height. Let $k$ be the sag in the middle. Then,

$k = y - c = x^2/2c$, where $2x$ is the span. |Refer Ex. 1 above

Let us consider the equilibrium of the portion $AC$ of the string. The forces acting on this portion are as follows:

(i) tension $T_0$ at $C$.

(ii) weight $W/2$ of $AC$ acting vertically downwards through the middle point $S$ of $AC$.

(iii) tension of the string at $A$.

(iv) reaction at $A$.

Since the string is tightly stretched, therefore,

$$AL = AS \text{ nearly}$$
$$= \ell/4$$

Hence, taking moments about $A$,

we get

$$T_0\,k = 1/2\ W \cdot \ell/4$$

$$\Rightarrow \quad T_0 = \ell W/8k \text{ nearly}$$

**Example 3:** A uniform measuring chain of length $\ell$ is tightly stretched over a river, the middle point just touching the surface of the water, while each of the extremities has an elevation $k$ above the surface. Show that the difference between the length of the measuring chain and the breadth of the river is $8k^2/3\ell$ nearly.

**Sol.**

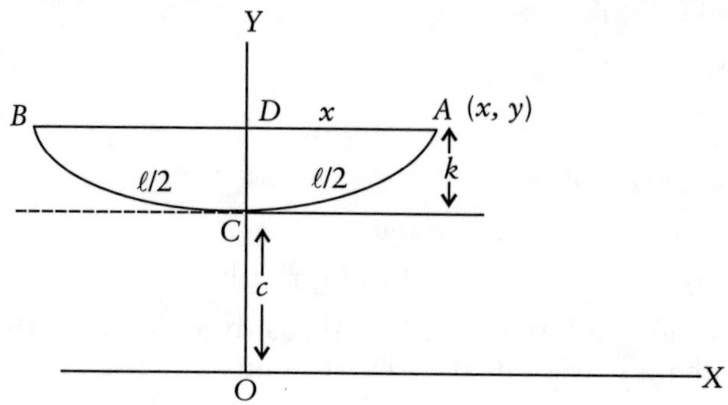


Let $ACB$ be the uniform chain of length $\ell$ hanging in the from of a catenary with vertex $C$ $(o, c)$ referred to the axes $OX$, $OY$ as shown in the figure. Length of arc $CA$ = length of arc $CB = \ell/2$.

Let the coordinates of $A$ be $(x, y)$.

We have, $s = c \sin h\ \alpha/c$

At the point $A$,

$\ell/2 = c \sin h\ x/c$ | $\because s = \ell/2$ at $A$

$$= c\left[\frac{x}{c} + \frac{1}{\lfloor 3}\frac{x^3}{c^3} + \ldots\right]$$

$$= x + \frac{x^3}{6c^2}$$ | $\because$ The chain is tightly stretched $\therefore$ $c$ is very large

$$\Rightarrow \quad \ell = 2x + \frac{x^3}{3c^2}$$

$$\Rightarrow \quad \ell - 2x = \frac{x^3}{3c^2} \text{ nearly} \qquad \ldots(1)$$

Now, $k$ = sag in the middle $= DC = y - c$

$= c \cos h\ x/c - c$ | $\because y = c \cos h\ x/c$

$= c\ [\cos h\ x/c - 1]$

$$= c\left[1 + \frac{1}{\lfloor 2}\frac{x^2}{\lfloor 2} + \frac{1}{\lfloor 4}\frac{x^4}{\lfloor 4} + \ldots\ldots - 1\right]$$

$\Rightarrow \quad x^2/2c$ nearly | $\because c$ is very large

$\Rightarrow \quad c = x^2/2k$ nearly ...(2)

Substituting the value of $c$ from (2) in (1), we get,

$$\ell - 2x = \frac{x^3}{3\left(\dfrac{x^2}{2k}\right)^2} = \frac{4k^2}{3x}$$

$$= \frac{4}{3}\frac{k^2}{\left(\dfrac{\ell}{2}\right)} \text{ nearly} \quad | \because \text{The chain is tightly stretched } \therefore x = \ell/2 \text{ nearly [From (1)]}$$

$$= 8k^2/3\ell \text{ nearly}$$

This is nearly the required difference between the length of the chain and the breadth of the river.

**Example 4:** A telegraph wire stretched between two poles at distance $a$ metres apart, sag $n$ metres in the middle. Prove that the tension at the ends is approximately

$$w\left(\frac{a^2}{8n} + \frac{7n}{6}\right)$$

**Sol.**

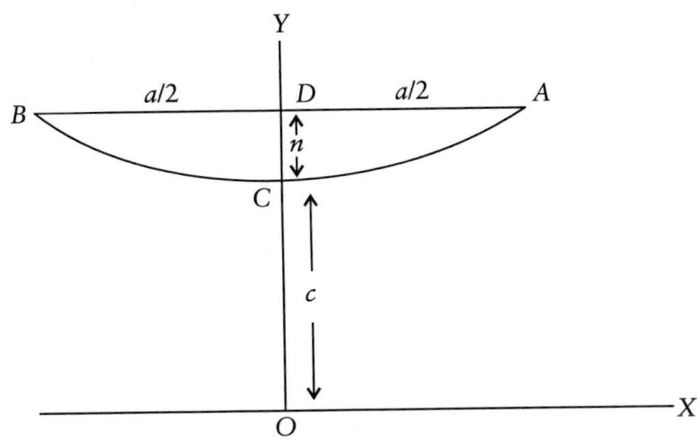


Let $ACB$ be the telegraph wire stretched between two poles $A$ and $B$ distance $a$ metres apart. Let C be its lowest point.

Let $OX$ and $OY$ be the coordinates axes as shown in the figure. Let OC = $c$. Then, $c$ is the parameter of the catenary.

Now, $n$ = sag in the middle $= y - c$

$$= c \cos h\, x/c - c \qquad | \because y = c \cos h\, x/c$$

$$= c\,(\cos h\, x/c - 1)$$

At the point $A$,

$$n = c\left(\cos h \frac{a}{2c} - c\right) \qquad | \because \text{At } A,\ x = a/2$$

$$= c\left[1+\frac{1}{\lfloor 2}\left(\frac{a}{2c}\right)^2+\frac{1}{\lfloor 4}\left(\frac{a}{2c}\right)^4+....-1\right]$$

$$= \frac{a^2}{8c}+\frac{a^4}{27.16c^3}+..... \qquad ...(1)$$

Since the wire is tightly stretched, therefore $c$ is very large so that

$n = a^2/8c$ to the first approximation

$$\Rightarrow \quad c = a^2/8n \qquad ...(2)$$

Substituting this value of $c$ in the term of (1), we get,

$$n = \frac{a^2}{8c}+\frac{a^4}{24.16}\left(\frac{8n}{a^2}\right)^3+.....$$

$$\Rightarrow \quad n = \frac{a^2}{8c}+\frac{4n^3}{3a^2} \text{ approximately}$$

$$\Rightarrow \quad \frac{a^2}{8c} = n-\frac{4n^3}{3a^2} \qquad \Rightarrow \quad = n\left(1-\frac{4n^2}{3a^2}\right)$$

$$\Rightarrow \quad c = \frac{a^2}{8c}\left(1-\frac{4n^2}{3a^2}\right)^{-1} \qquad \Rightarrow \quad = \frac{a^2}{8n}\left(1+\frac{4n^2}{3a^2}+...\right)$$

$$= \frac{a^2}{8n}\left(1+\frac{4n^2}{3a^2}\right) \qquad |\because n \text{ is small as compared with } a$$

$$= \frac{a^2}{8n}+\frac{n}{6} \text{ nearly} \qquad ...(3)$$

$\therefore$ Tension at the ends = Tension at $A$ (or $B$) $= wy$

$$= w\,(n + c) \qquad |\because y = n + c \text{ for the point } A \text{ (or } B)$$

$$= w\left\{n+\left(\frac{a^2}{8n}+\frac{n}{6}\right)\right\} \qquad |\text{From (3)}$$

$$= w\left(\frac{a^2}{8n}+\frac{7n}{6}\right) \text{ nearly} \qquad ...(4)$$

**Example 5:** *A uniform chain of length* $2\ell$ *has its ends attached to two points in the same horizontal line at a distance* $2a$ *apart. If* $\ell$ *is only a little greater than* $a$*, show that the tension of the chain is approximately equal to the weight of a length* $\sqrt{\frac{a^3}{6(\ell-a)}}$ *of the chain and that the sag or depression of the lowest point of the chain below its ends is nearly* $\frac{1}{2}\sqrt{6a(\ell-a)}$.

**Sol.**

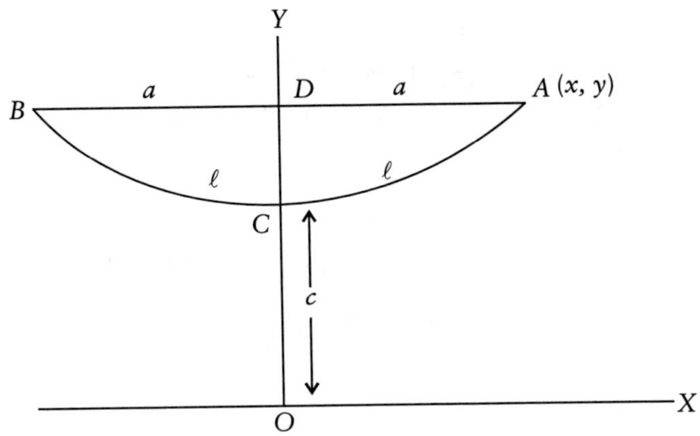


Let $ACB$ be a uniform chain of length $2\ell$ suspended from two points of support $A$ and $B$ in the same horizontal line at a distance $2a$ apart. Let C be the lowest point of the chain. Let $OC = c$. Then, $c$ is the parameter of the catenary. The coordinates axes are $OX$ and $OY$ as shown in the figure.

$$AD = BD = a$$

Since $\ell$ is only a little greater than $a$, therefore, the chain is tightly stretched and hence $c$ is vary large.

We have, $\quad s = c \sin h \, (x/c)$

For the point $A$,

$$\ell = c \sin h \frac{a}{c} \qquad \left| \because \text{At } A, \; s = \ell, x = a \right.$$

$$\Rightarrow \quad \ell = \left[\frac{a}{c} + \frac{1}{\lfloor 3}\left(\frac{a}{c}\right)^3 + \frac{1}{\lfloor 5}\left(\frac{a}{5}\right)^5 + \ldots\right] \qquad \left| \because \sin hx = x + \frac{x^3}{\lfloor 3} + \frac{x^5}{\lfloor 5} + \ldots\ldots \right.$$

$$\Rightarrow \quad \ell = a + \frac{a^3}{6c^2} \text{ nearly} \qquad | \text{ Retaining upto two terms only, } c \text{ being very large}$$

$$\Rightarrow \quad \ell - a = \frac{a^3}{6c^2} \qquad \Rightarrow \qquad c^2 = \frac{a^3}{6(\ell - a)}$$

$$\Rightarrow \quad c = \sqrt{\frac{a^3}{6(\ell - a)}} \qquad \ldots(1)$$

Since the chain is tightly stretched, therefore, the tension at any point of the chain can be taken nearly as the tension at the lowest point.

$\therefore$ Tension of the chain $\quad = T_0 \quad = wc$

$$= w\sqrt{\frac{a^3}{6(\ell - a)}} \text{ nearly}$$

$$= \text{weight of length } \sqrt{\frac{a^3}{6(\ell - a)}} \text{ of the chain nearly}$$

Also, sag in the middle

$$= CD \qquad = OD - OC \qquad = y - c$$

$$= c \cos h\,(x/c) - c \qquad = c\,[\cos h\,(x/c) - 1]$$

$$= c\,[\cos h\,(a/c) - 1] \qquad |\because \text{ At } A,\ x = a$$

$$= c\left[\left\{1 + \frac{1}{\underline{|2}}\left(\frac{a}{c}\right)^2 + \frac{1}{\underline{|4}}\left(\frac{a}{c}\right)^4 + \ldots\right\} - 1\right]$$

$$= a^2/2c \text{ nearly} \qquad |\text{neglecting other terms as } c \text{ is very large}$$

$$= \frac{a^2}{2}\sqrt{\frac{6(\ell - a)}{a^3}} \qquad |\text{From (1)}$$

$$= \frac{1}{2}\sqrt{6a(\ell - a)}$$

**Example 6:** $ACB$ is a telegraph wire, the straight line $AB$ being horizontal and of length $2\ell$ and $C$, the mid-point of the wire is at a distance h below $AB$. Show that the length of the wire is approximately

$$2\ell + \frac{4}{3}\frac{h^2}{\ell} - \frac{28}{45}\frac{h^4}{\ell^3}.$$

**Sol.**

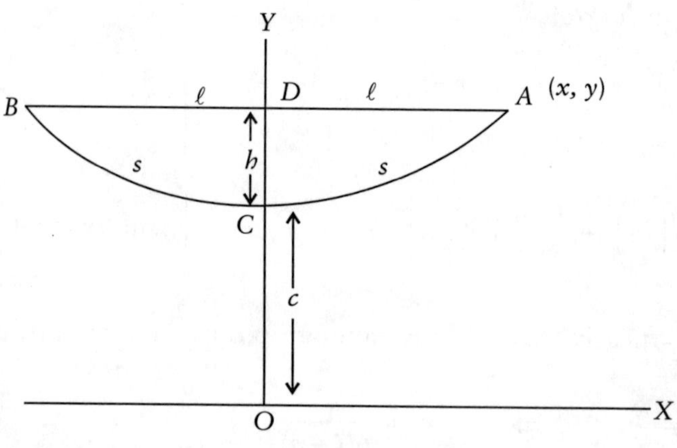


Let the length of the telegraph wire $ACB$ be $2s$ so that arc $= AC =$ arc $BC = s$.
$OX$, $OY$ are the coordinate axes as shown in the figure.
Let $OC = c$. Then, c is the parameter of the catenary.
Let the coordinates of $A$ be $(x, y)$.
We have,

$$\text{Sag} = DC$$

$$\Rightarrow \quad h = OD - OC \quad \Rightarrow \quad h = y - c$$

$$\Rightarrow \quad h = c \cos h\,(x/c) - c \qquad |\because y = c \cos h\, x/c$$

$$\Rightarrow \quad h = c\,[\cos h\,(\ell/c) - c] \qquad |\because \text{ At } A,\ x = \ell$$

$$= c\left[\left\{1+\frac{1}{\underline{|2}}\left(\frac{\ell}{c}\right)^2+\frac{1}{\underline{|4}}\left(\frac{\ell}{c}\right)^4+\ldots\ldots\right\}-1\right]$$

$$= \frac{\ell^2}{2c}+\frac{\ell^4}{24c^3}+\ldots\ldots \qquad \ldots(1)$$

Since for a telegraph wire, $c$ is very large, therefore,

$h = \ell^2/2c$ | to first approximation

$\Rightarrow \quad c = \ell^2/2h$ nearly ...(2)

Substituting this value of $c$ in second term of (1), we get

$$h = \frac{\ell^2}{2c}+\frac{\ell^4}{24}\frac{8h^3}{\ell^6} \text{ nearly}$$

$$= \frac{\ell^2}{2c}+\frac{h^3}{3\ell^2} \text{ nearly}$$

$$\Rightarrow \quad h-\frac{h^3}{3\ell^2}=\frac{\ell^2}{2c} \qquad \Rightarrow \qquad h\left(1-\frac{h^2}{3\ell^2}\right)=\frac{\ell^2}{2c}$$

$$\Rightarrow \quad \frac{1}{c}=\frac{2h}{\ell^2}\left(1-\frac{h^2}{3\ell^2}\right) \qquad \ldots(3)$$

Also, we have, $s = c \sin h\, x/c$

At the point $A$, $x = \ell$ $\quad \therefore\ s = c \sin h\, \ell/c$

$\Rightarrow \quad 2s = 2c \sin h\, \ell/c$

$$= 2c\left[\frac{\ell}{c}+\frac{1}{\underline{|3}}\frac{\ell^3}{c^3}+\frac{1}{\underline{|3}}\frac{\ell^5}{c^5}+\ldots\right]$$

$$= 2\ell+\frac{\ell^3}{3c^2}+\frac{\ell^5}{60c^4} \text{ nearly}$$

$$= 2\ell+\frac{\ell^3}{3}\left[\left(\frac{2h}{\ell^2}\right)^2\left(1-\frac{h^2}{3\ell^2}\right)^2\right]+\frac{\ell^5}{60}\left[\frac{2h}{\ell^2}\left(1-\frac{h^2}{3\ell^2}\right)^4\right] \qquad |\text{From (3)}$$

$$2\ell+\frac{4h^2}{3\ell}\left(1-\frac{2h^2}{3\ell^2}+\frac{h^4}{9\ell^4}\right)+\frac{\ell^5}{60}\frac{16h^4}{\ell^8}\left(1-\frac{h^2}{3\ell^2}\right)^4 \text{ nearly}$$

$$= 2\ell+\frac{4h^2}{3\ell}-\frac{h^4}{\ell^3}\left(\frac{8}{9}-\frac{4}{15}\right) \text{ nearly} \qquad |\text{neglecting other terms}$$

$$= 2\ell+\frac{4h^2}{3\ell}-\frac{28}{45}\frac{h^4}{\ell^3} \text{ nearly}$$

This gives the required approximate length of the wire.

## EXERCISE 1(B)

1. A telegraph wire is supported by two poles distance 40 metres apart. If the sag be 1/2 metre and the weight of the wire be one kilogram per metre, show that the horizontal pull on each pole is 400 kg.wt.
2. A heavy uniform string, 155 metre long, is suspended from two given points $A$ and $B$, 150 metres apart on the same horizontal plane. Show that the tension at the lowest point is approximately equal to 1.08 times the weight of the string.
3. Show that the maximum tension in a wire which weighs 0.05 kg. per metre and hangs with sag 1 metre in a horizontal span of 100 metres is about 62.5 kg. weight.
4. A telegraph wire has a span of 40 metres. Find the sag in the middle if the tension is not to exceed 400 kg.wt., assuming that 1 metre of wire weighs 1 kg.

   [**Ans.** 50 cm]
5. The ends of a tightly stretched cable weighing 1/2 lb. per yard are fixed to two points on a level 80 yards apart and the cable has a sag, at the middle, of 1 foot 4 inches. Show that the tension in the wire at the lowest point is 900 lbs. wt.
6. A telegraph wire has a span of 90 m. Find the sag in the middle if the tension does not exceed 175 kg. wt., assuming that 18 m of wire weighs 1 kg.

   [**Ans.** 9/28 m]
7. A telegraph wire is constructed of No. 8 iron wire which weighs 7.3 lbs. per 100 feet, the distance between the poles is 150 feet and the wire sags 1 foot in the middle. Show that it can be screwed upto a tension of about 205 lbs. wt.
8. A telegraph wire is supported by two poles distant 40 yards apart. If the sag be 1 foot and the weight of the wire half an ounce per foot, show that the horizontal pull on each pole is 1/2 cwt. nearly.

   [*Note*: 1 cwt. = 112 lbs.; 1 lb. = 1600 z]
9. A telegraph wire has a span of 88 feet. Find the sag in the middle if the tension is not to exceed 150 lbs., assuming that 200 feet of the wire weighs 1 lb.

   [**Ans.** 3.872 inches]
10. A telegraph wire is constructed of a wire which weighs 0.15 kg per metre, the distance between the points is 100 metres and wire sags 1 metre in the middle. Show that it can be screwed upto a tension of about 187.5 kg. wt.
11. A telegraph wire of length $\ell$ hangs between two posts on the same level at distance $a$ apart, the small sag at the centre being $b$. Show that

    $\ell - a = 8b^2/3a$ approximately

    Also, show that the least tension per unit area of section is

    $1/8 \,.\, wa^2/b$.

    where $w$ is weight per unit volume of the wire.

## 9. Suspension Bridge or Parabolic Chain

A suspension bridge consists of two chains hung up parallel to each other with their ends attached to two fixed points. From different points of these two chains, supporting rods are vertical by hung. These rods carry the roadway. The weight of the chains and rods is very small as compared to the weight of the roadway.

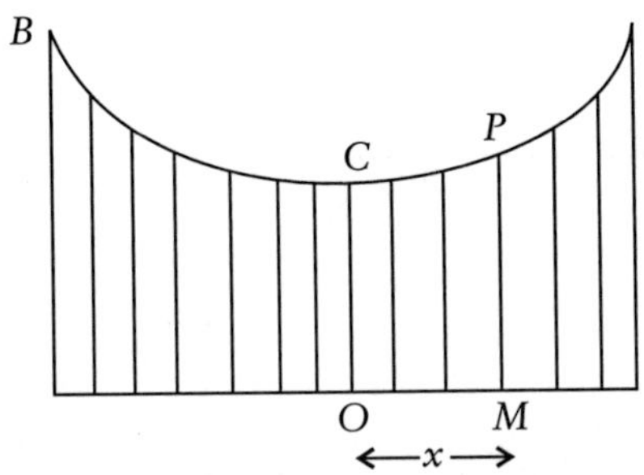


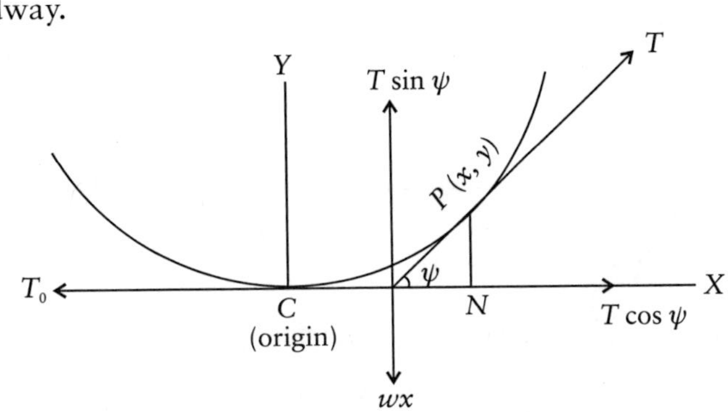


Let us consider the equilibrium of the portion $CP$ of the chain and part $OM$ of the roadway supported by it by means of the rods. Take the lowest point $C$ of the chain as the origin. The tension $T_0$ at $C$ and $T$ at $P$ support the weight of the length $OM$ of the roadway. Therefore, we can assume that the weight of portion $CP$ of the chain is proportional to the horizontal projection $CN$ of $CP$ on $CX$ where $CN = OM$. Let the horizontal and vertical lines through the lowest point $C$ be taken as $X$-axis and $Y$-axis respectively. Referred to these axes, let the coordinates of the point $P$ be $(x, y)$.

Now, resolving horizontally and vertically, we get, $\Rightarrow T\cos\psi = T_0$ ...(1)

$T\sin\psi = w\,CN = wx$ | $\because CN = OM = x$ ...(2)

Dividing (2) by (1), we get,

$$\Rightarrow \frac{dy}{dx} = \frac{wx}{T_0} \qquad \left|\because \tan\psi = \frac{dy}{dx}\right.$$

$$\Rightarrow T_0\,dy = wx\,dx$$ |separating the variables

Integration yields,

$$T_0 y = w\frac{x^2}{2} + k$$ where $k$ is an arbitrary constant of integration.

At the point $C$, $x = 0$, $y = 0$ | $\because$ $C$ is the origin

$$\therefore k = 0 \qquad \therefore T_0 y = wx^2/2 \qquad \Rightarrow \qquad x^2 = \frac{2T_0}{w}y$$

which is a parabola where vertex is $(0, 0)$ and latus rectum is $2T_0/w$.

Hence, the form of the chain is parabolic.

## 10. Heterogeneous Chain

Refer § 7. Take the lowest point $C$ as the origin. Let $w$ be the weight per unit length of the chain. Let $w$ be not a constant. Then, the chain is heterogeneous. Consider an infinitesimally small portion of length $ds$ of the chain. Then, its weight = $w\,ds$ [since for this elementary portion, we may regard $w$ as constant]

$\therefore$ Elementary weight $= w\, ds$

$\therefore$ Weight of $CP = \int_0^s w\, ds$ where arc length $CP = s$

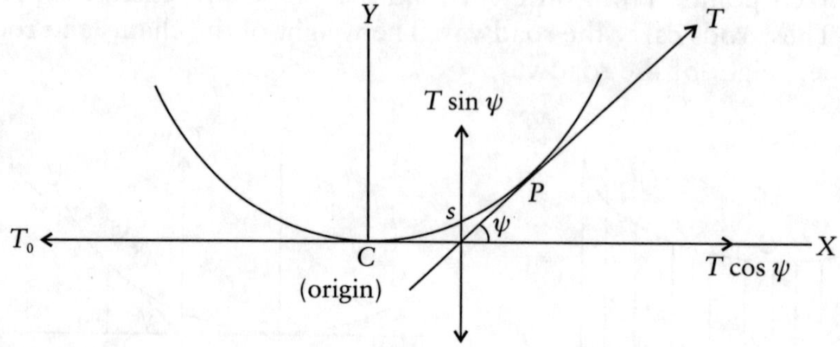


Resolving horizontally and vertically, we get

$$T \cos \psi = T_0 \quad \text{...(1)}$$

$$T \sin \psi = \int_0^s w\, ds \quad \text{...(2)}$$

Dividing (2) by (1), we get,

$$\tan \psi = \frac{\int_0^s w\, ds}{T_0}$$

$$\Rightarrow \quad T_0 \tan \psi = \int_0^s w\, ds \quad \text{...(3)}$$

Differentiating (3) with respect to $s$, we get

$$T_0 \sec^2 \psi \frac{d\psi}{ds} = w$$

$$\Rightarrow \quad \frac{T_0 \sec^2 \psi}{\rho} = w \qquad \left| \because \rho = \frac{ds}{d\psi} \right. \quad \text{...(4)}$$

$$\Rightarrow \quad \frac{T_0 \left(1 + y_1^2\right)}{\dfrac{\left(1 + y_1^2\right)^{3/2}}{y_2}} = w \text{ where } y_1 = \frac{dy}{dx} = \tan \psi, y_2 = \frac{d^2 y}{dx^2} \qquad \left| \because \rho = \frac{(1 + y_1^2)^{3/2}}{y_2} \right.$$

$$\Rightarrow \quad \frac{T_0 y_2}{\left(1 + y_1^2\right)^{\frac{1}{2}}} = w \quad \text{...(5)}$$

**Example:** If the chain is cycloidal, then is equation its $s = 4\, a \sin \psi$

$$\therefore \quad \rho = \frac{ds}{d\psi} = 4a \cos \psi \quad \text{...(6)}$$

$$\therefore \quad w = \frac{T_0}{\rho} \frac{1}{\cos^2 \psi} \qquad \text{|From (4)}$$

$$= \frac{T_0}{4a\cos\psi\cos^2\psi} \qquad \text{|From (6)}$$

$$= \frac{T_0}{4a\cos^3\psi}$$

$$= \frac{T_0}{4a\left(\frac{\rho}{4a}\right)^3} \qquad |\because \rho = 4a\cos\psi$$

$$= \frac{16a^2T_0}{\rho^3}$$

$$= \frac{16a^2T_0}{(16a^2 - s^2)^{3/2}} \qquad \left|\begin{array}{l}\because \rho^2 + s^2 = 16a^2 \\ \therefore \rho = (16a^2 - s^2)^{1/2}\end{array}\right.$$

At the vertex C, $s = 0$, $w = w_0$ (say)

$$\therefore w_0 = \frac{16a^2T_0}{(16a^2)^{3/2}} \qquad \text{...(7)}$$

Let at $s = a$, $w = w_1$

Then,

$$w_1 = \frac{16a^2T_0}{(16a^2 - a^2)^{3/2}}$$

$$\Rightarrow \quad w_1 = \frac{16a^2T_0}{(15a^2)^{3/2}} \qquad \text{...(8)}$$

Dividing (8) by (7), we get

$$\frac{w_1}{w_0} = \left(\frac{16}{15}\right)^{3/2} = \frac{10}{9} \text{ (approx.)}$$

## 11. Catenary of Uniform Strength

**Definition:** If a string is suspended from its two ends not lying in the same vertical line freely under gravity such that the tension at any point of the string is proportional to the area of cross-section at that point, then the shape occupied by the string is known as catenary of uniform strength.

Since the weight of an element at any point is proportional to the area of cross-section at that point, therefore, tension at any point of the catenary of uniform strength is proportional to its weight per unit length at that point, i.e.,

$$T \propto w$$

$$\Rightarrow \quad T = c\,w \qquad \text{where } c \text{ is constant.} \qquad \text{...(1)}$$

**Equation:** Let $ACB$ be a catenary of uniform strength. Take the lowest point $C$ as origin and the axes as shown in the figure. Consider the equilibrium of portion $CP$ (= $s$) of the string. We see that it is in equilibrium under the action of following three forces:

(i) Tension $T_0$ at $C$

(ii) Tension $T$ at $P$

(iii) Weight $\int_0^s w\,ds$ of the portion $CP$ of the string.

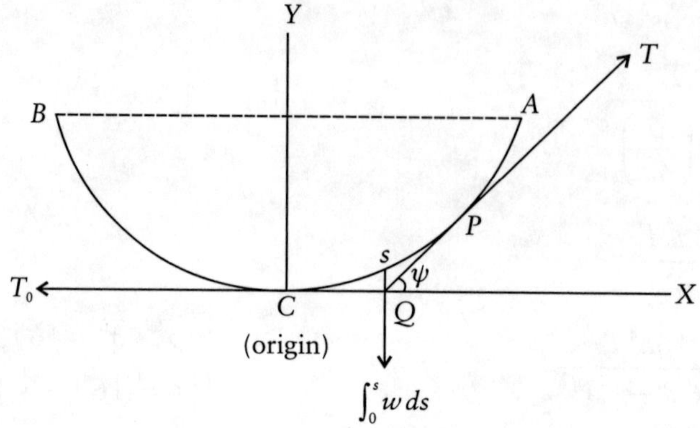


The directions of these forces are as shown in the figure. For equilibrium, these forces will meet at a point $Q$.

Now, resolving the forces horizontally and vertically, we get,

$$T \cos \psi = T_0 \quad \text{...(2)}$$

$$T \sin \psi = \int_0^s w\,ds \quad \text{...(3)}$$

Dividing (3) by (2), we get,

$$\tan \psi = \frac{\int_0^s w\,ds}{T_0} \quad \text{...(4)}$$

Differentiating (4) with respect to $s$, we get,

$$\sec^2 \psi \frac{d\psi}{ds} = \frac{w}{T_0}$$

$$= \frac{\left(\frac{T}{c}\right)}{T_0} \qquad |\because T = cw$$

$$= \frac{T}{cT_0}$$

$$= \frac{T_0 \sec \psi}{cT_0} \qquad | \text{ From (2)}$$

$$\Rightarrow \quad \frac{ds}{d\psi} = c \sec \psi \quad \text{...(5)}$$

$$\Rightarrow \quad ds = c \sec \psi \, d\psi$$

Integration yields,

$$s = c \log (\sec \psi + \tan \psi) + c_1$$

where $c_1$ is an arbitrary constant of integration.

At the lowest point C,

$$s = 0, \psi = 0 \therefore c_1 = 0$$

$$\therefore s = c \log (\sec \psi + \tan \psi) \quad ...(6)$$

(5) gives

$$\rho = c \sec \psi \qquad |\because \rho = ds/d\psi \quad ...(7)$$

From (7),

$$\sec \psi = \rho/c \quad ...(8)$$

$$\therefore \tan\psi = \sqrt{\sec^2 \psi - 1}$$

$$= \sqrt{\frac{\rho^2}{c^2} - 1}$$

$$= \frac{\sqrt{\rho^2 - c^2}}{c} \quad ...(9)$$

From (6), (8) and (9), we get

$$s = c \log \left(\frac{\rho}{c} + \frac{\sqrt{\rho^2 - c^2}}{c}\right)$$

$$\Rightarrow \quad s = c \log \left(\frac{\rho}{c} + \sqrt{\frac{\rho^2}{c^2} - 1}\right)$$

$$\Rightarrow \quad s = c \cos h^{-1}\left(\frac{\rho}{c}\right) \qquad \left|\because \cos h^{-1} x = \log\left(x + \sqrt{x^2 - 1}\right)\right.$$

$$\Rightarrow \quad \rho = c \cos h\left(\frac{s}{c}\right) \quad ...(10)$$

Again,

$$ds/d\psi = c \sec \psi \qquad |\text{From (5)}$$

$$\Rightarrow \quad \frac{ds}{dx}\frac{dx}{d\psi} = \frac{c}{\cos\psi}$$

$$\Rightarrow \quad \frac{1}{\cos\psi}\frac{dx}{d\psi} = \frac{c}{\cos\psi} \qquad \left|\because \cos\psi = \frac{dx}{ds}\right.$$

$$\Rightarrow \quad dx = c\, d\psi$$

Integrating, we get

$$x = c\,\psi + c_2$$

At the vertex C, $\psi = 0$, $x = 0$ $\therefore$ $c_2 = 0$

$\therefore$ $x = c\,\psi$ ...(11)

Also, $ds/d\psi = c \sec \psi$ |From (5)

$$\Rightarrow \quad \frac{ds}{dy}\frac{dy}{d\psi} = c \sec \psi$$

$$\Rightarrow \quad \frac{1}{\sin \psi}\frac{dy}{d\psi} = \frac{c}{\cos \psi} \qquad \Big| \because \sin \psi = \frac{dy}{ds}$$

$$\Rightarrow \quad \frac{dy}{\quad} = \tan \psi$$

$$\Rightarrow \quad dy = c \tan \psi \, d\psi$$

Integration gives,

$$y = c \log \sec \psi \qquad ...(12)$$

$$\Rightarrow \quad y = c \log \sec (x/c) \qquad \text{|From (11)} \qquad ...(13)$$

Equation (13) is called the cartesian equation of the catenary of uniform strength. The curve (13) is symmetrical about $Y$-axis and when $x = c\pi/2$, $y \to \infty$. Therefore, the curve has asymptotes as $x = \pm\, c\pi/2$. Hence, the span is $c\pi$.

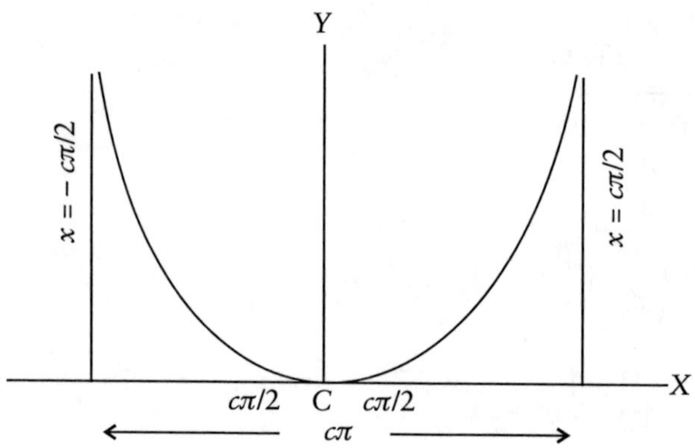


Moreover, from (2),

$$T = T_0 \sec \psi$$

$$= T_0\, \rho/c \qquad \text{|From (8)}$$

$$\Rightarrow \quad T \propto \rho \qquad ...(14)$$

Also, $T \propto w$ |From (1)

$\therefore$ From (12) and (1),

$$\rho \propto w \qquad ...(15)$$

*Note* 1: $c$ is called the parameter of catenary of uniform strength.

*Note* 2: The equations $x = c\psi$

$y = c \log (\sec \psi + \tan \psi)$ taken together may be named as the parametric equations of the catenary of uniform strength; $\psi$ being the parameter here.

## ILLUSTRATIVE EXAMPLES

**Example 1:** A heavy heterogeneous chain is suspended from two points freely under gravity. Show that the mass per unit length is proportional to $\sec^2 \psi/\rho$.

Or

A heavy heterogeneous chain is suspended from two points freely under gravity. Show that $\rho\, w \cos^2 \psi$ is constant at all points, the letters have their usual meanings.

**Sol.** Refer § 9.

We have the equation

$$\sec^2 \psi \frac{d\psi}{ds} = \frac{w}{T_0}$$

$$\Rightarrow \quad \frac{\sec^2 \psi}{\rho} = \frac{mg}{T_0} \qquad \Big|\because \rho = \frac{ds}{d\psi}$$

$$\Rightarrow \quad m = \frac{T_0 \sec^2 \psi}{\rho g}$$

$$\Rightarrow \quad m \alpha \frac{\sec^2 \psi}{\rho}; \; T_0 \text{ and } g \text{ being constants}$$

or

Refer § 9

We have the equation

$$\sec^2 \psi \frac{d\psi}{ds} = \frac{\mathrm{w}}{T_0}$$

$$\Rightarrow \quad \frac{1}{\cos^2 \psi} \frac{1}{\rho} = \frac{\mathrm{w}}{T_0} \qquad \Big|\because \rho = \frac{ds}{d\psi}$$

$$\Rightarrow \quad \rho\, w \cos^2 \psi = T_0 \text{ (constant)}$$

**Example 2:** Show that for a catenary of uniform strength $\cos \psi \cos h\, s/c = 1$.

**Sol.** Refer § 9

From equation (6), we have, $s = c \log (\sec \psi + \tan \psi)$

$\Rightarrow \quad \sec \psi + \tan \psi = e^{s/c} \quad \therefore \quad \sec \psi - \tan \psi = e^{-s/c}$

Adding, we get $\quad 2 \sec \psi = = e^{s/c} + e^{-s/c}$

$\Rightarrow \quad \sec \psi = e^{s/c} + e^{-s/c}/2 \quad \Rightarrow \quad \sec \psi = \cos h\, (s/c)$

$\Rightarrow \quad 1/\cos \psi = \cos h\, (s/c) \quad \Rightarrow \quad \cos \psi \cos h\, (s/c) = 1$

**Example 3:** Show that the mass per unit length at any point of a common catenary of uniform strength varies as the corresponding radius of curvature.

**Sol.** By definition of catenary of uniform strength, we have,

$w \,\alpha\, T$

$m \,\alpha\, T \qquad | \because w = mg \therefore w \,\alpha\, m$; $g$ being constant ...(1)

$$T \cos \psi = T_0 \quad \Rightarrow \quad T = T_0 \sec \psi$$

$\Rightarrow \quad T \propto \sec \psi \qquad | \because T_0$ is constant ...(2)

From (1) and (2), $m \propto \sec \psi$

$\Rightarrow \quad m \propto \rho/c \qquad | \because \rho = c \sec \psi \qquad \Rightarrow m \propto \rho \qquad | \because c$ is a constant

**Example 4:** Show that the form in which a chain hangs when the line density is given by $T_0/ag \sec^2 s/a$, $T_0$ being the tension at the lowest point and $s$ being measured from this point, is a circle of radius $a$.

**Sol.**

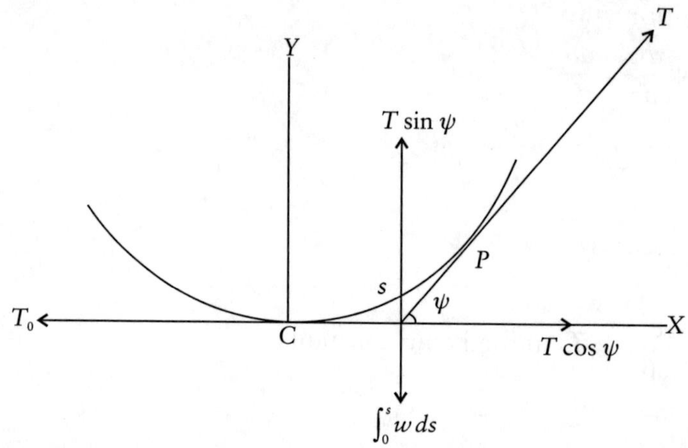


Line density $(m) = \dfrac{T_0}{ag}\sec^2\dfrac{s}{a} \qquad \Rightarrow \therefore w = mg = \dfrac{T_0}{a}\sec^2\dfrac{s}{a}$ ...(1)

Refer § 9,

$$T \cos \psi = T_0 \qquad ...(2)$$

$$T \sin\psi = \int_0^s w\,ds \qquad ...(3)$$

$\Rightarrow \quad T\sin\psi = \displaystyle\int_0^s \frac{T_0}{a}\sec^2\frac{s}{a}\,ds \qquad$ |From (1)

$$\Rightarrow \quad T\sin\psi = T_0 \tan\left(\frac{s}{a}\right)_0^s$$

$$\Rightarrow \quad T\sin\psi = T_0 \tan\frac{s}{a} \qquad ...(4)$$

Dividing (4) by (2), we get $\qquad \Rightarrow \tan \psi = \tan s/a$

$\Rightarrow \quad \psi = s/a \qquad \Rightarrow s = a\psi$

which is a circle of radius $a$.

**Example 5:** If the density as any point of a cord varies as the radius of curvature of the curve in which it hangs, show that the curve is the catenary of uniform strength.

**Sol.**

Here, density $\alpha$ $\rho$

$\Rightarrow \quad w \,\alpha\, \rho$ $\quad | \because w \,\alpha$ density

$\Rightarrow \quad w = \lambda \rho$ ...(1)

Also, $\quad w = \dfrac{T_0 \sec^2 \psi}{\rho}$ $\quad$ |Refer Ex. 1

$\Rightarrow \quad \lambda\rho = \dfrac{T_0 \sec^2 \psi}{\rho}$ $\quad$ |From (1)

$\Rightarrow \quad \lambda \rho^2 = T_0 \sec^2 \psi$

$\Rightarrow \quad \rho^2 = T_0/\lambda \sec^2 \psi$

$\Rightarrow \quad \rho = \sqrt{\dfrac{T_0}{\lambda}} \sec\psi \quad \Rightarrow \quad \rho = c \sec\psi \quad$ where $c = \sqrt{\dfrac{T_0}{\lambda}}$

$\Rightarrow \quad ds/d\psi = c \sec \psi$ $\quad |\because \rho = ds/d\psi$

$\Rightarrow \quad ds = c \sec \psi \, d\psi$

Integration yields, $\quad s = c \log(\sec \psi + \tan \psi) + C_1$

At the lowest point $C$,

$s = 0, \psi = 0 \therefore C_1 = 0 \qquad \therefore s = c \log(\sec \psi + \tan \psi)$

which is the intrinsic equations of a catenary of uniform strength.

Hence, the curve is the catenary of uniform strength.

**Example 6:** In a uniform string hanging under gravity the area of cross-section at any point is inversely proportion to the tension. Show that the curve is an arc of a parabola with its axis vertical.

**Sol.** $\quad A \,\alpha \dfrac{1}{\rho}$ $\quad$ |Given

We know that

$w \alpha\, A \qquad \therefore w \,\alpha\, 1/T$

$\Rightarrow \quad w = \lambda/T$ where $\lambda$ is a constant of proportionality

$\Rightarrow \quad \dfrac{T_0 \sec^2 \psi}{\rho} = \dfrac{\lambda}{T}$ $\quad$ |Refer Ex. 1

$\Rightarrow \quad \dfrac{T_0 \sec^2 \psi}{\rho} = \dfrac{\lambda}{T_0 \sec\psi}$ $\quad |\because T\cos\psi = T_0$

$\Rightarrow \quad T_0^2 \sec^3 \psi = \lambda\rho$

$$\Rightarrow \quad T_0^2 \left\{1 + \left(\frac{dy}{dx}\right)^2\right\}^{3/2} = \lambda \frac{\left\{1 + \left(\dfrac{dy}{dx}\right)^2\right\}^{3/2}}{\dfrac{d^2y}{dx^2}}$$

$$\Rightarrow \quad T_0^2 \frac{d^2y}{dx^2} = \lambda \quad \Rightarrow \quad \frac{d^2y}{dx^2} = \frac{\lambda}{T_0^2}$$

$$\Rightarrow \quad \frac{d^2y}{dx^2} = k_1 \text{ where } k_1 = \frac{\lambda}{T_0^2} = \text{constant}$$

Integrating both sides with respect to $x$,

We get,

$dy/dx = k_1x + k_2$ where $k_2$ is an arbitrary constant of integration.

At the lowest point C, $x = 0$, $dy/dx = 0$

$\therefore \; k_2 = 0$

$\therefore \; dy/dx = k_1 x \quad \Rightarrow dy = k_1 x\, dx$

Integration gives,

$y = k_1 x^2/2 + k_3$ where $k_3$ is an arbitrary constant of integration.

At the lowest point C, $x = 0$, $y = 0 \;\therefore\; k_3 = 0$

$\therefore \quad y = k_1 x^2/2$

$\Rightarrow \quad x^2 = (2/k_1)\, y \quad \Rightarrow x^2 = ay$ where $a = 2/k_1$

which is a parabola with vertex (0, 0), axis vertical and latus rectum $a$.

Hence, the curve is an arc of a parabola with its axis vertical.

**Example 7:** The distance between the points of support of a catenary of uniform strength is $a$ and the length of the chain is $\ell$. Show that the parameter $c$ must be found from $\tan h\,(\ell/4c) = \tan\,(a/4c)$.

**Sol.**

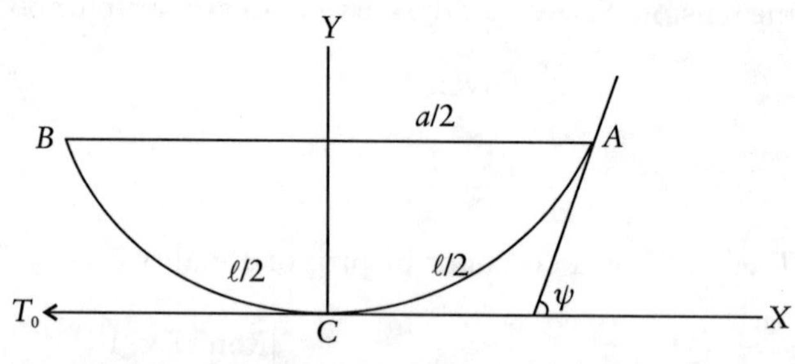


Equation of catenary of uniform strength is

$$y = c \log \sec (x/c) \qquad \text{...(1)}$$

$$\Rightarrow \quad \frac{dy}{dx} = \tan\frac{x}{c} = \tan\psi \quad \Rightarrow \quad \frac{x}{c} = \psi$$

$$\Rightarrow \quad x = c\psi \qquad \text{...(2)}$$

At the end $A$, $x = a/2$

$\therefore \quad a/2 = c\psi$

$$\Rightarrow \quad \psi = \frac{a}{2c} \qquad \text{...(3)}$$

We have, $s = c \log (\sec \psi + \tan \psi)$

$\Rightarrow$ $$s = c \log \tan\left(\frac{\pi}{4} + \frac{\psi}{2}\right)$$

At the end $A$, $s = \ell/2$

$\therefore$ $$\frac{\ell}{2} = c \log \tan\left(\frac{\pi}{4} + \frac{a}{4c}\right) \qquad \text{|From (3)}$$

$\Rightarrow$ $$e^{\ell/2c} = \tan\left(\frac{\pi}{4} + \frac{a}{4c}\right) \Rightarrow \frac{e^{\ell/2c}}{1} = \frac{1+\tan\frac{a}{4c}}{1-\tan\frac{a}{4c}}$$

Applying componendo and dividendo,

we get,

$$\frac{e^{\ell/2c}+1}{e^{\ell/2c}-1} = \frac{\left(1+\tan\frac{a}{4c}\right)+\left(1-\tan\frac{a}{4c}\right)}{\left(1+\tan\frac{a}{4c}\right)-\left(1-\tan\frac{a}{4c}\right)} \Rightarrow \frac{e^{\ell/4c}+e^{-\ell/4c}}{e^{\ell/4c}-e^{-\ell/4c}} = \frac{2}{2\tan\frac{a}{4c}}$$

$\Rightarrow$ $$\cot h\left(\frac{a}{4c}\right) = \cot\left(\frac{a}{4c}\right) \Rightarrow \tan h\left(\frac{\ell}{4c}\right) = \tan\left(\frac{a}{4c}\right)$$

**Example 8:** If a string hangs in the form of an ellipse whose major axis is horizontal, prove that its weight per unit length at any point is $T_0\, b^3/ab'y^2$, where $y$ is the depth of the point below the major axis and $b'$, the length of semi-conjugate diameter corresponding to that point.

**Sol.**

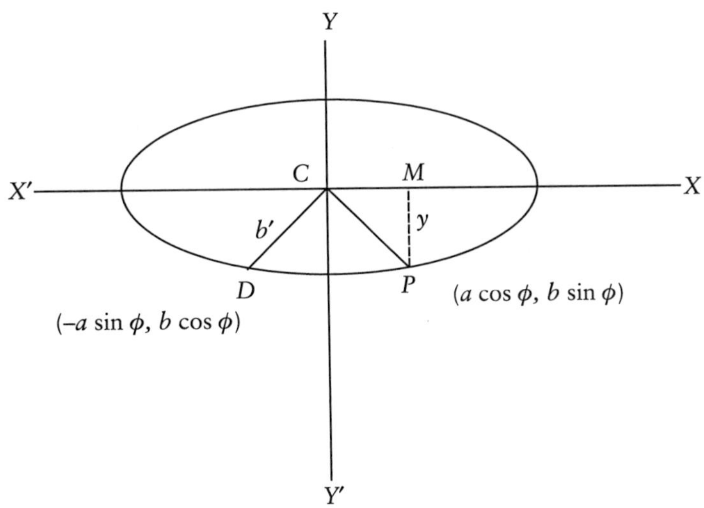


Let $D$ ($a \cos \phi$, $b \sin \phi$) be any point on the ellipse. The point conjugate to $P$ is $D$ ($-a \cos \phi$, $b \sin \phi$). Let $C$ (0, 0) be the centre of the ellipse.

$b'$ = length of semi-conjugate diameter $CD$

$$= a^2 \sin^2 \phi + b^2 \cos^2 \phi \qquad \ldots(1)$$

Also, $\rho_{\text{at}P} = \dfrac{CD^3}{ab}$ |From Differential Calculus

$$= \frac{b'^3}{ab} \qquad ...(2)$$

Equation of ellipse is

$$\frac{x^2}{a^2} + \frac{y^2}{b^2} = 1 \qquad ...(3)$$

Differentiating with respect to $x$, we get

$$\frac{2x}{a^2} + \frac{2y}{b^2}\frac{dy}{dx} = 0$$

$$\Rightarrow \quad \frac{dy}{dx} = -\frac{b}{a}\frac{x}{y}$$

$$\Rightarrow \quad \tan\psi = -\frac{b^2x}{a^2y} \qquad ...(4)$$

For a heterogeneous string,

$$w = \frac{T_0 \sec^2\psi}{\rho} \qquad \text{|Refer Ex. 1}$$

$$= \frac{T_0 ab \sec^2\psi}{CD^3} \qquad \text{|From (2)}$$

$$= \frac{T_0 ab}{b'^3}(1 + \tan^2\psi)$$

$$= \frac{T_0 ab}{b'^3}\left(1 + \frac{b^4x^2}{a^4y^2}\right) \qquad \text{|From (4)}$$

$$= \frac{T_0 ab}{b'^3}\left[1 + \frac{b^4a^2\cos^2\phi}{a^4b^2\sin^2\phi}\right] \qquad \left|\begin{array}{l}\because x = a\cos\phi,\\ y = b\sin\phi \text{ for point } P\end{array}\right.$$

$$= \frac{T_0 ab}{b'^3}\left(1 + \frac{b^2\cos^2\phi}{a^2\sin^2\phi}\right) \qquad \Rightarrow = \frac{T_0 ab}{b'^3}\left(\frac{a^2\sin^2\phi + b^2\cos^2\phi}{a^2\sin^2\phi}\right)$$

$$= \frac{T_0 ab}{b'^3}\frac{b'^2}{a^2\sin^2\phi} \qquad \text{|From (1)}$$

$$= \frac{T_0 b}{b' a \sin^2\phi} \qquad \Rightarrow = \frac{T_0 b^3}{ab'b^2\sin^2\phi} \qquad \Rightarrow = \frac{T_0 b^3}{aby^2}$$

**Example 9:** Show that mass per unit length of each point of a string acted upon by gravity only and suspended from two fixed points in order that it may hang in the form of a semi-circle with diameter horizontal, varies inversely as the square of the distance from that diameter.

**Sol.**

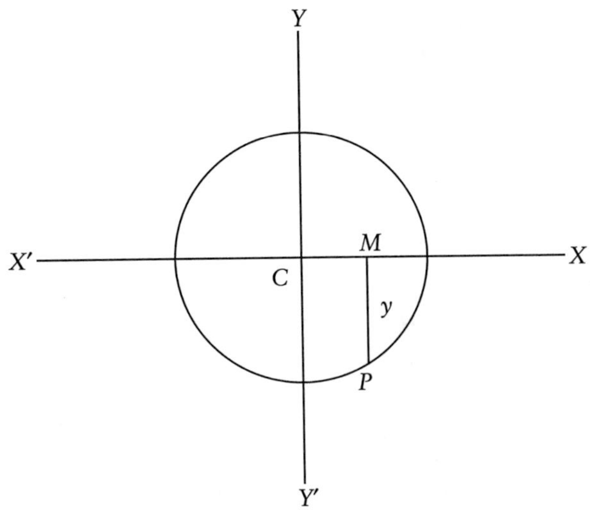


Let us take the horizontal diameter as the X-axis with its middle point as the origin and a vertical line through C as the Y-axis. Then, referred to these axes, the equation of the circle is

$$x^2 + y^2 = a^2 \qquad ...(1)$$

where $a$ is the radius of the circle.

Differentiating (1) with respect to $x$, we get,

$$2x + 2y\frac{dy}{dx} = 0 \quad \Rightarrow \frac{dy}{dx} = -\frac{x}{y} \quad \Rightarrow \tan\psi = -\frac{x}{y}$$

$$\Rightarrow \quad x = -y \tan\psi \qquad ...(2)$$

(1) and (2) give,

$$y^2 \tan^2\psi + y^2 = a^2 \quad \Rightarrow y^2 \sec^2\psi = a^2$$

$$\Rightarrow \quad \sec^2\psi = a^2/y^2 \qquad ...(3)$$

For a heterogeneous chain, we know that

$$w = \frac{T_0 \sec^2\psi}{\rho}$$

$$= \frac{T_0}{a}\frac{a^2}{y^2} \qquad |\because \rho = a \text{ for a circle of radius } a \text{ and from (3)}$$

$$= \frac{T_0 a}{y^2}$$

$$\Rightarrow \quad w \alpha \frac{1}{y^2} \qquad |\because T_0 \text{ is a constant}$$

where $y$ is the depth of the point below the horizontal diameter.

**Example 10:** A heavy string of variable density is hung up from two points. Prove that if $T_1$, $T_2$ and $T_3$ are tensions at points $A$, $B$ and $C$ where the inclinations of the tangents to the horizon are $\alpha-\beta$, $\alpha$, $\alpha+\beta$ and $w_1$, $w_2$ the weights of the parts of the string $AB$, $BC$ respectively, then

$$\frac{1}{T_1}+\frac{1}{T_3}=\frac{2\cos\beta}{T_2},\ \frac{T_1}{w_1}=\frac{T_3}{w_2}$$

**Sol.**

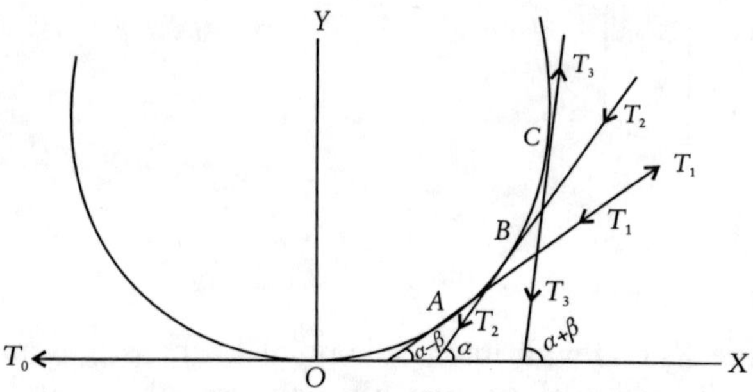


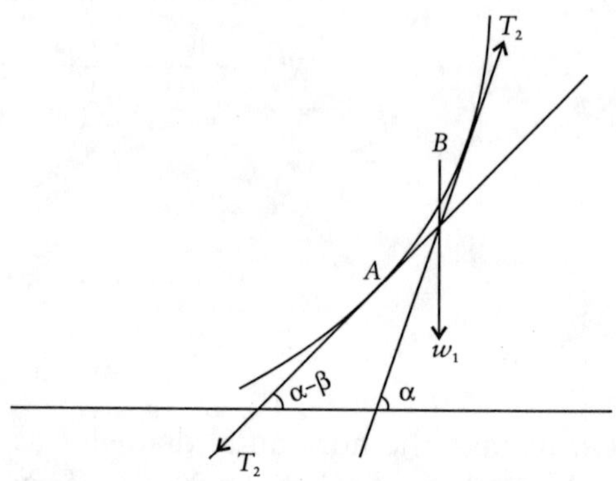


Let $O$ be the lowest point of the centenary. Let $T_1$, $T_2$ and $T_3$ be tensions at $A$, $B$ and $C$ respectively. Also, let $T_0$ be the tension at $O$.

Let us consider the equilibrium of the portion $OA$ of the string.

Resolving horizontally, we get,

$$T_1\cos(\alpha-\beta)=T_0 \qquad \text{...(1)}$$

Let us consider the equilibrium of the portion $OB$ of the string.

Resolving horizontally, we get,

$$T_2\cos\alpha=T_0 \qquad \text{...(2)}$$

Let us consider the equilibrium of the portion $OC$ of the string.

Resolving horizontally, we get,

$$T_3\cos(\alpha+\beta)=T_0 \qquad \text{...(3)}$$

Let us consider the equilibrium of the portion $AB$ of the string. Resolving vertically, we get,

$$T_2\sin\alpha-T_1\sin(\alpha-\beta)=w_1 \qquad \text{...(4)}$$

Let us consider the equilibrium of the portion $BC$ of the string. Resolving vertically, we get,

$$T_3\sin(\alpha+\beta)-T_2\sin\alpha=w_2 \qquad \text{...(5)}$$

(i) $\dfrac{1}{T_1}+\dfrac{1}{T_3}=\dfrac{1}{T_0}[\cos(\alpha-\beta)+\cos(\alpha+\beta)]=\dfrac{2\cos\alpha\cos\beta}{T_0}=\dfrac{2\cos\beta}{T_2}$ |From (2)

(ii) Multiplying (4) by $T_3$ and (5) by $T_1$ and subtracting, we get,

$$w_1T_3-w_2T_1=T_2T_3\sin\alpha-T_1T_3\sin(\alpha-\beta)-T_1T_3\sin(\alpha+\beta)+T_1T_2\sin\alpha$$

$$=T_1T_3\left(\frac{T_2\sin\alpha}{T_1}-\sin(\alpha-\beta)-\sin(\alpha+\beta)+\frac{T_2\sin\alpha}{T_3}\right)$$

$$= T_1T_3\left[\frac{\cos(\alpha-\beta)}{\cos\alpha}\sin\alpha - \sin(\alpha-\beta) - \sin(\alpha+\beta) + \frac{\cos(\alpha+\beta)}{\cos\alpha}\sin\alpha\right] \quad \text{|From (1), (2) and (3)}$$

$$= \frac{T_1T_3}{\cos\alpha}[\sin\alpha\cos(\alpha-\beta) - \cos\alpha\sin(\alpha-\beta) - \cos\alpha\sin(\alpha+\beta) + \sin\alpha\cos(\alpha+\beta)]$$

$$= \frac{T_1T_3}{\cos\alpha}[\sin\alpha\{\cos(\alpha-\beta) + \cos(\alpha+\beta)\} - \cos\alpha\{\sin(\alpha-\beta) + \sin(\alpha+\beta)\}]$$

$$= \frac{T_1T_3}{\cos\alpha}[(\sin\alpha 2\cos\alpha\cos\beta) - (\cos\alpha 2\sin\alpha\cos\beta)] = 0$$

$$\Rightarrow w_1 T_3 = w_2 T_1 \qquad \Rightarrow T_1/w_1 = T_3/w_2$$

## EXERCISE 1.3

1. A string hangs under gravity and it is loaded so that the weight of each element of it is proportional to the horizontal projection of that element. Show that it will hang in the form of a parabola.
2. Prove that the area of normal section at any point of a catenary of uniform strength is proportional to the radius of curvature.

   [Hint : $T \alpha A$

   $\Rightarrow T = \lambda A$

   $\Rightarrow T_0 \sec\psi = \lambda A \qquad | \because T\cos\psi = T_0$

   $\Rightarrow T_0 \rho/c = \lambda A \qquad | \because \rho = c\sec\psi$

   $\Rightarrow A = (T_0/\lambda c)\rho$

   $\Rightarrow A \alpha \rho$]
3. In the case of a catenary of uniform strength, show that mass per unit length is proportional to $\cos h\,(s/c)$.

   [Hint : $T = T_0 \sec\psi = T_0 \cos h\,(s/c) \quad | \because \cos\psi \cos h\,(s/c) = 1$

   $\Rightarrow T \alpha \cos h\,(s/c)$

   Again, $w \alpha T \Rightarrow m \alpha t \Rightarrow m \alpha \cos h\,(s/c)$]

Chapter 2

# Centre of Gravity

## 1. Centre of Gravity

We know that a rigid body is made up of a number of particles. Every particle is attracted by some force towards the centre of earth. Now the dimensions of the body are very small in comparison to the earth. So, the forces acting on different particles of the body form a system of parallel forces which has a resultant. This resultant is called the weight of the body. The point through which the line of action of the weight always passes, in whatsoever the position the body is placed, is called the centre of gravity of the body. The centre of gravity is abbreviated as C.G. It is also sometimes termed as centroid or centre of inertia.

If the body is removed away from the influence of gravity, there will be no centre of gravity of the body. But mass of the body is an inherent property of the body. Therefore, it will still have its centre of mass, which is the same as centre of gravity if gravity were there.

## 2. General Formula for Finding Centre of Gravity

Let the particles of weights $w_1, w_2, w_3, .....$ be placed at the points whose coordinates are $(x_1, y_1, z_1), (x_2, y_2, z_2), (x_3, y_3, z_3), .....$ respectively referred to rectangular system of coordinate axes $OX$, $OY$, $OZ$. Then, if $(\bar{x}, \bar{y}, \bar{z})$ are the coordinates of their C.G. referred to the same system of axes, we have

$$\bar{x} = \frac{\Sigma w_1 x_1}{\Sigma w_1} \qquad \Rightarrow \bar{y} = \frac{\Sigma w_1 y_1}{\Sigma w_1} \qquad \Rightarrow \bar{z} = \frac{\Sigma w_1 z_1}{\Sigma w_1}$$

Again, if the masses of the particles be $m_1, m_2, m_3, ......$ respectively, then

$$w_1 = m_1 g,\ w_2 = m_2 g,\ w_3 = m_3 g,\ .............$$

where $g$ is the force of attraction per unit mass due to gravity.

Hence, the C.G. of the system of particles is given by

$$\bar{x} = \frac{\Sigma m_1 g x_1}{\Sigma m_1 g} = \frac{\Sigma m_1 x_1}{\Sigma m_1}$$

Similarly,

$$\bar{y} = \frac{\Sigma m_1 g y_1}{\Sigma m_1 g} = \frac{\Sigma m_1 y_1}{\Sigma m_1}$$

and $$\bar{z} = \frac{\Sigma m_1 g z_1}{\Sigma m_1 g} = \frac{\Sigma m_1 z_1}{\Sigma m_1}$$

It shows that the centre of gravity coincides with the centre of mass.

*Note*: If all the particles are coplanar, i.e., lie in the same plane ($XY$ – plane say), then $\bar{z} = 0$. Hence, the centre of gravity $(\bar{x}, \bar{y})$ in this case is given by

$$\bar{x} = \frac{\Sigma w_1 x_1}{\Sigma w_1} = \frac{\Sigma m_1 x_1}{\Sigma m_1}$$

$$\bar{y} = \frac{\Sigma w_1 y_1}{\Sigma w_1} = \frac{\Sigma m_1 y_1}{\Sigma m_1}$$

## 3. Some Standard Results

(i) The C.G. of a thin uniform rod lies at its middle point.

(ii) The C.G. of a uniform triangular lamina lies at the point of concurrence of its three medians. By Geometry, C.G. divides each median in the ratio 1 : 2 from the base [or, in the ratio 2 : 1 from the vertex]

(iii) The C.G. of a uniform parallelogram lies at the point of intersection of its diagonals.

(iv) The C.G. of a circular wire or a circular disc is at its centre.

(v) The C.G. of a hollow cone lies on the line joining its vertex to the centroid of the base and divides it in the ratio 2 : 1 from the vertex.

(vi) The C.G. of a solid come lies on the line joining its vertex to the centroid of the base and divides it in the ratio 3 : 1 from the vertex.

(vii) The C.G. of a semi-circular arc of radius $a$ is at a distance $2a/\pi$ from the centre on the central radius.

(viii) The C.G. of a semi-circular lamina of radius $r$ is at a distance $4r/3\pi$ from the centre on the central radius.

## 4. Centre of Gravity by Integration

We know that if a number of particles of masses $m_1$, $m_2$, $m_3$, ..... be placed at the points $(x_1, y_1)$, $(x_2, y_2)$, $(x_3, y_3)$, ..... respectively, then the coordinates $(\bar{x}, \bar{y})$ of their C.G. are given by

$$\bar{x} = \frac{\Sigma m_1 g x_1}{\Sigma m_1 g}$$

$$\bar{y} = \frac{\Sigma m_1 g y_1}{\Sigma m_1 g}$$

If instead of discrete particles, we have a continuous distribution of matter, then the summation can be replaced by integration. Thus, if $dm$ is the mass of an element whose centroid is $(x, y)$, then in the above formula, we replace $\Sigma m_1 g$ by $\int g\, dm$, $\Sigma m_1 g\, x_1$ by $\int x\, g\, dm$ and $\Sigma m_1 g y_1$ by

$\int y\, g\, dm$, the integration being carried out throughout the matter whose C.G. $(\bar{x}, \bar{y})$ is to be determined. Thus, for continuous distribution of matter, we have

$$\bar{x} = \frac{\int x g\, dm}{\int g\, dm} = \frac{\int x\, dm}{\int dm}$$

and $$\bar{y} = \frac{\int y g\, dm}{\int g\, dm} = \frac{\int y\, dm}{\int dm} \text{ since } g \text{ is constant.}$$

## 5. Centre of Gravity of an Arc of a Given Curve

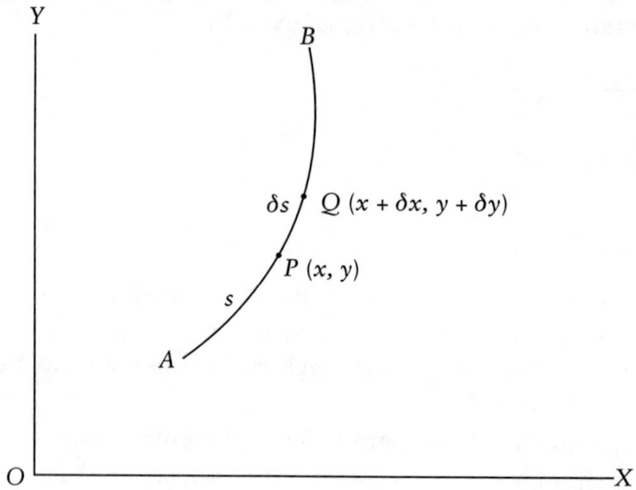


Let us consider the matter distributed in the form of arc $AB$ of a plane curve. The equation of the curve may be given by means of a cartesian equation or a polar equation or a pair of parametric equations. Let $P\,(x, y)$ and $Q\,(x + \delta x, y + \delta y)$ be any two neighbouring points on the arc $AB$. Let $A$ be a fixed point on the curve, arc $AP = s$ and arc $PQ = \delta s$. Let $\rho$ be the density of the arc of the curve at the point $P$. Then, $\rho$ may be considered constant from $P$ to $Q$ as arc $PQ = \delta s$ is very small. Hence, the mass $\delta m$ of the elementary arc $PQ$ is $\rho\, \delta s$. Also the centre of gravity of the elementary arc $PQ$ can be approximately taken as the point $P\,(x, y)$ because the point $Q$ is very close to $P$ so that arc $PQ$ is infinitesimally small.

Therefore, in case of the arc of uniform or non-uniform density, the co-ordinates $(\bar{x}, \bar{y})$ of the centre of gravity of the arc $AB$ are given by

$$\bar{x} = \frac{\int x\, dm}{\int dm} = \frac{\int x \rho\, ds}{\int ds}$$

$$\bar{y} = \frac{\int y\, dm}{\int dm} = \frac{\int y \rho\, ds}{\int \rho\, ds}$$

where in all the above integrals, the limits of integration are to be taken from one end $A$ of the arc $AB$, under consideration, to the other end $B$ of the arc $AB$.

If the distribution of matter is uniform, i.e., $\rho$ is constant, then the above formulae become

$$\bar{x} = \frac{\int x\, ds}{\int ds}$$

$$\bar{y} = \frac{\int y\, ds}{\int ds}$$

To perform above integrations, we have to substitute as from one of the following formulae, as the case may be:

1. In Cartesian coordinates

$$ds = \sqrt{1 + \left(\frac{dy}{dx}\right)^2}\ dx$$

$$ds = \sqrt{1 + \left(\frac{dx}{dy}\right)^2}\ dy$$

2. In Polar coordinates

$$ds = \sqrt{r^2 + \left(\frac{dr}{d\vartheta}\right)^2}\ d\vartheta$$

3. In Parametric coordinates

$$ds = \sqrt{\left(\frac{dx}{dt}\right)^2 + \left(\frac{dy}{dt}\right)^2}\ dt$$

## ILLUSTRATIVE EXAMPLES

**Example 1:** Find the centre of gravity of a circular arc subtending an angle $2\alpha$ at the centre. Hence or otherwise find the C.G. of the arc of a semi-circle.

**Sol.**

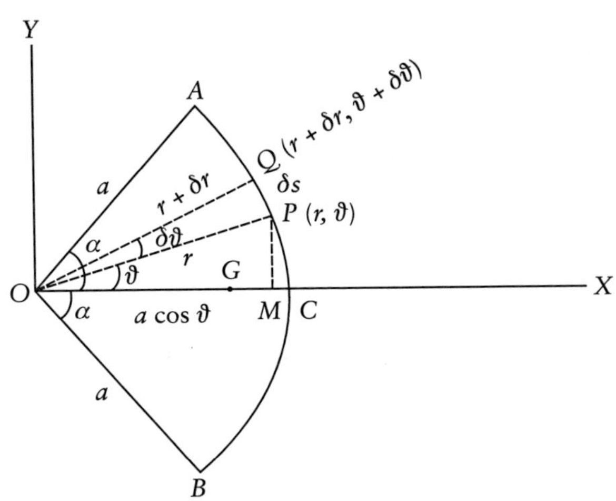

Let $AB$ be the circular arc subtending an angle $2\alpha$ at the centre O. We have to find the C.G. of the arc $ACB$ where $\angle AOB = 2\alpha$.

Take a point C on $AB$ such that arc $AC$ = arc $CB$. Then,

$$\angle AOC = \angle BOC = \alpha$$

Take the centre O of the circle as the pole and the symmetrical radius $OC$ as the initial line. We take two neighbouring points $P$ $(r, \vartheta)$ and $Q$ $(r + \delta r, \delta + \delta\vartheta)$ on the arc $ACB$. Let arc $PQ$ = $\delta s$. Then, $\delta s = a\delta\vartheta$, where $a$ is the radius of the circular arc. Let the certesian coordinates of $P$ by $(x, y)$. Then,

$$x = a \cos \theta$$

$$y = a \sin \vartheta$$

Therefore, the C.G. of the arc $PQ$ is $(x, y)$ or $(a \cos \vartheta, a \sin \vartheta)$.

Let $(\overline{x}, \overline{y})$ be the coordinates of the C.G. of the circular arc $AB$.

By symmetry, $\overline{y} = 0$

Now, $x = \dfrac{\int x\, dm}{\int dm}$

$$= \frac{\int x \rho ds}{\int \rho ds} \quad \Rightarrow = \frac{\int x\, ds}{\int ds} \qquad |\because \rho \text{ is constant}$$

$$= \frac{\int_{-\alpha}^{\alpha} a\cos\vartheta\, a d\vartheta}{\int_{-\alpha}^{\alpha} a d\vartheta} \quad \Rightarrow = \frac{a(\sin\vartheta)_{-\alpha}^{\alpha}}{(\vartheta)_{-\alpha}^{\alpha}} \quad \Rightarrow = \frac{a\{\sin\alpha - \sin(-\alpha)\}}{\alpha - (-\alpha)}$$

$$= 2a \sin \alpha/2\alpha \quad \Rightarrow = a \sin \alpha/\alpha$$

Hence, the required C.G. $G$ lies on the central radius $OC$ such that

$$OG = a \sin \alpha/\alpha$$

**Deduction:** If the given arc is semi-circular, then $\alpha = \pi/2$

$$\therefore OG = \frac{a \sin \frac{\pi}{2}}{\frac{\pi}{2}} = \frac{2a}{\pi}$$

Hence, the required C.G. $G$ lies on the symmetrical radius $OC$ such that $OG = 2a/\pi$.

**Example 2:** Find the centroid of the arc of the catenary $y = c \cos h\ (x/c)$ which is included between the origin and any point $(x, y)$

Or

Prove that the centroid of the arc of the catenary $y = c \cos h\ (x/c)$, which is included between the vertex and any point $(x, y)$, from the X-axis is $cx{+}ys/2s$.

**Sol.**

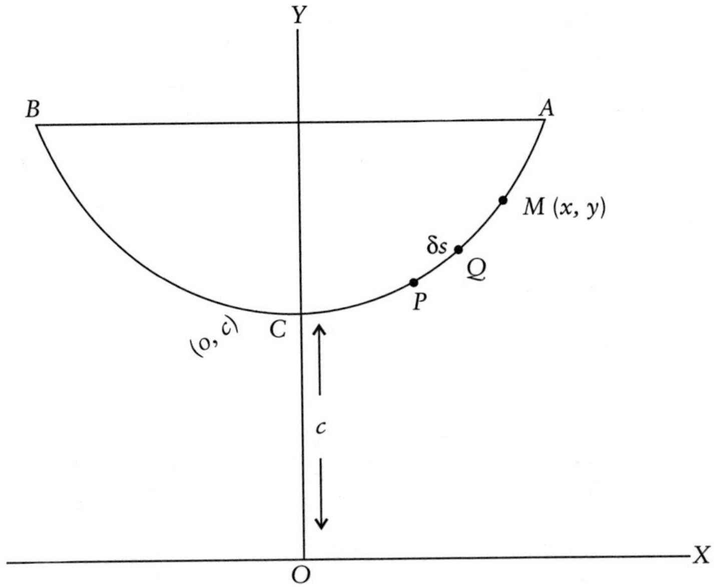


A $CB$ is a catenary. Let $M(x, y)$ be any point on the curve. We are to find out the C.G. of the arc $CM$, which is included between the vertex $C$ and any point $M(x, y)$.

The equation to the curve is

$$y = c \cos h\,(x/c) \qquad \text{...(1)}$$

$$\therefore \quad \frac{dy}{dx} = c \sin h\left(\frac{x}{c}\right)\frac{1}{c}$$

$$\Rightarrow \quad \frac{dy}{dx} = \sin h\left(\frac{x}{c}\right) \qquad \text{...(2)}$$

$$\therefore \quad \frac{ds}{dx} = \sqrt{1+\left(\frac{dy}{dx}\right)^2} \quad \Rightarrow \; = \sqrt{1+\sin h^2\left(\frac{x}{c}\right)} \qquad |\text{From (2)}$$

$$= \sqrt{\cos h^2\left(\frac{x}{c}\right)} \quad \Rightarrow \; = \cos h\left(\frac{x}{c}\right)$$

$$\Rightarrow \quad ds = \cos h\left(\frac{x}{c}\right)dx \qquad \text{...(3)}$$

Take an element $PQ$ of length $\delta s$ on the arc $CM$. Let $\rho$ be the mass per unit length of the arc $PQ$.

Let arc $PQ = \delta s$.

Then, mass of the elementary arc $PQ$

$$= \rho\, \delta s$$

Let the coordinates of C.G. of the arc $CM$ be $(\bar{x}, \bar{y})$. For the arc $CM$ of the catenary, $x$ varies from 0 to $x$.

$$\therefore \bar{x} = \frac{\int x\, dm}{\int dm} \qquad \Rightarrow \qquad = \frac{\int x \rho\, ds}{\int \rho\, ds}$$

$$= \frac{\int x\, ds}{\int ds} \qquad \Big|\because \rho \text{ is constant}$$

$$= \frac{\int_0^x x \cos h\left(\frac{x}{c}\right) dx}{\int_0^x \cos h\left(\frac{x}{c}\right) dx} \qquad \Big|\because \text{From}(3)$$

$$= \frac{\left[x c \sin h \frac{x}{c}\right]_0^x - \int_0^x 1.c \sin h \frac{x}{c}\, dx}{\left(c \sin h \frac{x}{c}\right)_0^x}$$

$$= \frac{cx \sin h\left(\frac{x}{c}\right) - c\left[c \cos h\left(\frac{x}{c}\right)\right]_0^x}{c \sin h\left(\frac{x}{c}\right)} \qquad \Rightarrow = \frac{x \sin h\left(\frac{x}{c}\right) - c\left(\cos h \frac{x}{c} - 1\right)}{\sin h\left(\frac{x}{c}\right)}$$

$$= x - c\frac{\left(\frac{y}{c} - 1\right)}{\left(\frac{s}{c}\right)} \qquad \Bigg|\because y = c \cos h\left(\frac{x}{c}\right),\ s = c \sin h\left(\frac{x}{c}\right) \qquad \Rightarrow = x - c\left(\frac{y - c}{s}\right)$$

and

$$\bar{y} = \frac{\int dm}{\int dm} \qquad \Rightarrow = \frac{\int y \rho\, ds}{\int \rho\, ds}$$

$$= \frac{\int y\, ds}{\int ds} \qquad \Big|\because \rho \text{ is constant}$$

$$= \frac{\int_0^x c \cos h\left(\frac{x}{c}\right) \cos h\left(\frac{x}{c}\right) dx}{\int_0^x \cos h\left(\frac{x}{c}\right) dx} \qquad \Rightarrow = \frac{\frac{c}{2}\int_0^x 2 \cos h^2\left(\frac{x}{c}\right) dx}{\left[c \sin h\left(\frac{x}{c}\right)\right]_0^x}$$

$$= \frac{\frac{c}{2}\int_0^x \left\{1 + \cos h\left(\frac{2x}{c}\right)\right\} dx}{c \sin h\left(\frac{x}{c}\right)} \qquad \Rightarrow = \frac{\frac{c}{2}\left[x + \frac{c}{2} \sin h\left(\frac{2x}{c}\right)\right]}{c \sin h\left(\frac{x}{c}\right)}$$

$$= \frac{\frac{1}{2}\left\{x + c\sin h\left(\frac{x}{c}\right)\cos h\left(\frac{x}{c}\right)\right\}}{\sin h\left(\frac{x}{c}\right)}$$

$$= \frac{\frac{1}{2}\left[x + c.\frac{s}{c}\frac{y}{c}\right]}{\frac{s}{c}} \qquad \left|\; \because y = c\cos h\left(\frac{x}{c}\right),\; s = c\sin h\left(\frac{x}{c}\right)\right.$$

$= cx + ys/2s$

**Example 3:** Find the centre of gravity of the arc of the parabola $y^2 = 4a\,x$ included between the vertex and the latus rectum.

**Sol.**

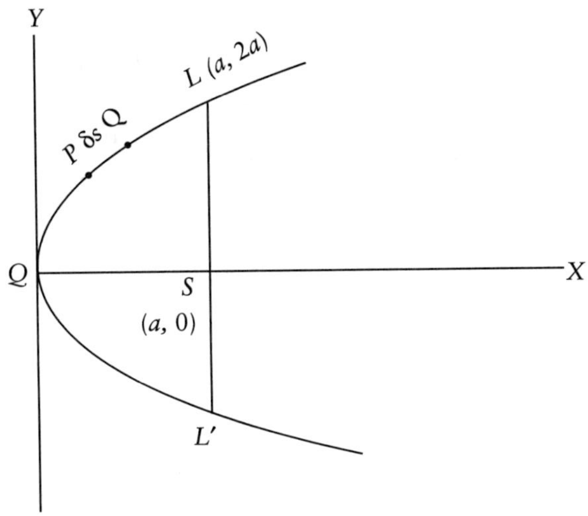


O(0, 0) is the vertex of the parabola. $L\ (a, 2a)$ is an extremity of the latus rectum $L\ SL'$ of this parabola. We are required to find out the C.G. of the arc $OL$.

At O, $x = 0$, $y = 0$

Equation of the parabola is

$$y^2 = 4\,ax \qquad ...(1)$$

Differentiating (1) with respect to $x$, we get

$$2y\frac{dy}{dx} = 4a \qquad \Rightarrow \frac{dy}{dx} = \frac{2a}{y}$$

$$\Rightarrow \qquad \frac{dx}{dy} = \frac{y}{2a} \qquad ...(2)$$

$$\therefore \qquad \frac{ds}{dy} = \sqrt{1 + \left(\frac{dx}{dy}\right)^2}$$

$$= \sqrt{1+\frac{y^2}{4a^2}} \qquad \Rightarrow = \frac{1}{2a}\sqrt{y^2+4a^2}$$

$$\therefore \qquad ds = \frac{1}{2a}\sqrt{y^2+4a^2}\,dy \qquad \text{...(3)}$$

Consider two neighbouring points $P(x, y)$ and $Q\ (x + \delta x, y + \delta y)$ on the arc $OL$. Let arc $PQ = \delta s$. Let $\rho$ be the mass per unit length of the arc $PQ$. Therefore, mass of the elementary arc $PQ = \rho\delta s$. Also, C.G. of the arc $PQ$ is $(x, y)$.

Let $(\bar{x}, \bar{y})$ be the required C.G. Then,

$$\bar{x} = \frac{\int x\,dm}{\int dm} \qquad \Rightarrow = \frac{\int x\rho ds}{\int \rho ds}$$

$$= \frac{\int x ds}{\int ds} \qquad |\because \rho \text{ is constant}$$

$$= \frac{\int_0^{2a} x\frac{ds}{dy}dy}{\int_0^{2a}\frac{ds}{dy}dy} \qquad \Rightarrow = \frac{\int_0^{2a} x.\frac{1}{2a}\sqrt{y^2+4a^2}\,dy}{\int_0^{2a}\frac{1}{2a}\sqrt{y^2+4a^2}\,dy} \qquad |\text{From (3)}$$

$$= \frac{\int_0^{2a}\frac{y^2}{4a}\sqrt{y^2+4a^2}\,dy}{\int_0^{2a}\sqrt{y^2+4a^2}\,dy} \qquad |\text{From (1)}$$

$$= \frac{\frac{1}{4a}\int_0^{2a} y^2\sqrt{y^2+4a^2}\,dy}{\int_0^{2a}\sqrt{y^2+4a^2}\,dy} \qquad \text{...(4)}$$

and, $$\bar{y} = \frac{\int y\,dm}{\int dm} \qquad \Rightarrow = \frac{\int y\rho ds}{\int \rho ds}$$

$$= \frac{\int y ds}{\int ds} \qquad |\because \rho \text{ is constant}$$

$$= \frac{\int_0^{2a} y\frac{ds}{dy}dy}{\int_0^{2a}\frac{ds}{dy}dy} \qquad \Rightarrow = \frac{\int_0^{2a}\frac{y}{2a}\sqrt{y^2+4a^2}\,dy}{\int_0^{2a}\frac{1}{2a}\sqrt{y^2+4a^2}\,dy} \qquad |\text{From (3)}$$

$$= \frac{\int_0^{2a} y\sqrt{y^2+4a^2}\,dy}{\int_0^{2a}\sqrt{y^2+4a^2}\,dy} \qquad \text{...(5)}$$

Numerator of $\bar{x} = \frac{1}{4a}\int_0^{2a} y^2\sqrt{y^2+4a^2}\,dy$

Put $\quad y = 2a \tan \vartheta$

$\therefore \quad dy = 2a \sec^2 \theta d\vartheta$

$$= \frac{1}{4a}\int_0^{\frac{\pi}{4}} 4a^2 \tan^2\vartheta\sqrt{4a^2\tan^2\vartheta + 4a^2}\,.2a\sec^2\vartheta\, d\vartheta$$

$$= 4a^3\int_0^{\frac{\pi}{4}} \tan^2\vartheta\sec^3\vartheta\, d\vartheta \qquad \Rightarrow = 4a^3\int^{-} (\sec^2\vartheta - 1)\sec^3\vartheta\, d\vartheta$$

$$= 4a^3\int_0^{\frac{\pi}{4}} (\sec^5\vartheta - \sec^3\vartheta)\, d\vartheta \qquad \Rightarrow = 4a^3\left[\int_0^{\frac{\pi}{4}} \sec^5\vartheta d\vartheta - \int_0^{\frac{\pi}{4}} \sec^3\vartheta d\vartheta\right]$$

$$= 4a^3\left[\left\{\left(\frac{\sec^3\vartheta\tan\vartheta}{4}\right)_0^{\frac{\pi}{4}} + \frac{3}{4}\int_0^{\frac{\pi}{4}}\sec^3\vartheta d\vartheta\right\} - \int_0^{\frac{\pi}{4}}\sec^3\vartheta d\vartheta\right]$$

$$\left|\because \int \sec^n\vartheta d\vartheta = \frac{\sec^{n-2}\vartheta\tan\vartheta}{n-1} + \frac{n-2}{n-1}\int\sec^{n-2}\vartheta d\vartheta\right.$$

$$= 4a^3\left[\frac{2\sqrt{2}}{4} - \frac{1}{4}\int_0^{\frac{\pi}{4}}\sec^3\vartheta d\vartheta\right]$$

$$= 4a^3\left[\frac{2\sqrt{2}}{4} - \frac{1}{4}\left\{\left(\frac{\sec\vartheta\tan\vartheta}{2}\right)_0^{\frac{\pi}{4}} + \frac{1}{2}\int_0^{\frac{\pi}{4}}\sec\vartheta d\vartheta\right\}\right]$$

$$= 4a^3\left[\frac{2\sqrt{2}}{4} - \frac{\sqrt{2}}{8} - \frac{1}{8}\{\log(\sec\vartheta\tan\vartheta)\}_0^{\pi/4}\right]$$

$$= 4a^3\left[\frac{2\sqrt{2}}{4} - \frac{\sqrt{2}}{8} - \frac{1}{8}\log\left(\sqrt{2}+1\right)\right]$$

$$= \frac{a^3}{2}\left[3\sqrt{2} - \log\left(\sqrt{2}+1\right)\right] \qquad \text{...(6)}$$

Numerator of $\bar{y} = \int_0^{2a} y\sqrt{y^2 + 4a^2}\, dy$

Put $\quad y^2 + 4a^2 = t^2$

$\therefore \quad 2y\, dy = 2t\, dt \qquad \Rightarrow y\, dy = t\, dt$

$$= \int_{2a}^{2\sqrt{2}a} t^2 dt \qquad \Rightarrow = \left(\frac{t^3}{3}\right)_{2a}^{2\sqrt{2}a}$$

$$= \frac{8a^3}{3}\left(2\sqrt{2} - 1\right) \qquad \text{...(7)}$$

Denominator of $\bar{x}$ (or $\bar{y}$)

$$= \int_0^{2a} \sqrt{y^2 + 4a^2}\, dy$$

$$= \left[\frac{1}{2}y\sqrt{y^2+4a^2}+\frac{1}{2}.4a^2\log\left\{y+\sqrt{y^2+4a^2}\right\}\right]_0^{2a}$$

$$= \frac{1}{2}\left[2a\sqrt{8a^2}+4a^2\log\left(2a+2\sqrt{2}a\right)-4a^2\log 2a\right]$$

$$= \frac{1}{2}\left[4\sqrt{2}a^2+4a^2\log\left(\frac{2a+2\sqrt{2}a}{2a}\right)\right]$$

$$= \frac{1}{2}\left[4\sqrt{2}a^2+4a^2\log\left(1+\sqrt{2}\right)\right]$$

$$= 2a^2\left[\sqrt{2}+\log\left(1+\sqrt{2}\right)\right] \qquad ...(8)$$

Hence,

$$\bar{x} = \frac{\frac{a^3}{2}\left[3\sqrt{2}-\log\left(\sqrt{2}+1\right)\right]}{2a^2\left[\sqrt{2}+\log\left(1+\sqrt{2}\right)\right]} \quad \Rightarrow = \frac{a}{4}\left\{\frac{3\sqrt{2}-\log\left(1+\sqrt{2}\right)}{\sqrt{2}+\log\left(1+\sqrt{2}\right)}\right\}$$

and

$$\bar{y} = \frac{\frac{8a^3}{3}\left(2\sqrt{2}+1\right)}{2a^2\left[\sqrt{2}+\log\left(1+\sqrt{2}\right)\right]} \quad \Rightarrow = \frac{4a}{3}\frac{2\sqrt{2}-1}{\sqrt{2}+\log\left(1+\sqrt{2}\right)}$$

**Example 4:** Find the position of the centroid of the arc of the cardioid $r = a\ (1 + \cos \vartheta)$ lying above the initial line.

**Sol.**

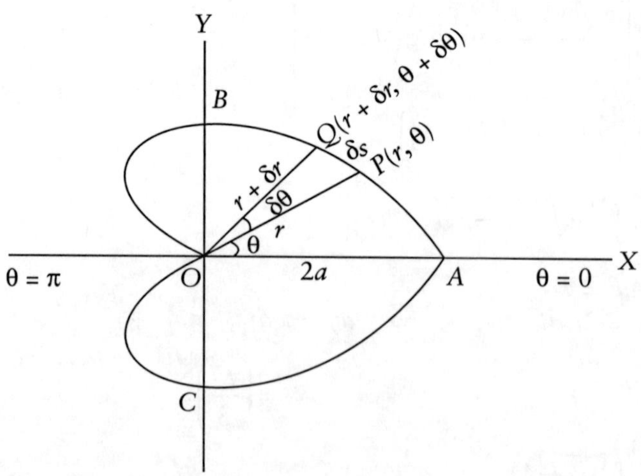


Let *OBAC O* be the cardioid. We are required to find the C.G. of the arc *OBA* lying above the initial line. We take two neighbouring points $P(r, \vartheta)$ and $Q(r + \delta r, \vartheta + \delta\vartheta)$ such that arc $PQ = \delta s$. Then mass of the elementary arc $PQ = e\ \delta s$ where $e$ is the mass per unit arc length of the cardioid. Its C.G. is at $(x, y)$ or $(r \cos \vartheta, r \sin \vartheta)$.

The arc $ABO$ extends from $\theta = 0$ (at $A$) to $\theta = \pi$ (at $O$)

Equation of the curve is

$$r = a\,(1 + \cos\theta) \qquad \text{...(1)}$$

Differentiating (1) with respect to $\theta$, we get

$$dr/d\theta = -\,a \sin\theta \qquad \text{...(2)}$$

$$\therefore \quad \frac{ds}{d\vartheta} = \sqrt{r^2 + \left(\frac{dr}{d\vartheta}\right)^2}$$

$$= \sqrt{a^2(1+\cos\vartheta)^2 + a^2\sin^2\vartheta} \qquad \text{|From (1) and (2)}$$

$$= a\sqrt{(1+\cos\vartheta)^2 + \sin^2\vartheta} \qquad \Rightarrow = a\sqrt{1+\cos\vartheta+2\cos\vartheta+\sin^2\vartheta}$$

$$= a\sqrt{2+2\cos\vartheta} \qquad \Rightarrow = a\sqrt{2(1+\cos\vartheta)}$$

$$= a\sqrt{4\cos^2\frac{\vartheta}{2}} \qquad \Rightarrow = 2a\cos\frac{\vartheta}{2}$$

$$\Rightarrow \quad ds = 2a\cos\frac{\vartheta}{2}\,d\vartheta \qquad \text{...(3)}$$

Let $(\bar{x}, \bar{y})$ be the required C.G. Then,
we have,

$$\bar{x} = \frac{\int x\,dm}{\int dm} = \frac{\int x\rho\,ds}{\int \rho\,ds}$$

$$= \frac{\int x\,ds}{\int ds} \qquad \text{| } \because \rho \text{ is constant}$$

$$= \frac{\int_0^\pi r\cos\theta\frac{ds}{d\theta}\,d\theta}{\int_0^\pi \frac{ds}{d\theta}\,d\theta} \qquad \text{| } \because x = r\cos\theta$$

$$= \frac{\int_0^\pi a(1+\cos\theta)\cos\theta\, 2a\cos\frac{\theta}{2}\,d\theta}{\int_0^\pi 2a\cos\frac{\theta}{2}\,d\theta} \qquad \text{| From (1) and (3)}$$

$$= \frac{a\int_0^\pi (1+\cos\theta)\cos\theta\cos\frac{\theta}{2}\,d\theta}{\int_0^\pi \cos\frac{\theta}{2}\,d\theta} \qquad \text{...(4)}$$

and $\bar{y} = \dfrac{\int y\,dm}{\int dm} \qquad = \dfrac{\int y\rho\,ds}{\int \rho\,ds}$

$= \dfrac{\int y\,ds}{\int ds}$ | $\because$ ρ is constant

$= \dfrac{\int_0^\pi r\sin\theta\, 2a\cos\frac{\theta}{2}\,d\theta}{\int_0^\pi 2a\cos\frac{\theta}{2}\,d\theta}$ | $\because y = r\sin\theta$ and from (3)

$= \dfrac{\int_0^\pi a(1+\cos\theta)\sin\theta\cos\frac{\theta}{2}\,d\theta}{\int_0^\pi \cos\frac{\theta}{2}\,d\theta}$ | From (1)

$$= \frac{a\int_0^\pi (1+\cos\theta)\sin\theta\cos\frac{\theta}{2}\,d\theta}{\int_0^\pi \cos\frac{\theta}{2}\,d\theta} \qquad ...(5)$$

Numerator of $\bar{x} = a\int_0^\pi (1+\cos\theta)\cos\theta\cos\frac{\theta}{2}\,d\theta$

$= a\int_0^\pi 2\cos^2\frac{\theta}{2}\left(2\cos^2\frac{\theta}{2}-1\right)\cos\frac{\theta}{2}\,d\theta \qquad = 2a\int_0^\pi \cos^3\frac{\theta}{2}\left(2\cos^2\frac{\theta}{2}-1\right)d\theta$

Put θ/2 = φ

$\therefore \quad 1/2\ d\theta = d\phi \qquad \Rightarrow d\theta = 2d\phi$

$= 2a\int_0^{\pi/2} \cos^3\phi\left(2\cos^2\phi-1\right)2d\phi$

$= 4a\left[2\int_0^{\pi/2}\cos^5\phi\,d\phi - \int_0^{\pi/2}\cos^3\phi\,d\phi\right]$

$= 4a\left[2\frac{4}{5}.\frac{2}{3}-\frac{2}{3}\right]$ | By Walli's Formula

$$= 8a\left(\frac{8}{15}-\frac{1}{3}\right) = \frac{8a}{5} \qquad ...(6)$$

Numerator of $\bar{y} = a\int_0^\pi (1+\cos\theta)\sin\theta\cos\frac{\theta}{2}\,d\theta$

$$= a\int_0^{\pi} 2\cos^2\frac{\theta}{2} 2\sin\frac{\theta}{2}\cos\frac{\theta}{2}\cos\frac{\theta}{2}d\theta \qquad = 4a\int_0^{\pi/2}\cos^4\theta\sin\frac{\theta}{2}\,d\theta$$

Put $\theta/2 = \phi$ $\quad\therefore$ $1/2\ d\theta = d\phi$ $\quad\Rightarrow d\theta = 2\ d\phi$

$$= 4a\int_0^{\pi/2}\cos^4\phi\sin\phi 2\ d\phi \qquad = 8a\int_0^{\pi/2}\cos^4\phi\sin d\phi$$

Put $\cos\phi = t$

$\therefore -\sin\phi\ d\phi = dt$

$\Rightarrow \sin\phi\ d\phi = -dt$

$$= -8a\int_1^0 t^4\,dt \qquad = 8a\int_0^1 t^4\,dt$$

$$= 8a\left(\frac{t^5}{5}\right)_0^1 \qquad = \frac{8a}{5} \qquad ...(7)$$

Denominator $\overline{x}$ = Denominator of $\overline{y}$

$$= \int_0^{\pi}\cos\frac{\theta}{2}d\theta \qquad = \left(2\sin\frac{\theta}{2}\right)_0^{\pi} = 2 \qquad ...(8)$$

$$\therefore\ \overline{x} = \frac{\frac{8}{5}a}{2} = \frac{4}{5}a \qquad \text{and} \qquad \overline{y} = \frac{\frac{8a}{5}}{2} = \frac{4}{5}a$$

**Example 5:** Prove that for the arc of the curve $x^{2/3} + y^{2/3} = a^{2/3}$, between two successive cusps, the centre of gravity $(\overline{x}, \overline{y})$ is given by

$\overline{x} = \overline{y} = 2/5a$

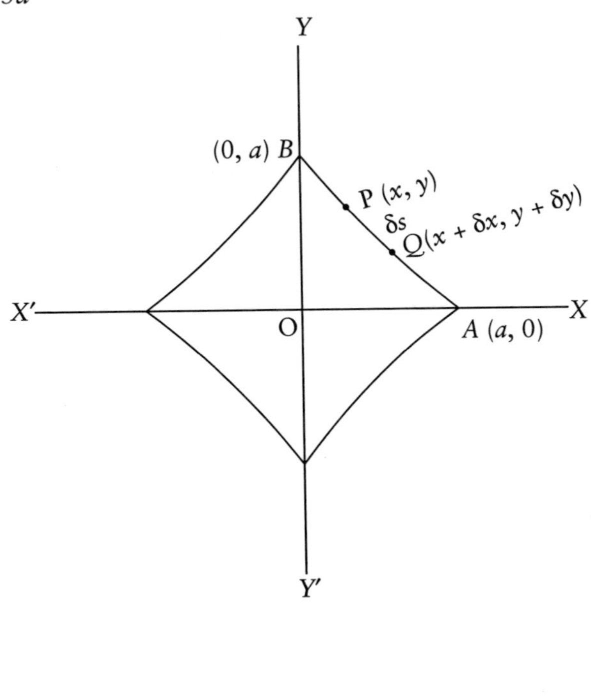

The equation of the curve is

$$x^{2/3} + y^{2/3} = a^{2/3} \quad ...(1)$$

$A(a, 0)$ and $B$ $(0, a)$ are the two successive cusps in the first quadrant. We are to find out the C.G. of the arc $AB$.

Since on interchanging $x$ and $y$, the equation of the curve remains unchanged, therefore, the curve (i) is symmetrical about the line $y = x$. Therefore, the arc $AB$ is symmetrical about the line $y = x$. So, its C.G. lies on this line. Therefore, $\bar{x} = \bar{y}$ ...(2)

where $(\bar{x}, \bar{y})$ are the coordinates of C.G. of the arc $AB$.

Differentiating (1) with repeat to $x$, and get

$$\frac{2}{3}x^{-1/3} + \frac{2}{3}y^{-1/3}\frac{dy}{dx} = 0 \qquad \Rightarrow dy/dx = -\,y^{1/3}/x^{1/3}$$

$$\therefore \qquad ds/dx = \sqrt{1+\left(\frac{dy}{dx}\right)^2} = \sqrt{1+\frac{y^{2/3}}{x^{2/3}}}$$

$$= \frac{\sqrt{x^{2/3}+y^{2/3}}}{x^{3}} = \frac{\sqrt{a^{2/3}}}{x^{3}} \qquad \text{| From (1)}$$

$$= \left(\frac{a}{x}\right)^{1/3} \qquad \Rightarrow ds = \left(\frac{a}{x}\right)^{1/3} dx \quad ...(3)$$

Take two neighbouring points $P(x, y)$ and $Q(x + \delta x, y + \delta y)$ on the arc $AB$. Let arc $PQ$ = $\delta s$. Then, $\delta s$ is the elementary arc of $AB$. It mass = $\rho\, ds$, where, $\rho$ is the mass for unit length of the arc $AB$. The C.G. of this elementary arc is at $P(x, y)$.

Now,

$$\bar{x} = \frac{\int x\,dm}{\int dm} = \frac{\int x\rho\, ds}{\int \rho ds}$$

$$= \frac{\int x\, ds}{\int ds} \qquad \text{|}\because \rho \text{ is constant}$$

$$= \frac{\int_0^a x\left(\frac{a}{x}\right)^{1/3} dx}{\int_0^a \left(\frac{a}{x}\right)^{1/3} dx} \qquad \text{|From (3)}$$

$$= \frac{\int_0^a x^{2/3} dx}{\int_0^a x^{-1/3} dx} = \frac{\frac{3}{5}\left(x^{5/3}\right)_0^a}{\frac{3}{2}\left(x^{2/3}\right)_0^a}$$

$$= \frac{2}{5}\frac{a^{5/3}}{a^{2/3}} = \frac{2}{5}a \quad ...(4)$$

Hence, $\bar{x} = \bar{y} = 2/5\ a$ | From (2) and (4)

**Example 6:** Find the centroid of the arc of he cycloid $x = a(\theta + \sin\theta)$, $y = a(1 - \cos\theta)$ which lies in the positive quadrant.

**Sol.**

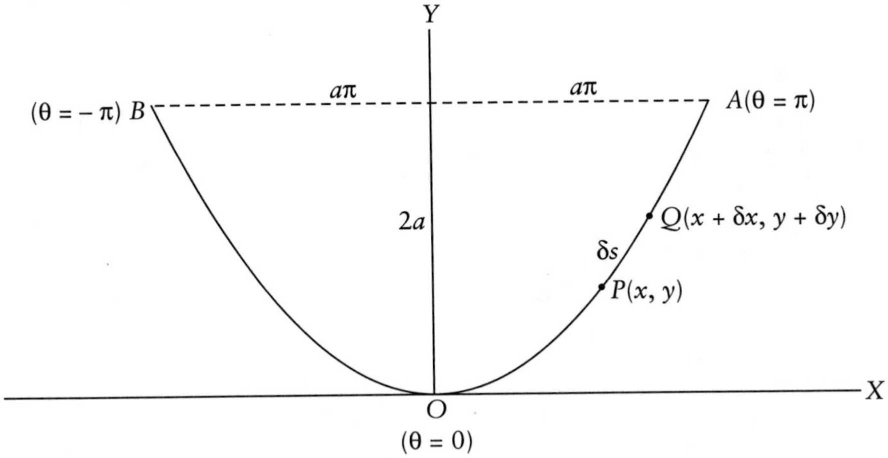


$OA$ is the arc of the cycloid which lies in the positive quadrant. We have to find the C.G. of arc $OA$. At O, $\theta = 0$ and at $A$, $\theta = \pi$.

O is the vertex of the cycloid and tangent at O is the $X$-axis.

Let us consider an element $PQ\ (= \delta s)$ of arc $OA$, where $P$ and $Q$ have coordinates $(x, y)$ and $(x + \delta x, + \delta y)$ respectively. Let $\rho$ be the mass per unit length of the arc. Then mass of element $PQ = \rho\ ds$. The C.G. of that elementary arc is at $P(x, y)$. Let $(\bar{x}, \bar{y})$ be the coordinates of C.G. of the arc $OA$.

The parametric equations of the cycloid are

$$x = a(\theta + \sin\theta \quad \ldots(1)$$

and, $$y = a(1 - \cos\theta) \quad \ldots(2)$$

$\therefore$ $$dx/d\theta = a(1 + \cos\theta)$$

and $$dy/d\theta = a\sin\theta$$

$\therefore$ $$ds/d\theta = \sqrt{\left(\frac{dx}{d\theta}\right)^2 + \left(\frac{dy}{d\theta}\right)^2} = \sqrt{a^2(1+\cos\theta)1 + a^2\sin^2\theta}$$

$$= a\sqrt{1+\cos^2\theta + 2\cos\theta + \sin^2\theta} = a\sqrt{2+2\cos\theta}$$

$$= a\sqrt{2(1+\cos\theta)} = a\sqrt{4\cos^2\frac{\theta}{2}}$$

$$= 2a\cos\frac{\theta}{2} \qquad \therefore\ ds = 2a\cos\frac{\theta}{2}d\theta \quad \ldots(3)$$

Now, $\bar{x} = \dfrac{\int x\, dm}{\int dm} \qquad = \dfrac{\int x\rho\, ds}{\int \rho\, ds}$

$= \dfrac{\int x\, ds}{\int ds}$ | $\because$ ρ is constant

$= \dfrac{\int_0^{\pi} x \frac{ds}{d\theta} d\theta}{\int_0^{\pi} \frac{ds}{d\theta} d\theta} \qquad = \dfrac{\int_0^{\pi} a(\theta + \sin\theta).2a\cos\frac{\theta}{2} d\theta}{\int_0^{\pi} 2a\cos\frac{\theta}{2} d\theta}$ | From (1) and (3)

$$= \frac{a\int_0^{\pi} (\theta + \sin\theta)\cos\frac{\theta}{2} d\theta}{\int_0^{\pi} \cos\frac{\theta}{2} d\theta} \qquad \text{...(4)}$$

and $\bar{y} = \dfrac{\int y\, dm}{\int dm} \qquad = \dfrac{\int y\rho\, ds}{\int \rho\, ds}$

$= \dfrac{\int y\, ds}{\int ds}$ | $\because$ ρ is constant

$= \dfrac{\int_0^{\pi} a(1-\cos\theta)2a\cos\frac{\theta}{2} d\theta}{\int 2a\cos\frac{\theta}{2} d\theta}$ | From (2) and (3)

$$= \frac{\int_0^{\pi} a(1-\cos\theta)\cos\frac{\theta}{2} d\theta}{\int_0^{\pi} \cos\frac{\theta}{2} d\theta} \qquad = \frac{2a\int_0^{\pi} \sin^2\frac{\theta}{2}\cos\frac{\theta}{2} d\theta}{\int_0^{\pi} \cos\frac{\theta}{2} d\theta} \qquad \text{...(5)}$$

Numerator of $\bar{x} = a\int_0^{\pi} (\theta + \sin\theta)\cos\frac{\theta}{2} d\theta$

Put $\theta = 2\phi$
$\therefore d\theta = 2d\phi$

$$= a\int_0^{\frac{\pi}{2}} (2\phi + \sin 2\phi)\cos\phi\, 2d\phi \qquad = 4a\int_0^{\pi/2} \phi\cos\phi\, d\phi + 2a\int_0^{\pi/2} \sin 2\phi\cos\phi\, d\phi$$

$$= 4a\left[(\phi\sin\phi)_0^{\pi/2} - \int_0^{\pi/2} \sin\phi\, d\phi\right] + 4a\int_0^{\pi/2} \sin\phi\cos\phi^2\, d\phi$$

$$= 4a\left[\frac{\pi}{2} + (\cos\phi)_0^{\pi/2}\right] + 4a\left(-\frac{\cos^3\phi}{3}\right)_0^{\pi/2} \qquad = 4a\left[\frac{\pi}{2} - 1\right] + \frac{4a}{3}$$

$$= 2a\pi - 4a + \frac{4a}{3} \qquad = 2a\pi - \frac{8a}{3} \qquad = \frac{2a}{3}(3\pi - 4) \qquad \text{...(6)}$$

Numerator of $\bar{y} = 2a\int_0^{\pi} \sin^2\frac{\theta}{2}\cos\frac{\theta}{2}d\theta$

Put $\theta/2 = \phi$
$\therefore\ d\theta = 2d\phi$

$$= 2a\int_0^{\pi/2} \sin^2\phi \cos\phi\, 2d\phi \qquad = 4a\int_0^{\pi/2} \sin^2\phi \cos\phi\, d\phi$$

$$= 4a\left(\frac{\sin^3\phi}{3}\right)_0^{\pi/2} \qquad = \frac{4a}{3} \qquad \text{...(7)}$$

Denominator of $\bar{x}$ = Denominator of $\bar{y}$

$$= \int_0^{\pi} \cos\frac{\theta}{2}d\theta \qquad = 2\left(\sin\frac{\theta}{2}\right)_0^{\pi} \qquad = 2 \qquad \text{...(8)}$$

Hence, $\bar{x} = \dfrac{\frac{2a}{3}(3\pi - 4)}{2} = \dfrac{a}{3}(3\pi - 4)$

and $\bar{x} = \dfrac{\frac{4a}{3}}{2} = \dfrac{2a}{3}$

**Example 7:** If $O$ is the pole of the lemniscate $r^2 = a^2 \cos 2\theta$ and $G$ is the centre of gravity of any arc $PQ$ of the curve, prove that $OG$ bisect the angle $POQ$.

Also prove that if the line joining the C.G. of the part of the curve which lies in the positive quadrant to the origin makes an angle $\gamma$ with the $X$-axis, then $\tan\gamma = \sqrt{2} - 1$.

**Sol.**

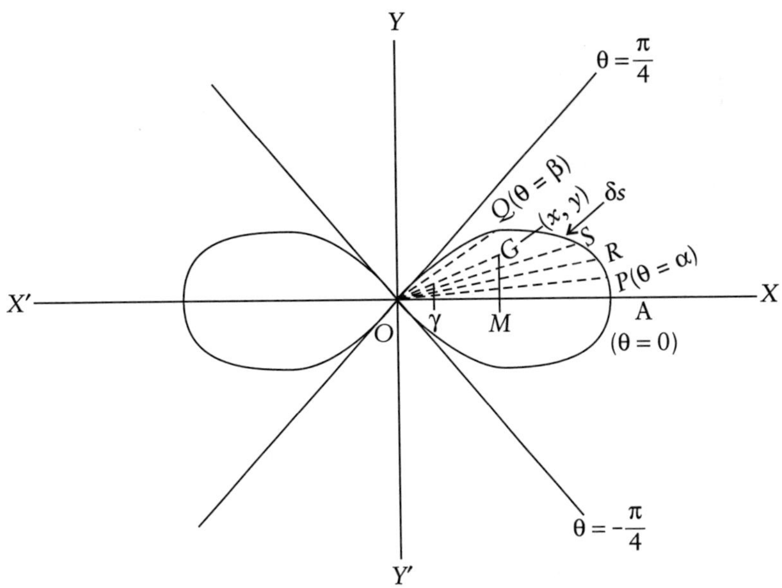

The lemniscate $r^2 = a^2 \cos 2\theta$ ...(1) has been shown in the figure. $O$ is the pole. As we pass from $A$ to $O$, $\theta$ varies from 0 to $\pi/4$. $PQ$ is any arc of the curve. At $P$, let $\theta = \alpha$ and at $Q$, let $\theta = \beta$.

Let $RS$ be an elementary arc of the length $\delta s$ when $R$ and $S$ are the points $(r, \theta)$ and $(r + \delta r, \theta + \delta\theta)$ respectively. For the point $R$, $x = r \cos \theta$ and $y = r \sin \theta$. Mass of the elementary arc $RS = \rho\, ds$.

The C.G. of the arc $RS$ is at $R$ $(r \cos \theta, r \sin\theta)$.

where $\rho$ is the mass per unit length.

From (1),

$$r^2 = a^2 \cos 2\theta$$

Differentiating with respect to $\theta$, we get

$$2r\frac{dr}{d\theta} = -2a^2 \sin 2\theta \qquad \Rightarrow \frac{dr}{d\theta} = -\frac{a^2}{r}\sin 2\theta$$

$$\therefore \quad \frac{ds}{d\theta} = \sqrt{r^2 + \left(\frac{dr}{d\theta}\right)^2} \qquad \Rightarrow = \sqrt{a^2 \cos 2\theta + \frac{a^4 \sin^2 2\theta}{r^2}}$$

$$= \sqrt{a^2 \cos 2\theta + \frac{a^4 \sin^2 2\theta}{a^2 \cos 2\theta}} \qquad | \text{ From (1)}$$

$$= \frac{a}{\sqrt{\cos 2\theta}} \qquad \Rightarrow \quad ds = \frac{a}{\sqrt{\cos 2\theta}}d\theta \qquad \text{...(2)}$$

Let $(\bar{x}, \bar{y})$ be the coordinates of the C.G. of the arc $PQ$. Then,

$$\bar{x} = \frac{\int x\, dm}{\int dm} = \frac{\int x\, \rho\, ds}{\int \rho\, ds} = \frac{\int x\, ds}{\int ds} \qquad | \because \rho \text{ is constant}$$

$$= \frac{\int_\alpha^\beta r \cos\theta \frac{a\,d\theta}{\sqrt{\cos 2\theta}}}{\int_\alpha^\beta \frac{a}{\sqrt{\cos 2\theta}} d\theta} \qquad \text{...(3)}$$

and

$$\bar{y} = \frac{\int y\, dm}{\int dm} = \frac{\int y \rho\, ds}{\int \rho\, ds} = \frac{\int y\, ds}{\int ds}$$

$$= \frac{\int_\alpha^\beta r \sin\theta \frac{a}{\sqrt{\cos 2\theta}} d\theta}{\int_\alpha^\beta \frac{a}{\sqrt{\cos 2\theta}} d\theta} \qquad \text{...(4)}$$

Let $OG$ make an angle $\gamma$ with the initial line $OX$. Then,

$$\tan \gamma = GM/OM \qquad = \frac{\bar{y}}{\bar{x}}$$

$$= \frac{\int_\alpha^\beta r\sin\theta \frac{a}{\sqrt{\cos 2\theta}} d\theta}{\int_\alpha^\beta r\cos\theta \frac{a}{\sqrt{\cos 2\theta}} d\theta} = \frac{\int_\alpha^\beta a\sqrt{\cos 2\theta}\,\sin\theta \frac{a}{\sqrt{\cos 2\theta}} d\theta}{\int_\alpha^\beta a\sqrt{\cos 2\theta}\,\cos\theta \frac{a}{\sqrt{\cos 2\theta}} d\theta} \quad |\text{From (1) and (2)}$$

$$= \frac{\int_\alpha^\beta \sin\theta\, d\theta}{\int_\alpha^\beta \cos\theta\, d\theta} = \frac{(-\cos\theta)_\alpha^\beta}{(\sin\theta)_\alpha^\beta} = \frac{\cos\alpha - \cos\beta}{\sin\beta - \sin\alpha}$$

$$= \frac{2\sin\frac{\alpha+\beta}{2}\sin\frac{\beta-\alpha}{2}}{2\cos\frac{\alpha+\beta}{2}\sin\frac{\beta-\alpha}{2}} = \tan\frac{\alpha+\beta}{2} \Rightarrow 4 = \frac{\alpha+\beta}{2} \quad ...(5)$$

$\therefore$ $\angle GOP = \angle GOX - \angle POX = \frac{\alpha+\beta}{2} - \alpha = \frac{\beta-\alpha}{2}$

$\angle GOQ = \angle QOX - \angle GOX = \beta - \frac{\alpha+\beta}{2} = \frac{\beta-\alpha}{2}$

$\therefore$ $\angle GOP = \angle GOQ \Rightarrow$ $OG$ bisects the angle $POQ$.

**Second Part**

If $P$ coincides with $A$ and $Q$ with $O$. Then

$\alpha = 0$ and $\beta = \pi/4$

$$\therefore \quad \tan\gamma = \frac{\cos\alpha - \cos\beta}{\sin\beta - \sin\alpha} = \frac{\cos 0 - \cos\frac{\pi}{4}}{\sin\frac{\pi}{4} - \sin 0}$$

$$= \frac{1 - \frac{1}{\sqrt{2}}}{\frac{1}{\sqrt{2}} - 0} = \sqrt{2} - 1$$

## EXERCISE 2(A)

1. Find the C.G. of a uniform circular wire of radius $a$ in the form of a quadrant of a circle.

   [**Ans.** $\bar{x} = \frac{2\sqrt{2}a}{\pi}$, $\bar{y} = 0$]

2. Find the C.G. of the arc of the parabola $y^2 = 4ax$ included between the vertex and the point whose abscissa is $at^2$.

   [**Ans.** $\bar{x} = \dfrac{\frac{a}{4}\left[t(1+2t^2)\sqrt{1+t^2} - \log\{t+\sqrt{1+t^2}\}\right]}{t\sqrt{1+t^2} + \log\{t+\sqrt{1+t^2}\}}$,

   $\bar{y} = \dfrac{\frac{4}{3}a\left[(1+t^2)^{3/2} - 1\right]}{t\sqrt{1+t^2} + \log\{t+\sqrt{1+t^2}\}}$ ]

3. Find the C.G. of the whole arc of the centroid $r = a\,(1 + \cos\theta)$.
   [**Ans.** $\bar{x} = 4a/5, \bar{y} = 0$]
4. Prove that the position of the centroid of the arc of the centroid $r = a\,(1 - \cos\theta)$ lying above the initial line is $(-4a/5, 4a/5)$.
5. Find the C.G. of an arc of the catenary $y = c \cos h\,(x/c)$.

[**Ans.** $$\bar{x} = \frac{\left[x_2 \sin h\left(\frac{x_2}{c}\right) - x_1 \sin h\left(\frac{x_1}{c}\right)\right] - c\left[\cos h\left(\frac{x_2}{c}\right) - \cos h\left(\frac{x_1}{c}\right)\right]}{\sin h\left(\frac{x_2}{c}\right) - \sin h\left(\frac{x_1}{c}\right)},$$

$$\bar{y} = \frac{1}{2}\left[\frac{(x_2 - x_1) + \frac{c}{2}\left\{\sin h\left(\frac{2x_2}{c}\right) - \sin h\left(\frac{2x_1}{c}\right)\right\}}{\sin h\left(\frac{x_2}{c}\right) - \sin h\left(\frac{x_1}{c}\right)}\right]$$]

6. Find the centroid of the arc of the curve $x = a\cos^3 t$, $y = a\sin^3 t$ lying in the first quadrant.
   [**Ans.** $\bar{x} = \bar{y} = 2/5\,a$]

## 6. Centre of the Gravity of a Plane Area

Let us consider the distribution of matter over a plane area. Here, we consider an elementary area $\delta A$ surrounding any point $P(x, y)$. Let $\rho$ be the areal density, i.e., mass per unit area containing the point $P$. Then, the elementary mass $\delta m = \rho\,\delta A$. [Note that $r$ varies from point to point.] Let $(\bar{x}, \bar{y})$ be the coordinates of the C.G. of the area under consideration. Then, we have

$$\bar{x} = \frac{\int x\,dm}{\int dm} = \frac{\int x\rho\,dA}{\int \rho\,dA}$$

and $$\bar{y} = \frac{\int y\,dm}{\int dm} = \frac{\int y\rho\,dA}{\int \rho\,dA}$$

If the density $\rho$ is constant throughout the plane area under consideration, then

$$\bar{x} = \frac{\int x\,dA}{\int dA} \quad \text{and} \quad \bar{y} = \frac{\int y\,dA}{\int dA}$$

The elementary area is chosen according to the nature of the problem. Here, the following cases arise:

**Case I:** When the equation of the bounding curve is in Cartesian coordinates.

(1) Let the plane area under consideration be bounded by a curve $y = f(x)$ and the ordinates $x = a$ and $x = b$. In this case, we take an elementary area $\delta A$ in the form of a narrows strip $PQKL$ whose length is $y$ and breadth $\delta x$.

$\therefore \quad \delta A = y\,\delta x$

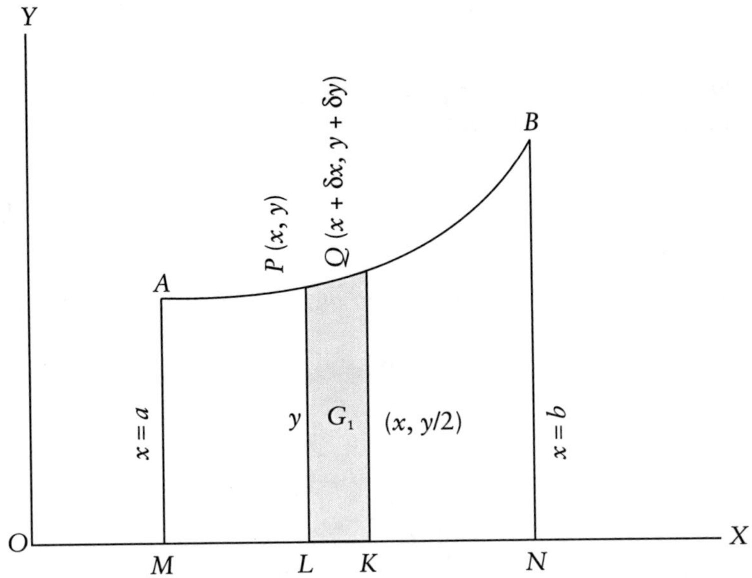


Let $G_1$ be the C.G. of this strip, where $G_1$ coincides with the middle point of $PL$ in the limit. Hence, the required C.G. $(\bar{x}, \bar{y})$ is given by

$$\bar{x} = \frac{\int_a^b x(y\,dx)}{\int_a^b y\,dx} \qquad \text{and} \qquad \bar{y} = \frac{\int_a^b \frac{y}{2}(y\,dx)}{\int_a^b y\,dx} = \frac{\frac{1}{2}\int_a^b y^2\,dx}{\int_a^b y\,dx}$$

(2) Let the plane area under consideration be bounded by a plane curve $x = f(y)$ and the abscissae $y = c$ and $y = d$. In this case, we take an elementary area $\delta A$ in the form of a narrow strip.

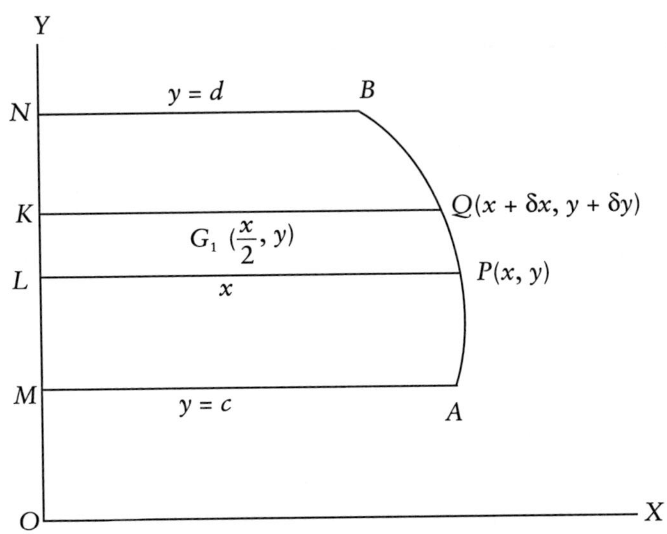

*PQKL* whose length is $x$ and breadth $\delta y$.

$\therefore \qquad \delta A = x\,\delta y$

Let $G_1$ be the C.G. of this strip, where $G_1$ coincides with the middle point of *PL* in the limit. Hence, the required C.G. $(\bar{x}, \bar{y})$ is given by

$$\bar{x} = \frac{\int_c^d \frac{x}{2}(x\,dy)}{\int_c^d x\,dy} = \frac{\frac{1}{2}\int_c^d x^2\,dy}{\int_c^d x\,dy} \quad \text{and} \quad \bar{y} = \frac{\int_c^d y(x\,dy)}{\int_c^d x\,dy}$$

**Case II:** When the equation of the bounding curve is in polar coordinates.

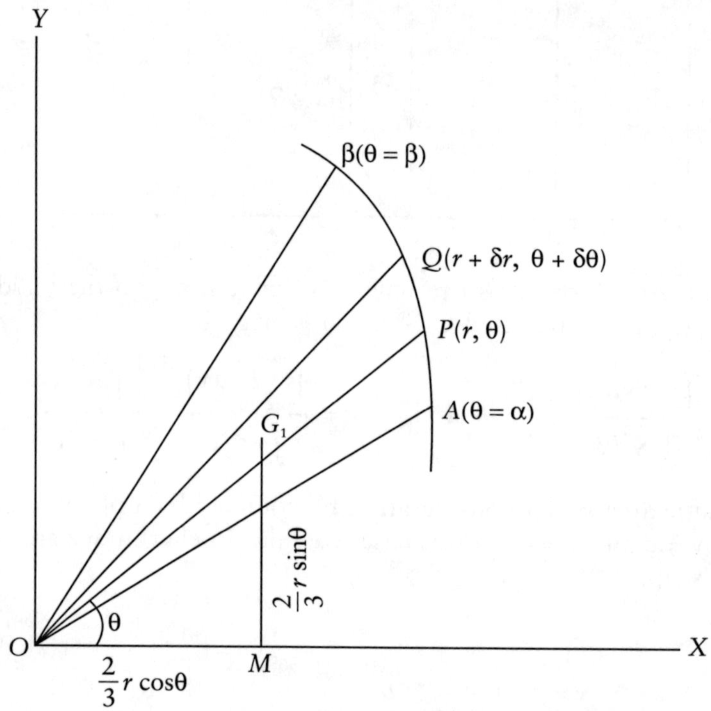


We have to find the position of centre of gravity of a sectorial area bounded by a curve $r = f(\theta)$ and two radii vectors $\theta = \alpha$ and $\theta = \beta$. In this case, we take an elementary area $\delta A$ in the form of a narrow sector *OPQ*, as shown in the figure.

Let the coordinates of *P* and *Q* be $(r, \theta)$ and $(r + \delta r, \theta + \delta\theta)$ respectively. Elementary sectorial area *POQ*

$= \delta A = 1/2 r^2\,\delta\theta. \qquad [\delta A = 1/2.\,r.\,r \sin\delta\theta.$

($\because$ Elementary sectorial area approximates to the area of $\Delta$ OPQ in limit)

$= 1/2\, r^2\,\delta\theta$ (to first order approximation).]

$\therefore$ Elementary mass $\delta m = \rho.\ 1/2\, r^2\,\delta\theta$ where $\rho$ is the mass per unit area.

Let $G_1$ be the C.G. of this elementary sectorial area. Then, $OG_1 = 2/3\ r$ in limit.

Let the coordinates of $G_1$ be $(x, y)$. Then,

$$x = OM = OG_1 \cos\theta = 2/3r \cos\theta$$

and $$y = G_1M = OG_1 \sin\theta = 2/3r \sin\theta$$

Hence, the required C.G. $(\bar{x}, \bar{y})$ is given by

$$\bar{x} = \frac{\int_\alpha^\beta \frac{2}{3} r\cos\theta\, \rho \frac{1}{2} r^2 d\theta}{\int_\alpha^\beta \rho \frac{1}{2} r^2 d\theta} = \frac{\frac{2}{3}\int_\alpha^\beta r^3 \cos\theta\, d\theta}{\int_\alpha^\beta r^2\, d\theta} \quad | \because \rho \text{ is constant}$$

and $$\bar{y} = \frac{\int_\alpha^\beta \frac{2}{3} r\sin\theta \rho \frac{1}{2} r^2 d\theta}{\int_\alpha^\beta \rho \frac{1}{2} r^2 d\theta} = \frac{\frac{2}{3}\int_\alpha^\beta r^3 \sin\theta\, d\theta}{\int_\alpha^\beta r^2 d\theta} \quad | \because \rho \text{ is constant}$$

**Note 1:** If the equations of the curve are given in parametric form, then we deal with this case as in case I. We simply change the variable with respect to which the integration is carried out by either $dx = dx/dt\ dt$ or $dy = dy/dt\ dt$

**Note 2:** If the given area is symmetrical about the initial line, then the C.G. will lie on the initial line and therefore we shall have $\bar{y} = 0$.

A similar proposition holds for symmetry about the line $Y$-axis and in that case $\bar{x} = 0$.

## ILLUSTRATIVE EXAMPLES

**Example 1:** Find the centre of gravity of the area bounded by the parabola $y^2 = 4ax$, the $X$-axis and the latus rectum.

**Sol.**

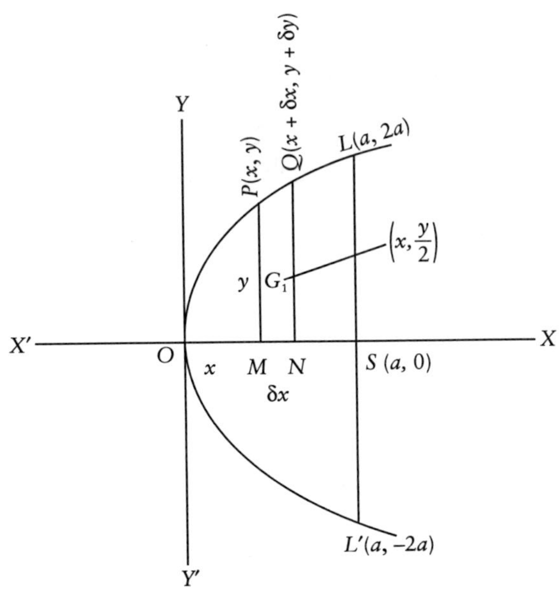

Equation of the parabola is $y^2 = 4ax$ ...(1)

$LSL'$ is the latus rectum of this parabola. It passes through the focus $S$ $(a, 0)$.

We are required to find out the C.G. of the area bounded by the parabola (1), $X$-axis and the latus rectum $LSL'$, i.e., the area $OLSO$.

Take two neighbouring points $P(x, y)$ and $Q$ $(x + \delta x, y + \delta y)$ on the curve. From $P$ and $Q$, draw perpendiculars $PM$ and $QN$ respectively on the $X$-axis. Take $PMNQ$ as the elementary area. Its height is $y$ and width is $\delta x$.

$\therefore$ Area of the elementary strip $= y\ \delta x$.

$\therefore$ Mass of the elementary strip $\delta m = \rho y\ \delta x$ where $\rho$ is the mass per unit area.

Also, the coordinates of C.G. $G_1$ of this elementary area are $(x, y/2)$.

Let $(\bar{x}, \bar{y})$ be he required C.G. then,

$$\bar{x} = \frac{\int x\, dm}{\int dm} = \frac{\int_0^a x\rho y\, dx}{\int_0^a \rho y\, dx}$$

$$= \frac{\int_0^a xy\, dx}{\int_0^a y\, dx} \qquad | \because \rho \text{ is constant} \qquad ...(2)$$

and

$$\bar{y} = \frac{\int \frac{y}{2} dm}{\int dm} = \frac{\int_0^a \frac{y}{2} \rho y\, dx}{\int_0^a \rho y\, dx}$$

$$= \frac{\frac{1}{2}\int_0^a y^2\, dx}{\int_0^a y\, dx} \qquad | \because \rho \text{ is constant} \qquad ...(3)$$

$$\text{Numerator of } \bar{x} = \int_0^a xy\, dx = \int_0^a x\, 2\sqrt{ax}\, dx \qquad | \because y^2 = 4\,ax$$

$$= 2\sqrt{a}\int_0^a x^{3/2} dx \Rightarrow 2\sqrt{a}\left(\frac{2}{5}x^{5/2}\right)_0^a = 2\sqrt{a}\frac{2}{5}a^{5/2} = \frac{4}{5}a^3 \qquad ...(4)$$

$$\text{Numerator of } \bar{y} = \frac{1}{2}\int_0^a y^2 dx$$

$$= \frac{1}{2}\int_0^a 4ax\, dx \qquad | \because y^2 = 4\,ax$$

$$= 2a\int_0^a x\, dx \Rightarrow = 2a\left(\frac{x^2}{2}\right)_0^a = a^3 \qquad ...(5)$$

Denominator of $\bar{x}$ = Denominator of $\bar{y}$

$$= \int_0^a y\, dx = \int_0^a 2\sqrt{ax}\, dx \qquad | \text{ From (1)}$$

$$= 2\sqrt{a}\int_0^a x^{1/2} dx \Rightarrow = 2\sqrt{a}\left(\frac{2}{3}x^{3/2}\right)_0^a = \frac{4}{3}a^2 \qquad ...(6)$$

Hence, $\bar{x} = \dfrac{\frac{4}{5}a^3}{\frac{4}{3}a^2} = \dfrac{3}{5}a$ and $\bar{y} = \dfrac{a^3}{\frac{4}{3}a^2} = \dfrac{3}{4}a$

**Example 2:** Find the centre of gravity of a plane lamina of uniform density in the form of a quadrant of an ellipse.

OR

Find the centre of gravity of a uniform lamina bounded by the coordinate axes and the arc of the ellipse $x^2/a^2 + y^2/b^2 = 1$ in the first quadrant.

**Sol.** The equation of the ellipse is

$$x^2/a^2 + y^2/b^2 = 1 \quad ...(1)$$

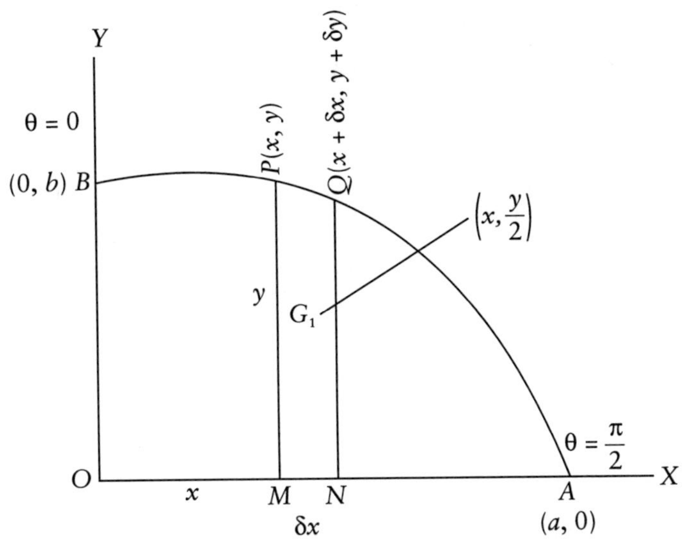


$OABO$ is the quadrant of ellipse lying in the positive quadrant.

Take two neighbouring points $P(x, y)$ and $Q(x + \delta x, y + \delta y)$ on the arc $AB$ of the ellipse. Consider an elementary area $PQNM$ in the form of a strip of height $PM$ (= $y$) and breadth $MN$ (= $\delta x$).

∴ Area of the elementary strip = $y\,\delta x$

∴ Mass of the elementary strip $\delta m = \rho y\,\delta x$

where $\rho$ is the mass per unit area.

Also, the coordinates of C.G. $G_1$ of this elementary area are $(x, y/2)$. Let $(\bar{x}, \bar{y})$ be the required C.G. Then,

$$\bar{x} = \frac{\int x\,dm}{\int dm} = \frac{\int_0^a x\,\rho y dx}{\int_0^a \rho y\,dx} = \frac{\int_0^a xy\,dx}{\int_0^a y\,dx} \quad | \because \rho \text{ is constant}$$

$$= \frac{\int_0^a x \frac{b}{a}\sqrt{a^2 - x^2}\, dx}{\int_0^a \frac{b}{a}\sqrt{a^2 - x^2}\, dx} \qquad \text{| From (1)}$$

$$= \frac{\int_0^a x\sqrt{a^2 - x^2}\, dx}{\int_0^a \sqrt{a^2 - x^2}\, dx} = \frac{\left[-\frac{1}{3}\left(a^2 - x^2\right)^{3/2}\right]_0^a}{\left[\frac{1}{2}x\sqrt{a^2 - x^2} + \frac{1}{2}a^2\sin^{-1}\left(\frac{x}{a}\right)\right]_0^a}$$

$$= \frac{\frac{a^3}{3}}{\frac{a^2 x}{4}} = \frac{4a}{3\pi} \qquad \text{and} \qquad \bar{y} = \frac{\int \frac{y}{2}\, dm}{\int dm}$$

$$= \frac{\int_0^a \frac{y}{2}\rho y\, dx}{\int_0^a \rho\, y\, dx} = \frac{\int_0^a y^2 dx}{\int_0^a y\, dx} \qquad \text{| } \because \rho \text{ is constant}$$

$$= \frac{\frac{1}{2}\int_0^a \frac{b^2}{a^2}\left(a^2 - x^2\right)dx}{\int_0^a \frac{b}{a}\sqrt{a^2 - x^2}\,dx} = \frac{\frac{b}{2a}\left(a^2 x - \frac{x^3}{3}\right)_0^a}{\left[\frac{1}{2}x\sqrt{a^2 - x^2} + \frac{1}{2}a^2\sin^{-1}\left(\frac{x}{a}\right)\right]_0^a}$$

$$= \frac{\frac{b}{2a}\cdot\frac{2a^3}{3}}{\frac{a^2\pi}{4}} = \frac{4b}{3\pi}$$

Hence, the required C.G. is given by $\left(\frac{4a}{3\pi}, \frac{4b}{3\pi}\right)$.

## Aliter

Parametric equations of the ellipse are

$x = a \sin\theta \qquad y = b \cos\theta$

At $B$, $x = 0$, $\theta = 0$. At $A$, $x = a$, $\theta = \pi/2$.

$$\bar{x} = \frac{\int_0^a x\,y\, dx}{\int_0^a y\, dx} = \frac{\int_0^{\frac{\pi}{2}} a\sin\theta\; b\cos\theta\; a\cos\theta\; d\theta}{\int_0^{\frac{\pi}{2}} b\cos\theta\; a\cos\theta\; d\theta}$$

$$= \frac{a\left(-\frac{\cos^3\theta}{3}\right)_0^{\pi/2}}{\frac{1}{2}\cdot\frac{\pi}{2}} \qquad \text{(By Walli's Formula)}$$

$$= \frac{\frac{a}{3}}{\frac{\pi}{4}} = \frac{4a}{3\pi} \qquad \text{and} \qquad \bar{y} = \frac{\frac{1}{2}\int_0^a y^2\,dx}{\int_0^a y\,dx}$$

$$= \frac{\frac{1}{2}\int_0^{\pi/2} b^2\cos\theta\, a\cos\theta\, d\theta}{\int_0^{\pi/2} b\cos\theta\, a\cos\theta\, d\theta} \qquad = \frac{\frac{b}{2}\int_0^{\pi/2}\cos^3\theta\, d\theta}{\int_0^{\pi/2}\cos^2\theta\, d\theta}$$

$$= \frac{\frac{b}{1}\cdot\frac{2}{3}}{\frac{1}{2}\cdot\frac{\pi}{2}} \qquad \text{(By Walli's Formula)}$$

$$= \frac{4b}{3\pi}$$

**Example 3:** Find the C.G. of the region bounded by the parabola $x^2 = 4\,ay$, $X$-axis and the ordinate $x = b$.

**Sol.**

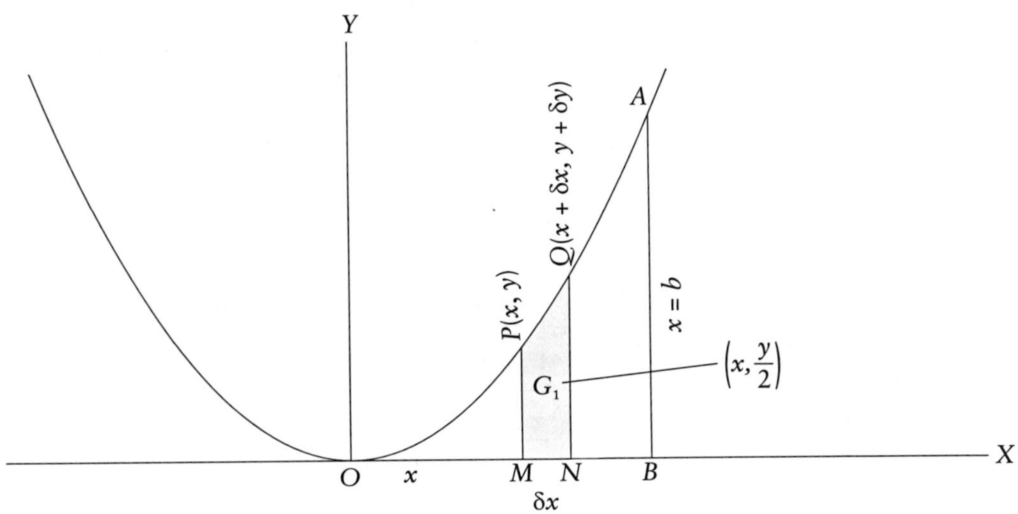


Equation of the parabola is

$$x^2 = 4\,ay \qquad ...(1)$$

We are to find out the C.G. of the area $OABO$.

Take two neighbouring points $P(x, y)$ and $Q(x + \delta x, y + \delta y)$ on the arc $OA$ of the parabola. Draw perpendiculars $PM$ and $QN$ on the $X$-axis. Take $PMNQ$ as the elementary area. Its height is $y$ and width is $\delta x$.

∴ Area of the elementary strip $= y\,\delta x$

∴ Mass of the elementary strip $\delta m$

$$= \rho\, y\, \delta x$$

where ρ is the mass per unit area. Also, the coordinates of C.G. $G_1$ of this elementary strip are $(x, y/2)$. Let $(\bar{x}, \bar{y})$ be the required C.G. Then,

$$\bar{x} = \frac{\int x\,dm}{\int dm} = \frac{\int_0^b x\rho y\,dx}{\int_0^b \rho y\,dx} = \frac{\int_0^b x y\,dx}{\int_0^b y\,dx} \qquad | \because \rho \text{ is constant}$$

$$= \frac{\int_0^b x\cdot\frac{x^2}{4a}dx}{\int_0^b \frac{x^2}{4a}dx} \qquad | \text{ From (1)}$$

$$= \frac{\int_0^b x^3\,dx}{\int_0^b x^2 dx} = \frac{\left(\frac{x^4}{4}\right)_0^b}{\left(\frac{x^3}{3}\right)_0^b} = \frac{\frac{b^4}{4}}{\frac{b^3}{3}} = \frac{3b}{4}$$

and

$$\bar{y} = \frac{\int \frac{y}{2}dm}{\int dm} = \frac{\int_0^b \frac{y}{2}\rho y\,dx}{\int_0^b \rho y\,dx} = \frac{\frac{1}{2}\int_0^b y^2\,dx}{\int_0^b y\,dx} \qquad | \because \rho \text{ is constant}$$

$$= \frac{\frac{1}{2}\int_0^b \left(\frac{x^2}{4a}\right)^2 dx}{\int_0^b \left(\frac{x^2}{4a}\right)dx} \qquad | \text{ From (1)}$$

$$= \frac{\frac{1}{8a}\int_0^b x^4 dx}{\int_0^b x^2 dx} = \frac{\frac{1}{8a}\left(\frac{x^5}{5}\right)_0^b}{\left(\frac{x^3}{3}\right)_0^b}$$

$$= \frac{\frac{1}{8a}\frac{b^5}{5}}{\frac{b^3}{3}} = \frac{3b^2}{40\,a}.$$

**Example 4:** Find the centre of gravity of the area of the curve $\left(\frac{x}{a}\right)^{2/3} + \left(\frac{x}{b}\right)^{2/3} = 1$ lying in the positive quadrant.

**Sol.**

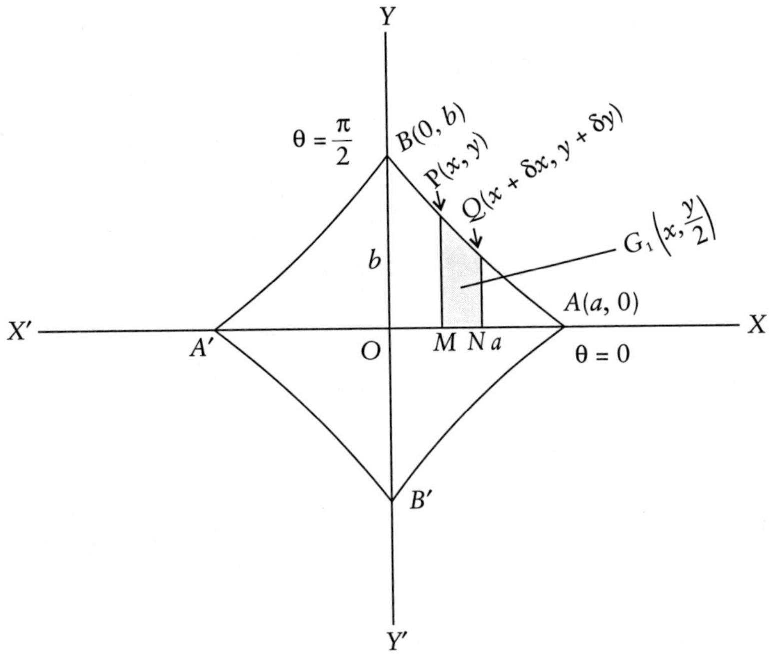


Equation of the curve is $\left(\frac{x}{a}\right)^{2/3}+\left(\frac{y}{b}\right)^{2/3}=1$ ...(1)

Its parametric equations are

$x = a\cos^3\theta$ ...(2)

$y = b\sin^3\theta$ ...(3)

We are to find out the C.G. of the area *OABO* of the curve lying in the positive quadrant.

At *A*, $x = a$, $\theta = 0$ $\Rightarrow$ At *B*, $x = 0$, $\theta = \pi/2$

Take two neighbouring points $P(x, y)$ and $Q(x + \delta x, y + \delta y)$ on the arc *AB*. From *P* and *Q*, draw perpendiculars *PM* and *QN* respectively on the *X*-axis. Take *PMNQ* as the elementary area. Its height is $y$ and width is $\delta x$.

∴ Area of the elementary strip $= y\,\delta x$

∴ Mass of the elementary strip $\delta m = \rho\, y\, \delta x$

where $\rho$ is the mass per unit area.

Also, the coordinates of C.G. $G_1$ of this elementary area are $(x, y/2)$. Let $(\bar{x}, \bar{y})$ be the required C.G. Then,

$$\bar{x} = \frac{\int x\,dm}{\int dm} = \frac{\int_0^a x\rho y\,dx}{\int_0^a \rho y\,dx}$$

$$= \frac{\int_0^a xy\,dx}{\int_0^a y\,dx} \qquad \mid \because \rho \text{ is constant} \qquad ...(4)$$

and $$\bar{y} = \frac{\int \frac{y}{2} dm}{\int dm} = \frac{\int_0^a \frac{y}{2} \rho y \, dx}{\int_0^a \rho y \, dx} = \frac{\frac{1}{2}\int_0^a y^2 \, dx}{\int_0^a y \, dx} \qquad ...(5)$$

$$\text{Numerator of } \bar{x} = \int_0^a x y \, dx = -\int_{\frac{\pi}{2}}^0 a\cos^3\theta \; b\sin^3\theta \; 3a\cos^2\theta \, \sin\theta \, d\theta$$

$$= 3a^2 b \int_0^{\pi/2} \sin^4\theta \cos^5\theta \, d\theta = 3a^2 b \frac{\left|\frac{5}{2}\right. \left|3\right.}{2\left|\frac{11}{2}\right.}$$

$$= \frac{3a^2 b \cdot \frac{3}{2} \cdot \frac{1}{2} \cdot \sqrt{\pi} \cdot 2}{2 \cdot \frac{9}{2} \cdot \frac{7}{2} \cdot \frac{5}{2} \cdot \frac{3}{2} \cdot \frac{1}{2} \cdot \sqrt{\pi}} = \frac{8a^2 b}{105} \qquad ...(6)$$

$$\text{Numerator of } \bar{y} = \frac{1}{2}\int_0^a y^2 dx = -\frac{1}{2}\int_{\frac{\pi}{2}}^a b^2 \sin^6\theta \left(3a \cos^2 \sin\theta\right) d\theta$$

$$= \frac{3ab^2}{2}\int_0^{\pi/2} \sin^7\theta \cos^2\theta \, d\theta = \frac{3ab^2}{2} \frac{\left|4\right. \left|\frac{3}{2}\right.}{\left|\frac{11}{2}\right.} = \frac{3ab^2}{4} \frac{3 \cdot 2 \cdot 1 \cdot \frac{1}{2} \cdot \sqrt{\pi}}{\frac{9}{2} \cdot \frac{7}{2} \cdot \frac{5}{2} \cdot \frac{3}{2} \cdot \frac{1}{2} \cdot \sqrt{\pi}}$$

$$= \frac{8ab^2}{105} \qquad ...(7)$$

Denominator of $\bar{x}$ = denominator of $\bar{y}$

$$= \int_0^a y \, dx = -\int_{\frac{\pi}{2}}^0 b\sin^3\theta \; 3a\cos^2\theta \, \sin\theta \, d\theta$$

$$= 3ab\int_0^{\pi/2} \sin^4\theta \cos^2\theta \, d\theta = 3ab \frac{\left|\frac{5}{2}\right. \left|\frac{3}{2}\right.}{2\left|4\right.} = \frac{3ab \cdot \frac{3}{2} \cdot \frac{1}{2} \cdot \sqrt{\pi} \frac{1}{2} \sqrt{\pi}}{2 \cdot 3 \cdot 2 \cdot 1}$$

$$= \frac{3ab\pi}{32} \qquad ...(8)$$

Hence, the required C.G. is given by

$$\bar{x} = \frac{\frac{8a^2 b}{105}}{\frac{3ab\pi}{32}} = \frac{256a}{315\pi} \quad \text{and} \quad \bar{y} = \frac{\frac{8ab^2}{105}}{\frac{3ab\pi}{32}} = \frac{256b}{315\pi}$$

**Example 5:** Find the C.G. of the area of the curve $\left(\frac{x}{a}\right)^{1/2} + \left(\frac{y}{b}\right)^{1/2} = 1$ between the curve and the coordinate axes.

**Sol.**

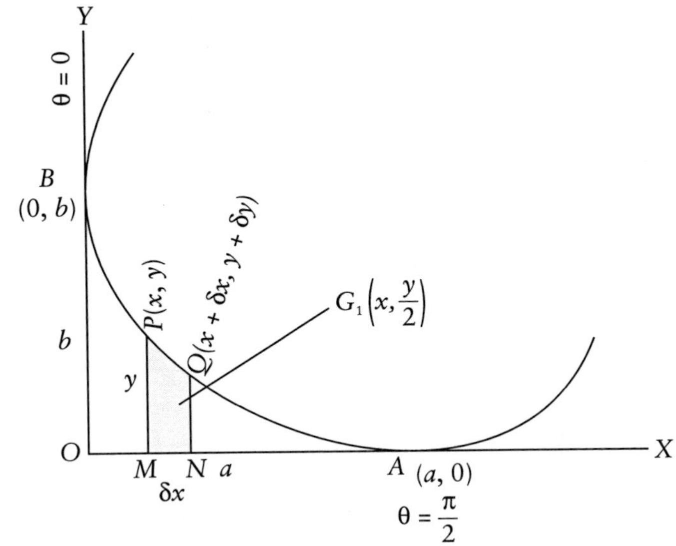


Equation of the curve is $\sqrt{\left(\frac{x}{a}\right)} + \sqrt{\left(\frac{y}{b}\right)} = 1$ ...(1)

Its parametric equations are

$x = a \sin^4\theta$ ...(2)

$y = b \cos^4\theta$ ...(3)

We are to find unit the C.G. of the area *OABO* between the curve (1) and the coordinate axes.

At *A*, $x = a, \theta = \pi/2$ $\Rightarrow$ At *B*, $x = 0, \theta = 0$

Take two neighbouring points $P(x, y)$ and $Q(x + \delta x, y + \delta y)$ on the curve *BA*. From *P* and *Q*, draw perpendiculars *PM* and *QN* respectively on the X-axis. Take *PMNQ* as the elementary area. Its height is $y$ and width is $\delta x$.

$\therefore$ Area of the elementary strip $= y\,\delta x$

$\therefore$ Mass of the elementary strip $\delta m = \rho\, y\, \delta x$

where $\rho$ is the mass per unit area. Also, the coordinates of C.G. $G_1$ of this elementary area are $(x, y/2)$. Let $(\bar{x}, \bar{y})$ be the required C.G. Then,

$$\bar{x} = \frac{\int x\,dm}{\int dm} = \frac{\int_0^a x\rho y\,dx}{\int_0^a \rho y\,dx}$$

$$= \frac{\int_0^a xy\,dx}{\int_0^a y\,dx} \qquad | \because \rho \text{ is constant}$$

$$= \frac{\int_0^{\pi/2} a\sin^4\theta \cdot b\cos^4\theta \cdot 4a\sin^3\theta\cos\theta\,d\theta}{\int_0^{\pi/2} b\cos^4\theta \cdot 4a\sin^3\theta\cos\theta\,d\theta}$$

$$= \frac{a\int_0^{\pi/2} \sin^3\theta \cos^5\theta \, d\theta}{\int_0^{\pi/2} \sin^4\theta \cos^5\theta \, d\theta} \quad \ldots(4)$$

and $\bar{y} = \dfrac{\int \frac{y}{2} dm}{\int dm} = \dfrac{\frac{1}{2}\int_0^a y\rho y \, dx}{\int_0^a \rho y \, dx}$

$$= \frac{\frac{1}{2}\int_0^a y^2 \, dx}{\int_0^a y \, dx} = \frac{\frac{1}{2}\int_0^{\pi/2} b^2 \cos^8\theta \; 4a\sin^3\theta \cos\theta \, d\theta}{\int_0^{\pi/2} b \cos^4\theta \cdot 4a\sin^3\theta \cos\theta \, d\theta}$$

$$= \frac{\frac{b}{2}\int_0^{\pi/2} \sin^3\theta \cos\theta \, d\theta}{\int_0^{\pi/2} \sin^3\theta \cos^5\theta \, d\theta} \quad \ldots(5)$$

Numerator of $\bar{x} = a\int_0^{\pi/2} \sin^7\theta \cos^5\theta \, d\theta \quad = \dfrac{a\lceil 4 \lceil 3}{2\lceil 7}$

$$= \frac{a \cdot 3 \cdot 2 \cdot 1, 2 \cdot 1}{2 \cdot 6 \cdot 5 \cdot 4, 3 \cdot 2 \cdot 1} = \frac{a}{120} \quad \ldots(6)$$

Numerator of $\bar{y} = \dfrac{b}{2}\int_0^{\pi/2} \sin^3\theta \cos^9\theta \, d\theta \quad = \dfrac{\frac{b}{2}\lceil 2 \lceil 5}{2\lceil 7}$

$$= \frac{\frac{b}{2} \cdot 4 \cdot 3 \cdot 2 \cdot 1}{2 \cdot 6 \cdot 5 \cdot 4 \cdot 3 \cdot 2 \cdot 1} = \frac{b}{120} \quad \ldots(7)$$

Denominator of $\bar{x}$ = Denominator *of* $\bar{y}$ $= \int_0^{\pi/2} \sin^3\theta \cos^5\theta \, d\theta$

$$= \frac{\lceil 2 \lceil 3}{2\lceil 5} = \frac{2}{2 \cdot 4 \cdot 3 \cdot 2 \cdot 1 \cdot} = \frac{1}{24} \quad \ldots(8)$$

Hence, the required C.G. is given by

$$\bar{x} = \frac{\frac{a}{120}}{\frac{1}{24}} = \frac{a}{5}$$

and

$$\bar{y} = \frac{\frac{b}{120}}{\frac{1}{24}} = \frac{b}{5}$$

**Example 6:** Find the centre of gravity of the area between the curve $y = c \cos h \, (x/c)$, the coordinate axes and the ordinate $x = a$.

**Sol.**

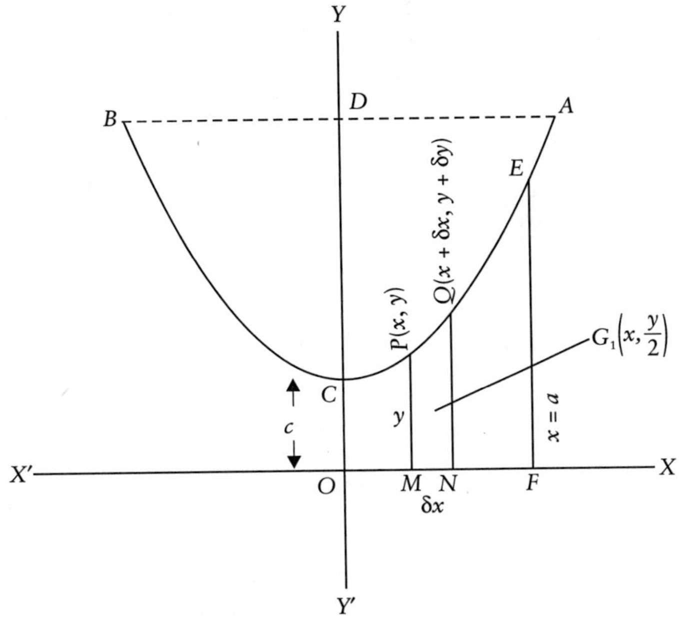


Equation of the given curve is

$$y = c \cos h \ (x/c) \qquad \text{...(1)}$$

It represents a catenary whose parameter is $c$. $EF$ is the ordinate $x = a$. We are to find out the C.G. of the area $CEFO$.

Take two neighbouring points $P(x, y)$ and $Q(x + \delta x, y + \delta y)$ on the arc $CE$. From $P$ and $Q$, draw perpendiculars $PM$ and $QN$ respectively on the $X$-axis. Take $PMNQ$ as the elementary area. Its height is $y$ and width is $\delta x$.

$\therefore$ Area of the elementary strip $= y \, \delta x$

$\therefore$ Mass of the elementary strip $\delta m = \rho \, y \, \delta x$

where $\rho$ is the mass per unit area. Also, the coordinates of C.G. $G_1$ of this elementary area are $(x, y/2)$. Let $(\bar{x}, \bar{y})$ be the required C.G. Then,

$$\bar{x} = \frac{\int x \, dm}{\int dm} = \frac{\int_0^a x \, \rho y \, dx}{\int_0^a \rho y \, dx}$$

$$= \frac{\int_0^a x y \, dx}{\int_0^a y \, dx} \qquad | \because \rho \text{ is constant}$$

$$= \frac{\int_0^a x c \cos h\left(\frac{x}{c}\right) dx}{\int_0^a c \cos h\left(\frac{x}{c}\right) dx} \qquad | \text{ From (1)}$$

$$= \frac{\int_0^a x\cos h\left(\frac{x}{c}\right)dx}{\int_0^a \cos h\left(\frac{x}{c}\right)dx} \qquad \Rightarrow \left[x\,c\sinh\left(\frac{x}{c}\right)\right]_0^a$$

$$= \frac{-\int_0^a 1\cdot c\sin h\left(\frac{x}{c}\right)dx}{\left[c\sin h\left(\frac{x}{c}\right)\right]_0^a} \qquad \Rightarrow = \frac{a\,c\sin h\left(\frac{a}{c}\right)-c\left[c\cos h\left(\frac{x}{c}\right)\right]_0^a}{c\sin h\left(\frac{a}{c}\right)}$$

$$= \frac{a\,c\sin h\left(\frac{a}{c}\right)-c^2\left[\cos h\left(\frac{a}{c}\right)-1\right]}{c\sin h\left(\frac{a}{c}\right)}$$

$$= a - c\cot h\left(\frac{a}{c}\right) + c\,\mathrm{cosec}\,h\left(\frac{a}{c}\right) \qquad \text{...(2)}$$

and

$$\bar{y} = \frac{\int \frac{y}{2}dm}{\int dm} = \frac{\int_0^a \frac{y}{2}\rho y\,dx}{\int_0^a \rho y\,dx}$$

$$= \frac{\frac{1}{2}\int_0^a y^2\,dx}{\int_0^a y\,dx} = \frac{\frac{1}{2}\int_0^a c^2\cos h^2\left(\frac{x}{c}\right)dx}{\int_0^a c\cos h\left(\frac{x}{c}\right)dx} \qquad |\text{From (1)}$$

$$= \frac{\frac{c}{4}\int_0^a\left(\cos h\frac{2x}{c}+1\right)dx}{\int_0^a \cos h\left(\frac{x}{c}\right)dx} = \frac{\frac{c}{4}\left[\frac{c}{2}\sin h\left(\frac{2x}{c}\right)+x\right]_0^a}{\left[c\sin h\left(\frac{x}{c}\right)\right]_0^a}$$

$$= \frac{\frac{c}{4}\left[\frac{c}{2}\sin h\left(\frac{2a}{c}\right)+a\right]}{c\sin h\left(\frac{a}{c}\right)} = \frac{\frac{1}{4}\left[c\sin h\left(\frac{a}{c}\right)\cos h\left(\frac{a}{c}\right)+a\right]}{\sin h\left(\frac{a}{c}\right)}$$

$$= \frac{1}{4}\left[c\cos h\left(\frac{a}{c}\right)+a\,\mathrm{cosec}\,h\left(\frac{a}{c}\right)\right] \qquad \text{...(3)}$$

**Example 7:** Find the position of the centroid of the area of the curve $ay^2 = x^3$ between the origin and $x = b$.

**Sol.**

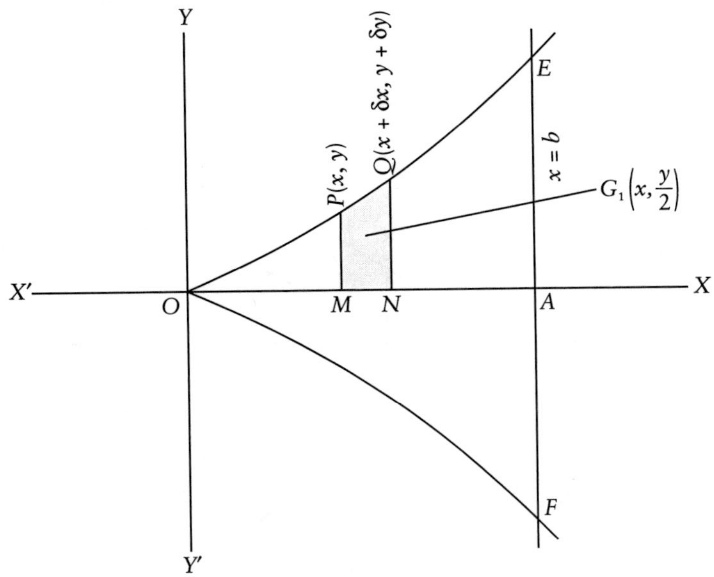


The equation of the given curve is

$$ay^2 = x^3 \qquad ...(1)$$

It has been traced as shown in the figure. $EF$ is the line $x = b$. We are to find the C.G. of the area $EOFAEO$. Let $(\bar{x}, \bar{y})$ be the coordinates of the C.G. of this area. Then, by symmetry, $\bar{x} = 0$ as C.G. will lie on $X$-axis.

Also, abscissa of the C.G. of the area $EOF\ AEO$ = abscissa of the C.G. of the area $OAEO$.

Take two neighbouring points $P(x, y)$ and $Q(x + \delta x, y + \delta y)$ on the arc $OE$. From $P$ and $Q$, draw perpendiculars $PM$ and $QN$ respectively on the $X$-axis. Take $PMNQ$ as the elementary area. Its height is $y$ and width is $\delta x$.

∴ Area of the elementary strip = $y\ \delta x$

∴ Mass of the elementary strip $\delta m = \rho\ y\ \delta x$

where $\rho$ is the mass per unit area. Also, the coordinates of C.G. $G_1$ of this elementary strip are $(x, y/2)$. Now, $\bar{x}$ = abscissa of the C.G. $G_1$ of the elementary strip $PMNQ$.

$$= \frac{\int x\, dm}{\int dm} = \frac{\int_0^b x \rho y\, dx}{\int_0^b \rho y\, dx} = \frac{\int_0^b x y\, dx}{\int_0^b y\, dx} \qquad | \because \rho \text{ is constant}$$

$$= \frac{\int_0^b x \frac{x^{3/2}}{a^{1/2}} dx}{\int_0^b \frac{x^{3/2}}{a^{1/2}} dx} = \frac{\int_0^b x^{5/2} dx}{\int_0^b x^{3/2} dx} = \frac{\frac{2}{7}\left(x^{7/2}\right)_0^b}{\frac{2}{5}\left(x^{5/2}\right)_0^b} = \frac{5}{7}\frac{b^{7/2}}{b^{5/2}} = \frac{5}{7}b$$

Hence, we have, $\bar{x} = 5/7\ b$

and $\bar{y} = 0.$

**Example 8:** Find the C.G. of the area included between the curve $y^2(2a - x) = x^3$ and its asymptote.

**Sol.**

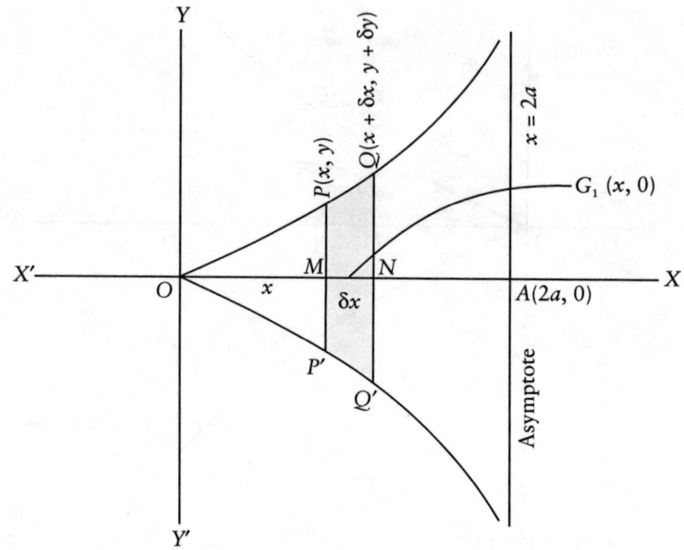


The equation of the given curve is $y^2(2a - x) = x^3$ ...(1)

It has been traced as shown in the figure. The asymptote of the curve (1) is the line $x = 2a$. We are to find the C.G. of the area included between the curve (1) and its asymptote $x = 2a$.

Take two neighbouring points $P(x, y)$ and $Q(x + \delta x, y + \delta y)$ on the curve. Consider an elementary strip $PP'Q'Q$ of length $PP'(= 2y)$ and breadth $MN\ (= \delta x)$. Then,

elementary area $= 2y\delta x$. $\quad\therefore\quad$ elementary mass $\delta m = \rho\, 2\, y\, \delta x$

where $\rho$ is the mass per unit area. Also, the coordinates of C.G. $G_1$ of the this strip are $(x, 0)$. Let $(\bar{x}, \bar{y})$ be the required C.G.

Then, by symmetry, $\bar{y} = 0$.

Now, $$\bar{x} = \frac{\int x\, dm}{\int dm} \quad \Rightarrow = \frac{\int_0^{2a} x\rho 2y\, dx}{\int \rho 2y\, dx}$$

$$= \frac{\int_0^{2a} x\, y\, dx}{\int_0^{2a} y\, dx} \qquad |\because \rho \text{ is constant}$$

$$= \frac{\int_0^{2a} x \cdot \frac{x^{3/2}}{\sqrt{2a - x}}\, dx}{\int_0^{2a} \frac{x^{3/2}}{\sqrt{2a - x}}\, dx} \qquad ...(2)$$

Numerator of $\bar{x} = \int_0^{2a} \frac{x^{5/2}}{\sqrt{2a - x}}\, dx$ $\qquad$ Put $x = 2a\sin^2\theta$ $\qquad \therefore\ dx = 4a\sin\theta\cos\theta\, d\theta$

$$= \int_0^{\pi/2} \frac{(2a)^{5/2} \sin^5 \theta}{\sqrt{2a - 2a \sin^2 \theta}} \cdot 4a \sin\theta \cos\theta \, d\theta \qquad = 16a^3 \int_0^{\pi/2} \sin^6 \theta \, d\theta$$

$$= 16a^3 \frac{5}{6} \cdot \frac{3}{4} \cdot \frac{1}{2} \cdot \frac{\pi}{2} \qquad \text{| By Walli's Formula}$$

$$= \frac{5\pi a^3}{2} \qquad \ldots(3)$$

Denominator of $\bar{x} = \int \frac{{}^{3/2}}{\sqrt{\ a \quad x}} dx$ Put $x = 2a \sin^2\theta$ $\therefore dx = 4a \sin\theta \cos\theta \, d\theta$

$$= \int_0^{\pi/2} \frac{(2a)^{3/2} \sin^3 \theta \cdot 4a \sin\theta \cos\theta \, d\theta}{\sqrt{2a - 2a \sin^2 \theta}}$$

$$= 8a^2 \int_0^{\pi/2} \sin^4 \theta \, d\theta \qquad = 8a^2 \frac{3}{4} \frac{1}{2} \cdot \frac{\pi}{2} \qquad \text{| By Walli's Formula}$$

$$= \frac{3\pi a^2}{2} \qquad \ldots(4)$$

Hence, $\bar{x} = \dfrac{\frac{5\pi a^3}{2}}{\frac{3\pi a^2}{2}} = \dfrac{5a}{3}$ and $\bar{y} = 0$.

**Example 9:** Find the centre of gravity of the area between the curve whose equation is $xy^2 = b^2 (a - x)$ and its asymptote.

**Sol.**

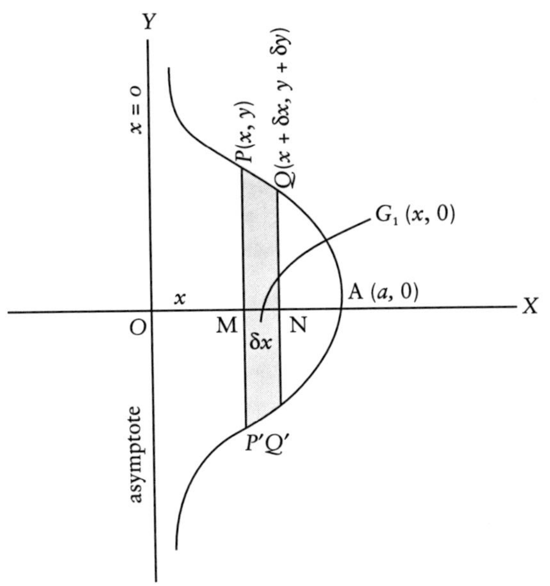


The equation of the given curve is $xy^2 = b^2(a - x)$ ...(1)

It has been traced as shown in the figure. The asymptote of the curve (1) is the $Y$-axis, i.e., $x = 0$. We are to find out the C.G. of the area included between the curve (1) and its asymptote $x = 0$.

Take two neighbouring points $P(x, y)$ and $Q(x + \delta x, y, \delta y)$ on the curve. Consider an elementary strip $PQ\ Q'P'$ of length $P'P'(=2y)$ and breadth $MN\ (=\delta x)$. Then,

$$\text{elementary area} = 2y\ \delta x.$$

$$\therefore \quad \text{elementary mass } \delta m = \rho\ 2y\ \delta x$$

where $\rho$ is the mass per unit area, Also, the coordinates of C.G. $G_1$ of this strip are $(x, 0)$. Let $(\bar{x}, \bar{y})$ be the required C.G. Then, by symmetry, $\bar{y} = 0$

Now, $$\bar{x} = \frac{\int x\, dm}{\int dm}$$

$$= \frac{\int_0^a x\rho 2y\, dx}{\int_0^a \rho 2y\, dx} = \frac{\int_0^a xy\, dx}{\int_0^a y\, dx} \qquad | \because \rho \text{ is constant}$$

$$= \frac{\int_0^a x \frac{b\sqrt{a-x}}{\sqrt{x}} dx}{\int_0^a \frac{b\sqrt{a-x}}{\sqrt{x}} dx}$$

$$= \frac{\int_0^a \sqrt{x}\sqrt{a-x}\, dx}{\int_0^a \sqrt{\frac{a-x}{x}} dx} \qquad \text{Put } x = a\sin^2\theta \qquad \therefore dx = 2a \sin\theta \cos\theta\, d\theta$$

$$= \frac{\int_0^{\pi/2} \sqrt{a}\sin\theta \sqrt{a - a\sin^2\theta}\ 2a\sin\theta\cos\theta\, d\theta}{\int_0^{\pi/2} \sqrt{\frac{a - a\sin^2\theta}{a\sin^2\theta}} \cdot 2a\sin\theta\cos\theta\, d\theta} = \frac{a\int_0^{\pi/2} \sin^2\theta\cos^2\theta\, d\theta}{\int_0^{\pi/2} \cos^2\theta\, d\theta}$$

$$\frac{a\overline{\left|\frac{3}{2}\right.}\overline{\left|\frac{3}{2}\right.}}{2\overline{|3}} \Big/ \frac{1}{2}\cdot\frac{\pi}{2} \qquad |\text{By Walli's Formula}$$

$$= \frac{\dfrac{a\frac{1}{2}\sqrt{\pi}\frac{1}{2}\sqrt{\pi}}{2\cdot 2\cdot 1}}{\dfrac{\pi}{4}} = \frac{a}{4}$$

and $\bar{y} = 0.$

**Example 10:** Find the C.G. of a loop of the curve $y^2(a + x) = x^2(a - x)$.

**Sol.**

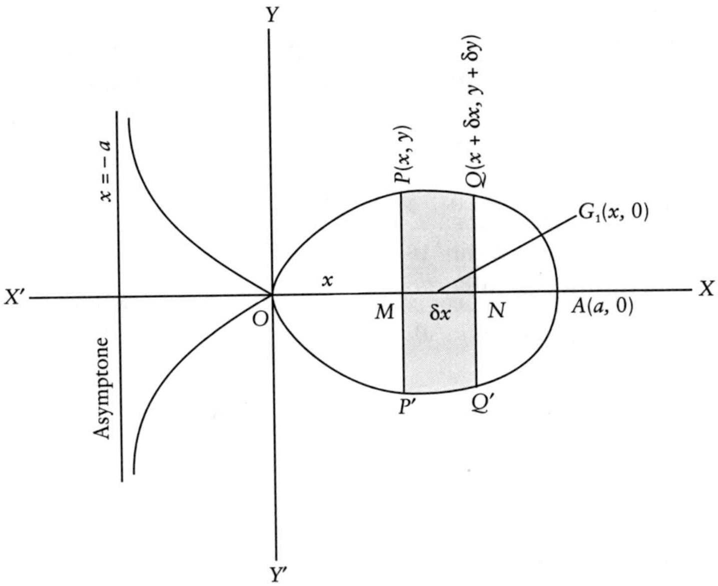


The equation of the given curve is $y^2(a + x) = x^2(a - x)$ ...(1)

It has been traced as shown in the figure.

The asymptote of the curve (1) is the line $x = -a$. We are to find and the C.G. of the loop $OPQ\ AQ'P'O$ of the curve (1).

Take two neighbouring points $P(x, y)$ and $Q(x + \delta x, y + \delta y)$ on the curve. Consider an elementary strip $PQQ'\ P'$ of length $PP'$ (= $2y$) and breadth $MN$(= $\delta x$). Then,

elementary area = $2y\ \delta x$.

$\therefore$ elementary mass $\delta m = \rho\ 2y\ \delta x$

where $\rho$ is the mass per unit area.

Also, the coordinates of C.G. $G_1$ of this strip are $(x, 0)$. Let $(\bar{x}, \bar{y})$ be the required C.G. Then, by symmetry $\bar{y} = 0$.

Now, $$\bar{x} = \frac{\int x\,dm}{\int dm} = \frac{\int_0^a x\rho 2y\,dx}{\int_0^a \rho 2y\,dx}$$

$$= \frac{\int_0^a xy\,dx}{\int_0^a y\,dx} \qquad | \because \rho \text{ is constant}$$

$$= \frac{\int_0^a x^2\sqrt{\frac{a-x}{a+x}}\,dx}{\int_0^a x\sqrt{\frac{a-x}{a+x}}\,dx} \qquad | \text{ From (1)}$$

$$= \frac{\int_0^a \frac{x^2(a-x)}{\sqrt{a^2-x^2}}dx}{\int_0^a \frac{x(a-x)}{\sqrt{a^2-x^2}}dx}$$ | Rationalising the numerators in the integrands in the numerator and the denominator.

Put $x = a \sin\theta$

$\therefore dx = \cos\theta \, d\theta$

$$= \frac{\int_0^{\pi/2} \frac{a^2 \sin^2\theta(a - a\sin\theta)a\cos\theta \, d\theta}{\sqrt{a^2 - a^2\sin^2\theta}}}{\int_0^{\pi/2} \frac{a\sin\theta(a - a\sin\theta)a\cos\theta \, d\theta}{\sqrt{a^2 - a^2\sin^2\theta}}} = \frac{a^3\left[\int_0^{\pi/2}\sin^2\theta \, d\theta - \int_0^{\pi/2}\sin^3\theta \, d\theta\right]}{a^2\left[\int_0^{\pi/2}\sin\theta - \int_0^{\pi/2}\sin^2\theta \, d\theta\right]}$$

$$= \frac{a\left[\frac{1}{2}\cdot\frac{\pi}{2} - \frac{2}{3}\right]}{1 - \frac{1}{2}\cdot\frac{\pi}{2}}$$ | By Walli's Formula $$= \frac{a\left(\frac{\pi}{4} - \frac{2}{3}\right)}{1 - \frac{\pi}{4}}$$

$$= a\left(\frac{3\pi - 8}{12}\right)\cdot\frac{4}{4-\pi} = \frac{a(3\pi - 8)}{3(4-\pi)}$$

and $\bar{y} = 0$.

**Example 11:** Find the C.G. of the area bounded by the curve $y = \sin x$, and the lines $x = 0$, $x = \pi$ and $y = 0$.

**Sol.**

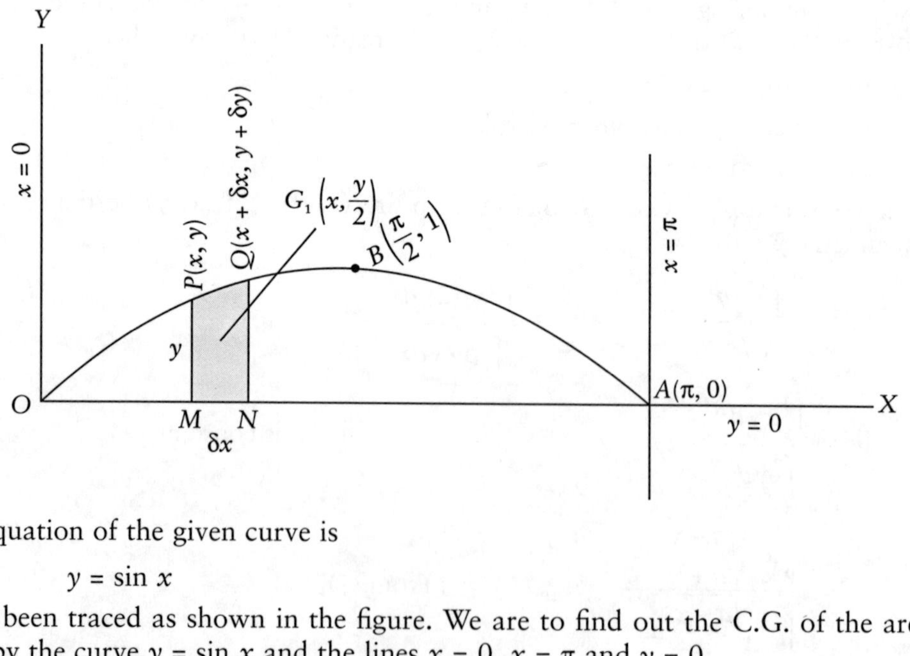


The equation of the given curve is

$$y = \sin x \quad \text{...(1)}$$

It has been traced as shown in the figure. We are to find out the C.G. of the area $OABO$ bounded by the curve $y = \sin x$ and the lines $x = 0$, $x = \pi$ and $y = 0$.

Take two neighbouring points $P(x, y)$ and $Q(x + \delta x, y + \delta y)$ on the curve. From $P$ and $Q$, draw perpendiculars $PM$ and $QN$ respectively on the $X$-axis. Take $PMNQ$ as the elementary area. Its height is $y$ and width is $\delta x$.

∴ Area of the elementary strip $= y\,\delta x$

∴ Mass of the elementary strip $\delta m = \rho\, y\, \delta x$

where ρ is the mass per unit area.

Also, the coordinates of C.G. $G_1$ of the elementary area are $(x, \pi/2)$. Let $(\bar{x}, \bar{y})$ be the required C.G. Then,

$$\bar{x} = \frac{\int x\,dm}{\int dm} = \frac{\int x\rho y\,dx}{\int \rho y\,dx}$$

$$= \frac{\int x y\,dx}{\int y\,dx} \qquad |\because \rho \text{ is constant}$$

$$= \frac{\int_0^\pi x\sin x\,dx}{\int_0^\pi \sin x\,dx} \qquad |\text{From (1)}$$

$$= \frac{[x(-\cos x)]_0^\pi - \int_0^\pi 1(-\cos x)\,dx}{(-\cos x)_0^\pi} = \frac{\pi + (\sin x)_0^\pi}{-\cos\pi + \cos 0} = \frac{\pi}{2}$$

and

$$\bar{y} = \frac{\int \frac{y}{2}\,dm}{\int dm} = \frac{\int_0^\pi \frac{y}{2}\rho y\,dx}{\int_0^\pi \rho y\,dx}$$

$$= \frac{\frac{1}{2}\int_0^\pi y^2\,dx}{\int_0^\pi y\,dx} \qquad |\because \rho \text{ is constant}$$

$$= \frac{\frac{1}{2}\int_0^\pi \sin^2 x\,dx}{\int_0^\pi \sin x\,dx} \qquad |\text{From (1)}$$

$$= \frac{\frac{1}{4}\int_0^\pi (1-\cos 2x)\,dx}{(-\cos x)_0^\pi} = \frac{\frac{1}{4}\left[x - \frac{\sin 2x}{2}\right]_0^\pi}{-\cos\pi + \cos 0} = \frac{\frac{\pi}{4}}{2} = \frac{\pi}{8}$$

Hence, $\bar{x} = \pi/2$ and $\bar{y} = \pi/8$.

**Example 12:** Find the centre of the gravity of the area between the curve $y = \cos x$ from $x = 0$ to $x = \pi/2$ bounded by the line $y = 0$.

**Sol.**

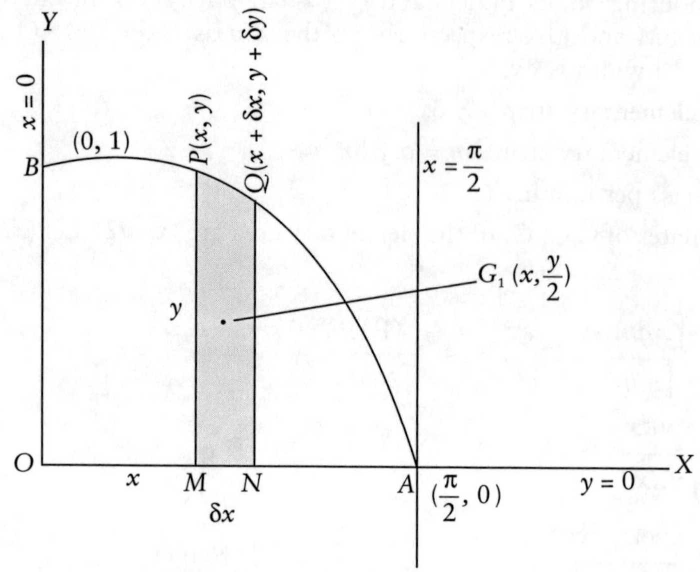


The equation of the given curve is $y = \cos x$ ...(1)

It has been traced as shown in the figure. We are to find that the C.G. of the area $OABO$ between the curve $y = \cos x$ from $x = 0$ to $x = \pi/2$ bounded by the line $y = 0$.

Take two neighbouring points $P(x, y)$ and $Q(x + \delta x, y + \delta y)$ on the curve. From $P$ and $Q$, draw perpendiculars $PM$ and $QN$ respectively on the $X$-axis. Take $PMNQ$ as the elementary area. It height is $y$ and width is $\delta x$.

$\therefore$ Area of the elementary strip $= y\ \delta x$

$\therefore$ Mass of the elementary strip $\delta m = \rho\ y\ \delta x$

where $\rho$ is the mass per unit area.

Also, the coordinates of C.G. $G_1$ of the elementary area are $(x, y/2)$. Let $(\bar{x}, \bar{y})$ be the required C.G. Then,

$$\bar{x} = \frac{\int x\,dm}{\int dm} = \frac{\int_0^{\pi/2} x\rho y\,dx}{\int_0^{\pi/2} \rho y\,dx} = \frac{\int_0^{\pi/2} xy\,dx}{\int_0^{\pi/2} y\,dx} \qquad | \because \rho \text{ is constant}$$

$$= \frac{\int_0^{\pi/2} x\cos x\,dx}{\int_0^{\pi/2} \cos x\,dx} \qquad |\text{From (1)}$$

$$= \frac{(x\sin x)_0^{\pi/2} - \int_0^{\pi/2} 1.\sin x\,dx}{(\sin x)_0^{\pi/2}} = \frac{\frac{\pi}{2} + (\cos x)_0^{\pi/2}}{1-0} = \pi/2 - 1.$$

$$\text{and } \bar{y} = \frac{\int \frac{y}{2}\,dm}{\int dm} = \frac{\frac{1}{2}\int_0^{\pi/2} y\rho y\,dx}{\int_0^{\pi/2} \rho y\,dx} \qquad |\text{From (1)}$$

$$= \frac{\frac{1}{2}\int_0^{\pi/2} y^2\,dx}{\int_0^{\pi/2} y\,dx} \qquad \Big|\ \because \rho \text{ is constant}$$

$$= \frac{\frac{1}{2}\int_0^{\pi/2} \cos^2 x\,dx}{\int_0^{\pi/2} \cos x\,dx} \qquad \Big|\text{From (1)}$$

$$= \frac{\frac{1}{4}\int_0^{\pi/2} (1+\cos 2x)\,dx}{(\sin x)_0^{\pi/2}} = \frac{\frac{1}{4}\left[x+\frac{\sin 2x}{2}\right]_0^{\pi/2}}{\sin\frac{\pi}{2}-\sin 0}$$

$$= \frac{\frac{1}{4}\left[\frac{\pi}{2}+\frac{1}{2}\sin\pi\right]}{1-0} = \pi/8$$

Hence, $\overline{x} = \pi/2 - 1$ and $\overline{y} = \pi/8$.

**Example 13:** Find the C.G. of the sector of a circle subtending an angle $2\alpha$ at the centre of the circle.

**Sol.**

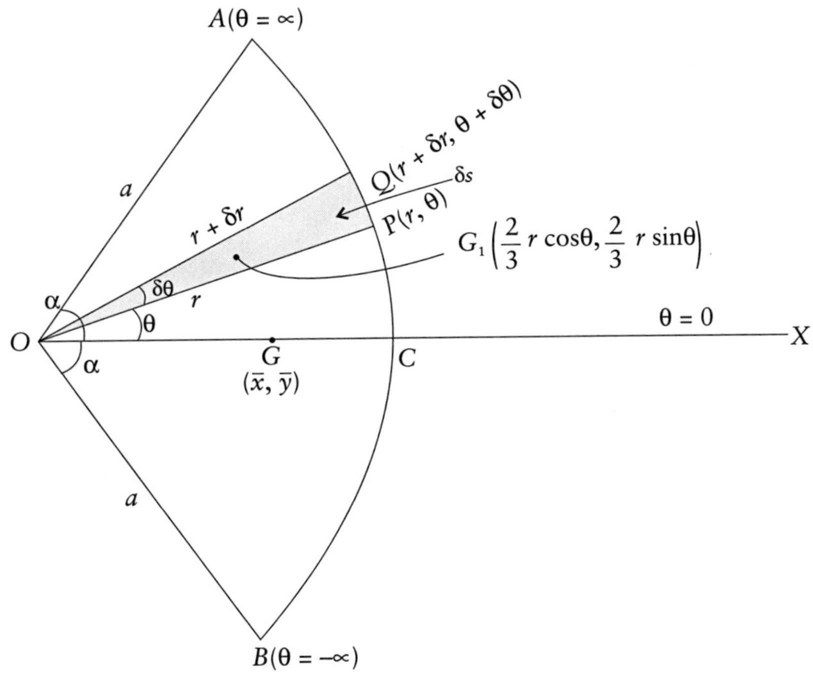


Take O as pole and $OX$ as the initial line.

Let the radius of the circle be $a$. Then, polar equation of the circle is $r = a$. ...(1)

We are to find unit the C.G. of the sector $OACBO$ of this circle which subtends an angle $2\alpha$ at the centre.

From the figure, we observe that the given sector is symmetrical about the line $OCX$. Hence, $\bar{y} = 0$ where $(\bar{x}, \bar{y})$ are the coordinates of C.G. of this sector.

Take an elementary area $\delta A$ in the form of a narrow sector $OPQ$, as shown in the figure, where the coordinates of $P$ and $Q$ are $(r, \theta)$ and $(r + \delta r, \theta + \delta\theta)$ respectively. Then, elementary sectorial area $OPQ = 1/2\ r^2\ \delta\theta$ ∴ elementary mass $\delta m = \rho\ 1/2\ r^2\ \delta\theta$ where $\rho$ in the mass per unit area.

Let $G_1$ be the C.G. of this elementary sectorial area. Then, $OG_1 = 2/3\ r$ is limit.

Let the coordinates of $G_1$ be $(x, y)$. Then, $x = 2/3\ r \cos\theta$ $\Rightarrow y = 2/3\ r \sin\theta$

Let $(\bar{x}, \bar{y})$ be the required C.G. Then,

$$\bar{x} = \frac{\int x\,dm}{\int dm} = \frac{\int_{-\alpha}^{\alpha} x\rho\frac{1}{2}r^2\,d\theta}{\int_{-\alpha}^{\alpha}\rho\frac{1}{2}r^2\,d\theta} = \frac{\int_{-\alpha}^{\alpha} x\frac{1}{2}r^2\,d\theta}{\int_{-\alpha}^{\alpha}\frac{1}{2}r^2\,d\theta} \qquad |\because \rho \text{ is constant}$$

$$= \frac{\int_{-\alpha}^{\alpha} x\,r^2\,d\theta}{\int_{-\alpha}^{\alpha} r^2\,d\theta} = \frac{\int_{-\alpha}^{\alpha}\frac{2}{3}r\cos\theta\,r^2 d\theta}{\int_{-\alpha}^{\alpha} r^2 d\theta} = \frac{\frac{2}{3}\int_{-\alpha}^{\alpha} a^3\cos\theta\,d\theta}{\int_{-\alpha}^{\alpha} a^2 d\theta} \qquad |\text{From (1)}$$

$$= \frac{\frac{2a}{3}\int_0^{\alpha}\cos\theta\,d\theta}{\int_0^{\alpha} d\theta} = \frac{2a}{3}\frac{\sin\alpha}{\alpha}$$

Hence, $\bar{x} = 2a/3\ \sin\alpha/\alpha$ and $\bar{y} = 0$.

**Example 14:** Find the C.G. of the segment of a circle that subtends an angle $2\alpha$ at the centre, the radius of the circle is $a$.

**Sol.**

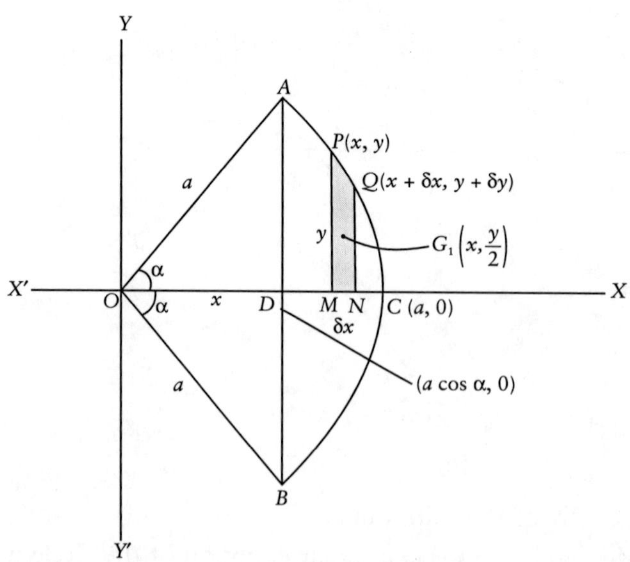


Let $ACBDA$ be a segment of a circle whose centre is O and radius is $a$. The axes of coordinates are as shown in the figure.

Equation of the circle is $x^2 + y^2 = a^2$ ...(1)

By symmetry, the C.G. of this segment will be on the symmetrical radius $OC$. Hence, $\bar{y} = 0$ where $(\bar{x}, \bar{y})$ are the coordinates of the C.G. of the segment.

$$\angle AOB = 2\alpha \quad \therefore \quad \angle AOC = \angle BOC = \alpha$$

Also, $x$-coordinate of the C.G. of the entire segment = $x$-coordinate of the C.G. of the semi-segment $ACDA$. | By symmetry

Take two neighbouring points $P(x, y)$ and $Q(x + \delta x, y + \delta y)$ on the arc $AC$. From $P$ and $Q$, draw perpendiculars $PM$ and $QN$ respectively on the X-axis. Take $PMNQ$ as the elementary area. It length is $y$ and width is $\delta x$.

$\therefore$ Area of the elementary strip = $y\ \delta x$

$\therefore$ Mass of the elementary strip $\delta m = \rho\ y\ \delta x$

where $\rho$ is the mass per unit area.

Also, the coordinates of C.G. $G_1$ of the elementary area are $(x, y/2)$.

Now, $x$ = $x$-coordinates of the C.G. of semi-segment $ACDA$.

$$\bar{x} = \frac{\int x\,dm}{\int dm} = \frac{\int_{a\cos\alpha}^{a} x\rho y\,dx}{\int_{a\cos\alpha}^{a} \rho y\,dx}$$

$$= \frac{\int_{a\cos\alpha}^{a} xy\,dx}{\int_{a\cos\alpha}^{a} y\,dx} \qquad \Big|\ \because \rho \text{ is constant}$$

$$= \frac{\int_{a\cos\alpha}^{a} x\sqrt{a^2 - x^2}\,dx}{\int_{a\cos\alpha}^{a} \sqrt{a^2 - x^2}\,dx} \qquad \Big|\ \text{From (1)}$$

$$= \frac{\left[-\frac{\left(a^2 - x^2\right)^{3/2}}{3}\right]_{a\cos\alpha}^{a}}{\left[\frac{1}{2}x\sqrt{a^2 - x^2} + \frac{1}{2}a^2 \sin\left(\frac{x}{a}\right)\right]_{a\cos\alpha}^{a}}$$

$$= \frac{\frac{\left(a^2 - a^2\cos^2\alpha\right)^{3/2}}{3}}{\frac{1}{2}a^2\left(\frac{\pi}{2}\right) - \frac{1}{2}a\cos\alpha\sqrt{a^2 - a^2\cos^2\alpha} - \frac{1}{2}a^2\sin^{-1}\left(\frac{a\cos\alpha}{a}\right)}$$

$$= \frac{2a^3\sin^3\alpha}{3a^2\left[\frac{\pi}{2} - \sin\alpha\sin\alpha - \left(\frac{\pi}{2} - \alpha\right)\right]}$$

$$\Big|\ \because \sin^{-1}(\cos\alpha) = \sin^{-1}\left\{\sin\left(\frac{\pi}{2} - \alpha\right)\right\} = \frac{\pi}{2} - \alpha$$

$$= \frac{2a}{3}\frac{\sin^3\alpha}{\alpha - \sin\alpha\cos\alpha}$$

and $\bar{y} = 0.$

*Note*: If a segment subtends angle $\pi/2$ at the centre, then $\alpha = \pi/4$. Hence,

$$\bar{x} = \frac{2a}{3}\frac{\sin^3\frac{\pi}{4}}{\frac{\pi}{4} - \sin\frac{\pi}{4}\cos\frac{\pi}{4}} = \frac{\frac{2a}{3}\frac{1}{2\sqrt{2}}}{\frac{\pi}{4} - \frac{1}{\sqrt{2}}\frac{1}{\sqrt{2}}} = \frac{\frac{a}{3\sqrt{2}}}{\frac{\pi - 2}{4}} = \frac{2\sqrt{2}}{3(\pi - 2)}$$

**Example 15:** Two parallel chords of a circle of radius $a$ subtend angles $2\alpha$ and $2\beta$ at the centre. Show that the C.G. of the disc between the chords in at a distance $\frac{2a^3\left(\sin^3\alpha - \sin^3\beta\right)}{3S}$ from the centre where $S$ is the area of the portion.

**Sol.**

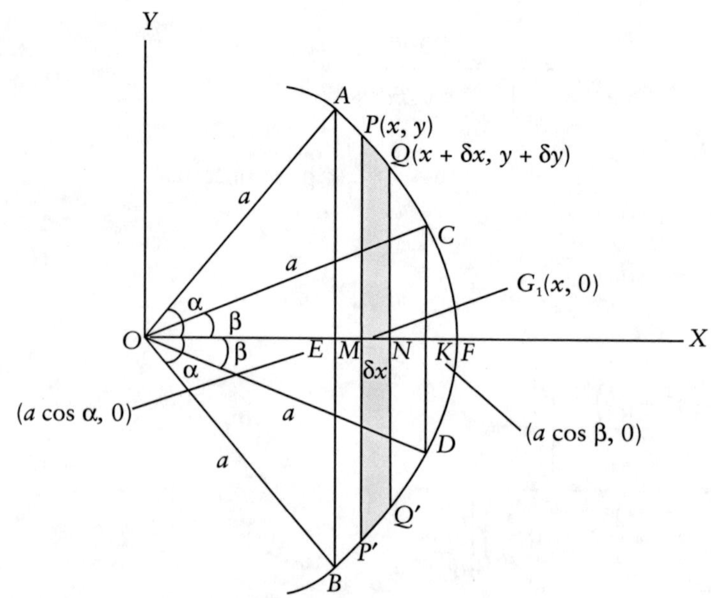


Equation of a circle whose centre is O and radius is $a$ is $x^2 + y^2 = a^2$...(1). Let two parallel chords $AB$ and $CD$ of this circle subtend angles $2\alpha$ and $2\beta$ respectively at the centre. Then, we have to find out the C.G. of the portion $ABDCA$.

Take two neighbouring points $P(x, y)$ and $Q(x + \delta x, y + \delta y)$ on the arc AC. Consider an elementary strip $PQQ'P'$ of length $PP'$ $(= 2y)$ and breadth $MN$ $(= \delta x)$. Then,

Area of the elementary strip $= 2y\,\delta x$

$\therefore$ Mass of the elementary strip $\delta m = \rho\, 2y\,\delta x$

where $\rho$ is the mass per unit area.

Also, the coordinates of C.G. $G_1$ of this strip are $(x, 0)$.

Let $(\bar{x}, \bar{y})$ be the required C.G. Then, from figure by symmetry,

$\overline{y} = 0$ as C.G. will be on the symmetrical radius $OEF$.

Now, $$\overline{x} = \frac{\int x\,dm}{\int dm} = \frac{\int_{a\cos\beta}^{a\cos\alpha} x\rho 2y\,dx}{\int_{a\cos\beta}^{a\cos\alpha} \rho 2y\,dx}$$

$$= \frac{\int_{a\cos\beta}^{a\cos\alpha} 2xy\,dx}{\int_{a\cos\beta}^{a\cos\alpha} 2y\,dx} \qquad \Big|\ \because \rho \text{ is constant}$$

$$= \frac{2}{S}\int_{a\cos\beta}^{a\cos\alpha} x\sqrt{a^2 - x^2}\,dx \qquad \Big|\ \text{From (1)}$$

where $S$ is the area of the portion $ABDCA$.

$$= \frac{2}{S}\left[-\frac{\left(a^2 - x^2\right)^{3/2}}{3}\right]_{a\cos\beta}^{a\cos\alpha} = \frac{2a^3}{3S}\left(\sin^3\alpha - \sin^3\beta\right)$$

Hence, $$\overline{x} = \frac{2a^3}{3S}\left(\sin^3\alpha - \sin^3\beta\right) \text{ and } \overline{y} = 0.$$

**Example 16:** Find the C.G. of the area bounded by the axis of Y, the cycloid $x = a(\theta + \sin\theta)$, $y = a(1 - \cos\theta)$ and its base.

**Sol.**

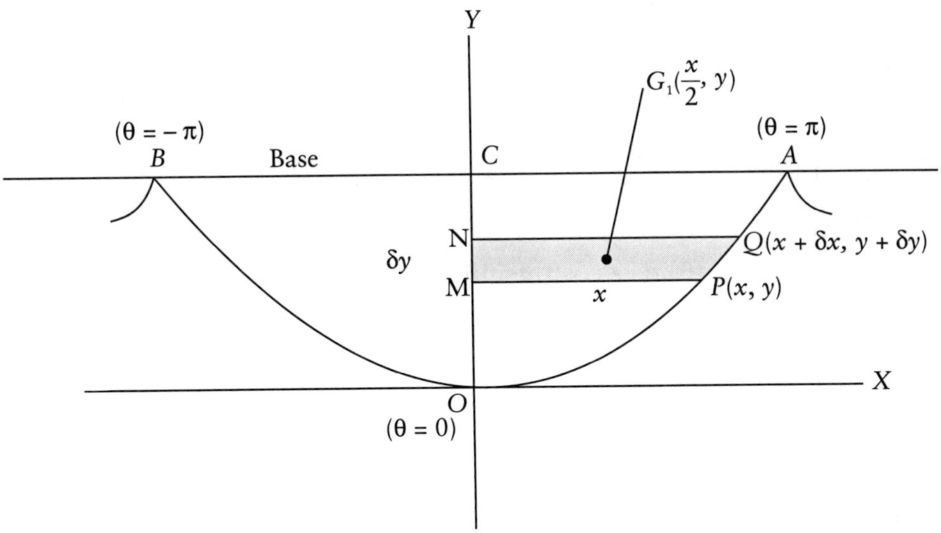


The parametric equations of the cycloid are

$$x = a(\theta + \sin\theta) \qquad ...(1)$$

$$y = a(1 - \cos\theta) \qquad ...(2)$$

The curve has been traced as shown in the figure. We are to find out the C.G. of the area OACO.

Take two neighbouring points $P(x, y)$ and $Q(x + \delta x, y + \delta y,)$ on the arc $OA$. From $P$ and $Q$, draw perpendiculars $PM$ and $QN$ respectively on the $Y$-axis. Take $PMNQ$ as the elementary area. It length is $x$ and breadth is $\delta y$.

∴ Area of the elementary strip = $x\,\delta y$

∴ Mass of the elementary strip $\delta m = \rho\, x\, \delta y$

where $\rho$ is the mass per unit area.

Also, the coordinates of C.G. $G_1$ of this elementary area are $(x/2, y)$. Let $(\bar{x}, \bar{y})$ be the required C.G. Then,

$$\bar{x} = \frac{\int \frac{x}{2}\, dm}{\int dm} = \frac{\int \frac{x}{2}\rho x\, dy}{\int \rho x\, dy}$$

$$= \frac{\frac{1}{2}\int x^2\, dy}{\int x\, dy} \qquad |\because \rho \text{ is constant}$$

$$= \frac{\frac{1}{2}\int_0^\pi a^2(\theta + \sin\theta)^2\, a\sin\theta\, d\theta}{\int_0^\pi a(\theta + \sin\theta) a\sin\theta\, d\theta}$$

$$= \frac{\frac{1}{2}\int_0^\pi (\theta + \sin\theta)^2 \sin\theta\, d\theta}{\int_0^\pi (\theta + \sin\theta)\sin\theta\, d\theta} \qquad \text{...(3)}$$

and

$$\bar{y} = \frac{\int y\, dm}{\int dm} = \frac{\int y\rho x\, dy}{\int \rho x\, dy}$$

$$= \frac{\int xy\, dy}{\int x\, dy} \qquad |\because \rho \text{ is constant}$$

$$= \frac{\int_0^\pi a(\theta + \sin\theta) a(1 - \cos\theta) a\sin\theta\, d\theta}{\int_0^\pi a(\theta + \sin\theta) a\sin\theta\, d\theta}$$

$$= \frac{\int_0^\pi (\theta + \sin\theta)(1 - \cos\theta)\sin\theta\, d\theta}{\int_0^\pi (\theta + \sin\theta)\sin\theta\, d\theta} \qquad \text{...(4)}$$

Numerator of $\bar{x} = \frac{a}{2}\int_0^\pi (\theta + \sin\theta)^2 \sin\theta\, d\theta$

$$= \frac{a}{2}\int_0^\pi (\theta^2 + 2\theta\sin\theta + \sin^2\theta)\sin\theta\, d\theta = \frac{a}{2}\left[\int_0^\pi \theta^2 \sin\theta\, d\theta + 2\int_0^\pi \theta\sin^2\theta\, d\theta + \int_0^\pi \sin^3\theta\, d\theta\right]$$

$$= \frac{a}{2}\left[\left\{\theta^2(-\cos\theta)\right\}_0^\pi - \int_0^\pi 2\theta(-\cos\theta)\, d\theta\right\} + \int_0^\pi \theta(1 - \cos 2\theta)\, d\theta + 2\int_0^{\pi/2} \sin^3\theta\, d\theta\right]$$

$$= \frac{a}{2}\left[\pi^2 + 2\int_0^\pi \theta\cos\theta\, d\theta + \int_0^\pi \theta\, d\theta - \int_0^\pi \theta\cos 2\theta\, d\theta + 2\frac{2}{3}\right] \qquad \text{| By Walli's Formula}$$

$$= \frac{a}{2}\left[\pi^2 + 2\left\{(\theta\sin\theta)_0^\pi - \int_0^\pi 1\cdot\sin\theta\, d\theta\right\} + \left(\frac{\theta^2}{2}\right)_0^\pi - \left\{\left(\frac{\theta\sin 2\theta}{2}\right)_0^\pi - \int_0^\pi 1\cdot\frac{\sin 2\theta}{2}\,d\theta\right\} + \frac{4}{3}\right]$$

$$= \frac{a}{2}\left[\pi^2 + 2(\cos\theta)_0^\pi + \frac{\pi^2}{2} - \left(\frac{\cos 2\theta}{4}\right)_0^\pi + \frac{4}{3}\right]$$

$$= \frac{a}{2}\left[\pi^2 - 4 + \frac{\pi^2}{2} + \frac{4}{3}\right] \qquad = \frac{a}{2}\left[\frac{3\pi^2}{2} - \frac{8}{3}\right] \qquad \ldots(5)$$

Numerator of $\overline{y}$

$$= a\int (\theta + \sin\theta)(1 - \cos\theta)\sin\theta\, d\theta \qquad = a\int_0^\pi (\theta + \sin\theta)(\sin\theta - \sin\theta\cos\theta)\, d\theta$$

$$= a\int_0^\pi \left(\theta + \sin\theta + \sin^2\theta - \theta\sin\theta\cos\theta - \sin^2\theta\cos\theta\right) d\theta$$

$$= a\left[\int_0^\pi \theta\sin\theta\, d\theta + \int_0^\pi \sin^2\theta\, d\theta - \int_0^\pi \theta\sin\theta\cos\theta\, d\theta - \int_0^\pi \sin^2\theta\cos\theta\, d\theta\right]$$

$$= a\left[\int_o^\pi \theta\sin\theta\, d\theta + 2\int_o^{\pi/2} \sin^2\theta\, d\theta - \frac{1}{2}\int_o^\pi \theta\sin 2\theta\, d\theta - \left(\frac{\sin^3\theta}{3}\right)_o^\pi\right]$$

$$= a\left[\{\theta(-\cos\theta)\}_0^\pi - \int_0^\pi 1\cdot(-\cos\theta)\, d\theta + 2\cdot\frac{1}{2}\cdot\frac{\pi}{2} - \frac{1}{2}\right.$$
$$\left.\left[\left\{\theta\left(-\frac{\cos 2\theta}{2}\right)\right\}_0^\pi - \int_0^\pi 1\cdot\left(-\frac{\cos 2\theta}{2}\right)d\theta\right]\right]$$

$$= a\left[\pi + (\sin\theta)_0^\pi + \frac{\pi}{2} + \frac{\pi}{4} - \left(\frac{\sin 2\theta}{4}\right)_0^\pi\right] \qquad = \frac{7\pi}{4}a \qquad \ldots(6)$$

Denominator of $x$ = Denominator of $y$

$$= \int_0^\pi (\theta + \sin\theta)\sin\theta\, d\theta \qquad = \int_0^\pi \theta\sin\theta\, d\theta + \int_0^\pi \sin^2\theta\, d\theta$$

$$= \{\theta(-\cos\theta)\}_0^\pi - \int_0^\pi 1(-\cos\theta)\, d\theta + 2\int_0^{\pi/2} \sin^2\theta\, d\theta$$

$$= \pi + (\sin\theta)_0^\pi + 2\cdot\frac{\pi}{4} \qquad \text{| By Walli's Formula}$$

$$= \pi + \frac{\pi}{2} \qquad = \frac{3\pi}{2} \qquad \ldots(7)$$

$$\therefore\ \bar{x} = \frac{\frac{a}{2}\left(\frac{3\pi^2}{2} - \frac{8}{3}\right)}{\frac{3\pi}{2}} = \frac{a}{3\pi}\left(\frac{9\pi^2 - 16}{6}\right) = \frac{a\left(9\pi^2 - 16\right)}{18\pi}$$

$$\text{and } \bar{y} = \frac{\frac{7\pi}{4}a}{\frac{3\pi}{2}} = \frac{7a}{6}$$

Hence, $\bar{x} = \dfrac{a\left(a\pi^2 - 16\right)}{18\pi}$ and $\bar{y} = 7/6\ a$.

**Example 17:** Find the position of the centroid of the area of the cardioid $r = a\ (1 + \cos\theta)$

**Sol.**

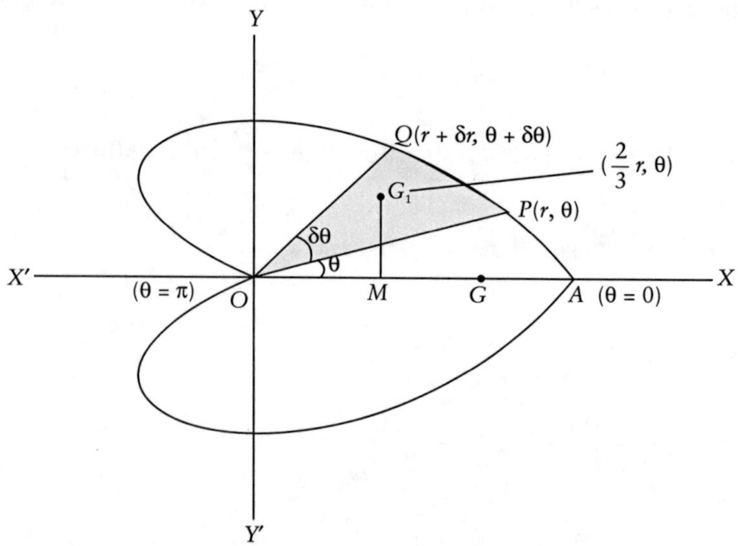


The equation of the cardioid is $r = a\ (1 + \cos\theta)$ ...(1)

It has been traced and shown in the figure. Since the figure is symmetrical about the initial line $OX$, therefore, its C.G. will be on the initial line. Hence, if $(\bar{x}, \bar{y})$ are the coordinates of the C.G., then $\bar{y} = 0$.

Also, $\bar{x}$ = abscissa of the C.G. of the entire cardioid = abscissa of the C.G. of the upper half area $OAPQO$ of the cardioid.

Take an elementary area in the form of a sector $POQ$ where coordinates of $P$ and $Q$ are $(r, \theta)$ and $(r + \delta r, \theta + \delta\theta)$ respectively.

$\therefore$ Elementary area = $1/2 r^2\ \delta\theta$

$\therefore$ Elementary mass $\delta m = \rho\ 1/2 r^2\ \delta\theta$

where $\rho$ is the mass per unit area.

Let $G_1$ be the C.G. of this elementary area. Then, the polar coordinates of $G_1$ are $(2/3r, \theta)$.

$\therefore \quad x = OM = 2/3\ r\cos\theta \qquad y = G_1M = 2/3\ r\sin\theta$

Now,

$$\bar{x} = \frac{\int x\,dm}{\int dm} = \frac{\int_0^\pi x\rho\frac{1}{2}r^2\,d\theta}{\int_0^\pi \rho\frac{1}{2}r^2\,d\theta}$$

$$= \frac{\int_0^\pi \frac{2}{3}r\cos\theta\frac{1}{2}r^2\,d\theta}{\int_0^\pi \frac{1}{2}r^2\,d\theta} \qquad |\because \rho \text{ is constant}$$

$$= \frac{=\frac{2}{3}\int_0^\pi r^3\cos\theta\,d\theta}{\int_0^\pi r^2\,d\theta} = \frac{\frac{2}{3}\int_0^\pi a^3(1+\cos\theta)^3\cos\theta\,d\theta}{\int_0^\pi a^2(1-\cos\theta)^2\,d\theta} \qquad | \text{ From(1)}$$

$$= \frac{\frac{2a}{3}\int_0^\pi (1+\cos\theta)^3\cos\theta\,d\theta}{\int_0^\pi (1+\cos\theta)^2\,d\theta} \qquad ...(2)$$

Numerator of $\bar{x} = \frac{2a}{3}\int_0^\pi (1+\cos\theta)^3\cos\theta\,d\theta$

$$= \frac{2a}{3}\int_0^\pi\left(2\cos^2\frac{\theta}{2}\right)^3\left(2\cos^2\frac{\theta}{2}-1\right)d\theta \qquad | \text{ Put } \theta/2 = \phi \quad | \therefore d\theta = 2d\phi$$

$$= \frac{2a}{3}\int_0^{\pi/2} 8\cos^6\phi\left(2\cos^2\phi-1\right)2d\phi = \frac{32a}{3}\int_0^{\pi/2}\left(2\cos^8\phi-\cos^6\phi\right)d\phi$$

$$= \frac{32a}{3}\left[2\cdot\frac{7}{8}\frac{5}{6}\cdot\frac{3}{4}\cdot\frac{1}{2}\frac{\pi}{2}-\frac{5}{6}\frac{3}{4}\cdot\frac{1}{2}\cdot\frac{\pi}{2}\right] \qquad | \text{By Walli's Formula}$$

$$= \frac{32a}{3}\left[\frac{5\pi}{32}\right]\left(\frac{7}{4}-1\right) = \frac{5\pi a}{4} \qquad ...(3)$$

Denominator of $\bar{x} = \int_0^\pi (1+\cos\theta)^2\,d\theta = \int_0^\pi\left(2\cos^2\frac{\theta}{2}\right)^2 d\theta = 4\int_0^\pi \cos^4\frac{\theta}{2}d\theta$

Put $\quad \theta/2 = \theta \qquad \therefore d\theta = 2d\phi$

$$= 4\int_0^{\pi/2}\cos^4\phi\ 2d\phi = 8\int_0^{\pi/2}\cos^4\phi\ d\phi = 8\cdot\frac{3}{4}\cdot\frac{1}{2}\cdot\frac{\pi}{2} \qquad | \text{By Walli's Formula}$$

$$= \frac{3\pi}{2} \qquad ...(4)$$

Hence, $\bar{x} = \dfrac{\frac{5\pi a}{4}}{\frac{3\pi}{2}} = \dfrac{5a}{6}$ and $\bar{y} = 0$, i.e., the C.G. $G$ lies on the initial line $OX$ such that $OG = 5a/6$.

**Example 18:** Find the C.G. of the area of a loop of Lemniscate of Bernoulli $r^2 = a^2 \cos 2\theta$.

**Sol.**

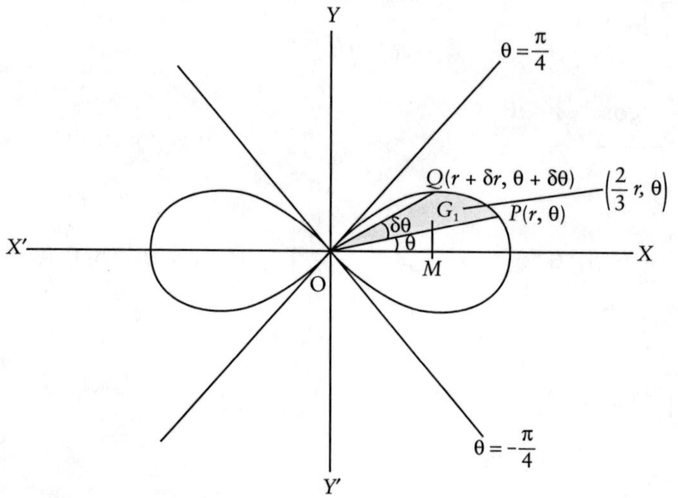


The equation of the Lemniscate of Bernoulli is

$$r^2 = a^2 \cos 2\theta \qquad ...(1)$$

It has been traced and shown in the figure. We have to find the C.G. of the area of a loop of (1).

For a loop, putting $r = 0$ in (1), we get

$$\cos 2\theta = 0 \quad \Rightarrow \cos 2\theta = \cos(\pm \pi/2) \quad \Rightarrow 2\theta = \pm \pi/2 \quad \Rightarrow \theta = \pm \pi/4$$

Hence, for a loop of the curve, $\theta$ varies from $-\pi/4$ to $\pi/4$.

Since the area of the loop is symmetrical about the initial line, therefore, $\bar{y} = 0$ where $(\bar{x}, \bar{y})$ are the coordinates of the C.G. of the area of the loop.

Take an elementary area $POQ$ in the form of a sector $POQ$ where the coordinates of $P$ and $Q$ are $(r, \theta)$ and $(r + \delta r, \theta + \delta\theta)$ respectively.

$\therefore$ Elementary area $= 1/2 r^2 \,\delta\theta$

$\therefore$ Elementary mass $\delta m = \rho\, 1/2 r^2 \,\delta\theta$

where $\rho$ is the mass per unit area.

Let $G_1$ be the C.G. of this elementary area. Then, the polar coordinates of $G_1$ are $(2/3\, r, \theta)$.

$\therefore \qquad x = OM = 2/3\, r \cos\theta \qquad\qquad y = G_1M = 2/3\, r \sin\theta$

Now,
$$x = \frac{\int x\,dm}{\int dm} = \frac{\int_{-\frac{\pi}{4}}^{\pi/4} x\rho \frac{1}{2} r^1 d\theta}{\int_{-\frac{\pi}{4}}^{\pi/4} \rho \frac{1}{2} r^2 d\theta} = \frac{\int_{-\frac{\pi}{4}}^{\pi/4} \frac{2}{3} r\cos\theta\, r^2 d\theta}{\int_{-\frac{\pi}{4}}^{\pi/4} r^2 d\theta} \qquad |\because \rho \text{ is constant}$$

$$= \frac{\frac{2}{3}\int_{-\frac{\pi}{4}}^{\pi/4} r^3 \cos\theta\, d\theta}{\int_{-\frac{\pi}{4}}^{\pi/4} r^2 d\theta} = \frac{\frac{2}{3}\int_{-\frac{\pi}{4}}^{\pi/4} a^3 \cos^{3/2} 2\theta \cos\theta\, d\theta}{\int_{-\frac{\pi}{4}}^{\pi/4} a^2 \cos 2\theta\, d\theta} \quad \text{| From (1)}$$

$$= \frac{\frac{4a}{3}\int_0^{\pi/4} \cos^{3/2} 2\theta \cos\theta\, d\theta}{2\int_0^{\pi/4} \cos 2\theta\, d\theta}$$

$$= \frac{\frac{2a}{3}\int_0^{\pi/4} \left(1 - 2\sin^2\theta\right)^{3/2} \cos\theta\, d\theta}{\left(\frac{\sin 2\theta}{2}\right)_0^{\pi/4}}$$

Put $\sqrt{2}\ \sin\theta = \sin\phi \qquad \therefore\ \sqrt{2}\cos\theta\ d\theta = \cos\phi\ d\phi$

$$\Rightarrow \cos\theta\ d\theta = \frac{\cos\phi}{\sqrt{2}} d\phi$$

$$= \frac{\frac{2a}{3}\int_0^{\pi/2} \left(1 - \sin^2\phi\right)^{3/2} \frac{\cos\phi}{\sqrt{2}} d\phi}{\frac{1}{2}} = \frac{4a}{3\sqrt{2}}\int_0^{\pi/2} \cos^4\phi\, d\phi$$

$$= \frac{2\sqrt{2}a}{3} \cdot \frac{3}{4} \cdot \frac{1}{2}\frac{\pi}{2} = \frac{\sqrt{2}\,\pi a}{8} \qquad \text{and} \qquad \bar{y} = 0.$$

Hence, the required C.G. is given by $\bar{x} = 1/8\ \pi\, a\sqrt{2}$ and $\bar{y} = 0$.

**Example 19:** Find the centre of gravity of the upper half of a loop of the Lemniscate of Bernoulli $r^2 = a^2 \cos 2\theta$.

**Sol.** Refer example 18.

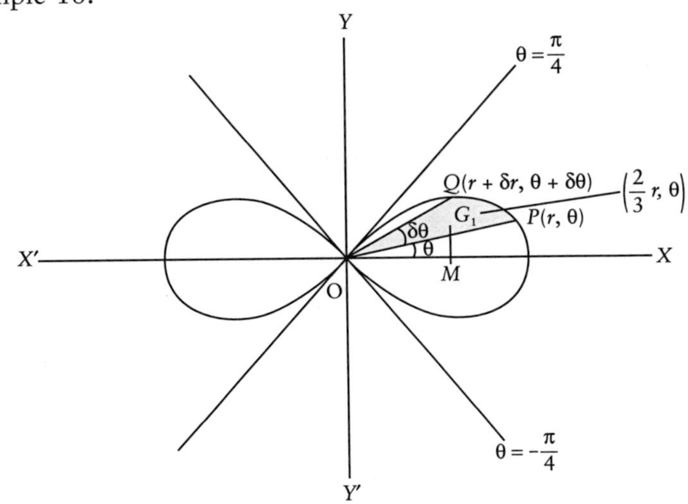


If we take the symmetry of the given curve about the initial line in consideration, we find that the abscissa of the C.G. of the upper half of a loop is the same as the abscissa of the whole loop. Let $(\bar{x}, \bar{y})$ be the coordinates of the C.G. of the upper half of a loop. Then,

$$\bar{x} = \frac{\pi a\sqrt{2}}{8} \qquad | \text{ As in Example 18} \qquad ...(1)$$

The limits of θ for the upper half of a loop are from θ = 0 to θ = π/4.

$$\therefore \quad \bar{y} = \frac{\int y\,dm}{\int dm} = \frac{\int_0^{\pi/4} y\rho\frac{1}{2}r^2\,d\theta}{\int_0^{\pi/4}\rho\frac{1}{2}r^2\,d\theta}$$

$$= \frac{\int_0^{\pi/4} yr^2\,d\theta}{\int_0^{\pi/4} r^2\,d\theta} \qquad | \because \rho \text{ is constant}$$

$$= \frac{\int_0^{\pi/4}\frac{2}{3}r\sin\theta\, r^2\,d\theta}{\int_0^{\pi/4} r^2 d\theta} = \frac{\frac{2}{3}\int_0^{\pi/4} r^3\sin\theta\,d\theta}{\int_0^{\pi/4} r^2 d\theta} = \frac{\frac{2}{3}\int_0^{\pi/4}\left\{a\sqrt{\cos 2\theta}\right\}^3\sin\theta\,d\theta}{\int_0^{\pi/4} a^2\cos 2\theta\,d\theta}$$

$$= \frac{\frac{2a}{3}\int_0^{\pi/4}\left(2\cos^2\theta - 1\right)^{3/2}\sin\theta\,d\theta}{\left(\frac{\sin 2\theta}{2}\right)_0^{\pi/4}}$$

Put $\sqrt{2}\,\cos\theta = \sec\phi$

$\therefore -\sqrt{2}\sin\theta\,d\theta = \sec\phi\tan\phi\,d\phi$

$\Rightarrow \sin\theta\,d\theta = -\dfrac{\sec\phi\tan\phi\,d\phi}{\sqrt{2}}$

$$= \frac{\frac{2a}{3}\int_{\pi/4}^{0}\left(\sec^2\phi - 1\right)^{3/2}\left(\frac{-\sec\phi\tan\phi}{\sqrt{2}}\right)d\phi}{\frac{1}{2}} = \frac{4a}{3\sqrt{2}}\int_0^{\pi/4}\tan^4\phi\sec\phi\,d\phi$$

$$= \frac{4a}{3\sqrt{2}}\int_0^{\pi/4}\left(\sec^2\phi - 1\right)^2\sec\phi\,d\phi = \frac{4a}{3\sqrt{2}}\int_0^{\pi/4}\left(\sec^4\phi - 2\sec^2\phi + 1\right)\sec\phi\,d\phi$$

$$= \frac{4a}{3\sqrt{2}}\int_0^{\pi/4}\left(\sec^5\phi - 2\sec^3\phi + \sec\phi\right)d\phi \qquad ...(2)$$

We know that,

$$\int \sec^n\phi\,d\phi = \frac{\sec^{n-2}\phi\tan\phi}{n-1} + \frac{n-2}{n-1}\int\sec^{n-2}\phi\,d\phi$$

$$\therefore \quad \int \sec^5\phi\,d\phi = \frac{\sec^3\phi\tan\phi}{4} + \frac{3}{4}\int\sec^3\phi\,d\phi \qquad ...(3)$$

$$\int \sec^3\phi\,d\phi = \frac{\sec\phi\tan\phi}{2} + \frac{1}{2}\int\sec\phi\,d\phi$$

$$= \frac{\sec\phi\tan\phi}{2} + \frac{1}{2}\log(\sec\phi + \tan\phi) \qquad ...(4)$$

From (3) and (4),

$$\int \sec^5 \phi \, d\phi = \frac{\sec^3 \phi \tan \phi}{4} + \frac{3}{8} \sec \phi \tan \phi + \frac{3}{8} \log(\sec \phi + \tan \phi) \quad ...(5)$$

Also, $\int \sec \phi \, d\phi = \log(\sec \phi + \tan \phi)$ ...(6)

$$\therefore \quad \bar{y} = \frac{4a}{3\sqrt{2}} \left[ \frac{\sec^3 \phi \tan \phi}{4} + \frac{3}{8} \sec \phi \tan \phi + \frac{3}{8} \log(\sec \phi + \tan \phi) \right.$$

$$\left. - \sec \phi \tan \phi - \log(\sec \phi + \tan \phi) + \log(\sec \phi + \tan \phi) \right]_0^{\pi/4}$$

$$= \frac{4a}{3\sqrt{2}} \left[ \frac{\sec^3 \phi \tan \phi}{4} - \frac{5}{8} \sec \phi \tan \phi + \frac{3}{8} \log(\sec \phi + \tan \phi) \right]_0^{\pi/4}$$

$$= \frac{4a}{3\sqrt{2}} \left[ \frac{(\sqrt{2})^3 \cdot 1}{4} - \frac{5}{8}(\sqrt{2}) \cdot 1 + \frac{3}{8} \log(\sqrt{2} + 1) \right]$$

$$= \frac{4a}{3\sqrt{2}} \frac{1}{8} \left[ 4\sqrt{2} - 5\sqrt{2} + 3\log(\sqrt{2} + 1) \right]$$

$$= \frac{a}{6\sqrt{2}} \left[ 3\log(\sqrt{2} + 1) - \sqrt{2} \right] \qquad = \frac{a\sqrt{2}}{\sqrt{12}} \left[ 3\log(\sqrt{2} + 1) - \sqrt{2} \right].$$

**Example 20:** Find the C.G. of a loop of the curve $r = a \cos 2\theta$.

**Sol.** For a loop of the curve,

$$r = 0 \quad \Rightarrow a \cos 2\theta = 0 \Rightarrow \cos 2\theta = 0 = \cos(\pm \pi/2)$$

$$\Rightarrow \quad 2\theta = \pm \pi/2 \qquad \Rightarrow \theta = \pm \pi/4$$

Let $(\bar{x}, \bar{y})$ be the coordinates the C.G. of the area of the loop. Then, due to symmetry of the area of the loop about the initial line, $\bar{y} = 0$. ...(1)

Refer Example 18.

$$\bar{x} = \frac{\int_0^{\pi/4} \frac{2}{3} r \cos \theta \frac{1}{2} r^2 \, d\theta}{\int_0^{\pi/4} \frac{1}{2} r^2 \, d\theta} = \frac{\frac{2}{3} \int_0^{\pi/4} a^3 \cos^3 2\theta \cos \theta \, d\theta}{\int_0^{\pi/4} a^2 \cos^2 2\theta \, d\theta}$$

$$= \frac{\frac{2a}{3} \int_0^{\pi/4} \cos^3 2\theta \cos \theta \, d\theta}{\int_0^{\pi/4} \cos^2 2\theta \, d\theta} \quad ...(2)$$

Numerator of $\bar{x} = \frac{2a}{3} \int_0^{\pi/4} \cos^3 2\theta \cos \theta \, d\theta$

$$= \frac{2a}{3} \int_0^{\pi/4} (1 - 2\sin^2 \theta)^3 \cos \theta \, d\theta$$

Put $\sqrt{2} \sin\theta = \sin\phi \therefore \sqrt{2} \cos\theta \, d\theta = \cos\phi \, d\phi$

$$\Rightarrow \cos\theta \, d\theta = \frac{\cos\phi \, d\phi}{\sqrt{2}}$$

$$= \frac{2a}{3}\int_0^{\pi/2}\left(1-\sin^2\phi\right)^3\frac{\cos\phi\, d\phi}{\sqrt{2}} \qquad = \frac{\sqrt{2}a}{3}\int_0^{\pi/2}\cos^7\phi\, d\phi$$

$$= \frac{\sqrt{2}a}{3}\frac{6}{7}\frac{4}{3}\cdot\frac{2}{3} \qquad \text{| By Walli's Formula}$$

$$= \frac{16\sqrt{2}a}{105} \qquad ...(3)$$

Denominator of $\bar{x} = \frac{1}{2}\int_0^{\pi/4}(1+\cos 4\theta)\, d\theta$

$$= \frac{1}{2}\left[\theta+\frac{\sin 4\theta}{4}\right]_0^{\pi/4} = \pi/8 \qquad ...(4)$$

$$\therefore \qquad \bar{x} = \frac{16\sqrt{2}\,a}{105} \Bigg| \frac{\pi}{8} = \frac{16\sqrt{2}a}{105}\frac{8}{\pi} = \frac{128\sqrt{2}a}{105\pi}$$

Hence, $\bar{x} = \dfrac{128\sqrt{2}a}{105\pi}$ and $\bar{y} = 0$.

## EXERCISE 2(B)

1. Find the centroid of the area enclosed by the parabola $y^2 = 4ax$ and the double ordinate $x = b$.

   [**Ans.** $\bar{x} = 3/5b$, $\bar{y} = 0$]
2. From that the C.G. of a lamina of uniform density in the form of a quadrant of a circle of radius $a$ is $(4a/3\pi, 4a/3\pi)$.
3. Find the centre of gravity of the area of the curve $x^{2/3} + y^{2/3} = a^{2/3}$ lying in the positive quadrant.

   OR

   Find the coordinates of the C.G. of a quadrant of the area of the curve $x^{2/3} + y^{2/3} = a^{2/3}$, bounded by the axes of coordinates.

   [**Ans.** $256a/3\pi$, $256a/3\pi$]
4. Show that the C.G. of the area of the curve $y = \sin x$ included between $X$-axis and lines $x = 0$ and $x = \pi/2$ is $(1, \pi/16)$.
5. Find the C.G. of a uniform lamina in the shape of a sector of a circle of radius $a$ with the angle at the centre equal to 60°.

   [**Ans.** $\bar{x} = 2a/\pi$, $\bar{y} = 0$]
6. Find the C.G. of a uniform semi-circular disc of radius $a$.

   [**Ans.** $\bar{x} = 4a/3\pi$, $\bar{y} = 0$]
7. Find the centre of gravity of the area of the cardioid $r = a\,(1 - \cos\theta)$.

   [**Ans.** $\bar{x} = -5a/6$, $\bar{y} = 0$]

8. Find the C.G. of the area of a loop of the curve $r = a\cos 3\theta$ containing the initial line.

[**Ans.** $\bar{x} = \dfrac{81\sqrt{3}a}{80\pi}$, $\bar{y} = 0$ ]

9. Find the C.G. of the area of a loop of the curve $r = a\sin 2\theta$, which lies in the positive quadrant, the density being supposed uniform.

[**Ans.** $\bar{x} = 128a/105\pi$, $\bar{y} = 128a/105\pi$]

## 7. Centre of Gravity of a Solid of Revolution

Let the solid be generated by the revolution of the area enclosed by the curve $y = f(x)$, the X-axis and ordinates at $x = a$ and $x = b$ about the X-axis as the axis of revolution.

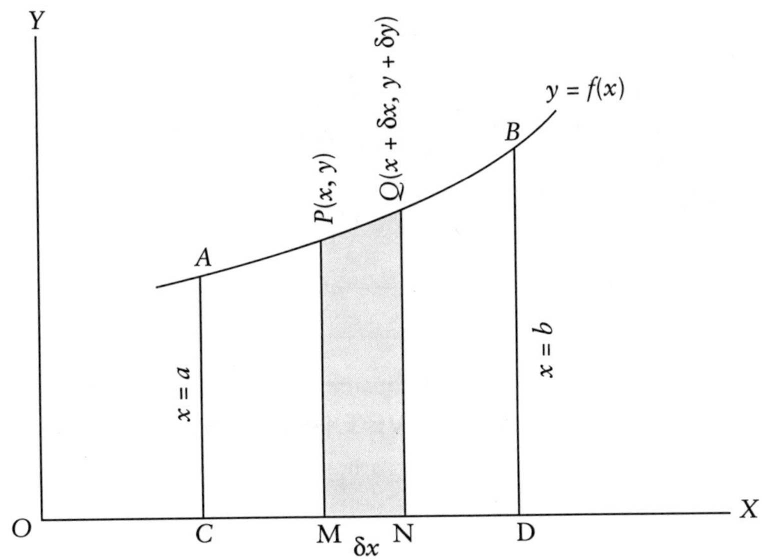


Take two neighbouring points $P(x, y)$ and $Q(x + \delta x, y + \delta y)$ on the arc $AB$ of the curve $y = f(x)$. From $P$ and $Q$, draw perpendiculars $PM$ and $QN$ respectively to the X-axis. If we revolve the area between the curve $y = f(x)$, the X-axis and ordinates at $x = a$ and $x = b$ about the X-axis, then the elementary strip $PQNM$, whose height is $y$ and breadth is $\delta x$, will generate an elementary disc of small thickness $\delta x$ and circular base of area $\pi y^2$ whose volume is $\pi y^2 \delta x$. It $\rho$ is the density per unit volume, then mass $\delta m$ of this elementary disc is $\rho\pi y^2\,\delta x$. The centre of gravity of this elementary disc may be taken at the point $M(x, 0)$ as MN (= $\delta x$) is infinitesimally small. Therefore, if $(\bar{x}, \bar{y})$ is the required C.G. then by symmetry $\bar{y} = 0$ since C.G. of the solid of revolution lies on the X-axis as it is symmetrical about the X-axis, i.e., the X-axis is the axis of symmetry.

Also $$\bar{x} = \frac{\int x\,dm}{\int dm} = \frac{\int_a^b x\rho\pi y^2 dx}{\int_a^b \rho\pi y^2 dx} = \frac{\int_a^b x y^2 dx}{\int_a^b y^2 dx} \qquad |\because \rho \text{ is constant}$$

wherey = $f(x)$.

If the solid be generated by the revolution of the area enclosed by the curve $x = f(y)$, the $Y$-axis and the abscissae at $y = c$ and $y = d$ about the $Y$-axis as the axis of revolution, then as above mass of the elementary disc is $\rho\, \pi\, x^2\, \delta y$ where $e$ is the mas per unit volume. Here, the axis of symmetry is $Y$-axis. Therefore, if $(\bar{x}, \bar{y})$ are the coordinates of the required C.G., then in this case $\bar{x} = 0$.

Also, $$\bar{y} = \frac{\int y\, dm}{\int dm} = \frac{\int_c^d y \rho \pi x^2 dy}{\int_c^d \rho \pi x^2 dy} = \frac{\int_c^d y x^2 dy}{\int_c^d x^2 dy} \quad \Big| \because \rho \text{ is constant}$$

where $x = f(y)$.

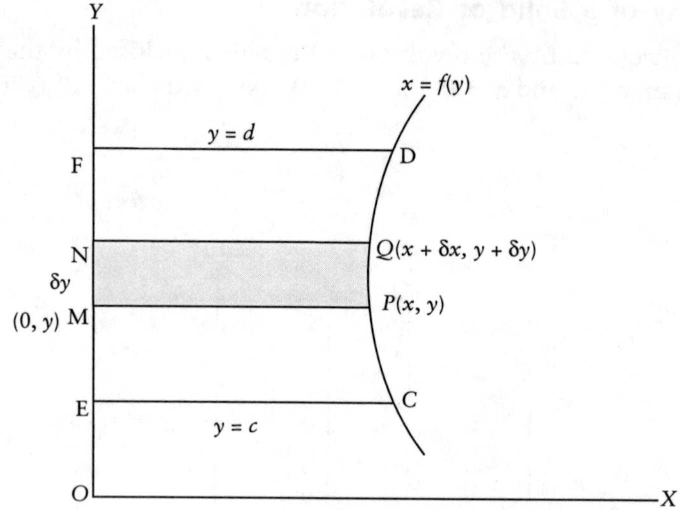


## ILLUSTRATIVE EXAMPLES

**Example 1:** Find the C.G. of a solid uniform hemisphere of radius $a$.

**Sol.**

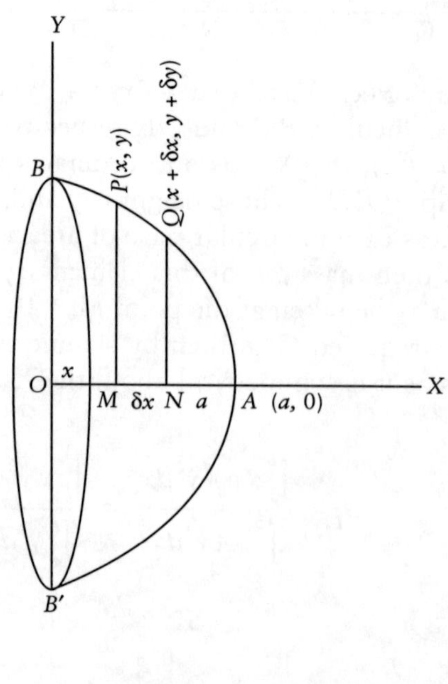

We know that the hemisphere is generated by the revolution of the quadrant of the circle $AOB$ through four right angles about the bounding radius $OA$.

Take O as origin, $OA$ as the $X$-axis and $OB$ as the $Y$-axis. Then the equation to the generating circle is $x^2 + y^2 = a^2$. ...(1)

Take two neighbouring points $P(x, y)$ and $Q(x + \delta x, y + \delta y)$ on the generating circle.

From $P$ and $Q$, draw $PM$ and $QN$ as perpendiculars respectively to the $X$-axis. Take $PMNQ$ as the elementary area of height $y$ and breadth $\delta x$. If this elementary area is revolved about the $X$-axis, an elementary disc is formed whose area of circular base is $\pi y^2$ and whose infinitesimally small thickness is $\delta x$.

$\therefore$ Volume of elementary disc $= \pi y^2\, \delta x$

$\therefore$ Mass of elementary disc $\delta m = \rho\, \pi y^2\, \delta x$

where $\rho$ is the density.

Also, the C.G. of this elementary disc may be taken as the point $M\ (x, 0)$, since $MN\ (= \delta x)$ is very small.

Let $(\bar{x}, \bar{y})$ denote the C.G. of the hemisphere. Then, $\bar{y} = 0$ as $X$-axis is the axis of symmetry.

Also
$$\bar{x} = \frac{\int x\, dm}{\int dm} = \frac{\int_0^a x\, \rho\, \pi y^2 dx}{\int_0^a \rho \pi y^2 dx}$$

$$= \frac{\int_0^a x y^2 dx}{\int_0^a y^2 dx} \qquad |\because \rho \text{ is constant}$$

$$= \frac{\int_0^a x(a^2 - x^2) dx}{\int_0^a (a^2 - x^2)\, dx} \qquad |\text{From (1)}$$

$$= \frac{\left(\frac{a^2 x^2}{2} - \frac{x^4}{4}\right)_0^a}{\left(a^2 x - \frac{x^3}{3}\right)_0^a} = \frac{\frac{a^4}{2} - \frac{a^4}{4}}{a^3 - \frac{a^3}{3}}$$

$$= \frac{\frac{a^4}{4}}{\frac{2a^3}{3}} = \frac{3}{8} a$$

Hence, the C.G. of a uniform hemisphere of radius $a$ lies on its symmetrical radius at a distance $3a/8$ from the centre.

**Example 2:** Find the centre of gravity of the segment of a sphere of radius $a$ cut off by a plane at a distance $c$ from the centre.

**Sol.**

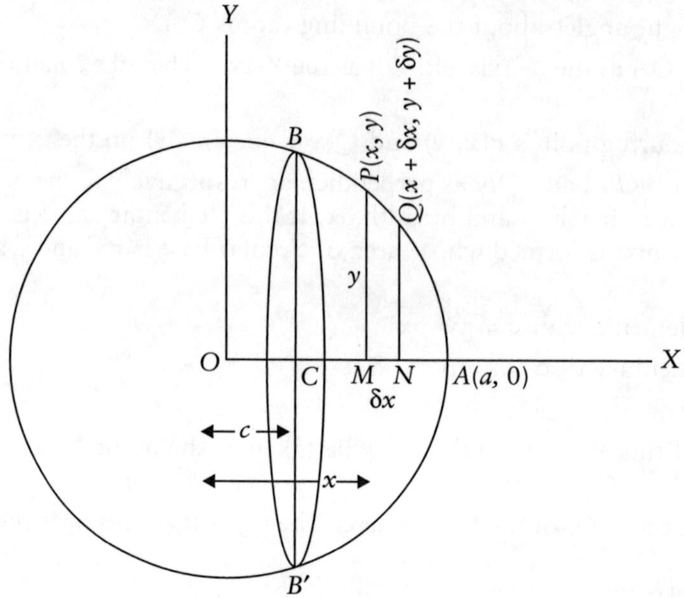


Let O be the centre of the sphere of radius $a$. Take $OX$ as the $X$-axis where $OX$ is perpendicular to the base of the segment. Let $OX$ meet the segment at $C$ and the curved sphere of the sphere at $A$. Then,

$$OC = c$$

and $$OA = a$$

Take two neighbouring points $P(x, y)$ and $Q(x + \delta x, y + \delta y)$ on the sphere as shown in the figure.

Volume of elementary disc formed $= \pi y^2 \, \delta x$

$\therefore$ Mass of elementary disc $\delta m = \rho \, \pi \, y^2 \delta x$

where $\rho$ is the density.

Also, the C.G. of this elementary disc may be taken as $M(x, 0)$ as $MN(= \delta x)$ is very small.

Let $(\bar{x}, \bar{y})$ denote the C.G. of the segment of the sphere. Then, $\bar{y} = 0$ as $X$-axis is the axis of symmetry.

Also,
$$\bar{x} = \frac{\int x\, dm}{\int dm} = \frac{\int_c^a x \rho \pi y^2 \, dx}{\int_c^a \rho \pi y^2 \, dx} = \frac{\int_c^a x y^2 \, dx}{\int_c^a y^2 \, dx} \qquad | \because \rho \text{ is uniform}$$

$$= \frac{\int_c^a x\left(a^2 - x^2\right) dx}{\int_c^a \left(a^2 - x^2\right) dx} \qquad |\because x^2 + y^2 = a^2 \qquad = \frac{\left(a^2 \dfrac{x^2}{2} - \dfrac{x^4}{4}\right)_c^a}{\left(a^2 x - \dfrac{x^3}{3}\right)_c^a}$$

$$= \frac{\left(\frac{a^4}{2}-\frac{a^4}{4}\right)-\left(\frac{a^2c^2}{2}-\frac{c^4}{4}\right)}{\left(a^3-\frac{a^3}{3}\right)-\left(a^2c-\frac{c^3}{3}\right)} = \frac{\frac{a^4}{4}+\frac{c^4}{4}-\frac{a^2c^2}{2}}{\frac{2a^3}{3}+\frac{c^3}{3}-a^2c} = \frac{\frac{1}{4}\left(a^4+c^4-2a^2c^2\right)}{\frac{1}{3}\left(2a^3+c^3-3a^2c\right)}$$

$$= \frac{3}{4}\frac{\left(a^2-c^2\right)^2}{(2a+c)\left(a^2-2ac+c^2\right)} = \frac{3\,(a-c)^2\,(a+c)^2}{4\,(2a+c)(a-c)^2} = \frac{3}{4}\frac{(a+c)^2}{2a+c}.$$

**Example 3:** Find the centre of gravity of a solid figure formed by revolving a quadrant of an ellipse about its major axis.

**Sol.**

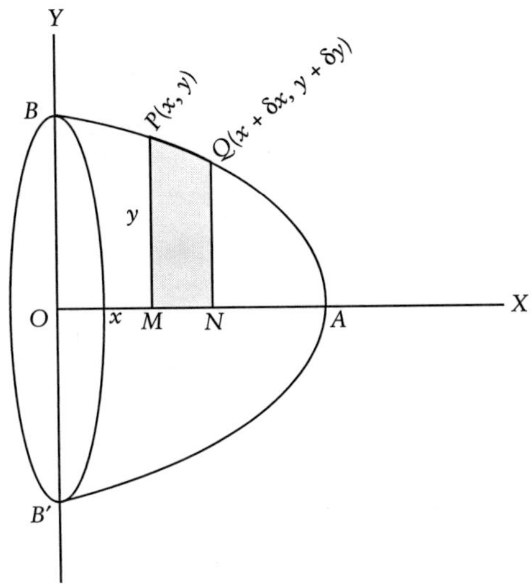


Let the equation to the ellipse be $\frac{x^2}{a^2}+\frac{y^2}{b^2}=1$ ...(1)

Let the solid be formed by revolving the quadrant $AOB$ of the ellipse (1) about the major axis $OX$.

Take two neighbouring points $P(x, y)$ and $Q(x + \delta x, y + \delta y)$ on the ellipse. From $P$ and $Q$, draw perpendiculars $PM$ and $QN$ respectively on the $X$-axis.

Volume of the elementary disc formed by revolving the elementary area $PMNQ$ about the $X$-axis.

$$= \pi\, y^2\, \delta x$$

$\therefore$ Mass of the elementary disc $\delta m$

$$= \rho\, \pi\, y^2\, \delta x$$

where $\rho$ is the density.

Also, the C.G. of this elementary disc may be taken as $M(x, 0)$ as $MN(= \delta x)$ is very small.

Let $(\bar{x}, \bar{y})$ denote the C.G. of the solid of revolution. Then, $\bar{y} = 0$ as $X$-axis is the axis of symmetry.

Also, $$\bar{x} = \frac{\int x\,dm}{\int dm} = \frac{\int_0^a x\rho\pi y^2\,dx}{\int_0^a \rho\pi y^2\,dx}$$

$$= \frac{\int_0^a x y^2\,dx}{\int_0^a y^2\,dx} \qquad \mid \because \rho \text{ is uniform}$$

$$= \frac{\int_0^a x b^2\left(1-\frac{x^2}{a^2}\right)dx}{\int_0^a b^2\left(1-\frac{x^2}{a^2}\right)dx} \qquad \mid \text{From (1)}$$

$$= \frac{\int_0^a x\left(1-\frac{x^2}{a^2}\right)dx}{\int_0^a \left(1-\frac{x^2}{a^2}\right)dx} = \frac{\left(\frac{x^2}{2}-\frac{x^4}{4a^2}\right)_0^a}{\left(x-\frac{x^3}{3a^2}\right)_0^a}$$

$$= \frac{\frac{a^2}{2}-\frac{a^2}{4}}{a-\frac{a}{3}} = \frac{a^2}{4}\cdot\frac{3}{2a} = \frac{3}{8}a$$

**Example 4:** Find the centre of gravity of the volume formed by revolving the parabola $y^2 = 4ax$, cut off by the ordinate $x = h$ about the axis of $X$.

**Sol.**

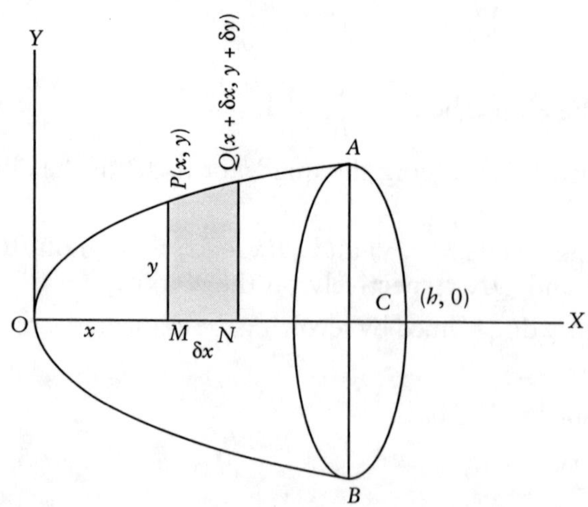


Equation of the parabola is

$$y^2 = 4ax \qquad \text{...(1)}$$

The portion $AOBCA$ of (1) is revolved about the axis of $X$, where $OC = h$.

Take two neighbouring point $P(x, y)$ and $Q(x + \delta x, y + \delta y)$ on the curve. From $P$ and $Q$, draw perpendicular $PM$ and $QN$ respectively on the $X$-axis.

Volume of the elementary disc formed by revolving the elementary area $PMNQ$ about $X$-axis $= \pi y^2 \delta x$.

$\therefore$ Mass of the elementary disc $\delta m = \rho \pi y^2 \delta x$

where $\rho$ is the density.

Also, the C.G. of the elementary disc may be taken as $M(x, 0)$ as $MN(= \delta x)$ is vary small.

Let $(\bar{x}, \bar{y})$ denote the C.G. of the solid of revolution. Then, $\bar{y} = 0$ as $X$-axis is the axis of symmetry.

Also, $$\bar{x} = \frac{\int x\,dm}{\int dm} = \frac{\int_0^h x \rho \pi y^2 dx}{\int_0^h \rho \pi y^2 dx}$$

$$= \frac{\int_0^h x y^2 dx}{\int_0^h y^2 dx} \qquad |\because \rho \text{ is uniform}$$

$$= \frac{\int_0^h x\, 4ax\, dx}{\int_0^h 4ax\, dx} \qquad |\text{From (1)}$$

$$= \frac{\int_0^h x^2\, dx}{\int_0^h x\, dx} = \frac{\left(\frac{x^3}{3}\right)_0^h}{\left(\frac{x^2}{2}\right)_0^h} = \frac{\frac{h^3}{3}}{\frac{h^2}{2}} = \frac{2h}{3}$$

Hence, the required C.G. is given by $\bar{x} = 2h/3$ and $\bar{y} = 0$.

**Example 5:** Find the centre of gravity of the solid formed by the revolution of the area bounded by the parabola $y^2 = 4ax$, the $X$-axis and the latus rectum about the latus rectum.

**Sol.**

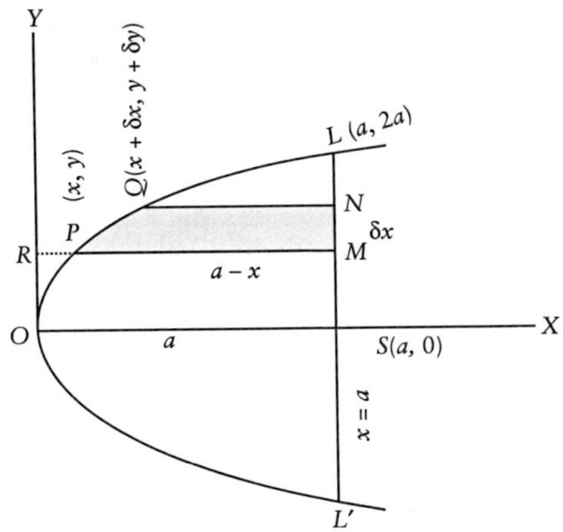

The given parabola is $y^2 = 4ax$ ...(1)

$O$ is the vertex and $LSL'$ is the latus rectum of the parabola. We have to revolve the area $LOS$ about the line $LSL'$.

Take two neighbouring points $P(x, y)$ and $Q(x + \delta x, y + \delta y)$ on the parabola. From $P$ and $Q$, draw perpendiculars $PM$ and $QN$ respectively on the line $LSL'$. Also, draw $PR \perp OY$. Then,

$$PR = x \qquad PM = RM - PR = OS - PR = a - x$$

We have to find the C.G. of the solid generated by the revolution of the area $LPOSL$ about the latus rectum.

Take $PMNQ$ as the elementary area. Its length is $(a - x)$ and width is $\delta y$. When the elementary strip $PMNQ$ revolves round $LSL'$, a disc is formed whose thickness is $\delta y$ and area of circular base is $\pi(a - x)^2$.

$\therefore$ Volume of the elementary disc $= \pi(a - x)^2\, \delta y$

$\therefore$ Mass of the elementary disc $\delta m$ $= \rho\pi(a - x)^2\, \delta y$

Also, the C.G. of this elementary disc may be taken as $M(a, y)$ as $MN(= \delta y)$ is very small. Let $(\bar{x}, \bar{y})$ denote the C.G. of the solid of revolution. Then, $\bar{x} = a$ as $x = a$ is the axis of symmetry.

Also,
$$\bar{y} = \frac{\int y\,dm}{\int dm} = \frac{\int_0^{2a} y\rho\pi(a-x)^2 dy}{\int_0^{2a} \rho\pi(a-x)^2 dy}$$

$$= \frac{\int_0^{2a} y(a-x)^2 dy}{\int_0^{2a} (a-x)^2 dy} \qquad \Big| \because \rho \text{ is uniform}$$

$$= \frac{\int_0^{2a} y\left(a - \frac{y^2}{4a}\right)^2 dy}{\int_0^{2a} \left(a - \frac{y^2}{4a}\right)^2 dy} \quad \Big|\text{From (1)} \quad = \frac{\int_0^{2a} y(4a^4 - y^2)^2\, dy}{\int_0^{2a} (4a^2 - y^2)^2\, dy}$$

$$= \frac{\int_0^{2a} y\left(16a^4 + y^4 - 8a^2y^2\right)dy}{\int_0^{2a} \left(16a^4 + y^4 - 8a^2y^2\right)dy} = \frac{\int_0^{2a} \left(16a^4 y + y^5 - 8a^2y^3\right)dy}{\int_0^{2a} \left(16a^4 + y^4 - 8a^2y^2\right)dy}$$

$$= \frac{\left(8a^4y^2 + \frac{y^6}{6} - 2a^2y^4\right)_0^{2a}}{\left(16a^4y + \frac{y^5}{5} - \frac{8a^2y^3}{3}\right)_0^{2a}} = \frac{32a^6 + \frac{32}{3}a^6 - 32a^6}{32a^5 + \frac{32a^5}{5} - \frac{64a^5}{3}}$$

$$= \frac{\frac{32}{3}a^6}{32a^5\left(1 + \frac{1}{5} - \frac{2}{3}\right)} = \frac{a}{3 \cdot \frac{8}{15}} = \frac{5}{8}a$$

**Example 6:** Find the centre of gravity of a solid right circular cone.

**Sol.** We know that the right circular cone is generated by revolving the right angled triangle *OAB* about *OA*. Let *O* be the origin and *OA* the *X*-axis. If $\angle BOA = \alpha$, then the equation of *OB* is $y = x \tan \alpha$. ...(1)

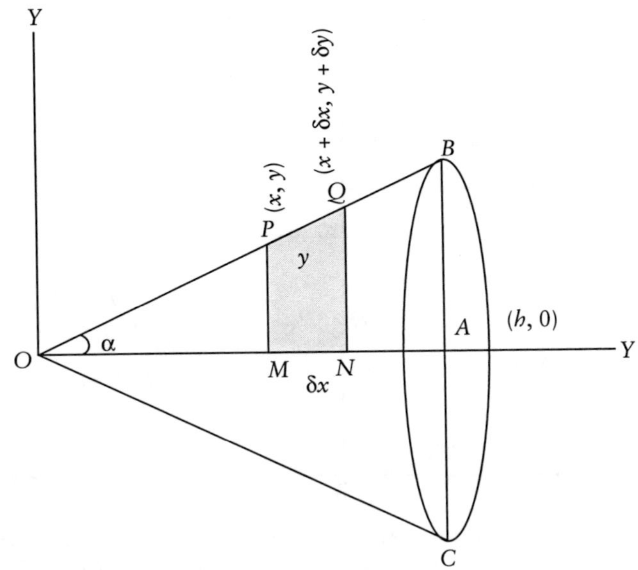


Take two neighbouring points $P(x, y)$ and $Q(x + \delta x, y + \delta y)$ on the line *OB*. From *P* and *Q*, draw perpendiculars *PM* and *QN* respectively on the *X*-axis. Then, mass $\delta m$ of the elementary disc generated by the revolution of the elementary area *PMNQ* about the *X*-axis $= \rho\, \pi\, y^2 \delta x$, where $\rho$ is the mass per unit volume.

Let $OA = h$ be the height of the cone.

The C.G. of this disc may be taken as the point $M(x, 0)$ as $MN(= \delta x)$ is very small.

Let $(\bar{x}, \bar{y})$ be the coordinates of the C.G. of the right circular cone. Then, $\bar{y} = 0$ as C.G. lies on the *X*-axis which is the axis of symmetry.

Also, $$\bar{x} = \frac{\int x\, dm}{\int dm} = \frac{\int_0^h x \rho \pi y^2\, dx}{\int_0^h \rho \pi y^2\, dx} = \frac{\int_0^h x y^2\, dx}{\int_0^h y^2\, dx} \qquad | \because \rho \text{ is uniform}$$

$$= \frac{\int_0^h x x^2 \tan^2 \alpha\, dx}{\int_0^h x^2 \tan^2 \alpha\, dx} \qquad | \text{ From (1)}$$

$$= \frac{\int_0^h x^3 dx}{\int_0^h x^2\, dx} = \frac{\left(\dfrac{x^4}{4}\right)_0^h}{\left(\dfrac{x^3}{3}\right)_0^h} = \frac{\dfrac{h^4}{4}}{\dfrac{h^3}{3}} = \frac{3}{4}h.$$

Hence, the C.G. of a solid right circular cone of height $h$ lies on its axis at a distance 3/4 $h$ from the vertex.

**Example 7:** Find the C.G of the volume formed by the revolution of the cycloid $x = a(\theta + \sin\theta)$, $y = a(1 - \cos\theta)$ about the axis of Y.

**Sol.**

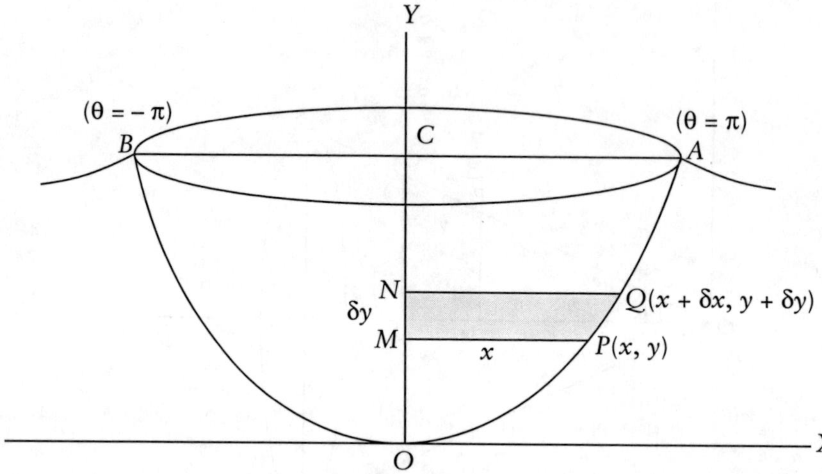


The required solid is formed by the revolution of the area $OACO$ about the $Y$-axis. Take two neighbouring points $P(x, y)$ and $Q(x + \delta x, y + \delta y)$ on the arc $OA$ of the cycloid. From $P$ and $Q$, draw perpendiculars $PM$ and $QN$ respectively on the $Y$-axis. Take $PMNQ$ as the elementary strip whose length is $x$ and breadth is $\delta y$.

When this elementary strip revolves about the axis of $Y$, a disc of small thickness $\delta y$ and circular base of area $\pi x^2$ is formed. The volume of this elementary disc is $\pi x^2 \delta y$. It $\rho$ is the mass per unit volume, then the mass $\delta m$ of this elementary disc is $\rho \pi x^2 \delta y$. C.G. of this disc may be taken as the point $M(0, y)$, since $\delta y$ is very small.

The perametric equations of the cycloid are

$$x = a(\theta + \sin\theta) \quad ...(1)$$

$$y = a(1 - \cos\theta) \quad ...(2)$$

Let $(\bar{x}, \bar{y})$ be the required C.G. Then, $\bar{x} = 0$ | By Symmetry

as C.G. lies on the $Y$-axis which is the axis of symmetry.

Also, $$\bar{y} = \frac{\int y\,dm}{\int dm} = \frac{\int_{\theta=0}^{\pi} y\rho\pi x^2\,dy}{\int_{\theta=0}^{\pi} \rho\pi x^2\,dy} = \frac{\int_{\theta=0}^{\pi} yx^2 dy}{\int_{\theta=0}^{\pi} x^2 dy}$$ | $\because \rho$ is uniform

Numerator of $\bar{y} = \int_{\theta=0}^{\pi} yx^2 dy = \int_{\theta=0}^{\pi} yx^2 \frac{dy}{d\theta} d\theta$

$$= \int_0^{\pi} a(1-\cos\theta)a^2(\theta+\sin\theta)^2 \cdot a\sin\theta\, d\theta$$

$$= a^4 \int_0^{\pi} (\sin\theta - \sin\theta\cos\theta)\left(\theta^2 + \sin^2\theta + 2\theta\,\sin\theta\right) d\theta$$

$$= a^4\int_0^{\pi}\left(\theta^2\sin\theta+\sin^3\theta+2\theta\sin^2\theta-\theta^2\sin\theta\cos\theta-\sin^3\theta\cos\theta-2\theta\sin^2\theta\cos\theta\right)d\theta$$

$$= a^4\int_0^{\pi}\left(\theta^2\sin\theta+\sin^3\theta+\theta(1-\cos2\theta)-\frac{\theta^2}{2}\sin2\theta-\sin^3\theta-2\theta\sin^2\theta\cos\theta\right)d\theta$$

$$= a^4\Bigg[\left\{\theta^2(-\cos\theta)\right\}_0^{\pi}-\int_0^{\pi}2\theta(-\cos\theta)d\theta+2\int_0^{\pi/2}\sin^3\theta\,d\theta$$

$$+\left(\frac{\theta^2}{2}\right)_0^{\pi}-\left(\theta\frac{\sin2\theta}{2}\right)_0^{\pi}+\int_0^{\pi}\frac{\sin2\theta}{2}d\theta$$

$$-\left[\frac{1}{2}\theta^2\left(\frac{-\cos2\theta}{2}\right)\right]_0^{\pi}+\frac{1}{2}\int_0^{\pi}2\theta\left(-\frac{\cos2\theta}{2}\right)d\theta-\left(\frac{\sin^4\theta}{4}\right)_0^{\pi}-2\left(\theta\frac{\sin^3\theta}{3}\right)_0^{\pi}$$

$$+2\int_0^{\pi}\frac{\sin^3\theta}{3}d\theta\Bigg]$$

$$= a^4\left[\pi^2+2\int_0^{\pi}\theta\cos\theta\,d\theta+2\cdot\frac{2}{3}+\frac{\pi^2}{2}-\left(\frac{\cos2\theta}{4}\right)_0^{\pi}+\frac{\pi^2}{4}-\frac{1}{2}\int_0^{\pi}\theta\cos2\theta\,d\theta+\frac{4}{3}\int_0^{\pi/2}\sin^3\theta\,d\theta\right]$$

$$= a^4\Bigg[\pi^2+2(\theta\sin\theta)_0^{\pi}-2\int_0^{\pi}\sin\theta\,d\theta+\frac{4}{3}+\frac{\pi^2}{2}+\frac{\pi^2}{4}-\frac{1}{2}$$

$$\left(\theta\frac{\sin2\theta}{2}\right)_0^{\pi}+\frac{1}{2}\int_0^{\pi}\frac{\sin2\theta}{2}d\theta+\frac{4}{3}\cdot\frac{2}{3}\Bigg]$$ | By Walli's Formula

$$= a^4\left[\pi^2+2(\cos\theta)_0^{\pi}+\frac{4}{3}+\frac{\pi^2}{2}+\frac{\pi^2}{4}-\left(\frac{\cos2\theta}{8}\right)_0^{\pi}+\frac{8}{9}\right]$$

$$= a^4\left[\pi^2-4+\frac{4}{3}+\frac{\pi^2}{2}+\frac{\pi^2}{4}+\frac{8}{9}\right] = a^4\left[\frac{7\pi^2}{4}-\frac{16}{9}\right] = \frac{a^4}{36}\left[63\pi^2-64\right] \quad ...(4)$$

Denominator of $\bar{y} = \int_0^{\pi}x^2dy = \int_0^{\pi}x^2\frac{dy}{d\theta}d\theta = \int_0^{\pi}a^2(\theta+\sin\theta)^2\,a\sin\theta\,d\theta$

$$= a^3\int_0^{\pi}\left(\theta^2+\sin^2\theta+2\theta\sin\theta\right)\sin\theta\,d\theta = a^3\int_0^{\pi}\left(\theta^2\sin\theta+\sin^3\theta+2\theta\sin^2\theta\right)d\theta$$

$$= a^3\int_0^{\pi}\left\{\theta^2\sin\theta+\sin^3\theta+\theta(1-\cos2\theta)\right\}d\theta$$

$$= a^3\int_0^{\pi}\left(\theta^2\sin\theta+\sin^3\theta+\theta+\theta-\theta\cos2\theta\right)d\theta$$

$$= a^3\Bigg[\left\{\theta^2(-\cos\theta)\right\}_0^{\pi}-\int_0^{\pi}2\theta(-\cos\theta)d\theta+2\int_0^{\pi/2}\sin^3\theta\,d\theta+\left(\frac{\theta^2}{2}\right)_0^{\pi}$$

$$-\left(\theta\frac{\sin2\theta}{2}\right)_0^{\pi}+\int_0^{\pi}\frac{\sin2\theta}{2}d\theta\Bigg]$$

$$= a^3\left[\pi^2 + 2\int_0^\pi \theta\cos\theta\, d\theta + 2\cdot\frac{2}{3} + \frac{\pi^2}{2} - \left(\frac{\cos 2\theta}{4}\right)_0^\pi\right]$$

$$= a^3\left[\pi^2 + 2(\theta\ \sin\theta)_0^\pi - 2\int_0^\pi \sin\theta\ d\theta + \frac{4}{3} + \frac{\pi^2}{2}\right]$$

$$= a^3\left[\pi^2 + 2(\cos\theta)_0^\pi + \frac{4}{3} + \frac{\pi^2}{2}\right] = a^3\left[\pi^2 - 4 + \frac{4}{3} + \frac{\pi^2}{2}\right] = a^3\left[\frac{3\pi^2}{2} - \frac{8}{3}\right]$$

$$= a^3\left[\frac{9\pi^2 - 16}{6}\right] \qquad ...(5)$$

From (3), (4) and (5), we get

$$\bar{y} = \frac{\frac{a^4}{36}\left(63\pi^2 - 64\right)}{\frac{a^4}{6}\left(9\pi^2 - 16\right)} = \frac{a}{6}\left(\frac{63\pi^2 - 64}{9\pi^2 - 16}\right)$$

**Example 8:** Find the centroid of the volume formed by the revolution of the cardioid $r = a(1 + \cos\theta)$ about the initial line.

**Sol.**

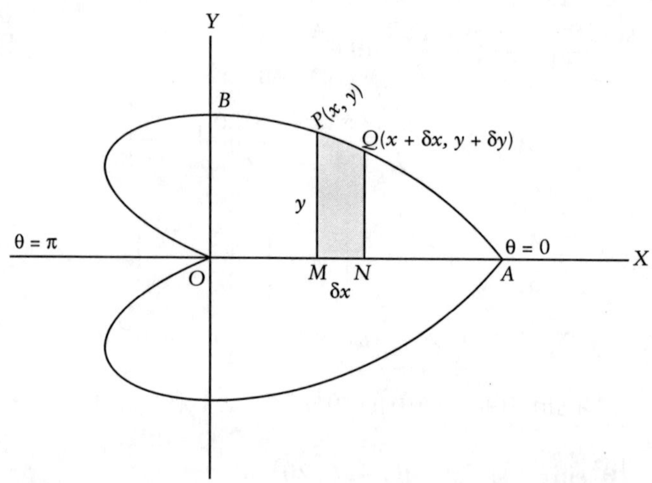


The equation of the cardioid

$$r = a(1 + \cos\theta) \qquad ...(1)$$

It has been traced and shown in the figure. Take the initial line $OA$ as the $X$-axis and a line through O at right angles to $OA$ as $Y$-axis. The required solid is formed by the revolution of the area $OABO$ about the $X$-axis.

Take two neighbouring points $P(x, y)$ and $Q(x + \delta x, y + \delta y)$ on the curve. Let the polar coordinates of $P$ be $(r, \theta)$. Then,

$x = r \cos \theta$ ...(2)

$y = r \sin \theta$ ...(3)

Draw perpendiculars *PM* and *QN* respectively from *P* and *Q* on *X*-axis.

Take an elementary strip *PQNM* of height *y* and width $\delta x$. When this strip is revolved about the initial line, then an elementary disc in generated whose thickness is $\delta x$ and area of circular base is $\pi y^2$.

$\therefore$ Volume of this elementary disc $= \pi y^2 \, \delta x$

Let $\rho$ the mass per unit volume. Then, mass of the elementary disc $\delta m$

$= \rho \, \pi \, y^2 \, \delta x$

Also, the C.G. of this disc may be taken as the point $M(x, 0)$ because $MN(= \delta x)$ is very small. Let $(\bar{x}, \bar{y})$ be the required C.G. Then,

$\bar{y} = 0$ | By Symmetry ...(4)

as C.G. lies on the *X*-axis which is the axis of symmetry.

Also, $$\bar{x} = \frac{\int x\, dm}{\int dm} = \frac{\int x \rho \pi y^2 dx}{\int \rho \pi y^2 dx}$$

$$= \frac{\int x y^2 dx}{\int y^2 dx}$$ | $\because \rho$ is uniform ...(5)

Now, $x = r \cos\theta$ | From (2)

$= a(1 + \cos\theta) \cos\theta$ | From (1) ...(6)

$y = r \sin\theta$ | From (3)

$= a(1 + \cos\theta) \sin\theta$ | From (1) ...(7)

From (5), (6) and (7), we get

$$\bar{x} = \frac{\int_0^{\pi} a(1+\cos\theta)\cos\theta \; a^2(1+\cos\theta)^2 \sin^2\theta \; a(-\sin\theta - 2\sin\theta\cos\theta)d\theta}{\int_0^{\pi} a^2(1+\cos\theta)^2 \sin^2\theta \; a(-\sin\theta - 2\sin\theta\cos\theta)d\theta} \quad \text{...(8)}$$

Numerator of $\bar{x} = -a^4 \int_0^{\pi} (1+\cos\theta)^3 \sin^3\theta(1+2\cos\theta)\cos\theta \, d\theta$

$$= -a^4 \int_0^{\pi} 8\cos^6\frac{\theta}{2} \, 8\sin^3\frac{\theta}{2}\cos^3\frac{\theta}{2}\left(1+4\cos^2\frac{\theta}{2}-2\right)\left(2\cos^2\frac{\theta}{2}-1\right)d\theta$$

$$= -64a^4 \int_0^{\pi} \sin^3\frac{\theta}{2}\cos^9\frac{\theta}{2}\left(4\cos^2\frac{\theta}{2}-1\right)\left(2\cos^2\frac{\theta}{2}-1\right)d\theta$$

Put $\theta/2 = \phi$

$\therefore d\theta = 2d\phi$

$$= -128a^4 \int_0^{\pi} \sin^3\phi\cos^9\phi\left(4\cos^2\phi-1\right)\left(2\cos^2\phi-1\right)d\phi$$

$$= -128a^4 \int_0^{\pi 2} \sin^3\phi\cos^9\phi\left(8\cos^4\phi-6\cos^2\phi+1\right)d\phi$$

$$= -128a^4\left[8\int_0^{\pi/2}\sin^3\phi\cos^{13}\phi\,d\phi - 6\int_0^{\pi/2}\sin^3\phi\cos^{11}\phi\,d\phi + \int_0^{\pi/2}\sin^3\phi\cos^9\phi\,d\phi\right]$$

$$= -128a^4\left[\frac{8\Gamma2\,\Gamma7}{2\Gamma9} - 6\frac{\Gamma2\,\Gamma6}{2\Gamma8} + \frac{\Gamma2\,\Gamma5}{2\Gamma7}\right] = -128a^4\left[\frac{8}{2\times8\times7} - \frac{6}{2\times7\times6} + \frac{1}{2\times6\times5}\right]$$

$$= -128a^4\left[\frac{1}{14} - \frac{1}{14} + \frac{1}{60}\right] = -\frac{32}{15}a^4 \qquad \ldots(9)$$

Denominator of $\bar{x}$ $= -a^3\int_0^{\pi}(1+\cos\theta)^2\sin^3\theta(1+2\cos\theta)\,d\theta$

$$= -a^3\int_0^{\pi} 4\cos^4\frac{\theta}{2}\,8\sin^3\frac{\theta}{2}\cos^3\frac{\theta}{2}\left\{1+2\left(2\cos^2\frac{\theta}{2}-1\right)\right\}d\theta$$

$$= -a^3\int_0^{\pi} 32\sin^3\frac{\theta}{2}\cos^7\frac{\theta}{2}\left(4\cos^2\frac{\theta}{2}-1\right)d\theta \qquad \text{Put } \theta/2 = \phi \quad \therefore\ d\theta = 2d\phi$$

$$= -64a^3\int_0^{\pi/2}\sin^3\phi\cos^7\phi\left(4\cos^2\phi - 1\right)d\phi$$

$$= -64a^3\left[4\int_0^{\pi/2}\sin^3\phi\cos^9\phi\,d\phi - \int_0^{\pi/2}\sin^3\phi\cos^7\phi\,d\phi\right] = -64a^3\left[4\frac{\Gamma2\,\Gamma5}{2\Gamma7} - \frac{\Gamma2\,\Gamma4}{2\Gamma6}\right]$$

$$= -64a^3\left[\frac{4}{2\cdot6\cdot5} - \frac{1}{2\cdot5\cdot4}\right] = -64a^3\left[\frac{1}{15} - \frac{1}{40}\right] = -64a^3\,\frac{8-3}{120} = \frac{-8}{3}a^3$$

From (8), (9) and (10), we get $\bar{x} = -\frac{32}{15}a^4 \Big/ -\frac{8}{3}a^3 = \frac{4a}{3}$

Hence, the required C.G. is given by $\bar{x} = 4a/3$, $\bar{y} = 0$.

## EXERCISE 2(C)

1. Find the centre of gravity of a segment of height $h$ of a sphere of radius $a$.
   [**Ans.** $\bar{x} = 3/4\ (2a - h)^2/3a - h$, $\bar{y} = 0$]
2. Show that the C.G. of the solid formed by revolving the quadrant of a circle of radius $a$ about the $X$-axis is given by
   $\bar{x} = 3a/8$, $\bar{y} = 0$.
3. Show that the C.G. of the solid formed by revolving the quadrant of a circle of radius $a$ about the $Y$-axis is given by
   $\bar{x} = 0$, $\bar{y} = 3a/8$.
4. Find the C.G. of the volume of the part of sphere of radius a included between two parallel planes which are at distances $b$ and $c$ ($b < c$) from the centre.
   $\bar{x} = 0$, $\bar{y} = 3a/8$.
   [**Ans.** $\bar{x} = 3/4\ (a^2 - b^2)^2 - (a^2 - c^2)^2/3a^2\ (c - b) - (c^3 - b^3)$, $\bar{y} = 0$]

   or

$$\left[\bar{x} = \frac{3}{4}\frac{(c+b)(2a^2 - b^2 - c^2)}{3a^2 - (c^2 + cb + b^2)},\ \bar{y} = 0\right]$$

5. Find the centre of gravity of a solid figure formed by revolving a quadrant of an ellipse about its minor axis.

   [**Ans.** $\bar{x} = 0, \bar{y} = 3b/8$]

6. Find the C.G. of the solid formed by the revolution of the portion of the parabola $y^2 = 4ax$ bounded by its latus rectum about the X-axis.

   [**Ans.** $\bar{x} = 2/3\ a, \bar{y} = 0$]

7. Prove that the centroid of the volume formed by the revolution of the curve $r = a(1 - \cos\theta)$ about the initial line is $(-4a/5, 0)$.

8. Find the distance of C.G. of solid semi-circular cone from its axis.

   [**Ans.** At a distance $r/\pi$ from the axis, $r$ being the radius of the base].

## 8. Centre the Gravity of a Sphere of Revolution

Let the surface be generated by the revolution of the arc of the curve $y = f(x)$ lying between the ordinates

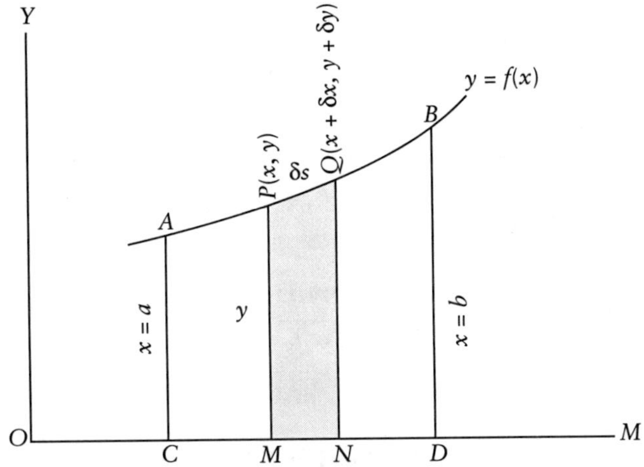


$x = a$ and $x = b$ about the axis of X as the axis of revolution. Take two neighbouring points $P(x, y)$ and $Q(x + \delta x, y + \delta y)$ on the arc $AB$ of the curve. From $P$ and $Q$, draw perpendiculars $PM$ and $QN$ respectively to the X-axis. Let arc $PQ = \delta s$.

If the arc $PQ$ is revolved about the X-axis, is would generated the curved surface of an elementary disc whose radius is $PM(= y)$ and thickness is $PQ(= \delta s)$.

$\therefore$ Area of the curved surface of this elementary disc $= 2\pi y\ \delta s$

$\therefore$ Its mass $\delta m = \rho\ 2\ \pi y\ \delta s$ where $\rho$ is mass per unit area of the curved space.

Let $(\bar{x}, \bar{y})$ be the required C.G. Then,

$$\bar{y} = 0 \quad | \text{ By symmetry about the axis of revolution, i.e., X-axis.}$$

Also,
$$\bar{x} = \frac{\int x\,dm}{\int dm} = \frac{\int x\rho 2\pi y\,ds}{\int \rho 2\pi y\,ds} = \frac{\int xy\,ds}{\int y\,ds} \quad | \because \rho \text{ is uniform}$$

where $ds$ can be expressed in terms of $dx$, $dy$, $dr$, $d\theta$ or $dt$ as is required in the problem under consideration.

If the surface is generated by the revolution of the arc of the curve $x = f(y)$ lying between the abscissae $y = c$ and $y = d$ about the axis of $Y$ as the axis of revolution, then as above mass of the elementary disc $= \rho \pi x^2 \delta y$ where $\rho$ is the mass per unit area of the curved surface.

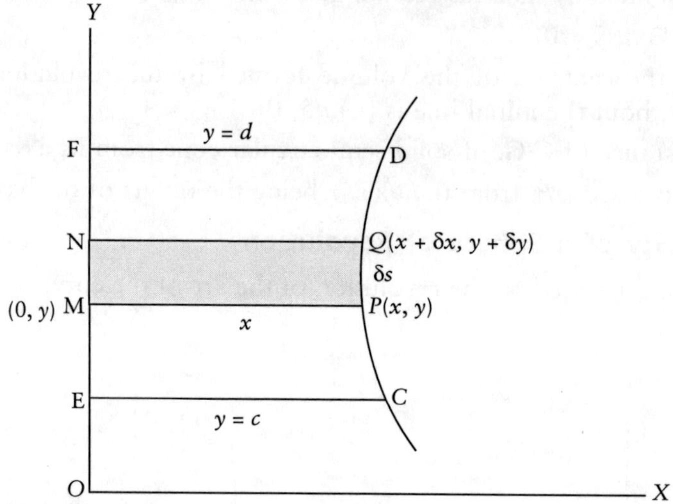


Here, the axis of symmetry is $Y$-axis. Therefore, if $(x, y)$ are the coordinates of the required C.G., Then in this case $\bar{x} = 0$

and $$\bar{y} = \frac{\int y\,dm}{\int dm} = \frac{\int y\rho 2\pi x\,ds}{\int \rho 2\pi x\,ds} = \frac{\int xy\,ds}{\int x\,ds} \qquad |\because \rho \text{ is uniform}$$

where $x = f(y)$.

## ILLUSTRATIVE EXAMPLES

**Example 1:** Find the C.G. of a zone of a sphere.

**Sol.**

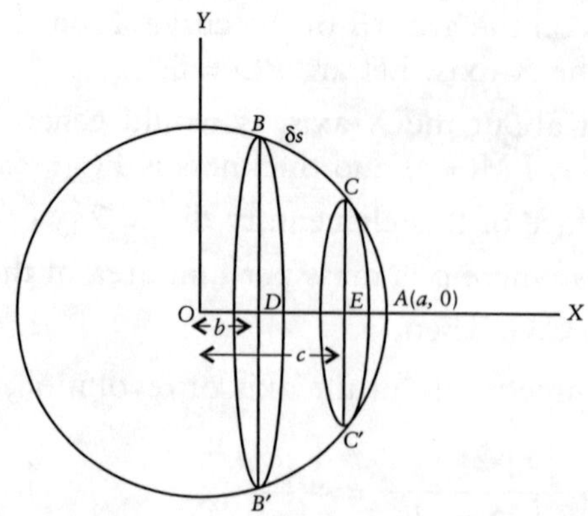

Let the spherical zone $BCC'B'$ be formed by the revolution of the arc $BC$ of the generating circle whose radius is $a$ (say).

Reformed to the axes of coordinates as shown in the figure, the equation of the generating circle is

$$x^2 + y^2 = a^2 \qquad ...(1)$$

Differentiating (1) with repeat to $x$, we set $2x + 2y\, dy/dx = 0$

$$\Rightarrow \qquad dy/dx = -\, x/y \qquad ...(2)$$

$$\therefore \qquad ds/dx = \sqrt{1+\left(\frac{dy}{dx}\right)^2} = \sqrt{1+\left(\frac{-x}{y}\right)^2} \qquad \text{| From (2)}$$

$$= \sqrt{\frac{x^2+y^2}{y^2}} = a/y \qquad \text{| From (1)} \qquad ...(3)$$

Mass of the elementary zone $\delta m = \rho \cdot 2\pi y\, \delta s$

where $\rho$ is the mass per unit surface area. Its C.G. is at the point $(x, 0)$ as $\delta s$ is very small.

Let $D$ and $E$ be the centres of the plane ends of the zone such that $OD = b$ and $OE = c$. Let the required C.G. be $(\overline{x}, \overline{y})$.

Then, $\overline{y} = 0$ | By symmetry about $OX$, the axis of revolution

$$\text{Also,} \qquad \overline{x} = \frac{\int x\, dm}{\int dm} = \frac{\int x \rho 2\pi y\, ds}{\int \rho 2\pi y\, ds} = \frac{\int x y\, ds}{\int y\, ds} \qquad \text{| } \because \rho \text{ is uniform}$$

$$= \frac{\int_b^c xy \frac{ds}{dx} dx}{\int_b^c y \frac{ds}{dx} dx} = \frac{\int_b^c xy \frac{a}{y} dx}{\int_b^c y \frac{a}{y} dx} \qquad \text{| From (3)}$$

$$= \frac{\int_b^c x\, dx}{\int_b^c dx} = \frac{\left(\frac{x^2}{2}\right)_b^c}{(x)_b^c} = \frac{\frac{c^2-b^2}{2}}{c-b} = \frac{b+c}{2}$$

Hence, the C.G. bisects the height of the zone of the sphere.

**Example 2:** Show that the centre of gravity of a lune of a sphere of angle $2\alpha$ is at a distance $\pi/4\ a \sin \alpha/\alpha$ from its axis.

**Sol.** We know that the lune of angle $2\alpha$ is the surface area generated by the revolution of the semi-circular arc $ACB$ about the diameter $AB$ through an angle $2\alpha$. The diameter $AB$ is the axis of this lune.

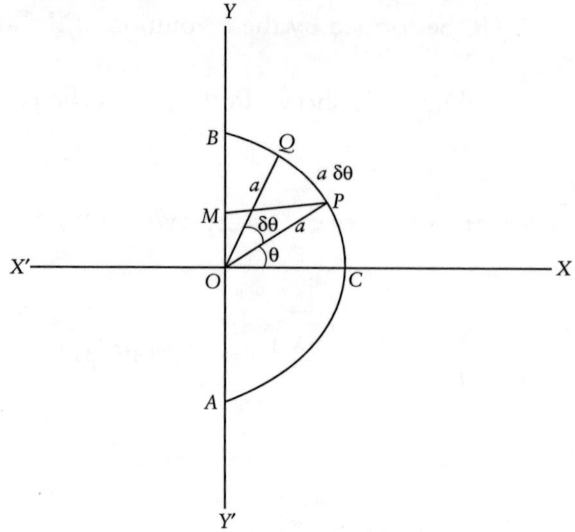


Let the radius of the circle be $a$. Let us consider an elementary arc $PQ = a\,\delta\theta$. As the semi-circular arc $ACB$ revolves about the diameter $AB$ though an angle $2\alpha$, point $P$ will generate an arc of radius $PM = a\cos\theta$. Arc $PQ$ will generate a ring of radius $a\cos\theta$ and small thickness $\delta s (= a\delta\theta)$. Elementary surface area $= 2\,\pi\,a\cos\theta\,a\,\delta\theta$. Elementary mass $\delta m = \rho\,2\,\pi\,a\cos\theta\,a\,\delta\theta = 2\pi\,\rho\,a^2\cos\theta\,\delta\theta$, where $\rho$ is the mass per unit surface area.

The distance of C.G. of the arc so formed from $AB$ is

$$= (\text{Radius of the arc})\,\frac{\sin\alpha}{\alpha} = (a\cos\theta)\,\frac{\sin\alpha}{\alpha}$$

Hence, the distance of C.G. $(\bar{x}, \bar{y})$ of the lune from $AB$ is given by

$$\bar{x} = \frac{\int_{-\frac{\pi}{2}}^{\frac{\pi}{2}} (a\cos\theta)\frac{\sin\alpha}{\alpha}\,2\pi\rho\,a^2\cos\theta\,d\theta}{\int_{-\frac{\pi}{2}}^{\frac{\pi}{2}} 2\pi\rho\,a^2\cos\theta\,d\theta} = \frac{\frac{a\sin\alpha}{\alpha}\,2\int_0^{\frac{\pi}{2}}\cos^2\theta\,d\theta}{2\int_0^{\frac{\pi}{2}}\cos\theta\,d\theta} \qquad |\because \rho \text{ is uniform}$$

$$= \frac{\frac{a\sin\alpha}{\alpha}\cdot\frac{1}{2}\cdot\frac{\pi}{2}}{(\sin\theta)_0^{\frac{\pi}{2}}} \qquad |\text{By Walli's Formula}$$

$$= \frac{\pi}{4}\left(\frac{a\sin\alpha}{\alpha}\right)$$

Also, $\bar{y} = 0$ |By symmetry

**Note:** Lune is defined as the part of the surface of a sphere bounded by any two diametrical planes. The angle between these planes is called the angle of the lune. The diameter in which the two diametrical planes intersect is called the axis of the lune.

**Example 3:** Find the centre of gravity of a thin right conical shell of uniform density.

**Sol.**

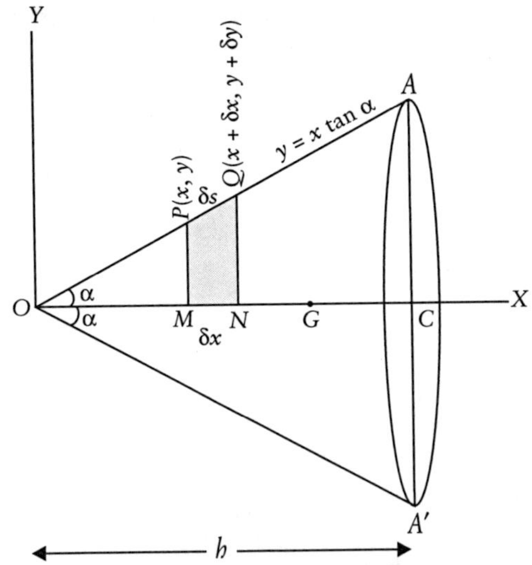


The conical shell $OAA'$ is generated by the revolution of the line $OA$ about $OX$ through four right angles. Let $OA$ make an angle $\alpha$ with $OX$. Then, referred to $O$ as origin and the coordinate axes as shown in the figure, the equation of line $OA$ is $y = x \tan \alpha$ ...(1)

Take two neighbouring points $P(x, y)$ and $Q(x + \delta x, y + \delta y)$ on line $OA$ such that arc length $PQ = \delta s$. When elementary arc $PQ$ revolves about $OX$, it generates a ring of radius $y$ and small thickness $\delta s$.

∴ Surface area of the elementary ring $= 2\pi y \, \delta s$

Let $\rho$ be the surface density. Then, elementary mass $\delta m = \rho \, 2 \, \pi \, y \, \delta s$.

Also, the C.G. of this elementary ring is at $M\ (x, 0)$ as $\delta s$ is very small.

Let $h$ be the height of the conical shell and $(\bar{x}, \bar{y})$ be the coordinates of its C.G. Then,

$$\bar{y} = 0 \qquad \text{| By symmetry}$$

and
$$\bar{x} = \frac{\int x \, dm}{\int dm} = \frac{\int_{x=0}^{h} x \rho 2\pi y \, ds}{\int_{x=0}^{h} \rho 2\pi y \, ds} = \frac{\int_0^h x y \frac{ds}{dx} dx}{\int_0^h y \frac{ds}{dx} dx} \qquad \text{| } \because \rho \text{ is uniform}$$

$$= \frac{\int_0^h x y \sqrt{1 + \left(\frac{dy}{dx}\right)^2} \, dx}{\int_0^h y \sqrt{1 + \left(\frac{dy}{dx}\right)^2} \, dx} = \frac{\int_0^h x \cdot x \tan \alpha \sqrt{1 + \tan^2 \alpha} \, dx}{\int_0^h x \tan \alpha \sqrt{1 + \tan^2 \alpha} \, dx}$$

$$= \frac{\int_0^h x^2 \, dx}{\int_0^h x \, dx} = \frac{\left(\frac{x^3}{3}\right)_0^h}{\left(\frac{x^2}{2}\right)_0^h} = \frac{\frac{x^3}{3}}{\frac{h^2}{2}} = \frac{2}{3} h$$

Hence the required C.G. is given by $\overline{x} = 2h/3$ and $y = 0$.

**Example 4:** If $A$ and $B$ be the centres and $r_1$ and $r_2$ the radii of the plane ends of the frustum of a hollow right circular cone of uniform density, show that its centre of gravity divides the axis AB in the ratio $(r_1 + 2r_2) : (r_2 + 2r_1)$.

**Sol.**

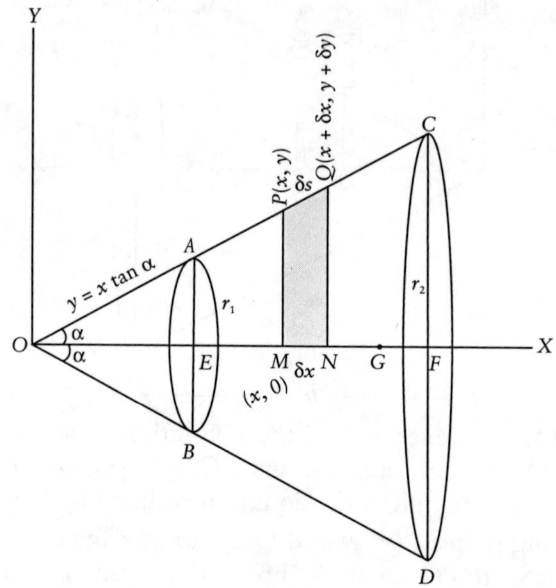


Let $ACDB$ be the frustum of a hollow right circular cone of semi-vertical angle $\alpha$ with $E$ and $F$ as the centres of plane ends.

Let $AE = r_1$ and $CF = r_2$ be the radii of plane ends. Then, referred to $O$ as origin and the coordinate axes as shown in the figure, the equation of line $OAC$ is

$$y = x \tan \alpha \quad \text{...(1)}$$

From figure,

$$OE = r_1 \cot \alpha \quad \text{...(2)}$$

$$OF = r_2 \cot \alpha \quad \text{...(3)}$$

Take two neighbouring points $P(x, y)$ and $Q(x + \delta x, y + \delta y)$ on line $AC$ such that when arc length $PQ = \delta s$ revolves about $OX$, it generates a ring of radius $y$ and small thickness $\delta s$.

$\therefore$ Surface area of the elementary ring $= 2\pi y \, \delta s$

Let $\rho$ be the surface density. Then, elementary mass $\delta m = \rho 2 \, \pi y \, \delta s$

Also, the C.G. of this elementary ring is at $M(x, 0)$ as $\delta s$ is very small.

Let $(\overline{x}, \overline{y})$ be the required C.G. Then, $\overline{y} = 0$ | By symmetry ...(4)

and $$\overline{x} = \frac{\int x \, dm}{\int dm} = \frac{\int_{x=r_1 \cot\alpha}^{r_2 \cot\alpha} x \rho 2\pi y \, ds}{\int_{x=r_1 \cot\alpha}^{r_2 \cot\alpha} \rho 2\pi y \, ds}$$

$$= \frac{\int_{r_1 \cot\alpha}^{r_2 \cot\alpha} x\, y \frac{ds}{dx} dx}{\int_{r_2 \cot\alpha}^{r_2 \cot\alpha} y \frac{ds}{dx} dx} \qquad \Big|\ \because \rho \text{ is uniform}$$

$$= \frac{\int_{r_1 \cot\alpha}^{r_2 \cot\alpha} x \cdot y \sqrt{1+\left(\frac{dy}{dx}\right)^2}\, dx}{\int_{r_1 \cot\alpha}^{r_2 \cot\alpha} y \sqrt{1+\left(\frac{dy}{dx}\right)^2}\, dx} = \frac{\int_{r_1 \cot\alpha}^{r_2 \cot\alpha} x \cdot x \tan\alpha \sqrt{1+\tan^2\alpha}\, dx}{\int_{r_1 \cot\alpha}^{r_2 \cot\alpha} x \tan\alpha \sqrt{1+\tan^2\alpha}\, dx} \qquad \Big|\ \text{From (1)}$$

$$= \frac{\int_{r_1 \cot\alpha}^{r_2 \cot\alpha} x^2 dx}{\int_{r_1 \cot\alpha}^{r_2 \cot\alpha} x\, dx} = \frac{\left(\frac{x^3}{3}\right)_{r_1 \cot\alpha}^{r_2 \cot\alpha}}{\left(\frac{x^2}{2}\right)_{r_1 \cot\alpha}^{r_2 \cot\alpha}} = \frac{2}{3}\frac{\left(r_2^2 - r_1^3\right)\cot^3\alpha}{\left(r_2^2 - r_1^2\right)\cot^2\alpha}$$

$$= \frac{2}{3}\frac{\left(r_2^2 + r_2 r_1 + r_1^2\right)\cot\alpha}{r_1 + r_1} \qquad \therefore\ OG = \frac{2}{3}\frac{r_2^2 + r_2 r_1 + r_1^2}{r_2 + r_1}\cot\alpha \qquad \text{...(5)}$$

where $G$ is the C.G. of the frustum.

$$\therefore \qquad EG = OG - OE$$

$$= \frac{2}{3}\frac{r_2^2 + r_2 r_1 + r_1^2}{r_2 + r_1}\cot\alpha - r_1 \cot\alpha = \frac{2r_2^2 + 2r_2 r_1 + 2r_1^2 - 3r_2 r_1 - 3r_1^2}{3(r_2 + r_1)}\cot\alpha$$

$$= \frac{2r_2^2 - r_2 r_1 - r_1^2}{3(r_2 + r_1)}\cot\alpha \qquad \text{...(6)}$$

and

$$GF = OF - OG$$

$$= r_2 \cot\alpha - \frac{2}{3}\frac{r_2^2 + r_2 r_1 + r_1^2}{r_2 + r_1}\cot\alpha = \frac{3r_2^2 + 3r_2 r_1 - 2r_2^2 - 2r_2 r_1 - 2r_1^2}{3(r_2 + r_1)}\cot\alpha$$

$$= \frac{r_2^2 + r_2 r_1 - 2r_1^2}{3(r_2 + r_1)}\cot\alpha \qquad \text{...(7)}$$

$$\therefore \qquad \frac{EG}{GF} = \frac{2r_2^2 - r_2 r_1 - r_1^2}{r_2^2 + r_2 r_1 - 2r_1^2} = \frac{2r_2^2 - 2r_2 r_1 + r_2 r_1 - r_1^2}{r_2^2 + 2r_2 r_1 - r_2 r_1 - 2r_1^2}$$

$$= \frac{2r_2(r_2 - r_1) + r_1(r_2 - r_1)}{r_2(r_2 + 2r_1) - r_1(r_2 - 2r_1)} = \frac{2r_2 + r_1}{r_2 + 2r_1}$$

$$\therefore \qquad EF : GF = (r_1 + 2r_2) : (r_2 + 2r_1)$$

**Example 5:** A parabola revolves round its axis. Find the centroid of the portion of the surface between the vertex and a plane perpendicular to the axis at a distance $h$ from the vertex, $4a$ being the latus rectum.

OR

Find the C.G. of the surface formed by the revolution about the axis of $X$, of the portion of the parabola $y^2 = 4ax$ cut off by the ordinate $x = h$.

**Sol.**

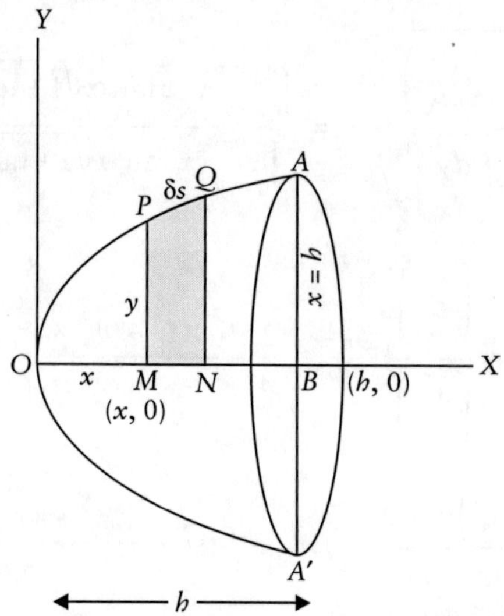


Let the equation of the generating parabola be $y^2 = 4ax$ ...(1)

Take two neighbouring points $P(x, y)$ and $Q(x + \delta x, y + \delta y)$ on the parabola (1) such that arc length $PQ = \delta s$. Draw $PM$ and $QN$ perpendiculars respectively to the $X$-axis.

When the elementary arc $PQ$ revolves about $OX$, it generates a ring of radius $y$ and small thickness $\delta s$.

$\therefore$ Surface area of the elementary ring $= 2\pi\, y\, \delta s$

Let $\rho$ be the surface density. Then, elementary mass $\delta m = \rho\, 2\, \pi y\, \delta s$

Also, the C.G. of this elementary ring is at $M\ (x, 0)$ as $\delta s$ is very small. Let $BA$ be the ordinates $x = h$. Let $(\bar{x}, \bar{y})$ be the required C.G. Then,

$$\bar{y} = 0 \qquad \text{| By symmetry} \qquad ...(2)$$

and
$$\bar{x} = \frac{\int x\, dm}{\int dm} = \frac{\int_{x=0}^{h} x \cdot \rho 2\pi y\, ds}{\int_{x=0}^{h} \rho 2\pi y\, ds} = \frac{\int_{x=0}^{h} x y\, ds}{\int_{x=0}^{h} y\, ds} \qquad | \because \rho \text{ is uniform}$$

$$= \frac{\int_0^h x y \frac{ds}{dx} dx}{\int_0^h y \frac{ds}{dx} dx} = \frac{\int_0^h x \cdot 2\sqrt{ax}\sqrt{1+\left(\frac{dy}{dx}\right)^2}\, dx}{\int_0^h 2\sqrt{ax}\sqrt{1+\left(\frac{dy}{dx}\right)^2}\, dx} \qquad | \text{ From (1)}$$

$$= \frac{\int_0^h x^{3/2}\sqrt{1+\left(\frac{dy}{dx}\right)^2}\,dx}{\int_0^h x^{1/2}\sqrt{1+\left(\frac{dy}{dx}\right)^2}\,dx} \qquad ...(3)$$

Differentiating (1) with respect to $x$, we get

$$2y\,.\,dy/dx = 4a \qquad \Rightarrow dy/dx = 2a/y \qquad \Rightarrow dy/dx = \frac{2a}{2\sqrt{ax}} \quad |\text{From (1)}$$

$$\Rightarrow \qquad dy/dx = \sqrt{\frac{a}{x}} \qquad ...(4)$$

From (3) and (4),

$$\bar{x} = \frac{\int_0^h x^{3/2}\sqrt{1+\frac{a}{x}}\,dx}{\int_0^h x^{1/2}\sqrt{1+\frac{a}{x}}\,dx} = \frac{\int_0^h x\sqrt{x+a}\,dx}{\int_0^h \sqrt{x+a}\,dx} = \frac{\left[x\frac{2}{3}(x+a)^{3/2}\right]_0^h - \int_0^h \frac{2}{3}(x+a)^{3/2}\,dx}{\left[\frac{2}{3}(x+a)^{3/2}\right]_0^h}$$

$$= \frac{h(h+a)^{3/2} - \frac{2}{5}\left[(x+a)^{3/2}\right]_0^h}{(h+a)^{3/2}-a^{3/2}} = \frac{h(h+a)^{3/2} - \frac{2}{5}\left[(h+a)^{3/2}-a^{3/2}\right]}{(h+a)^{3/2}-a^{3/2}}$$

**Example 6:** Find the centre of gravity of the surface formed by the revolution of the cycloid $x = a(\theta + \sin\theta)$, $y = a(1 - \cos\theta)$ about the axis of $Y$.

**Sol.** The given parametric equations of the cycloid are

$$x = a(\theta + \sin\theta) \qquad ...(1)$$

$$y = a(1 - \cos\theta) \qquad ...(2)$$

From (1) and (2), we get,

$$dx/d\theta = a(1 + \cos\theta) \qquad \Rightarrow dy/d\theta = a\sin\theta$$

$$\therefore \qquad ds/d\theta = \sqrt{\left(\frac{dx}{d\theta}\right)^2 \left(\frac{dy}{d\theta}\right)^2} = \sqrt{a^2(1+\cos\theta)^2 + a^2\sin^2\theta}$$

$$= a\sqrt{1+\cos^2\theta+2\cos\theta+\sin^2\theta} = a\sqrt{2+2\cos\theta}$$

$$= a\sqrt{2(1+\cos\theta)} = a\sqrt{4\cos^2\frac{\theta}{2}} = 2a\cos\frac{\theta}{2}$$

$$\Rightarrow \qquad ds = 2\,a\cos\theta/2\,d\theta \qquad ...(3)$$

At 0, $\theta = 0$ and at $A$, $\theta = \pi$.

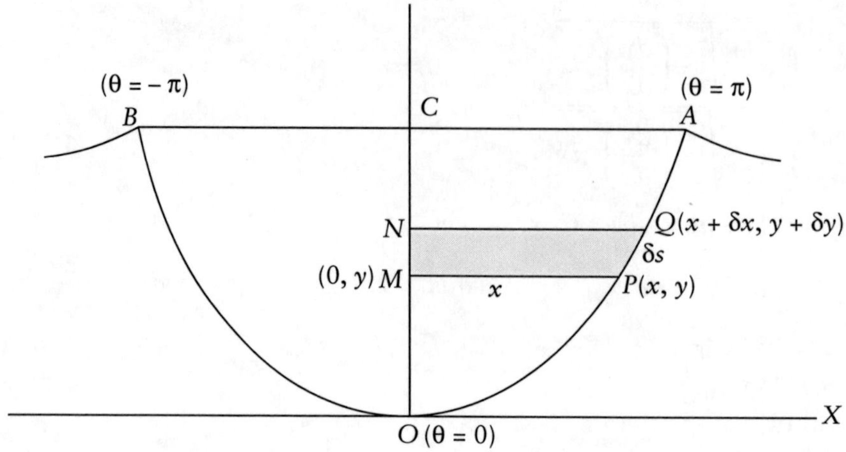


From figure, we see that the cycloid is symmetrical about $OY$. Therefore, the surface formed by revolving the whole cycloid about $OY$ is the same as that revolving arc of the cycloid lying in the positive quadrant.

Take two neighbouring points $P(x, y)$ and $Q(x + \delta x, y + \delta y)$ on the arc $OA$ of the cycloid. Let arc $PQ = \delta s$. Draw $PM$ and $QN$ perpendiculars respectively to $OY$.

When the elementary arc $PQ$ revolves about $OY$, it generates a ring of radius $x$ and small thickness $\delta s$.

$\therefore$ Surface area of the elementary ring $= 2\pi x\ \delta s$

Let $\rho$ be the surface density. Then, elementary mass $\delta m = \rho\ 2\pi x\ \delta s$

Also, the C.G. of this elementary ring is at $M(0, y)$ as $\delta s$ is very small.

Let $(\bar{x}, \bar{y})$ be the required C.G. then,

$$\bar{x} = 0 \qquad \text{| By symmetry} \qquad \ldots(4)$$

And
$$\bar{y} = \frac{\int y\,dm}{\int dm} = \frac{\int_{\theta=0}^{\pi} y\rho 2\pi x\,ds}{\int_{\theta=0}^{\pi} \rho 2\pi x\,ds} = \frac{\int_{\theta=0}^{\pi} y\ x\,ds}{\int_{\theta=0}^{\pi} x\,ds} \qquad |\because \rho \text{ is uniform}$$

$$= \frac{\int_0^{\pi} a(1-\cos\theta)\ a(\theta+\sin\theta)2a\cos\frac{\theta}{2}d\theta}{\int_0^{\pi} a(\theta+\sin\theta)\ 2a\cos\frac{\theta}{2}d\theta}$$

$$= \frac{a\int_0^{\pi}(1-\cos\theta)\ (\theta+\sin\theta)\cos\frac{\theta}{2}d\theta}{\int_0^{\pi}(\theta+\sin\theta)\cos\frac{\theta}{2}d\theta} \qquad \ldots(5)$$

Numerator of $\bar{y} = a\int_0^{\pi}(1-\cos\theta)\ (\theta+\sin\theta)\cos\frac{\theta}{2}d\theta$ Put $\theta/2 = \phi$ $\therefore d\theta = 2d\phi$

$$= 2a\int_0^{\pi/2}(1-\cos 2\phi)\ (2\phi+\sin 2\phi)\cos\phi\ d\phi$$

$$= 2a\int_0^{\pi/2}\left(2\sin^2\phi\right)(2\phi+2\sin\phi\cos\phi)\cos\phi\,d\phi$$

$$= 8a\int_0^{\pi/2}\sin^2\phi(\phi+\sin\phi\cos\phi)\cos\phi\,d\phi$$

$$= 8a\left[\int_0^{\pi/2}\phi\sin^2\phi\cos\phi\,d\phi+\int_0^{\pi/2}\sin^3\phi\cos^2\phi\,d\phi\right]$$

$$= 8a\left[\left(\phi\frac{\sin^3\phi}{3}\right)_0^{\pi/2}-\int_0^{\pi/2}\frac{\sin^3\phi}{3}d\theta+\frac{\sqrt{2}\,\Gamma\frac{3}{2}}{\Gamma 2\,\Gamma\frac{7}{2}}\right]$$

$$= 8a\left[\frac{\pi}{6}-\frac{1}{3}\cdot\frac{2}{3}+\frac{\frac{1}{2}\sqrt{\pi}}{2\cdot\frac{5}{2}\cdot\frac{3}{2}\cdot\frac{1}{2}\cdot\sqrt{\pi}}\right] \qquad \text{| By Walli's Formula}$$

$$= 8a\left(\frac{\pi}{6}-\frac{2}{9}+\frac{2}{15}\right) = \frac{8a}{90}(15\pi-20+12)$$

$$= \frac{4a(15\pi-8)}{45} \qquad \text{...(6)}$$

Denominator of $\bar{y} = \int_0^{\pi}(\theta+\sin\theta)\cos\frac{\theta}{2}d\theta$ Put $\theta/2 = \phi$ $\therefore\ d\theta = 2\,d\phi$

$$= \int_0^{\pi}(2\phi+\sin 2\phi)\cos\phi\,2d\phi = \int_0^{\pi/2}(2\phi+2\sin\phi\cos\phi)\cos\phi\,2d\phi$$

$$= 4\int_0^{\pi/2}\left(\phi\cos\phi+\sin\phi\cos^2\phi\right)d\phi = 4\left[\int_0^{\pi/2}\phi\cos\phi\,d\phi+\int_0^{\pi/2}\sin\phi\cos^2\phi\,d\phi\right]$$

$$= 4\left[(\phi\sin\phi)_0^{\pi/2}-\int_0^{\pi/2}\sin\phi\,d\phi+\left(\frac{-\cos^3\phi}{3}\right)_0^{\pi/2}\right] = 4\left[\frac{\pi}{2}-(-\cos\phi)_0^{\pi/2}+\frac{1}{3}\right]$$

$$= 4\left[\frac{\pi}{2}-1+\frac{1}{3}\right] = 4\left[\frac{\pi}{2}-\frac{2}{3}\right] = \frac{2}{3}(3\pi-4) \qquad \text{...(7)}$$

From (4), (5) and (6), we get

$$\bar{y} = \frac{\frac{4a(15\pi-8)}{45}}{\frac{2}{3}(3\pi-4)} = \frac{2a}{15}\left(\frac{15\pi-8}{3\pi-4}\right).$$

Hence, the required C.G. is given by

$$\bar{x} = 0 \text{ and } \bar{y} = \frac{2a}{15}\left(\frac{15\pi-8}{3\pi-4}\right)$$

**Example 7:** Find the C.G. of the surface formed by the revolution of the cardioid $r = a(1 + \cos\theta)$ about its axis.

**Sol.**

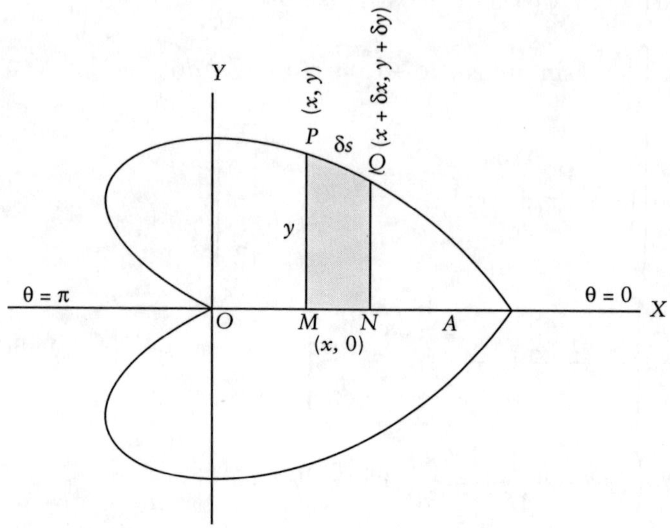


We have to find out the C.G. of the surface formed by the revolution of the cardioid

$$r = a(1 + \cos\theta) \qquad ...(1)$$

about OX.

Take two neighbouring points $P(x, y)$ and $Q(x + \delta x, y + \delta y)$ on the curve. From $P$ and $Q$ draw perpendiculars $PM$ and $QN$ respectively to $OX$. Let arc $PQ = \delta s$.

When the elementary arc $\delta s$ revolves about $OX$, it generates a ring of radius $y$ and small thickness $\delta s$.

$\therefore$ Surface area of the elementary ring $= 2\,\pi\, y\, \delta s$

Let $\rho$ be the surface density. Then, elementary mass $\delta m = \rho\, 2\,\pi\, y\, \delta s$.

Also, the C.G. of this elementary ring is at $M(x, 0)$ as $\delta s$ is very small.

Let $(\bar{x}, \bar{y})$ be the required C.G. Then, $\bar{y} = 0$ | By symmetry

and $$\bar{x} = \frac{\int x\,dm}{\int dm} = \frac{\int_{\theta=0}^{\pi} x\rho 2\pi y\,ds}{\int_{\theta=0}^{\pi} \rho 2\pi y\,ds} = \frac{\int_0^{\pi} xy\frac{ds}{d\theta}d\theta}{\int_0^{\pi} y\frac{ds}{d\theta}d\theta} = \frac{\int_0^{\pi} xy\sqrt{r^2+\left(\frac{dr}{d\theta}\right)^2}\,d\theta}{\int_0^{\pi} y\sqrt{r^2+\left(\frac{dr}{d\theta}\right)^2}\,d\theta}$$

$$= \frac{\int_0^{\pi} r\cos\theta\, r\sin\theta\sqrt{a^2(1+\cos\theta)^2+(-a\cos\theta)^2}\,d\theta}{\int_0^{\pi} r\sin\theta\sqrt{a^2(1+\cos\theta)^2+(-a\cos\theta)^2}\,d\theta} \qquad \text{| From (1)}$$

$$= \frac{\int_0^\pi r^2 \sin\theta \cos\theta a\sqrt{1+\cos^2\theta+2\cos\theta+\sin^2\theta}\ d\theta}{\int_0^\pi r \sin\theta a\sqrt{1+\cos^2\theta+2\cos\theta+\sin^2\theta}\ d\theta}$$

$$= \frac{\int_0^\pi a^2 (1+\cos\theta)^2 \sin\theta\cos\theta a\sqrt{2(1+\cos\theta)}\ d\theta}{\int_0^\pi a^2 (1+\cos\theta)\sin\theta\sqrt{2(1+\cos\theta)}\ d\theta} \qquad \text{| From (1)}$$

$$= \frac{\int_0^\pi a^3 (1+\cos\theta)^2 \sin\theta\cos\theta\ 2\cos\frac{\theta}{2}\ d\theta}{\int_0^\pi a^2 (1+\cos\theta)\sin\theta\ 2\cos\frac{\theta}{2}\ d\theta}$$

$$= \frac{a\int_0^\pi \left(2\cos^2\frac{\theta}{2}\right)^2 2\sin\frac{\theta}{2}\cos\frac{\theta}{2}\left(2\cos^2\frac{\theta}{2}-1\right)\cos\frac{\theta}{2}\ d\theta}{\int_0^\pi \left(2\cos^2\frac{\theta}{2}\right)\left(2\sin\frac{\theta}{2}\cos\frac{\theta}{2}\right)\cos\frac{\theta}{2}\ d\theta}$$

$$= \frac{2a\int_0^\pi \cos^6\frac{\theta}{2}\left(2\cos^2\frac{\theta}{2}-1\right)\sin\frac{\theta}{2}\ d\theta}{\int_0^\pi \cos^4\frac{\theta}{2}\sin\frac{\theta}{2}\ d\theta}$$

Put $\theta/2 = \phi$
$\therefore\ d\theta = 2\ d\phi$

$$= \frac{2a\int_0^{\pi/2} \cos^6\phi\left(2\cos^2\phi-1\right)\sin\phi 2d\phi}{\int_0^{\pi/2} \cos^4\phi\sin\phi\cdot 2d\phi}$$

$$= \frac{4a\left[2\int_0^{\pi/2} \cos^8\phi\ \sin\phi\, d\phi - \int_0^{\pi/2} \cos^6\phi\ \sin\phi\, d\phi\right]}{2\int_0^{\pi/2} \cos^4\phi\sin\phi\, d\phi}$$

$$= \frac{2a\left[2\left(\frac{-\cos^9\phi}{9}\right)_0^{\pi/2} - \left(\frac{-\cos^7\phi}{7}\right)_0^{\pi/2}\right]}{\left(\frac{-\cos^5\phi}{5}\right)_0^{\pi/2}}$$

$$= \frac{2a\left(\frac{2}{9}-\frac{1}{7}\right)}{\frac{1}{5}} = 2a\frac{5}{63}\cdot\frac{5}{1} = \frac{50a}{63}$$

Hence, the required C.G. is given by

$$\bar{x} = \frac{50a}{63},\ \bar{y} = 0.$$

**Example 8:** Find the C.G. of the surface formed by the revolution of one loop of the lemnisate of Bernoulli $r^2 = a^2 \cos 2\theta$ about the initial line.

**Sol.**

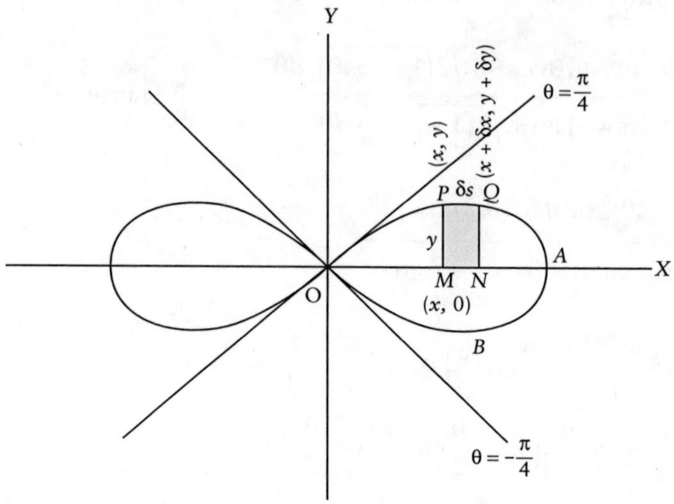


The equation of Lemniscate of Bernoulli is $r^2 = a^2 \cos 2\theta$ ...(1)

For one loop of the curve, put $r = 0$

$\Rightarrow \quad \cos 2\theta = 0 = \cos(\pm \pi/2) \Rightarrow 2\theta = \pm \pi/2 \quad \Rightarrow \theta = \pm \pi/4$

Hence, there lies a loop between the lines $\theta = -\pi/4$ and $\theta = \pi/4$.

We are to find the C.G. of the surface formed by the revolution of one loop of the curve (1) about the initial line. The surface of revolution obtained by the revolution of one loop *OBAQPO* about the initial line will be the same as the surface of revolution obtained by the revolution of the arc *OA* of the curve about the initial line since the curve (1) is symmetrical about the initial line.

Take two neighbouring points $P(x, y)$ and $Q(x + \delta x, y + \delta y)$ on the curve. From *P* and *Q* draws perpendiculars *PM* and *QN* respectively on *OX*. Let arc $PQ = \delta s$.

When the elementary arc *PQ* revolves about *OX*, it generates a ring of radius *y* and small thickness $\delta s$.

$\therefore$ Surface area of the elementary ring $= 2\pi y \,\delta s$

Let $\rho$ be the surface density. Then, elementary mass $\delta m = \rho\, 2\pi y\, \delta s$

Also, the C.G. of this elementary ring is at $M(x, 0)$ as $\delta s$ is very small.

Let $(\bar{x}, \bar{y})$ be the required C.G. Then,

$\bar{y} = 0$ | By symmetry [**Note** that *y* coordinate of the C.G. of the elementary ring is 0.] ...(2)

and $$\bar{x} = \frac{\int x\,dm}{\int dm} = \frac{\int_{\theta=0}^{\pi/4} x\rho 2\pi y\,ds}{\int_{\theta=0}^{\pi/4} \rho 2\pi y\,ds} = \frac{\int_0^{\pi/4} xy\frac{ds}{d\theta}d\theta}{\int_0^{\pi/4} y\frac{ds}{d\theta}d\theta}$$ | $\because \rho$ is uniform

Differentiating (1) with respect to $\theta$, we get $2r\, dr/d\theta = -2a^2 \sin 2\theta$

$$\Rightarrow \quad dr/d\theta = -a^2 \sin 2\theta / r \qquad \therefore \quad ds/d\theta = \sqrt{r^2 + \left(\frac{dr}{d\theta}\right)^2}$$

$$= \sqrt{a^2 \cos 2\theta + \frac{a^4 \sin^2 2\theta}{r^2}} \qquad = \frac{\sqrt{r^2 a^2 \cos 2\theta + a^4 \sin^2 2\theta}}{r}$$

$$= \frac{\sqrt{\left(a^2 \cos 2\theta\right)^2 + a^4 \sin^2 2\theta}}{r} = \frac{a^2\sqrt{\cos^2 2\theta + \sin^2 2\theta}}{r} = \frac{a^2}{r} \qquad \ldots(4)$$

From (3) and (4), we get

$$\bar{x} = \frac{\int_0^{\pi/4} r\cos\theta\, r\sin\theta \frac{a^2}{r} d\theta}{\int_0^{\pi/4} r\cos\theta \frac{a^2}{r} d\theta} = \frac{\int_0^{\pi/4} r \frac{\sin 2\theta}{2} d\theta}{\int_0^{\pi/4} \sin\theta\, d\theta}$$

$$= \frac{\frac{a}{2}\int_0^{\pi/4} \sqrt{\cos 2\theta}\, \sin 2\theta\, d\theta}{\left(-\cos\theta\right)_0^{\pi/4}} \qquad \Big| \text{From (1)}$$

Put $\cos 2\theta = t \therefore -2 \sin 2\theta\, d\theta = dt$
$\Rightarrow \sin 2\theta\, d\theta = -\, dt/2$

$$= \frac{\frac{a}{2}\int_1^0 \sqrt{t}\left(-\frac{dt}{2}\right)}{\left(-\cos\frac{\pi}{4} + \cos 0\right)} = \frac{\frac{a}{4}\int_0^1 \sqrt{t}\, dt}{1 - \frac{1}{\sqrt{2}}} = \frac{\frac{a}{4}\cdot\frac{2}{3}\left(t^{3/2}\right)_0^1}{\frac{\sqrt{2}-1}{\sqrt{2}}}$$

$$= \frac{a}{6}\cdot\frac{\sqrt{2}}{\sqrt{2}-1} = \frac{a}{3\sqrt{2}(\sqrt{2}-1)} = \frac{a\left(\sqrt{2}+1\right)}{3\sqrt{2}\left(2-1\right)\left(\sqrt{2}+1\right)}$$

$$= \frac{a\left(\sqrt{2}+1\right)}{3\sqrt{2}} = \frac{a\sqrt{2}\left(\sqrt{2}+1\right)}{3\sqrt{2}\sqrt{2}} = \frac{a\left(2+\sqrt{2}\right)}{6}$$

Hence, the required C.G. is given by

$$\bar{x} = \frac{a\left(2+\sqrt{2}\right)}{6}, \quad \bar{y} = 0.$$

## EXERCISE 2(D)

1. Show that the C.G. of the surface of a spherical segment bisects its height.
2. Find the C.G. of a thin uniform hemispherical shell.

   [**Ans.** At the mid-point of the symmetrical radius]

## 9. Centre of Gravity of the Sum or Difference of Two Bodies (by Integration)

To find the C.G. of an area enclosed between two curves $y = f_1(x)$, $y = f_2(x)$ and the ordinates $x = a$ and $x = b$.

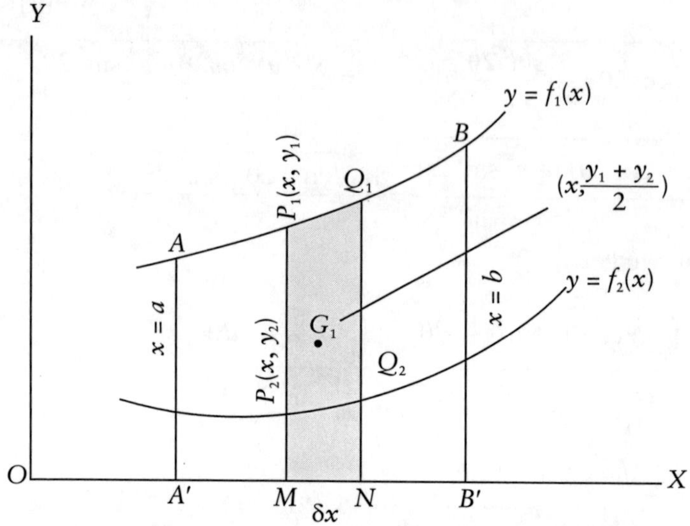


Let $AB$ and $CD$ be the given curves $y = f_1(x)$ and $y = f_2(x)$ respectively. Let $AA'$ and $BB'$ be the given ordinates $x = a$ and $x = b$ respectively. We are required to find out the C.G. of the area $ABCD$ enclosed by the given curves and the given ordinates.

Take two neighbouring points $P_1$ and $Q_1$ on the curve $y = f_1(x)$. From $P_1$ and $Q_1$, draw perpendiculars $P_1M$ and $Q_1N$ respectively on the $X$-axis intersecting the curve $y = f_2(x)$ at $P_2$ and $Q_2$ respectively.

Let $P_1M = y_1$ and $P_2M = y_2$.

Let $OM = x$. Then, the coordinates of the point $P_1$ and $P_2$ are $(x, y_1)$ and $(x, y_2)$ respectively. Since the points $P_1$ and $P_2$ lie on the curves $y = f_1(x)$ and $y = f_2(x)$ respectively, therefore,

$$y_1 = f_1(x) \quad \text{...(1)}$$

and, $$y_2 = f_2(x) \quad \text{...(2)}$$

Let $MN = \delta x$. Consider an elementary area $P_1Q_1\,Q_2P_2$.

Its area $= (y_1 - y_2)\delta x$. Elementary mass $\delta m = \rho(y_1 - y_2)\delta x$ where $\rho$ is mass per unit area. The C.G. of this elementary area will be at the point $G_1 \left\{x, \frac{y_1 + y_2}{2}\right\}$ since $\delta x$ is very small and height of $G_1$ above $OX$

$$= P_2M + 1/2\ P_1P_2 = y_2 + 1/2\ (y_1 - y_2) = 1/2\ (y_1 + y_2)$$

If $(\bar{x}, \bar{y})$ is the required C.G., then,

$$\bar{x} = \frac{\int x\, dm}{\int dm} = \frac{\int_a^b x\, \rho(y_1 - y_2)\, dx}{\int_a^b \rho(y_1 - y_2)\, dx}$$

$$= \frac{\int_a^b x(y_1 - y_2)\,dx}{\int_a^b (y_1 - y_2)\,dx} \qquad | \because \rho \text{ is uniform} \qquad ...(3)$$

and
$$\bar{y} = \frac{\int y\,dm}{\int dm} = \frac{\int_a^b \left(\frac{y_1 + y_2}{2}\right)\rho(y_1 - y_2)\,dx}{\int_a^b \rho(y_1 - y_2)\,dx}$$

$$= \frac{\frac{1}{2}\int_a^b (y_1^2 - y_2^2)\,dx}{\int_a^b (y_1 - y_2)\,dx} \qquad | \because \rho \text{ is uniform} \qquad ...(4)$$

where $y_1$ and $y_2$ are given by (1) and (2) respectively.

## 10. C.G. of the Sum or Difference of Two Bodies (by Geometrical Method)

1. C.G. of a compound body

or

C.G. of a composite body

Find the C.G. of a body, when C.G. of its two parts are known.

Let a body be made up of two parts $A$ and $B$ of respective weights $W_1$ and $W_2$. Let $G_1$ and $G_2$ be the C.G. of the two parts $A$ and $B$ respectively. Then, the weights $W_1$ and $W_2$ will act through $G_1$ and $G_2$ respectively. We are to find out the C.G. of the composite body $A + B$.

Let $W$ be the whole weight of the composite body. Then,

$$W = W_1 + W_2 \qquad ...(1)$$

The resultant weight $W$ will pass

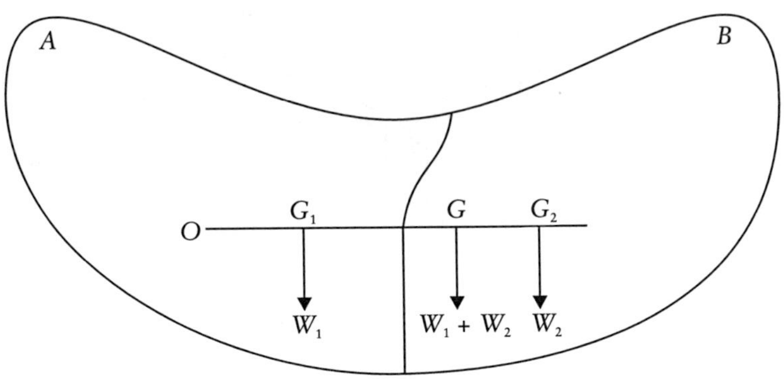


through a point $G$ on the line $G_1\,G_2$ such that $W_1 \cdot G_1G = W_2\,G_2G$ ...(2)

| By law of parallel forces

Take a point $O$ on line $G_1G_2$.

Taking moments about $O$, we get $(W_1 + W_2)\,OG = W_1 \cdot OG_1 + W_2 \cdot OG_2$

$$\therefore \qquad OG = \frac{W_1 \cdot OG_1 + W_2 \cdot OG_2}{W_1 + W_2} \qquad ...(3)$$

If $\qquad OG_1 = x_1$, $OG_2 = x_2$ and $OG = \overline{x}$, then,

$$\overline{x} = \frac{W_1 x_1 + W_2 x_2}{W_1 + W_2} \qquad ...(4)$$

**(2) C.G. of the difference of two bodies**

or

**C.G. of a part of the body**

We are to find out the C.G. of a body $B$ which may be considered as a body $B_1$ of weight $W_1$ with its C.G. at $G_1$ minus a body $B_2$ of weight $W_2$ with its C.G. at $G_2$. Let referred to a system of coordinate axes, the coordinates of $G_1$ and $G_2$ are $(x_1, y_1)$ and $(x_2, y_2)$ respectively.

Let the coordinates of C.G. $G$ of the remaining part (remainder) be $(\overline{x}, \overline{y})$. Let us consider the weight $W_2$ acting though $G_2$ as $- W_2$; it being made of negative matter [the whole body is made of positive matter] so that if these two are compounded then we get the remaining part whose C.G. is found as follows.

Then, by taking moments about $Y$-axis and $X$-axis separately, we obtain

$$(W_1 - W_2)\,\overline{x} = W_1x_1 - W_2x_2 \quad \text{and } (W_1 - W_2)\,\overline{y} = W_1y_1 - W_2y_2$$

$$\Rightarrow \qquad \overline{x} = \frac{W_1x_1 - W_2x_2}{W_1 - W_2} \quad \text{and } \overline{y} = \frac{W_1y_1 - W_2y_2}{W_1 - W_2}$$

## ILLUSTRATIVE EXAMPLES

**Example 1:** Find the position of the centroid of the area enclosed by $y = mx$ and $y^2 = 4ax$.

**Sol.**

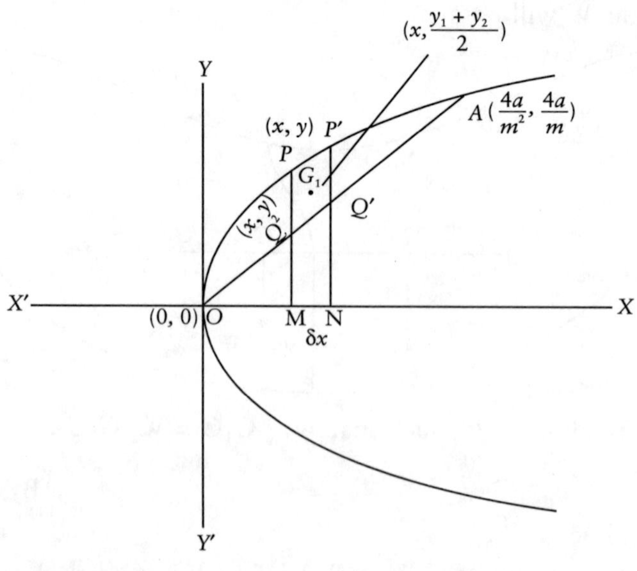

The equation of the parabola is

$$y^2 = 4ax \quad ...(1)$$

The equation of the straight line is

$$y = mx \quad ...(2)$$

It is a straight line passing through the origin $O$.

Solving equations (1) and (2), we find that the two curves intersect at $O(0, 0)$ and $A\left(\frac{4a}{m^2}, \frac{4a}{m}\right)$.

Let the coordinates of $P$ and $Q$ be $(x, y_1)$ and $(x, y_2)$ respectively. Then,

$$y_1 = \sqrt{4ax} \quad ...(3)$$

and $$y_2 = mx \quad ...(4)$$

Take a neighbouring point $P'$ on (1) and draw perpendicular $P'N$ from $P'$ to $OX$ intersecting (2) at $Q'$. Let $MN = \delta x$. Elementary area $= PP'Q'Q = (y_1 - y_2)\delta x$ where $\rho$ is mass per unit area.

Also, C.G. $G_1$ of the elementary area $PP'Q'Q$ is at $\left(x, \frac{y_1 + y_2}{2}\right)$ as $\delta x$ is very small.

Let the C.G. of the enclosed area $OQQ'AP'PO$ be $G(\bar{x}, \bar{y})$. Then,

$$\bar{x} = \frac{\int x\, dm}{\int dm} = \frac{\int_{x \text{ for } O}^{x \text{ for } A} x\rho(y_1 - y_2)\, dx}{\int_{x \text{ for } O}^{x \text{ for } A} \rho(y_1 - y_2)\, dx}$$

$$= \frac{\int_0^{\frac{4a}{m^2}} x(y_1 - y_2)\, dx}{\int_0^{\frac{4a}{m^2}} (y_1 - y_2)\, dx} \quad |\because \rho \text{ is uniform} \quad ...(3)$$

$$= \frac{\int_0^{\frac{4a}{m^2}} x\left(\sqrt{4ax} - mx\right) dx}{\int_0^{\frac{4a}{m^2}} \left(\sqrt{4ax} - mx\right) dx} \quad |\text{From (3) and (4)}$$

$$= \frac{\int_0^{\frac{4a}{m^2}} \left(2\sqrt{a}\, x^{3/2} - mx^2\right) dx}{\int_0^{\frac{4a}{m^2}} \left(2\sqrt{a}\, x^{1/2} - mx\right) dx} = \frac{\left(2\sqrt{a} \cdot \frac{2}{5} x^{5/2} - m\frac{x^3}{3}\right)_0^{\frac{4a}{m^2}}}{\left(2\sqrt{a} \cdot \frac{2}{5} x^{3/2} - m\frac{x^2}{2}\right)_0^{\frac{4a}{m^2}}}$$

$$= \frac{\frac{4\sqrt{a}}{5}\left(\frac{4a}{m^2}\right)^{5/2} - \frac{m}{3}\left(\frac{4a}{m^2}\right)^3}{\frac{4\sqrt{a}}{3}\left(\frac{4a}{m^2}\right)^{3/2} - \frac{m}{2}\left(\frac{4a}{m^2}\right)^2} = \frac{\frac{4\sqrt{a}}{5} \cdot \frac{32a^{5/2}}{m^5} - \frac{64}{3}\frac{a^3}{m^5}}{\frac{4\sqrt{a}}{5} \cdot \frac{8a^{3/2}}{m^3} - \frac{8a^2}{m^3}}$$

$$= \frac{\frac{128a^3}{5m^5} - \frac{64a^3}{3m^5}}{\frac{32a^2}{m^3} - \frac{8a^2}{m^3}} = \frac{\frac{a^3}{m^5}\left(\frac{128}{5} - \frac{64}{3}\right)}{\frac{a^2}{m^3}\left(\frac{32}{3} - 8\right)} = \frac{\frac{a}{m^5}\left(\frac{384-320}{15}\right)}{\left(\frac{8}{3}\right)} = \frac{a}{m^2}\frac{64}{15}\cdot\frac{3}{8} = \frac{8a}{5m^2}$$

and $$\bar{y} = \frac{\int y\,dm}{\int dm} = \frac{\int_0^{\frac{4a}{m^2}} \frac{y_l + y_2}{2}\rho(y_1 - y_2)\,dx}{\int_0^{\frac{4a}{m^2}} \rho(y_1 - y_2)\,dx} = \frac{\frac{1}{2}\int_0^{\frac{4a}{m^2}} (y_1^2 - y_2^2)\,dx}{\int_0^{\frac{4a}{m^2}} (y_1 - y_2)\,dx} \qquad | \because \rho \text{ is uniform}$$

$$= \frac{\frac{1}{2}\int_0^{\frac{4a}{m^2}} (4ax - m^2x^2)\,dx}{\int_0^{\frac{4a}{m^2}} (\sqrt{4ax} - mx)\,dx} = \frac{\frac{1}{2}\left(4a\frac{x^2}{2} - \frac{m^2x^3}{3}\right)_0^{\frac{4a}{m^2}}}{\left(2\sqrt{a}\frac{2}{3}x^{3/2} - \frac{mx^2}{2}\right)_0^{\frac{4a}{m^2}}} = \frac{\frac{1}{2}\left[2a\left(\frac{4a}{m^2}\right)^2 - \frac{m^2}{3}\left(\frac{4a}{m^2}\right)^3\right]}{\frac{4\sqrt{a}}{3}\left(\frac{4a}{m^2}\right)^{3/2} - \frac{m}{2}\left(\frac{4a}{m^2}\right)^2}$$

$$= \frac{\frac{1}{2}\left[\frac{32a^3}{m^4} - \frac{64a^3}{3m^4}\right]}{\frac{32a^2}{3m^3} - \frac{8a^2}{m^3}} = \frac{\frac{16a^3}{m^4} - \frac{32a^3}{3m^4}}{\frac{32a^2}{3m^3} - \frac{8a^2}{m^3}} = \frac{\frac{a^3}{m^4}\left(16 - \frac{32}{3}\right)}{\frac{a^2}{m^3}\left(\frac{32}{3} - 8\right)} = \frac{\frac{a}{m}\cdot\frac{16}{3}}{\frac{8}{3}} = \frac{2a}{m}$$

Hence, the required C.G. is given by

$$\bar{x} = \frac{8a}{5m^2}, \quad \bar{y} = \frac{2a}{m}.$$

**Example 2:** Find the position of the centroid of the area enclosed by $y^2 = ax$ and $x^2 = by$.

**Sol.**

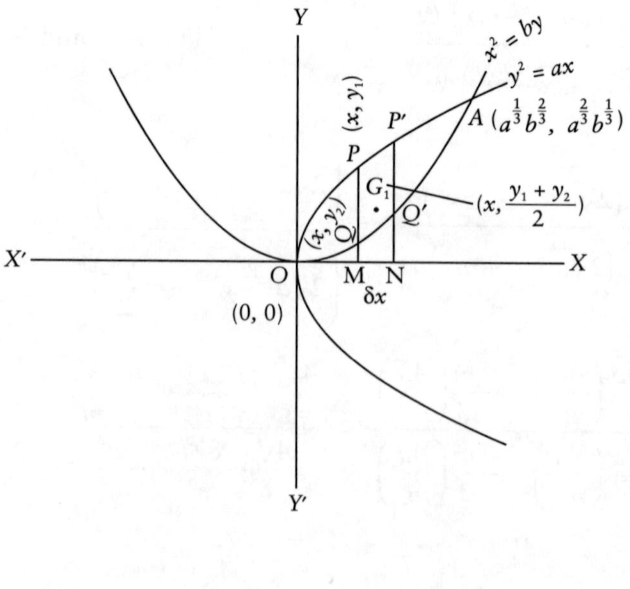

The parabolas

$$y^2 = ax \qquad \text{...(1)}$$

and

$$x^2 = by \qquad \text{...(2)}$$

have been traced and shown in the figure.

Solving equations (1) and (2), we find that the two parabolas intersect at the points O(0, 0) and $A\left(a^{\frac{1}{2}} b^{\frac{2}{3}}, a^{\frac{2}{3}} b^{\frac{1}{3}}\right)$.

Let the coordinates of $P$ and $Q$ be $(x, y_1)$ and $(x, y_2)$ respectively. Then,

$$y_1^2 = ax \qquad \text{...(3)}$$

and

$$x^2 = by_2 \qquad \text{...(4)}$$

Take a neighbouring point $P'$ on (1) and draw perpendicular $P'N$ From $P'$ on $OX$ intersecting (2) at $Q'$. Let $MN = \delta x$. Elementary area = $PP'Q'Q = (y_1 - y_2)\,\delta x$ where $\rho$ is mass per unit area.

Also, C.G. $G_1$ of the elementary area $PP'Q'Q$ is at $\left(x, \dfrac{y_1 + y_2}{2}\right)$ as $\delta x$ is very small.

Let the C.G. of the enclosed area $OQQ'AP'PO$ be $G(\bar{x}, \bar{y})$. Then,

$$\bar{x} = \frac{\int x\,dm}{\int dm} = \frac{\int_{x \text{ for } O}^{x \text{ for } A} x\rho(y_1 - y_2)\,dx}{\int_{x \text{ for } O}^{x \text{ for } A} \rho(y_1 - y_2)\,dx} = \frac{\int_0^{a^{\frac{1}{3}} b^{\frac{2}{3}}} x(y_1 - y_2)\,dx}{\int_0^{a^{\frac{1}{3}} b^{\frac{2}{3}}} (y_1 - y_2)\,dx} \qquad | \because \rho \text{ is uniform}$$

$$= \frac{\int_0^{a^{\frac{1}{3}} b^{\frac{2}{3}}} x\left(\sqrt{ax} - \dfrac{x^2}{b}\right)dx}{\int_0^{a^{\frac{1}{3}} b^{\frac{2}{3}}} \left(\sqrt{ax} - \dfrac{x^2}{b}\right)dx} \qquad | \text{From (3) and (4)} \qquad \text{...(5)}$$

$$\text{Numerator of } \bar{x} = \int_0^{a^{\frac{1}{3}} b^{\frac{2}{3}}} \left(\sqrt{a}\,x^{3/2} - \frac{1}{b}x^3\right)dx = \left(\sqrt{a}\,\frac{2}{5}x^{3/2} - \frac{1}{b}\frac{x^4}{4}\right)_0^{a^{\frac{1}{2}} b^{\frac{2}{3}}}$$

$$= \frac{2\sqrt{a}}{5} a^{\frac{5}{6}} b^{\frac{5}{3}} - \frac{a^{\frac{4}{3}} b^{\frac{8}{3}}}{4b} = \frac{2}{5} a^{\frac{4}{3}} b^{\frac{5}{3}} - \frac{a^{\frac{4}{3}} b^{\frac{5}{3}}}{4}$$

$$= \frac{3}{20} a^{\frac{4}{3}} b^{\frac{5}{3}} \qquad \text{...(6)}$$

$$\text{Denominator of } \bar{x} = \int_0^{a^{\frac{1}{3}} b^{\frac{2}{3}}} \left(\sqrt{ax} - \frac{x^2}{b}\right)dx = \left(\sqrt{a}\,\frac{2}{3}x^{\frac{3}{2}} - \frac{x^3}{3b}\right)_0^{a^{\frac{1}{3}} b^{\frac{2}{3}}} = \frac{2\sqrt{a}}{3} a^{\frac{1}{2}} b - \frac{ab^2}{3b}$$

$$= \frac{2ab}{3} - \frac{ab}{3} = \frac{ab}{3} \qquad \text{...(7)}$$

$$\therefore \qquad \bar{x} = \frac{\frac{3}{20}a^{\frac{4}{3}}b^{\frac{5}{3}}}{\frac{ab}{3}} = \frac{9}{20}a^{\frac{1}{3}}b^{\frac{2}{3}} \qquad ...(8)$$

$$\text{Again,} \qquad \bar{y} = \frac{\int y\,dm}{\int dm} = \frac{\int_0^{a^{\frac{1}{3}}b^{\frac{2}{3}}} \frac{y_1+y_2}{2}\rho(y_1-y_2)\,dx}{\int_0^{a^{\frac{1}{3}}b^{\frac{2}{3}}} \rho(y_1-y_2)\,dx} = \frac{\frac{1}{2}\int_0^{a^{\frac{1}{3}}b^{\frac{2}{3}}} (y_1^2-y_2^2)\,dx}{\int_0^{a^{\frac{1}{3}}b^{\frac{2}{3}}} (y_1-y_2)\,dx} \qquad |\because \rho \text{ is uniform}$$

$$= \frac{\frac{1}{2}\int_o^{a^{\frac{1}{3}}b^{\frac{2}{3}}} \left(ax - \frac{x^4}{b^2}\right)dx}{\int_o^{a^{\frac{1}{3}}b^{\frac{2}{3}}} \left(\sqrt{ax} - \frac{x^2}{b}\right)dx} \qquad |\text{From (3) and (4)} \qquad ...(9)$$

$$\text{Numerator } \bar{y} = \frac{1}{2}\int_0^{a^{\frac{1}{3}}b^{\frac{2}{3}}} \left(ax - \frac{x^4}{b^2}\right)dx = \frac{1}{2}\left[\frac{ax^2}{2} - \frac{x^5}{5b^2}\right]_0^{a^{\frac{1}{3}}b^{\frac{2}{3}}}$$

$$= \frac{1}{2}\left[\frac{a}{2}\cdot a^{2/3}b^{4/3} - \frac{a^{\frac{5}{3}}b^{\frac{10}{3}}}{5b^2}\right] = \frac{1}{2}\left[\frac{a^{5/3}b^{4/3}}{2} - \frac{a^{\frac{5}{3}}b^{\frac{4}{3}}}{5}\right]$$

$$= \frac{3a^{5/3}b^{4/3}}{20} \qquad ...(10)$$

$$\text{Denominator of } \bar{y} = \text{Denominator of } \bar{x} = \frac{ab}{3} \qquad ...(11)$$

$$\therefore \qquad \bar{y} = \frac{\frac{3}{20}a^{\frac{5}{3}}b^{\frac{4}{3}}}{\frac{ab}{3}}$$

$$= \frac{9}{20}a^{\frac{2}{3}}b^{\frac{1}{3}} \qquad ...(12)$$

Hence, the required C.G. is given by

$$\bar{x} = \frac{9}{20}a^{\frac{1}{3}}b^{\frac{2}{3}}, \quad \bar{y} = \frac{9}{20}a^{\frac{2}{3}}b^{\frac{1}{3}}$$

**Example 3:** Find the centroid of the portion of an ellipse cut off by a line joining the extremities of the major and minor axis.

**Sol.**

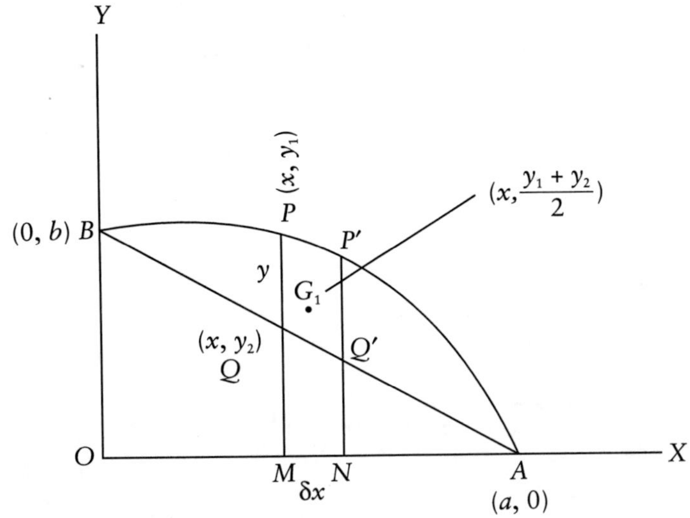


Let the equation of the ellipse be

$$\frac{x^2}{a^2} + \frac{y^2}{b^2} = 1 \qquad ...(1)$$

Then, $A \to (a, 0)$ and $B \to (0, b)$

The equation of line joining the extremities $A(a, 0)$ $B(0, b)$ is

$$\frac{x}{a} + \frac{y}{b} = 1 \qquad ...(2)$$

We are to find the C.G. of the area included between the ellipse and the line $AB$.

Let the coordinates of $P$ and $Q$ be $(x, y_1)$ and $(x, y_2)$ respectively. Then,

$$\frac{x^2}{a^2} + \frac{y_1^2}{b^2} = 1 \qquad ...(3)$$

and $$\frac{x}{a} + \frac{y_2}{b} = 1 \qquad ...(4)$$

Take a neighbouring point $P'$ on (1) and draw perpendicular $P'N$ from $P'$ on $OX$ intersecting (2) at $Q$. Let $MN = \delta x$.

Elementary area $PP'Q'Q = (y_1 - y_2)\delta x$

$\therefore$ Elementary mass $\delta m = \rho(y_1 - y_2)\delta x$ where $\rho$ is mass per unit area.

Also, C.G. $G_1$ of the elementary area $PP'Q'Q$ is at $\left(x, \dfrac{y_1 + y_2}{2}\right)$ as $\delta x$ is very small.

Let the required C.G. be $(\bar{x}, \bar{y})$. Then,

$$\bar{x} = \frac{\int x\,dm}{\int dm} = \frac{\int_0^a x\rho(y_1 - y_2)\,dx}{\int_0^a \rho(y_1 - y_2)\,dx} = \frac{\int_0^a x(y_1 - y_2)\,dx}{\int_0^a (y_1 - y_2)\,dx} \qquad | \because \rho \text{ is uniform}$$

$$= \frac{\int_0^a x\left\{\frac{b}{a}\sqrt{a^2 - x^2} - \frac{b}{a}(a - x)\right\}dx}{\int_0^a \left\{\frac{b}{a}\sqrt{a^2 - x^2} - \frac{b}{a}(a - x)\right\}dx} \qquad | \text{From (3) and (4)}$$

$$= \frac{\int_0^a x\left\{\sqrt{a^2 - x^2} - (a - x)\right\}dx}{\int_0^a \left\{\sqrt{a^2 - x^2} - (a - x)\right\}dx} \qquad \text{...(5)}$$

Numerator of $\bar{x} = \int_0^a x\left\{\sqrt{a^2 - x^2} - (a - x)\right\}dx = \int_0^a x\sqrt{a^2 - x^2}\,dx - \int_0^a (ax - x^2)\,dx$

$$= \left[-\frac{(a^2 - x^2)^{\frac{3}{2}}}{3}\right]_0^a - \left(\frac{ax^2}{2} - \frac{x^3}{3}\right)_0^a = \frac{a^3}{3} - \left(\frac{a^3}{2} - \frac{a^3}{3}\right) = \frac{a^3}{6} \qquad \text{...(6)}$$

Denominator of $\bar{x} = \int_0^a \left\{\sqrt{a^2 - x^2} - (a - x)\right\}dx$

$$= \left[\frac{1}{2}x\sqrt{a^2 - x^2} + \frac{1}{2}a^2 \sin^2\left(\frac{x}{a}\right)\right]_0^a - \left(ax - \frac{x^2}{2}\right)_0^a = \frac{a^2}{2}\frac{\pi}{2} - \left(a^2 - \frac{a^2}{2}\right)$$

$$= \frac{a^2\pi}{4} - \frac{a^2}{2} = \frac{a^2(\pi - 2)}{4} \qquad \text{...(7)}$$

$$\therefore \qquad \bar{x} = \frac{\frac{a^3}{6}}{\frac{a^2(\pi - 2)}{4}} - \frac{2}{3}\frac{a}{(\pi - 2)} \qquad \text{...(8)}$$

Also, $$\bar{y} = \frac{\int y\,dm}{\int dm} = \frac{\int_0^a \left(\frac{y_1 + y_2}{2}\right)\rho(y_1 - y_2)\,dx}{\int_0^a \rho(y_1 - y_2)\,dx} = \frac{\frac{1}{2}\int_0^a (y_1^2 - y_2^2)\,dx}{\int_0^a (y_1 - y_2)\,dx} \qquad | \because \rho \text{ is uniform}$$

$$= \frac{\frac{1}{2}\int_0^a \left\{\frac{b^2}{a^2}(a^2 - x^2) - \frac{b^2}{a^2}(a - x)^2\right\}dx}{\int_0^a \left\{\frac{b}{a}\sqrt{a^2 - x^2} - \frac{b}{a}(a - x)\right\}dx} \qquad | \text{From (3) and (4)}$$

$$= \frac{\frac{b}{2a}\int_0^a \left\{\left(a^2 - x^2\right) - (a - x)^2\right\} dx}{\int_0^a \left\{\sqrt{a^2 - x^2} - (a - x)\right\} dx} \quad ...(9)$$

Numerator of $\bar{y} = \frac{b}{2a}\int_0^a \left\{\left(a^2 - x^2\right) - (a - x)^2\right\} dx$

$$= \frac{b}{2a}\int_0^a \left(-2x^2 + 2ax\right) dx$$

$$= \frac{b}{a}\int_0^a \left(ax - x^2\right) dx = \frac{b}{a}\left(\frac{ax^2}{2} - \frac{x^3}{3}\right)_0^a$$

$$= \frac{b}{a}\frac{a^3}{6} = \frac{a^2 b}{6} \quad ...(10)$$

Denominator of $\bar{y}$ = Denominator of $\bar{x}$

$$= \frac{a^2(\pi - 2)}{4} \quad ...(11)$$

$$\therefore \quad \bar{y} = \frac{a^2 b}{6} \cdot \frac{4}{a^2(\pi - 2)} = \frac{2b}{3(\pi - 2)} \quad ...(12)$$

Hence, the required C.G. given by

$$\bar{x} = \frac{2a}{3(\pi - 2)}, \quad \bar{y} = \frac{2b}{3(\pi - 2)}$$

**Example 4:** Find the position of the centre of gravity of the area enclosed by the curves $y^2 = ax$ and $y^2 = 2ax - x^2$ on the positive side of the X-axis.

**Sol.** Equation of the first curve is

$$y^2 = ax \quad ...(1)$$

It represents a parabola.

Equation of the second curve is

$$y^2 = 2ax - x^2 \quad ...(2)$$

$$\Rightarrow \quad (x - a)^2 + y^2 = a^2$$

It represents a circle whose centre is $(a, 0)$ and radius is $a$.

Solving equations (1) and (2), we find that the two curves intersect at O(0, 0) and $A(a, a)$. Therefore, limits of integration for $x$ are from $x = 0$ to $x = a$.

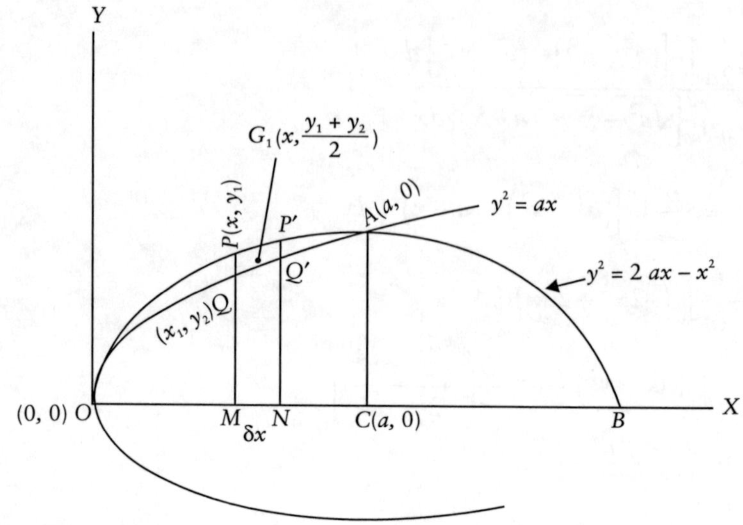


We are to find the C.G. of the area enclosed by the curves (1) and (2). Let the coordinates of $P$ and $Q$ be $(x, y_1)$ and $(x, y_2)$ respectively. Then,

$$y_1^2 = 2ax - x^2 \qquad \text{...(3)}$$

and

$$y_2^2 = ax \qquad \text{...(4)}$$

Take a neighbouring point $P'$ on (1) and draw perpendicular $P'N$ from $P'$ on $OX$ intersecting (2) in $Q'$. Let $MN = \delta x$.

Elementary area $PP'Q'Q = (y_1 - y_2)\delta x$

$\therefore$ Elementary mass $\delta m = \rho\,(y_1 - y_2)\,\delta x$, where $\rho$ is mass per unit area.

Also, C.G. of the elementary area $PP'Q'Q$ is at $\left(x, \dfrac{x_1 + y_2}{2}\right)$ as $\delta x$ is very small.

Let the required C.G. be $(\bar{x}, \bar{y})$. Then,

$$\bar{x} = \frac{\int x\,dm}{\int dm} = \frac{\int_0^a x\rho(y_1 - y_2)\,dx}{\int_0^a \rho(y_1 - y_2)\,dx}$$

$$= \frac{\int_0^a x(y_1 - y_2)\,dx}{\int_0^a (y_1 - y_2)\,dx} \qquad |\because \rho \text{ is uniform}$$

$$= \frac{\int_0^a x\left(\sqrt{2ax - x^2} - \sqrt{ax}\right)dx}{\int_0^a \left(\sqrt{2ax - x^2} - \sqrt{ax}\right)dx} \qquad |\text{From (3) and (4)} \qquad \text{...(5)}$$

Numerator of $\bar{x} = \int_0^a x\left(\sqrt{2ax - x^2} - \sqrt{ax}\right)dx = \int_0^a x\sqrt{2ax - x^2}\,dx - \sqrt{a}\int_0^a x^{\frac{3}{2}}\,dx$

$$= \int_0^a x\sqrt{a^2-(a-x)^2}\,dx - \frac{2}{5}\sqrt{a}\left(x^{\frac{5}{2}}\right)_0^a = \int_0^a x\sqrt{a^2-(a-x)^2}\,dx - \frac{2a^3}{5}$$

Put $a - x = a\sin\theta$
$\therefore -dx = a\cos\theta\, d\theta$
$\Rightarrow dx = -a\cos\theta\, d\theta$

$$= \int_{\frac{\pi}{2}}^0 a(1-\sin\theta)\sqrt{a^2-a^2\sin^2\theta}\,(-a\cos\theta\, d\theta) - \frac{2a^3}{5}$$

$$= a^3\int_0^{\pi/2}(1-\sin\theta)\cos^2\theta\, d\theta - \frac{2a^3}{5}$$

$$= a^3\left[\int_0^{\pi/2}\cos^2 d\theta - \int_0^{\pi/2}\sin\theta\cos^2\theta\, d\theta\right] - \frac{2a^3}{5}$$

$$= a^3\left[\frac{1}{2}\frac{\pi}{2} + \left(\frac{\cos^3\theta}{3}\right)_0^{\pi/2}\right] - \frac{2a^3}{5}$$ | By Walli's Formula

$$= a^3\left[\frac{\pi}{4}-\frac{1}{3}\right] - \frac{2a^3}{5} = a^3\left(\frac{\pi}{4}-\frac{1}{3}-\frac{2}{5}\right) = a^3\left(\frac{\pi}{4}-\frac{11}{15}\right)$$

$$= \frac{(15\pi-44)a^3}{60} \quad \text{...(6)}$$

Denominator of $\bar{x} = \int_0^a\left(\sqrt{2ax-x^2}-\sqrt{ax}\right)dx = \int_0^a\sqrt{a^2-(a-x)^2}\,dx - \sqrt{a}\frac{2}{3}\left(x^{\frac{3}{2}}\right)_0^a$

$$= \int_0^a\sqrt{a^2-(a-x)^2}\,dx - \frac{2}{3}a^2$$

Put $a - x = a\sin\theta$
$\therefore -dx = a\cos\theta\, d\theta$
$\Rightarrow dx = -a\cos\theta\, d\theta$

$$= \int_{\frac{\pi}{2}}^0\sqrt{a^2-a^2\sin^2\theta}\,(-a\cos\theta)d\theta - \frac{2}{3}a^2 = \int_0^{\frac{\pi}{2}} a^2\cos^2\theta\, d\theta - \frac{2a^2}{3}$$

$$= a^2\frac{\pi}{4} - \frac{2a^2}{3}$$ | By Walli's Formula

$$= \left(\frac{3\pi-8}{12}\right)a^2 \quad \text{...(7)}$$

$$\therefore \quad \bar{x} = \frac{\frac{(15\pi-44)a^3}{60}}{\left(\frac{3\pi-8}{12}\right)a^2} = \left(\frac{15\pi-44}{3\pi-8}\right)\frac{a}{5} \quad \text{...(8)}$$

Also, $\bar{y} = \dfrac{\int y\,dm}{\int dm} = \dfrac{\int_0^a \left(\dfrac{y_1+y_2}{2}\right)\rho(y_1-y_2)\,dx}{\int_0^a \rho(y_1-y_2)\,dx} = \dfrac{\frac{1}{2}\int_0^a (y_1+y_2)\,dx}{\int_0^a (y_1-y_2)\,dx}$ | $\because$ ρ is uniform

$$= \frac{\frac{1}{2}\int_0^a \left[\left(2ax-x^2\right)-ax\right]dx}{\left(\dfrac{3\pi-8}{12}\right)a^2}$$ | From (3), (4) and (7)

$$= \frac{\frac{1}{2}\int_0^a \left(ax-x^2\right)dx}{\left(\dfrac{3\pi-8}{12}\right)a^2} = \frac{6}{(3\pi-8)a^2}\int_0^a \left(ax-x^2\right)dx$$

$$= \frac{6}{(3\pi-8)a^2}\left[\frac{ax^2}{2}-\frac{x^3}{3}\right]_0^a = \frac{6}{(3\pi-8)a^2}\left(\frac{a^3}{2}-\frac{a^3}{3}\right) = \frac{a}{3\pi-8} \qquad ...(9)$$

Hence, the required C.G. is given by

$$\bar{x} = \left(\frac{15\pi-44}{3\pi-8}\right)\frac{a}{5},\ \bar{y} = \frac{a}{3\pi-8}.$$

**Example 5:** Find the C.G. of the area enclosed by the circle $x^2 + y^2 = a^2$ and the parabola $y^2 = 4ax$ on the positive side of the axis of $X$.

**Sol.**

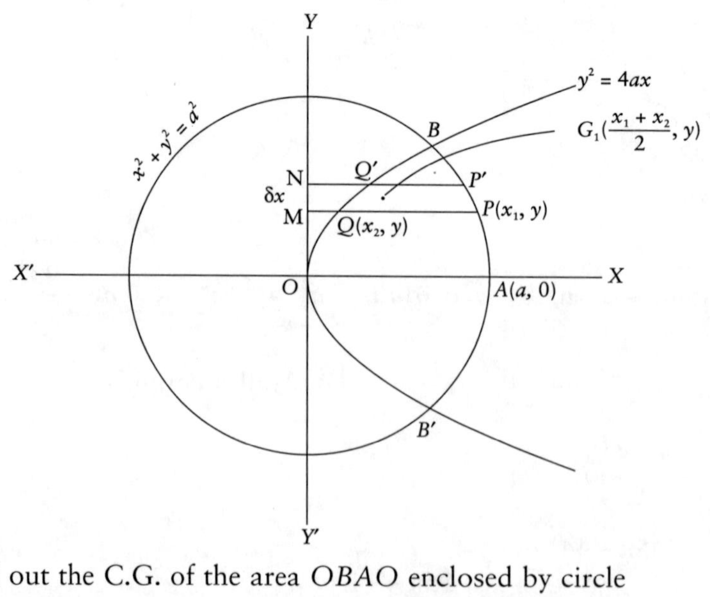


We are to find out the C.G. of the area *OBAO* enclosed by circle

$$x^2 + y^2 = a^2 \qquad ...(1)$$

and the parabola

$$y^2 = 4ax \qquad \text{...(2)}$$

on the positive side of the axis of X. Solving (1) and (2), we get

$$\frac{y^4}{16a^2} + y^2 = a^2 \quad \Rightarrow y^4 + 16a^2y^2 = 16a^4 \quad \Rightarrow (y^2 + 8a^2) = 80\,a^4$$

$$\Rightarrow \quad y^2 + 8a^2 = \pm 4\sqrt{5}\,a^2 \quad \Rightarrow y^2 = -8a^2 \pm 4\sqrt{5}\,a^2$$

$\Rightarrow \quad y^2 = -8a^2 + 4\sqrt{5}\,a^2$ neglecting negative sign as $y^2$ cannot be negative.

Hence, the $y$-coordinate of the points of intersection $B$ and $B'$ of (1) and (2) is given by

$$y^2 = -8a^2 + 4\sqrt{5}\,a^2$$

$$= 4a^2\left(\sqrt{5} - 2\right)$$

$$= b^2 \text{(say)} \qquad \text{...(3)}$$

Let the coordinates of $P$ and $Q$ be $(x_1, y)$ and $(x_2, y)$ respectively. Then,

$$x_1^2 + y^2 = a^2 \qquad \text{...(4)}$$

and $$y^2 = 4ax_2 \qquad \text{...(5)}$$

Take a neighbouring point $P'$ on (1) and draw perpendicular $P'N$ from $P'$ on $OY$ intersecting (2) in $Q'$. Let $MN = \delta y$

Elementary area $PP'\,Q'Q = (x_1 - x_2)\delta y$

$\therefore$ Elementary mass $\delta m = \rho(x_1 - x_2)\delta y$ where $\rho$ is mass per unit area.

Also, C.G. $G_1$ of the elementary area $PP'Q'Q$ is at $\left(\dfrac{x_1 + x_2}{2}, y\right)$

Let the required C.G. be $(\bar{x}, \bar{y})$. Then,

$$\bar{x} = \frac{\int x\,dm}{\int dm} = \frac{\int_0^b \frac{x_1 + x_2}{2}\rho(x_1 - x_2)\,dy}{\int_0^b \rho(x_1 - x_2)\,dy} = \frac{\frac{1}{2}\int_0^b \left(x_1^2 - x_2^2\right)dy}{\int_0^b (x_1 - x_2)\,dy} \qquad |\because \rho \text{ is uniform}$$

$$= \frac{\frac{1}{2}\int_0^b \left(a^2 - y^2 - \frac{y^4}{16a^2}\right)dy}{\int_0^b \left(\sqrt{a^2 - y^2} - \frac{y^2}{4a}\right)dy} = \frac{\frac{1}{2}\left[a^2y - \frac{y^3}{3} - \frac{y^5}{80a^2}\right]_0^b}{\left[\frac{1}{2}y\sqrt{a^2 - y^2} + \frac{1}{2}a^2\sin^{-1}\left(\frac{y}{a}\right) - \frac{y^3}{12a}\right]_0^b}$$

$$= \frac{\frac{1}{2}\left[a^2b - \frac{b^3}{3} - \frac{b^5}{80a^2}\right]}{\frac{1}{2}b\sqrt{a^2 - b^2} + \frac{1}{2}a^2\sin^{-1}\left(\frac{b}{a}\right) - \frac{b^3}{12a}}$$

$$= \frac{a^2 b - \frac{b^3}{3} - \frac{b^5}{80a^2}}{b\sqrt{a^2 - b^2} + a^2 \sin^{-1}\left(\frac{b}{a}\right) - \frac{b^3}{6a}} = \frac{\frac{b}{240a^2}\left[240a^4 - 80a^2 b^2 - 3b^4\right]}{b\sqrt{a^2 - b^2} + a^2 \sin^{-1}\left(\frac{b}{a}\right) - \frac{b^3}{6a}}$$

$$= \frac{b\left[240a^4 - 80a^2 b^2 - 3b^4\right]}{40a\left[6ab\sqrt{a^2 - b^2} + 6a^3 \sin^{-1}\left(\frac{b}{a}\right) - b^3\right]} \quad ...(6)$$

and $$\bar{y} = \frac{\int y\,dm}{\int dm} = \frac{\int_0^b y\rho(x_1 - x_2)\,dy}{\int_0^b \rho(x_1 - x_2)\,dy} = \frac{\int_0^b y(x_1 - x_2)\,dy}{\int_0^b (x_1 - x_2)\,dy} \quad | \because \rho \text{ is uniform}$$

$$= \frac{\int_0^b y\left(\sqrt{a^2 - y^2} - \frac{y^2}{4a}\right)dy}{\int_0^b \left(\sqrt{a^2 - y^2} - \frac{y^2}{4a}\right)dy} = \frac{\left[-\frac{1}{3}\left(a^2 - y^2\right)^{\frac{3}{2}} - \frac{y^4}{16a}\right]_0^b}{\frac{1}{2}b\sqrt{a^2 - b^2} + \frac{1}{2}a^2 \sin^{-1}\left(\frac{b}{a}\right) - \frac{b^3}{12a}} \quad | \text{From } \bar{x}$$

$$= \frac{\frac{1}{3}a^3 - \frac{1}{3}\left(a^2 - b^2\right)^{\frac{3}{2}} - \frac{b^4}{16a}}{\frac{1}{2}b\sqrt{a^2 - b^2} + \frac{1}{2}a^2 \sin^{-1}\left(\frac{b}{a}\right) - \frac{b^3}{12a}} = \frac{2\left[\frac{1}{3}a^3 - \frac{1}{3}\left(a^2 - b^2\right)^{\frac{3}{2}} - \frac{b^4}{16a}\right]}{b\sqrt{a^2 - b^2} + a^2 \sin^{-1}\left(\frac{b}{a}\right) - \frac{b^3}{6a}}$$

$$= \frac{16a^4 - 16a\left(a^2 - b^2\right)^{\frac{3}{2}} - b^4}{24a\left[b\sqrt{a^2 - b^2} + a^2 \sin^{-1}\left(\frac{b}{a}\right) - \frac{b^3}{6a}\right]} \quad | \text{where } b^2 = 4a^2\left(\sqrt{5} - 2\right) \text{ From [(3)]} \quad ...(7)$$

**Example 6:** Find the centre of gravity of the area between the arc of the semi-cycloid $x = a(\theta + \sin\theta)$ and $y = a(1 - \cos\theta)$ and the circumference of the circle $x^2 + y^2 - 2ay = 0$

**Sol.**

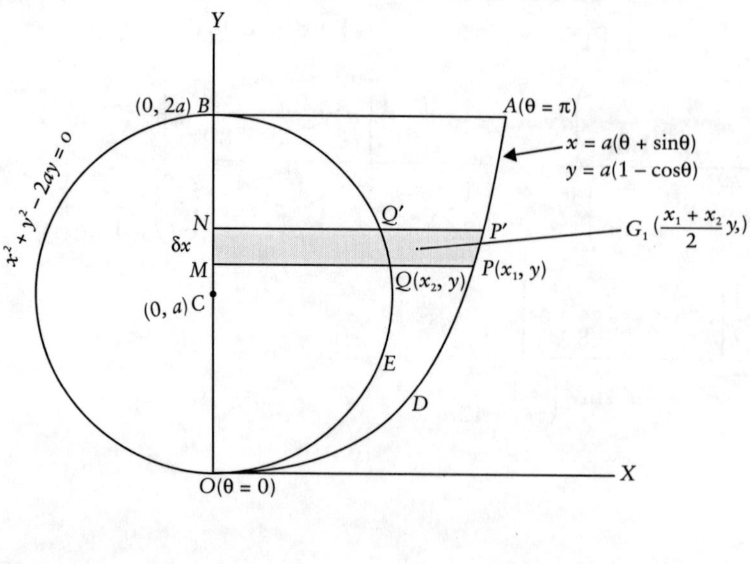

The parametric equation of the semi-cycloid are

$$x = a(\theta + \sin\theta) \quad \text{...(1)}$$

$$y = a(1 - \cos\theta) \quad \text{...(2)}$$

The given equation of the circle is

$$x^2 + y^2 - 2ay = 0$$

$$\Rightarrow \quad x^2 + (y - a)^2 = a^2 \quad \text{...(3)}$$

It represents a circle whose centre is $C(0, a)$ and radius is $a$.

The parametric equations of the circle (3) are

$$x = a \sin\theta \quad \text{...(4)}$$

$$y = a(1 - \cos\theta) \quad \text{...(5)}$$

The two curves meet at O (0, 0).

At O, $\theta = 0$

At $A$, $\theta = \pi$

We are to find the C.G. of the area $ODABEO$.

Let the coordinates of $P$ and $Q$ be $(x_1, y)$ and $(x_2, y)$ respectively. Then,

$$x_1 = a(\theta + \sin\theta) \quad \text{...(6)}$$

$$x_2 = a \sin\theta \quad \text{...(7)}$$

Take a neighbouring point $P'$ on the semi-cycloid and draw perpendicular $P'N$ from $P'$ on $OY$ intersecting the circle in $Q'$. Let $MN = \delta y$.

Elementary area $PP'Q'Q = (x_1 - x_2)\delta y$

$\therefore$ Elementary mass $\delta m = \rho\,(x_1 - x_2)\delta y$ where $\rho$ is the mass per unit area.

Also, C.G. $G_1$ of the elementary area $PP'Q'Q$ is at $\left(\frac{x_1 + x_2}{2}, y\right)$ as $\delta y$ is very small.

Let the required C.G. be $(\bar{x}, \bar{y})$. Then,

$$\bar{x} = \frac{\int x\,dm}{\int dm} = \frac{\int_{y=0}^{2a} \frac{x_1 + x_2}{2}\rho(x_1 - x_2)\,dy}{\int_{y=0}^{2a} \rho(x_1 - x_2)\,dy}$$

$$= \frac{\frac{1}{2}\int_0^{\pi}\left(x_1^2 - x_2^2\right)\frac{dy}{d\theta}\,d\theta}{\int_{y=0}^{2a}(x_1 - x_2)\frac{dy}{d\theta}\,d\theta} \qquad |\because \rho \text{ is uniform} \quad \text{...(8)}$$

$$\text{Numerator of } \bar{x} = \frac{1}{2}\int_0^{\pi}\left(x_1^2 - x_2^2\right)\frac{dy}{d\theta}\,d\theta = \frac{1}{2}\int_0^{\pi}\left[a^2(\theta + \sin\theta)^2 - a^2\sin^2\theta\right]a\sin\theta\,d\theta$$

$$= \frac{a^3}{2}\int_0^{\pi}\left(\theta^2 + 2\theta\sin\theta\right)\sin\theta\,d\theta = \frac{a^3}{2}\int_0^{\pi}\left(\theta^2\sin\theta + 2\theta\sin^2\theta\right)d\theta$$

$$= \frac{a^3}{2}\int_0^\pi \theta^2 \sin\theta \, d\theta + \frac{a^3}{2}\int_0^\pi \theta(1-\cos 2\theta)\, d\theta$$

$$= \frac{a^3}{2}\left[\left\{\theta^2(-\cos\theta)\right\}_0^\pi - \int_0^\pi 2\theta(-\cos\theta)\, d\theta\right] + \frac{a^3}{2}\int_0^\pi \theta \, d\theta - \frac{a^3}{2}\int_0^\pi \theta\cos 2\theta \, d\theta$$

$$= \frac{a^3}{2}\left[\pi^2 + 2\int_0^\pi \theta\cos\theta \, d\theta\right] + \frac{a^3}{2}\left(\frac{\theta^2}{2}\right)_0^\pi - \frac{a^3}{2}\left[\left(\theta\frac{\sin 2\theta}{2}\right)_0^\pi - \int_0^\pi \frac{\sin 2\theta}{2} d\theta\right]$$

$$= \frac{a^3}{2}\left[\pi \ + 2\{\theta\sin\theta\} \ - 2\int \ \sin\theta \ \ \theta\right] + \frac{a^3\pi^3}{4} + \frac{a^3}{4}\left(\frac{-\cos 2\theta}{2}\right)$$

$$= \frac{a^3}{2}\left[\pi^2 + 2(\cos\theta)_o^\pi\right] + \frac{a^3\pi^2}{4} = \frac{a^3}{2}(\pi^2 - 4) + \frac{a^3\pi^2}{4}$$

$$= \frac{a^3}{4}\left[2\pi^2 - 8 + \pi^2\right] = \frac{a^3(3\pi^2 - 8)}{4} \qquad ...(9)$$

Denominator of $\bar{x} = \int_0^\pi (x_1 - x_2)\frac{dy}{d\theta} d\theta = \int_0^\pi \left[a(\theta + \sin\theta) - a\sin\theta\right] a\sin\theta \, d\theta$

$$= a^2\int_0^\pi \theta\sin\theta \, d\theta = a^2\left[\left\{\theta(-\cos\theta)\right\}_0^\pi - \int_0^\pi (-\cos\theta)\, d\theta\right]$$

$$= a^2\pi \qquad ...(10)$$

$$\therefore \qquad \bar{x} = \frac{\dfrac{a^3(3\pi^2-8)}{4}}{a^2\pi} = \frac{(3\pi^2 - 8)a}{4\pi} \qquad ...(11)$$

Also, $\bar{y} = \dfrac{\int y\, dm}{\int dm} = \dfrac{\int_0^{2a} y\rho(x_1 - x_2)\, dy}{\int_0^{2a} \rho(x_1 - x_2)\, dy}$

$$= \frac{\int_0^{2a} y(x_1 - x_2)\, dy}{\int_0^{2a} (x_1 - x_2)\, dy} \qquad | \because \rho \text{ is uniform}$$

Denominator of $\bar{y} = \int_0^{2a} y(x_1 - x_2)\, dy$

$$= \int_0^\pi y(x_1 - x_2)\frac{dy}{d\theta} d\theta = \int_0^\pi a(1 - \cos\theta)\left[a(\theta + \sin\theta) - a\sin\theta\right] a\sin\theta \, d\theta$$

$$= a^3\int_0^\pi (1 - \cos\theta)\theta\sin\theta \, d\theta = a^3\int_0^\pi \theta\sin\theta \, d\theta - \frac{a^3}{2}\int_0^\pi \theta\sin 2\theta \, d\theta$$

$$= a^3\left[\left\{\theta(-\cos\theta)\right\}_0^\pi - \int_0^\pi (-\cos\theta)\, d\theta\right] - \frac{a^3}{2}\left[\left\{\theta\left(\frac{-\cos 2\theta}{2}\right)\right\}_0^\pi - \int_0^\pi \left(\frac{-\cos 2\theta}{2}\right) d\theta\right]$$

$$= a^3\pi - \frac{a^3}{2}\left[\frac{-\pi}{2}\right] = a^3\pi + \frac{a^3\pi}{4} = \frac{5a^3\pi}{4} \qquad ...(12)$$

Denominator of $\bar{y}$ = Denominator of $\bar{x} = a^2\pi$ | From (10) ...(13)

$$\therefore \quad \bar{y} = \frac{\frac{5a^3\pi}{4}}{a^2\pi} = \frac{5a}{4} \qquad ...(14)$$

Hence, the required C.G. is given by

$$\bar{x} = \frac{3\pi^2 - 8}{4\pi}, \quad \bar{y} = \frac{5a}{4}.$$

**Example 7:** A piece of wire of given length $\ell$ is bent into the form of a circular quadrant and its two bounding radii. Show that the distance of the C.G. of the whole from the centre of the circle is $\dfrac{6\sqrt{2}\,\ell}{(4+\pi)^2}$.

**Sol.** *OACBO* is a piece of wire of given length $\ell$ which is bent into the form of a circular quadrant *OAB* with its two bounding radii *OA* and *OB*.

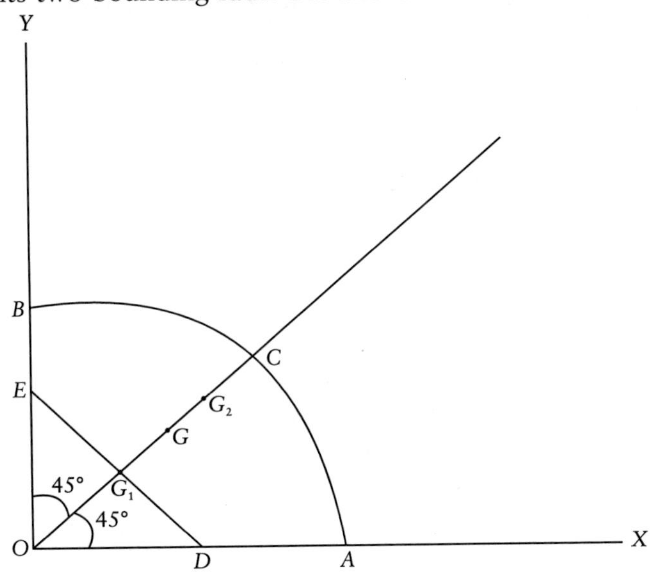


Let the radii of the quadrant OAB be $a$. Then,

$$\ell = OA + OB + \text{arc } ACB = a + a + \pi a/2$$
$$= 2a + \pi a/2 = a/2(\pi + 4) \qquad ...(1)$$

C.G. $G_2$ of the arc *ACB* lies on the symmetrical radius *OC* such that

$$OG_2 = \frac{a\sin\frac{\pi}{4}}{\frac{\pi}{4}} \qquad \Big| \text{From } \bar{x} = \frac{a\sin\alpha}{\alpha}$$

$$= \frac{2\sqrt{2}\,a}{\pi} = \frac{2\sqrt{2}}{\pi} \cdot \frac{2\ell}{\pi + 4} \qquad \text{| From (1)}$$

$$= \frac{4\sqrt{2}\,\ell}{\pi(\pi + 4)} \qquad \ldots(2)$$

C.G. of the straight portion $OA$ lies on the mid-point $D$ of $OA$.

C.G. of the straight portions $OB$ lies on the mid-point $E$ of $OB$.

∴ C.G. $G_1$ of the two portions $OA$ and $OB$ taken together lies on the symmetrical radius $OC$ such that

$$OG_1 = \frac{a}{2}\cos 45° \qquad \text{| By symmetry} = \frac{a}{2\sqrt{2}} = \frac{2\ell}{(\pi + 4)2\sqrt{2}} \qquad \text{| From (1)}$$

$$= \frac{\ell\sqrt{2}}{2(\pi + 4)} \qquad \ldots(3)$$

Let $G$ be the required C.G. Then, $G$ lies on the symmetrical radius $OC$ such that

$$OG = \frac{W_1 x_1 + W_2 x_2}{W_1 + W_2} \text{ where}$$

$W_1$ = combined weight of bounding radii $OA$ and $OB$

= $wa + wa$ where $w$ is weight per unit length

$$= 2wa = \frac{2w \cdot 2\ell}{\pi + 4} = \frac{4lw}{\pi + 4} \qquad \text{| From (1)}$$

$$x_1 = OG_1 = \frac{\ell\sqrt{2}}{2(\pi + 4)} \qquad \text{| From (3)}$$

$W_2$ = weight of the arc $ACB$

$$= \frac{\pi a}{2} w = \frac{\pi}{2} \cdot \frac{2\ell}{\pi + 4} w \qquad \text{| From (1)}$$

$$= \frac{\pi\ell}{\pi + 4} w \Rightarrow x_2 = OG_2 = \frac{4\sqrt{2}\,\ell}{\pi(\pi + 4)} \qquad \text{| From (2)}$$

$$\therefore \qquad OG = \frac{\frac{4\ell w}{\pi + 4} \cdot \frac{\ell\sqrt{2}}{2(\pi + 4)} + \frac{\pi \ell w}{\pi + 4} \cdot \frac{4\sqrt{2}\,\ell}{\pi(\pi + 4)}}{\frac{4\ell w}{\pi + 4} + \frac{\pi \ell w}{\pi + 4}} = \frac{\frac{2\sqrt{2}\,\ell^2 w}{(\pi + 4)^2} + \frac{4\sqrt{2}\,\ell^2}{(\pi + 4)^2}}{\frac{\ell w}{\pi + 4}(4 + \pi)}$$

$$= \frac{\frac{6\sqrt{2}\,\ell^2 w}{(\pi + 4)^2}}{lw} = \frac{6\sqrt{2}\,\ell}{(\pi + 4)^2}.$$

**Example 8:** A square hole is punched out of a circular lamina, the diagonal of the square being a radius of the circle. Show that the C.G. of the remainder is at a distance $\frac{a}{(8\pi - 4)}$ from the centre of the circle, where $a$ is the diameter of the circle.

**Sol.** Let $\rho$ be the surface density. Then,

$$m_1 = \text{mass of the circular lamina} = \pi\left(\frac{a}{2}\right)^2 \rho = \frac{\pi a^2 \rho}{4}$$

$x_1$ = distance of the C.G. of the circular lamina from O.

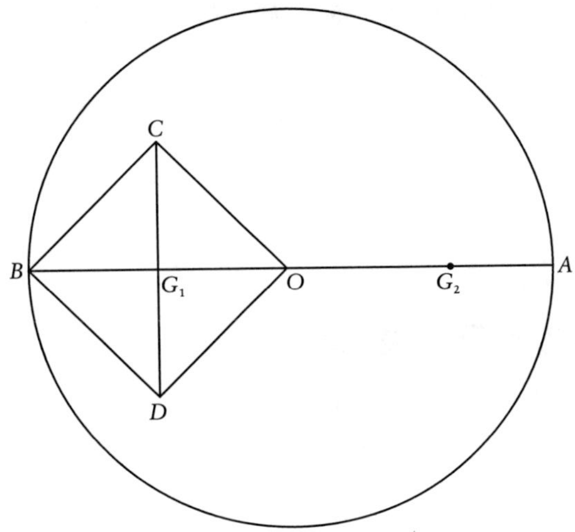


$= 0$ | By symmetry

$m_2$ = mass of the square hole

$$= \rho\left(\frac{OB}{\sqrt{2}}\right)^2 = \rho\left(\frac{a}{2\sqrt{2}}\right)^2 = \frac{a^2\rho}{8}$$

$x_2$ = distance of the C.G. of the square hole from O.

$$= OG_1 = \frac{OB}{2} = \frac{OA}{2} = \frac{\frac{a}{2}}{2} = \frac{a}{4}$$

Hence, the distance of the C.G. $G_2$ of the remainder from O

$$= OG_2 = \frac{m_1 x_1 - m_2 x_2}{m_1 - m_2} = \frac{\frac{\pi a^2 \rho}{4} \cdot 0 - \frac{a^2 \rho}{8}\frac{a}{4}}{\frac{\pi a^2 \rho}{4} - \frac{a^2 \rho}{8}}$$

$$= -\frac{a}{4(2\pi - 1)} = -\frac{a}{(8\pi - 4)}.$$

The negative sign shows that the C.G. lies on the side of O other than $B$, i.e., it lies on $OA$.

**Example 9:** Find the position of the centre of gravity of the area enclosed by the curves

$$x^2 + y^2 - 2ax = 0 \qquad \text{and } x^2 + y^2 - 2bx = 0$$

on the positive side of the $X$-axis.

**Sol.** The first curve is

$$x^2 + y^2 - 2ax = 0 \qquad \Rightarrow (x - a)^2 + y^2 = a^2$$

It represents a circle whose centre is $C(a, 0)$ and radius is $a$.

The second curve is

$$x^2 + y^2 - 2bx = 0 \ (x - b)^2 + y^2 = b^2$$

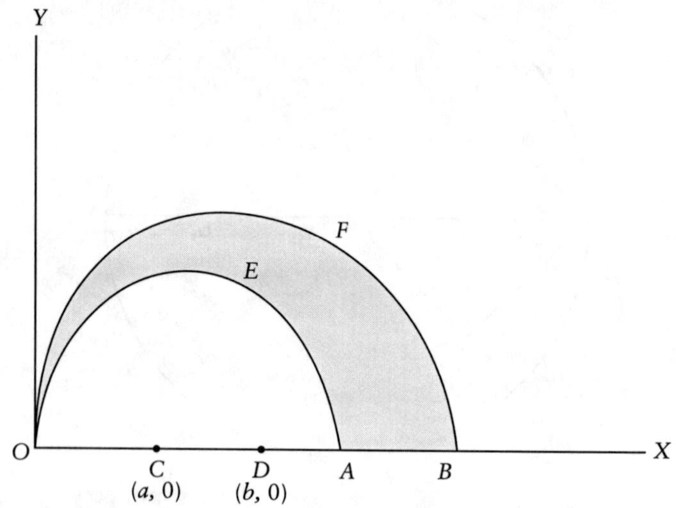


It represents a circle whose centre is $D(b, 0)$ and radius is $b$.

Assume that $b > a$.

Let $\rho$ be the surface density. Then,

$$m_1 = \text{mass of the semi-circle } OEA = \rho \cdot \frac{\pi a^2}{2}$$

Coordinates of its C.G. are $\left(a, \frac{4a}{3\pi}\right)$

so that $x_1 = a$ and $y_1 = \frac{4a}{3\pi}$

$$m_2 = \text{mass of the semi-circle } OFB = \rho \frac{\pi b^2}{2}$$

Coordinates of its C.G. are $\left(b, \frac{4b}{3\pi}\right)$ so that $x_2 = b$, $y_2 = \frac{4b}{3\pi}$

Let $(\bar{x}, \bar{y})$ be the required C.G. Then,

$$\bar{x}_2 = \frac{m_2x_2 - m_1x_1}{m_2 - m_2} = \frac{\rho\pi\frac{b^2}{2}b - \rho\pi\frac{a^2}{2}\cdot a}{\rho\pi\frac{b^2}{2} - \rho\pi\frac{a^2}{2}} = \frac{b^3 - a^3}{b^2 - a^2} = \frac{a^2 + ab + b^2}{a + b}$$

and $$\bar{y} = \frac{m_2y_2 - m_1y_1}{m_2 - m_1} = \frac{\rho\pi\frac{b^2}{2}\frac{4b}{3\pi} - \rho\pi\frac{a^2}{2}\frac{4a}{3\pi}}{\rho\pi\frac{b^2}{2} - \rho\pi\frac{a^2}{2}} = \frac{4}{3\pi}\frac{b^3 - a^3}{b^2 - a^2} = \frac{4}{3\pi}\cdot\frac{a^3 + ab + b^2}{a + b}$$

Hence, the required C.G. is given by

$$\bar{x} = \frac{a^2 + ab + b^2}{a + b}, \quad \bar{y} = \frac{4}{3\pi}\cdot\frac{a^2 + ab + b^2}{a + b}.$$

**Example 10:** Find the vertical angle of the cone in order that the centre of gravity of its whole surface including its plane base may coincide with centre of gravity of its volume.

**Sol.**

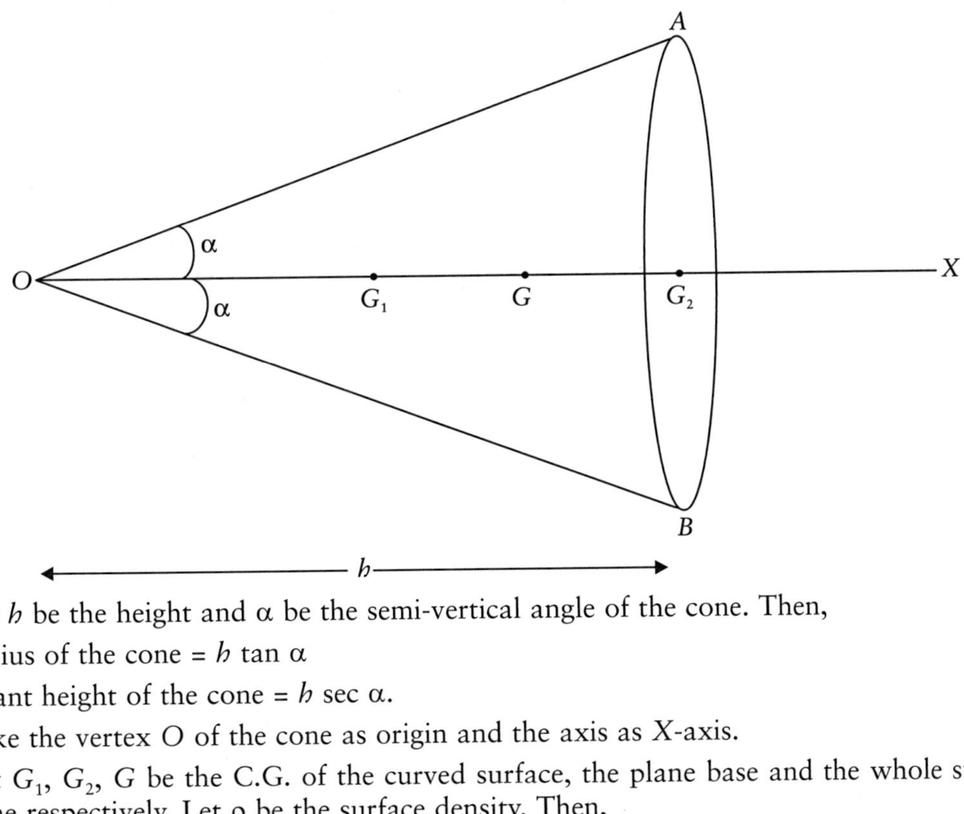


Let $h$ be the height and $\alpha$ be the semi-vertical angle of the cone. Then,

radius of the cone = $h \tan \alpha$

and, slant height of the cone = $h \sec \alpha$.

Take the vertex O of the cone as origin and the axis as $X$-axis.

Let $G_1$, $G_2$, $G$ be the C.G. of the curved surface, the plane base and the whole surface of the cone respectively. Let $\rho$ be the surface density. Then,

$$m_1 = \text{mass of the curved surface} = (\pi\, r\, \ell)\rho$$

$x_1$ = distance of the C.G. of the curved surface from vertex O

$= \frac{2}{3}h$. $\qquad m_2$ = mass of the plane base = $\pi r^2 \rho$

and $\quad x_2$ = distance of the C.G. of the plane base from vertex O = $h$

∴ Distance of C.G. of the whole surface from vertex O = $\bar{x}$

$$= \frac{m_1x_2 + m_2x_2}{m_1 + m_2} = \frac{(\pi r \ell)\rho \frac{2}{3}h + \pi r^2 \rho\, h}{(\pi r \ell)\rho + \pi r^2 \rho} = \frac{h\left(\frac{2}{3}\ell - r\right)}{\ell + r} \qquad ...(1)$$

Also, distance of the C.G. of the volume of the cone from vertex O. $= \frac{3}{4}h$ ...(2)

If the C.G. of the whole surface coincides with the C.G. of the volume, then the distances (1) and (2) will be the same.

$$\therefore \quad \frac{h\left(\frac{2}{3}\ell + r\right)}{\ell + r} = \frac{3}{4}h \quad \Rightarrow 4\left(\frac{2}{3}\ell + r\right) = 3(\ell + r) \quad \Rightarrow -\ell + 4r = 3\ell + 3r$$

$$\Rightarrow \quad r = \frac{1}{3}\ell \quad \Rightarrow h\tan\alpha = \frac{1}{3}h\sec\alpha \quad \Rightarrow \tan\alpha = \frac{\sec\alpha}{3}$$

$$\Rightarrow \quad \frac{\sin\alpha}{\cos\alpha} = \frac{1}{3\cos\alpha} \Rightarrow \sin\alpha = \frac{1}{3} \quad \Rightarrow \alpha = \sin^{-1}\left(\frac{1}{3}\right) \quad \Rightarrow 2\alpha = 2\sin^{-1}\left(\frac{1}{3}\right)$$

Hence, the vertical angle of the cone is given by $2\sin^{-1}\left(\frac{1}{3}\right)$.

**Example 11:** A solid right cone has its base scooped out so that the hollow is a right cone on the same base. How much must it be scooped out so that the C.G. of the remainder may coincide with the vertex of the latter?

**Sol.**

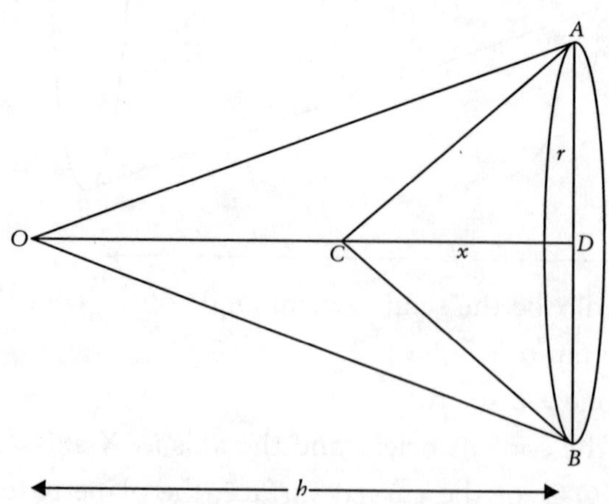


Let $h$ be the height of the bigger cone $AOB$. Let $x$ be the height of the cone $ACB$ scooped out from the bigger cone $AOB$. Let $r$ be the radius of the common base. Let $\rho$ be the surface density. If $\bar{x}$ is the distance of the C.G. of the remainder from C, then we have

$$\bar{x} = \frac{m_1 x_1 - m_2 x_2}{x_1 - x_2} \text{ where}$$

$m_1$ = Mass of the bigger cone $AOB = \left(\frac{1}{3}\pi r^2 h\right)\rho$

$x_1$ = distance of the C.G. of the bigger cone $AOB$ from $D = \frac{1}{4}h$

$m_2$ = mass of the smaller cone $ACB = \left(\frac{1}{3}\pi r^2 x\right)\rho$

and $x_2$ = distance of the C.G. of the smaller cone $ACB$ from $D = \frac{1}{4}x$

$$\therefore \quad \bar{x} = \frac{\left(\frac{1}{3}\pi r^2 h\right)\rho \frac{1}{4}h - \left(\frac{1}{3}\pi r^2 x\right)\rho \frac{1}{4}x}{\left(\frac{1}{3}\pi r^2 h\right)\rho - \left(\frac{1}{3}\pi r^2 x\right)\rho} = \frac{\frac{1}{4}(h^2 - x^2)}{h - x} = \frac{h + x}{4} \qquad | \because h \neq x$$

If the C.G. of the remainder coincides with the vertex $C$ of the smaller cone, then,

$$\bar{x} = x \Rightarrow \frac{h+x}{4} = \alpha \Rightarrow h + x = 4x \Rightarrow h = 3x \Rightarrow x = \frac{1}{3}h$$

Hence, the height of the cone scooped out is one-third of the height of the given cone.

**Example 12:** Show how to cut a cone out of a uniform cylinder whose base coincides with that of the cylinder, so that the centre of gravity of the remaining solid many coincide with the vertex of the cone?

**Sol.**

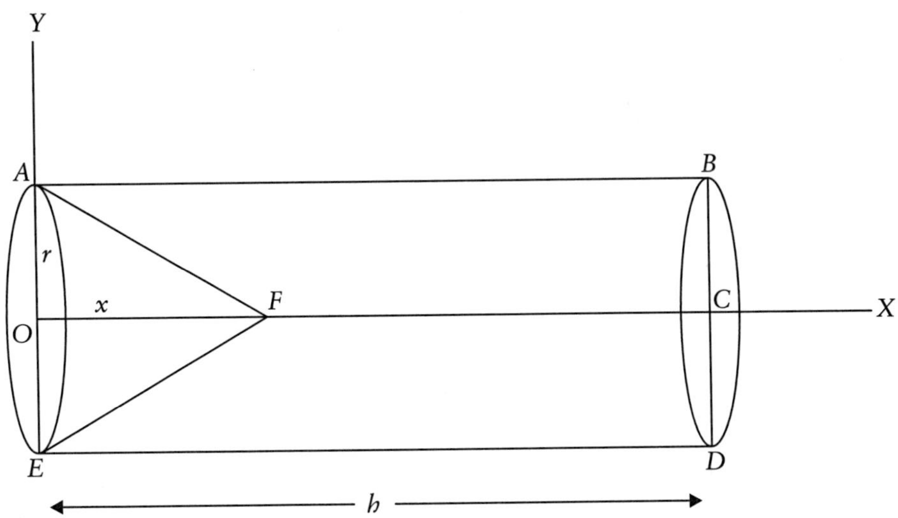


Let $r$ be the radius of the base of the cylinder. Let $h$ be its height. Let $x$ be the height of the cone $FAE$ cut out.

Take O as origin, the axis $OFC$ of the cylinder as $X$-axis and a line $OY$ through O and perpendicular to $X$-axis as the $Y$-axis. Let $\rho$ be the surface density.

Let $\overline{x}$ be the distance of the C.G. of the remaining solid from O. Then,

$$\overline{x} = \frac{m_1x_1 - m_2x_2}{m_1 - m_2} \quad \text{where} \qquad m_1 = \text{mass of the cylinder} = \pi\, r^2\, h\, \rho$$

$$x_1 = \text{distance of the C.G. of the cylinder from O.} = \frac{1}{2}h$$

$$m_2 = \text{mass of the cone } FAE \text{ cut out} = \frac{1}{3}\pi r^2 x\rho$$

and $$x_2 = \text{distance of the C.G. of the cone } FAE \text{ cut out} = \frac{1}{4}x$$

$$\therefore \qquad \overline{x} = \frac{(\pi r^2 h)\rho\frac{1}{2}h - \left(\frac{1}{3}\pi r^2 x\right)\rho\frac{1}{4}x}{(\pi r^2 h)\rho - \left(\frac{1}{3}\pi r^2 x\right)\rho} = \frac{\frac{1}{2}h^2 - \frac{1}{12}x^2}{h - \frac{1}{3}x} = \frac{6h^2 - x^2}{12h - 4x}.$$

If the C.G. of the remaining solid coincides with $F$, the vertex of the cone, then

$$\overline{x} = x \;\Rightarrow\; \frac{6h^2 - x^2}{12h - 4x} = x \Rightarrow 6h^2 - x^2 = 12hx - 4x^2 \Rightarrow x^2 - 4hx + 2h^2 = 0$$

$$\therefore \qquad x = \frac{4h \pm \sqrt{16x^2 - 8a^2}}{2} = \frac{4h \pm 2\sqrt{2}\,h}{2} = \left(2 \pm \sqrt{2}\right)h$$

Discarding the +ve sign as $x < h$, we get $x = \left(2 - \sqrt{2}\right)h$

Hence, the height of the cone cut out is $\left(2 - \sqrt{2}\right)$ times the height of the cylinder.

**Example 13:** A body consists of a cone and a hemisphere on the same base. Find the position of the C.G. of the solid formed.

Also, find the semi-vertical angle of the cone, so that the centre of gravity may be at the centre of the base.

**Sol.**

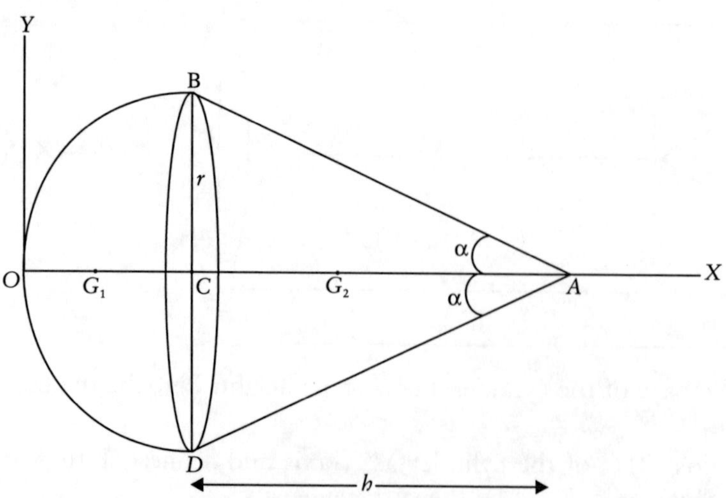

Let $ABODA$ be a body consisting of a cone and a hemisphere on the same base $BD$.

Let $r$ be radius of the hemisphere and $h$ be the height of the cone $ABD$. Let $\rho$ be the surface density.

Let $\bar{x}$ be the distance of the C.G. of the body from O. Then, $\bar{x} = \dfrac{W_1x_1 + W_2x_2}{W_1 + W_2}$ where

$$W_1 = \text{weight of the hemisphere } OBDO = \frac{2}{3}\pi r^3 \rho g$$

$$x_1 = \text{distance of the C.G. of the hemisphere } OBDO \text{ from } O$$

$$= \frac{5}{8}r \qquad \left|\; \because OG_1 = OC - G_1C = r - \frac{3}{8}r = \frac{5}{8}r \right.$$

$$W_2 = \text{weight of the solid cone} = \frac{1}{3}\pi r^2 h\, \rho g$$

and $x_2$ = distance of the C.G. of the solid cone from O.

$$= OC + \frac{1}{4}h = r + \frac{1}{4}h$$

$$\therefore \quad \bar{x} = \frac{\left(\frac{2}{3}\pi r^3 \rho g\right)\frac{5}{8}r + \left(\frac{1}{3}\pi r^2 h\, \rho g\right)\left(r + \frac{1}{4}h\right)}{\left(\frac{2}{3}\pi r^3 \rho g\right) + \left(\frac{1}{3}\pi r^2 h\, \rho g\right)}$$

$$= \frac{\frac{5}{4}r^2 + h\left(r + \frac{1}{4}h\right)}{2r + h} = \frac{5r^2 + 4hr + h^2}{4(2r + h)}.$$

**Second Part**

If the C.G. of the body is at the centre of the base, then, $\bar{x} = r$

$$\Rightarrow \quad \frac{5r^2 + 4hr + h^2}{4(2r + h)} = r \quad \Rightarrow 5r^2 + 4hr + h^2 = 8r^2 + 4hr \quad \Rightarrow h^2 = 3r^2$$

$$\Rightarrow \quad \frac{r^2}{h^2} = \frac{1}{3} \quad \Rightarrow \frac{r}{h} = \frac{1}{\sqrt{3}} \quad \Rightarrow \tan\alpha = \frac{1}{\sqrt{3}}$$

$$\Rightarrow \quad \tan\alpha = \tan 30^\circ \quad \Rightarrow \alpha = 30^\circ$$

Hence, the semi-vertical angle of the cone in this case is 30°.

**Example 14:** Two tangents are drawn to a circle of a radius a subtending an angle 2α at the centre. Prove that the C.G. of the area bounded by the tangents and the smaller arc between them is at a distance from the centre equal to $\frac{a}{3}\cdot\frac{\tan^2\alpha\sin\alpha}{\tan\alpha-\alpha}$.

**Sol.**

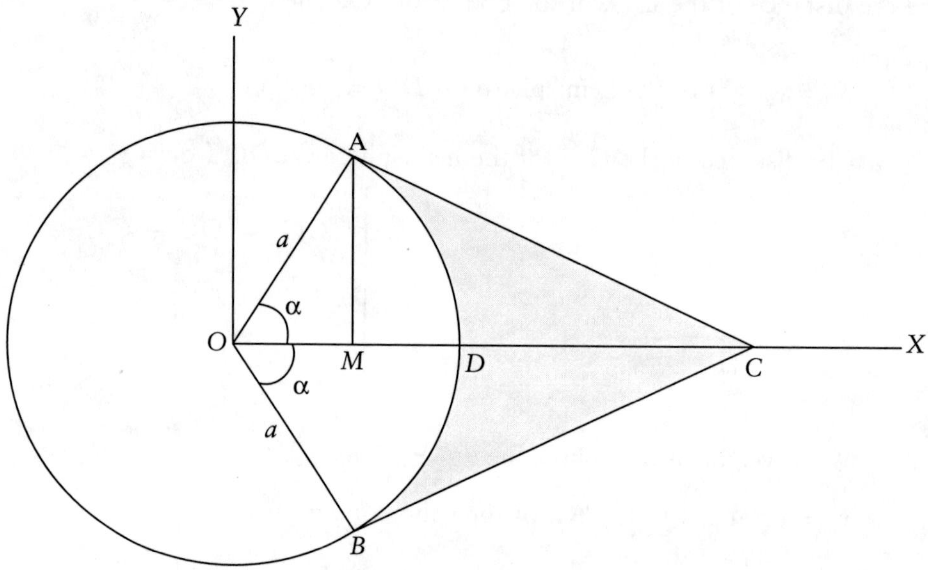


We are required to find out the C.G. of the shaded area as shown in the figure. Take $O$ as origin, $OC$ as $X$-axis and a line through $O$ perpendicular to $OC$ as $Y$-axis. Let the radius of the circle be $a$. By symmetry, the C.G. will lie on $OC$.

Shaded area = Area of $\Delta OAC$ + Area of $\Delta OBC$ – Area of sector $OADBO$

Area of $\Delta OAC = \frac{1}{2}\cdot OA\cdot AC = \frac{1}{2}\cdot a\cdot a\tan\alpha = \frac{a^2\tan\alpha}{2}$ = Area of $\Delta OBC$

Area of sector $OADBO = a^2\alpha$

Let ρ be the surface density. Then, $m_1$ = Sum of the masses of $\Delta OAC$ and $\Delta OBC$

$$= \left(\frac{1}{2}a^2\tan\alpha+\frac{1}{2}a^2\tan\alpha\right)\rho = (a^2\tan\alpha)\rho$$

By symmetry, the distance of the C.G. of the whole figure $OACBO$ from $OY$ = Distance of the C.G. of $\Delta OAC$ from $OY$.

Let the abscissae of the vertices O, A, C of $\Delta OAC$ be $x_1$, $x_2$, $x_3$ respectively. Then,

$z_1$ = distance of the C.G. of the whole area $OACBO$ from $OY$.

= distance of C.G. of $\Delta OAC$ from $OY$.

$$= \frac{1}{3}(x_1+x_2+x_3) = \frac{1}{3}(0+OM+OC) = \frac{1}{3}(0+a\cos\alpha+a\sec\alpha)$$

$$= \frac{1}{3}a(\cos\alpha+\sec\alpha)$$ $m_2$ = mass of the sectorial area $OADBO = (a^2\alpha)\rho$

and $\quad z_2$ = distance of the C.G. of the sectorial area from $OY = \dfrac{2}{3}\dfrac{a\sin\alpha}{\alpha}$

Let $\overline{x}$ be distance of the required C.G. from $OY$. Then,

$$\overline{x} = \frac{m_1 z_1 - m_2 z_2}{m_1 - m_2} = \frac{\left(a^2\tan\alpha\right)\rho\,\frac{1}{3}a(\cos\alpha+\sec\alpha) - \left(a^2\alpha\right)\rho\,\frac{2}{3}\frac{a\sin\alpha}{\alpha}}{\left(a^2\tan\alpha\right)\rho - \left(a^2\alpha\right)\rho} = \frac{a}{3}\frac{\tan\alpha(\cos\alpha+\sec\alpha) - 2\sin\alpha}{\tan\alpha - \alpha}$$

$$= \frac{\frac{a}{3}\left\{\frac{\sin\alpha}{\cos\alpha}\left(\cos\alpha + \frac{1}{\cos\alpha}\right) - 2\sin\alpha\right\}}{\tan\alpha - \alpha} = \frac{\frac{a\sin\alpha}{3\cos^2\alpha}\left\{\left(\cos^2\alpha + 1\right) - 2\cos^2\alpha\right\}}{\tan\alpha - \alpha}$$

$$= \frac{\frac{a\sin\alpha}{3\cos^2\alpha}\left(1 - \cos^2\alpha\right)}{\tan\alpha - \alpha} = \frac{\frac{a}{3}\frac{\sin\alpha}{\cos^2\alpha}\sin^2\alpha}{\tan\alpha - \alpha} = \frac{a\tan^2\alpha\sin\alpha}{3(\tan\alpha - \alpha)}$$

Hence, the required distance is

$$\frac{a\tan^2\alpha\sin\alpha}{3(\tan\alpha - \alpha)}.$$

**Example 15:** A sphere of radius $a$ is inscribed in a cone of vertical angle $2\alpha$. Show that the distance between the centre of the sphere and the centre of gravity of that part of the volume of the cone which lies between its vertex and the nearer part of the surface of the sphere is $\dfrac{a(1+\sin\alpha)^2}{4\sin\alpha}$.

**Sol.**

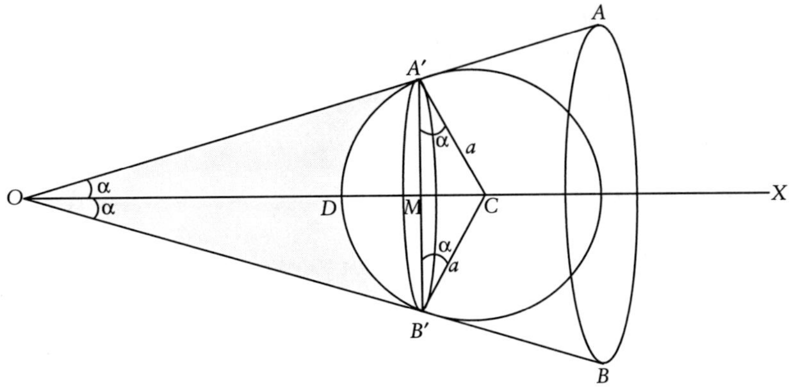


Let $a$ be the radius of the sphere whose centre is $C$. $OA'DB'O$ is the part of the volume of the cone which lies between its vertex O and the nearer part $A'DB'$ of the surface of the sphere. By symmetry, the C.G. of this part of volume of the cone will lie on $OX$.

Let ρ be the surface density.

**For smaller cone *OA′B′***

Radius of the base = $A'M = a\cos\alpha$

Height $OM = OA'\cos\alpha = a\cot\alpha\cos\alpha$

$\therefore$ $m_1$ = mass of the smaller cone $OA'B'$

$$= \frac{1}{3}\pi(a\cos\alpha)^2\, a\cot\alpha\cos\alpha\,\rho = \frac{1}{3}\pi a^3\cos^3\alpha\cot\alpha\,\rho$$

$x_1$ = distance of the C.G. of the smaller cone $OA'B'$ from $C$

$$= CM + \frac{1}{4}OM$$

| ∵ C.G. of the solid cone divides the axis in the ratio 3 : 1 from the vertex

$$= a\sin\alpha + \frac{1}{4}a\cot\alpha\cos\alpha$$

$m_2$ = mass of the segment $A'DB$ of the sphere

$$= \pi h^2\left(a - \frac{1}{3}h\right)\rho \text{ where } h \text{ is the height of the segment}$$

$$= \pi\,(a - a\sin\alpha)^2\left\{a - \frac{1}{3}(a - a\sin\alpha)\right\}\rho \qquad \Big|\because h = a - a\sin\alpha$$

$$= \frac{1}{3}\pi a^3(1-\sin\alpha)^2(2+\sin\alpha)\rho$$

and $x_2$ = Distance of the C.G. of the segment $A'DB'$ from $C$

$$= \frac{3}{4}\frac{(2a-h)^2}{3a-h} = \frac{3a}{4}\frac{(1+\sin\alpha)^2}{2+\sin\alpha} \qquad \Big|\because h = a - a\sin\alpha$$

Let $\bar{x}$ be the distance of the required C.G. from $C$. Then,

$$\bar{x} = \frac{m_1x_1 - m_2x_2}{m_1 - m_2} \qquad \text{...(1)}$$

Numerator of $\bar{x} = m_1x_1 - m_2x_2$

$$= \frac{1}{3}\pi a^3\cos^3\alpha\cot\alpha\,\rho\left\{a\sin\alpha + \frac{1}{4}a\cot\alpha\cos\alpha\right\}$$

$$-\frac{1}{3}\pi a^3(1-\sin\alpha)^2(2+\sin\alpha)\rho\left\{\frac{3a}{4}\frac{(1+\sin\alpha)^2}{2+\sin\alpha}\right\}$$

$$= \frac{\pi a^4\cos^4\alpha}{3\sin\alpha}\left\{\frac{4\sin^2\alpha+\cos^2\alpha}{4\sin\alpha}\right\}\rho - \frac{\pi a^4}{4}\cos^4\alpha\,\rho$$

$$= \frac{\pi a^4 \cos^4 \alpha \rho}{4} \left\{ \frac{4\sin^2 \alpha + \cos^2 \alpha}{3\sin^2 \alpha} - 1 \right\} = \frac{\pi a^4 \cos^4 \alpha \rho}{12 \sin^2 \alpha} \quad \text{...(2)}$$

Denominator of $\bar{x} = \frac{1}{3}\pi a^3 \cos^3 \alpha \cot \alpha \rho - \frac{1}{3}\pi a^3 (1-\sin\alpha)^2 (2+\sin\alpha)\rho$

$$= \frac{\pi a^3}{3}\left[\cos^3 \alpha \cot \alpha - \left(2 - 3\sin\alpha + \sin^3 \alpha\right)\right]\rho$$

$$= \frac{\pi a^3}{3\sin\alpha}\left[\cos^4 \alpha - 2\sin\alpha + 3\sin^2 \alpha - \sin^4 \alpha\right]\rho$$

$$= \frac{\pi a^3}{3\sin\alpha}\left[\left(\cos^2 \alpha - \sin^2 \alpha\right)\left(\cos^2 \alpha + \sin^2 \alpha\right) - 2\sin\alpha + 3\sin^2 \alpha\right]\rho$$

$$= \frac{\pi a^3}{3\sin\alpha}\left[\cos^2 \alpha - \sin^2 \alpha - 2\sin\alpha + 3\sin^2 \alpha\right]\rho$$

$$= \frac{\pi a^3}{3\sin\alpha}\left[\cos^2 \alpha + 2\sin^2 \alpha - 2\sin\alpha\right]\rho = \frac{\pi a^3}{3\sin\alpha}\left[1 - 2\sin\alpha + \sin^2 \alpha\right]\rho$$

$$= \frac{\pi a^3 (1-\sin\alpha)^2}{3\sin\alpha}\rho \quad \text{...(3)}$$

$$\therefore \quad \bar{x} = \frac{\pi a^4 \cos^4 \alpha\rho}{12\sin^2 \alpha} \cdot \frac{3\sin\alpha}{\pi a^3 (1-\sin\alpha)^2 \rho} = \frac{a}{4}\frac{\left(1-\sin^2 \alpha\right)^2}{\sin\alpha(1-\sin\alpha)^2} \quad \left|\because \cos^2\alpha = 1 - \sin^2\alpha\right.$$

$$= \frac{a(1+\sin\alpha)^2}{4\sin\alpha}$$

## EXERCISE 2(E)

1. Find the locus of the centroid of the area of the parabola $y^2 = 4ax$ cut off by a variable straight line passing through the vertex.

   [**Ans.** $y^2 = 5/2ax$, which is a parabola]

   [**Hint:** Refer Ex. 1

   $$\bar{x} = \frac{8a}{5m^2}, \quad \bar{y} = \frac{2a}{m}$$

   Eliminate $m$, we get $\bar{y}^2 = \frac{5}{2}a\bar{x}$

   Hence, the locus]

2. Find the C.G. of a thin homogeneous plate covering the area enclosed by the curves $y^2 = 8x$ and $x^2 = y$.

   [**Ans.** $\bar{x} = 9/10$, $\bar{y} = 9/5$]

3. Find the C.G. of the area enclosed by the curves $y^2 = 4ax$ and $x^2 = 4by$.
[**Ans.** $\bar{x} = 9/5a^{1/3}b^{2/3}$, $\bar{y} = 9/5\ a^{2/3}b^{1/3}$]
4. Find the C.G. of the area bounded by the parabola $y^2 = 8x$ and $x^2 = 8y$.
[**Ans.** $\bar{x} = 18/5 = \bar{y}$]
5. Find the position of the centroid of the area enclosed by the parabolas $y^2 = x$ and $x^2 = 2y$.
[**Ans.** $\bar{x} = 9/20\ (2)^{2/3}$, $\bar{y} = 9/20\ (2)^{1/3}$]
6. Find the centre of gravity of the volume formed by revolving the area bounded by the parabolas $y^2 = 4ax$ and $x^2 = 4by$ about the axis of $X$.
[**Ans.** $\bar{x} = 20/9a^{1/3}b^{2/3}$, $\bar{y} = 0$]

[**Hint:** $\bar{x} = \dfrac{\int_0^{4a^{\frac{1}{3}}b^{\frac{2}{3}}} x\left(y_1^2 - y_2^2\right)dx}{\int_0^{4a^{\frac{1}{3}}b^{\frac{2}{3}}} \left(y_1^2 - y_2^2\right)dx}$ where $y_1^2 = 4ax$ and $x^2 = 4by_2$]

7. A uniform bowl has for its inner and outer surfaces concentric hemispheres of radii $a$ and $b$. Prove that the distance of its centre of gravity from the geometric centre is $\dfrac{3}{8}\dfrac{(a+b)(a^2+b^2)}{a^2+ab+b^2}$.
[**Hint:** Required distance

$$= \frac{\left(\frac{2}{3}\pi a^3 \rho g\right)\left(\frac{3a}{8}\right) - \left(\frac{2}{3}\pi b^3 \rho g\right)\left(\frac{3b}{8}\right)}{\frac{2}{3}\pi a^3 \rho g - \frac{2}{3}\pi b^3 \rho g}]$$

8. From a circular disc of radius $r$, is cut out a circle described on a radius of the disc as diameter. Find the centre of gravity of the remainder.
[**Ans.** C.G. lies on the negative side of $X$-axis at a distance $r/6$ from the centre]
9. A bowl in the shape of a spherical segment is 18 inches deep and 4 feet in diameter at the top. It is filled with water to a depth of 15 inches. Find the centre of gravity of the bowl and water assuming the surface density of the material of the bowl to be 8.75 times that of water.
[**Ans.** C.G. lies on the symmetrical radius 35/4 inches below the top of the bowl]

## 11. Centre of Gravity when Density Varies

When the density $\rho$ is not uniform, i.e., when $\rho$ varies from point to point, we cannot cancel $\rho$ from the integrals occurring is the numerator and the denominator of $\bar{x}$ and $\bar{y}$. Also, in this case if the body is in the form of a plane lamina, we cannot consider the elementary area in the form of a strip since we cannot find out the elementary mass. To solve the purpose we divide the lamina into infinitesimally small elements of the second order and evaluate the numerators and the denominators of $\bar{x}$ and $\bar{y}$ by making use of double integrals. The procedure adopted has been explained below:

(i) **In Cartesian coordinates**

In the case of Cartesian curves, we consider an infinitesimally small element $\delta x\ \delta y$ at any point $P(x, y)$ lying in the area whose C.G. is to be determined. This elementary area is included between two very close lines parallel to $X$-axis and $Y$-axis through two neighbouring points $P(x, y)$ and $Q(x + \delta x, y + \delta y)$. Let $\rho$ be the density at the point $P$. Then, the mass $\delta m$ of the elementary area $\delta x\ \delta y$ can be taken as $\rho \delta x\ \delta y$ as the density at every point of this elementary area can be taken as the same as that at the point P$(x, y)$.

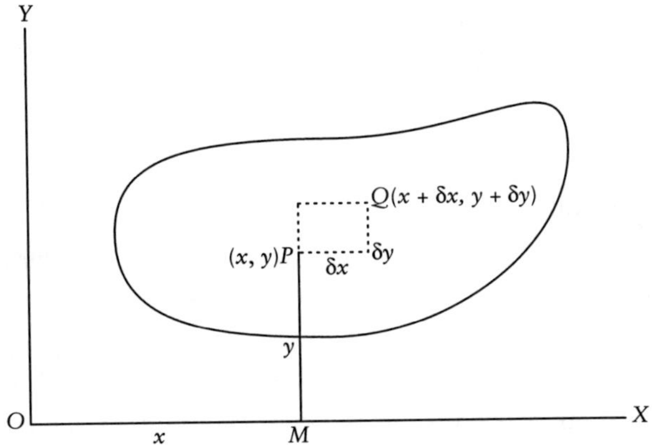


Let $(\overline{x}, \overline{y})$ be the required C.G. of the whole area under consideration. Then, we have,

$$\overline{x} = \frac{\iint x \rho\, dx\, dy}{\iint \rho\, dx\, dy} \qquad \text{and} \qquad \overline{y} = \frac{\iint y \quad dx\, dy}{\iint \quad dx\, dy}$$

Here, the limits of integration are so chosen that the whole area under consideration is covered.

If the equation of the curve is given in the form $y = f(x)$, then we first integrate with respect to $y$ between the limits say 0 to $y$ (on the curve) and finally integrate with respect to $x$ after substituting the value of $y$ in term of $x$ between the required limits of $x$, say $x = a$ to $x = b$.

(ii) **In Polar coordinates**

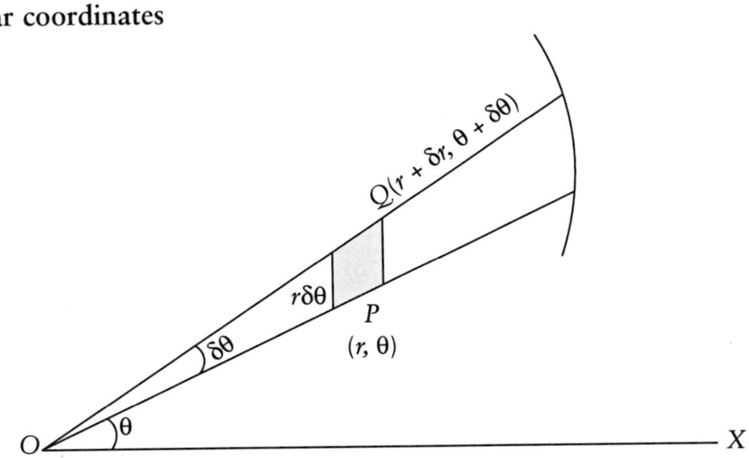

In case of the polar curves, we consider an infinitesimally small element $r\delta\theta\ \delta r$ at any point $P(r, \theta)$ lying in the area whose C.G. is to be determined. This elementary area is included between two very close radii vectors and two very close arcs at $P(r, \theta)$ and $Q(r + \delta r, \theta + \delta\theta)$ respectively. Let $\rho$ be the density at the point $P$. Then, the mass $\delta m$ of the elementary area $r\delta\theta\ \delta r$ can be taken as $\rho r\ \delta\theta\ \delta r$ as the density at every point of the elementary area can be taken as the same as that at the point $P$ whose cartesian coordinates are $(r \cos \theta, r \sin\theta)$.

Let $(\bar{x}, \bar{y})$ be the required C.G. of the where area under consideration. Then, we have,

$$\bar{x} = \frac{\iint r\cos\theta\ \rho\ r\ d\theta\ dr}{\iint \rho\ r\ d\theta\ dr}$$

and
$$\bar{y} = \frac{\iint r\sin\theta\ \rho\ r\ d\theta\ dr}{\iint \rho\ r\ d\theta\ dr}$$

Here, the limits of integration are so chosen that the whole area under consideration is covered.

If the equation of the curve is given by $r = f(\theta)$, then we first integrate with respect to $r$ between the limits 0 to $r$ (on the curve) and finally integrate with respect to $\theta$ after substituting the value of $r$ in term of $\theta$ between the required limits of $\theta$, say $\theta = \alpha$ to $\theta = \beta$.

**Note:** We adopt the similar procedure in the case of solids and surfaces of revolution when the density varies.

The illustrative examples given below explain the whole procedure.

## ILLUSTRATIVE EXAMPLES

**Example 1:** If the density of a circular arc varies as the $n$th power of the distance from a point O on the arc, show that the centroid of the circle divides the diameter through O in the ratio $(n + 1) : 1$.

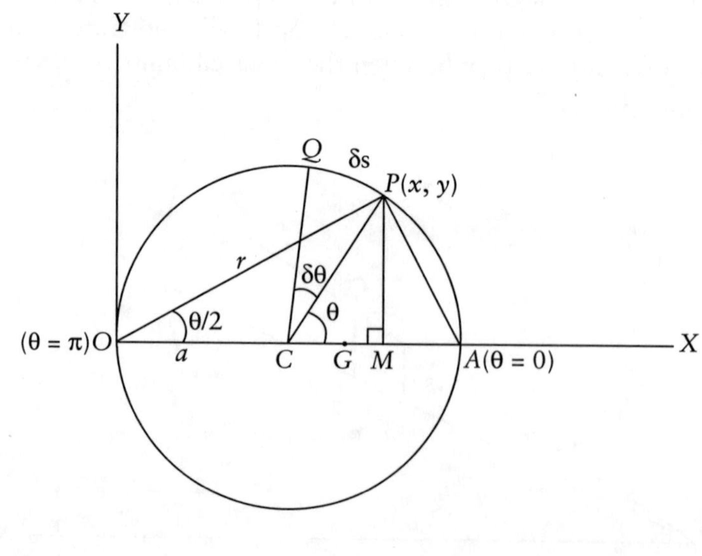

Let us consider a circle where radius is $a$. $O$ is any point on the circle. Take $O$ as origin, the diameter $OA$ through $O$ as the $X$-axis and a line through $O$ perpendicular to $OX$ as the $Y$-axis. Let $C$ be the centre of the circle. Then,

$$OC = CA = a \qquad \therefore \qquad OA = 2a$$

Let $\angle PCA = \theta$

Then, by simple geometry, $\angle POC = \theta/2$

Let $OP = r$

Then,

$$r = 2a\cos\frac{\theta}{2} \qquad \Big| \text{From right triangle } OPA \qquad ...(1)$$

Take a point $Q$ neighbouring to $P(x, y)$ such that arc $PQ = \delta s$. Then,

$$\delta s = a\delta\theta \qquad \Big| \because s = a\theta \text{ for a circle of radius } a \qquad ...(2)$$

Let $\rho$ be the density at $P$. Then, $\rho \propto r^n$

$$\Rightarrow \qquad \rho = \lambda\, r^n$$

$$\Rightarrow \qquad \rho = \lambda\left(2a\cos\frac{\theta}{2}\right)^n \qquad \Big| \text{From (1)} \qquad ...(3)$$

From right triangle $OMP$,

$$x = OM = OP\cos\frac{\theta}{2} = r\cos\frac{\theta}{2} = 2a\cos^2\frac{\theta}{2} \qquad \Big| \text{From (1)} \qquad ...(4)$$

Let $(\bar{x}, \bar{y})$ be the required C.G. Then, $\bar{y} = 0$ | By symmetry

and
$$\bar{x} = \frac{\int x\,dm}{\int dm} = \frac{\int x\rho\,ds}{\int \rho\,ds}$$

$$= \frac{\int_0^\pi 2a\cos^2\frac{\theta}{2}\lambda\left(2a\cos\frac{\theta}{2}\right)^n a\,d\theta}{\int_0^\pi \left(2a\cos\frac{\theta}{2}\right)^n a\,d\theta} \qquad \Big| \text{From (4), (3) and (2)}$$

$$= \frac{2a\int_0^\pi \cos^{n+2}\frac{\theta}{2}\,d\theta}{\int_0^\pi \cos^n\frac{\theta}{2}\,d\theta} \qquad \text{Put } \frac{\theta}{2} = \phi \quad \therefore\ d\theta = 2d\phi$$

$$= \frac{2a\int_0^{\pi/2} \cos^{n+2}\phi\; 2d\phi}{\int_0^\pi \cos^n\phi\; 2d\phi} = \frac{2a\int_0^{\pi/2} \cos^{n+2}\phi\; d\phi}{\int_0^\pi \cos^n\phi\; d\phi}$$

$$= \frac{\dfrac{2a\Gamma\left(\frac{n+3}{2}\right)\Gamma\left(\frac{1}{2}\right)}{2\Gamma\left(\frac{n+4}{2}\right)}}{\dfrac{\Gamma\left(\frac{n+1}{2}\right)\Gamma\left(\frac{1}{2}\right)}{2\Gamma\left(\frac{n+2}{2}\right)}} = \frac{2a\Gamma\left(\frac{n+3}{2}\right)\Gamma\left(\frac{n+2}{2}\right)}{\Gamma\left(\frac{n+4}{2}\right)\Gamma\left(\frac{n+1}{2}\right)}$$

$$= \frac{2a\Gamma\left(\left(\frac{n+1}{2}\right)+1\right)\Gamma\left(\frac{n+2}{2}\right)}{\Gamma\left(\left(\frac{n+2}{2}\right)+1\right)\Gamma\left(\frac{n+1}{2}\right)} = \frac{2a\left(\frac{n+1}{2}\right)\Gamma\left(\frac{n+1}{2}\right)\Gamma\left(\frac{n+2}{2}\right)}{\left(\frac{n+2}{2}\right)\Gamma\left(\frac{n+2}{2}\right)\Gamma\left(\frac{n+1}{2}\right)} \qquad \left|\ \because \Gamma(p+1) = p\Gamma(p)\right.$$

$$= 2a\left(\frac{n+1}{n+2}\right) \qquad \therefore OG = 2a\left(\frac{n+1}{n+2}\right)$$

$$\therefore \qquad GA = OA - OG = 2a - 2a\left(\frac{n+1}{n+2}\right)$$

$$= \frac{2a}{n+2} \qquad \therefore \frac{OG}{GA} = \frac{n+1}{1}$$

$$\Rightarrow \qquad OG : GA = (n+1) : 1$$

Hence, the centroid of the circle divides the diameter though O in the ratio $(n + 1) : 1$.

**Example 2:** The density at any point of a circular lamina varies as the $n$th power of the distance from a point O in the circumference. Show that the centre of gravity of the lamina divides the diameter through O in the ratio $(n + 2) : 2$.

**Sol.**

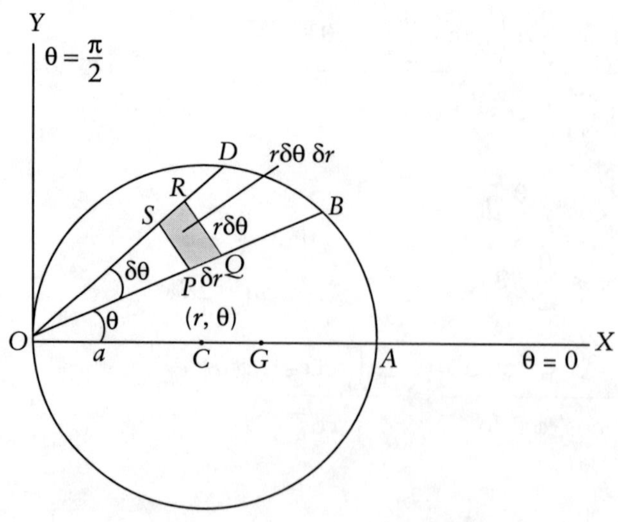

Let us consider a circle with centre $C$ and radius $a$. O is a point on the circumference of the circle. Take O as pole and the diameter $OCA$ through O as the initial line. Then, the polar equation of the circle is $r = 2a \cos\theta$ ...(1)

Consider on element $PQRS$ of area $r\delta\theta\, \delta r$ at $P(r, \theta)$. Then, density at $P \propto \rho^n$

$\Rightarrow$ density at $P = \lambda r^n$

$\therefore$ Elementary mass $\delta m = \rho r\, d\theta\, \delta r = \lambda r^n \; r\delta\theta\, \delta r = \lambda r^{n+1}\, \delta\theta\, \delta r$

The C.G. of this elementary area is at $P(r \cos\theta, r \sin\theta)$.

Since the circular lamina is symmetrical about $OX$, therefore the centroid $G$ of the lamina will lie on $OAX$. Thus, if $(\bar{x}, \bar{y})$ be the required C.G., then

$$\bar{y} = 0 \qquad \text{| By symmetry}$$

Also, due to symmetry, we may conclude that the abscissa of the C.G. of the upper half is the same as the abscissa of the C.G. of the whole lamina. For the upper half, $\theta$ varies from 0 to $\pi/2$. Hence,

$$\bar{x} = \frac{\int x\, dm}{\int dm} = \frac{\int_0^{\pi/2}\int_0^{2a\cos\theta} r\cos\theta\, \lambda r^{n+1}\, d\theta\, dr}{\int_0^{\pi/2}\int_0^{2a\cos\theta} \lambda r^{n+1}\, d\theta\, dr} \qquad \text{| At O, } r = 0; \text{ At } B, r = 2a\cos\theta$$

$$= \frac{\int_0^{\pi/2}\int_0^{2a\cos\theta} r^{n+2}\cos\theta\, d\theta\, dr}{\int_0^{\pi/2}\int_0^{2a\cos\theta} r^{n+1}\, d\theta\, dr} = \frac{\int_0^{\pi/2}\left(\frac{r^{n+3}}{n+3}\right)_0^{2a\cos\theta}\cos\theta\, d\theta}{\int_0^{\pi/2}\left(\frac{r^{n+3}}{n+3}\right)_0^{2a\cos\theta} d\theta}$$

$$= \frac{2a\left(\frac{n+2}{n+3}\right)\int_0^{\pi/2}\cos^{n+4}\theta\, d\theta}{\int_0^{\pi/2}\cos^{n+2}\theta\, d\theta} = \frac{2\,\frac{n+2}{n+3}\cdot\frac{n+3}{n+4}\cdot\frac{n+1}{n+2}\cdot\frac{n-1}{n}\cdots}{\frac{n+1}{n}\cdot\frac{n-1}{n}\cdots} \qquad \text{| By Walli's Formula}$$

$$= 2a\left(\frac{n+2}{n+4}\right) \quad \Rightarrow OG = 2a\left(\frac{n+2}{n+4}\right)$$

$$\therefore \quad AG = OA - OG = 2a - 2a\left(\frac{n+2}{n+4}\right) = 2a\left(\frac{2}{n+4}\right)$$

$$\therefore \quad \frac{OG}{AG} = \frac{n+2}{2} \quad \Rightarrow OG : AG = (n+2) : 2$$

Hence, the centre of gravity of the lamina divides the diameter through O in the ratio $(n + 2) : 2$.

**Example 3:** Find the distance of the C.G. of the area of the cardioid $r = a(1 + \cos\theta)$ from its cusp, when the density varies as the $n$th power of the distance from O.

**Sol.** The equation of the cardioid is $r = a(1 + \cos\theta)$ ...(1)

Take O as pole and $OAX$ as the initial line. O is a cusp.

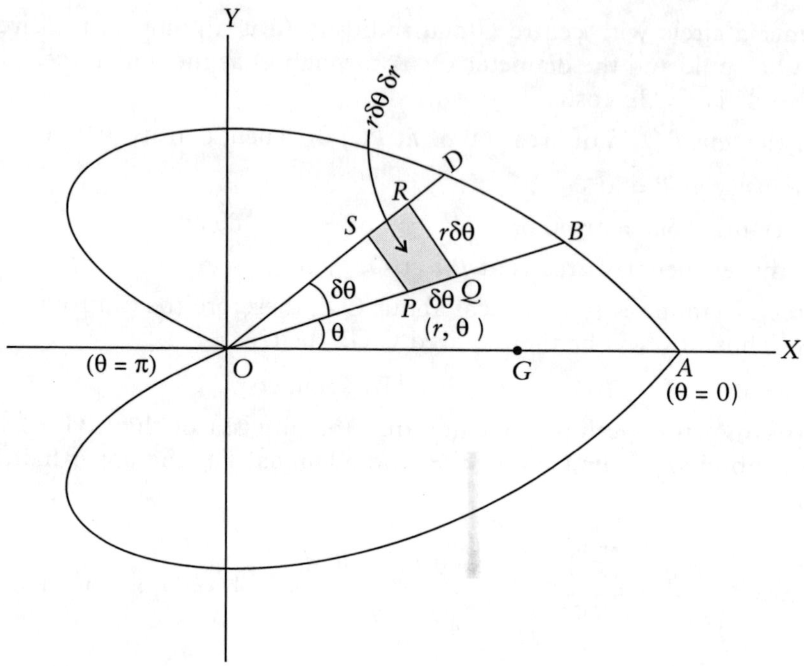


Consider on element $PQRS$ of area $r\delta\theta\ \delta r$ at $P(r, \theta)$. Then,

density at $P\ \alpha\ r^n$

$\Rightarrow$ density at $P = \lambda r^n$

$\therefore$ Elementary mass $\delta m = \rho\, r\ \delta\theta\ \delta r = \lambda r^n\ r\ \delta\theta\ \delta r = \lambda r^{n+1}\ \delta\theta\ \delta r$

The C.G. of this elementary area is at $P(r \cos\theta, r \sin\theta)$.

Since the curve is symmetrical about the initial line, therefore the C.G. $G$ of the cardioid will lie on $OAX$. Thus, if $(\bar{x}, \bar{y})$ be the required C.G. Then $\bar{y} = 0$.

Also, due to symmetry we may conclude that the abscissa of the C.G. of the upper half is the same as the abscissa of the C.G. of the whole cardioid.

For the upper half, $\theta$ varies from 0 to $\pi$.

Hence,

$$\bar{x} = \frac{\int x\,dm}{\int dm} = \frac{\int_0^\pi \int_0^{a(1+\cos\theta)} r\cos\theta \cdot \lambda r^{n+1}\, d\theta\, dr}{\int_0^\pi \int_0^{a(1+\cos\theta)} \lambda r^{n+1}\, d\theta\, dr} \qquad \begin{array}{|l} \text{At } A,\ \theta = \theta; \\ \text{At } O,\ \theta = \pi \end{array}$$

$$= \frac{\int_0^\pi \int_0^{(1+\cos\theta)} r \quad \cos\theta\, d\theta\, dr}{\int_0^\pi \int_0^{(1+\cos\theta)} r \quad d \quad dr} = \frac{\int_0^\pi \left(\frac{r^{n+3}}{n+3}\right)_0^{a(1+\cos\theta)} \cos\theta\, d\theta}{\int_0^\pi \left(\frac{r^{n+2}}{n+2}\right)_0^{a(1+\cos\theta)} d\theta}$$

$$= \frac{a\left(\frac{n+2}{n+3}\right)\int_0^{\pi}(1+\cos\theta)^{n+3}\cos\theta\,d\theta}{\int_0^{\pi}(1+\cos)^{n+2}\,d\theta}$$

$$= \frac{\frac{a(n+2)}{n+3}\int_0^{\pi}\left(2\cos^2\frac{\theta}{2}\right)^{n+3}\left(2\cos^2\frac{\theta}{2}-1\right)d\theta}{\int_0^{\pi}\left(2\cos^2\frac{\theta}{2}\right)^{n+2}d\theta}$$

Put $\frac{\theta}{2} = \phi$

$\therefore\ d\theta = 2d\phi$

$$= \frac{\frac{2a(n+2)}{n+3}\int_0^{\pi/2}\left(2\cos^{2n+8}\phi - \cos^{2n+6}\phi\right)d\phi}{\int_0^{\pi/2}\cos^{2n+4}\phi\,d\phi}$$

$$= \frac{\frac{2a(n+2)}{n+3}\left[2\int_0^{\pi/2}\cos^{2n+8}\theta\,d\phi - \int_0^{\pi/2}\cos^{2n+6}\phi\,d\phi\right]}{\int_0^{\pi/2}\cos^{2n+4}\theta\,d\phi}$$

$$= \frac{\frac{2a(n+2)}{n+2}\left[\left\{2\frac{2n+7}{2n+8}\,\frac{2n+5}{2n+6}\,\frac{2n+3}{2n+4}.....\right\} - \left\{\frac{2n+5}{2n+6}\,\frac{2n+3}{2n+4}.....\right\}\right]}{\frac{2n+3}{2n+4}\cdot\frac{2n+1}{2n+2}}$$

$$= \frac{2a(n+2)}{n+3}\left[2\left(\frac{2n+7}{2n+5}\right)\left(\frac{2n+5}{2n+6}\right) - \frac{2n+5}{2n+6}\right]$$

$$= \frac{2a(n+2)(2n+5)}{(n+3)(2n+6)}\left[\frac{2n+7}{n+4} - 1\right]$$

$$= \frac{2a(n+2)(2n+5)(n+3)}{(n+3)(2n+6)(n+4)} = \frac{a(n+2)(2n+5)}{(n+3)(n+4)}$$

Hence, the required distance is given by

$$\frac{a(n+2)(2n+5)}{(n+3)(n+4)}.$$

**Example 4:** Find the centre of mass of a circular arc $AB$ of uniform section, density varying as the length of the arc measured from the extremity $A$.

**Sol.** Let O be the centre of the circular arc $AB$.

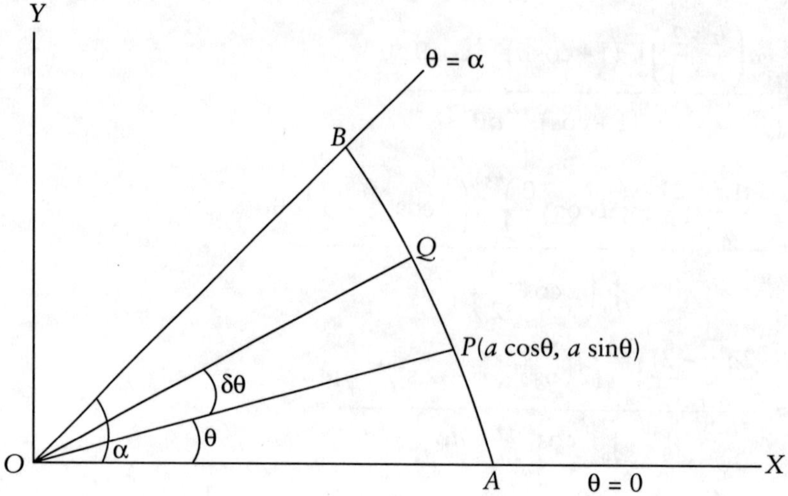


Let $\angle AOB = \alpha$

Take $O$ as pole and $OA$ as the initial line.

Take an elementary arc $PQ$ such that $\angle POA = \theta$ and $\angle POQ = \delta\theta$.

Let arc $AP = s$. Then, $s = a\,\theta \quad \therefore\ \delta s = a\,\delta\theta$

Density at $P \propto s$

$\therefore$ Density at $P = \lambda\, s = \lambda\, a\, \theta$

$\therefore$ Elementary mass $\delta m = \lambda\, a\theta\, a\, \delta\theta = \lambda a^2\theta\, \delta\theta$.

The C.G. of this elementary area is at $P(a\cos\theta, a\sin\theta)$ referred to $OA$ and a line through $O$ perpendicular to $OA$ as the coordinate axes.

Let $(\bar{x}, \bar{y})$ be the required C.G. Then,

$$\bar{x} = \frac{\int x\,dm}{\int dm} = \frac{\int_0^{\alpha} a\cos\theta\, \lambda a^2\theta\, d\theta}{\int_0^{\alpha} \lambda a^2\theta\, d\theta} = \frac{a\int_0^{\alpha} \theta\cos\theta\, d\theta}{\int_0^{\alpha} \theta\, d\theta}$$

$$= \frac{a\left[(\theta\sin\theta)_0^{\alpha} - \int_0^{\alpha}\sin\theta\, d\theta\right]}{\left(\frac{\theta^2}{2}\right)_0^{\alpha}} = \frac{a\left[\alpha\sin\alpha + (\cos\theta)_0^{\alpha}\right]}{\frac{\alpha^2}{2}} = \frac{2a(\alpha\sin\alpha + \cos\alpha - 1)}{\alpha^2}$$

and

$$\bar{y} = \frac{\int y\,dm}{\int dm} = \frac{\int_0^{\alpha} a\sin\theta\, \lambda a^2\theta\, d\theta}{\int_0^{\alpha} \lambda a^2\theta\, d\theta} = \frac{a\int_0^{\alpha} \theta\sin\theta\, d\theta}{\int_0^{\alpha} \theta\, d\theta}$$

$$= \frac{a\left[\{\theta(-\cos\theta)\}_0^{\alpha} - \int_0^{\alpha}(-\cos\theta)\, d\theta\right]}{\left(\frac{\theta^2}{2}\right)_0^{\alpha}} = \frac{2a[-\alpha\cos\alpha \cdot + \sin\alpha]}{\alpha^2}$$

Hence, the required C.G. $(\overline{x}, \overline{y})$ is given by

$$\overline{x} = \frac{2a(\alpha\sin\alpha + \sin\alpha - 1)}{\alpha^2}$$

and
$$\overline{y} = \frac{2a(\sin\alpha - \alpha\cos\alpha)}{\alpha^2}.$$

**Example 5:** If $a$ is the radius of the generating circle of a cycloidal arc, and the density of the arc varies as the $n$th power of the arc measured from vertex, show that the C.G. lies on the axis at a distance $\frac{2a(n+1)}{n+3}$ from the vertex.

**Sol.** $O$ is the vertex, $AB$ is the base and $OC$ is the axis of the cycloidal arc.

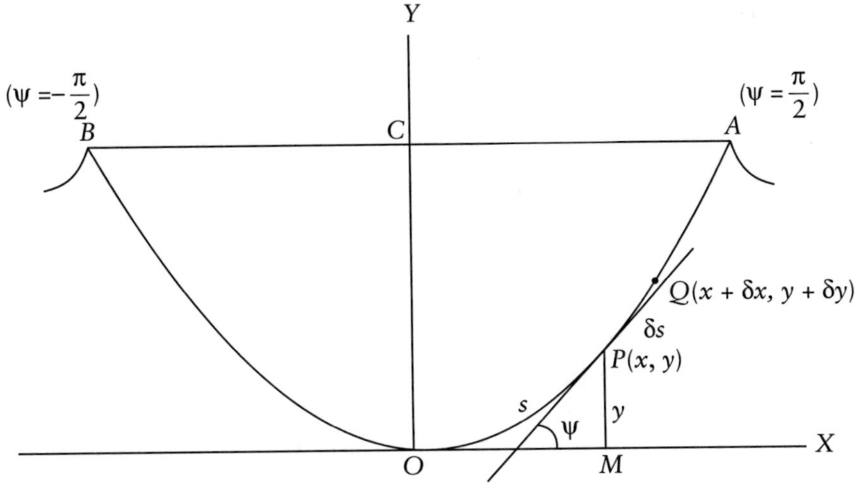


The intrinsic equation of the cycloidal arc is

$$x = 4a\sin\Psi \qquad ...(1)$$

Also, the relation between $s$ and $y$ for this arc is

$$s^2 = \delta\, ay \qquad ...(2)$$

Here, arc $OP = s$, arc $PQ = \delta s$, $y$ is the ordinate of $P$ and $\Psi$ is the angle which the tangent at the point $P$ makes with $X$-axis.

From (1),

$$\delta s = 4\,a\cos\Psi\,\delta\Psi \qquad ...(3)$$

Density at $P \propto s^n$

$$\Rightarrow \qquad \rho = \lambda\, s^n \qquad ...(4)$$

$\therefore$ Elementary mass $\delta m$ = mass of the elementary arc $PQ = \rho\,\delta s = 4\lambda\, a\, s^n \cos\Psi\,\delta\Psi$

The C.G. of this elementary arc $PQ$ is at $P(x, y)$ as $\delta s$ is very small.

Also, for the cycloidal arc $BOA$, $\Psi$ varies from $\Psi = -\frac{\pi}{2}$ to $\Psi = \frac{\pi}{2}$.

Let $(\bar{x}, \bar{y})$ be the required C.G. Then, $\bar{x} = 0$ | By symmetry

and $$\bar{y} = \frac{\int y\,dm}{\int dm}$$

$$= \frac{\int_{\frac{-\pi}{2}}^{\frac{\pi}{2}} y\,4\lambda a s^n \cos\Psi\,d\Psi}{\int_{\frac{-\pi}{2}}^{\frac{\pi}{2}} 4\lambda a s^n \cos\Psi\,d\Psi} = \frac{\int_{\frac{-\pi}{2}}^{\frac{\pi}{2}} y s^n \cos\Psi\,d\Psi}{\int_{\frac{-\pi}{2}}^{\frac{\pi}{2}} s^n \cos\Psi\,d\Psi}$$

$$= \frac{\int_{\frac{-\pi}{2}}^{\frac{\pi}{2}} \frac{s^2}{8a}\cdot s^n \cos\Psi\,d\Psi}{\int_{\frac{-\pi}{2}}^{\frac{\pi}{2}} (4a\sin\Psi)^n \cos\Psi\,d\Psi}$$ | From (2)

$$= \frac{\frac{1}{8a}\int_{\frac{-\pi}{2}}^{\frac{\pi}{2}} (4a\sin\Psi)^{n+2} \cos\Psi\,d\Psi}{\int_{\frac{-\pi}{2}}^{\frac{\pi}{2}} (4a\sin\Psi)^n \cos\Psi\,d\Psi}$$ | From (1)

$$= \frac{\frac{16a^2}{8a}\int_{\frac{-\pi}{2}}^{\frac{\pi}{2}} \sin^{n+2}\Psi\cos\Psi\,d\Psi}{\int_{\frac{-\pi}{2}}^{\frac{\pi}{2}} \sin^n\Psi\cos\Psi\,d\Psi}$$

Ordinate of the C.G. of the whole cycloidal arc $BOA$ = ordinate of the C.G. of the half cylinder arc $OA$.

$$= \frac{2a\left[\frac{\sin^{n+3}\Psi}{n+3}\right]_0^{\frac{\pi}{2}}}{\left[\frac{\sin^{n+1}\Psi}{n+1}\right]_0^{\frac{\pi}{2}}} = 2a\left(\frac{n+1}{n+3}\right) = \frac{2a\int_0^{\frac{\pi}{2}} \sin^{n+2}\cos\Psi\,d\Psi}{\int_0^{\frac{\pi}{2}} \sin^n\Psi\cos\Psi\,d\Psi}$$

**Example 6:** If the density at any point of an arc of a uniform circular wire varies as its distance from the central radius, prove that the centre of mass is at a point on the central radius, mid-way between the chord and the arc.

**Sol.**

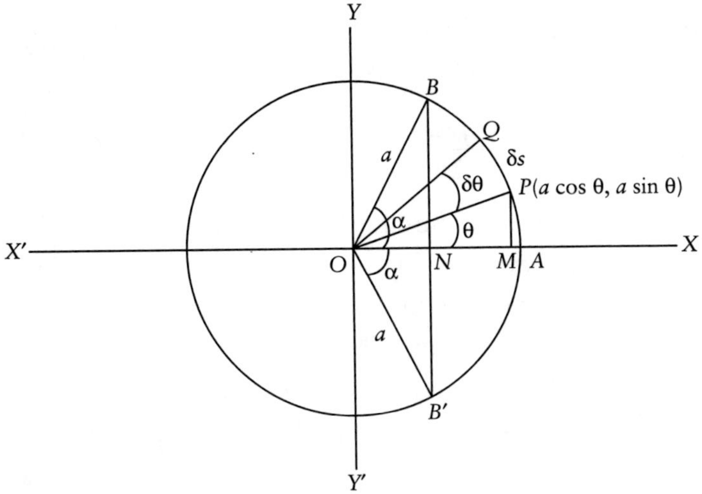


Let $BAB'$ be a uniform circular wire of radius $a$ and centre $O$. $OA$ is the central radius.

Let $\angle BOB' = 2\alpha$

Then, $\angle BOA = \angle B'OA = \alpha$

Consider an elementary arc $PQ(= \delta s)$ such that $\angle POA = \theta$ and $\angle QOP = \delta\theta$.

$\because \quad s = a\theta \quad$ | For a circle of radius $a$

$\therefore \quad \delta s = a\delta\theta \quad$ ...(1)

Density at $P \propto PM$

$\Rightarrow \quad \rho = \lambda\, PM$

$\Rightarrow \quad \rho = \lambda\, a \sin\theta \quad$ ...(2)

$\therefore$ Elementary mass $\delta m$

$= \text{Mass of the elementary arc } PQ = a\,\delta\theta\,\lambda\,a\sin\theta = \lambda a^2 \sin\theta\,\delta\theta$

The C.G. of this elementary arc is at $P(a\cos\theta, a\sin\theta)$ referred to $OA$ and a line through $O$ perpendicular to $OA$ as axes.

Since the arc $BAB'$ is symmetrical about the central radius $OA$, therefore, its C.G. $G$ will lie on $OA$.

Let $(x, y)$ be the required C.G. of the arc $BAB'$. Then,

$\bar{y} = 0 \quad$ | By symmetry

and
$$\bar{x} = \frac{\int x\,dm}{\int dm} = \frac{\int_{-\alpha}^{\alpha} a\cos\theta\,\lambda a^2 \sin\theta\,d\theta}{\int_{-\alpha}^{\alpha} \lambda a^2 \sin\theta\,d\theta} = \frac{a\int_{-\alpha}^{\alpha} \sin\theta\cos\theta\,d\theta}{\int_{-\alpha}^{\alpha} \sin\theta\,d\theta}$$

$$= \frac{\frac{a}{2}\int_{-\alpha}^{\alpha} \sin 2\theta\,d\theta}{\int_{-\alpha}^{\alpha} \sin\theta\,d\theta} = \frac{\frac{a}{2}\int_{0}^{\alpha} \sin 2\theta\,d\theta}{\int_{0}^{\alpha} \sin\theta\,d\theta}$$

| Abscissa of the C.G. of the whole arc $BAB'$ = Abscissa of the C.G. of the upper half arc $BA$.

$$= \frac{\frac{a}{2}\left(\frac{-\cos 2\theta}{2}\right)_0^{\alpha}}{(-\cos\theta)_0^{\alpha}} = \frac{a}{4}\,\frac{1-\cos 2\alpha}{1-\cos\alpha} = \frac{a}{4}\cdot\frac{2\sin^2\alpha}{1-\cos\alpha} = \frac{a}{2}\,\frac{1-\cos 2\alpha}{1-\cos\alpha}$$

$$= \frac{a}{2}(1+\cos\alpha) = \frac{a+a\cos\alpha}{2} = \frac{OA+ON}{2} \qquad \Rightarrow OG = \frac{OA+ON}{2}$$

Hence, $G$ is a point on the central radius, mid-way between the chord $BB'$ and the arc $BAB'$.

**Example 7:** Find the centre of gravity of a semi-circular lamina when the density at any point.

(i) Varies as the distance from the centre

(ii) Varies as the square of the distance from the centre

(iii) Varies as the cube of the distance from the centre

(iv) Varies as the square of the distance from the bounding diameter

(v) Varies as the distance from one end of the bounding diameter.

**Sol.**

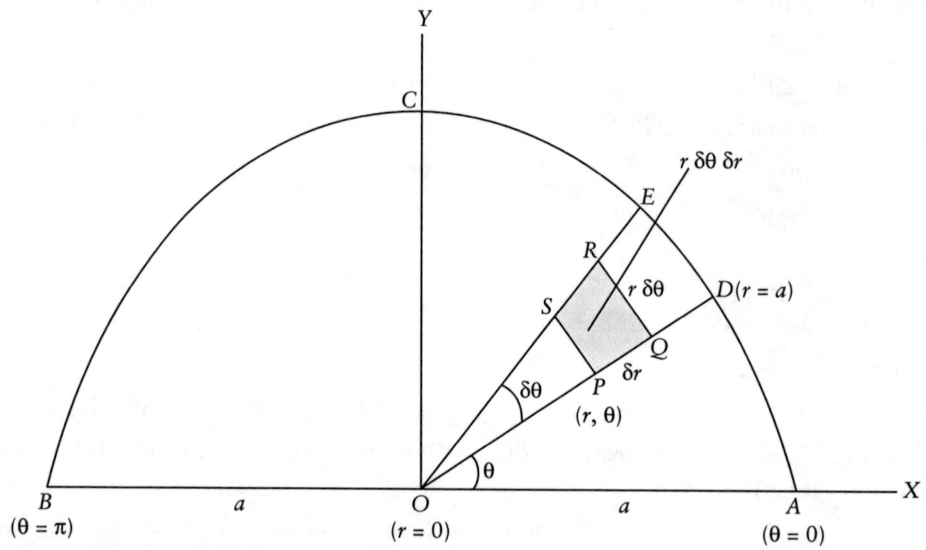


Let O be the centre of the semi-circular lamina. $AB$ is its bounding diameter. Take O as pole and $OA$ as initial line. Then, the polar equation of semi-circle is $r = a$.

Take a point $P(r, \theta)$ inside the semi-circle. Consider an elementary area $PQRS$ at $P$ such that $PQ = \delta r$, $PS = r\,\delta\theta$ where $\angle POS = \delta\theta$.

$\therefore$ Elementary area $\delta s = r\,\delta\theta\,\delta r$

Since the element $PQRS$ is very small, therefore, density at any point of the element $PQRS$ can be taken as the same as the density at $P$.

(i) $\rho \propto OP \quad \Rightarrow \rho = \lambda OP$, where $\lambda$ is a constant. $\quad \Rightarrow \quad \rho = \lambda r$

$\therefore$ Elementary mass $\delta m = \rho\,\delta s = \lambda r \cdot r\delta\theta\,\delta r = \lambda r^2\,\delta\theta\,\delta r$

Also, the C.G. of this elementary area is at $P(r\cos\theta, r\sin\theta)$ referred to the coordinate axes as shown in the figure.

Let $(\bar{x}, \bar{y})$ be the required C.G. Then,

$$\bar{x} = 0 \qquad \text{| By symmetry}$$

and
$$\bar{y} = \frac{\int y\,dm}{\int dm} = \frac{\int_{\theta=0}^{\pi}\int_{r=0}^{a} r\sin\theta\,\lambda r^2\,d\theta\,dr}{\int_{\theta=0}^{\pi}\int_{r=0}^{a} \lambda r^2\,d\theta\,dr} \qquad \text{| At O, } r = 0\text{; at } D,\ r = a$$

$$= \frac{\int_{\theta=0}^{\pi}\int_{r=0}^{a} r^3\sin\theta\,d\theta\,dr}{\int_{\theta=0}^{\pi}\int_{r=0}^{a} r^2\,d\theta\,dr} = \frac{\int_0^{\pi}\left(\frac{r^4}{4}\right)_0^a \sin\theta\,d\theta}{\int_0^{\pi}\left(\frac{r^3}{3}\right)_0^a d\theta} = \frac{\int_0^{\pi}\frac{a^4}{4}\sin\theta\,d\theta}{\int_0^{\pi}\frac{a^3}{3}d\theta}$$

$$= \frac{\frac{3a}{4}\int_0^{\pi}\sin\theta\,d\theta}{\int_0^{\pi}d\theta} = \frac{\frac{3a}{4}(-\cos\theta)_0^{\pi}}{(\theta)_0^{\pi}} = \frac{3a}{2\pi}$$

(ii) $\rho \,\alpha\, OP^2 \quad \Rightarrow \rho = \lambda\, OP^2 \quad \Rightarrow \rho = \lambda\, r^2$

$\therefore$ Elementary mass $\delta m = \rho\delta s = \lambda\, r^2\, r\,\delta\theta\,\delta r = \lambda r^3\,\delta\theta\,\delta r$

Also, the C.G. of the this elementary area is at $P(r\cos\theta, r\sin\theta)$ referred to $OX$ and $OY$ as the axes.

Let $(\bar{x}, \bar{y})$ be the required C.G. Then, $\bar{x} = 0$ | By symmetry

and
$$\bar{y} = \frac{\int y\,dm}{\int dm} = \frac{\int_{\theta=0}^{\pi}\int_{r=0}^{a} r\sin\theta\,\lambda r^3\,d\theta\,dr}{\int_{\theta=0}^{\pi}\int_{r=0}^{a} \lambda r^3\,d\theta\,dr} \qquad \text{| At O, } r = 0\text{; at } D,\ r = a$$

$$= \frac{\int_{\theta=0}^{\pi}\int_{r=0}^{a} r^4\sin\theta\,d\theta\,dr}{\int_{\theta=0}^{\pi}\int_{r=0}^{a} r^3\,d\theta\,dr} = \frac{\int_0^{\pi}\left(\frac{r^5}{5}\right)_0^a \sin\theta\,d\theta}{\int_0^{\pi}\left(\frac{r^4}{4}\right)_0^a d\theta} = \frac{\frac{4a}{5}\int_0^{\pi}\sin\theta\,d\theta}{\int_0^{\pi}d\theta}$$

$$= \frac{\frac{4a}{5}(-\cos\theta)_0^{\pi}}{(\theta)_0^{\pi}} = \frac{8a}{5\pi}$$

(iii) $\rho \,\alpha\, OP^3 \quad \Rightarrow \rho = \lambda\, OP^3 \quad \Rightarrow \rho = \lambda\, r^3$

$\therefore$ Elementary mass $\delta m = \rho\,\delta s \quad = \lambda\, r^3\, r\,\delta\theta\,\delta r \quad = \lambda\, r^4\,\delta\theta\,\delta r$

Also, the C.G. of this elementary area is at $P(r\cos\theta, r\sin\theta)$ referred to $OX$ and $OY$ as axes.

Let $(\bar{x}, \bar{y})$ be the required C.G. Then, $\bar{x} = 0$ | By symmetry

and
$$\bar{y} = \frac{\int y\,dm}{\int dm} = \frac{\int_{\theta=0}^{\pi}\int_{r=0}^{a} r\sin\theta\,\lambda r^4\,d\theta\,dr}{\int_{\theta=0}^{\pi}\int_{r=0}^{a} \lambda r^4\,d\theta\,dr} \qquad \text{| At O, } r = 0\text{; at } D,\ r = a$$

$$= \frac{\int_{\theta=0}^{\pi}\int_{r=0}^{a} r^5 \sin\theta \, d\theta \, dr}{\int_{\theta=0}^{\pi}\int_{r=0}^{a} r^4 \, d\theta \, dr} = \frac{\int_0^{\pi}\left(\frac{r^6}{6}\right)_0^a \sin\theta \, d\theta}{\int_0^{\pi}\left(\frac{r^5}{5}\right)_0^a d\theta} = \frac{\frac{5a}{6}\int_0^{\pi}\sin\theta \, d\theta}{\int_0^{\pi} d\theta} = \frac{5a}{3\pi}.$$

(iv) $\rho \propto (r \sin\theta)^2$ $\qquad \rho = \lambda r^2 \sin^2\theta$

$\therefore$ Elementary mass $\delta m = \rho \, \delta s \quad = \lambda r^2 \sin^2\theta \, r\delta\theta \, \delta r \quad = \lambda r^3 \sin^2\theta \, \delta\theta \, \delta r$

Also, the C.G. of the this elementary area is at $P(r \cos\theta, r \sin\theta)$ referred to $OX$ and $OY$ as the axes.

Let $(\bar{x}, \bar{y})$ be the required C.G. Then, $\bar{x} = 0$ | By symmetry

and $$\bar{y} = \frac{\int y \, dm}{\int dm} = \frac{\int_{\theta=0}^{\pi}\int_{r=0}^{a} r\sin\theta \, \lambda r^3 \sin^2\theta \, d\theta \, dr}{\int_{\theta=0}^{\pi}\int_{r=0}^{a} \lambda r^3 \sin^2\theta \, d\theta \, dr}$$ | At O, $r = 0$; at $D$, $r = a$

$$= \frac{\int_{\theta=0}^{\pi}\int_{r=0}^{a} r^4 \sin^3\theta \, d\theta \, dr}{\int_{\theta=0}^{\pi}\int_{r=0}^{a} r^3 \sin^2\theta \, d\theta \, dr} = \frac{\int_0^{\pi}\left(\frac{r^5}{5}\right)_0^a \sin^3\theta \, d\theta}{\int_0^{\pi}\left(\frac{r^4}{4}\right)_0^a \sin^2\theta \, d\theta} = \frac{\frac{4a}{5}\int_0^{\pi}\sin^3\theta \, d\theta}{\int_0^{\pi}\sin^2\theta \, d\theta}$$

$$= \frac{\frac{4a}{5} 2\int_0^{\pi/2}\sin^3\theta \, d\theta}{2\int_0^{\pi/2}\sin^2\theta \, d\theta} = \frac{\frac{4a}{5}\cdot\frac{2}{3}}{\frac{1}{2}\cdot\frac{\pi}{2}}$$ | By Walli's Formula $\Rightarrow = \frac{32a}{15\pi}$

(v) Take $O$ as pole and the bounding diameter $OA$ as the initial line. Then, the polar equation of the semi-circle is $r = 2a \cos\theta$

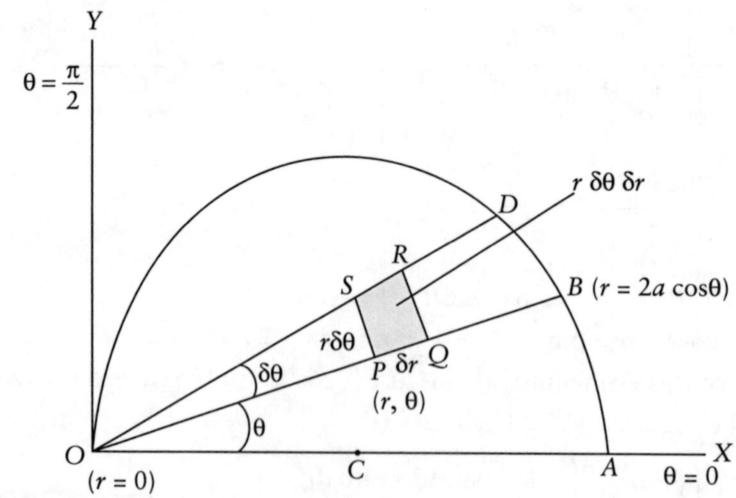

$$\rho \propto r \quad \Rightarrow \quad \rho = \lambda r$$

∴ Elementary mass $\delta m = \rho\, \delta s = \lambda r\, r\delta\theta\, \delta r = \lambda r^2\, \delta\theta\, \delta r$

Also, the C.G. of this elementary area is at $P(r \cos\theta, r \sin\theta)$ referred to $OX$ and $OY$ as the axes.

Let $(\bar{x}, \bar{y})$ be the required C.G. Then, $\bar{x} = \dfrac{\int x\, dm}{\int dm}$

$$= \frac{\int_{\theta=0}^{\pi/2}\int_{r=0}^{2a\cos\theta} r\cos\theta\, \lambda r^2\, d\theta\, dr}{\int_{\theta=0}^{\pi/2}\int_{r=0}^{2a\cos\theta} \lambda r^2\, d\theta\, dr} \qquad \Big| \text{At O, } r = 0; \text{ at } B, r = 2a\cos\theta$$

$$= \frac{\int_{\theta=0}^{\pi/2}\int_{r=0}^{2a\cos\theta} r^3\cos\theta\, d\theta\, dr}{\int_{\theta=0}^{\pi/2}\int_{r=0}^{2a\cos\theta} r^2\, d\theta\, dr} = \frac{\int_0^{\pi/2}\left(\frac{r^4}{4}\right)_0^{2a\cos\theta}\cos\theta\, d\theta}{\int_0^{\pi/2}\left(\frac{r^3}{3}\right)_0^{2a\cos\theta} d\theta}$$

$$= \frac{\frac{3}{4}\cdot(2a)\int_0^{\pi/2}\cos^5\theta\, d\theta}{\int_0^{\pi/2}\cos^3\theta\, d\theta} = \frac{\frac{3a}{2}\cdot\frac{4}{5}\cdot\frac{2}{3}}{\frac{2}{3}} \qquad \Big| \text{By Walli's Formula}$$

$$= \frac{6a}{5} \text{ and } \bar{x} = \frac{\int y\, dm}{\int dm}$$

$$= \frac{\int_{\theta=0}^{\pi/2}\int_{r=0}^{2a\cos\theta} r\sin\theta\, \lambda r^2\, d\theta\, dr}{\int_{\theta=0}^{\pi/2}\int_{r=0}^{2a\cos\theta} \lambda r^2\, d\theta\, dr} = \frac{\int_{\theta=0}^{\pi/2}\int_{r=0}^{2a\cos\theta} r^3\sin\theta\, d\theta\, dr}{\int_{\theta=0}^{\pi/2}\int_{r=0}^{2a\cos\theta} r^2\, d\theta\, dr}$$

$$= \frac{\int_0^{\pi/2}\left(\frac{r^4}{4}\right)_0^{2a\cos\theta}\sin\theta\, d\theta}{\int_0^{\pi/2}\left(\frac{r^3}{3}\right)_0^{2a\cos\theta} d\theta} = \frac{\frac{3}{4}\cdot 2a\int_0^{\pi/2}\cos^4\theta\sin\theta\, d\theta}{\int_0^{\pi/2}\cos^3\theta\, d\theta}$$

$$= \frac{\frac{3a}{2}\left(-\frac{\cos^5\theta}{5}\right)_0^{\pi/2}}{\frac{2}{3}} \qquad \Big| \text{By Walli's Formula}$$

$$= \frac{\frac{3a}{2}\frac{1}{5}}{\frac{2}{3}} = \frac{9a}{20}$$

**Example 8:** Find the centre of gravity of a semi-circular plate of radius a whose mass per unit area at any point varies as $\sqrt{a^2 - r^2}$, where $r$ is the distance of the point from the centre.

**Sol.**

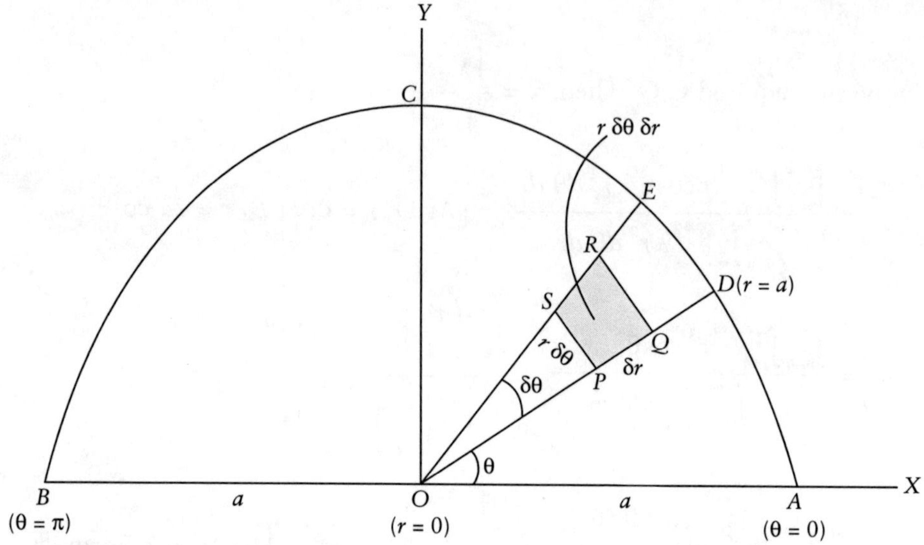


Let $O$ be the centre of the semi-circular plate. $AB$ is the bounding diameter. Take $O$ as pole and $OA$ as initial line.

Then, the polar equation of the semi-circle is $r = a$ ...(1)

Take a point $P(r, \theta)$ inside the semi-circle. Consider an elementary area $PQRS$ at $P$ such that $PQ = \delta r$, $PS = r\delta\theta$ where $\angle POS = \delta\theta$.

$\therefore$ Elementary area $\delta s = r\delta\theta\,\delta r$.

Since the element $PQRS$ is very small, therefore, density at any point of the element $PQRS$ can be taken the same as the density at $P$.

$$\rho \propto \sqrt{a^2 - r^2} \quad \Rightarrow \quad \rho = \lambda\sqrt{a^2 - r^2}, \text{ where } \lambda \text{ is a constant.}$$

$\therefore$ Elementary mass $\delta m = \rho\delta s \quad = \lambda\sqrt{a^2 - r^2}\; r\delta\vartheta\delta r$

Also, the C.G. of this elementary area is at $P(r\cos\theta, r\sin\theta)$ referred to the Cartesian axes as shown in the figure.

Let $(\bar{x}, \bar{y})$ be the required C.G. Then, $\bar{x} = 0$ | By symmetry

and
$$\bar{y} = \frac{\int y\,dm}{\int dm} = \frac{\int_{\theta=0}^{\pi}\int_{r=0}^{a} r\sin\theta\,\lambda\sqrt{a^2 - r^2}\; r\,d\theta\,dr}{\int_{\theta=0}^{\pi}\int_{r=0}^{a} \lambda\sqrt{a^2 - r^2}\; r\,d\theta\,dr} \quad | \therefore \text{ At O, } r = 0; \text{ at } D, r = a$$

$$= \frac{\int_{\theta=0}^{\pi}\int_{r=0}^{a} r^2\sqrt{a^2 - r^2}\,\sin\theta\,d\theta\,dr}{\int_{\theta=0}^{\pi}\int_{r=0}^{a} r\sqrt{a^2 - r^2}\;d\theta\,dr} = \frac{\int_{r=0}^{a}(-\cos\theta)_0^{\pi}\,r^2\sqrt{a^2 - r^2}\,dr}{\int_{r=0}^{a}(\theta)_0^{\pi}\,r\sqrt{a^2 - r^2}\,dr}$$

$$= \frac{\frac{2}{\pi}\int_0^a r^2\sqrt{a^2-r^2}\,dr}{\int_0^a r\sqrt{a^2-r^2}\,dr} \qquad \text{Put } r = a\sin\phi \quad \therefore\ dr = a\cos\phi\,d\phi$$

$$= \frac{\frac{2}{\pi}\int_0^{\pi/2} a^2\sin^2\phi\sqrt{a^2-a^2\sin^2\phi}\;a\cos\phi\,d\phi}{\int_0^{\pi/2} a\sin\phi\sqrt{a^2-a^2\sin^2\phi}\;a\cos\phi\,d\phi} = \frac{\frac{2a}{\pi}\int_0^{\pi/2}\sin^2\phi\cos^2\phi\,d\phi}{\int_0^{\pi/2}\sin\phi\cos^2\phi\,d\phi}$$

$$= \frac{\dfrac{\frac{2a}{\pi}\,\Gamma\frac{3}{2}\,\Gamma\frac{3}{2}}{2\Gamma 3}}{\dfrac{\Gamma 1\,\Gamma\frac{3}{2}}{2\Gamma\frac{5}{2}}} = \frac{\frac{2a}{\pi}\frac{1}{2}\Gamma\frac{1}{2}}{2\cdot 2\cdot 1}\cdot\frac{2\cdot\frac{3}{2}\cdot\frac{1}{2}\Gamma\frac{1}{2}}{1} = \frac{3a}{8}.$$

Hence, the required C.G. is given by $\bar{x} = 0,\ \bar{y} = \frac{3a}{8}$.

**Example 9:** Find the centre of gravity of a plate in the form of a quadrant of an ellipse, the density at any point of plate varying as the product of the distance from $OA$ and $OB$.

**Sol.**

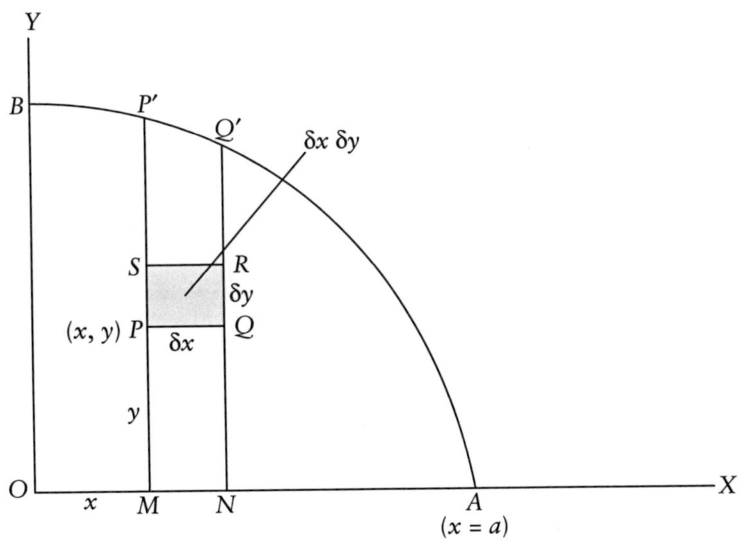


Let the equation of the ellipse be $\frac{x^2}{a^2}+\frac{y^2}{b^2}=1$

Take a point $P(x, y)$ inside the quadrant of the ellipse. Consider an element $\delta x\,\delta y$ at $P$. Since the element is very small, therefore the density at any point of the element can be taken as the same as the density at $P$.

Therefore,

$\rho$ = density at any point of the element $PQRS$
= density at $P = \lambda\, xy$, where $\lambda$ is a constant.

Elementary area = $\delta s = \delta x\ \delta y$

$\therefore$ Elementary mass $\delta m$ = Mass of the element $PQRS = \rho\ \delta s = \lambda\ \delta xy\ \delta x\ \delta y$

Also, the C.G. of the elementary area is at $P(x, y)$ referred to the coordinate axes as shown in the figure since $\delta x$ and $\delta y$ are very small.

For the quadrant $AOB$ of the ellipse (1), $x$ varies from 0 to $a$ and $y$ varies from 0 to $\frac{b}{a}\sqrt{a^2 - x^2}$.

Let $(\overline{x}, \overline{y})$ be the required C.G. Then,

$$\overline{x} = \frac{\int x\,dm}{\int dm} = \frac{\int_{x=0}^{a}\int_{y=0}^{\frac{b}{a}\sqrt{a^2-x^2}} x\,\lambda\,xy\,dx\,dy}{\int_{x=0}^{a}\int_{y=0}^{\frac{b}{a}\sqrt{a^2-x^2}} \lambda\,xy\,dx\,dy} = \frac{\int_{x=0}^{a}\int_{y=0}^{\frac{b}{a}\sqrt{a^2-x^2}} x^2y\,dx\,dy}{\int_{x=0}^{a}\int_{y=0}^{\frac{b}{a}\sqrt{a^2-x^2}} xy\,dx\,dy}$$

$$= \frac{\int_0^a \left(\frac{y^2}{2}\right)^{\frac{b}{a}\sqrt{a^2-x^2}} x^2\,dx}{\int_0^a \left(\frac{y^2}{2}\right)^{\frac{b}{a}\sqrt{a^2-x^2}} x\,dx} = \frac{\int_0^a x^2\left(a^2 - x^2\right)dx}{\int_0^a x\left(a^2 - x^2\right)dx} = \frac{a^2\left(\frac{x^3}{3}\right)_0^a - \left(\frac{x^5}{5}\right)_0^a}{a^2\left(\frac{x^2}{2}\right)_0^a - \left(\frac{x^4}{4}\right)_0^a}$$

$$= \frac{\frac{a^5}{3} - \frac{a^5}{5}}{\frac{a^4}{2} - \frac{a^4}{4}} = \frac{\frac{2}{15}a^5}{\frac{1}{4}a^4} = \frac{8a}{15}$$

and,

$$\overline{y} = \frac{\int y\,dm}{\int dm} = \frac{\int_{x=0}^{a}\int_{y=0}^{\frac{b}{a}\sqrt{a^2-x^2}} y\,\lambda\,xy\,dx\,dy}{\int_{x=0}^{a}\int_{y=0}^{\frac{b}{a}\sqrt{a^2-x^2}} \lambda\,xy\,dx\,dy} = \frac{\int_{x=0}^{a}\int_{y=0}^{\frac{b}{a}\sqrt{a^2-x^2}} xy^2\,dx\,dy}{\int_{x=0}^{a}\int_{y=0}^{\frac{b}{a}\sqrt{a^2-x^2}} xy\,dx\,dy}$$

$$= \frac{\int_0^a \left(\frac{y^3}{3}\right)_0^{\frac{b}{a}\sqrt{a^2-x^2}} x\,dx}{\int_0^a \left(\frac{y^2}{2}\right)_0^{\frac{b}{a}\sqrt{a^2-x^2}} x\,dx} = \frac{\frac{2b}{3a}\int_0^a x\left(a^2 - x^2\right)^{3/2}dx}{\int_0^a x\left(a^2 - x^2\right)dx}$$

Put $x = a\sin\theta$
$\therefore\ dx = a\cos\theta\ d\theta$

$$= \frac{\frac{2b}{3a}\int_0^{\pi/2} a\sin\theta\left(a^2 - a^2\sin^2\theta\right)^{3/2} a\cos\theta\,d\theta}{\int_0^{\pi/2} a\sin\theta\left(a^2 - a^2\sin^2\theta\right) a\cos\theta\,d\theta} = \frac{\frac{2b}{3a}\int_0^{\pi/2}\sin\theta\cos^4\theta\,d\theta}{\int_0^{\pi/2}\sin\theta\cos^3\theta\,d\theta}$$

$$= \frac{\frac{2b}{3a}\left(\frac{-\cos^5\theta}{5}\right)_0^{\pi/2}}{\left(\frac{-\cos^4\theta}{4}\right)_0^{\pi/2}} = \frac{2b}{3}\cdot\frac{4}{5} = \frac{8b}{15}.$$

**Example 10:** Find the coordinates of the centre of gravity of a lamina is the shape of a quadrant of the curve $\left(\frac{x^{\frac{2}{3}}}{a}\right)+\left(\frac{y^{\frac{2}{3}}}{b}\right)$, the density being given by $\rho = k\,xy$.

**Sol.**

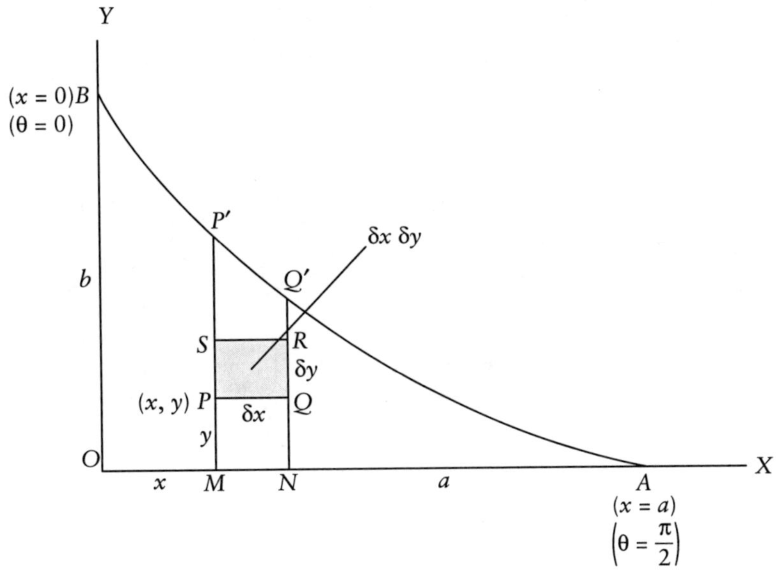


The equation of the curve is

$$\left(\frac{x}{a}\right)^{\frac{2}{3}} + \left(\frac{y}{b}\right)^{\frac{2}{3}} = 1$$

It parametric equation can be taken as

$$x = a\sin^3\theta \qquad ...(2)$$

$$y = b\cos^3\theta \qquad ...(3)$$

Take a point $P(x, y)$ inside the quadrant of the given curve. Consider an element $\delta x\,\delta y$ at $P$. Since the element is very small, therefore, the density at any point of the element can be taken as the same as the density at $P$. Therefore,

$$\rho = \text{density at any point of the element } PQRS = \text{density at } P = k\,xy$$

Elementary area $= \delta s = \delta x\,\delta y$

$\therefore$ Elementary mass $\delta m$

$$= \text{mass of the element } PQRS = \rho\,\delta s = k\,xy\,\delta x\,\delta y$$

Also, the C.G. of the elementary area is at $P(x, y)$ referred to $OX$ and $OY$ as the coordinate axes as shown in the figure since $\delta x$ and $\delta y$ are very small.

For the quadrant of the curve (1), $x$ varies from 0 to $a$ and $y$ varies from O to $y$.

Let $(x, y)$ be the required coordinates of C.G. Then,

$$\bar{x} = \frac{\int x\,dm}{\int dm} = \frac{\int_{x=0}^{a}\int_{y=0}^{y} x\,kxy\,dx\,dy}{\int_{x=0}^{a}\int_{y=0}^{b} kxy\,dx\,dy} = \frac{\int_{x=0}^{a}\int_{y=0}^{y} x^2 y\,dx\,dy}{\int_{x=0}^{a}\int_{y=0}^{b} xy\,dx\,dy} = \frac{\int_0^a \left(\frac{y^2}{2}\right)_0^y x^2\,dx}{\int_0^a \left(\frac{y^2}{2}\right)_0^y x\,dx}$$

$$= \frac{\int_0^b x^2 y^2\,dx}{\int_0^b xy^2\,dx} = \frac{\int_{\theta=0}^{\pi/2} a^2 \sin^6\theta\, b^2 \cos^6\theta\, 3a\sin^2\theta\cos\theta\,d\theta}{\int_{\theta=0}^{\pi/2} a\sin^3\theta\, b^2\cos^6\theta\, 3a\sin^2\theta\cos\theta\,d\theta} \quad \Big| \text{From (2) and (3)}$$

$$= \frac{a\int_0^{\pi/2} \sin^8\theta\cos^7\theta\,d\theta}{\int_{\theta=0}^{\pi/2} \sin^5\theta\cos^7\theta\,d\theta} = \frac{\dfrac{a\,\Gamma\frac{9}{2}\,\Gamma 4}{2\,\Gamma\frac{17}{2}}}{\dfrac{\Gamma 3\,\Gamma 4}{2\,\Gamma 7}} = \frac{a\,\Gamma\frac{9}{2}\,\Gamma 7}{\Gamma\frac{17}{2}\,\Gamma 3} = \frac{a\,\Gamma\frac{9}{2}\; 6\cdot 5\cdot 4\cdot 3\cdot \Gamma 3}{\frac{15}{2}\cdot\frac{13}{2}\cdot\frac{11}{2}\cdot\frac{9}{2}\,\Gamma\frac{9}{2}} = \frac{128a}{429}$$

and

$$\bar{y} = \frac{\int y\,dm}{\int dm} = \frac{\int_{x=0}^{a}\int_{y=0}^{y} y\,kxy\,dx\,dy}{\int_{x=0}^{a}\int_{y=0}^{y} kxy\,dx\,dy} = \frac{\int_{x=0}^{a}\int_{y=0}^{y} xy^2\,dx\,dy}{\int_{x=0}^{a}\int_{y=0}^{y} xy\,dx\,dy}$$

$$= \frac{\int_0^a \left(\frac{y^3}{3}\right)_0^y x\,dx}{\int_0^a \left(\frac{y^2}{2}\right)_0^y x\,dx} = \frac{\frac{2}{3}\int_0^a xy^3\,dx}{\int_0^a xy^2\,dx}$$

$$= \frac{\frac{2}{3}\int_{\theta=0}^{\pi/2} a\sin^3\theta \cdot b^3\cos^9\theta\, 3a\sin^2\theta\cos\theta\,d\theta}{\int_{\theta=0}^{\pi/2} a\sin^3\theta\, b^2\cos^6\theta\, 3a\sin^2\theta\cos\theta\,d\theta} \quad \Big| \text{From (2) and (3)}$$

$$= \frac{\frac{2b}{3}\int_0^{\pi/2} \sin^5\theta\cos^{10}\theta\,d\theta}{\int_0^{\pi/2} \sin^5\theta\cos^7\theta\,d\theta} = \frac{\dfrac{2b}{3}\dfrac{\Gamma 3\,\Gamma\frac{17}{2}}{2\,\Gamma\frac{17}{2}}}{\dfrac{\Gamma 3\,\Gamma 4}{2\,\Gamma 7}} = \frac{2b}{3}\,\frac{\Gamma\frac{11}{2}\,\Gamma 7}{\Gamma\frac{17}{2}\,\Gamma 4}$$

$$= \frac{\frac{2b}{3}\,\overline{\left|\frac{11}{2}\right.}\;6\cdot 5\cdot 4\,\overline{|4}}{\frac{15}{2}\cdot\frac{13}{2}\cdot\frac{11}{2}\,\overline{\left|\frac{11}{2}\right.}\;\overline{|4}} = \frac{128b}{429}.$$

**Example 11:** Find the centre of gravity of a sector of a sphere, the semi-vertical angle of whose cone is $\alpha$.

**Sol.** Let $OAB$ be a sector of a circle of radius $a$ such that angle of the sector is $\alpha$. When this sector is revolved about the initial line, it will generated the given sector of the sphere.

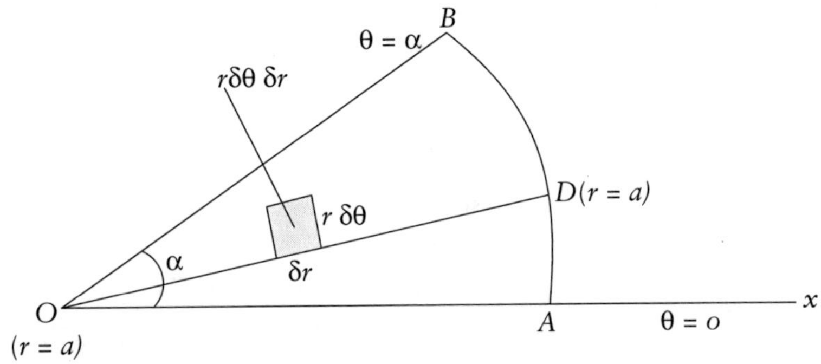


Take a point $P(r, \theta)$ inside this sector and then consider an element $r\delta\theta\ \delta r$ at the point $P(r, \theta)$.

When this element is revolved about the initial line, it will generate a mig of radius $r \sin\theta$ and symmetrical area $r\delta\theta\ \delta r$. It C.G. will be on the $X$-axis at a distance $r \cos\theta$ from the origin.

Elementary mass.

$= $ Mass of the ring generated $= \rho\ \delta\upsilon$

$= \rho\ 2\pi\ r \sin\theta\ r\delta\theta\ \delta r$, where $\rho$ is mass per unit volume.

Let $(\bar{x}, \bar{y})$ be the required C.G. then, $\bar{y} = 0$ | By symmetry

and $$\bar{x} = \frac{\int x\, dm}{\int dm}$$

$$= \frac{\int_{r=0}^{a}\int_{\theta=0}^{\alpha} r\cos\theta\ \rho\ 2\pi r\sin\theta\ r\ d\theta\ dr}{\int_{r=0}^{a}\int_{\theta=0}^{\alpha} \rho\ 2\pi r\sin\theta\ r\, d\theta\ dr} \qquad \text{| At O, } r = 0\text{; at } D,\ r = a$$

$$= \frac{\int_{r=0}^{a}\int_{\theta=0}^{\alpha} r^3 \sin\theta\ \cos\theta\, d\theta\ dr}{\int_{r=0}^{a}\int_{\theta=0}^{\alpha} r^2 \sin\theta\, d\theta\ dr} = \frac{\left(\frac{r^4}{4}\right)_o^a \left(\frac{\sin^2\theta}{2}\right)_0^\alpha}{\left(\frac{r^3}{3}\right)_0^a \left(-\cos\theta\right)_0^\alpha} = \frac{3a}{8}\frac{\sin^2\alpha}{1-\cos\alpha} = \frac{3a}{8}\frac{1-\cos^2\alpha}{1-\cos\alpha}$$

$$= \frac{3a}{8}\frac{(1-\cos\alpha)(1+\cos\alpha)}{1-\cos\alpha} = \frac{3a}{8}(1+\cos\alpha).$$

**Example 12:** Find the centre of gravity of a hemisphere is which the density is proportional to the $n$th power of the distance from the centre. Hence, show that the C.G. divides the radius perpendicular to the plane surface is the ratio $(n + 3)$: $(n + 5)$.

**Sol.** We know that a hemisphere is generated by the revolution of the quadrant $OAB$ of the circle about the bounding radius $OA$. Let the radius of the hemisphere be $a$. Then, the radius of the generating circle is $a$.

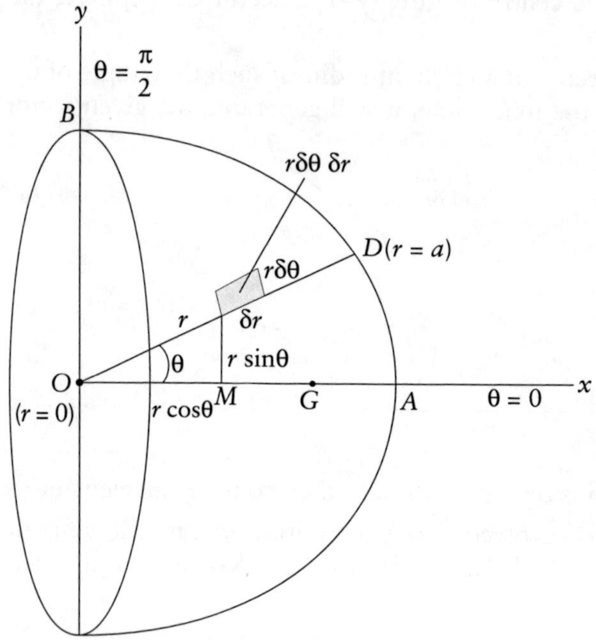


Take O as pole and bounding radius $OA$ as the initial line. Then, the polar equation of the generating circle is $r = a$.

Take a point $P(r, \theta)$ inside the quadrant $OAB$. Consider an elementary area $r\delta\theta\ \delta r$ at the point $P$.

When this element is revolved about $OA$, it will generate a circular ring whose radius is $r \sin\theta$ and cross-sectorial area is $r\delta\theta\ \delta r$.

$\therefore$ Elementary volume $= 2\ \pi\ r \sin\theta\ r\delta\theta\ \delta r$

$= 2\ \pi\ r^2 \sin\theta\ \delta\theta\ \delta r$

Density at any point of this element = Density at $P = \lambda\ (OP)^n = \lambda\ r^n$

$\therefore$ Elementary mass $= \lambda\ r^n\ 2\pi r^2 \sin\theta\ \delta\theta\ \delta r = \lambda \cdot 2\pi r^{n+2} \sin\theta\ \delta\theta\ \delta r$

Also, the C.G. of this elementary ring is at $M(r\cos\theta, \theta)$.

Let $(\bar{x}, \bar{y})$ be the required C.G. Then,

$\bar{y} = 0$ | By symmetry

and
$$\bar{x} = \frac{\int x\,dm}{\int dm} = \frac{\int_{\theta=0}^{\pi/2}\int_{r=0}^{a} r\cos\theta\ \lambda\ 2\pi r^{n+2} \sin\theta\ d\theta\, dr}{\int_{\theta=0}^{\pi/2}\int_{r=0}^{a} \lambda \cdot 2\pi r^{n+2} \sin\theta\ d\theta\, dr}$$

$$= \frac{\int_{\theta=0}^{\pi/2}\int_{r=0}^{a} r^{n+3}\sin\theta\cos\theta\, d\theta\, dr}{\int_{\theta=0}^{\pi/2}\int_{r=0}^{a} r^{n+2}\sin\theta\, d\theta dr} = \frac{\int_0^{\pi/2}\left(\frac{r^{n+4}}{n+4}\right)_0^a \sin\theta\cos\theta\, d\theta}{\int_0^{\pi/2}\left(\frac{r^{n+3}}{n+3}\right)\sin\theta\, d\theta}$$

$$= \left(\frac{n+3}{n+4}\right)a\frac{\int_0^{\pi/2}\sin\theta\cos\theta\, d\theta}{\int_0^{\pi/2}\sin\theta\, d\theta} = \left(\frac{n+3}{n+4}\right)a\frac{\left(\frac{\sin^2\theta}{2}\right)_0^{\pi/2}}{(-\cos\theta)_0^{\pi/2}} = \frac{(n+3)a}{2(n+4)}$$

Hence, the required C.G. is given by

$$\bar{x} = \frac{(n+3)a}{2(n+4)}, \quad \bar{y} = 0$$

$$\therefore \quad OG = \frac{n+3}{n+4}\frac{a}{2} \qquad \therefore \qquad GA = GA - OG$$

$$= a - \frac{n+3}{n+4}\frac{a}{2} = \frac{a}{2}\frac{n+5}{n+4}$$

$\therefore \quad OG : GA = (n + 3) : (n + 5).$

**Example 13:** Find the centre of gravity of a sphere when the density varies as the $n$th power of the distance from a point on the surface.

**Sol.** We know that the sphere is generated by revolving the semi-circle $OABO$ about its bounding diameter $OA$.

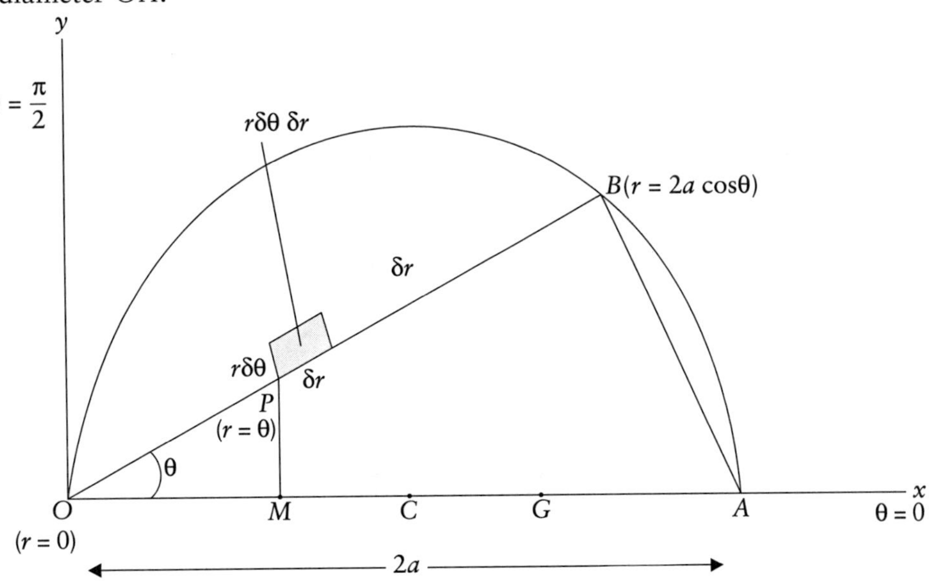


Take O, the end of the bounding diameters $OA$, as the pole and $OA$ as the initial line.

Let the radius of the semi-circle be $a$. Then, polar equation of the generating semi-circle is

$$r = 2a\cos\theta \qquad ...(1)$$

Take a point $P(r, \theta)$ inside the semi-circle. Consider an elementary area $r\delta\theta\,\delta r$ as the point $P(r, \theta)$.

When this element is revolved about the initial line $OX$, it will generate a ring of volume.

$$2\pi\, r\sin\theta\, r\delta\theta\,\delta r$$

Density at any point of this element

= Density at $P = \lambda r^n$, where $\lambda$ is a constant.

∴ Elementary mass $\delta m = \lambda r^n\, 2\pi r\sin\theta\, r\delta\theta\,\delta r = 2\pi\lambda r^{n+2}\sin\theta\,\delta\theta\,\delta r$

Also, the C.G. of the elementary ring is at $M(r\cos\theta, 0)$.

Let $(\bar{x}, \bar{y})$ be the required C.G. Then, $\bar{y} = 0$ | By symmetry

and $\bar{x} = \dfrac{\int x\,dm}{\int dm}$

$$= \frac{\int_{\theta=0}^{\pi/2}\int_{r=0}^{2a\cos\theta} r\cos\theta\, 2\pi\lambda r^{n+2}\sin\theta\, d\theta\, dr}{\int_{\theta=0}^{\pi/2}\int_{r=0}^{2a\cos\theta} r\pi\lambda r^{n+2}\sin\theta\, d\theta\, dr} \quad \text{| At O, } r = 0;\text{ at } D,\ r = 2a\cos\theta$$

$$= \frac{\int_{\theta=0}^{\pi/2}\int_{r=0}^{2a\cos\theta} r^{n+3}\sin\theta\cos\theta\, d\theta\, dr}{\int_{\theta=0}^{\pi/2}\int_{r=0}^{2a\cos\theta} r^{n+2}\sin\theta\, d\theta\, dr} = \frac{\int_0^{\pi/2}\left(\frac{r^{n+4}}{n+4}\right)_0^{2a\cos\theta}\sin\theta\cos\theta\, d\theta}{\int_0^{\pi/2}\left(\frac{r^{n+3}}{n+3}\right)_0^{2a\cos\theta}\sin\theta\, d\theta}$$

$$= \frac{2a\left(\frac{n+3}{n+4}\right)\int_0^{\pi/2}\cos^{n+5}\theta\sin\theta\, d\theta}{\int_0^{\pi/2}\cos^{n+3}\theta\sin\theta\, d\theta} = \frac{2a\left(\frac{n+3}{n+4}\right)\left(-\frac{\cos^{n+6}\theta}{n+6}\right)_0^{\pi/2}}{\left(-\frac{\cos^{n+4}\theta}{n+4}\right)_0^{\pi/2}}$$

$$= 2a\left(\frac{n+3}{n+4}\right)\left(\frac{n+4}{n+6}\right) = 2a\left(\frac{n+3}{n+6}\right)$$

$$\Rightarrow OG = 2a\left(\frac{n+3}{n+6}\right) \qquad \therefore GA = OA - OG = 2a - 2a\left(\frac{n+3}{n+6}\right) = 2a\left(\frac{3}{n+6}\right)$$

$$\therefore \quad OG : GA = (n+3) : 3$$

## EXERCISE 2(F)

1. Find the centre of gravity of a rod whose density varies as the square of the distance from one end.

   [**Ans.** At a distance $\dfrac{3a}{4}$ from the given end; $a$ being the length of the rod]

2. The mass per unit length at any point of a straight beam of length $l$ is $\rho\left(1+\frac{x}{l}\right)$, where $x$ is the distance of the point from one end of the been. Find (i) the mass of the beam and (ii) the position of its centre of gravity.

$\left[\textbf{Ans.}\ \text{(i)}\ \frac{3}{2}\rho l \quad \text{(ii)}\ \bar{x} = \frac{5}{9}l\right]$

3. If the density of a circular arc varies as the square of the distance from a point O on the arc, shows that the centroid divides the diameter through O in the ratio 3 : 1.

4. Find the centre of gravity of a solid hemisphere when density varies directly as the distance from the centre.

$\left[\textbf{Ans.}\ \bar{x} = \frac{2}{5}a,\ \bar{y} = 0\right]$

5. Find the centre of gravity of a solid hemisphere when density varies inversely as the distance from the centre.

$\left[\textbf{Ans.}\ \bar{x} = \frac{a}{3},\ \bar{y} = 0\right]$

6. Find the C.G. of a solid hemisphere when density at any point varies directly as the square of the distance from the centre.

OR

Find the C.G. of a solid hemisphere when density as any point varies directly as the square of the distance from the centre of the whole sphere.

$\left[\textbf{Ans.}\ \bar{x} = \frac{5a}{12},\ \bar{y} = 0\right]$

7. Show that the C.G. of a sphere, the density at any point of which varies inversely as the square of the distance from a fixed point on the surface of the sphere, bisects the radius through the fixed point.

[**Hint:** Refer Ex. 13

Put $n = -2$

$$\therefore\ OG = \frac{a}{2} = \frac{OC}{2}$$

$\Rightarrow$ C.G. $G$ bisects $OC$, the radius through the fixed point O]

## MISCELLANEOUS ILLUSTRATIVE EXAMPLES

**Example 1:** A thin uniform rod of length $l$ is bent into the form of a circular arc whose radius $a$ is large compared to $l$. Prove that the displacement of the C.G. is $\frac{l^2}{24a}$ approximately.

**Sol.**

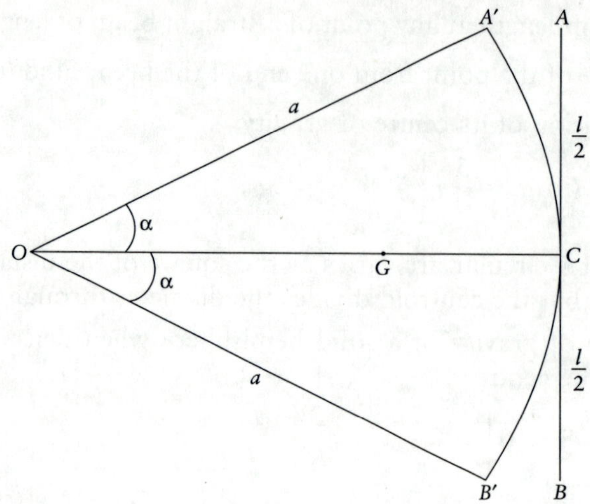


Let $AB$ be a thin uniform rod of length $l$ with $C$ as its mid-point so that $AC = BC = \dfrac{l}{2}$. $A'CB'$ is the position of the rod when it is bent into the form of a circular arc whose radius is $a$ where $a >>> l$. Let the arc $A'CB'$ subtend an angle $2\alpha$ at the centre $O$. Let $G$ be the C.G. of the arc $A'CB'$. Then,

$$OG = \frac{a \sin \alpha}{\alpha}$$

$$= \frac{a}{\alpha}\left[\alpha - \frac{\alpha^3}{\alpha} + \text{terms containing higher powers of } \alpha\right] \qquad ...(1)$$

For a circular arc, we know that

$$\text{angle} = \frac{\text{arc}}{\text{radius}}$$

Therefore, for circular arc $A'CB'$, we have

$$2\alpha = \frac{l}{a}$$

$$\Rightarrow \quad \alpha = \frac{l}{2a} \qquad ...(2)$$

Since $a$ is large compared to $l$, therefore, $\dfrac{l}{2a}$ is small. Hence, $\alpha$ is small.

Therefore, neglecting the terms containing higher powers of $\alpha$, we have from (1),

$$OG = \frac{a}{\alpha}\left(\alpha - \frac{\alpha^3}{\underline{|3}}\right) = a - \frac{a\,\alpha^2}{6}$$

$$= a - \frac{a}{6}\left(\frac{l}{2a}\right)^2 \qquad \text{| From (1)}$$

$$= a - \frac{l^2}{24a} \qquad \text{| From (3)}$$

Originally, the rod $AB$ was straight. Therefore, its C.G. was at $C$ where $OC = a$.

Hence, the required displacement of the C.G. = $CG$

$$= OC - OG$$

$$= a - \left(a - \frac{l^2}{24a}\right) \qquad = \frac{l^2}{24a} \text{ approximately}$$

**Example 2:** A uniform wire is bent into the form of a triangle. If $x$, $y$, $z$ are the distance of its C.G. from the three sides and $r$ the in-radius of the triangle, then show that

$$r^3 + r^2 (x + y + z) - 4xyz = 0$$

**Sol.** Let the triangle be $ABC$ in which $BC = a$, $CA = b$ and $AB = c$.

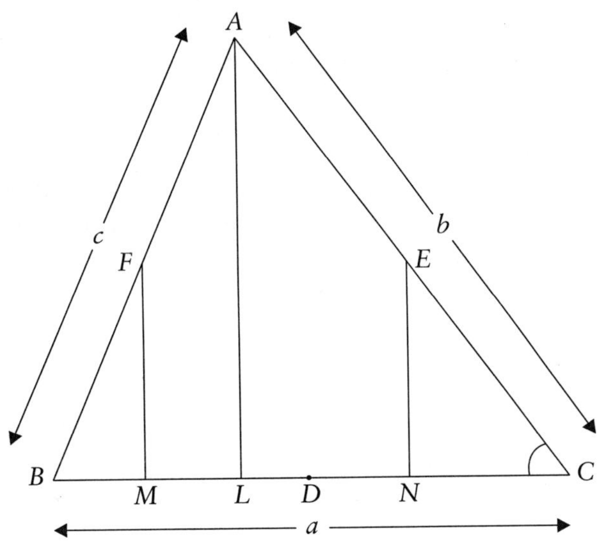


Let $\lambda$ be the line density. Then, the masses of sides $BC$, $CA$ and $AB$ are $\lambda a$, $\lambda b$ and $\lambda c$ respectively acting at their middle points $D$, $E$ and $F$. The distance of the middle points $E$ and $F$ from the side $a$

$$= \frac{b \sin C}{2} \qquad | \because EN = FM \text{ (by geometry)}$$

$$= \frac{S}{a} \qquad | \because S = \frac{1}{2} ab \sin C$$

where $S$ is the area of the triangle $ABC$.

Hence, taking moments about the side $a$, we get

$$x = \frac{\frac{S}{a}\cdot\lambda b + \frac{S}{a}\cdot\lambda c + 0\cdot\lambda a}{\lambda a+\lambda b+\lambda c} = \frac{S(b+c)}{a(a+b+c)} = \frac{S(b+c)}{a(2s)} \qquad |\therefore 2s = a + b + c$$

$$= \frac{r}{2}\left(\frac{b+c}{a}\right) \qquad |\therefore r = \frac{S}{s}$$

Similarly,

$$y = \frac{r}{2}\left(\frac{c+a}{b}\right) \quad \text{and} \quad z = \frac{r}{2}\left(\frac{a+b}{c}\right)$$

$\therefore \quad r^3 + r^2 (x + y + z) - 4xyz$

$$= r^3 + \frac{r^3}{2}\left[\frac{b+c}{a} + \frac{c+a}{b} + \frac{a+b}{c}\right] - 4\cdot\frac{r^3}{8}\left(\frac{b+c}{a}\right)\left(\frac{c+a}{b}\right)\left(\frac{a+b}{c}\right)$$

$$= r^3 + \frac{r^3}{2abc}\left[bc(b+c)+ca(c+a)ab(a+b)\right] - \frac{r^3}{2abc}(b+c)(c+a)(a+b)$$

$$= \frac{r^3}{2abc}\Big[2abc + b^2c + bc^2 + c^2a + ca^2 + a^2b + ab^2$$
$$-abc - cb^2 - a^2b - ab^2 - c^2a - c^2b - ca^2 - abc\Big] = 0$$

**Example 3:** A thin uniform rod is bent at one end to form a walking stick surmounted by a semi-circular handle. The straight portion $AB$ is of length $2l$ and the portion $BC$, which is semi-circular of radius $a < l$. The straight line joining the ends $B$ and C is perpendicular to $AB$. The stick hangs with the point $C$ supported on a horizontal table. Prove that the straight part makes an angle $\theta$ with the vertical where

$$\tan\theta = \frac{a(\pi a + 4l)}{2(l^2 - a^2)}$$

**Sol.**

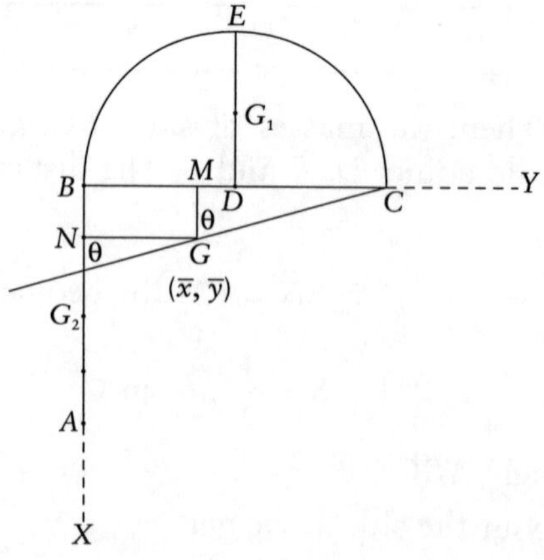

Take $BA$ as $X$-axis and $BC$ as $Y$-axis. The centre of gravity of the semi-circular portion $BECB$ is at $G_1\left(-\frac{2a}{\pi}, a\right)$ and that of the straight portion $BA$ is at $G_2(l, 0)$. The weights acting at these points are $a\pi w$ and $2lw$ respectively where $w$ is weight per unit length.

Let the resultant centre of gravity be $G(\bar{x}, \bar{y})$. Then,

$$\bar{x} = \frac{\left(-\frac{2a}{\pi}\right)a\pi w + l(2l)w}{a\pi w + 2lw} = \frac{2(l^2 - a^2)}{a\pi + 2l} \quad ...(1)$$

and $$\bar{y} = \frac{(a)a\pi w + (0)2lw}{a\pi w + 2lw} = \frac{a^2\pi}{a\pi + 2l} \quad ...(2)$$

When the stick is hung from the point $C$, then clearly in the position of equilibrium, $G$ will be vertically below $C$, i.e., C.G. will be a vertical line. Let $AB$ make an angle $\theta$ with C.G. Then,

$$\tan\theta = \frac{CM}{MG}$$

where $M$ is the foot of the perpendicular from $G$ on $BC$.

$$= \frac{BC - BM}{BN} = \frac{2a - \bar{y}}{\bar{x}} = \frac{2a - \frac{a^2\pi}{a\pi + 2l}}{\frac{2(l^2 - a^2)}{a\pi + 2l}} = \frac{a^2\pi + 4al}{2(l^2 - a^2)} = \frac{a(a\pi + 4l)}{2(l^2 - a^2)}.$$

**Example 4:** Two pieces of the same uniform wire, one a semi-circle and the other an arc of a circle subtending an angle $2\theta(<\pi)$ at its centre, are placed so as to form a crescent. If $\theta$ is such that the C.G. is on the inner arc, show that it is given by the equation

$$\sin^2\theta + \sin\theta = \frac{1}{2}\pi\sin\theta(1 - \cos\theta) + \theta$$

**Sol.**

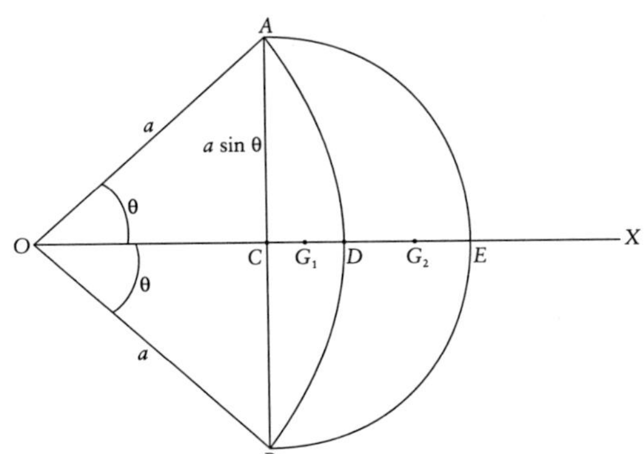


$AEB$ is the semi-circular piece of wire on $AB$ as diameter, $C$ being the centre.

$ADB$ is another piece of wire subtending an angle $2\theta$ at its centre $O$. $OCDE$ is the symmetrical radius of the two arcs.

By symmetry, the combined C.G. must lie on $OCDE$. According to the problem, it must coincide with $D$.

Let $OP = a$,

Then, from right triangle $OCA$, $AC = a \sin\theta = b$(say)

Let $G_1$ and $G_2$ be the centroids of the arcs $ADB$ and $AEB$ respectively. Then,

$$x_1 = OG_1 = \frac{a\sin\theta}{\theta} \qquad CG_2 = \frac{b\sin\alpha}{\alpha} = \frac{a\sin\theta\,\sin\frac{\pi}{2}}{\frac{\pi}{2}} \qquad \because\ \alpha = \frac{\pi}{2}$$

$$= \frac{2a\sin\theta}{\pi} \qquad \therefore \qquad x_2 = OG_2 = OC + CG_2 = a\cos\theta + \frac{2a\sin\theta}{\pi}$$

Let $w$ be the weight per unit length of the wire. Then,

$w_1$ = weight of the wire $ADB = (2a\,\theta)w$

$w_2$ = weight of the wire $AEB = (\pi\, b)w = \pi\, a \sin\theta\, w$

Let the combined C.G. of the two wires be at a distance $\bar{x}$ from O. Then,

$$\bar{x} = \frac{w_1x_1 + w_2x_2}{w_1 + w_2} = \frac{2a\theta w\left(\frac{a\sin\theta}{\theta}\right) + \pi a\sin\theta w\cdot\left(a\cos + \frac{2a\sin\theta}{\pi}\right)}{2a\theta w + \pi a\sin\theta w}$$

$$= \frac{2a\sin\theta + \pi a\sin\theta\cos\theta + 2a\sin^2\theta}{2\theta + \pi\sin\theta} \qquad \Rightarrow\ 2\theta + \pi\sin\theta = 2\sin\theta + \pi\sin\theta\cos\theta + 2\sin^2\theta$$

$$\Rightarrow\ \sin^2\theta + \sin\theta = -\frac{1}{2}\pi\sin\theta\cos\theta + \frac{1}{2}\pi\sin\theta + \theta \qquad \Rightarrow\ \sin^2\theta + \sin\theta = \frac{1}{2}\pi\sin\theta(1-\cos\theta) + \theta$$

**Example 5:** An isosceles triangular lamina is such that its mass per unit area at any point varies as the sum of the perpendicular distances of the point from equal sides of the triangle. Prove that the distance of the C.G. from the vertex is 3/4 of the altitude.

**Sol.**

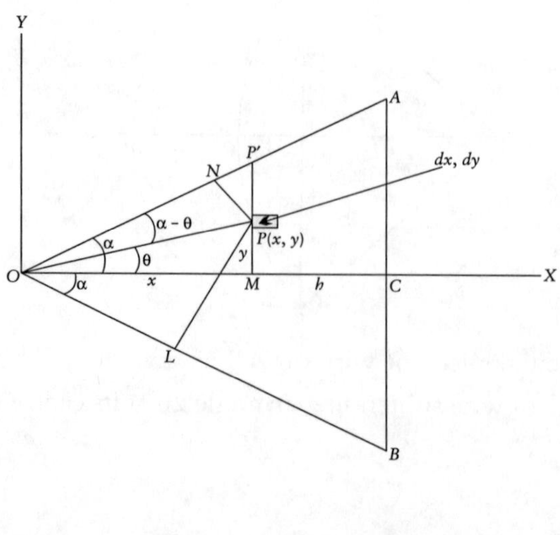

Let $OAB$ be an isosceles triangular lamina in which $OA = OB$; $OA$ and $OB$ being the equal sides. Let the altitude of this triangle be $OC(= h)$.

Let us consider an elementary area $dxdy$ at $P(x, y)$. Draw the perpendiculars $PL$ and $PN$ from $P$ to the equal sides $OB$ and $OA$ respectively. Let $\angle POX = \theta$ and $\angle AOC = \angle BOC = \alpha$

Let $\rho$ be the density at $P$. Then, $\rho = \lambda\ (PN + PL) = \lambda\ \{OP \sin(\alpha - \theta) + OP \sin(\alpha + \theta)\}$

$$= \lambda \cdot OP \cdot 2\sin\alpha \cos\theta = 2\lambda\ OP \sin\alpha \cos\theta = 2\lambda\ OP \sin\alpha\ \frac{OM}{OP}$$

$$= 2\lambda\ OM \sin\alpha = 2\lambda\ x \sin\alpha \qquad ...(1)$$

Take O as origin and the horizontal and vertical lines $OX$ and $OY$ through O as $X$-axis and $Y$-axis respectively.

Then, equation of the line $OA$ is $y = x \tan \alpha$ ...(2)

Let $(\bar{x}, \bar{y})$ be the coordinates of the required C.G. Then, $y = 0$ | By symmetry

and, $$\bar{x} = \frac{\int x\,dm}{\int dm} = \frac{\int_{x=0}^{h}\int_{y=0}^{x\tan\alpha} x\rho\ dx\ dy}{\int_{x=0}^{h}\int_{y=0}^{x\tan\alpha} \rho\ dx\ dy} = \frac{\int_0^h\int_0^{x\tan\alpha} x\,2\lambda x \sin\alpha\,dx\ dy}{\int_0^h\int_0^{x\tan\alpha} 2\lambda x \sin\alpha\,dx\,dy} \qquad \text{| From (1)}$$

$$= \frac{\int_0^h\int_0^{x\tan\alpha} x^2\ dx\ dy}{\int_0^h\int_0^{x\tan\alpha} x\,dx\,dy} = \frac{\int_0^h x^2\,(y)_0^{x\tan\alpha}\ dx}{\int_0^h x\,(y)_0^{x\tan\alpha}\ dx} = \frac{\int_0^h x^3 \tan\alpha\,dx}{\int_0^h x^2 \tan\alpha\,dx}$$

$$= \frac{\int_0^h x^3 dx}{\int_0^h x^2 dx} = \frac{\left(\frac{x^4}{4}\right)_0^h}{\left(\frac{x^3}{3}\right)_0^h} = \frac{\frac{h^4}{4}}{\frac{h^3}{3}} = \frac{3}{4}h$$

**Example 6:** An isosceles triangular lamina is such that its mass per unit area at any point is proportional to the product of the distances of the point from the equal sides of the triangle. Prove that the distance of the C.G. from the vertex is $\frac{4}{5}$ of the altitude.

**Sol.**

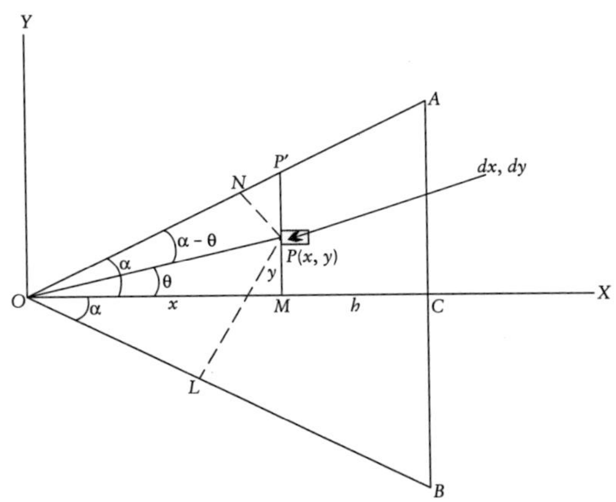

Let $OAB$ be an isosceles triangular lamina in which $OA = OB$; $OA$ and $OB$ being the equal sides. Let the altitude of this triangle be $OC(= h)$.

Let us consider an elementary area $dxdy$ at $P(x, y)$. Draw the perpendiculars $PL$ and $PN$ from $P$ to the equal sides $OB$ and $OA$ respectively. Let $\angle POX = \theta$ and $\angle AOC = \angle BOC = \alpha$.

Let $\rho$ be the density $P$. Then,

$$\rho = \lambda\, PN\, PL = \lambda\, OP \sin(\alpha - \theta)\, OP \sin(\alpha + \theta) = \lambda\, OP^2 (\sin^2\alpha - \sin^2\theta)$$

$$= \lambda\, OP^2 \left(\sin^2\alpha - \frac{PM^2}{OP^2}\right) \qquad \Big| \text{From } \Delta\, PMO$$

$$= \lambda\, OP^2 \left(\sin^2\alpha - \frac{y^2}{OP^2}\right) = \lambda\,(OP^2 \sin^2\alpha - y^2) = \lambda\,\{(x^2 + y^2)\sin^2\alpha - y^2\}$$

$$= \lambda\,\{x^2 \sin^2\alpha - y^2(1 - \sin^2\alpha)\} = \lambda\,(x^2\sin^2\alpha - y^2\cos^2\alpha) \qquad \text{...(1)}$$

Take $O$ as origin and the horizontal and vertical lines $OX$ and $OY$ through $O$ as $X$-axis and $Y$-axis respectively.

Then, equation of the line $OA$ is $y = x \tan\alpha$ ...(2)

Let $(\bar{x}, \bar{y})$ be the coordinates of the required C.G. Then,

$$\bar{y} = 0 \qquad \Big| \text{By symmetry about } X\text{-axis}$$

and

$$\bar{x} = \frac{\int x\, dm}{\int dm} = \frac{\int_{x=0}^{h}\int_{y=0}^{x\tan\alpha} x\,\rho\, dx\, dy}{\int_{x=0}^{h}\int_{y=0}^{x\tan\alpha} \rho\, dx\, dy}$$

$$= \frac{\int_{x=0}^{h}\int_{y=0}^{x\tan\alpha} x\,\lambda(x^2\sin^2\alpha - y^2\cos^2\alpha)\, dx\, dy}{\int_{x=0}^{h}\int_{h=0}^{x\tan\alpha} \lambda(x^2\sin^2\alpha - y^2\cos^2\alpha)\, dx\, dy} \qquad \Big| \text{From (1)}$$

$$= \frac{\int_0^h\int_0^{x\tan\alpha} (x^3\sin^2\alpha - xy^2\cos^2\alpha)\, dx\, dy}{\int_0^h\int_0^{x\tan\alpha} (x^2\sin^2\alpha - y^2\cos^2\alpha)\, dx\, dy}$$

$$= \frac{\int_0^h \left(x^3\sin^2\alpha\; y - \alpha\cos^2\alpha \dfrac{y^3}{3}\right)_0^{x\tan\alpha} dx}{\int_0^h \left(x^2\sin^2\alpha\; y - \cos^2\alpha \dfrac{y^3}{3}\right)_0^{x\tan\alpha} dx}$$

$$= \frac{\int_0^h \left(x^3\sin^2\alpha\; x\tan\alpha - x\cos^2\alpha \dfrac{x^3\tan^3\alpha}{3}\right) dx}{\int_0^h \left(x^2\sin^2\alpha\; x\tan\alpha - \dfrac{\cos^2\alpha}{3} x^3\tan^3\alpha\right) dx}$$

$$= \frac{\int_0^h \left( x^4 \sin^2 \alpha \tan\alpha - \frac{x^4}{3} \sin^2 \alpha \tan\alpha \right) dx}{\int_0^h \left( x^3 \sin^2 \alpha \tan\alpha - \frac{x^3}{3} \sin^2 \alpha \tan\alpha \right) dx}$$

$$= \frac{\int_0^h \left( x^4 - \frac{x^4}{3} \right) dx}{\int_0^h \left( x^3 - \frac{x^3}{3} \right) dx} = \frac{\int_0^h \frac{2}{3} x^4 dx}{\int_0^h \frac{2}{3} x^3 dx} = \frac{\int_0^h x^4 dx}{\int_0^h x^3 dx} = \frac{\left( \frac{x^5}{5} \right)_0^h}{\left( \frac{x^4}{4} \right)_0^h} = \frac{\frac{h^5}{5}}{\frac{h^4}{4}} = \frac{4}{5} h .$$

**Example 7:** Find the centre of gravity of half of a solid right circular cone bounded by a plane through its axis.

**Sol.**

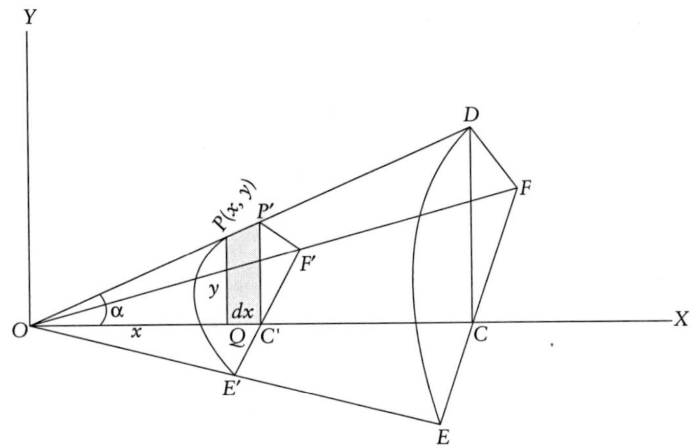


The above figure represents a semi-circular cone $OEF$ bounded by a plane through its axis. Let us consider an elementary strip $PQ$ of height $y$ and breadth $dx$. When this strip is rotated through two right angles about $OCX$, then it generates a semi-circular disc of mass $dm = 1/2\ \pi\ y^2\ dx\ \rho$ ...(1)

Take O as origin and the horizontal and vertical lines $OX$ and $OY$ through O as the axis of $X$ and axis of $Y$ respectively.

Referred to these axes, the coordinates of the centroid of this elementary semi-circular plate will be $\left( x, \frac{4y}{3\pi} \right)$. [We know that the C.G. of a semi-circular plane lies on its central radius at a distance $\frac{4a}{3\pi}$, where $a$ is the radius of the semi-circle.]

Let the semi-vertical angle of the cone be $\alpha$. Then, we have, $y = x \tan \alpha$ ...(2)

Let the height of the cone be $h$. Let $(\bar{x}, \bar{y})$ be the coordinates of the required C.G. Then,

$$\bar{x} = \frac{\int x\, dm}{\int dm} = \frac{\int_{x=0}^{h} x \frac{1}{2} \pi\, y^2\, dx\, \rho}{\int_{x=0}^{h} \frac{1}{2} \pi\, y^2\, dx\, \rho} \qquad \text{| From (1)}$$

$$= \frac{\int_0^h x y^2\, dx}{\int_0^h y^2\, dx} = \frac{\int_0^h x (x\tan\alpha)^2\, dx}{\int_0^h (x\tan\alpha)^2\, dx} \qquad \text{| From (2)}$$

$$= \frac{\int_0^h x^3\, dx}{\int_0^h x^2\, dx} = \frac{\left(\frac{x^4}{4}\right)_0^h}{\left(\frac{x^3}{3}\right)_0^h} = \frac{\frac{h^4}{4}}{\frac{h^3}{3}} = \frac{3}{4}h$$

$$\text{and, } \bar{y} = \frac{\int_{x=0}^h \frac{4y}{3\pi}\frac{1}{2}\pi y^2\, dx\, \rho}{\int_{x=0}^h \frac{1}{2}\pi y^2\, dx\, \rho} \qquad \text{| From (1)}$$

$$= \frac{\frac{4}{3\pi}\int_0^h y^3\, dx}{\int_0^h y^2\, dx} = \frac{\frac{4}{3\pi}\int_0^h x^3 \tan^3\alpha\, dx}{\int_0^h x^2 \tan^2\alpha\, dx} \qquad \text{| From (2)}$$

$$= \frac{\frac{4\tan\alpha}{3\pi}\int_0^h x^3 dx}{\int_0^h x^2 dx} = \frac{\frac{4\tan\alpha}{3\pi}\left(\frac{x^4}{4}\right)_0^h}{\left(\frac{x^3}{3}\right)_0^h} = \frac{\frac{4\tan\alpha}{3\pi}\frac{h^4}{4}}{\frac{h^3}{3}} = \frac{h\tan\alpha}{\pi} = \frac{\text{Radius of the base}}{\pi}$$

**Example 8:** Find the centre of gravity of a semi-conical shell of uniform thickness and density.

**Sol.** The semi-conical shell *OEF* is generated by the revolution of the straight line *CD* about *OX* through two right angles. *OE* and *OF* are the two extreme positions of the line *OD*. Clearly, the C.G. of this semi-conical shell will lie in the plane *OCD* which is perpendicular to the plane *OEF*.

Let us consider an elementary arc *PP′* of arc length $ds = dx \sec \alpha$ ...(1) of the generating line *OD*, where $\alpha$ is the semi-vertical angle of the conical shell.

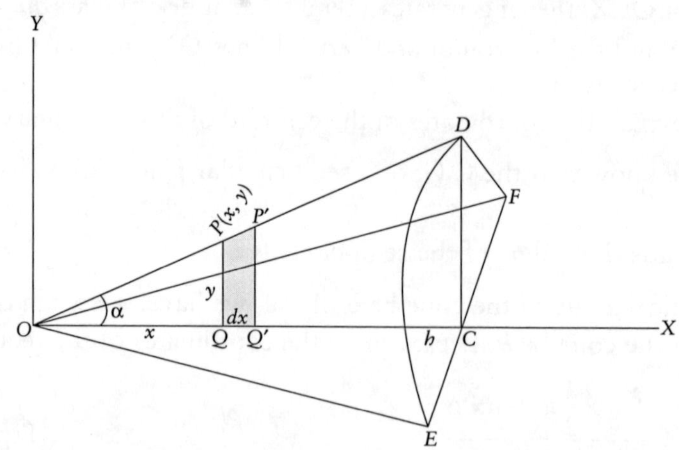

Take O as origin and the horizontal and the vertical lines $OX$ and $OY$ through O as X-axis and Y-axis respectively. Referred to these axes, let the coordinates of ρ be $(x, y)$. Then,

$$y = x \tan \alpha \qquad ...(2)$$

The elementary arc $PP'$ will generate a semi-circular arc of mass

$$dm = 2\pi y \, ds \, \rho$$

$$= 2\pi \, x \tan \alpha \, dx \sec \alpha \, \rho \qquad \text{| From (1) and (2)}$$

where ρ is the surface density.

We know that the C.G. of this elementary semi-circular ring will be at $\left[x, \frac{2y}{\pi}\right]$, i.e., at $\left[x, \frac{2x\tan\alpha}{\pi}\right]$. | From (2)

[We know that the C.G. of a semi-circular arc lies on the central radius at a distance $\frac{2r}{\pi}$ from the centre, where $r$ is the radius of the arc.]

Let the height of the shell be $OC$ (= $h$). Let $(\bar{x}, \bar{y})$ be the coordinates of the required C.G. referred to coordinate axes $OX$ and $OY$. Then,

$$\bar{x} = \frac{\int x\,dm}{\int dm} = \frac{\int_{x=0}^{h} x\, 2\pi\, x\tan\alpha\, dx \sec\alpha\, \rho}{\int_{x=0}^{h} 2\pi\, x\tan\alpha\, dx\sec\alpha\,\rho} = \frac{\int_0^h x^2\,dx}{\int_0^h x\,dx}$$

$$= \frac{\left(\frac{x^3}{3}\right)_0^h}{\left(\frac{x^2}{2}\right)_0^h} = \frac{\frac{h^3}{3}}{\frac{h^2}{2}} = \frac{2}{3}h \qquad \text{and,} \qquad \bar{y} = \frac{\int y\,dm}{\int dm}$$

$$= \frac{\int_{x=0}^{h} 2\frac{x\tan\alpha}{\pi}\, 2\pi\, x\tan\alpha\, dx\sec\alpha\,\rho}{\int_{x=0}^{h} 2\pi\, x\tan\alpha\, dx\sec\alpha\,\rho} = \frac{2\tan\alpha}{\pi}\frac{\int_0^h x^2\,dx}{\int_0^h x\,dx}$$

$$= \frac{2\tan\alpha}{\pi}\frac{\left(\frac{x^3}{3}\right)_0^h}{\left(\frac{x^2}{2}\right)_0^h} = \frac{2\tan\alpha}{\pi}\frac{\frac{h^3}{3}}{\frac{h^2}{2}} = \frac{4h\tan\alpha}{3\pi}$$

$$= \frac{4r}{3\pi}. \qquad \text{| } \because r = h\tan\alpha \text{ [= Radius of the base]}$$

**Example 9:** If the density at any point of a circular disc whose radius is $a$, varies directly as the distance from the centre and a circle described on the radius as diameter be cut out, prove that the centre of inertia of the remainder will be at a distance $\frac{6a}{(15\pi - 10)}$, from the centre.

**Sol.**

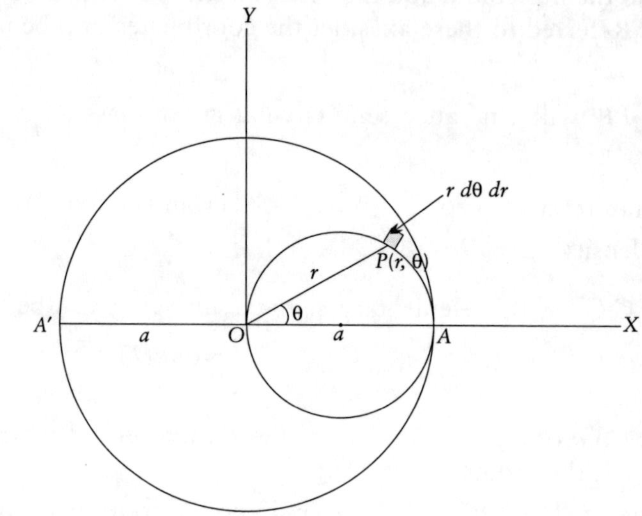


Take O, the centre of circular disc of radius $a$, as origin and the horizontal and vertical lines $OX$ and $OY$ through $O$ as X-axis and Y-axis respectively. Then,

$$r = a \qquad ...(1)$$

and, the equation of the smaller circle is

$$r = a\cos\theta \qquad ...(2)$$

Let $\rho$ be the density at any point $P(r, \theta)$. Then,

$$\rho = \lambda r \qquad ...(3)$$

Now,

$m_1$ = mass of the bigger cycle

$$= \int_{\theta=0}^{2\pi}\int_{r=0}^{a} \lambda r \cdot r d\theta\, dr = \lambda\int_0^{2\pi}\left(\frac{r^3}{3}\right)_0^a d\theta = \frac{\lambda a^3}{3}\int_0^{2\pi} d\theta = \frac{2\pi\lambda a^3}{3}$$

$x_1$ = distance of the C.G. of the bigger circle from $O$

$= 0$ | By symmetry

$x_2$ = Mass of the smaller circle

$$= 2\int_{\theta=0}^{\pi/2}\int_{r=0}^{a\cos\theta} \lambda r\, r d\theta\, ds = 2\lambda\int_0^{\pi/2}\left(\frac{r^3}{3}\right)_0^{a\cos\theta} d\theta = \frac{2\lambda a^3}{3}\int_0^{\pi/2}\cos^3\theta\, d\theta$$

$$= \frac{2\lambda a^3}{3}\cdot\frac{2}{3}$$ | By Walli's Formula

$$= \frac{4\lambda a^3}{9}$$

$x_2$ = distance of the C.G. of the smaller circle from $O$

$$= \frac{2\int_{\theta/0}^{\pi/2}\int_{r=0}^{a\cos\theta} r\cos\theta\cdot\lambda r\cdot r d\theta\, dr}{2\int_{\theta=0}^{\pi/2}\int_{r=0}^{a\cos\theta}\lambda r\, r d\theta\, dr} = \frac{2\lambda\int_0^{\pi/2}\left(\frac{r^4}{4}\right)_0^{a\cos\theta}\cos\theta\, d\theta}{\text{mass of the smaller circle}} = \frac{\frac{\lambda a^4}{2}\int_0^{\pi/2}\cos^5\theta\, d\theta}{\frac{4\lambda a^3}{9}}$$

$$= \frac{9a}{8}\int_0^{\pi/2}\cos^5\theta\, d\theta = \frac{9a}{8}\cdot\frac{4}{5}\cdot\frac{2}{3} \qquad \text{| By Walli's Formula}$$

$$= \frac{3a}{5}$$

Hence, the distance of the C.G. of the remainder is given by

$$\bar{x} = \frac{m_1 x_1 - m_2 x_2}{m_1 - m_2} = \frac{\frac{2\pi\lambda a^3}{3}(0) - \frac{4\lambda a^3}{9}\cdot\frac{3a}{5}}{\frac{2\pi\lambda a^3}{3} - \frac{4\lambda a^3}{9}} = -\frac{\frac{4}{15}a}{\frac{2}{9}(3\pi - 2)} = -\frac{6a}{15\pi - 10}$$

The negative sign simply signifies the fact that the C.G. lies on the negative side of $X$-axis, i.e., on $XO$ produced.

**Example 10:** If the density at any point of a sphere of radius $a$ varies directly as the distance from the centre and a sphere described on the radius as diameter be cut out, show that the centre of gravity of the remainder is at a distance $\frac{4a}{63}$ from the centre.

**Sol.** The solid under consideration here is generated by revolving the semi-circle on $A'A$ as diameter from which a semi-circle described on $OA$ as diameter is removed.

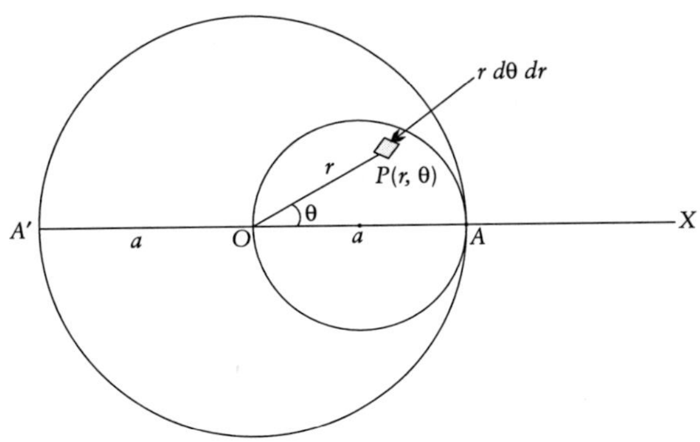


Take O as pole and $OX$ as the initial line. Then, the equation of the bigger circle is $r = a$ ...(1)
and, the equation of the smaller circle is

$$r = a\cos\theta \qquad ...(2)$$

Volume of the ring generated by revolving the element $r\, d\theta\, dr$ about the initial line

$$= (2\pi r\sin\theta)\, r\, d\theta\, dr$$

Also, density at any point of this element

$$= \text{density at } P(r, \theta) = \lambda(OP) = \lambda r$$

$\therefore$ $m_1$ = mass of the bigger sphere

$$= \int_{\theta=0}^{\pi}\int_{r=0}^{a} \lambda r(2\pi\, r\sin\theta) r d\theta\, dr = 2\pi\lambda\int_0^{\pi}\left(\frac{r^4}{4}\right)_0^a \sin\theta\, d\theta = \frac{\pi\lambda a^4}{2}(-\cos\theta)_0^{\pi} = \pi\lambda a^4$$

$m_2$ = mass of the smaller circle

$$= \int_{\theta=0}^{\pi/2}\int_{r=0}^{a\cos\theta} \lambda r(2\pi r\sin\theta) r\, d\theta\, dr = 2\pi\lambda\int_0^{\pi/2}\left(\frac{r^4}{4}\right)_0^{a\cos\theta} \sin\theta\, d\theta$$

$$= \frac{\pi\lambda a^4}{2}\int_0^{\pi/2}\cos^4\theta\sin\theta\, d\theta = \frac{\pi\lambda a^4}{2}\left(-\frac{\cos^5\theta}{5}\right)_0^{\pi/2} = \frac{\pi\lambda a^4}{10}$$

$x_1$ = distance of C.G. of the bigger sphere from $O$

= 0 | By symmetry

$x_2$ = distance of C.G. of the smaller sphere from $O$

$$= \frac{\int_{\theta=0}^{\pi/2}\int_{r=0}^{a\cos\theta} a\cos\theta\, \lambda r\cdot 2\pi r\sin\theta\, r\, d\theta\, dr}{\int_{\theta=0}^{\pi/2}\int_{r=0}^{a\cos\theta} \lambda r\cdot 2\pi r\sin\theta\, r\, d\theta\, dr} = \frac{\int_0^{\pi/2}\left(\frac{r^5}{5}\right)_0^{a\cos\theta}\cos\theta\sin\theta\, d\theta}{\int_0^{\pi/2}\left(\frac{r^4}{4}\right)_0^{a\cos\theta}\sin\theta\, d\theta}$$

$$= \frac{\frac{4a}{5}\int_0^{\pi/2}\cos^6\theta\sin\theta\, d\theta}{\int_0^{\pi/2}\cos^4\theta\sin\theta\, d\theta} = \frac{\frac{4a}{5}\left(-\frac{\cos^7\theta}{7}\right)_0^{\pi/2}}{\left(-\frac{\cos^5\theta}{5}\right)_0^{\pi/2}} = \frac{\frac{4a}{5}\left(\frac{1}{7}\right)}{\left(\frac{1}{5}\right)} = \frac{4a}{5}\cdot\frac{5}{7} = \frac{4a}{7}$$

Hence, the distance of the C.G. of the remainder from O is given by

$$\bar{x} = \frac{m_1 x_1 - m_2 x_2}{m_1 - m_2} = \frac{\lambda\pi a^4(a) - \frac{\lambda\pi a^4}{10}\cdot\frac{4a}{7}}{\lambda\pi a^4 - \frac{\lambda\pi a^4}{10}} = -\frac{4\lambda\pi a^5}{70}\cdot\frac{10}{9\lambda\pi a^4} = \frac{-4a}{63}$$

The negative sign simply shows that the C.G. is on the negative side of $X$-axis, i.e., on $XO$ produced.

## EXERCISE 2(G)

1. Find the position of the centre of gravity of a uniform piece of wire bent in the form of a semi-circle with its diameter.

   [**Ans.** At a distance $\frac{2a}{\pi+2}$ from the centre O on the symmetrical radius $OC$]

2. From a semi-circular lamina of radius $r$, a circular lamina of radius $\frac{r}{2}$ is removed. Find the position of the C.G. of the remainder.

   [**Ans.** $\frac{(16-3\pi)r}{6\pi}$ from the centre on the symmetrical diameter]

3. A circular hole of radius 1 cm is cut from a uniform circular disc of radius 2 cm, so that the C.G. of the remaining portion lies on the circumference of the hole. Find the distance between the centres of the hole and disc.

4. A circular disc of radius $a$ whose density is proportional to the distance from the centre, has a hole cut in it bounded by a circle of diameter $b$ which passes through the centre. Show that the distance from the centre of the disc of the C.G. of the remaining portion is $\frac{6b^4}{15\pi a^3 - 10b^3}$.

5. Find the C.G. of the volume formed by revolving the area bounded by the parabolas $y^2 = 4ax$ and $x^2 = 4by$ about the axis of X.

   $$\left[\textbf{Ans. } \bar{x} = \frac{20}{9} a^{\frac{1}{3}} b^{\frac{2}{3}}, \ \bar{y} = 0\right]$$

   $$\left[\textbf{Hint: } \bar{x} = \frac{\int_{x=0}^{4a^{\frac{1}{3}}b^{\frac{2}{3}}} \int_{y=y_1}^{y_2} x\rho 2\pi y \, dx\, dy}{\int_{x=0}^{4a^{\frac{1}{3}}b^{\frac{2}{3}}} \int_{y=y_1}^{y_2} \rho 2\pi y \, dx\, dy}\right.$$

   where $y_1^2 = \frac{x^2}{4b}$

   and $y_2^2 = 4ax$]

6. A hollow right circular cone without base, of mass $M$ and made of thin metallic sheet is placed with its axis vertical and vertex downwards. Water is poured into it upto the depth of one half of the vertical height. Show that for the C.G. of the cone and water to lie at the surface of the water, the mass of water poured should be $\frac{4}{3}M$.

7. A portion of an anchor ring is formed by the revolution of a circular area of radius $a$ about a line in its plane at a distance $c$ from its centre, where $c > a$. If $2\alpha$ be the angle through which it revolves, prove that the centre of gravity is at a distance $\left[\frac{4c^2 + a^2}{4c}\right]\left(\frac{\sin\alpha}{\alpha}\right)$ from the line.

   Deduce the position of the centre of gravity of the volume formed by the revolution of a circle of radius $a$ through the right angles about a tangent line.

   $$\left[\textbf{Ans. } \frac{5a}{2\pi}\right]$$

8. A portion of a uniform thin spherical shell is bounded by a plane circular rim. When the shell is freely suspended from a point in the rim, the radius through the lowest point of the rim is horizontal. Show that the plane bounding the shell is at a distance from the centre equal to two-thirds of the radius.
9. Prove that the centre of inertia of a circular disc, the density of which varies inversely as the fourth power of the distance from an external point O in the plane, is the inverse point of O with respect to the boundary of the disc.

## 12. Centre of Gravity (Three Dimensional)

### (i) In Cartesian Coordinates

Let the equation of the surface of the solid be given in cartesian coordinates.

Let $P(x, y, z)$ be any point of the volume. Let $Q(x + \delta x, y + \delta y, z + \delta z)$ be another point of the volume very close to $P$. Then, the volume of the elementary parallelepiped bounded by the planes through $P$ and $Q$ parallel to the coordinate planes $XOY$, $YOZ$ and $ZOX$ is given by $\delta v = \delta x\ \delta y\ \delta z$. Let $\rho$ be the mass density of this volume. Then, elementary mass $dm = \rho\ dv$

$= \rho\ dx\ dy\ dx$

Let $(\bar{x}, \bar{y}, \bar{z})$ be the coordinates of the C.G. of the entire volume under consideration. Then, using the fundamental formulae to determine the coordinates of the C.G., we have,

$$\bar{x} = \frac{\int x\,dm}{\int dm} = \frac{\iiint x\rho\,dx\,dy\,dz}{\iiint \rho\,dx\,dy\,dz}\ ;\ \bar{y} = \frac{\int y\,dm}{\int dm} = \frac{\iiint y\rho\,dx\,dy\,dz}{\iiint \rho\,dx\,dy\,dz}$$

and,
$$\bar{z} = \frac{\int z\,dm}{\int dm} = \frac{\iiint z\rho\,dx\,dy\,dz}{\iiint \rho\,dx\,dy\,dz}$$

The limits of integration are taken such that the whole volume of the solid under consideration is included.

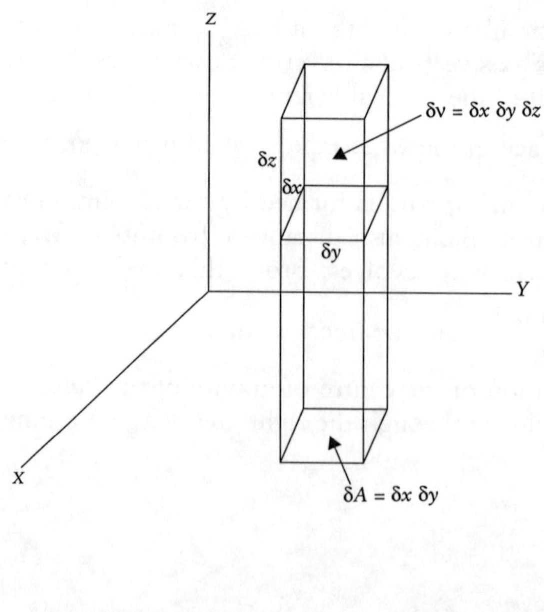

## (ii) In Polar Coordinates

Let the equation of the surface of the solid be given in polar coordinates. Let $P(r, \theta, \phi)$ be any point of the volume.

Let the cartesian coordinates of $P$ be$(x, y, z)$. Here, $OP = r$; $\theta$ is the angle which $OP$ makes with the $Z$-axis and $\phi$ is the angle which the projection of $OP$ on $YOZ$ plane makes with the $X$-axis.

Then, from Analytical Geometry, we have the transformation:

$$x = r \sin\theta \cos\phi \qquad y = r \sin\theta \cos\phi \qquad z = r \cos\phi$$

Also, elementary volume here $\delta v = \delta r \cdot r\delta\theta \cdot r \sin\theta \, \delta\phi$

Let $\rho$ denote the mass density of this volume. Then,

elementary mass $dm = \rho \, dv = \rho \, dr \cdot rd\theta \cdot r \sin\theta \, d\phi = \rho \, r^2 \sin\theta \, dr \, d\theta \, d\phi$

Let $(\bar{x}, \bar{y}, \bar{z})$ be the coordinates of the C.G. of the whole volume under consideration. Then, as in (i), we have,

$$\bar{x} = \frac{\int x \, dm}{\int dm} = \frac{\iiint r\sin\theta\cos\phi \; \rho r^2 \sin\theta \, dr \, d\theta \, d\phi}{\iiint \rho r^2 \sin\theta \, dr \, d\theta \, d\phi} = \frac{\iiint \rho r^3 \sin^2\theta\cos\phi \, dr \, d\theta \, d\phi}{\iiint \rho r^2 \sin\theta \, dr \, d\theta \, d\phi}$$

$$\bar{y} = \frac{\int y \, dm}{\int dm} = \frac{\iiint r\sin\theta\sin\phi \; \rho r^2 \sin\theta \, dr \, d\theta \, d\phi}{\iiint \rho r^2 \sin\theta \, dr \, d\theta \, d\phi} = \frac{\iiint \rho r^3 \sin^2\theta\sin\phi \, dr \, d\theta \, d\phi}{\iiint \rho r^2 \sin\theta \, dr \, d\theta \, d\phi}$$

and

$$\bar{z} = \frac{\int z \, dm}{\int dm} = \frac{\iiint r\cos\theta \; \rho r^2 \sin\theta \, dr \, d\theta \, d\phi}{\iiint \rho r^2 \sin\theta \, dr \, d\theta \, d\phi} = \frac{\iiint \rho r^3 \sin^2\theta\cos\phi \, dr \, d\theta \, d\phi}{\iiint \rho r^2 \sin\theta \, dr \, d\theta \, d\phi}$$

The limits of integration are taken such that the whole volume of the solid under consideration is included.

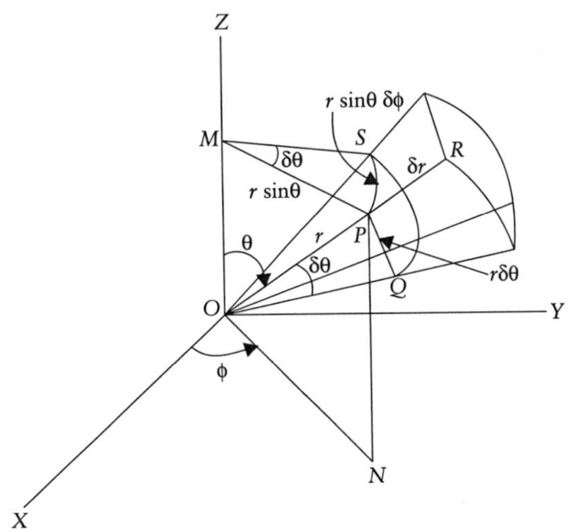

## 13. Dirichlet's Integral

The following result is done to Dirichlet and proves to be very useful in certain problem. According to this integral,

$\iiint_V x^{l-1}\, y^{m-1}\, z^{n-1}\, dx\, dy\, dz = \dfrac{\Gamma l\, \Gamma m\, \Gamma n}{\Gamma(l+m+n+1)}$ where $V$ denotes the closed region bounded by the coordinate planes and the plane $x + y + z = 1$, i.e., $V$ is given by $x \geq 0$, $y \geq 0$, $z \geq 0$ and $x + y + z \leq 1$.

### ILLUSTRATIVE EXAMPLES

**Example 1:** Find the centre of gravity of the positive octant of the solid ellipsoid $\dfrac{x^2}{a^2} + \dfrac{y^2}{b^2} + \dfrac{z^2}{c^2} = 1$ which is of constant density.

**Sol.** In the positive octant, $x$, $y$, $z$ are all positive. Also, for the region under consideration

$$\frac{x^2}{a^2} + \frac{y^2}{b^2} + \frac{z^2}{c^2} \leq 1$$

Put $\qquad \dfrac{x^2}{a^2} = X, \dfrac{y^2}{b^2} = Y$ and $\dfrac{z^2}{a^2} = Z.$

Then,

$$x = aX^{\frac{1}{2}};\ y = bY^{\frac{1}{2}} \quad \text{and,} \quad z = cZ^{\frac{1}{2}}$$

$$\therefore \quad dx = \frac{1}{2}aX^{-\frac{1}{2}}\, dX;\ dy = \frac{1}{2}bY^{-\frac{1}{2}}\, dY \quad \text{and} \quad dz = \frac{1}{2}cZ^{-\frac{1}{2}}\, dZ$$

Thus, we have $X \geq 0$, $\Rightarrow Y \geq 0$, $\Rightarrow Z \geq 0$

and $\qquad X + Y + Z \leq 1$

Now, $$\bar{x} = \frac{\iiint x\, dx\, dy\, dz}{\iiint dx\, dy\, dz} \qquad |\because \rho \text{ is constant}$$

$$= \frac{\iiint aX^{\frac{1}{2}}\, \frac{1}{2}aX^{-\frac{1}{2}}\, dX\, \frac{1}{2}bY^{-\frac{1}{2}}\, dY\, \frac{1}{2}cZ^{-\frac{1}{2}} dZ}{\iiint \frac{1}{2}aX^{-\frac{1}{2}}\, dX\, \frac{1}{2}bY^{-\frac{1}{2}}\, dY\, \frac{1}{2}cZ^{-\frac{1}{2}} dZ}$$

$$= \frac{a\iiint X^{1-1}\, Y^{\frac{1}{2}-1}\, Z^{\frac{1}{2}-1}\, dX\, dY\, dZ}{\iiint X^{\frac{1}{2}-1}\, Y^{\frac{1}{2}-1}\, Z^{\frac{1}{2}-1}\, dX\, dY\, dZ}$$

$$= \frac{\dfrac{a\Gamma(1)\,\Gamma\left(\frac{1}{2}\right)\Gamma\left(\frac{1}{2}\right)}{\Gamma\left(1+\frac{1}{2}+\frac{1}{2}+1\right)}}{\dfrac{\Gamma\left(\frac{1}{2}\right)\Gamma\left(\frac{1}{2}\right)\Gamma\left(\frac{1}{2}\right)}{\Gamma\left(\frac{1}{2}+\frac{1}{2}+\frac{1}{2}+1\right)}} \qquad \text{| By Dirichlet's Integral}$$

$$= \frac{a\Gamma(1)}{\Gamma\left(\frac{1}{2}\right)}\frac{\Gamma\left(\frac{5}{2}\right)}{\Gamma(3)} = \frac{a\cdot 1\cdot\frac{3}{2}\cdot\frac{1}{2}\Gamma\left(\frac{1}{2}\right)}{\Gamma\left(\frac{1}{2}\right)\cdot 2\cdot 1} = \frac{3a}{8}$$

Similarly, $\bar{y} = \dfrac{3b}{8}$ and $\bar{z} = \dfrac{3c}{8}$

Hence, the required C.G. is $\left(\dfrac{3a}{8}, \dfrac{3b}{8}, \dfrac{3c}{8}\right)$.

**Example 2:** Find the C.G. of the solid bounded by the surface $\left(\dfrac{x}{a}\right)^{2/3} + \left(\dfrac{y}{b}\right)^{2/3} + \left(\dfrac{z}{c}\right)^{2/3} = 1$ in the positive octant.

**Sol.** In the positive octant, $x, y, z$ are all positive. Also, for the region under consideration $\left(\dfrac{x}{a}\right)^{2/3} + \left(\dfrac{y}{b}\right)^{2/3} + \left(\dfrac{z}{c}\right)^{2/3} \le 1$

Put $\left(\dfrac{x}{a}\right)^{2/3} = X$, $\left(\dfrac{y}{b}\right)^{2/3} = Y$ and $\left(\dfrac{z}{c}\right)^{2/3} = Z$

Then, $\quad x = aX^{3/2}, \; y = bY^{3/2} \quad$ and $\quad z = cZ^{3/2}$

$\therefore \quad dx = \dfrac{3}{2}aX^{\frac{1}{2}}\,dX, \; dy = \dfrac{3}{2}bY^{\frac{1}{2}}\,dY \quad$ and $\quad dz = \dfrac{3}{2}cZ^{\frac{1}{2}}\,dZ$

Thus, we have $\quad X \ge 0, \quad \Rightarrow Y \ge 0, \quad \Rightarrow Z \ge 0$

Now, $$\bar{x} = \frac{\iiint x\,dx\,dy\,dz}{\iiint dx\,dy\,dz} \qquad |\because \rho \text{ is constant}$$

$$= \frac{\iiint aX^{\frac{3}{2}}\,\frac{3}{2}aX^{\frac{1}{2}}\,dX\,\frac{3}{2}\,bY^{\frac{1}{2}}\,dY\,\frac{3}{2}\,cZ^{\frac{1}{2}}dZ}{\iiint \frac{3}{2}aX^{\frac{1}{2}}\,dX\,\frac{3}{2}bY^{\frac{1}{2}}\,dY\,\frac{3}{2}\,cZ^{\frac{1}{2}}dZ} = \frac{a\iiint X^{3-1}\,Y^{\frac{3}{2}-1}\,Z^{\frac{3}{2}-1}dX\,dY\,dZ}{\iiint X^{\frac{3}{2}-1}\,Y^{\frac{3}{2}-1}\,Z^{\frac{3}{2}-1}\,dX\,dY\,dZ}$$

$$= \frac{\dfrac{a\Gamma(3)\,\Gamma\left(\frac{3}{2}\right)\Gamma\left(\frac{3}{2}\right)}{\Gamma\left(3+\frac{3}{2}+\frac{3}{2}+1\right)}}{\dfrac{\Gamma\left(\frac{3}{2}\right)\Gamma\left(\frac{3}{2}\right)\Gamma\left(\frac{3}{2}\right)}{\Gamma\left(\frac{3}{2}+\frac{3}{2}+\frac{3}{2}+1\right)}} \qquad \text{| By Dirichlet's Integral}$$

$$= a\frac{\Gamma(3)}{\Gamma(7)}\cdot\frac{\Gamma\left(\frac{11}{2}\right)}{\Gamma\left(\frac{3}{2}\right)} = \frac{a\cdot 2\cdot 1\cdot\frac{9}{2}\cdot\frac{7}{2}\cdot\frac{5}{2}\cdot\frac{3}{2}}{6\cdot 5\cdot 4\cdot 3\cdot 2\cdot 1\cdot} = \frac{21}{128}a$$

Similarly, $\bar{y} = \frac{21}{128}b$ and $\bar{z} = \frac{21}{128}c$

Hence, the required C.G. is $\left(\frac{21}{128}a, \frac{21}{128}b, \frac{21}{128}c\right)$.

**Example 3:** Find the C.G. of the positive octant of an ellipsoid $\frac{x^2}{a^2}+\frac{y^2}{b^2}+\frac{z^2}{c^2}=1$, if density at any point vary as $x^l y^m z^n$.

Consider the cases when

(i) $l = m = n = 0$ (ii) $l = m = n = 1$

(iii) $l = m = n = 2$ (iv) $l = 1, m = 2, n = 3$

**Sol.** Here, $\rho = \lambda x^l y^m z^n$ ...(1)

In the positive octant, $x$, $y$, $z$ are all positive. Also, for the region under consideration

$$\frac{x^2}{a^2}+\frac{y^2}{b^2}+\frac{z^2}{c^2} \le 1$$

Put $\frac{x^2}{a^2} = X, \frac{y^2}{b^2} = Y$ and $\frac{z^2}{a^2} = Z$

Then, $x = aX^{\frac{1}{2}}, \quad y = bY^{\frac{1}{2}}, z = cZ^{\frac{1}{2}}$

$\therefore \quad dx = \frac{1}{2}aX^{-\frac{1}{2}}dX, \quad dy = \frac{1}{2}bY^{-\frac{1}{2}}dY, \quad dz = \frac{1}{2}cY^{-\frac{1}{2}}dZ$

Thus, we have $X \ge 0, \quad Y \ge 0, \quad Z \ge 0$

and $X + Y + Z \le 1$

Now, $$\bar{x} = \frac{\iiint x\, \rho\, dx\, dy\, dz}{\iiint \rho\, dx\, dy\, dz}$$

$$= \frac{\iiint x \lambda\, x^l\, y^m\, z^n\, dx\, dy\, dz}{\iiint \lambda\, x^l\, y^m\, z^n\, dx\, dy\, dz} \qquad \Big| \text{From (1)}$$

$$= \frac{\iiint x^{l \times 1}\, y^m\, z^n\, dx\, dy\, dz}{\iiint x^l\, y^m\, z^n\, dx\, dy\, dz} \qquad \Big| \because \alpha \text{ is constant}$$

$$= \frac{\iiint \left(aX^{\frac{1}{2}}\right)^{l+1} \left(bY^{\frac{1}{2}}\right)^m \left(cZ^{\frac{1}{2}}\right)^n \frac{1}{2} aX^{-\frac{1}{2}}\, dX \frac{1}{2} bY^{-\frac{1}{2}}\, dY \frac{1}{2} cZ^{-\frac{1}{2}}\, dZ}{\iiint \left(aX^{\frac{1}{2}}\right)^{l} \left(bY^{\frac{1}{2}}\right)^m \left(cZ^{\frac{1}{2}}\right)^n \frac{1}{2} aX^{-\frac{1}{2}}\, dX \frac{1}{2} bY^{-\frac{1}{2}}\, dY \frac{1}{2} cZ^{-\frac{1}{2}}\, dZ}$$

$$= \frac{a \iiint X^{\left(\frac{l}{2}+1\right)-1}\, Y^{\left(\frac{m}{2}+\frac{1}{2}\right)-1}\, Z^{\left(\frac{n}{2}+\frac{1}{2}\right)-1}\, dX\, dY\, dZ}{\iiint X^{\left(\frac{l}{2}+\frac{1}{2}\right)-1}\, Y^{\left(\frac{m}{2}+\frac{1}{2}\right)-1}\, Z^{\left(\frac{n}{2}+\frac{1}{2}\right)-1}\, dX\, dY\, dZ} = \frac{\dfrac{a\,\Gamma\left(\frac{l}{2}+1\right)\Gamma\left(\frac{m}{2}+\frac{1}{2}\right)\Gamma\left(\frac{n}{2}+\frac{1}{2}\right)}{\Gamma\left(\frac{l}{2}+1+\frac{m}{2}+\frac{1}{2}+\frac{n}{2}+\frac{1}{2}+1\right)}}{\dfrac{\Gamma\left(\frac{l}{2}+\frac{1}{2}\right)\Gamma\left(\frac{m}{2}+\frac{1}{2}\right)\Gamma\left(\frac{n}{2}+\frac{1}{2}\right)}{\Gamma\left(\frac{l}{2}+\frac{1}{2}+\frac{m}{2}+\frac{1}{2}+\frac{n}{2}+\frac{1}{2}+1\right)}} \qquad \Big| \text{By Dirichlet's Integral}$$

$$= \frac{a\,\Gamma\left(\frac{l}{2}+1\right)}{\Gamma\left(\frac{l}{2}+\frac{1}{2}\right)} \frac{\Gamma\left(\frac{l+m+n+5}{2}\right)}{\Gamma\left(\frac{l+m+n+6}{2}\right)}$$

Similarly,

$$\bar{y} = \frac{b\,\Gamma\left(\frac{m}{2}+1\right)}{\Gamma\left(\frac{m}{2}+\frac{1}{2}\right)} \cdot \frac{\Gamma\left(\frac{l+m+n+5}{2}\right)}{\Gamma\left(\frac{l+m+n+6}{2}\right)}$$

and $$\bar{z} = \frac{c\,\Gamma\left(\frac{n}{2}+1\right)}{\Gamma\left(\frac{n}{2}+\frac{1}{2}\right)} \cdot \frac{\Gamma\left(\frac{l+m+n+5}{2}\right)}{\Gamma\left(\frac{l+m+n+6}{2}\right)}$$

## Particular Cases

(i) When $l = m = n = 0$, then

$$\bar{x} = \frac{a\Gamma(1)\Gamma\left(\frac{5}{2}\right)}{\Gamma\left(\frac{1}{2}\right)\Gamma(3)} = \frac{1\cdot\frac{3}{2}\cdot\frac{1}{2}\Gamma\left(\frac{1}{2}\right)}{\Gamma\left(\frac{1}{2}\right)\cdot 2\cdot 1} = \frac{3}{8}a, \quad \bar{y} = \frac{3}{8}b, \qquad \bar{z} = \frac{3}{8}c$$

(ii) When $l = m = n = 1$, then

$$\bar{x} = \frac{a\Gamma\left(\frac{3}{2}\right)\Gamma(4)}{\Gamma(1)\Gamma\left(\frac{9}{2}\right)} = \frac{a\Gamma\left(\frac{3}{2}\right)\cdot 3\cdot 2\cdot 1\Gamma(1)}{\Gamma(1)\cdot\frac{1}{2}\cdot\frac{5}{2}\cdot\frac{3}{2}\cdot\Gamma\left(\frac{3}{2}\right)} = \frac{16}{35}a, \ \bar{y} = \frac{16}{35}b, \ \bar{z} = \frac{16}{35}c$$

(iii) When $l = m = n = 2$, then

$$\bar{x} = \frac{a\Gamma(2)\Gamma\left(\frac{11}{2}\right)}{\Gamma\left(\frac{3}{2}\right)\Gamma(6)} = \frac{a\cdot 1\cdot\Gamma(1)\frac{9}{2}\cdot\frac{7}{2}\cdot\frac{5}{2}\cdot\frac{3}{2}\cdot\Gamma\left(\frac{3}{2}\right)}{\Gamma\left(\frac{3}{2}\right)5\cdot 4\cdot 3\cdot 2\cdot 1\Gamma(1)}$$

$$= \frac{63}{128}a, \ \bar{y} = \frac{63}{128}b, \ \bar{z} = \frac{63}{128}c$$

(iv) When $l = 1$, $m = 2$, $n = 3$, then

$$\bar{x} = \frac{a\Gamma\left(\frac{3}{2}\right)\Gamma\left(\frac{11}{2}\right)}{\Gamma(1)\Gamma(6)} = \frac{a\frac{1}{2}\Gamma\left(\frac{1}{2}\right)\cdot\frac{9}{2}\cdot\frac{7}{2}\cdot\frac{5}{2}\cdot\frac{3}{2}\cdot\frac{1}{2}\Gamma\left(\frac{1}{2}\right)}{1\cdot 5\cdot 4\cdot 3\cdot 2\cdot 1} = \frac{63\pi}{512}a, \ \bar{y} = \frac{63b}{128}, \ \bar{z} = \frac{189\pi}{1024}c.$$

**Example 4:** Find the C.G. of a portion of the solid $z^2 = xy$ which is cut off by fine planes $x = y = z = 0$, $x = a$, $y = b$.

**Sol.** Here, the limits of $z$ are from $z = 0$ to $z = \sqrt{xy}$;
the limits of $y$ are from $y = 0$ to $y = b$;
the limits of $x$ are from $x = 0$ to $x = a$.
Therefore,

$$\bar{x} = \frac{\int_0^a\int_0^b\int_0^{\sqrt{xy}} x\,dx\,dy\,dz}{\int_0^a\int_0^b\int_0^{\sqrt{xy}} dx\,dy\,dz} = \frac{\int_0^a\int_0^b x\,dx\,dy(z)_0^{\sqrt{xy}}}{\int_0^a\int_0^b dx\,dy(z)_0^{\sqrt{xy}}} = \frac{\int_0^a\int_0^b x^{\frac{3}{2}}y^{\frac{1}{2}}dx\,dy}{\int_0^a\int_0^b x^{\frac{1}{2}}y^{\frac{1}{2}}dx\,dy}$$

$$= \frac{\left(\frac{2}{5}x^{\frac{5}{2}}\right)_0^a\left(\frac{2}{3}y^{\frac{3}{2}}\right)_0^b}{\left(\frac{2}{3}x^{\frac{3}{2}}\right)_0^a\left(\frac{2}{3}y^{\frac{3}{2}}\right)_0^b} = \frac{3}{5}\frac{a^{\frac{5}{2}}b^{\frac{3}{2}}}{a^{\frac{3}{2}}b^{\frac{3}{2}}} = \frac{3}{5}a$$

$$\overline{y} = \frac{\int_0^a\int_0^b\int_0^{\sqrt{xy}} y\,dx\,dy\,dz}{\int_0^a\int_0^b\int_0^{\sqrt{xy}} dx\,dy\,dz} = \frac{\int_0^a\int_0^b y\,dx\,dy\,(z)_0^{\sqrt{xy}}}{\int_0^a\int_0^b dx\,dy(z)_0^{\sqrt{xy}}} = \frac{\int_0^a\int_0^b x^{\frac{1}{2}}\,y^{\frac{3}{2}}\,dx\,dy}{\int_0^a\int_0^b x^{\frac{1}{2}}\,y^{\frac{1}{2}}dx\,dy}$$

$$= \frac{\left(\frac{2}{3}x^{\frac{3}{2}}\right)_0^a\left(\frac{2}{5}y^{\frac{5}{2}}\right)_0^b}{\left(\frac{2}{3}x^{\frac{3}{2}}\right)_0^a\left(\frac{2}{3}y^{\frac{3}{2}}\right)_0^b} = \frac{3}{5}\frac{a^{\frac{3}{2}}\,b^{\frac{5}{2}}}{a^{\frac{3}{2}}\,b^{\frac{3}{2}}} = \frac{3}{5}b$$

$$\overline{z} = \frac{\int_0^a\int_0^b\int_0^{\sqrt{xy}} z\,dx\,dy\,dz}{\int_0^a\int_0^b\int_0^{\sqrt{xy}} dx\,dy\,dz} = \frac{\int_0^a\int_0^b dx\,dy\left(\frac{z^2}{2}\right)_0^{\sqrt{xy}}}{\int_0^a\int_0^b dx\,dy(z)_0^{\sqrt{xy}}} = \frac{\frac{1}{2}\int_0^a\int_0^b xy\,dx\,dy}{\int_0^a\int_0^b x^{\frac{1}{2}}\,y^{\frac{1}{2}}dx\,dy}$$

$$= \frac{\frac{1}{2}\left(\frac{x^2}{2}\right)_0^a\left(\frac{y^2}{2}\right)_0^b}{\left(\frac{2}{3}x^{\frac{3}{2}}\right)_0^a\left(\frac{2}{3}y^{\frac{3}{2}}\right)_0^b} = \frac{\frac{1}{2}\frac{a^2}{2}\frac{b^2}{2}}{\frac{2}{3}a^{\frac{3}{2}}\frac{2}{3}b^{\frac{3}{2}}} = \frac{9}{32}a^{\frac{1}{2}}\,b^{\frac{1}{2}}.$$

**Example 5:** Find the C.G. of the volume enclosed between the surfaces $\frac{x^2}{a^2}+\frac{y^2}{b^2} = 1$, $z = 0$ and $lx + my + nz = 1$.

**Sol.** Here, the limits of $z$ are from $z = 0$ to $z = \frac{1-lx-my}{n}$;

the limits of $y$ are from $-y$ to $y$ where $y = \frac{b}{a}\sqrt{a^2-x^2}$;
the limits of $x$ are from $x = -a$ to $x = a$.

Hence,

$$\overline{x} = \frac{\iint\int_0^z x\,dx\,dy\,dz}{\iint\int_0^z dx\,dy\,dz} = \frac{\iint x\,dx\,dy(z)_0^z}{\iint dx\,dy(z)_0^z} = \frac{\iint x\,z\,dx\,dy}{\iint z\,dx\,dy} = \frac{\int_{-a}^a\int_{-y}^y x\left(\frac{1-lx-my}{n}\right)dx\,dy}{\int_{-a}^a\int_{-y}^y\left(\frac{1-lx-my}{n}\right)dx\,dy}$$

$$= \frac{2\int_{-a}^a\int^y x(1\quad lx)\,dx\,dy}{2\int_{-a}^a\int^y(1\quad lx)\,dx\,dy}$$

|Other integrals vanish, integrands being odd functions of $y$

$$= \frac{\int_{-a}^a x(1-lx)y\,dx}{\int_{-a}^a(1-lx)y\,dx} = \frac{\int_{-a}^a x(1-lx)\frac{b}{a}\sqrt{a^2-x^2}\,dx}{\int_{-a}^a(1-lx)\frac{b}{a}\sqrt{a^2-x^2}\,dx}$$

$$= \frac{\int -lx^2\sqrt{a^2\quad x^2}\,dx}{\int \sqrt{a^2\quad x^2}\,dx}$$

|Other integrals vanish, integrands being odd functions of $x$

$$= \frac{-l\int_0^a x^2\sqrt{a^2-x^2}\,dx}{\int_0^a \sqrt{a^2-x^2}\,dx}$$

Put $x = a\sin\theta$
$\therefore\ dx = a\cos\theta\, d\theta$

$$= \frac{-l\int^{/2} a^2\sin^2\theta\sqrt{a^2-a^2\sin^2\theta}\ a\cos\theta\, d\theta}{\int^{/2}\sqrt{a^2-a^2\sin^2\theta}\ a\cos\theta\, d\theta}$$

When $x = 0$, $\theta = 0$;
When $x = a$, $\theta = \frac{\pi}{2}$

$$= \frac{-a^2 l\int_0^{\pi/2}\sin^2\theta\cos^2\theta\, d\theta}{\int_0^{\pi/2}\cos^2\theta\, d\theta} = \frac{\dfrac{-a^2 l\,\overline{\left|\frac{3}{2}\right.}\,\overline{\left|\frac{3}{2}\right.}}{2\,\overline{\left|3\right.}}}{\frac{1}{2}\cdot\frac{\pi}{2}}$$

| Using Wallis Formula

$$= \frac{-a^2 l\cdot\frac{1}{2}\overline{\left|\frac{1}{2}\right.}\cdot\frac{1}{2}\overline{\left|\frac{1}{2}\right.}\cdot}{2\cdot(2\cdot 1)}\ \frac{2\cdot 2}{\pi} = \frac{-a^2 l}{4}$$

Similarly, $\bar{y} = \dfrac{-b^2 m}{4}$ | Replacing $a$ by $b$ and $l$ by $m$

$$\bar{z} = \frac{\iiint_0^z z\,dx\,dy\,dz}{\iiint_0^z dx\,dy\,dz} = \frac{\iint\frac{1}{2}z^2 dx\,dy}{\iint z\,dx\,dy} = \frac{\frac{1}{2}\int_{-a}^{a}\int_{-y}^{y}\left(\frac{1-lx-my}{n}\right)^2 dx\,dy}{\int_{-a}^{a}\int_{-y}^{y}\left(\frac{1-lx-my}{n}\right)dx\,dy}$$

$$= \frac{\frac{1}{2n}\int_{-a}^{a}\int_{-y}^{y}\left\{(1-lx)^2+m^2y^2-2m(1-lx)y\right\}dx\,dy}{\int_{-a}^{a}\int_{-y}^{y}(1-lx-my)\,dx\,dy}$$

$$= \frac{\frac{1}{2n}\cdot 2\int_{-a}^{a}\int_0^{y}\left[(1-lx)^2+m^2y^2\right]dx\,dy}{2\int_{-a}^{a}\int_0^{y}(1-lx)\,dx\,dy}$$

| Other integrals vanish, integrands being odd functions of $y$

$$= \frac{\frac{1}{2n}\int_{-a}^{a}\left[(1-lx)^2 y+\frac{m^2y^3}{3}\right]dx\,dy}{\int_{-a}^{a}(1-lx)y\,dx\,dy}$$

$$= \frac{\frac{1}{2n}\int_{-a}^{a}\left[(1-lx)^2\frac{b}{a}\sqrt{a^2-x^2}+\frac{m^2}{3}\frac{b^3}{a^3}\left(a^3-x^3\right)^{3/2}\right]dx}{\int_{-a}^{a}(1-lx)\frac{b}{a}\sqrt{a^2-x^2}\,dx}$$

$$= \frac{\frac{1}{2n}\cdot 2\int_0^a \left[\left(1-l^2x^2\right)\sqrt{a^2-x^2}+\frac{m^2b^2}{3a^2}\left(a^2-x^2\right)^{3/2}\right]dx}{2\int_0^a \sqrt{a^2-x^2}\,dx}$$

Other integrals vanish, integrands being odd functions of $x$

Put $x = a \sin\theta$
$\therefore\ dx = a \cos\theta\ d\theta$

$$= \frac{\frac{1}{2n}\int_0^{\pi/2}\left[\left(1-l^2a^2\sin^2\theta\right)a\cos\theta+\frac{m^2b^2}{3a^2}a^3\cos^3\theta\right]a\cos\theta\,d\theta}{\int_0^{\pi/2} a\cos\theta\ a\cos\theta\,d\theta}$$

$$= \frac{\frac{1}{2n}\int_0^{\pi/2}\left[\cos^2\theta+a^2l^2\sin^2\theta\cos^2\theta+\frac{1}{3}m^2b^2\cos^4\theta\right]d\theta}{\int_0^{\pi/2}\cos^2\theta\,d\theta}$$

$$= \frac{\frac{1}{2n}\left[\frac{1}{2}\cdot\frac{\pi}{2}+a^2l^2\,\frac{\Gamma\left(\frac{3}{2}\right)\Gamma\left(\frac{3}{2}\right)}{2\Gamma(3)}+\frac{1}{3}m^2b^2\,\frac{3}{4}\cdot\frac{1}{2}\cdot\frac{\pi}{2}\right]}{\frac{1}{2}\cdot\frac{\pi}{2}}$$

$$= \frac{1}{2n}\cdot\frac{4}{\pi}\left[1+a^2l^2\,\frac{\frac{1}{2}\Gamma\left(\frac{1}{2}\right)\frac{1}{2}\Gamma\left(\frac{1}{2}\right)}{2(2\cdot 1)}+m^2b^2\,\frac{\pi}{16}\right] = \frac{1}{2n}\cdot\frac{4}{\pi}\left[1+\frac{a^2l^2\pi}{16}+\frac{m^2b^2\pi}{16}\right]$$

$$= \frac{1}{2n}\left[1+\frac{a^2l^2}{4}+\frac{m^2b^2}{4}\right] = \frac{a^2l^2+b^2m^2+4}{8n}.$$

**Example 6:** Find the C.G. of the volume enclosed by $x^2 + y^2 = a^2$, $z = 0$, $z = x \tan\alpha + h$.

OR

Find the C.G. of the volume cut off from the cylinder $x^2 + y^2 = a^2$ by the planes $z = 0$ and $z = x \tan\alpha + h$.

**Sol.** Consider an element $dx\ dy\ dz$ of the volume.

Here,

limits of $z$ are from $z = 0$ to $z = x \tan\alpha + h$;

limits of $y$ are from $y = -\sqrt{a^2-x^2}$ to $y = -\sqrt{a^2-x^2}$;

limits of $x$ are from $x = -a$ to $x = a$.

Therefore,

$$\bar{x} = \frac{\iint\int_0^z x\,dx\,dy\,dz}{\iint\int_0^z dx\,dy\,dz}$$

$| \because \rho$ is constant

where $z = x\tan\alpha + h$

$$= \frac{\iint x(z)_0^z\,dx\,dy}{\iint (z)_0^z\,dx\,dy} = \frac{\iint x\,z\,dx\,dy}{\iint z\,dx\,dy}$$

$$= \frac{\int_{-a}^{a}\int_{-y}^{y} x(x\tan\alpha + h)\,dx\,dy}{\int_{-a}^{a}\int_{-y}^{y}(x\tan\alpha + h)\,dx\,dy}$$

where $y = \sqrt{a^2 - x^2}$

$$= \frac{\int_{-a}^{a} x(x\tan\alpha + h)(y)_{-y}^{y}\,dx}{\int_{-a}^{a}(x\tan\alpha + h)(y)_{-y}^{y}\,dx} = \frac{\int_{-a}^{a} x(x\tan\alpha + h)2y\,dx}{\int_{-a}^{a}(x\tan\alpha + h)2y\,dx}$$

$$= \frac{\int_{-a}^{a} x(x\tan\alpha)\sqrt{a^2 - x^2}\,dx}{\int_{-a}^{a}(x\tan\alpha + h)\sqrt{a^2 - x^2}\,dx}$$

$$= \frac{2\int_0^a x^2\tan\alpha\sqrt{a^2 - x^2}\,dx}{\int_0^a h\sqrt{a^2 - x^2}\,dx}$$

By property of difinite integrals $\int_{-a}^{a} f(x)\,dx = 2\int_{-a}^{a} f(x)\,dx$ if $f(x)$ is an even function of $x$ and $= 0$ if $f(x)$ is an odd function of $x$

$$= \frac{\frac{\tan\alpha}{h}\int_0^a x^2\sqrt{a^2 - x^2}\,dx}{\int_0^a \sqrt{a^2 - x^2}\,dx}$$

Put $x = a\sin\theta$

$\therefore dx = a\cos\theta\,dx$

$$= \frac{\frac{\tan\alpha}{h}\int_0^{\pi/2} a^2\sin^2\theta\sqrt{a^2 - a^2\sin^2\theta}\cdot a\cos\theta\,d\theta}{\int_0^{\pi/2}\sqrt{a^2 - a^2\sin^2\theta}\;a\cos\theta\,d\theta} = \frac{\frac{a^2\tan\alpha}{h}\int_0^{\pi/2}\sin^2\theta\cos^2\theta\,dx}{\int_0^{\pi/2}\cos^2\theta\,d\theta}$$

$$= \frac{a^2\tan\alpha}{h}\,\frac{\dfrac{\overline{\left|\frac{3}{2}\right.}\;\overline{\left|\frac{3}{2}\right.}}{2\overline{|3}}}{\dfrac{1}{2}\cdot\dfrac{\pi}{2}}$$

| By Wallis Formula

$$= \frac{4a^2 \tan\alpha}{\pi h} \frac{\frac{1}{2}\sqrt{\pi}\frac{1}{2}\sqrt{\pi}}{2\cdot(2\cdot 1)} = \frac{a^2 \tan\alpha}{4h} \qquad \bar{y} = \frac{\int_{-a}^{a}\int_{-y}^{y}\int_{0}^{x\tan\alpha+h} y\,dx\,dy\,dz}{\int_{-a}^{a}\int_{-y}^{y}\int_{0}^{x\tan\alpha+h} dx\,dy\,dz}$$

$$= 0$$

$\because$ integrand in the numerator is an odd function of $y$

$$\bar{z} = \frac{\iiint_0^z \bar{z}\,dx\,dy\,dz}{\iiint_0^z dx\,dy\,dz} = \frac{\iint\left(\frac{z^2}{2}\right)_0^{x\tan\alpha+h} dx\,dy}{\iint (z)_0^{x\tan\alpha+h}\,dx\,dy}$$

$$= \frac{\frac{1}{2}\iint_{-y}^{y}(x\tan\alpha+h)^2\,dx\,dy}{\iint_{-y}^{y}(x\tan\alpha+h)\,dx\,dy} = \frac{\frac{1}{2}\int_{-a}^{a}(x\tan\alpha+h)^2(y)_{-y}^{y}\,dx}{\int_{-a}^{a}(x\tan\alpha+h)(y)_{-y}^{y}}$$

$$= \frac{\frac{1}{2}\int_{-a}^{a}2(x\tan\alpha+h)^2 y\,dx}{\int_{-a}^{a}2(x\tan\alpha+h)y\,dx} = \frac{\frac{1}{2}\int_{-a}^{a}\left(x^2\tan^2\alpha+2h\,x\tan\alpha+h^2\right)\sqrt{a^2-x^2}\,dx}{\int_{-a}^{a}(x\tan\alpha+h)\sqrt{a^2-x^2}\,dx}$$

$$= \frac{\frac{1}{2}\cdot 2\int_0^a\left(x^2\tan^2\alpha+h^2\right)\sqrt{a^2-x^2}\,dx}{2\int_0^a h\sqrt{a^2-x^2}\,dx}$$

Other integrals vanish integrands being odd functions of $x$

$$= \frac{\frac{1}{2}\int_0^a\left(x^2\tan^2\alpha+h^2\right)\sqrt{a^2-x^2}\,dx}{\int_0^a h\sqrt{a^2-x^2}\,dx}$$

Put $x = a\sin\theta$
$\therefore\ dx = a\cos\theta\,d\theta$

$$= \frac{\frac{1}{2}\int_0^{\pi/2}\left(a^2\sin^2\theta\tan^2\alpha+h^2\right)a\cos\theta\; a\cos\theta\,d\theta}{\int_0^{\pi/2} h\; a\cos\theta\; a\cos\theta\,d\theta}$$

$$= \frac{\frac{1}{2h}\left[a^2\tan^2\alpha\int_0^{\pi/2}\sin^2\theta\cos^2\theta\,d\theta + h^2\int_0^{\pi/2}\cos^2\theta\,d\theta\right]}{\int_0^{\pi/2}\cos^2\theta\,d\theta}$$

$$= \frac{\frac{1}{2h}a^2\tan^2\alpha\int_0^{\pi/2}\sin^2\theta\cos^2\theta\,d\theta}{\int_0^{\pi/2}\cos^2\theta} + \frac{h}{2} = \frac{a^2\tan^2\alpha}{2h}\,\frac{\frac{\Gamma\frac{3}{2}\,\Gamma\frac{3}{2}}{2\Gamma 3}}{\frac{1}{2}\cdot\frac{\pi}{2}} + \frac{h}{2} = \frac{a^2\tan^2\alpha}{8h} + \frac{h}{2}.$$

**Example 7:** Find the C.G. of the volume cut off from the cylinder $x^2 + y^2 = 2ax$ by the planes $z = mx$ and $z = nx$.

**Sol.** Here,
limits of $z$ are from $z = mx$ to $z = nx$;
limits of $y$ are from $y = -\sqrt{2ax - x^2}$ to $y = \sqrt{2ax - x^2}$;
limits of $x$ are from $x = 0$ to $x = 2a$;
Let the required C.G. be at $(\bar{x}, \bar{y}, \bar{z})$. Then,

$$\bar{x} = \frac{\iiint \rho x \, dx \, dy \, dz}{\iiint \rho \, dx \, dy \, dz} = \frac{\iiint x \, dx \, dy \, dz}{\iiint dx \, dy \, dz} \qquad \Big| \because \rho \text{ is constant}$$

$$= \frac{\iint x(z)_{mx}^{nx} \, dx \, dy}{\iint (z)_{mx}^{nx} \, dx \, dy} = \frac{\int_0^{2a}\int_{-y}^{y} x(n-m)x \, dx \, dy}{\int_0^{2a}\int_{-y}^{y} (n-m)x \, dx \, dy} \qquad \text{where } y = \sqrt{2ax - x^2}$$

$$= \frac{\int_0^{2a}\int_{-y}^{y} x^2 \, dx \, dy}{\int_0^{2a}\int_{-y}^{y} x \, dx \, dy} = \frac{2\int_0^{2a}\int_0^{y} x^2 \, dx \, dy}{2\int_0^{2a}\int_0^{y} x \, dx \, dy} = \frac{\int_0^{2a}\int_0^{y} x^2 \, dx \, dy}{\int_0^{2a}\int_0^{y} x \, dx \, dy} = \frac{\int_0^{2a} x^2 (y)_0^{\sqrt{2ax-x^2}} \, dx}{\int_0^{2a} x(y)_0^{\sqrt{2ax-x^2}} \, dx}$$

$$= \frac{\int_0^{2a} x^2 \sqrt{2ax - x^2} \, dx}{\int_0^{2a} x\sqrt{2ax - x^2} \, dx}$$

Put $x = 2a \sin^2\theta$
$\therefore dx = 4a \sin\theta \cos\theta \, d\theta$

$$= \frac{\int_0^{\pi/2} 4a^2 \sin^4\theta \sqrt{4a^2 \sin^2\theta - 4a^2 \sin^4\theta} \; 4a \sin\theta \cos\theta \, d\theta}{\int_0^{\pi/2} 2a \sin^2\theta \sqrt{4a^2 \sin^2\theta - 4a^2 \sin^4\theta} \; 4a \sin\theta \cos\theta \, d\theta}$$

$$= \frac{2a\int_0^{\pi/2} \sin^6\theta \cos^2\theta \, d\theta}{\int_0^{\pi/2} \sin^4\theta \cos^2\theta \, d\theta} = \frac{2a \dfrac{\Gamma\frac{7}{2}\,\Gamma\frac{3}{2}}{2\Gamma 5}}{\dfrac{\Gamma\frac{5}{2}\,\Gamma\frac{3}{2}}{2\Gamma 4}} = \frac{2a\,\Gamma\frac{5}{2}\,\Gamma\frac{5}{2}}{4\,\Gamma\frac{5}{2}} = \frac{5a}{4}$$

$$\bar{y} = \frac{\int_0^{2a}\int_{-y}^{y}\int_{mn}^{nx} y \, dx \, dy \, dz}{\int_0^{2a}\int_{-y}^{y}\int_{mn}^{nx} dx \, dy \, dz} = 0 \qquad \Big| \therefore \text{ integrand in the numerator is an odd function of } y$$

$$\bar{z} = \frac{\int_0^{2a}\int_{-y}^{y}\int_{mx}^{nx} z \, dx \, dy \, dz}{\int_0^{2a}\int_{-y}^{y}\int_{mx}^{nx} dx \, dy \, dz} = \frac{\int_0^{2a}\int_{-y}^{y} \left(\frac{z^2}{2}\right)_{mx}^{nx} dx \, dy}{\int_0^{2a}\int_{-y}^{y} (z)_{mx}^{nx} \, dy \, dz} = \frac{\frac{1}{2}\int_0^{2a}\int_{-y}^{y} (n^2 - m^2)x^2 dx \, dy}{\int_0^{2a}\int_{-y}^{y} (n-m)x \, dx \, dy}$$

$$= \frac{\frac{n+m}{2}\int_0^{2a}\int_{-y}^{y} x^2 dx \, dy}{\int_0^{2a}\int_{-y}^{y} x \, dx \, dy}$$

$$= \frac{\left(\frac{n+m}{2}\right) 2\int_0^{2a}\int_0^{y} x^2 dx\, dy}{2\int_0^{2a}\int_0^{y} x\, dx\, dy}$$ | ∴ integrands are even functions of $y$

$$= \frac{\frac{m+n}{2}\int_0^{2a} x^2 (y)_0^y\, dx}{\int_0^{2a} x(y)_0^y\, dx} = \frac{\frac{m+n}{2}\int_0^{2a} x^2 y\, dx}{\int_0^{2a} xy\, dx}$$

$$= \frac{\frac{m+n}{2}\int_0^{2a} x^2\sqrt{2ax - x^2}\, dx}{\int_0^{2a} x\sqrt{2ax - x^2}\, dx}$$ Put $x = 2a \sin^2\theta$

$\therefore\ dx = 4a \sin\theta \cos\theta\, d\theta$

$$= \frac{\frac{m+n}{2}\int_0^{2a} 4a^2 \sin^4\theta\sqrt{4a^2\sin^2\theta - 4a^2\sin^4\theta}\ 4a\sin\theta\cos\theta\, d\theta}{\int_0^{2a} 2a\sin^2\theta\sqrt{4a^2\sin^2\theta - 4a^2\sin^4\theta}\ 4a\sin\theta\cos\theta\, d\theta}$$

$$= \frac{(m+n)a\int_0^{\pi/2}\sin^6\theta\cos^2\theta\, d\theta}{\int_0^{\pi/2}\sin^4\theta\cos^2\theta\, d\theta} = (m+n)a\frac{\dfrac{\left|\frac{7}{2}\right.\left|\frac{3}{2}\right.}{2\left|5\right.}}{\dfrac{\left|\frac{5}{2}\right.\left|\frac{3}{2}\right.}{2\left|4\right.}} = (m+n)a\frac{5}{2}\frac{1}{4} = \frac{5(m+n)a}{8}.$$

**Example 8:** Find the C.G. of the volume enclosed by the elliptic cylinder $2x^2 + y^2 = 2ax$ and the planes $z = mx$, $z = nx$.

**Sol.** $2x^2 + y^2 = 2ax$

$$\Rightarrow \quad x^2 + \frac{y^2}{2} = ax \quad \Rightarrow x^2 - ax + \frac{y^2}{2} = 0 \quad \Rightarrow x^2 - ax + \frac{a^2}{4} + \frac{y^2}{2} = \frac{a^2}{4}$$

$$\Rightarrow \quad \left(x - \frac{a}{2}\right)^2 + \frac{y^2}{2} = \frac{a^2}{4} \quad \Rightarrow \frac{\left(x - \frac{a}{2}\right)^2}{\left(\frac{a}{2}\right)^2} + \frac{y^2}{\left(\frac{a^2}{2}\right)} = 1$$

Here,

the limits of $z$ are from $z = mn$ to $z = nx$;

the limits of $y$ are from $y = -\sqrt{2ax - 2x^2}$ to $y = \sqrt{2ax - 2x^2}$;

the limits of $x$ are from $x = 0$ to $x = a$.

Let the required C.G. be at $(\overline{x}, \overline{y}, \overline{z})$.

Then,

$$\overline{x} = \frac{\iiint x\rho\, dx\, dy\, dz}{\iiint \rho\, dx\, dy\, dz} = \frac{\iiint x\, dx\, dy\, dz}{\iiint dx\, dy\, dz}$$ | ∵ ρ is constant

$$= \frac{\iint x\,dx\,dy\,(z)_{mx}^{nx}}{\iint dx\,dy\,(z)_{mx}^{nx}} = \frac{\iint x(n-m)x\,dx\,dy}{\iint (n-m)x\,dx\,dy}$$

$$= \frac{\int_0^a \int_{-y}^{y} x^2\,dx\,dy}{\int_0^a \int_{-y}^{y} x\,dx\,dy} \qquad \text{where } y = \sqrt{2ax - 2x^2}$$

$$= \frac{\int_0^a x^2 (y)_{-y}^{y}\,dx}{\int_0^a x(y)_{-y}^{y}\,dx} = \frac{\int_0^a x^2\,2y\,dx}{\int_0^a x\,2y\,dx} = \frac{\int_0^a x^2 y\,dx}{\int_0^a x\,y\,dx}$$

$$= \frac{\int_0^a x^2\sqrt{2ax-2x^2}\,dx}{\int_0^a x\sqrt{2ax-2x^2}\,dx} = \frac{\int_0^a x^2\sqrt{ax-x^2}\,dx}{\int_0^a x\sqrt{ax-x^2}\,dx}$$

Put $x = a\sin^2\theta$

$\therefore\ dx = 2a\sin\theta\cos\theta\,d\theta$

$$= \frac{\int_0^{\pi/2} a^2\sin^4\theta\sqrt{a^2\sin^2\theta - a^2\sin^4\theta}\cdot 2a\sin\theta\cos\theta\,d\theta}{\int_0^{\pi/2} a\sin^2\theta\sqrt{a^2\sin^2\theta - a^2\sin^4\theta}\cdot 2a\sin\theta\cos\theta\,d\theta} = \frac{a\int_0^{\pi/2}\sin^6\theta\cos^2\theta\,d\theta}{\int_0^{\pi/2}\sin^4\theta\cos^2\theta\,d\theta}$$

$$= \frac{\dfrac{\Gamma\frac{7}{2}\,\Gamma\frac{3}{2}}{2\,\Gamma 5}}{\dfrac{\Gamma\frac{5}{2}\,\Gamma\frac{3}{2}}{2\,\Gamma 4}} = a\frac{5}{2}\frac{1}{4} = \frac{5a}{8} \qquad \bar{y} = 0$$

| By symmetry

$$\bar{z} = \frac{\iiint z\,dx\,dy\,dz}{\iiint dx\,dy\,dz} = \frac{\iint\left(\frac{z^2}{2}\right)_{mx}^{nx} dx\,dy}{\iint (z)_{mx}^{nx}\,dx\,dy} = \frac{\frac{1}{2}\iint (n^2-m^2)x^2\,dx\,dy}{\iint (n-m)x\,dx\,dy}$$

$$= \frac{\frac{m+n}{2}\iint x^2\,dx\,dy}{\iint x\,dx\,dy} = \frac{m+n}{2}\cdot\frac{5a}{8}$$

| See the calculation for $\bar{x}$

$$= \frac{5(m+n)a}{16}.$$

**Example 9:** Find the position of the centroid of the volume included between the surface $\frac{x^2}{a^2}+\frac{y^2}{b^2}-\frac{z^2}{c^2}=1$, $x = 0$ and $z = \pm c$.

**Sol.** Here,

the limits of $y$ are from $-y$ to $y$ where $y = b\sqrt{1+\frac{z^2}{c^2}-\frac{x^2}{a^2}}$;

the limits of $x$ are from $x = 0$ to $a\sqrt{1+\dfrac{z^2}{c^2}}$;

the limits of $z$ are from $z = -c$ to $z = c$.

Let the required C.G. be at $(\bar{x}, \bar{y}, \bar{z})$. Then,

$$\bar{x} = \frac{\iint\int_{-y}^{y} x\,dx\,dy\,dz}{\iint\int_{-y}^{y} dx\,dy\,dz} \qquad \because \rho \text{ is constant}$$

where $y = b\sqrt{1+\dfrac{z^2}{c^2}-\dfrac{x^2}{a^2}}$

$$= \frac{\iint x\,dx\,dz\,(y)_{-y}^{y}}{\iint dx\,dz\,(y)_{-y}^{y}} = \frac{\iint x\,dx\,dz\,2y}{\iint dx\,dz\,2y} = \frac{\iint_{x=0}^{a\sqrt{1+\frac{z^2}{c^2}}} x\sqrt{1+\dfrac{z^2}{c^2}-\dfrac{x^2}{a^2}}\,dx\,dz}{\iint_{x=0}^{a\sqrt{1+\frac{z^2}{c^2}}} \sqrt{1+\dfrac{z^2}{c^2}-\dfrac{x^2}{a^2}}\,dx\,dz}$$

$$= \frac{\int_{z=-c}^{c}\left[-\dfrac{a^2}{3}\left(1+\dfrac{z^2}{c^2}-\dfrac{x^2}{a^2}\right)^{3/2}\right]_0^{a\sqrt{1+\frac{z^2}{c^2}}} dz}{\int_{z=-c}^{c}\left[\dfrac{1}{2}\cdot\dfrac{x}{a}\sqrt{1+\dfrac{z^2}{c^2}-\dfrac{x^2}{a^2}}+\dfrac{1}{2}\left(1+\dfrac{z^2}{c^2}\right)\sin^{-1}\dfrac{\left(\dfrac{x}{a}\right)}{\sqrt{1+\dfrac{z^2}{c^2}}}\right]_0^{a\sqrt{1+\frac{z^2}{c^2}}} dz}$$

$$= \frac{\int_{-c}^{c}\dfrac{a^2}{3}\left(1+\dfrac{z^2}{c^2}\right)^{3/2} dz}{\int_{-c}^{c}\dfrac{a}{2}\left(1+\dfrac{z^2}{c^2}\right)\dfrac{\pi}{2}dz} = \frac{\dfrac{4a}{3\pi}\int_{-c}^{c}\left(1+\dfrac{z^2}{c^2}\right)^{3/2} dz}{\int_{-c}^{c}\left(1+\dfrac{z^2}{c^2}\right)dz}$$

$$= \frac{\dfrac{4a}{3\pi}2\int_{0}^{c}\left(1+\dfrac{z^2}{c^2}\right)^{3/2} dz}{2\int_{0}^{c}\left(1+\dfrac{z^2}{c^2}\right)dz} \qquad \therefore \text{ Integrands are even functions of } z$$

$$= \frac{\dfrac{4a}{3\pi}\int_{0}^{c}\left(1+\dfrac{z^2}{c^2}\right)^{3/2} dz}{\int_{0}^{c}\left(1+\dfrac{z^2}{c^2}\right)dz}$$

Put $z = c\tan\theta$ in the numerator

$\therefore\ dz = c\sec^2\theta\, d\theta$

$$= \frac{\frac{4a}{3\pi}\int_0^{\pi/4} \sec^3\theta\, c\sec^2\theta\, d\theta}{\left(z+\frac{z^3}{3c^2}\right)_0^c} = \frac{4a}{3\pi}\cdot\frac{3}{4}\int_0^{\pi/4} \sec^5\theta\, d\theta = \frac{a}{\pi}\int_0^{\pi/4} \sec^5\theta\, d\theta$$

Using reduction formula for $\int \sec^n\theta\, d\theta$ as follows:

$$\int \sec^n\theta\, d\theta = \frac{\sec^{n-2}\theta\tan\theta}{n-1}+\frac{n-2}{n-1}\int \sec^{n-2}\theta\, d\theta$$

$$= \frac{a}{\pi}\left[\left(\frac{\sec^3\theta\tan\theta}{4}\right)_0^{\pi/4}+\frac{3}{4}\int_0^{\pi/4}\sec^3\theta\, d\theta\right]$$

$$= -\left[\frac{2\sqrt{2}}{4}+\frac{3}{4}\int^{/4} \sec\ \theta\ \theta\right] = \frac{a}{\pi}\left[\frac{2\sqrt{2}}{4}+\frac{3}{4}\left\{\left(\frac{\sec\theta\tan\theta}{2}\right)_0^{\pi/4}+\frac{1}{2}\int_0^{\pi/4}\sec\theta\, d\theta\right\}\right]$$

$$= \frac{a}{\pi}\left[\frac{2\sqrt{2}}{4}+\frac{3\sqrt{2}}{8}+\frac{3}{8}\{\log(\sec\theta+\tan\theta)\}_0^{\pi/4}\right] = \frac{a}{\pi}\left[\frac{2\sqrt{2}}{4}+\frac{3\sqrt{2}}{8}+\frac{3}{8}\log\left(\sqrt{2}+1\right)\right]$$

$$= \frac{a}{\pi}\left[\frac{7\sqrt{2}}{8}+\frac{3}{8}\log\left(\sqrt{2}+1\right)\right] = \frac{a}{8\pi}\left[7\sqrt{2}+3\log\left(\sqrt{2}+1\right)\right]$$

Again since the region under consideration is symmetrical about the $X$-axis (i.e., $Y = 0 = Z$), we have

$$\bar{y} = 0 = \bar{z}.$$

**Example 10:** Find the centroid of the volume included between the following surfaces:

$\frac{y^2}{b^2}+\frac{z^2}{c^2}-\frac{2x}{a} = 0$, $x = 2a$, $y = 0$ and $z = 0$.

**Sol.** Here,

The limits of $z$ are from $z = 0$ to $z = c\sqrt{\frac{2x}{a}-\frac{y^2}{b^2}}$;

The limits of $y$ are from $y = 0$ to $y = b\sqrt{\frac{2x}{a}}$;

The limits of $x$ are from $x = 0$ to $x = 2a$

Let the required C.G. be at $(\bar{x}, \bar{y}, \bar{z})$. Then,

$$\bar{x} = \frac{\iiint x\, dx\, dy\, dz}{\iiint dx\, dy\, dz} \qquad \mid \because \rho \text{ is constant}$$

$$= \frac{\iint x(z)_0^z\, dx\, dy}{\iint (z)_0^z\, dx\, dy} = \frac{\iint xc\sqrt{\frac{2x}{a}-\frac{y^2}{b^2}}\, dx\, dy}{\iint c\sqrt{\frac{2x}{a}-\frac{y^2}{b^2}}\, dx\, dy} \qquad \mid \because z = c\sqrt{\frac{2x}{a}-\frac{y^2}{b^2}}$$

$$= \frac{\iint x\sqrt{\frac{2x}{a} - \frac{y^2}{b^2}}\,dx\,dy}{\iint \sqrt{\frac{2x}{a} - \frac{y^2}{b^2}}\,dx\,dy} = \frac{\iint x\sqrt{\frac{1}{b^2}\left(\frac{2b^2x}{a} - y^2\right)}dx\,dy}{\iint \sqrt{\frac{1}{b^2}\left(\frac{2b^2x}{a} - y^2\right)}dx\,dy}$$

$$= \frac{\iint x\sqrt{\frac{2b^2x}{a} - y^2}\,dx\,dy}{\iint \sqrt{\frac{2b^2x}{a} - y^2}\,dx\,dy} = \frac{\int_0^{2a}\left[\frac{1}{2}y\sqrt{\frac{2b^2x}{a} - y^2} + \frac{1}{2}\cdot\frac{2b^2x}{a}\sin^{-1}\left\{\frac{y}{\sqrt{2}b\sqrt{\frac{x}{a}}}\right\}\right]_0^{b\sqrt{\frac{2x}{a}}}}{\int_0^{2a}\left[\frac{1}{2}y\sqrt{\frac{2b^2x}{a} - y^2} + \frac{1}{2}\cdot\frac{2b^2x}{a}\sin^{-1}\left\{\frac{y}{\sqrt{2}b\sqrt{\frac{x}{a}}}\right\}\right]_0^{b\sqrt{\frac{2x}{a}}}}$$

$$= \frac{\int_0^{2a} x\frac{x}{a}\frac{\pi}{2}dx}{\int_0^{2a}\frac{x}{a}\frac{\pi}{2}dx} = \frac{\int_0^{2a} x^2\,dx}{\int_0^{2a} x\,dx} = \frac{\left(\frac{x^3}{3}\right)_0^{2a}}{\left(\frac{x^2}{2}\right)_0^{2a}} = \frac{8a^3}{3}\cdot\frac{2}{4a^2} = \frac{4a}{3}$$

$$\bar{y} = \frac{\iiint y\,dx\,dy\,dz}{\iiint dx\,dy\,dz} = \frac{\iint y(z)_0^z\,dx\,dy}{\iint (z)_0^z\,dx\,dy} = \frac{\iint yc\sqrt{\frac{2x}{a} - \frac{y^2}{b^2}}\,dx\,dy}{\iint c\sqrt{\frac{2x}{a} - \frac{y^2}{b^2}}\,dx\,dy} \quad \Big|\because\; z = c\sqrt{\frac{2x}{a^2} - \frac{y^2}{b^2}}$$

$$= \frac{\iint y\sqrt{\frac{2x}{a} - \frac{y^2}{b^2}}\,dx\,dy}{\iint \sqrt{\frac{2x}{a} - \frac{y^2}{b^2}}\,dx\,dy} = \frac{\iint y\sqrt{\frac{2x}{a} - \frac{y^2}{b^2}}\,dx\,dy}{\iint \frac{1}{b}\sqrt{\frac{2b^2x}{a} - y^2}\,dx\,dy}$$

$$= \frac{\int_0^{2a}\left[-\frac{b^2}{3}\left(\frac{2x}{a} - \frac{y^2}{b^2}\right)^{3/2}\right]_0^{b\sqrt{\frac{2x}{a}}}dx}{\frac{1}{b}\int_0^{2a}\left\{\frac{1}{2}y\sqrt{\frac{2b^2x}{a} - y^2} + \frac{1}{2}\cdot\frac{2b^2x}{a}\sin^{-1}\frac{y}{\sqrt{2}\,b\sqrt{\frac{x}{a}}}\right\}_0^{b\sqrt{\frac{2x}{a}}}dx} = \frac{\frac{b^2}{3}\int_0^{2a}\left(\frac{2x}{a}\right)^{3/2}}{\frac{1}{b}\int_0^{2a}\frac{b^2x}{a}\frac{\pi}{2}dx}$$

$$= \frac{\frac{b^2}{3}\frac{2\sqrt{2}}{a^{3/2}}\int_0^{2a} x^{3/2}\,dx}{\frac{b\pi}{2a}\int_0^{2a} x\,dx} = \frac{\frac{4\sqrt{2}\,b}{3\sqrt{a}\,\pi}\int_0^{2a} x^{3/2}\,dx}{\int_0^{2a} x\,dx} = \frac{4\sqrt{2}\,b}{3\sqrt{a}\,\pi}\frac{\left(\frac{2}{5}x^{5/2}\right)_0^{2a}}{\left(\frac{x^2}{2}\right)_0^{2a}}$$

$$= \frac{4\sqrt{2}\,b}{3\sqrt{a}\,\pi}\frac{\frac{2}{5}(2a)^{5/2}}{\frac{1}{2}(2a)^2} = \frac{4\sqrt{2}\,b}{3\sqrt{a}\,\pi}\frac{4}{5}\sqrt{2a} = \frac{32b}{15\pi}$$

Again, we see that the equation of the given surface remains unchanged by interchanging $b$ and $c$ and also $y$ and $z$. Therefore, the value of $\bar{z}$ can be immediately obtained from $\bar{y}$ by writing $c$ for $b$. Hence, $\bar{z} = \frac{32c}{15\pi}$.

**Example 11:** Find the C.G. of the portion of the paraboloid $y^2 + z^2 = 4mx$ which is cut off by the three planes $x = a$, $y = 0$, $z = 0$.

**Sol.** Here,

the limits of $z$ are from $z = 0$ to $z = \sqrt{4mx - y^2}$;

the limits of $y$ are from $y = 0$ to $y = \sqrt{4mx}$;

the limits of $x$ are from $x = 0$ to $y = a$;

Let the required C.G. be at $(\bar{x}, \bar{y}, \bar{z})$.

Then,

$$\bar{x} = \frac{\int_0^a\int_0^{\sqrt{4mx}}\int_0^{\sqrt{4mx-y^2}} x\,dx\,dy\,dz}{\int_0^a\int_0^{\sqrt{4mx}}\int_0^{\sqrt{4mx-y^2}} dx\,dy\,dz} \qquad |\because \rho \text{ is constant} \qquad ...(1)$$

Numerator of $\bar{x}$

$$= \int_0^a\int_0^{\sqrt{4mx}} x\sqrt{4mx - y^2}\,dx\,dy = \int_0^a x\left[\frac{1}{2}y\sqrt{4mx-y^2} + \frac{1}{2}\cdot 4mx\sin^{-1}\frac{y}{\sqrt{4mx}}\right]_0^{\sqrt{4mx}} dx$$

$$= \int_0^a x\cdot 2mx\sin^{-1}(1)\,dx = \int_0^a x\times 2mx\times\frac{\pi}{2}dx = \pi m\int_0^a x^2\,dx = \pi m\left(\frac{x^3}{3}\right)_0^a$$

$$= \frac{\pi m a^3}{3} \qquad ...(2)$$

Denominator of $\bar{x}$

$$= \int_0^a\int_0^{\sqrt{4mx}} \sqrt{4mx - y^2}\,dx\,dy = \int_0^a\left[\frac{1}{2}y\sqrt{4mx-y^2} + \frac{1}{2}\cdot 4mx\sin^{-1}\frac{y}{\sqrt{4mx}}\right]_0^{\sqrt{4mx}} dx$$

$$= \int_0^a 2mx \cdot \frac{\pi}{2} dx = \pi m \frac{a^2}{2} \qquad \text{...(3)}$$

From (1), (2) and (3)

$$\bar{x} = \frac{\frac{\pi m a^3}{3}}{\pi m \frac{a^2}{2}} = \frac{2}{3}a \quad \bar{y} = \frac{\int_0^a \int_0^{\sqrt{4mx}} \int_0^{\sqrt{4mx-y^2}} y \, dx \, dy \, dz}{\int_0^a \int_0^{\sqrt{4mx}} \int_0^{\sqrt{4mx-y^2}} dx \, dy \, dz} \qquad \text{...(4)}$$

Numerator of $\bar{y}$

$$= \int_0^a \int_0^{\sqrt{4mx-y^2}} y\sqrt{4mx-y^2} \, dx \, dy = \int_0^a \left[ -\frac{\left(4mx-y^2\right)^{3/2}}{3} \right]_0^{\sqrt{4mx}} dx$$

$$= \frac{1}{3}\int_0^a (4mx)^{3/2} dx = \frac{(4m)^{3/2}}{3}\left(\frac{2}{5}x^{5/2}\right)_0^a = \frac{8m^{3/2}}{3} \cdot \frac{2}{5} a^{5/2}$$

$$= \frac{16}{15} m^{3/2} a^{5/2} \qquad \text{...(5)}$$

Denominator of $\bar{y}$ = Denominator of $\bar{x} = \frac{\pi m a^2}{2}$ | From (3) ...(6)

From (4), (5) and (6),

$$\bar{y} = \frac{\frac{16}{15} m^{3/2} a^{5/2}}{\frac{\pi m a^2}{2}} = \frac{32}{15}\sqrt{am}, \; \bar{z} = \frac{\int_0^a \int_0^{\sqrt{4mx}} \int_0^{\sqrt{4mx-y^2}} z \, dx \, dy \, dz}{\int_0^a \int_0^{\sqrt{4mx}} \int_0^{\sqrt{4mx-y^2}} dx \, dy \, dz} \qquad \text{...(7)}$$

Numerator of $\bar{z}$

$$= \int_0^a \int_0^{\sqrt{4mx}} \left(\frac{z^2}{2}\right)_0^{\sqrt{4mx-y^2}} dx \, dy = \frac{1}{2}\int_0^a \int_0^{\sqrt{4mx}} \left(4mx - y^2\right) dx \, dy$$

$$= \frac{1}{2}\int_0^a \left(4mx\, y - \frac{y^3}{3}\right)_0^{\sqrt{4mx}} dx = \frac{1}{2}\int_0^a \left\{4mx\sqrt{4mx} - \frac{4mx\sqrt{4mx}}{3}\right\} dx$$

$$= \frac{8}{3} m\sqrt{m} \int_0^a x^{3/2} dx = \frac{8}{3} m^{3/2} \frac{2}{5}\left(x^{3/2}\right)_0^a = \frac{16}{15} m^{3/2} a^{5/2} \qquad \text{...(8)}$$

Denominator of $\bar{z}$ = Denominator of $\bar{x}$

$$= \frac{\pi m a^2}{2} \qquad \text{| From (3)} \qquad \text{...(9)}$$

From (7), (8) and (9),

$$\bar{z} = \frac{\frac{16}{15} m^{3/2} a^{5/2}}{\pi \frac{ma^2}{2}} = \frac{32}{15\pi}\sqrt{am}.$$

**Example 12:** Find the C.G. of the portion of the solid cone $y^2 + z^2 = \beta^2 x^2$ cut off by the planes $ZX$, $XY$ and a given plane parallel to $YZ$ plane.

**Sol.** Let the given plane parallel to $YZ$ plane be $x = a$.

Here, limits of $z$ are from $z = 0$ to $z = \sqrt{\beta^2 x^2 - y^2}$;

limits of $y$ are from $y = 0$ to $y = \beta x$;

limits of $x$ are from $x = 0$ to $x = a$.

Let the required C.G. from be at $(\bar{x}, \bar{y}, \bar{z})$. Then,

$$\bar{x} = \frac{\int_0^a \int_0^{\beta x} \int_0^z x\,dx\,dy\,dz}{\int_0^a \int_0^{\beta x} \int_0^z dx\,dy\,dz} \qquad | \because \rho \text{ is constant}$$

where, $z = \sqrt{\beta^2 x^2 - y^2}$

$$= \frac{\int_0^a \int_0^{\beta x} x\sqrt{\beta^2 x^2 - y^2}\,dx\,dy}{\int_0^a \int_0^{\beta x} \sqrt{\beta^2 x^2 - y^2}\,dx\,dy} \qquad \text{Put } y = \beta x \sin\theta \quad \therefore dy = \beta x \cos\theta\,d\theta$$

$$= \frac{\int_0^a \int_0^{\pi/2} x\,dx\sqrt{\beta^2 x^2 - \beta^2 x^2 \sin^2\theta}\;\beta x\cos\theta\,d\theta}{\int_0^a \int_0^{\pi/2} dx\sqrt{\beta^2 x^2 - \beta^2 x^2 \sin^2\theta}\;\beta x\cos\theta\,d\theta} = \frac{\int_0^a \int_0^{\pi/2} x^3 dx\cos^2\theta\,d\theta}{\int_0^a \int_0^{\pi/2} x^2 dx\cos^2\theta\,d\theta}$$

$$= \frac{\int_0^a x^3 \cdot \frac{1}{2} \cdot \frac{\pi}{2}\,dx}{\int_0^a x^2 \frac{1}{2}\frac{\pi}{2}\,dx} \qquad | \text{ By Walli's Formula}$$

$$= \frac{\int_0^a x^3\,dx}{\int_0^a x^2\,dx} = \frac{\left(\frac{x^4}{4}\right)_0^a}{\left(\frac{x^3}{3}\right)_0^a} = \frac{3}{4}a$$

$$\bar{y} = \frac{\int_0^a \int_0^{\beta x} \int_0^z y\,dx\,dy\,dz}{\int_0^a \int_0^{\beta x} \int_0^z dx\,dy\,dz} = \frac{\int_0^a \int_0^{\beta x} yz\,dx\,dy}{\int_0^a \int_0^{\beta x} z\,dx\,dy}$$

$$= \frac{\int_0^a \int_0^{\beta x} y\sqrt{\beta^2 x^2 - y^2}\,dx\,dy}{\int_0^a \int_0^{\beta x} \sqrt{\beta^2 x^2 - y^2}\,dx\,dy} \qquad \text{Put } y = \beta x \sin\theta \quad \therefore dy = \beta x \cos\theta\,d\theta$$

$$= \frac{\int_0^a \int_0^{\pi/2} dx\, \beta x \sin\theta \sqrt{\beta^2 x^2 - \beta^2 x^2 \sin^2\theta}\ \ \beta x \cos\theta\, d\theta}{\int_0^a \int_0^{\pi/2} dx \sqrt{\beta^2 x^2 - \beta^2 x^2 \sin^2\theta}\ \ \beta x \cos\theta\, d\theta}$$

$$= \frac{\beta \int_0^a \int_0^{\pi/2} x^3 \sin\theta \cos^2\theta\, dx\, d\theta}{\int_0^a \int_0^{\pi/2} x^2 \cos^2\theta\, dx\, d\theta} = \frac{\beta \int_0^a x^3 \left(\frac{-\cos^3\theta}{3}\right)_0^{\pi/2} dx}{\int_0^a x^2 \cdot \frac{1}{2} \cdot \frac{\pi}{2} dx} = \frac{\frac{4\beta}{3\pi} \int_0^a x^3\, dx}{\int_0^a x^2\, dx}$$

$$= \frac{4\beta}{3\pi} \frac{\left(\frac{x^4}{4}\right)_0^a}{\left(\frac{x^3}{3}\right)_0^a} = \frac{4\beta}{3\pi} \frac{\frac{a^4}{4}}{\frac{a^3}{3}} = \frac{4\beta}{3\pi} \frac{3a}{4} = \frac{\beta a}{\pi}$$

Again, we see that the equation of the given surface remain unchanged on interchanging $y$ and $z$. Hence,

$$\bar{z} = \bar{y} = \frac{\beta a}{\pi}$$

**Example 13:** Find the centre of gravity of a hemisphere whose density varies as the distance from a given point on its plane edge.

**Sol.** Take the given point $O$ on the plane edge of the hemisphere of radius $a$(say) as origin. The diameter of the base through $O$ as the $Y$-axis, the tangent at $O$ to the circular base as the $X$-axis and a line normal to the plane base through $O$ as the $Z$-axis.

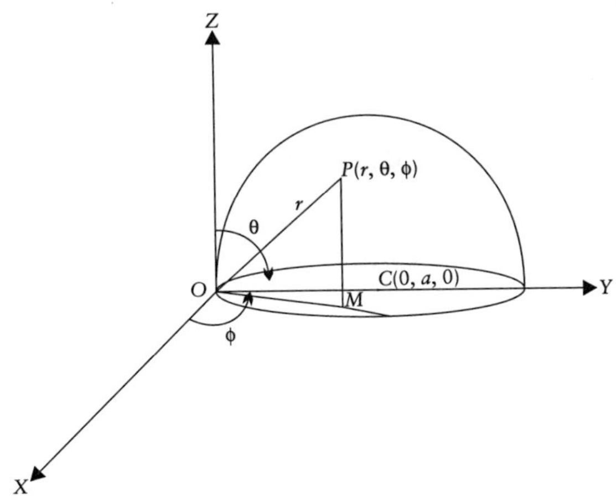


Then, the equation of the hemisphere is $x^2 + (y - a)^2 + z^2 = a^2$

$$\Rightarrow \qquad x^2 + y^2 + z^2 - 2ay = 0 \qquad ...(1)$$

Let $P$ be any point in the volume of the hemisphere. Let $OP = r$ and $\angle ZOP = \theta$. Draw perpendicular $PM$ to the plane base of the hemisphere which is obviously $XY$ plane.

Let $\angle XOM = \phi$

Then, the spherical polar coordinates of $P$ are $(r, \theta, \phi)$.

The relations between the cartesian and polar coordinates are given by

$$x = r\sin\theta\cos\phi \qquad \text{| Refer § 12 (ii)}$$

$$y = r\sin\theta\cos\phi \qquad z = r\cos\theta$$

Using those, the spherical polar equation of the hemisphere becomes

$$r^2 - 2ar\sin\theta\sin\theta = 0 \quad \Rightarrow \quad r - 2a\sin\theta\sin\theta = 0 \qquad ...(2)$$

For the entire volume of the hemisphere,

limits of $r$ are from $r = 0$ to $r = 2a\sin\theta\sin\phi$

limits of $\phi$ are from $\phi = 0$ to $\phi = \pi$

limits of $\theta$ are from $\theta = 0$ to $\theta = \dfrac{\pi}{2}$

Let $\rho$ be the density at the point $P(r, \theta, \phi)$. Then, $\rho = \lambda r$

Let the required C.G. be at $(\bar{x}, \bar{y}, \bar{z})$.

Since the given hemisphere is symmetrical about the $YZ$-plane (i.e. the plane $x = 0$), therefore, we have $\bar{x} = 0$

Also,

$$\bar{y} = \frac{\iiint \rho r^3 \sin^2\theta\sin\phi\, dr\, d\theta\, d\phi}{\iiint \rho r^2 \sin\theta\, dr\, d\theta\, d\phi} \qquad \text{| Refer § 12 (ii)}$$

$$= \frac{\iiint \lambda r r^3 \sin^2\theta\sin\phi\, dr\, d\theta\, d\phi}{\iiint \lambda r r^2 \sin\theta\, dr\, d\theta\, d\phi} = \frac{\int_{\theta=0}^{\pi/2}\int_{\phi=0}^{\pi}\int_{r=0}^{2a\sin\theta\sin\phi} r^4 \sin^2\theta\sin\phi\, dr\, d\theta\, d\phi}{\int_{\theta=0}^{\pi/2}\int_{\phi=0}^{\pi}\int_{r=0}^{2a\sin\theta\sin\phi} r^3 \sin\theta\, dr\, d\theta\, d\phi}$$

$$= \frac{\int_0^{\pi/2}\int_0^{\pi}\left(\dfrac{r^5}{5}\right)_0^{2a\sin\theta\sin\phi} \sin^2\theta\sin\phi\, d\theta\, d\phi}{\int_0^{\pi/2}\int_0^{\pi}\left(\dfrac{r^4}{4}\right)_0^{2a\sin\theta\sin\phi} \sin\theta\, d\theta\, d\phi} = \frac{\dfrac{8a}{5}\int_0^{\pi/2}\int_0^{\pi} \sin^7\theta\sin^6\phi\, d\theta\, d\phi}{\int_0^{\pi/2}\int_0^{\pi} \sin^5\theta\sin^4\phi\, d\theta\, d\phi}$$

$$= \frac{\dfrac{8a}{5}\int_0^{\pi/2} \sin^7\theta\, d\theta \cdot 2\int_0^{\pi/2} \sin^6\theta\, d\phi}{\int_0^{\pi/2} \sin^5\theta\, d\theta \cdot 2\int_0^{\pi/2} \sin^4\theta\, d\phi} \qquad \text{| By property of definite integrals}$$

$$= \frac{\dfrac{8a}{5}\cdot\dfrac{6}{7}\cdot\dfrac{4}{5}\cdot\dfrac{2}{3}\cdot\dfrac{5}{6}\cdot\dfrac{3}{4}\cdot\dfrac{1}{2}\cdot\dfrac{\pi}{2}}{\dfrac{4}{5}\cdot\dfrac{2}{3}\cdot\dfrac{3}{4}\cdot\dfrac{1}{2}\cdot\dfrac{\pi}{2}} \qquad \text{| By Walli's Formula}$$

$$= \frac{8a}{7}$$

$$\bar{z} = \frac{\iiint \rho r^3 \sin\theta\cos\theta\, dr\, d\theta\, d\phi}{\iiint \rho r^2 \sin\theta\, dr\, d\theta\, d\phi} = \frac{\iiint \lambda r\, r^3 \sin\theta\cos\theta\, dr\, d\theta\, d\phi}{\iiint \lambda r\, r^2 \sin\theta\, dr\, d\theta\, d\phi}$$

$$= \frac{\int_{\theta=0}^{\pi/2}\int_{\phi=0}^{\pi}\int_{r=0}^{2a\sin\theta\,\sin\phi} r^4 \sin\theta\cos\theta\, dr\, d\theta\, d\phi}{\int_{\theta=0}^{\pi/2}\int_{\phi=0}^{\pi}\int_{r=0}^{2a\sin\theta\,\sin\phi} r^3 \sin\theta\, dr\, d\theta\, d\phi} = \frac{\int_0^{\pi/2}\int_0^{\pi}\left(\frac{r^5}{5}\right)_0^{2a\sin\theta\,\sin\phi} \sin\theta\cos\theta\, d\theta\, d\phi}{\int_0^{\pi/2}\int_0^{\pi}\left(\frac{r^4}{4}\right)_0^{2a\sin\theta\,\sin\phi} \sin\theta\, dr\, d\theta\, d\phi}$$

$$= \frac{\frac{8a}{5}\int_0^{\pi/2} \sin^6\theta\cos\theta\, d\theta \int_0^{\pi} \sin^5\phi\, d\phi}{\int_0^{\pi/2} \sin^5\theta\, d\theta \int_0^{\pi} \sin^4\phi\, d\phi}$$

$$= \frac{\frac{8a}{5}\left(\frac{\sin^7\theta}{7}\right)_0^{\pi/2} 2\int_0^{\pi/2} \sin^5\phi\, d\phi}{\int_0^{\pi/2} \sin^5\theta\, d\theta\, 2\int_0^{\pi} \sin^4\phi\, d\phi} \qquad \text{|By property of Definite Integrals}$$

$$= \frac{\frac{8a}{5}\cdot\left(\frac{1}{7}\right)\left(\frac{4}{5}\cdot\frac{2}{3}\right)}{\left(\frac{4}{5}\cdot\frac{2}{3}\right)\cdot\left(\frac{3}{4}\cdot\frac{1}{2}\cdot\frac{\pi}{2}\right)} \qquad \text{| By Walli's Formula}$$

$$= \frac{128a}{105\pi}.$$

**Example 14:** A right circular cone is scooped out of a solid homogeneous sphere, the vertex of the cone being in the surface of the sphere and its axis being a diameter of the sphere. Find the C.G. of the remainder.

**Sol.**

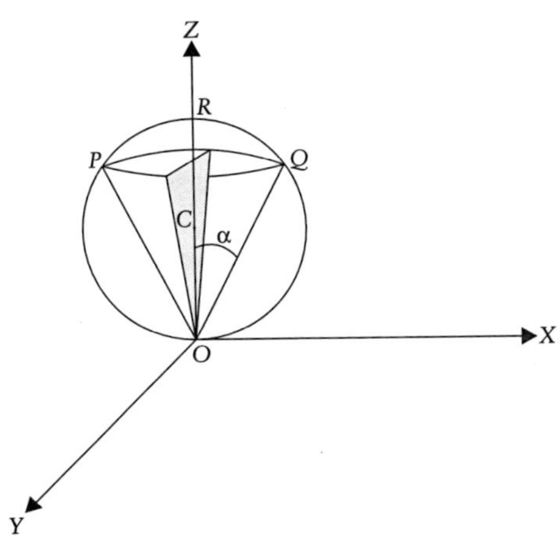

Let the radius of the sphere be $a$. Let $C$ be the centre of the sphere lying on $Z$-axis. Let $\alpha$ be the semi-vertical angle of the cone scooped out of the sphere. Let O be the vertex of the cone lying in the surface of the sphere.

Let the diameter $OR$ of the sphere coincide with the axis of the cone.

The equation of the sphere is

$$r = 2a\cos\theta \qquad \text{(in polar coordinates)}$$

and

$$x^2+y^2+z^2 = 2az \qquad \text{(in cartesian coordinates)}$$

The equation of the cone is

$$\theta = \alpha \qquad \text{(in polar coordinates)}$$

and

$$x^2+y^2 = z^2\tan^2\alpha \qquad \text{(in cartesian coordinates)}$$

Let $M_1$ be the mass of the sphere. Then,

$$M_1 = \frac{4}{3}\pi a^3\,\rho \text{ where } \rho \text{ is the density.}$$

Let $M_2$ be the mass common to the sphere and the cone.

## Determination of $M_2$

Consider an element of volume $\delta r\cdot r\delta\theta\cdot r\sin\theta\,\delta\phi$ at a point $= r^2\sin\theta\,\delta r\,\delta\theta\,\delta\phi$.

$P(r, \theta, \phi)$. Then,

$$M_2 = 4\int_{\phi=0}^{\pi/2}\int_{\theta=0}^{\alpha}\int_{r=0}^{2a\cos\theta}\rho\, r^2\sin\theta\, dr\, d\theta\, d\phi$$

$$= 4\rho\int_{\phi=0}^{\pi/2}\int_0^{\alpha}\left(\frac{r^3}{3}\right)_0^{2a\cos\theta}\sin\theta\, d\theta\, d\phi = \frac{32a^3\rho}{3}\int_0^{\pi/2}\int_0^{\alpha}\cos^3\theta\sin\theta\, d\theta\, d\phi$$

$$= \frac{32a^3\rho}{3}\frac{\pi}{2}\left(\frac{-\cos^4\theta}{4}\right)_0^{\alpha} = \frac{16\pi a^3}{3}\rho\left(\frac{1-\cos^4\alpha}{4}\right) = \frac{4\rho\pi a^3}{3}(1-\cos^4\alpha)$$

Now, the C.G. of the sphere lies at its centre $C$, i.e., $OC = a$.

Let the C.G. of mass $M_2$ lie at $G'$.

$$\text{Then, } OG' = \frac{\iiint r\cos\theta\,\rho r^2\sin\theta\, dr\, d\theta\, d\phi}{\iiint \rho r^2\sin\theta\, dr\, d\theta\, d\phi}$$

$$= \frac{4\int_{\phi=0}^{\pi/2}\int_{\theta=0}^{\alpha}\int_{r=0}^{2a\cos\theta} r^3\sin\theta\cos\theta\, dr\, d\theta\, d\phi}{4\int_{\phi=0}^{\pi/2}\int_{\theta=0}^{\alpha}\int_{r=0}^{2a\cos\theta} r^2\sin\theta\, dr\, d\theta\, d\phi} \qquad \because \rho \text{ is constant}$$

$$= \frac{\int_0^{\pi/2}\int_0^{\alpha}\left(\frac{r^4}{4}\right)_0^{2a\cos\theta}\sin\theta\cos\theta\, d\theta\, d\phi}{\int_0^{\pi/2}\int_0^{\alpha}\left(\frac{r^3}{3}\right)_0^{2a\cos\theta}\sin\theta\, dr\, d\theta\, d\phi}$$

$$= \frac{\frac{3}{4}\cdot(2a)\cdot\int_0^{\pi/2}\int_0^{\alpha}\cos^5\theta\sin\theta\,d\theta\,d\phi}{\int_0^{\pi/2}\int_0^{\alpha}\cos^3\theta\sin\theta\,d\theta\,d\phi} = \frac{\frac{3a}{2}\frac{\pi}{2}\left(-\frac{\cos^6\theta}{6}\right)_0^{\alpha}}{\frac{\pi}{2}\left(-\frac{\cos^4\theta}{4}\right)_0^{\alpha}}$$

$$= \frac{\frac{3a}{2}\frac{1}{6}\left(1-\cos^6\alpha\right)}{\frac{1}{4}\left(1-\cos^4\alpha\right)} = a\left(\frac{1-\cos^6\alpha}{1-\cos^4\alpha}\right)$$

Let the C.G. of the remainder lie at $G$.

$$\text{Then, } OG = \frac{M_1(OC)-M_2(OG')}{M_1-M_2}$$

$$= \frac{\left(\frac{4}{3}\pi a^3\rho\right)(a)-\left(\frac{4\rho\pi a^3}{3}\right)\int^{(1-\cos^4\alpha)}\left(\frac{1-\cos^6\alpha}{1-\cos^4\alpha}\right)a}{\frac{4}{3}\pi a^3\rho-\frac{4}{3}\pi a^3\rho\left(1-\cos^4\alpha\right)} = \frac{\frac{4}{3}\pi a^3\rho\left[1-\left(1-\cos^6\alpha\right)\right]}{\frac{4}{3}\pi a^3\rho\left[1-\left(1-\cos^4\alpha\right)\right]}$$

$$= a\frac{\cos^6\alpha}{\cos^4\alpha} = a\cos^2\alpha.$$

## EXERCISE 2(H)

1. Find the C.G. of the portion of the sphere $x^2 + y^2 + z^2 = a^2$ cut off by three planes $x = 0$, $y = 0$, $z = 0$ in the position octant, density of the sphere being constant.

   [**Ans.** $\left(\frac{3a}{8},\frac{3a}{8},\frac{3a}{8}\right)$]

2. Find the centre of gravity of the positive octant of an ellipsoid (solid) $\frac{x^2}{a^2}+\frac{y^2}{b^2}+\frac{z^2}{c^2} = 1$, if the density vary as $x^3 y^2 z^3$.

   [**Ans.** $\left(\frac{693a\pi}{4096},\frac{231b}{512},\frac{693c\pi}{4096}\right)$]

3. Find the C.G. of the solid bounded by the ellipsoid $\frac{x^2}{a^2}+\frac{y^2}{b^2}+\frac{z^2}{c^2} = 1$ in the positive octant, if the density at any point varies as $x y^2 z^3$.

   [**Ans.** $\left(\frac{63\pi a}{512},\frac{63b}{128},\frac{189\pi c}{1024}\right)$]

4. Find the C.G. of the volume enclosed by the planes $x = 0$, $y = 0$, $z = 0$ and $x + y + z = a$.

   [**Hint:** Limits of $z$ are from $z = 0$ to $z = a - x - y$

   Limits of $y$ are from $y = 0$ to $y = a - x$ Limits of $x$ are from $x = 0$ to $x = a$]

   $\left[\textbf{Ans. } \bar{x} = \frac{a}{4} = \bar{y} = \bar{z}\right]$

5. Find the centre of gravity of the volume cut off from the first octant by the plane $x + 2y + 4z = 8$.

$$\left[\textbf{Ans. } \bar{x} = 2, \bar{y} = 1, \bar{z} = \frac{1}{2}\right]$$

[**Hint:** Limits of $z$ are from $z = 0$ to $z = \dfrac{8 - x - 2y}{4}$.

Limits of $y$ are from $y = 0$ to $y = 8–x/2$

Limits of $x$ are from $x = 0$ to $x = 8$]

6. Find the centroid of the solid of uniform density bounded above by the plane $z = 4$ and below by the paraboloid $z = x^2 + y^2$.

$$\left[\textbf{Ans. } \bar{x} = \bar{y} = 0, \bar{z} = \frac{17}{6}\right]$$

7. Find the C.G. of the portion of solid sphere contained in a right cone whose vertex is the centre of the sphere; density varying as the $n$th power of the distance from the centre; $\alpha$ being the semi-vertical angle of the cone.

$$\left[\textbf{Ans. } \bar{x} = 0 = \bar{y},\ \bar{z} = \frac{n+3}{n+4} \cdot \frac{a}{2}(1 + \cos\alpha)\right]$$

8. Find the C.G. of the portion of the elliptic paraboloid $\dfrac{x^2}{a^2} + \dfrac{y^2}{b^2} = \dfrac{2z}{c}$ included between the planes $ZX$ and $YZ$ and a plane perpendicular to $Z$-axis at a distance $b$ from the vertex.

$$\left[\textbf{Ans. } \bar{x} = \frac{4a}{3}, \bar{y} = \frac{32b}{15\pi}, \bar{z} = \frac{32c}{15\pi}\right]$$

9. A body is formed of the portion of a uniform solid sphere of radius $a$, which is cut off by a circular cylinder of diameter $a$ passing through the centre of the sphere. Show that the centre of gravity of the portion that lies within the cylinder is at a distance $\dfrac{12a}{(15\pi - 20)}$ from the centre of the sphere.

Chapter
3

# Virtual Work

## 1. Work

A force is said to do work when its point of application undergoes a displacement from one position to another. Work is a scalar quantity. If the force acting upon the point is of constant nature, i.e., its magnitude and direction both remain constant throughout the course, then the amount of work done by the force is equal to the product of the magnitude of the force with the distance through which the point of application is displaced in the direction of the force.

Let a force of magnitude $F$ act at a point $O$. Let the magnitude of force be represented by $OB$. Suppose the point of application $O$ is displaced from $O$ to $P$ in a direction making an angle $\theta$ with the direction of the force $F$. Draw a perpendicular $PM$ from $P$ on the line of action of the force $F$. If $W$ denotes the amount of work done by the force $F$, then,

$$W = \text{Force} \times \text{Displacement in the direction of force} = F \times OM = F \times OP \cos\theta$$

$$= \text{Force} \times \text{Projection of the displacement in the direction of force}$$

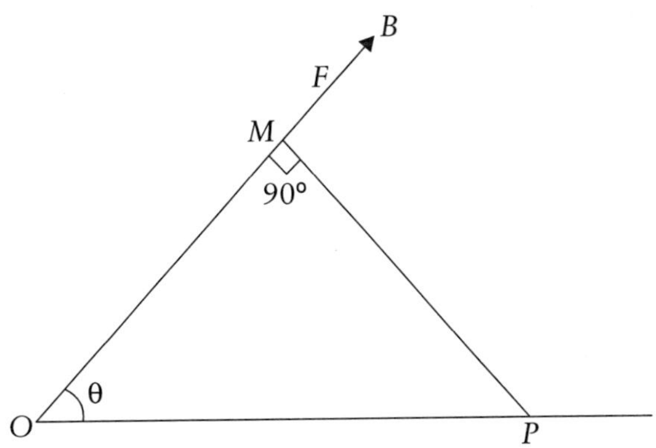


Again, $W = F \times OP \cos\theta = OP \times F \cos\theta$

$= \text{Actual displacement} \times \text{Resolved part of the force in the direction of the actual displacement}$

## 2. Positive and Negative Work

Work is said to be positive if the direction of the force is the same as the direction of displacement. However, if the directions of the force and the displacement are opposite to each other, then the work is said to be negative.

(i) When $\theta$ is acute, $\cos\theta$ is positive. Hence, the work done by the force is positive.

(ii) When $\theta$ is obtuse, $\cos\theta$ is negative. Hence, the work done by the force is negative.

(iii) When $\theta = 90°$, $\cos\theta = \cos 90° = 0$. Hence, the work done by the force $= F \times OP \times \cos 90° = F \times OP \times 0 = 0$, i.e. a force does no work when its point of application gets displaced at right angles to the direction of the force.

Moreover, a force does no work when its point of application is not displacement at all.

## 3. Power

The power of a working agent is defined as the amount of work done by it, if it worked uniformly for unit time. In other words, we can say that the power of a working agent is defined as the rate of its doing work.

## 4. Energy

Energy of a working agent is defined as its capacity to do the work. There are several types of energy as follows:

1. Mechanical energy
2. Chemical energy
3. Electrical energy
4. Heat energy
5. Light energy, etc.

## 5. Mechanical Energy

Mechanical energy of a body is the energy possessed by it due to its position or motion. Accordingly, the mechanical energy is of two types as follows:

(i) Potential Energy

(ii) Kinetic Energy

The potential energy of a body is defined as its capacity of doing work due to its position.

The kinetic energy of a body is defined as its capacity of doing work due to its motion.

## 6. Theorem

The work done by a force in displacing a particle from one position to another is equal to the algebraic sum of the works done by the resolved parts of the force.

**Proof**

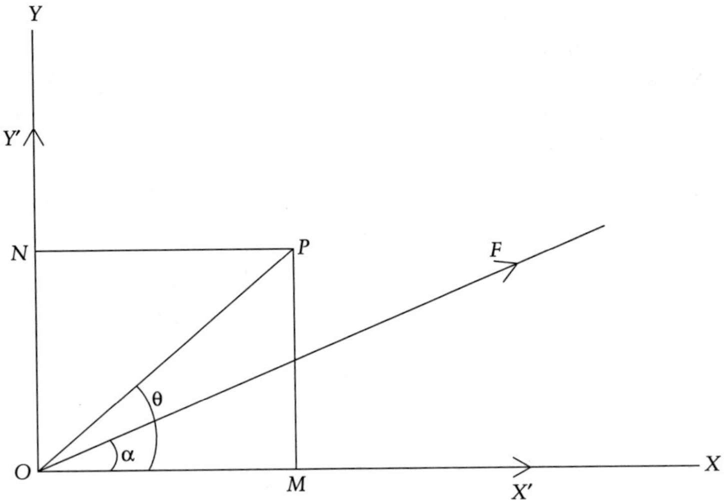


Let a force $F$ acting on a particle, placed at $O$, displace it from $O$ to $P$, such that $OP$ makes an angle $\theta$ with the $X$-axis. Let $F$ make an angle $\theta$ with the $X$-axis. Then, the resolved parts of the force $F$ along the $X$-axis and $Y$-axis are $X' = F\cos\alpha$ and $Y' = F\sin\alpha$ respectively.

From the above figure, it is clear that $OM$ and $ON$ are the projections of the displacement $OP$ in the directions of the $X$-axis and the $Y$-axis respectively.

Now,

$$\text{Work done by } F = F \cdot OP\cos(\theta - \alpha) \quad \text{...(i)}$$

$$\begin{aligned}\text{Work done by } X' &= X' \cdot OM \\ &= F\cos\alpha \cdot OP\cos\theta \\ &= F \cdot OP\cos\theta\cos\alpha \quad \text{...(ii)}\end{aligned}$$

$$\begin{aligned}\text{and, work done by } Y' &= Y' \cdot ON \\ &= F\sin\alpha \cdot OP\sin\theta \\ &= F \cdot OP\sin\theta\sin\alpha \quad \text{...(iii)}\end{aligned}$$

$\therefore$ Algebraic sum of the works done by $X'$ and $Y'$

$$\begin{aligned}&= F \cdot OP\cos\theta\cos\alpha + F \cdot OP\sin\theta\sin\alpha \\ &= F \cdot OP(\cos\theta\cos\alpha + \sin\theta\sin\alpha) \\ &= F \cdot OP(\theta - \alpha) \quad \text{...(iv)} \\ &= \text{Work done by } F\end{aligned}$$

This proves the theorem.

### 7. Theorem

The algebraic sum of the works done by a number of coplanar forces acting on a particle for any displacement of the particle, is equal to the work done by their resultant.

## Proof

Let $R$ be the resultant of a number of coplanar forces $F_1, F_2, F_3$, ....... acting on a particle, placed at O. Let the resolved parts of these forces along two mutually perpendicular directions $OX$ and $OY$ be $X_1, X_2, X_3$, .... and $Y_1, Y_2, Y_3$, .... respectively. Let the particle be displaced from $O$ to $P$. Then, the resolved parts of the displacement $OP$ in the directions $OX$ and $OY$ are $OP\cos\theta$ and $OP\sin\theta$ respectively, where $\theta = \angle POX$.

Now, from §6 Theorem, we have Work done by $R$ = Work done by $\Sigma X_1$ + Work done by $\Sigma Y_1$.

$= (\Sigma X_1)\, OP\cos\theta + (\Sigma Y_1)\, OP\sin\theta$

= (Sum of the works done by the resolved parts of $F_1, F_2, F_3$, ..... along $OX$)
+ (Sum of the works done by the resolved parts of $F_1, F_2, F_3$, ..... along $OY$)

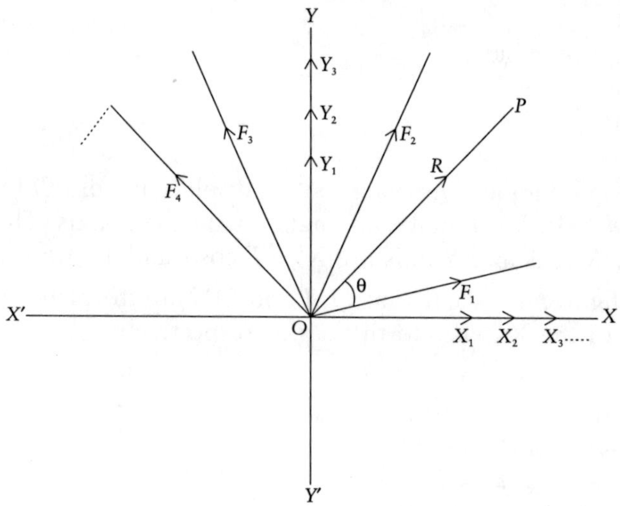


= Algebraic sum of the works done by $F_1, F_2\ F_3$,..... | From § 6 Theorem

## Corollary

If the forces are in equilibrium, then their resultant $R = 0$ and, therefore, the work done = 0.

## 8. Virtual Displacement and Virtual Work

If a number of coplanar forces acting on a body displace it through some distance, then we say that these forces do some work actually. But if a body is in equilibrium under the action of a number of coplanar forces, then it means that there is no displacement of the body and consequently, we say that these forces do not work.

Since the forces in equilibrium do not undergo actual displacement, therefore, they do no actual work.

However, it is found convenient in some statical problems to suppose that the body undergoes an infinitesimally small imaginary displacement, called virtual displacement, and then find the work done in causing this imaginary displacement. Since the body is not actually displaced, the work done is called virtual work. Thus, the virtual work is the amount of work that would have been done if the actual displacements had actually been taken place.

Hence, the virtual work done by a force

= Force × Projection of the virtual displacement of its point of application in the direction of the force.

OR

= Virtual displacement × Resolved part of the force in the direction of the virtual displacement of its point of application.

Since the virtual displacements are infinitesimally small, therefore, the magnitudes of the acting forces can be taken to be constant during the displacement.

**Note:** The definition of virtual work is exactly the same as that of work with the only difference that the virtual displacement is infinitesimally small.

## 9. Principle of Virtual Work for a System of Coplanar Forces Acting on a Particle

**Statement:** The necessary and sufficient condition that a particle acted upon by a number of coplanar forces be in equilibrium is that the algebraic sum of the virtual works done by the forces in any arbitrary small virtual displacement consistent with the geometrical conditions of the system is zero.

**Proof:** Let a number of coplanar forces $F_1$, $F_2$, $F_3$,..... act on a particle resting in equilibrium at $O$. Take two mutually perpendicular lines $OX$ and $OY$ through $O$ as the axes of $X$ and $Y$ respectively. Then, all the forces can be resolved along $OX$ and $OY$. Let $X_1$, $Y_1$; $X_2$, $Y_2$; $X_3$, $Y_3$;..... etc. be the resolved parts of the forces $F_1$, $F_2$, $F_3$, ..... etc. respectively along the directions of $OX$ and $OY$. Let $X'$ and $Y'$ be the resolved parts of their resultant $R$ along the directions of $OX$ and $OY$. Then,

$$X' = X_1 + X_2 + X_3 + \ldots\ldots\ldots\ldots = \Sigma X_1, \quad Y' = Y_1 + Y_2 + Y_3 + \ldots\ldots\ldots\ldots = \Sigma Y_1$$

and $$R^2 = X'^2 + Y'^2$$

Since the particle is in equilibrium, therefore, the resultant of the forces is zero, i.e., $R = 0$

$$\Rightarrow X' = 0, Y' = 0$$

### The Condition is Necessary

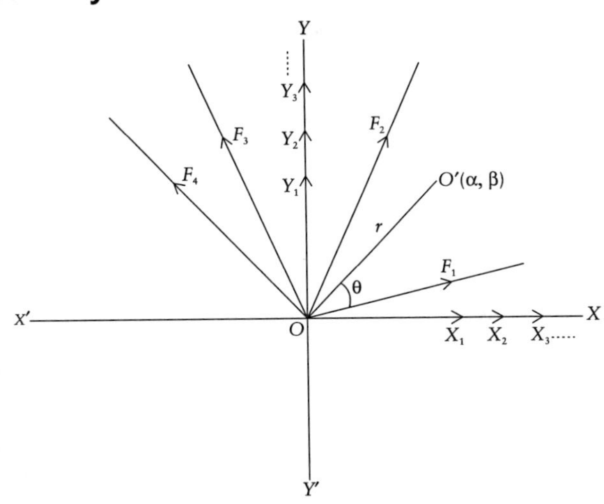

Let the particle at O be given an arbitrary small virtual displacement to a point $O'$ $(\alpha, \beta)$ in the plane of the forces consistent with the geometrical conditions of the system such that $OO' = r$. Then, resolved part of this displacement along $OX = \alpha$

and, resolved part of this displacement along $OY = \beta$

Now, the virtual work done by the forces

$$= \alpha X' + \beta Y'$$

$$= 0 \qquad \Big| \because X' = Y' = 0$$

Hence, the condition is necessary.

### The Condition is Sufficient

Since the virtual work done by the forces is zero for all arbitrary small displacements, therefore, let us imagine two virtual displacements $r$ and $r'$ where resolved parts along the axes $OX$ and $OY$ are $\alpha$, $\beta$ and $\alpha'$, $\beta'$ respectively.

According to the given condition,

$$\alpha X' + \beta Y' = 0$$

and $$\alpha' X' + \beta' Y' = 0$$

These equations imply

$$X' = 0 = Y'$$

i.e., the particle is in equilibrium.

Hence, the condition is sufficient.

**Note:** 'Consistent with the geometrical conditions of the system' signifies the following two facts:

(i) An arbitrarily small virtual displacement given to the particle does not change its geometry, i.e., the shape and size of the body, considered as a particle, does not change.

(ii) By virtue of this arbitrarily small virtual displacement, under consideration, no force of the system vanishes.

## 10. Principle of Virtual Work for a System of Coplanar Forces Acting at Different Points of Solid Body

**Statement:** The necessary and sufficient condition that a rigid body acted upon by a number of coplanar forces be in equilibrium is that the algebraic sum of the virtual works done by the forces in an arbitrarily small virtual displacement consistent with the geometrical conditions of the system is zero.

### Necessary Condition

**Proof:** Let a rigid body be acted upon by a number of coplanar forces $F_1, F_2, F_3, \ldots\ldots$, etc. acting at different points $A_1, A_2, A_3, \ldots\ldots$, etc. respectively of the rigid body. Let the rigid body be in equilibrium due to these coplanar forces. Take an arbitrary point O. Take two fixed rectangular axes $OX$ and $OY$ in the plane of the forces. Let the coordinates of the points $A_1, A_2, A_3, \ldots\ldots$ be $(x_1, y_1), (x_2, y_2), (x_3, y_3), \ldots\ldots$ respectively referred to there coordinate axes. Let the resolved parts of the forces $F_1, F_2, F_3, .....$, etc. along the coordinate axes $OX$ and $OY$ be $X_1, Y_1$; $X_2, Y_2$; $X_3, Y_3, .....$, etc. respectively. Further, let us suppose that the body is given an arbitrary small virtual displacement as a consequence of which the point $A_1$ gets displaced to the point $R$.

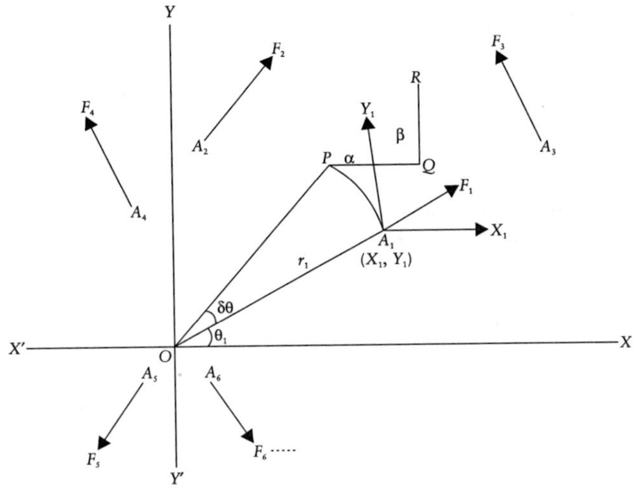


Any plane rotation of a rigid body can be considered as a small rotation, say $\delta\theta$, about $O$, a translation $\alpha$ parallel to $OX$ and lastly a translation $\beta$ parallel to $OY$. In these successive displacements, the point $A_1$ occupies the position $P$, $Q$, $R$ respectively. Let the polar coordinates of $A_1$, taking $O$ as pole and $OX$ as initial line, be $(r_1, \theta_1)$.

Then,

$$x_1 = r_1 \cos\theta_1$$

and $$y_1 = r_1 \sin\theta_1$$

The coordinates of $R$ are $\{r_1 \cos(\theta_1 + \delta\theta) + \alpha, r_1 \sin(\theta_1 + \delta\theta) + \beta\}$. Let the coordinates of $R$ be denoted by $\{x_1 + \delta x_1, y_1 + \delta y_1\}$. Then,

$$\begin{aligned} x_1 + \delta x_1 &= r_1\cos(\theta_1 + \delta\theta) + \alpha \\ &= r_1\cos\theta_1 \cos\delta\theta - r_1\sin\theta_1 \sin\delta\theta + \alpha \\ &= r_1\cos\theta_1 \cdot 1 - r_1\sin\theta_1 \cdot \delta\theta + \alpha \\ &= x_1 - y_1\, \delta\theta + \alpha \end{aligned}$$

| $\because$ $\cos\delta\theta \to 1$ and $\sin\delta\theta \to \delta\theta$ as $\delta\theta$ is very small

$\Rightarrow$ $\delta x_1 = \alpha - y_1\, \delta\theta$ to a first approximation.

$$\begin{aligned} y_1 + \delta y_1 &= r_1\sin(\theta_1 + \delta\theta) + \beta \\ &= r_1\sin\theta_1 \cos\delta\theta + r_1\cos\theta_1 \sin\delta\theta + \beta \\ &= r_1\sin\theta_1 \cdot 1 + r_1\cos\theta_1 \cdot \delta\theta + \beta \\ &= y_1 + x_1\, \delta\theta + \beta \end{aligned}$$

| retaining first powers of $\delta\theta$

$\Rightarrow$ $\delta y_1 = \beta + x_1\, \delta\theta$ to a first approximation.

Thus, the resolved parts of the displacement along the axes $OX$ and $OY$ are

$$\delta x_1 = \alpha - y_1\delta\theta$$

and $\delta y_1 = \beta + x_1\delta\theta$ respectively.

$\therefore$ Virtual work done by the force $F_1$ acting at $A_1$

$$= X_1(\alpha - y_1\delta\theta) + Y_1(\beta + x_1\delta\theta)$$

$$= \alpha X_1 + \beta y_1 + \delta\theta\,(Y_1x_1 - X_1y_1)$$ | Internal action and reaction do no virtual work

Since the body is rigid, therefore, under the aforesaid arbitrarily small virtual displacement, every point of the body will suffer the same translation and rotation.

Consequently,

$$\delta x_2 = \alpha - y_2\delta\theta \qquad \delta y_2 = \beta + x_2\delta\theta; \qquad \delta x_3 = \alpha - y_3\delta\theta \qquad \delta y_3 = \beta + x_3\delta\theta, \text{ ....., etc.}$$

$\therefore$ Virtual work done by the force $F_2$ acting at $A_2$

$$= X_2(\alpha - y_2\,\delta\theta) + Y_2(\beta + x_2\,\delta\theta) = \alpha X_2 + \beta Y_2 + \delta\theta\,(Y_2x_2 - X_2y_2);$$

Virtual work done by the force $F_3$ acting at $A_3$

$$= X_3(\alpha - y_3\,\delta\theta) + y_3(\beta + x_3\,\delta\theta) = \alpha X_3 + \beta Y_3 + \delta\theta\,(Y_3x_3 - X_3y_3), \text{ ....., etc.}$$

Algebraic sum of the virtual works done by the system of forces acting upon the rigid body

$$= \alpha\,\Sigma X_1 + \beta\,\Sigma Y_1 + \delta\theta\,\Sigma\,(Y_1x_1 - X_1y_1) = \alpha\,X + \beta Y + \delta\theta \cdot G$$

where $G$ = Sum of the moments of the forces about $O$

$$= 0$$ | Since the body is in equilibrium, therefore, $X = Y = G = 0$

Hence, the condition is necessary.

## Sufficient Condition

Let us assume that the algebraic sum of the virtual works done by the forces for any arbitrarily small virtual displacement consistent with the geometrical conditions of the system is zero. Then,

$$\alpha X + \beta Y + \delta\theta.\ G = 0 \qquad \text{...(1)}$$

for arbitrary values of $\alpha$, $\beta$ and $\delta\theta$.

## This equation is known as the equation of virtual work

Sin $\alpha$, $\beta$ and $\delta\theta$ are independent of each other, let us take a displacement in which $\beta = 0$, $\delta\theta = 0$, $\alpha \neq 0$.

Then, (1) gives $\alpha X = 0 \qquad \Rightarrow X = 0$ ...(2)

Similarly, by taking $\alpha = 0$, $\delta\theta = 0$, $\beta \neq 0$,

we have from (1), $\beta Y = 0 \qquad \Rightarrow Y = 0$ ...(3)

Again, by taking $\alpha = 0$, $\beta = 0$, $\delta\theta \neq 0$, we obtain from (1),

$\delta\theta \cdot G = 0 \qquad \Rightarrow G = 0$ ...(4)

Hence, $X = Y = G = 0$, i.e., the body is in equilibrium.

### 11. Work Done by Tension $T$ of an Extensible String of Length $l$ during a Small Displacement

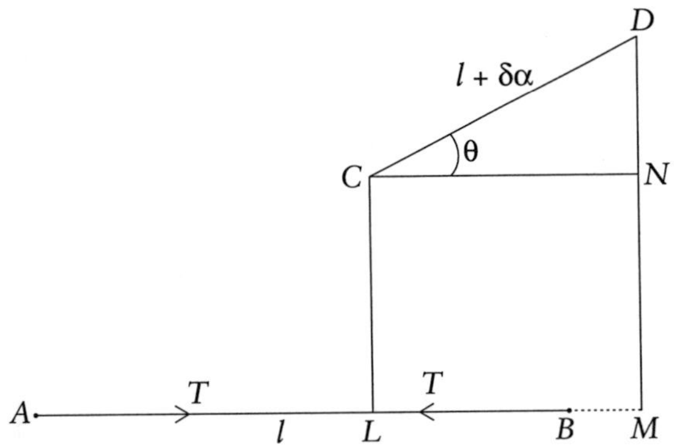


Let $T$ and $T$ be the tensions in the extensible string $AB(= l)$ at the ends $A$ and $B$ along $AB$ and $BA$ respectively. Let the string $AB$ undergo an arbitrary small virtual displacement, consistent with the geometrical conditions of the system, such that the new positions of $A$ and $B$ are $C$ and $D$ respectively.

Let $CD = l + \delta\alpha$ and $CD$ be inclined to $AB$ at a small angle $\theta$.

From $C$ and $D$, draw perpendiculars $CL$ and $DM$ on $AB$. Also, draw $CN \perp$ to $DM$.

$\therefore$ Virtual work done by the tension $T$ in the extensible string $AB$

= Algebraic sum of the virtual works done by $T$ at $A$ and $T$ at $B$

$\because$ Tension $T$ in the string $AB$ is equivalent to a force $T$ at $A$ in the direction of $AB$ and a force $T$ at $B$ in the direction of $BA$

$$= T \cdot AL - T \cdot BM = T(AB - LB) - T(LM - LB) = T(AB - LM)$$

$$= T(AB - CN) = T(AB - CD\cos\theta) = T\{l - (l + \delta l)\cos\theta\}$$

$$= T\left\{l + (l + \delta l)\left(1 - \frac{\theta^2}{\underline{|2}} + \ldots\right)\right\}$$

$$= -T\,\delta l$$

$\because$ $\theta$ is very small

$\therefore$ its higher powers (> 1) can be neglected

**Note:** If the string $AB$ is inelastic (or inextensible), then $\delta l = 0$. Consequently, the virtual work done by the tension of such a string = 0.

### 12. Work Done by Thrust $T$ in an Extensible Light Rod of Length $l$

This case is similar to that of tension in an extensible string. The only difference is that here we have $T$ at $A$ in the direction $BA$ and $T$ at $B$ in the direction $AB$, i.e., the directions of $T$'s are reversed.

Hence, the virtual work done by the thrust $T$ in the light rod $AB$ when it is displaced from the position $AB$ to $CD = (-T)\ AL + T \cdot BM$

| Here, $T$ at $A$ is acting along $LA$. So, we take the negative sign

$= +\ T\ \delta l$ | Refer § 11

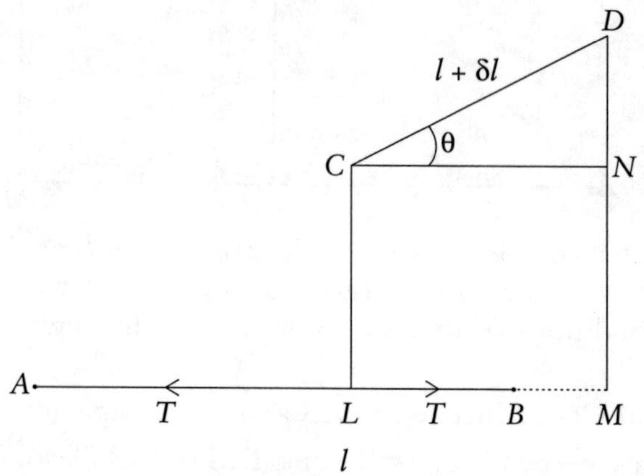


**Note:** If the rod $AB$ is inelastic (or inextensible), then $\delta l = 0$. Consequently, the virtual work done by thrust of such a rod = 0.

## 13. Forces which can be Omitted in Forming the Equation of Virtual Work

If a body in equilibrium be acted upon by a number of forces and an arbitrary small virtual displacement be given to the body, then the virtual work done by certain forces, listed below, is zero. As such, such forces can be omitted while forming the equation of virtual work.

(1) **The tension of an inextensible string:** It has been shown in § 11 (Note) that the virtual work done in this case will be zero.

(2) **The thrust of an inextensible light rod:** It has been shown in § 12 (Note) that the virtual work done in this case will be zero.

(3) **Reaction $R$ of any smooth surface with which the body is in contact:** Let the point of contact of the body with the smooth surface be $P$. Then, the reaction $R$ acts at $P$ normal to the surface. Now, if the point $P$ is displaced to $P'$, then $PP'$ will be perpendicular to the direction of the reaction $R$. Hence, the virtual work done by the reaction $R$ is zero [since the displacement along the direction of the force is zero].

(4) **Reaction at any point of contact with a fixed surface on which the body rolls without sliding:** In this case, the point of contact of the body with the surface is always at rest momentarily. Hence, it does not undergo any displacement. Consequently, the virtual work done by the normal reaction or the force of friction at the point of contact is zero.

(5) **Reaction at a fixed point or a fixed axis about which the body rotates:** In this case, the point of application or the axis of rotation does not undergo any displacement (as it is fixed) and hence the virtual work done is zero.

(6) **Mutual action and reaction between two bodies whose equilibrium is considered together:** Since the action and reaction are equal and opposite, therefore, the virtual works done by them are also equal and opposite. Hence, the sum of their virtual works is zero. Actually, the work done by one is balanced by the other.

## 14. Procedure to Solve the Problems Based on Virtual Work

(i) Draw the diagram of the system and mark only those forces showing their directions which contribute to the virtual work.

(ii) Replace the string by two forces $T$ and $T$ acting inwards. If $l$ is the length of the string in equilibrium, then the virtual work done by the tension in the string is $-T\,\delta l$.

(iii) Replace the rod by two forces $T$ and $T$ acting outwards. If $l$ is the length of the rod, then the work done by the thrust in the rod is $+\,Tdl$.

(iv) Find the distances of the points of application of all other forces acting on the system from a fixed point or a fixed line or a fixed plane. If $x$ is the distance of the point of application of a force $F$ from a fixed point, then after virtual displacement has been given, this distance becomes $x + \delta x$ so that the virtual displacement is $\delta x$. Consequently, the work done by the force is $F \cdot \delta x$.

This work done will be positive or negative according as the distance is measured in the direction of $F$ or in the direction opposite to $F$.

(v) In the end, equate the algebraic sum of the virtual works done by individual forces to zero. What we get is called the equation of virtual work.

(vi) Write down the geometrical equations involved in the problem under consideration.

With the help of the above points, we can get the required result.

## ILLUSTRATIVE EXAMPLES

### Problems on Simple Frameworks of Rods

**Example 1:** Four uniform rods are freely jointed at their extremities and form a parallelogram $ABCD$, which is suspended by the point $A$ and is kept in shape by a string $AC$. Prove that the tension of the string is equal to half of the whole weight.

**Sol.** Let ABCD be a parallelogram formed by four uniform rods freely joined at their extremities $A$, $B$, $C$ and $D$ suspended by the point $A$ and is kept in shape by a string $AC$. Let $W$ be the weight of each rod. Then, their combined weight will act at $O$, the point of intersection of the diagonals. Let $T$ be the tension in the string $AC$.

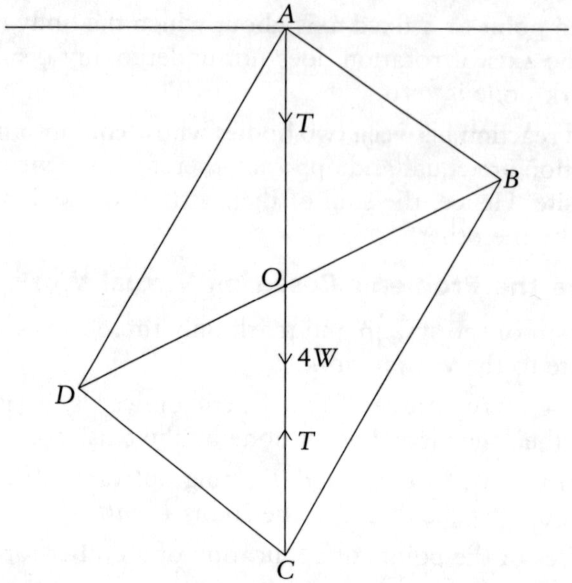


Replace the string $AC$ by two equal and opposite forces $T$, $T$ acting at $A$ and $C$ in the directions $AC$ and $CA$ respectively. Let $AC = l$. Then, $AO = \frac{l}{2}$. Let the distances be measured from the point of suspension $A$ of the parallelogram.

Let the system be given a small virtual displacement such that $l$ changes to $l + \delta l$. Then, the equation of virtual work is

$$4W\,\delta(AO) - T\,\delta(AC) = 0$$

$$\Rightarrow \quad 4W\,\delta\left(\frac{l}{2}\right) - T\,\delta(l) = 0$$

$$\Rightarrow \quad (2W - T)\,\delta(l) = 0$$

$$\Rightarrow \quad 2W - T = 0 \qquad \Big|\because \delta(l) \neq 0$$

$$\Rightarrow \quad T = 2W$$

$$\Rightarrow \quad T = \frac{1}{2}\,(4W)$$

$\Rightarrow$ $T$ = Half of the whole weight.

**Example 2:** A square framework formed of uniform heavy rods of equal weight $W$ jointed together is hung up by one corner. A weight $W$ is suspended from each of the three lower corners and the shape of the square is preserved by a light rod along the horizontal diagonal. Find the thrust in the light rod.

**Sol.** Let $ABCD$ be the square framework formed of four uniform heavy rods each of weight $W$. The framework is hung up by one corner $A$. Its shape is preserved by a horizontal rod $BD$. Three weights $W$ each are suspended from the three lowers ends $B$, $C$ and $D$.

Let the thrust in the horizontal rod $BD$ be $T$.

Replace the rod $BD$ by two equal and opposite forces $T$ and $T$ acting at $B$ and $D$ along $DB$ and $BD$ respectively.

The system is hung from $A$ and we shall measure the distances downwards and hence the work done by the weight at $O$ will be positive.

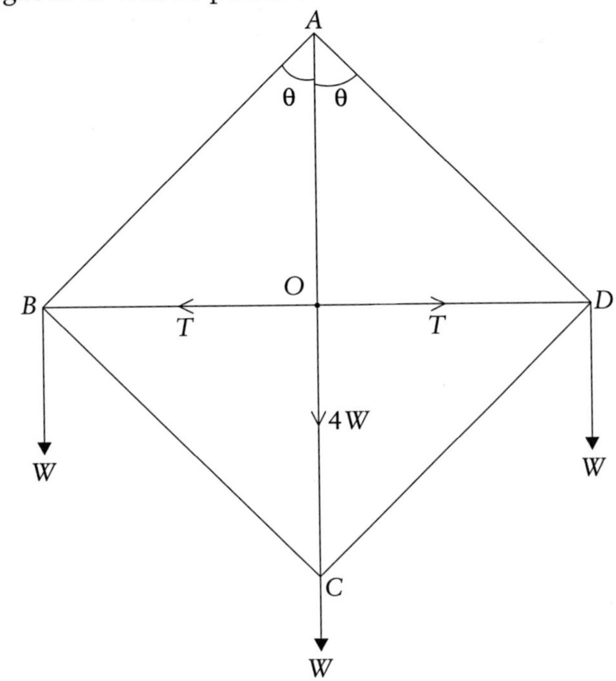


Let $a$ be the length of each rod.

Let $\angle BAD = 2\theta$

Then, $\angle BAO = \angle DAO = \theta$

$AO = a\cos\theta \quad \Rightarrow AC = 2a\cos\theta \quad \Rightarrow BO = a\sin\theta \quad \Rightarrow BD = 2a\sin\theta$

Now give the system a small virtual displacement so that $\theta$ increases to $\theta + \delta\theta$.

Hence, the equation of virtual work is

$6W\,\delta(AO) + W\,\delta(AC) + T\,\delta(BD) = 0$

$\Rightarrow \quad 6W\,\delta(a\cos\theta) + W\,\delta(2a\cos\theta) + T\,\delta(2a\sin\theta) = 0$

$\Rightarrow \quad -6W\,a\sin\theta\,\delta\theta - 2W\,a\sin\theta\,\delta\theta + T\,2a\cos\theta\,\delta\theta = 0$

$\Rightarrow \quad [-6W\,a\sin\theta - 2W\,a\sin\theta + T\,2a\cos\theta]\,\delta\theta = 0 \quad \Rightarrow [-8W\,a\sin\theta + T\,2a\cos\theta]\,\delta\theta = 0$

$\Rightarrow \quad -8W\,a\sin\theta + T\,2a\cos\theta = 0 \quad \Rightarrow T = 4W\tan\theta$

In the position of equilibrium, $\theta = 45°$

$\therefore \quad T = 4W.$

**Example 3:** Four equal heavy uniform rods are freely jointed so as to form a rhombus which is freely suspended by one angular point, and the middle points of the two upper rods are connected by a light rod so that the rhombus cannot collapse. Prove that the tension of this light rod is $4W \tan\theta$, where $W$ is the weight of each rod and $2\theta$ is the angle of the rhombus at the point of suspension.

**Sol.** Let $ABCD$ be the rhombus suspended from the point $A$. Let O be the point of intersection of the diagonals. Then, the total weight $4W$ of the four rods acts vertically downwards at $O$. Let $E$ and $F$ be the mid-points of the two upper rods $AB$ and $AC$ respectively. Let $E$ and $F$ be connected by a light rod $EF$. Let $T$ be the thrust in the rod $EF$.

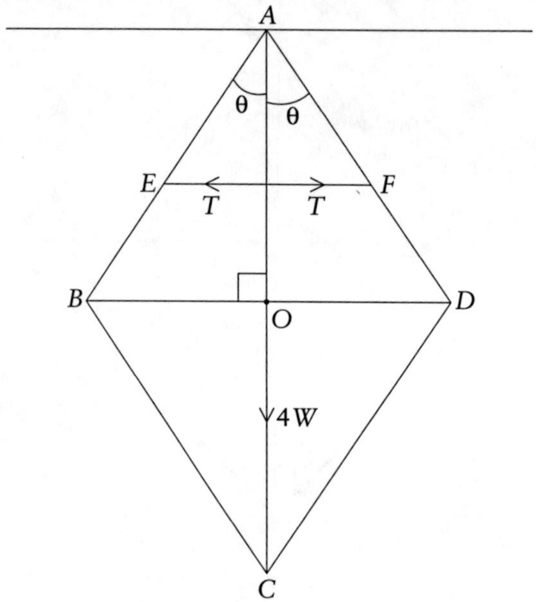


Replace the rod $EF$ by a force $T$ at $E$ acting in the direction $FE$ and a force $T$ at $F$ acting in the direction $EF$.

Since the point of suspension is fixed, therefore, we shall measure the distances from the fixed point $A$ in writing down the equation of the virtual work. Let each rod forming the rhombus $ABCD$ be of length $2a$. Then,

$EF$ = length of the rod

$= \frac{1}{2} BD$ | By geometry

$= BO$ | By geometry

$= 2\,a \sin\theta = l(\text{say})$ ...(1)

where $\angle BAO = \angle DAO = \theta$

and $AO = 2\,a \cos\theta$ ...(2)

Let the system be given an arbitrary small virtual displacement consistent with the geometrical conditions such that $\theta$ becomes $\theta + \delta\theta$ and $l$ becomes $l + \delta l$.

Then, the equation of virtual work is

$$4W\,\delta\,(AO) + T \cdot \delta l = 0$$

$\Rightarrow \; 4W\,\delta(2a\cos\theta) + T\,\delta(2a\sin\theta) = 0$ $\qquad \Rightarrow 4W(-2a\sin\theta\,\delta\theta) + T(2a\cos\theta\,\delta\theta) = 0$

$\Rightarrow \; (2a\cos\theta)\,T = 8aW\sin\theta$ $\qquad \Big|\; \because \delta\theta \neq 0$

$\Rightarrow \; T = 4W\tan\theta$

**Example 4:** Four equal uniform rods are jointed to form a rhombus $ABCD$, which is placed in a vertical plane with $AC$ vertical and $A$ resting on a horizontal plane. The rhombus is kept in position in which angle $BAC = \theta$, by a light string joining $B$ and $D$. Show that its tension is $2W\tan\theta$, where $W$ is the weight of each rod.

**Sol.**

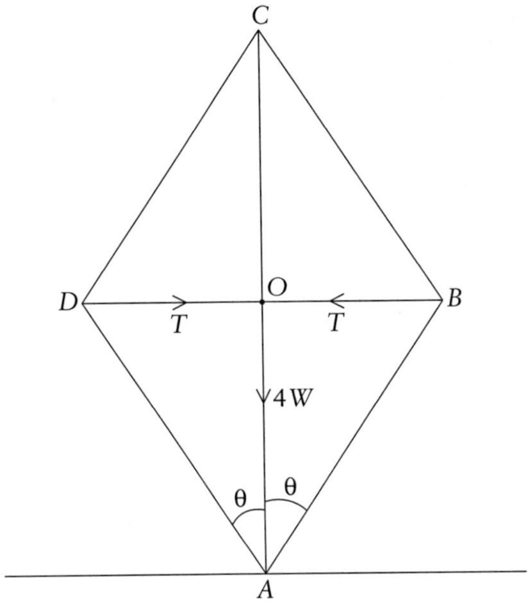


Since the point $A$ rests on a horizontal table, therefore, $A$ is a fixed point and we shall measure the distances from $A$ in writing down the equation of virtual work. Let $a$ be the length of each rod forming the rhombus $ABCD$. Let $T$ be the tension in the string $BD$.

Since the rods are uniform, therefore, the combined weight $4W$ of the four rods will act vertically downwards at $O$, the point of intersection of the diagonals.

Replace the string $BD$ by a force $T$ at $B$ acting along $BD$ and a force $T$ at $D$ acting along $DB$.

Now, $\qquad AO = a\cos\theta \qquad \ldots(1)$

$\qquad BD = 2OB = 2a\sin\theta = l\text{(say)} \qquad \ldots(2)$

Let the system be given an arbitrarily small virtual displacement consistent with the geometrical conditions such that $\theta$ becomes $\theta + \delta\theta$ and $l$ becomes $l + \delta l$.

Then, the equation of virtual work is

$-\,4W\,\delta(AO) - T\,\delta l = 0$ $\qquad$ | Since the weight $4W$ is acting at O which is a point above the fixed point O, therefore, virtual work done by $4W$ is negative

$\Rightarrow \; 4W\,\delta(AO) + T\,\delta l = 0 \qquad \Rightarrow 4W\,\delta(a\cos\theta) + T\,\delta(2a\sin\theta) = 0$

$\Rightarrow \; 4W\,(-a\sin\theta\,\delta\theta) + T\,(2a\cos\theta\,\delta\theta) = 0$

$\Rightarrow \; -4aW\sin\theta + 2aT\cos\theta = 0$ | $\because \delta\theta \neq 0$

$\Rightarrow \; -2W\sin\theta + T\cos\theta = 0 \qquad \Rightarrow T\cos\theta = 2W\sin\theta \quad \Rightarrow T = 2W\tan\theta.$

**Example 5:** Four rods of equal weight $w$ form a rhombus, with smooth hinges at the joints. The frame is suspended by the point $A$, and a weight $W$ is attached to $C$. A stiffening rod of negligible weight joins the mid-points of $AB$ and $AD$, keeping these inclined at an angle $\alpha$ to $AC$. Show that the thrust in the stiffening rod is $(2W + 4w)\tan\alpha$.

**Sol.** Let $O$ be the point of intersection of the diagonals. Then the combined weight $4w$ of the four rods will act vertically downwards at $O$.

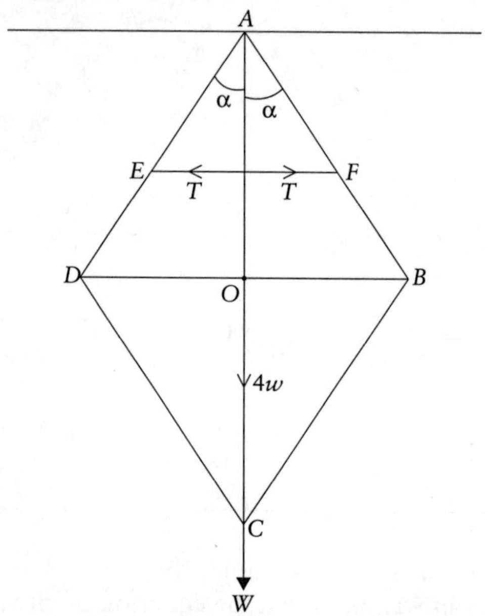


Let $E$ and $F$ be the mid-points of $AD$ and $AB$ respectively. Then $EF$ is stiffening (inelastic) rod. A weight $W$ is attached at $C$. Let $T$ be the thrust in the rod $EF$. Replace the rod $EF$ by a force $T$ at $E$ acting along $FE$ and a force $T$ at $F$ acting along $EF$.

Since the point of suspension $A$ is fixed, therefore, the distances will be measured from $A$.

Let each side of the rhombus $ABCD$ be $a$.

Now,

$$AO = a\cos\alpha \qquad \text{...(1)}$$

$$AC = 2AO = 2a\cos\alpha \qquad \text{...(2)}$$

$$EF = \text{Length of the rod}$$

$$= \frac{1}{2}DB \qquad \text{| By geometry}$$

$$= \frac{1}{2}\cdot(2OD) \qquad \text{| By geometry}$$

$$= OD = AD \sin \alpha$$

$$= a \sin \alpha = l \text{ (say)} \qquad ...(3)$$

where $\angle DAO = \angle BAO = \alpha$

Let the system be given a small virtual displacement such that $\alpha$ becomes $\alpha + \delta\alpha$ and $l$ becomes $l + \delta\alpha$.

Then, the equation of virtual work is $4w\ \delta(AO) + W\ \delta(AC) + T\ \delta l = 0$

$\Rightarrow\ 4w\ \delta(a \cos \alpha) + W\ \delta(2a \cos \alpha) + T\ \delta\theta(a \sin \alpha) = 0$

$\Rightarrow\ 4w\ (-\ a \sin \alpha\ \delta\alpha) + W\ (-2a \sin \alpha\ \delta\alpha) + T\ a \cos \alpha\ \delta\alpha = 0$

$\Rightarrow\ -\ 4w \sin \alpha - 2aW \sin \alpha + T\ a \cos \alpha = 0 \qquad | \because \delta\alpha \neq 0$

$\Rightarrow\ T = (2W + 4w)\tan \alpha.$

**Example 6:** Four equal uniform rods, each of weight $w$, are freely jointed to form a rhombus $ABCD$. The framework is suspended freely from $A$ and weight $W$ is attached to each of the joints $B$, $C$ and $D$. If two horizontal forces each of magnitude $P$ acting at $B$ and $D$ keep the angle $BAD$ equal to 120°, prove that

$$P = 2(W + w)\ \sqrt{3}$$

**Sol.** Let $ABCD$ be the given framework suspended freely from $A$. The total weight $4w$ of the four rods acts at O, the point of intersection of the diagonals of the rhombus. The weights $W$ at $D$ and $W$ at $B$ are equilibrium to a weight $2W$ at O. Thus, a total weight $(4w + 2W)$ is concentrated at O. A weight $W$ acts at C.

Let each side of the rhombus be $a$.

Since $A$ is fixed, therefore, the distances will be measured from $A$.

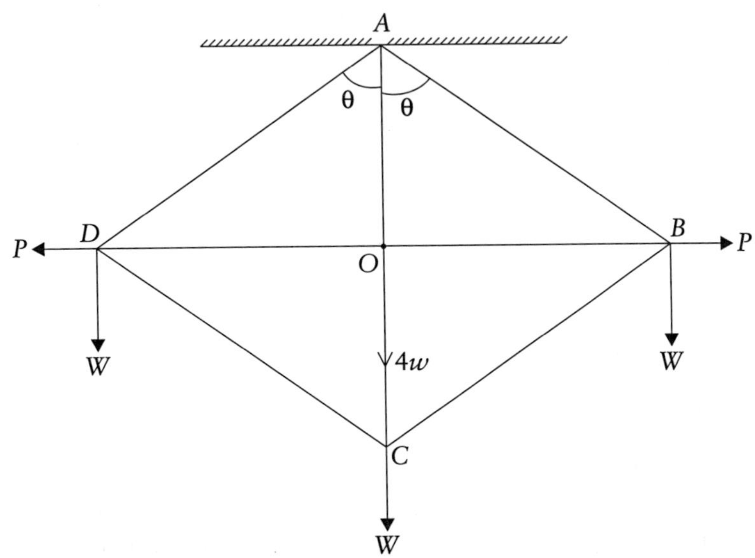

Now,

$$AO = a\cos\theta \qquad ...(1)$$
$$AC = 2AO = 2a\cos\theta \qquad ...(2)$$
$$BD = 2BO$$
$$= 2a\sin\theta = l \text{ (say)} \qquad ...(3)$$

Let the system be given a small virtual displacement such that $\theta$ becomes $\theta + \delta\theta$ and $l$ becomes $l + \delta l$.

Then, the equation of virtual work is

$$(4w + 2W)\,\delta(AO) + W\,\delta(AC) + P\,\delta(BD) = 0$$
$$\Rightarrow (4w + 2W)\,\delta(a\cos\theta) + W\,\delta(2a\cos\theta) + P\,\delta(2a\sin\theta) = 0$$
$$\Rightarrow (4w + 2W)(-a\sin\theta\,\delta\theta) + W(-2a\sin\theta\,\delta\theta) + P(2a\cos\theta\,\delta\theta) = 0$$
$$\Rightarrow (4w + 2W)(-\sin\theta) + W(-2\sin\theta) + P(2\cos\theta) = 0$$
$$\Rightarrow P\cos\theta = (2w + W)\sin\theta + W\sin\theta = 2(W + w)\sin\theta$$
$$\Rightarrow P = 2(W + w)\tan\theta$$

In the position of equilibrium,

$$\angle BAD = 120^\circ \quad \Rightarrow 2\theta = 120^\circ \quad \Rightarrow \theta = 60^\circ$$
$$\therefore \quad P = 2(W + w)\tan 60^\circ = 2(W + w)\sqrt{3}$$

**Example 7:** Four uniform rods, each of weight $W$, are freely jointed to form a square $ABCD$, the side $AB$ is fixed in a vertical position with $A$ upper most and the figure is kept in shape by a string, joining the middle points of $AD$, $DC$. Prove that the tension of the string is $4\sqrt{2}\ W$.

**Sol.** The combined weight $4W$ of the four rods acts at $O$, the centre of the given square. Let $E$ and $F$ be the mid-points of $AD$ and $CD$. Then, $EF$ is the string. Let $T$ be the tension in the string.

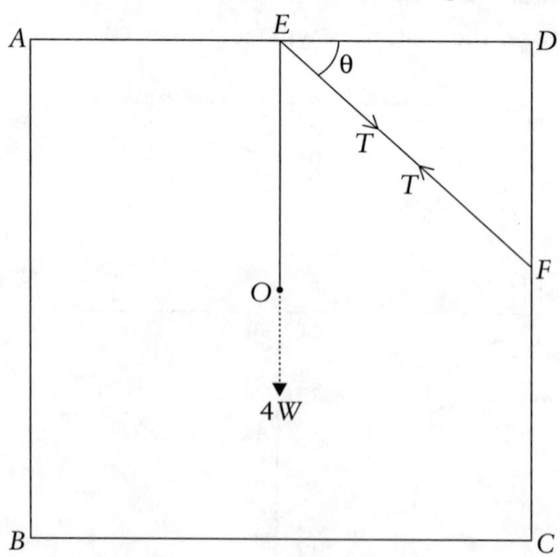


Since side $AB$ is fixed, therefore, $A$ is fixed. Since $AB$ is a fixed vertical line, therefore, $AD$ is a fixed horizontal line. So, the distance will be measured from this fixed horizontal line.

Let each side of the square $ABCD$ be $2a$.

Now,

$$EO = DF = ED \tan\theta = a \tan\theta \quad ...(1)$$

$$EF = ED \sec\theta = a \sec\theta = l \quad \text{| say} \quad ...(2)$$

Let the system be given a small virtual displacement such that $\theta$ becomes $\theta + \delta\theta$ and $l$ becomes $l + \delta l$.

Then, the equation of virtual work is

$$4W\,\delta(EO) - T\,\delta l = 0$$

$$\Rightarrow \; 4W\,\delta(a \tan\theta) - T\,\delta(a \sec\theta) = 0 \qquad \Rightarrow 4W\,(a \sec^2\theta\,\delta\theta) - T\,(a \sec\theta \tan\theta\,\delta\theta) = 0$$

$$\Rightarrow \; 4aW \sec^2\theta - Ta \sec\theta \tan\theta = 0 \qquad | \because \delta\theta \neq 0$$

$$\Rightarrow \; T = \frac{4W \sec\theta}{\tan\theta} = 4W \operatorname{cosec}\theta$$

In the position of equilibrium,

$\theta = 45^\circ$ (since the framework is a square)

$$\therefore \quad T = 4W \operatorname{cosec} 45^\circ = 4\sqrt{2}\,W$$

**Example 8:** A string of length $a$, forms the shorter diagonal of a rhombus formed by four uniform rods, each of length $b$ and weight $W$, which are hinged together. If one of the rods is supported in a horizontal position, prove that the tension of the string is $\dfrac{2W\left(2b^2 - a^2\right)}{b\sqrt{4b^2 - a^2}}$.

**Sol.** Let $ABCD$ be the given rhombus. The rod $AB$ is supported in a horizontal position. $AC$ is the shorter diagonal of the rhombus. It is occupied by a string of length $a$.

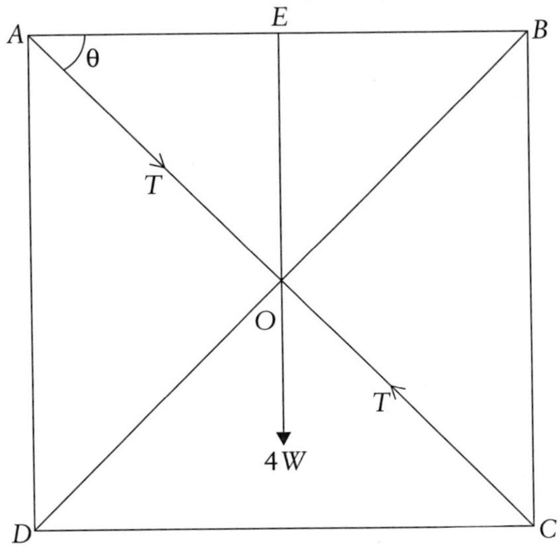


So, $AC = a$ ...(1)

Let O be the C.G. of the rhombus. Therefore, the combined weight $4W$ of four rods acts vertically downwards through O.

Replace the string $AC$ by a force $T$ at $A$ in the direction $AC$ and a force $T$ at C in the direction $CA$.

Then, $AO = OC = \dfrac{a}{2}$ | By geometry ...(2)

$$AO = AB\cos\theta = b\cos\theta \quad ...(3)$$

$$AC = 2AO = 2b\cos\theta \quad ...(4)$$

$$EO = AO\sin\theta = b\cos\theta\sin\theta$$

$$= \frac{b}{2}(2\sin\theta\cos\theta)$$

$$= \frac{b}{2}\sin 2\theta \quad ...(5)$$

Let the system be given a small virtual displacement such that θ become θ + δθ whereas the side remains unchanged.

Then, the equation of virtual work is $4W\,\delta(EO) - T\,\delta(AC) = 0$

$$\Rightarrow \quad 4W\,\delta\left(\frac{b}{2}\sin 2\theta\right) - T\,\delta(2b\cos\theta) = 0$$

$$\Rightarrow \quad 4bW\cos 2\theta\,\delta\theta + 2b\,T\sin\theta\,\delta\theta = 0$$

$$\Rightarrow \quad 4bW\cos 2\theta + 2b\,T\sin\theta = 0 \qquad |\because \delta\theta \neq 0$$

$$\Rightarrow \quad T = -2W\frac{\cos 2\theta}{\sin\theta}$$

$$\Rightarrow \quad = \frac{-2W(2\cos^2\theta - 1)}{\sin\theta} \quad ...(6)$$

In the position of equilibrium.

$$AO = \frac{a}{2}$$

$$\therefore \quad \cos\theta = \frac{a}{2b} \quad ...(7)$$

$$\therefore \quad \sin\theta = \sqrt{1-\cos^2\theta}$$

$$= \sqrt{1-\frac{a^2}{4b^2}} = \frac{\sqrt{4b^2-a^2}}{2b} \quad ...(8)$$

On putting the values of cosθ and sinθ from equations (7) and (8) respectively in equation (6), we get

$$T = \frac{-2W\left(2\frac{a^2}{4b^2}-1\right)}{\frac{\sqrt{4b^2-a^2}}{2b}} = \frac{2W\left(2b^2-a^2\right)}{2b^2}\cdot\frac{2b}{\sqrt{4b^2-a^2}} = \frac{2W\left(2b^2-a^2\right)}{b\sqrt{4b^2-a^2}}.$$

**Example 9:** A rhombus $ABCD$ is formed of four equal uniform rods jointed together and suspended from $A$. It is kept in position by a light rod joining the middle points of $BC$ and $CD$. Prove that if $T$ be the thrust in this rod and $W$ is the weight of the rhombus, then,

$$T = W\tan\frac{A}{2}$$

**Sol.** Let $O$ be the point of intersection of the diagonals of the rhombus $ABCD$. Then, the weight of the rhombus acts vertically downwards at $O$.

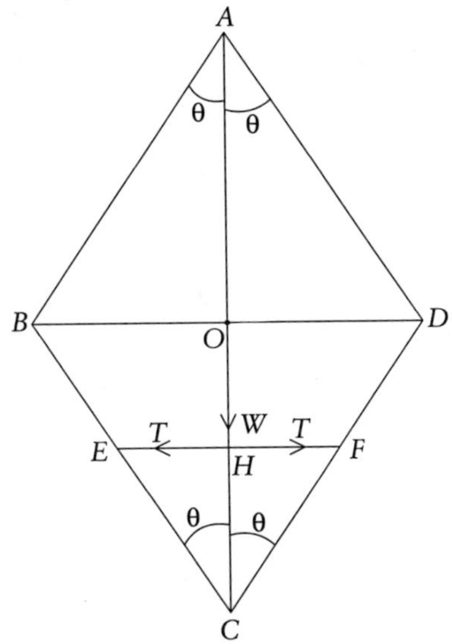


Let $E$ and $F$ be the mid-points of the light rods $BC$ and $CD$. Then, $EF$ is the light rod.

Replace the rod $EF$ by a force $T$ at $E$ in the direction of $FE$ and a force $T$ at $F$ in the direction $EF$.

Since the point of suspension $A$ is fixed, therefore, the distances will be measured from $A$.

Let each side of the rhombus be $a$.

Then,

$$AO = a\cos\theta \qquad \text{...(1)}$$

$$EF = 2EH \qquad \text{| By geometry}$$

$$= 2EC\sin\theta = a\sin\theta \qquad \left|\because EC = \frac{1}{2}BC = \frac{1}{2}a\right.$$

$$= l \text{ (say)} \qquad \text{...(2)}$$

Let the system be given a small virtual displacement such that θ becomes θ + δθ and $l$ becomes $l + \delta l$.

Then, the equation of virtual work is

$W\,\delta(AO) + T\,\delta l = 0$

$\Rightarrow\ W\,\delta(a\cos\theta) + T\,\delta(a\sin\theta) = 0 \qquad \Rightarrow W(-a\sin\theta\,\delta\theta) + T(a\cos\theta\,\delta\theta) = 0$

$\Rightarrow\ -a\,W\sin\theta + a\,T\cos\theta = 0 \qquad \mid \because \delta\theta \neq 0$

$\Rightarrow\ -W\sin\theta + T\cos\theta = 0 \Rightarrow T\cos\theta = W\sin\theta \qquad \Rightarrow T = W\tan\theta$

In the position of equilibrium,

$$\theta = \frac{A}{2}$$

$$\therefore\quad T = W\tan\frac{A}{2}.$$

**Example 10:** Four equal rods, each of weight $W$, are jointed together to form a rhombus $ABCD$. The whole system hangs from a fixed point $A$ and is kept in shape by a horizontal thrust in $BD$. A weight $w$ hangs from $C$. Find the thrust in $BD$.

**Sol.**

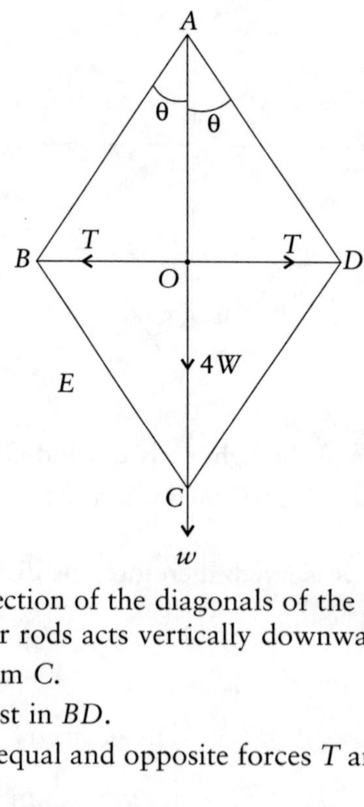


Let O be the point of intersection of the diagonals of the given rhombus $ABCD$. Then, the combined weight $4W$ of the four rods acts vertically downwards at $O$.

A weight $w$ is suspended from $C$.

Let $T$ be the horizontal thrust in $BD$.

Replace the rod $BD$ by two equal and opposite forces $T$ and $T$ acting at $B$ and $D$ along $DB$ and $BD$ respectively.

Since $A$ is the fixed point, therefore, the distances will be measured from $A$. Let each side of the rhombus $ABCD$ be $a$. Then,

$$AO = AB \cos\theta = a\cos\theta \quad ...(1)$$

$$AC = 2\,AO \quad \text{| by geometry}$$

$$= 2\,a\cos\theta \quad ...(2)$$

$$BD = 2\,BO \quad \text{| by geometry}$$

$$= 2\,AB\sin\theta$$

$$= 2\,a\sin\theta = l \text{ (say)} \quad ...(3)$$

Let the system be given a small virtual displacement such that $\theta$ becomes $\theta + \delta\theta$ and $l$ be comes $l + \delta l$.

Then, the equation of virtual work is $4\,W\,\delta\,(AO) + w\,\delta\,(AC) + T\,.\,\delta l = 0$

$\Rightarrow \quad 4\,w\,\delta\,(a\cos\theta) + w\,\delta\,(2a\cos\theta) + T\delta\,(2a\sin\theta) = 0$

$\Rightarrow \quad 4\,w\,(-a\sin\theta\,\delta\theta) + w\,(-2a\sin\theta\,\delta\theta) + T\,(2a\cos\theta\,\delta\theta) = 0$

$\Rightarrow \quad -4a\,W\sin\theta - 2a\,w\sin\theta + 2a\,T\cos\theta = 0 \qquad | \because \delta\theta \neq 0$

$\Rightarrow \quad T\cos\theta = 2W\sin\theta + w\sin\theta$

$\Rightarrow \quad T = (2\,W + w)\tan T$

In the position of equilibrium,

$$\theta = A/2$$

$\therefore\ T = (2\,W + w)\tan A/2$

**Example 11:** Two uniform rods $AB$, $BC$ of weights $w$ and $w'$ are smoothly jointed at $B$ and their middle points are jointed by a cord. The rods are held in a vertical plane with their ends, $A$, $C$ resting on a smooth horizontal plane. Prove that the tension in the cord is

$$(w + w')\cos A\cos C/\sin B$$

**Sol.** Let $E$ and $F$ be the mid-points of the rods $AB$ and $BC$ respectively. Then, the weights $w$ and $w'$ of the rods $AB$ and $BC$ will act at $E$ and $F$ respectively.

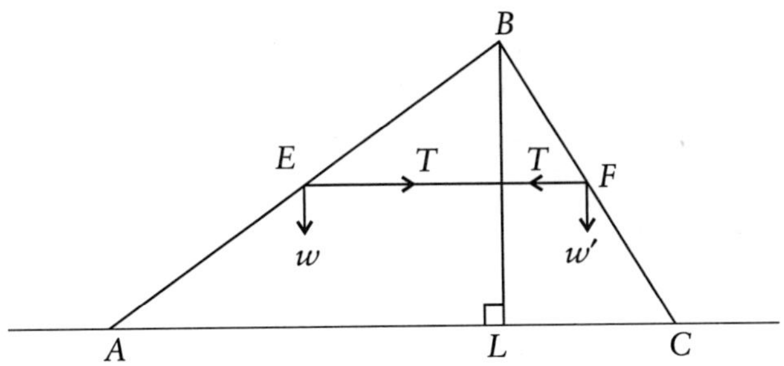


$E$ and $F$ are jointed by a cord (string) $EF$. Let $T$ be the tension in the string $EF$. Replace the string $EF$ by two inward forces $T$ and $T$ acting at $E$ and $F$.

Let in $\Delta\,ABC$,

$$BC = a \qquad \Rightarrow CA = b \qquad \Rightarrow AB = c$$

From $B$ draw perpendicular $BL$ to $AC$. Then,

$$EF = 1/2\,AC \quad \text{| by geometry}$$

$$= 1/2\,(AL + LC)$$

$$= 1/2\,(c\cos A + a\cos C) \quad ...(1)$$

Also, vertical distances of $E$ and $F$ from $AC$

$= 1/2\ BL$ | by geometry

$= 1/2\ c \sin A$ ...(2)

Since the ends $A$ and $C$ of the rods rest on a smooth horizontal plane, therefore, the distances will be measured from $AC$.

Let the system be given a small virtual displacement such that $A$ becomes $A + \delta A$ and $C$ becomes $C + \delta C$. Then, the equation of virtual work is

$$-(w + w')\, \delta\, (BL/2) - T\delta\, (EF) = 0$$

| Since the distances of $E$ and $F$ from $AC$ are measured upwards while the weights $w$ and $w'$ acts vertically downwards, therefore works done by them are negative

$\Rightarrow\ (w + w')\, \delta\, (1/2\ c \sin A) + T\delta\, \{1/2\, (c \cos A + a \cos C)\} = 0$

$\Rightarrow\ (w + w')\, c \cos A\, \delta A + T\, (-\, c \sin A\, \delta A - a \sin C\ \ \delta C) = 0$

$\Rightarrow\ \{(w + w')\, c \cos A - T\, c \sin A\}\, \delta A = T\, a \sin C\ \ \delta C)$ ...(3)

Now, from $\Delta\ ABL$,

$BL = AB \sin A = c \sin A$ ...(4)

From $\Delta\ CBL$,

$BL = BC \sin C = a \sin C$ ...(5)

From (4) and (5), equating the two values of $BL$,we get

$c \sin A = a \sin C$

$\Rightarrow\ c \cos A\, \delta A = a \cos C\ \ \delta C$ ...(6)

To eliminate $\delta A$ and $\delta C$, dividing (3) by (6), we get

$$\frac{(w + w')c \cos A - Tc \sin A}{c \cos A} = \frac{Ta \sin C}{a \cos C}$$

$\Rightarrow\ T \cos A \sin C = (w + w') \cos A \cos C - T \sin A \cos C$

$\Rightarrow\ T\, (\cos A \sin C\ + \sin A \cos C) = (w + w') \cos A \cos C$

$\Rightarrow\ T \sin\, (A + C) = (w + w') \cos A \cos C$

$$T = \frac{(w + w')\cos A \cos C}{\sin(A + C)}$$

$$= \frac{(w + w')\cos A \cos C}{\sin(\pi - B)} \qquad |\because A + B + C = \pi$$

$$\frac{(w\quad w')\cos A \cos C}{\sin}$$

**Example 12:** Two uniform rods $AB$ and $AC$, smoothly jointed at $A$, are in equilibrium in a vertical plane. $B$ and $C$ rest on a smooth horizontal plane and the mid-points of $AB$ and $AC$ are connected by a string. Show that the tension of the string is $w/\tan B + \tan C$, where $w$ is the total weight of the rods $AB$ and $AC$, $B$ and $C$ are the inclinations of the rods $AB$ and $AC$ to the horizontal.

**Sol.** Let $E$ and $F$ be the mid-points of the rods $AB$ and $AC$ respectively. Then, their weights say $w_1$ and $w_2$ will act vertically downwards at $E$ and $F$ respectively.

$w = w_1 + w_2$ | Given ...(1)

Let $T$ be the tension in the string $EF$. Replace the string $EF$ by two inward forces $T$ at $E$ and $T$ at $F$.

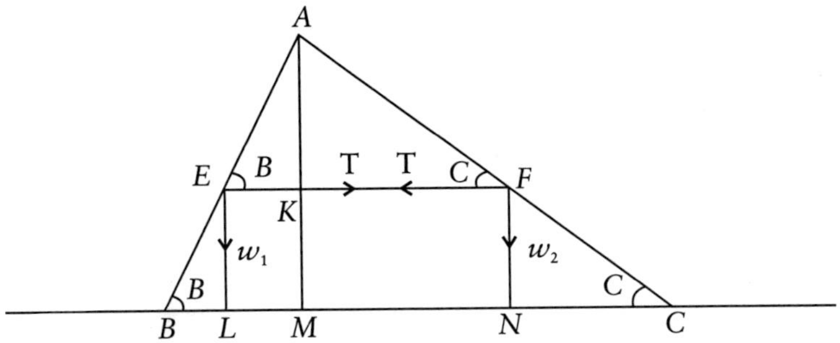


Let $AB = 2\,c$ and AC = $2b$.

Since $BC$ is a fixed horizontal line, therefore, the distances will be measured from $BC$.

Now,

$$EL = BE \sin B = c \sin \text{B} \quad ...(2)$$

$$FN = CF \sin C = b \sin \text{C} \quad ...(3)$$

$$EF = EK + KF = AE \cos B + AF \cos C$$

$$= c \cos B + b \cos C \quad ...(4)$$

Let the system be given a small virtual displacement such that $B$ becomes $B + \delta B$ and $C$ becomes $C + \delta C$. Then, the equation of virtual work is

$$- w_1\, \delta(EL) - w_2\, \delta(FN) - T\, \delta(EF) = 0$$

(Note that the reactions at $B$ and $C$ do no work)

The distances of $E$ and $F$ are measured from $BC$ upwards while the weight $w_1$ and $w_2$ act vertically downwards. Therefore, the works done by the weights are negative.

$\Rightarrow \quad w_1\, \delta\,(c \sin B) + w_2\, \delta\,(b \sin C) + T\, \delta\,(c \cos B + b \cos C) = 0$

$\Rightarrow \quad w_1\,(c \cos B)\, \delta B + w_2\,(b \cos C)\ \ \delta C + T\,(- c \sin B\, \delta B - b \sin C\, \delta C) = 0$

$\Rightarrow \quad (c\, w_1 \cos B - CT \sin B)\, \delta B = (bT \sin C - b\, w_2 \cos C)\, \delta C$ ...(5)

Now, from $\Delta\, AEK$,

$$AK = AE \sin B = c \sin B \quad ...(6)$$

from $\Delta\, AFK$, $\Rightarrow AK = AF \sin C$

$$= b \sin C \quad ...(7)$$

From (6) and (7), equating the two values of $AK$, we get

$$c \sin B = b \sin C$$

$\Rightarrow \quad c \cos B\, \delta B = b \cos c\, \delta C$ ...(8)

To eliminate $\delta B$ and $\delta C$, dividing (5) by (8), we get

$$\frac{w_1 \cos B - T \sin B}{\cos B} = \frac{T \sin C - w_2 \cos C}{\cos C}$$

$\Rightarrow \quad T(\sin C \cos B + \sin B \cos C) = (w_1 + w_2) \cos B \cos C$

Dividing both sides by cos $B$ cos $C$, we get

$$T(\tan C + \tan B) = w_1 + w_2$$

$$\Rightarrow \quad T = \frac{w_1 + w_2}{\tan B + \tan C}$$

$$= \frac{w}{\tan B + \tan C} \qquad \text{|From (1)}$$

**Example 13:** Five weightless rods of equal length are jointed together to form a rhombus $ABCD$ with one diagonal $BD$. If a weight $w$ be attached to C and the system be suspended from $A$, show that there is a thrust in $BD$ equal to $\frac{w}{\sqrt{3}}$.

**Sol.**

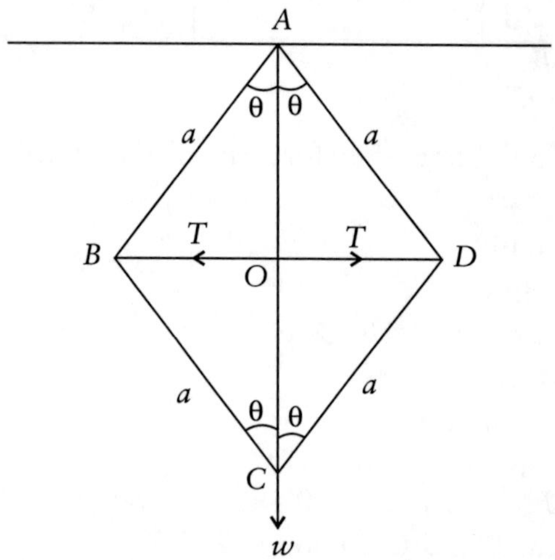


Let O be the point of intersection of the diagonals of the rhombus $ABCD$. Since the system is suspended from $A$ and a weight $w$ is attached at C, therefore, $AC$ must be vertical.

Since $A$ is fixed, therefore the, distances will be measured from $A$.

Let each side of the rhombus $ABCD$ be $a$ and be inclined at an angle θ to the vertical. Let $T$ be the thrust in the rod. Replace this rod $BD$ by a force $T$ at $B$ in the direction $DB$ and a force $T$ at $D$ in the direction $BD$.

Now,

$$AC = 2\,AO \qquad \text{|by geometry}$$

$$= 2\,a \cos\theta \qquad \ldots(1)$$

$$BD = 2\,BO \qquad \text{| by geometry}$$

$$= 2\,a \sin\theta = \ell \text{ (say)} \qquad \ldots(2)$$

Let the system be given a small virtual displacement such that θ changes to θ + δθ and $\ell$ changes to $\ell + \delta\ell$.

Then, the equation of virtual work is $w\,\delta(AC) + T\,\delta\ell = 0$

$\Rightarrow\quad w\,\delta\,(2\,a\cos\theta) + T\delta\,(2\,a\sin\theta) = 0$

$\Rightarrow\quad w\,(-2\,a\sin\theta\;\;\delta\theta) + T\,(2\,a\cos\theta\;\delta\theta) = 0$

$\Rightarrow\quad w\,(-2\,a\sin\theta) + T\,(2\,a\cos\theta) = 0 \qquad\qquad |\because \delta\theta \neq 0$

$\Rightarrow\quad w\sin\theta = T\cos\theta \qquad \Rightarrow T = w\tan\theta$

In the position of equilibrium, $\Delta\,ABD$ is equilateral, since the rods $AB$, $AD$ and $BD$ are of equal length.

$\therefore\qquad \angle\,BAD = 60° \qquad \Rightarrow 2\,\theta = 60° \qquad \Rightarrow \theta = 30°$

$$\Rightarrow\qquad T = w\tan 30° = \frac{w}{\sqrt{3}}$$

**Example 14:** Six equal rods $AB$, $BC$, $CD$, $DE$, $EF$ and $FA$ are each of weight $w$ and are freely jointed at their extremities to form a regular hexagon. The rod $AB$ is fixed in a horizontal position and the middle points of $AB$ and $DE$ are jointed by a string. Prove that its tension is $3w$.

**Sol.** The combined weight $6w$ of the rods will act at O, i.e., the centre of the hexagon. Let $T$ be the tension of the string $LM$, where $L$ and $M$ are the mid-points of $AB$ and $DE$ respectively.

Since $AB$ is fixed in a horizontal position, therefore, the distances will be measured from $AB$.

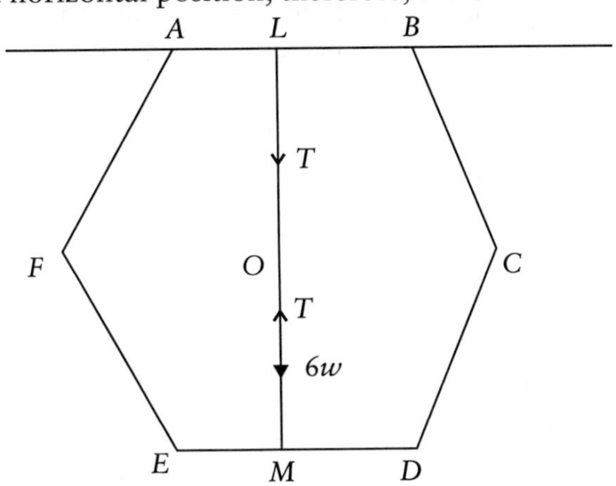


Let $OL = x$. Then, $LM + 2\;OL = 2x = \ell$ (say).

Let the system be given a small virtual displacement consistent with the geometrical conditions such that $x$ becomes $x = \delta x$ and $\ell$ becomes $\ell + \delta\ell$.

Then, the equation of virtual work is $6w\;\delta(OL) - T\,\delta\,(LM) = 0$

$\Rightarrow\quad 6w\;\delta(x) - T\,\delta\,(2x) = 0 \qquad\qquad \Rightarrow 6w\;\delta x - 2T\,\delta x = 0$

$\Rightarrow\quad 6w - 2T = 0 \qquad\qquad\qquad\qquad |\because \delta x \neq 0$

$\Rightarrow\quad 2T - 6w \qquad\qquad \Rightarrow T = 3w$

**Example 15:** Six equal heavy beams, freely jointed at their ends to form a hexagon, are placed in a vertical plane with one beam resting on a horizontal plane. The middle points of the two upper-slant beams, which are inclined at angle $\theta$ to the horizon, are connected by a light cord. Find the tension in terms of $w$ and $\theta$, where $w$ is the weight of each beam.

**Sol.**

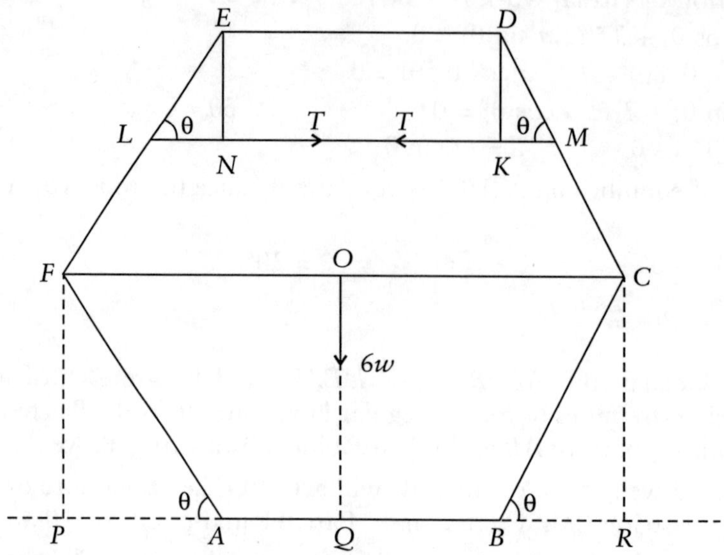


Let $T$ be the tension in the string $LM$ where $L$ and $M$ are the mid-points of $EF$ and $DC$ respectively. The combined weight $6w$ of six beams acts vertically downwards at O, the centre of the hexagon.

Since $AB$ is fixed in a horizontal position, therefore, the distances will be measured from $AB$.

Let each side of the hexagon be $2a$.

From O, draw perpendicular $OQ$ to $AB$.

Then,

$$OQ = CR = BC \sin \theta = 2a \sin \theta \qquad ...(1)$$

$$LM = LN + NK + KM = a \cos \theta + 2a + a \cos \theta$$

$$= 2a(1 + \cos \theta) = \ell \text{ (say)} \qquad ...(2)$$

Let the system be given a small virtual displacement, consistent with the geometrical conditions, such that $\theta$ becomes $\theta + \delta\theta$ and $\ell$ becomes $\ell + \delta\ell$.

Then, the equation of virtual work is

$$-6w\,\delta(OQ) - T\,\delta(LM) = 0$$

| In $-6w\,\delta(OQ)$, negative sign shows that the
| distance is being measured in the opposite
| direction of $6w$.

$\Rightarrow \quad 6w\,\delta(OQ) + T\,\delta(LM) = 0 \qquad \Rightarrow 6w\,\delta(2a \sin \theta) + T\,\delta\{2a(1 + \cos \theta)\} = 0$

$\Rightarrow \quad 12\,aw \cos \theta\,\delta\theta - 2aT \sin \theta\,\delta\theta = 0 \qquad \Rightarrow 12\,aw \cos \theta - 2aT \sin \theta = 0 \qquad | \because \delta\theta \neq 0$

$\Rightarrow \quad T \sin \theta = 6w \cos \theta \qquad \Rightarrow T = 6w \cot \theta$

**Example 16:** Six equal light rods are jointed to form a regular hexagon which is suspended at $A$ and $F$, so that $AF$ is horizontal. A light rod $BE$, also peeps the frame in shape and is of such a length that the rods ending in the point $B$, $E$ are inclined at an angle of 45° to the vertical. Equal weights are suspended from $B$, $C$, $D$, $E$. Find the stress in $BE$.

**Sol.** Let $ABCDEF$ be the regular hexagon suspended at corners $A$ and $F$ such that $AF$ is horizontal. Since $AF$ is fixed, therefore, the distances will be measured from $AF$ in the vertically downwards direction. $BE$ is the light rod connecting the corners $B$ and $E$.

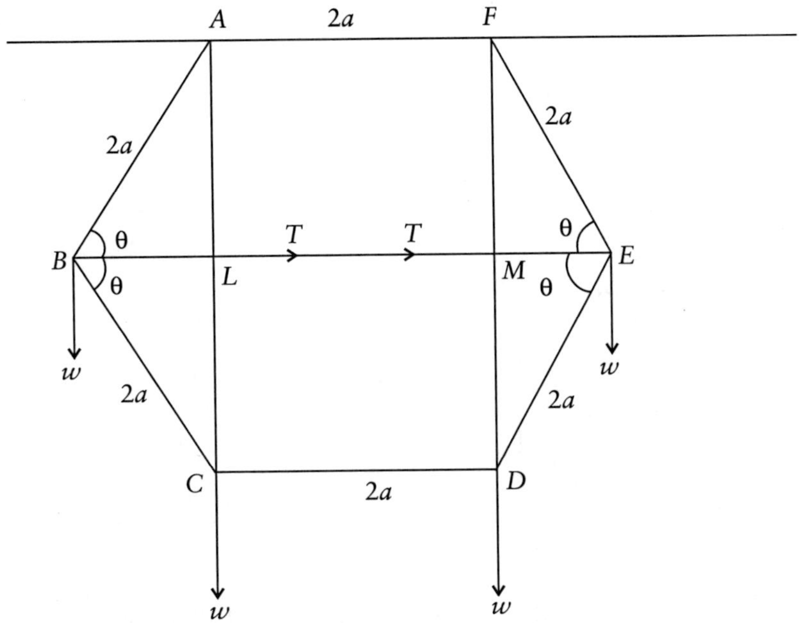


Let $T$ be the thrust in this rod. Let $2a$ be the length of each rod. Let $\angle ABE = \theta$.

Then,

$$BE = BL + LM + ME = 2a\cos\theta + 2a + 2a\cos\theta$$

$$= 2a + 4a\cos\theta = \ell \text{ (say)} \quad \ldots(1)$$

$$AL = 2a\cos\theta \quad \ldots(2)$$

$$AC = 2\,AL = 4a\sin\theta \quad \ldots(3)$$

Replace the rod $BE$ by two outward forces $T$, $T$ at $B$ and $E$ along $EB$ and $BE$ respectively.

Let the system be given a small virtual displacement consistent with the geometrical conditions such that $\theta$ becomes $\delta + \delta\theta$ and $\ell$ becomes $\ell + \delta\ell$.

Then, the equation of virtual work is

$$2w\,\delta(AL) + 2w\,\delta(AC) + T\,\delta(BE) = 0$$

$$\Rightarrow \quad 2w\,\delta(2a\sin\theta) + 2w\,\delta(4a\sin\theta) + T\delta\,(2a + 4a\cos\theta) = 0$$

$$\Rightarrow \quad 4w\,a\cos\theta\,\delta\theta + 8w\,a\cos\theta\,\delta\theta - 4a\,T\sin\theta\,\delta\theta = 0$$

$$\Rightarrow \quad 12w\,a\cos\theta\,\delta\theta - 4a\,T\sin\theta\,\delta\theta = 0$$

$$\Rightarrow \quad 12w\,a\cos\theta - 4a\,T\sin\theta = 0 \qquad |\because \delta\theta \neq 0$$

$$\Rightarrow \quad 3w\cos\theta - T\sin\theta = 0 \qquad \Rightarrow T = 3w\cot\theta$$

In the position of equilibrium,

$$\theta = 45^\circ \qquad \Rightarrow T = 3w\cot 45^\circ = 3w$$

**Example 17:** A regular *ABCDEF* consists of six equal rods each of weight $w$ and are freely jointed together. The hexagon rests in a vertical plane and *AB* is in contact with a horizontal table. If $C$ and $F$ be connected by a light string, prove that the tension in the string is $\frac{w}{\sqrt{3}}$.

**Sol.**

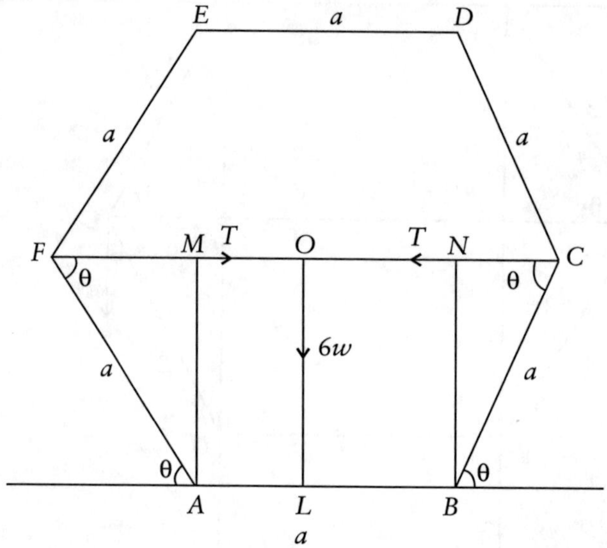


Let *ABCDEF* be the regular hexagon resting in a vertical plane with *AB* in contact with a horizontal table. The total weight $6w$ of six rods will act vertically downwards through $O$, the centre of gravity of the hexagon. *CF* is a light string by which the corners $C$ and $F$ are connected. Let $T$ be the tension in the string. Let $\theta$ be the inclination of the lower slant rods with the horizontal.

Since *AB* is fixed, therefore the distances will be measured from *AB*. Let $a$ be each side of the hexagon.

Then, $OL = a \sin \theta$ ...(1)

$$FC = FM + MN + NC = a \cos \theta + a + a \cos \theta = a + 2a \cos \theta$$

$$= a\,(1 + 2 \cos \theta) = \ell \text{ (say)} \quad \text{...(2)}$$

Replace the string *FC* by two inward forces $T$, $T$ at $F$ and $C$ along *FC* and *CF* respectively.

Let the system be given a small virtual displacement, such that $\theta$ becomes $\theta + \delta\theta$ and $\ell$ becomes $\ell + \delta\ell$.

Then, the equation of virtual work is

$$-\,6\,w\,\delta(OL) - T\,\delta\ell = 0$$

| Since the weight $6w$ is acting at O, a point above the
| fixed level *AB*, therefore, virtual work done by
| $6w$ is negative

$\Rightarrow \quad 6w\,\delta(OL) + T\,\delta\ell = 0 \qquad \Rightarrow 6w\,\delta(a \sin \theta) + T\,\delta\,\{a\,(1 + 2 \cos \theta)\} = 0$

$\Rightarrow \quad 6a\,w \cos \theta\,\delta\theta - 2\,a\,T \sin \theta\,\delta\theta = 0 \qquad \Rightarrow 6a\,w \cos \theta - 2\,a\,T \sin \theta = 0 \qquad | \because \delta\theta \neq 0$

$\Rightarrow \quad 3w \cos\theta - T\sin\theta = 0 \qquad \Rightarrow \qquad T = 3\,w \cot\theta$

In the position of equilibrium

$$\theta = 60°$$

$$\therefore \quad T = 3\,w \cot 60° = 3\,w\,\frac{1}{\sqrt{3}} = \frac{\sqrt{3}}{w}$$

**Example 18:** Six equal bars are freely jointed at their extremities forming a regular hexagon *ABCDEF*, which is kept in shape by vertical strings joining the middle points of *BC*, *CD* and *AF*, *FE* respectively, the side *AB* being held horizontal and upper-most. Prove that the tension of each string is three times the weight of a bar.

**Sol.** Let $w$ be the weight of each bar. Then, combined weight 6 bars = $6w$ and it will act at *O*, the centre of the hexagon.

Let *L*, *M*, *N*, *P* be the mid-points of *AF*, *FE*, *BC*, *CD* respectively. *LM* and *NP* are the two strings.

By symmetry, the tension in each string is the same, say *T*.

Since *AB* is horizontal,therefore, the distances will be measured from *AB*.

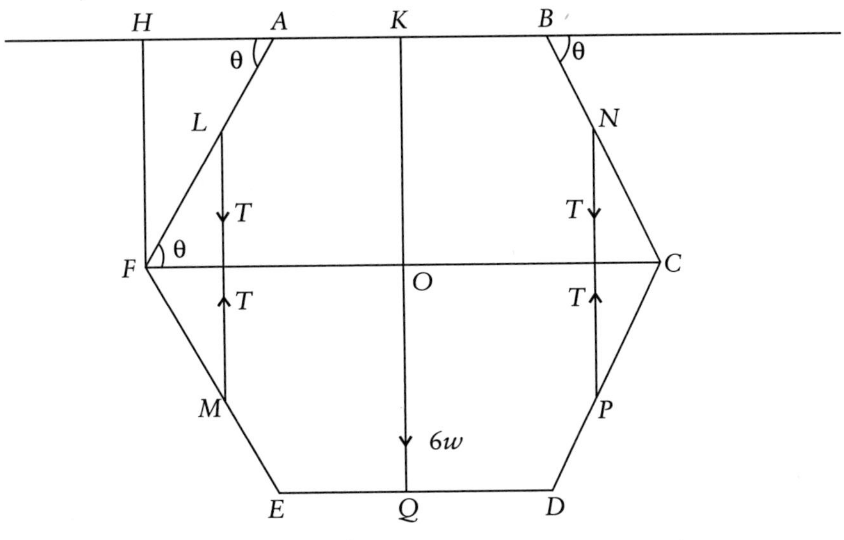


Let each side of the hexagon be $a$. Then,

$$OK = FH = FA\sin\theta = a\sin\theta \qquad \text{...(1)}$$

$$NP = LM = 2\,LN = 2\,LF\sin\theta$$

$$= 2 \cdot a/2 \sin\theta$$

$$= a\sin\theta = \ell \text{ (say)} \qquad \text{...(2)}$$

where the inclination of each of the upper slant rods with the horizontal is $\theta$.

Replace the string *LM* by a force *T* at *L* in the direction *LM* and a force *T* at *M* in the direction *ML*. Similarly, replace the string *NP* by a force *T* at *N* in the direction *NP* and a force *T* at *P* in the direction *PN*. It will keep the shape maintained in the position of equilibrium.

Let the system be given a small virtual displacement such that $\theta$ becomes $\theta + \delta\theta$ and $\ell$ becomes $\ell + \delta\ell$.

Then, the equation of virtual work is

$6w\,\delta\,(OK) - T\,\delta\ell - T\,\delta\ell = 0 \quad \Rightarrow 6w\,\delta\,(a \sin\theta) - 2T\,\delta\,(a\sin\theta) = 0$

$\Rightarrow \quad 6w\,a\cos\theta\,\delta\theta - 2T\,a\cos\theta\,\delta\theta = 0 \quad \Rightarrow 6w\,a\cos\theta - 2T\,a\cos\theta = 0 \qquad |\because \delta\theta \neq 0$

$\Rightarrow \quad T = 3w$

**Example 19:** Three equal uniform rods $AB$, $BC$, $CD$, each of weight $w$, are freely jointed together at $B$ and $C$ and rest in a vertical plane; $A$ and $D$ being in contact with a smooth horizontal table. Two equal light strings $AC$, $BD$ help to support it so that $AB$ and $CD$ are each inclined at an angle $\alpha$ to the horizontal. Show that of a weight $w$ be placed on $BC$ at its middle point, the tension of each string will be $(w + 1/2W)\cos\alpha\,\text{cosec}\,\alpha/2$

**Sol.** Let $G_1$, $G_2$ and $G_3$ be the middle points of the rods $AB$, $BC$ and $CD$ respectively. Then, the weights $w$, $w$ and $w$ of these rods act at $G_1$, $G_2$ and $G_3$ respectively. The weight $W$ is placed at the middle point $G_2$ of $BC$. $AC$ and $BD$ are two equal light strings.

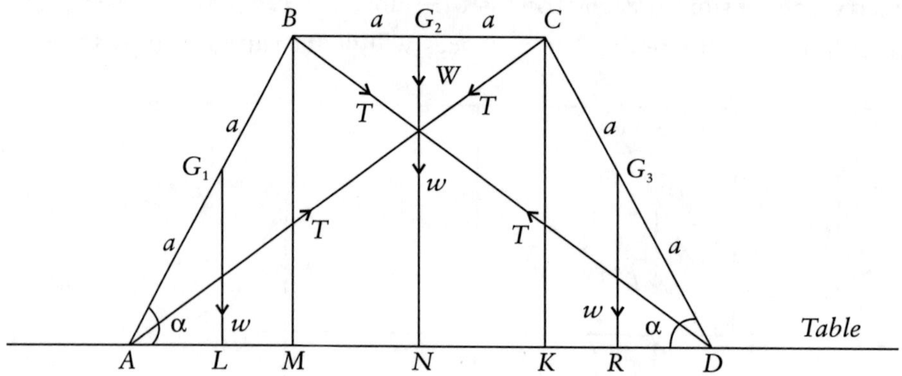


$\angle BAD = \angle CDA = \alpha$ (say) |Given

Let the lengths of the given rods $AB$, $BC$ and $CD$ be $2a$ each, since the rods are of equal length. Draw perpendiculars $G_1L$, $BM$, $G_2N$, $CK$ and $G_3R$ from $G_1$, $B$, $G_2$, $C$ and $G_3$ respectively on $AD$. Then,

$G_1L = AG_1 \sin\alpha = a\sin\alpha \qquad ...(1)$

$G_2N = BM = AB\sin\alpha = 2a\sin\alpha \qquad ...(2)$

$G_3R = DG_3\sin\alpha = a\sin\alpha \qquad ...(3)$

$AD = AM + MK + KD = AB\cos\alpha + BC + DC\cos\alpha = 2a\cos\alpha + 2a + 2a\cos\alpha$

$= 2a + 4a\cos\alpha \qquad ...(4)$

From $\Delta\,ABD$,

$BD^2 = AB^2 + AD^2 - 2AB \cdot AD \cdot \cos\alpha$ |by cosine formula

$= (2a)^2 + (2a + 4a\cos\alpha)^2 - 2\,(2a)\,(2a + 4a\cos\alpha)\cos\alpha$

$= 4a^2 + 4a^2 + 16a^2\cos^2\alpha + 16a^2\cos\alpha - 8a^2\cos\alpha - 16a^2\cos^2\alpha$

$= 8a^2 + 8a^2\cos\alpha = 8a^2(1 + \cos\alpha) = 8a^2(2\cos^2\alpha/2) = 16a^2\cos^2\alpha/2$

$\Rightarrow \quad BD = 4a^2\cos^2\alpha/2 = AC = \ell$ (say) $\qquad ...(1)$

Since $A$ and $D$ are in contact with a smooth horizontal table, therefore, the line $AD$ is fixed. Hence, the distances will be measured from $AD$.

By symmetry, the tensions in the strings $AC$ and $BD$ will be the same. Let $T$ be the tension in each of the strings $AC$ and $BD$.

Replace the strings by inwards forces $T$ at $A$ along $AC$, $T$ at $C$ along $CA$; $T$ and $B$ along $BD$, $T$ at $D$ along $DB$.

Let the system be given a small virtual displacement such that $\alpha$ changes to $\alpha + \delta\alpha$ and $\ell$ changes to $\ell + \delta\ell$.

Then, the equation of virtual work is

$$- w\delta\,(G_1L) - (w + W)\,\delta\,(G_2N) - T\,(G_3R) - T\,\delta\,(AC) - \alpha\,\delta(BD) = 0$$

|Since the directions of $LG_1$, $NG_2$ and $RG_3$ are vertically | upwards while the weights act vertically downwards, | therefore the works done by them will be negative.

$$\Rightarrow w\delta\,(a \sin\alpha) + (w + W)\,\delta\,(2a \sin\alpha) + w\delta\,(a \sin\alpha) - T\,\delta\,(4\,a \cos\alpha/2) - T\,\delta(4a \cos\alpha/2) = 0$$

|Using (1), (2), (3) and (5)

$$\Rightarrow \quad (4w + 2W)\,\delta\,(a \sin\alpha) + 8a\,T\delta(\cos\alpha/2) = 0$$

$$\Rightarrow \quad (2w + W)\,\delta\,(\sin\alpha) + 4\,T\delta(\cos\alpha/2) = 0 \Rightarrow (2w + W)\cos\alpha\,\delta\alpha - 2\,T \sin\alpha/2\,\delta\alpha = 0$$

$$\Rightarrow \quad (2w + W)\cos\alpha - 2\,T \sin\alpha/2\,\delta\alpha = 0 \qquad |\because \delta\alpha \neq 0$$

$$\Rightarrow \quad T = \frac{(2w + W)\cos\alpha}{2\sin\dfrac{\alpha}{2}} \quad \Rightarrow T = \left(w + \frac{W}{2}\right)\cos\alpha\,\text{cosec}\frac{\alpha}{2}$$

**Example 20:** A step-ladder has a pair of legs, which are jointed by a hinge at the top, and are connected by a cord attached at one-third of the distance from lower end to the top. If the weight of each leg be $w_1$ and acts at their middle points and if a man of weight $W$ be two-thirds the way up the ladder, show that the tension in the cord is

$1/2\,(W + 3/2\,w_1)\tan\alpha$, $\alpha$ being the inclination of each leg to the vertical.

**Sol.**

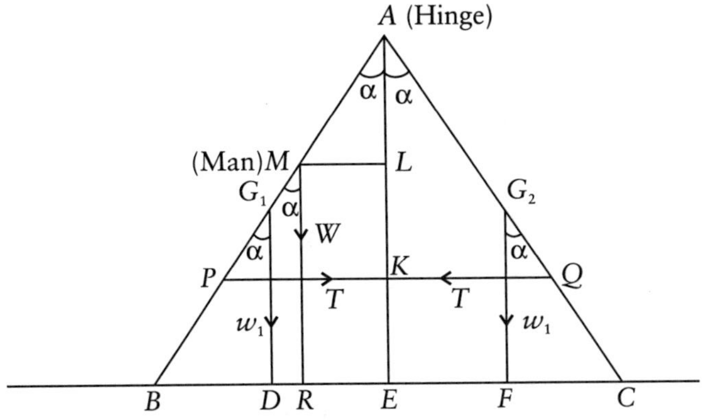

$AB$ and $AC$ are the legs of the step-ladder, which are jointed by a hinge $A$ at the top. Let $G_1$ and $G_2$ be the mid-points of legs $AB$ and $AC$ respectively. Then, their weights $w_1$ and $w_2$ act at $G_1$ and $G_2$ respectively.

$P$ and $Q$ are joined by a cord such that $BP = CQ = 1/3\ AB = 1/3\ AC$. $M$ is the position of the man such that $BM = 2/3AB$ so that $AM = 1/3\ AB$.

Let $AB = AC = 3a$

Then,

$$AM = 1/3(3a) = a \quad \text{...(1)}$$

$$BM = 2a \quad \text{...(2)}$$

$$BP = 1/3\ (AB) = 3a/3 = a = CQ \quad \text{...(3)}$$

$$AP = 2a = AQ \quad \text{...(4)}$$

$$AG_1 = BG_1 = 1/2\ AB = 3a/2 \quad \text{...(5)}$$

$$AG_2 = CG_2 = 1/2\ AC = 3a/2 \quad \text{...(6)}$$

Since $BC$ is fixed, therefore, the distances will be measured from $BC$.

Let $T$ be the tension in the string $PQ$. Replace the string $PQ$ by two inward forces $T$ at $P$ along $PQ$ and $T$ at $Q$ along $QP$. Draw perpendiculars $G_1D$, $MR$, $AE$, $G_2F$ from $G_1$, $M$, $A$, $G_2$ respectively on $BC$

Now,

$$G_1D = BG_1 \cos\alpha = 3a/2 \cos\alpha \quad \text{...(7)}$$

$$G_2F = G_1D = 3a/2 \cos\alpha \quad \text{...(8)}$$

$$MR = BM \cos\alpha = 2a \cos\alpha \quad \text{...(9)}$$

$$PQ = 2\ PK = 2AP \sin\alpha = 4a \sin\alpha = \ell \text{ (say)} \quad \text{...(10)}$$

Let the system be given a small virtual displacement such that $\alpha$ changes to $\alpha + \delta\alpha$ and $\ell$ changes to $\ell + \delta\ell$.

Then, the equation of virtual work is

$$-w_1\ \delta(G_1D) - W\ \delta\ (MR) - w_1\ \delta\ (G_2F) - T\ \delta\ (PQ) = 0$$

Since the directions of $DG_1$, $RM$ and $FG_2$ are opposite to the directions of $w_1$, $W$ and $w$ acting vertically downwards at $G_1$, $M$ and $G_2$ respectively, therefore the works done by the weights are negative.

$\Rightarrow \quad w_1\ \delta\ (3a/2 \cos\alpha) + W\ \delta\ (2a \cos\alpha) + w_1\ \delta\ (3a/2 \cos\alpha) + T\ \delta\ (4a \sin\alpha) = 0$

|From (7), (8), (9) and (10)

$\Rightarrow \quad w_1\ \delta\ (-3a/2 \sin\alpha\ \delta\alpha) + W\ (-2a \sin\alpha\ \delta\alpha) + w_1\ (-3a/2 \sin\alpha\ \delta\alpha) + T\ (4a \cos\alpha\ \delta\alpha) = 0$

$\Rightarrow \quad w_1\ (-3a \sin\ \delta\alpha) + W\ (-2a \sin\alpha\ \delta\alpha) + T\ (4a \cos\alpha\ \delta\alpha) = 0$

$\Rightarrow \quad w_1\ (-3a \sin\alpha) + W\ (-2a \sin\alpha) + T\ (4a \cos\alpha) = 0 \qquad |\because \delta\alpha \neq 0$

$\Rightarrow \quad (3w_1 + 2W) \sin\alpha = 4\ T \cos\alpha$

$\Rightarrow \quad T = 1/2\ (W + 3/2w_1) \tan\alpha$

**Example 21:** Two equal uniform rods $AB$ and $AC$, each of length $2b$, are freely jointed at $A$ and rest on a smooth vertical circle of radius $a$. Show that if $2\theta$ be the angle between them, then $b \sin^3\theta = a \cos\theta$

**Sol.** $AB$ and $AC$ are two equal uniform rods.

$AB = AC = 2b$ |Given

Let $w$ be the weight of each rod. Let $G_1$ and $G_2$ the centres of gravity of the rods $AB$ and $AC$ respectively. Then, the weights $w$ and $w$ act at $G_1$ and $G_2$ respectively. Therefore, the combined weight $2w$ of the two rods will act vertically downwards at $G$, the middle point of $G_1G_2$.

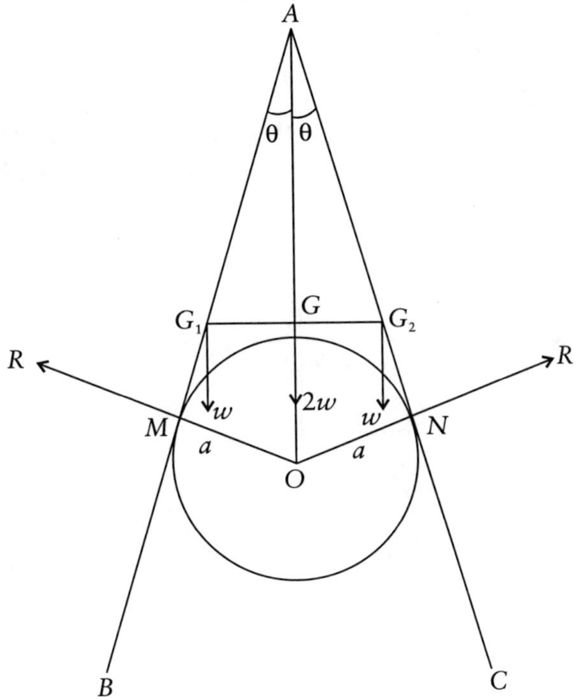


Since the given circle is fixed, therefore, its centre, say O, is fixed. Thus we shall measure the distances from the fixed point O.

$\angle BAC = 2\theta$ |Given

$\therefore \quad \angle BAO = \angle CAO = \theta$ | by geometry

$AG_1 = G_1 B = 1/2\ AB = 1/2\ (2b) = b$

From $\Delta\ AON$,

$AO = ON \text{ cosec } \theta = a \text{ cosec } \theta$

From $\Delta A\ G\ G_1$,

$AG = AG_1 \cos \theta = b \cos \theta$

$\therefore \quad OG = AO - AG$

$= a \text{ cosec } \theta - b \cos \theta$ ...(1)

Let the system be given a small virtual displacement such that $\theta$ becomes $\theta + \delta\theta$.

Then, the equation of virtual work is

$-\ 2w\ \delta(OG) = 0$ | $\because$ $G$ lies above $O$

$\Rightarrow \quad \delta\ (OG) = 0$ | $\because$ $w \neq 0$

[The reactions $R$ and $R$ at $M$ and $N$ will do no work since the reactions are perpendicular to the rods while the displacements are along the rods.]

$\Rightarrow \quad \delta\,(a \operatorname{cosec}\theta - b\cos\theta) = 0$ |From (1)

$\Rightarrow \quad (-a \operatorname{cosec}\theta \cot\theta + b\sin\theta)\,\delta\theta = 0$

$\Rightarrow \quad -a \operatorname{cosec}\theta\cot\theta + b\sin\theta = 0$ | $\because \delta\theta \neq 0$

$\Rightarrow \quad b\sin\theta = a\cos\theta/\sin^2\theta$

$\Rightarrow \quad b\sin^3\theta = a\cos\theta$

**Example 22:** Two smooth fixed rods $OA$, $OB$ are inclined downwards at equal angles $\alpha$ to the horizontal. Two equal uniform rods $AC$, $CB$, hinged together at $C$, have rings at the ends $A$, $B$ which can slide on $OA$, $OB$. Prove that, in equilibrium, the inclination $\theta$ of the movable rods to the horizontal is given by

$$\tan\theta = 1/2 \cot\alpha$$

**Sol.**

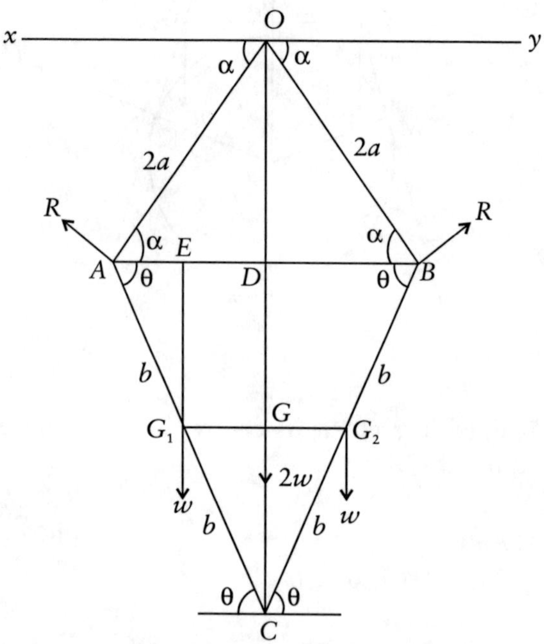


Since rods $OA$ and $OB$ are inclined downwards at equal angles $\alpha$ to the horizontal, therefore,

$OA = OB$ |by geometry

Let $OA = OB = 2a$

$\angle CAB = \angle CBA = \theta$ |Given

Let $AC = BC = 2b$

Let $G_1$ and $G_2$ be the mid-joints of the rods $CA$ and $CB$ respectively. Then, their weights say $w$ and $w$ will act at $G_1$ and $G_2$ respectively.

Therefore, the combined weight $2w$ of the two rods will act vertically downwards through $G$, the mid-point of $G_1G_2$.

Now, from $\Delta\ OAD$,

$$AD = OA \cos \alpha = 2a \cos \alpha \quad ...(1)$$

From $\Delta\ ACD$,

$$AD = AC \cos \theta = 2a \cos \theta \quad ...(2)$$

From (1) and (2), equating the two values of $AD$, we have

$$2a \cos \alpha = 2b \cos \theta$$

$$\Rightarrow \quad a \cos \alpha = b \cos \theta \quad ...(3)$$

$$OG = OD + DG = OD + EG_1$$

$$= OA \sin \alpha + AG_1 \sin \theta = 2a \sin \alpha + b \sin \theta$$

$$= 2\left(\frac{b\cos\theta}{\cos\alpha}\right) \sin \alpha + b \sin \theta \qquad | \text{ From (3)}$$

$$= 2b \tan \alpha \cos \theta + b \sin \theta \quad ...(4)$$

Since the rods $OA$ and $OB$ are fixed, therefore, $O$ is also fixed. Hence, the distances will be measured from $O$.

Let the system be given a small virtual displacement such that $\theta$ changes to $\theta + \delta\theta$.

The only force which will contribute towards the virtual work is the combined weight $2w$ of the rods acting at $G$. [The weights of the rods $OA$ and $OB$ will do no work, since the rods $OA$ and $OB$ are fixed. Also, the reactions $R$ and $R$ on the rings $A$ and $B$ will do no work, since they act normally to the rods while the displacements are along the rods.]

Now, since the directions of $OG$ (i.e., the direction from the fixed point O to the point of application G of $2w$) is the same as the direction of the line of action of $2w$ (vertically downwards), therefore, the work done by $2w$ will be positive.

Hence, the equation of the virtual work is

$$2w\ \delta(OG) = 0$$

$$\Rightarrow \quad \delta(OG) = 0 \qquad | \because w \neq 0$$

$$\Rightarrow \quad \delta(2b \tan \alpha \cos \theta + b \sin \theta) = 0 \qquad |\text{From (4)}$$

$$\Rightarrow \quad -2b \tan \alpha \sin \theta\ \delta\theta + b \cos \theta\ \delta\theta = 0$$

$$\Rightarrow \quad (-2b \tan \alpha \sin \theta + b \cos \theta)\ \delta\theta = 0$$

$$\Rightarrow \quad -2b \tan \alpha \sin \theta + b \cos \theta = 0 \qquad | \because \delta\theta \neq 0$$

$$\Rightarrow \quad 2 \tan \alpha \sin \theta = \cos \theta \qquad | \because b \neq 0$$

$$\Rightarrow \quad \tan \theta = 1/2 \cot \alpha$$

**Example 23:** Four equal uniform bars, each of weight $w$, are jointed together so as to form a rhombus. This is suspended vertically from one of its joints and a sphere of weight $P$ is balanced inside the rhombus so as to keep it from collapsing. Show that if $2\theta$ be the angle at the fixed point in the position of equilibrium, then

$$\frac{\sin^3\theta}{\cos\theta} = \frac{Pr}{4a(P+2w)},$$

where $r$ is the radius of the sphere and $2a$ is the length of each bar.

**Sol.**

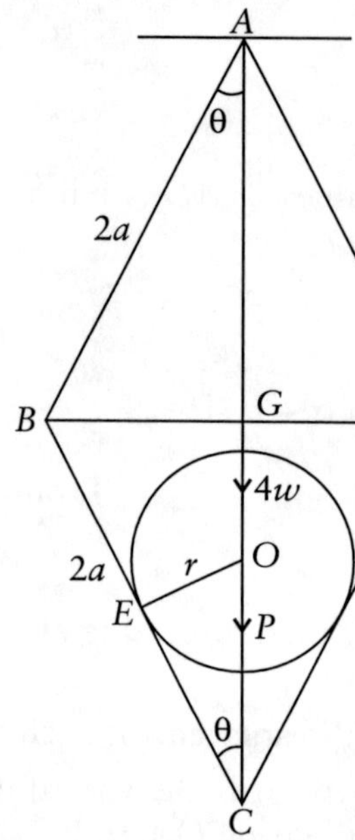


$AB$, $BC$, $CD$ and $DA$ are four equal uniform bars, each of weight $w$, jointed together so as to form a rhombus $ABCD$. It is suspended from one of its joints $A$. A sphere with centre $O$, radius $r$ and weight $P$ keeps the framework from collapsing. The combined weight $4w$ of the four rods will act at $G$, the C.G. of the rhombus $ABCD$. The weight $P$ of the sphere acts at $O$.

Since $A$ is fixed, therefore the distances will be measured from $A$.

Now,

$$AG = AB \cos\theta = 2a \cos\theta \qquad \ldots(1)$$

$$AO = AC - OC = 2AG - OC$$

$$= 2\,(2a\cos\theta) - r\,\text{cosec}\,\theta \qquad |\text{From (1)}$$

$$= 4a\cos\theta - r\,\text{cosec}\,\theta \qquad \ldots(2)$$

Let the system be given a small virtual displacement such that $\theta$ changes to $\theta + \delta\theta$ while the lengths of the rods of the rhombus remain unchanged.

Then, the equation of virtual work is $4w\,\delta\,(AG) + P\,\delta(AO) = 0$

Since the directions of $AG$ and $AO$, i.e., the directions from the fixed point $A$ to the points of application $G$ and $O$ of $4w$ and $P$ respectively, are same (vertically downwards) as the directions of the lines of action of $4w$ and $P$, therefore, the works done by $4w$ and $P$ will be both positive.

$$\Rightarrow \quad 4w\,\delta(2a\cos\theta) + P\,\delta(4a\cos\theta - r\,\text{cosec}\,\theta) = 0 \qquad |\text{From (1) and (2)}$$

$$\Rightarrow \quad 4w\,(-2a\sin\theta\,\delta\theta) + P\,(-4a\sin\theta\,\delta\theta + r\,\text{cosec}\,\theta\cot\theta\,\delta\theta) = 0$$

$$\Rightarrow \quad [-8a\,w\sin\theta + P\,(-4a\sin\theta + r\,\text{cosec}\,\theta\cot\theta)]\,\delta\theta = 0$$

$$\Rightarrow \quad -8a\,w\sin\theta + P\,(-4a\sin\theta + r\,\text{cosec}\,\theta\cot\theta) = 0 \qquad |\because \delta\theta \neq 0$$

$$\Rightarrow \quad 4a\sin\theta\,(P + 2w) = r\,P\,\text{cosec}\,\theta\cot\theta$$

$$= rP\frac{1}{\sin\theta}\frac{\cos\theta}{\sin\theta} \qquad\qquad \Rightarrow \frac{\sin^3\theta}{\cos\theta} = \frac{Pr}{4a(P+2w)}$$

$$= \frac{rP\cos\theta}{\sin^2\theta}$$

**Example 24:** Four uniform rods, each of length $a$ and weight $w$ are smoothly jointed together to form a rhombus $ABCD$. The rhombus is kept in shape by a light strut $BD$ and hung from $A$. A uniform circular disc of radius $r$ and weight $w'$ is placed inside the triangle $BCD$ with its place vertical and its smooth rim in contact with $BC$ and $CD$, its highest point is below $BD$. If angle $BAC$ is $\theta$, show that the thrust in $BD$ is $(2w + w')\tan\theta - w'r/2a\sin^2\theta$.

**Sol.**

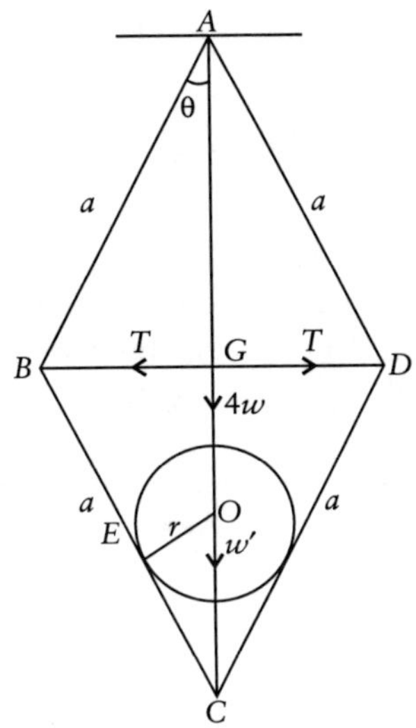


The combined weight $4w$ of the four rods will act at $G$, the C.G. of the rhombus $ABCD$. The weight $w'$ will act $O$, the centre of the disc.

We know that strut is a piece of wood or metal used as a support. So, let $T$ be the trust in the given strut $BD$. Replace this by a force $T$ at $B$ along $DB$ and a force $T$ at $D$ along $BD$.

Now,

$$AG = a\cos\theta \qquad ...(1)$$

$$AO = AC - OC = 2AG - OC$$

$$= 2a\cos\theta - r\,\text{cosec}\,\theta \qquad |\text{Refer Ex. 23} \qquad ...(2)$$

$$BD = 2\,BG = 2\,a\sin\theta = \ell \text{ (say)} \qquad ...(3)$$

Since $A$ is fixed, therefore the distances will be measured from $A$.

Let the system be given a small virtual displacement such that $\theta$ changes to $\theta + \delta\theta$ and $\ell$ changes to $\ell + \theta\ell$.

Then, the equation of virtual work is

$$4w\,\delta(AG) + w'\,\delta(AO) + T\,\delta\,(BD) = 0 \qquad |\text{Refer Ex. 23}$$

$\Rightarrow \quad 4w\,\delta(a\cos\theta) + w'\,\delta(2a\cos\theta - r\,\text{cosec}\,\theta) + T\delta\,(2a\sin\theta) = 0$ |From (1), (2) and (3)

$\Rightarrow \quad 4w\,(-a\sin\theta\,\delta\theta) + w'\,(-2a\sin\theta\,\delta\theta + r\,\text{cosec}\,\theta\cot\theta)\delta\theta + T\,(2a\cos\theta\,\delta\theta) = 0$

$\Rightarrow \quad \delta\theta\,[-4a\,w\sin\theta - 2a\,w'\sin\theta + r\,\text{cosec}\,\alpha\cot\theta\,w' + 2a\cos\theta T] = 0$

$\Rightarrow \quad -4a\,w\sin\theta - 2a\,w'\sin\theta + r\,\text{cosec}\,\alpha\cot\theta\,w' + 2a\cos\theta T = 0$ $\quad |\because \delta\theta \neq 0$

$$\Rightarrow \quad T\,(2a\cos\theta) = 2a\,(2w + w')\sin\theta - rw'\frac{\cos\theta}{\sin^2\theta}$$

$$\Rightarrow \quad T = (2w + w')\tan\theta - \frac{w'r}{2a\sin^2\theta}$$

**Example 25:** Two equal rods, each of weight $w\ell$ and length $\ell$, are hinged together and placed astride a smooth horizontal cylindrical peg of radius $r$. Then the lower ends are tied together by a string and the rods are left at the same inclinations $\phi$ to the horizontal. Prove that the tension in the string is

$$w\,(r\sec^2\phi - 1/2\,\ell\cot\phi),$$

and if the string is slack, show that

$$\tan^3\phi + \tan\phi = \ell/2r.$$

**Sol.** $AB$ and $AC$ are the two equal rods, each of length $\ell$ and weight $w\ell$. They are hinged together at $A$. Let $G_1$ and $G_2$ be the mid-points of the rods $AB$ and AC respectively. Then, their weights $w\ell$ and $w\ell$ will act at $G_1$ and $G_2$ respectively.

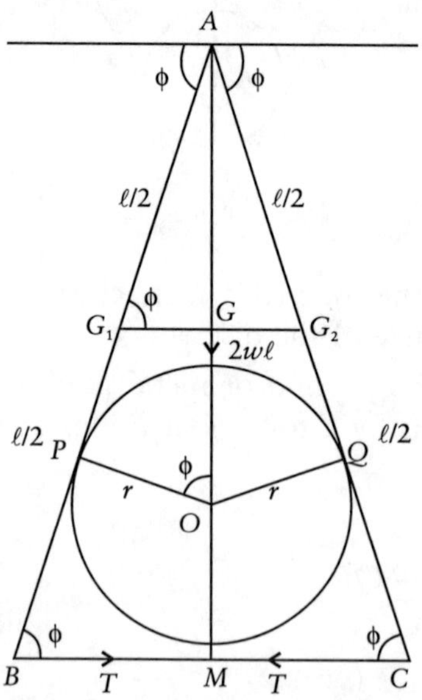


Therefore, their combined weight $2w\ell$ will act $G$, where $G$ is the mid-point of $G_1G_2$.

$B$ and $C$ are joined by a string. Let $T$ be the tension in the string. Replace the string $BC$ by two inwards forces $T$, $T$ at $B$ and $C$ along $BC$ and $CB$ respectively.

Since the point O is fixed as it is the centre of the fixed cylinder, therefore, the distances will be measured from O.

From figure,

$$AG_1 = BG_1 = \ell/2 \quad ...(1)$$

$$AG = AG \sin\phi = \ell/2 \sin\phi \quad ...(2)$$

$$AO = OP \sin\phi = r \sec\phi \quad ...(3)$$

$$\therefore \quad OG = AO - AG = r\sec\phi - \ell/2 \sin\phi \quad ...(4)$$

$$BC = 2\,M = 2\,AB\cos\phi = 2\ell\cos\phi = \lambda \text{ (say)} \quad ...(5)$$

Let the system be given a small virtual displacement such that $\phi$ changes to $\phi + \delta\phi$ and the length of the string $\lambda$ changes to $\lambda + \delta\lambda$.

Then, the equation of virtual work is

$$-2w\ell\,\delta(OG) - T\,\delta(BC) = 0 \qquad |\because G \text{ lies above O.}$$

$$\Rightarrow \quad 2w\ell\,\delta(OG) + T\,\delta(BC) = 0$$

$$\Rightarrow \quad 2w\ell\,\delta(r\sec\phi - \ell/2 \sin\phi) + \delta\,(2\ell\cos\phi) = 0$$

$$\Rightarrow \quad 2w\ell\,(r\sec\phi\tan\phi\,\delta\phi - \ell/2\cos\phi\,\delta\phi + T\,(-2\ell\sin\phi\,\delta\phi) = 0$$

$$\Rightarrow \quad \delta\phi\,[2w\ell\,r\sec\phi\tan\phi - w\ell\cos\phi - 2\,T\ell\sin\phi] = 0$$

$$\Rightarrow \quad 2w\ell\,r\sec\phi\tan\phi - w\ell\cos\phi - 2T\ell\sin\phi \qquad |\because \delta\phi \neq 0$$

$$\Rightarrow \quad 2\,T\sin\phi = 2wr\sec\phi\tan\phi - w\ell\cos\phi$$

$$= w(2r\sec\phi\tan\phi - \ell\cos\phi) \qquad |\because \ell \neq 0$$

$$= w\left(2r\frac{1}{\cos\phi}\frac{\sin\phi}{\cos\phi} - \ell\cos\phi\right)$$

$$\Rightarrow \quad T = w\,(r\sec^2\phi - \ell/2\cot\phi)$$

When the string becomes slack, $T = 0$

$$\therefore \quad w(r\sec^2\phi - \ell/2\cot\phi) = 0$$

$$\Rightarrow \quad r\sec^2\phi - \ell/2\cot\phi = 0 \qquad |\because w \neq 0$$

$$\Rightarrow \quad r\sec^2\phi = \ell/2\cot\phi \qquad \Rightarrow r\,(1 + \tan^2\phi) = \ell/2\tan\phi \Rightarrow \ell/2r = \tan\phi + \tan^3\phi$$

## EXERCISE 3(A)

1. Four equal heavy uniform rods are hanged together to form a rhombus $ABCD$ and the frame is suspended from $A$. The corners $A$ and $C$ are connected by an elastic string to prevent the frame from collapsing. Find the tension in the string.

   [**Ans.** 1/2 weight of rods.]

2. Four uniform rods are jointed to form a rectangle $ABCD$. $AB$ is fixed in the vertical position with $A$ upper must and the rectangle is kept in shape by a string joining $A$ and $C$. Find the tension of the string, where it is given that $AB = 2a$, $BC = 2b$ and $w$ is the weight of the rectangle.

   [**Ans.** $T = \dfrac{w\sqrt{a^2+b^2}}{2a}$ ]

3. A regular hexagon $ABCDEF$ is composed of six equal heavy uniform rods jointed together, and two opposite angles $C$ and $F$ are connected by a string which is horizontal, $AB$ being in contact with the horizontal plane. At the middle point of the opposite rod $DE$, a weight $w'$ is placed. If $w$ is the weight of each rod, show that the tension of the string is

$$\frac{3w + w'}{\sqrt{3}}$$

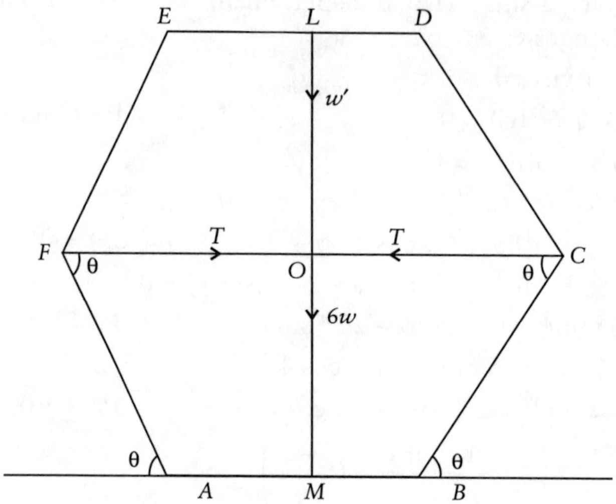


[**Hint:** The equation of virtual work is

$$-6w\,(OM) - w'\,\delta\,(LM) - T\,(FC) = 0$$

$$\Rightarrow \quad -6w\,\delta\,(a \sin\theta) - w'\,\delta\,(2a \sin\theta) - T\,(a + 2a\cos\theta) = 0]$$

4. If two equal uniform rods connected by a smooth hinge are placed over the circumference of a smooth vertical circle, show that in the position of equilibrium, the inclination of either rod to the vertical is given by $\operatorname{cosec}^2\theta \cot\theta = \ell/a$, where $2\ell$ is the length of the rod and $2a$ is the diameter of the circle.

   [**Hint.** Refer Ex. 21 (solved). Put $b = \ell$ simply)

5. A uniform rectangular plate $ABCD$ of weight $w$ hangs from $A$. If a weight $w'$ be suspended from $B$, prove that in the position of equilibrium, the inclination $\theta$ of the diagonal $AC$ to the vertical is given by

$$\tan\theta = \frac{2w'ab}{w(a^2 + b^2) + 2w'a^2}$$

   where $AB = a$ and $AD = b$.

6. A framework $ABC$ consists of three light rods of which $AB$, $AC$ are each of length $\lambda a$ and $BC$ of length $\mu a$, freely jointed together. It rests with $BC$ horizontal, $A$ below $BC$, and the rods $AB$, $AC$ over smooth legs $D$ and $E$ in same horizontal line at a distance

*Va* apart. A weight *w* is suspended from *A*. Show, by principle of virtual work, that the stress in *BC* is

$$\frac{2\lambda^2 V}{\mu^2\sqrt{4\lambda^2-\mu^2}}\cdot w$$

Problem on bodies resting on pegs or inclined planes.

## ILLUSTRATIVE EXAMPLES

**Example 1:** Four equal rods, each of length $2a$ and weight $w$ are freely jointed to form a square *ABCD* which is kept in shape by a light rod *BD* and is supported in a vertical plane with *BD* horizontal, *A* above *C* and *AB*, *AD* in contact with two fixed smooth pegs which are at a distance $2b$ apart on the same level. Find the stress in the rod *BD*.

**Solution.**

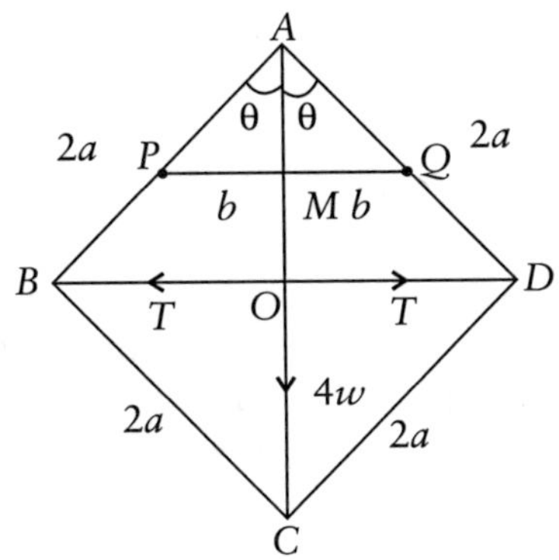


Let *ABCD* be a square formed by four equal rods *AB*, *BC*, *CD* and *DA*, each of weight *w* and length $2a$. *BD* is a light rod connecting the vertices *B* and *D* to preserve the shape of the square framework. *P* and *Q* are two fixed pegs such that $PQ = 2b$. Since *P* and *Q* are fixed, therefore, line *PQ* is fixed. Therefore, the distances will be measured from *PQ*.

Replace the rod *BD* by two forces *T* at *B* along *DB* and *T* at *D* along *BD*, where α is the thrust in the rod *BD*.

Le $\angle BAO = \theta$, where O is the C.G. of the square frame work *ABCD*. The combined weight $4w$ of the four rods acts at O vertically downwards.

Let *M* be the mid-point of *PQ*. Then, $PM = MQ = b$

Now, in $\Delta\, PAM$,

$$AM = b\cot\theta \qquad \text{...(1)}$$

In $\Delta\, BAO$,

$$AO = AB\cos\theta = 2a\cos\theta \qquad \text{...(2)}$$

$$\therefore \quad MO = AO - AM$$

$$= 2a\cos\theta - b\cot\theta \qquad |\text{From (1) and (2)} \qquad \text{...(3)}$$

$$BD = 2BO = 2AB\sin\theta = 2(2a\sin\theta) = 4a\sin\theta \qquad \text{...(4)}$$

Let the system be given a small virtual displacement such that θ be comes $\theta + \delta\theta$, consistent with the geometrical conditions.

Then the equation of virtual work is

$$4w\,\delta(MO) + T\,\delta(BD) = 0$$

$\Rightarrow \quad 4w\,\delta(2a\cos\theta - b\cot\theta) + T\,\delta(4a\sin\theta) = 0$ |From (3) and (4)

$\Rightarrow \quad 4w\,(-2a\sin\theta + b\,\mathrm{cosec}^2\,\theta)\,\delta\theta + T(4a\cos\theta)\,\delta\theta = 0$

$\Rightarrow \quad \delta\theta\,[4w\,(-2a\sin\theta + b\,\mathrm{cosec}^2\,\theta) + T(4a\cos\theta)] = 0$

$\Rightarrow \quad 4w\,(-2a\sin\theta + b\,\mathrm{cosec}^2\,\theta) + T(4a\cos\theta) = 0$ $|\because \delta\theta \neq 0$

$\Rightarrow \quad 4a\,T\cos\theta = 4w\,(2a\sin\theta - b\,\mathrm{cosec}^2\,\theta)$

$\Rightarrow \quad T = \dfrac{w(2a\sin\theta - b\,\mathrm{cosec}^2\theta)}{a\cos\theta}$

In the position of equilibrium, $\theta = 45°$

$$\therefore \quad T = \frac{w(2a\sin 45° - b\,\mathrm{cosec}^2\,45°)}{a\cos 45°}$$

$$= \frac{w\left\{(2a\dfrac{1}{\sqrt{2}} - b(\sqrt{2})^2\right\}}{\dfrac{a}{\sqrt{2}}} = \frac{w(2a - 2\sqrt{2}\,b)}{a} = \frac{2w(a - \sqrt{2}\,b)}{a}$$

**Example 2:** A rhombus is formed of four rods each of weight $w$ and length $\ell$ with smooth joints. It rests symmetrically with its upper sides in contact with two smooth pegs at the same level and at a distance $2a$ apart. A weight $w'$ is hung at the lowest point. If the sides of the rhombus make an angle $\theta$ with the vertical, prove that

$$\sin^3\theta = \frac{a(4w + w')}{\ell(4w + 2w')}$$

**Sol.**

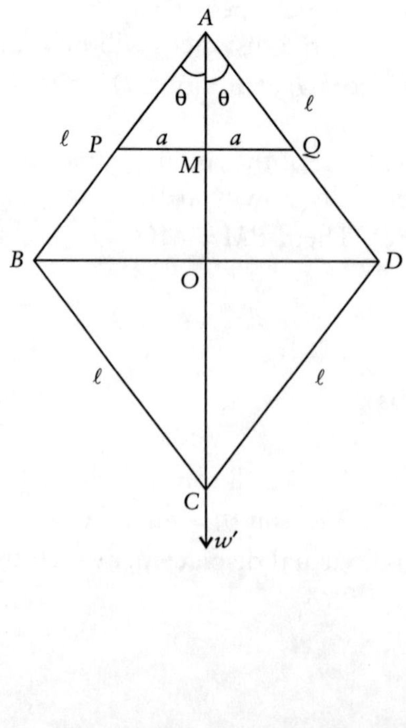

Let $ABCD$ be the rhombus formed by four rods $AB$, $BC$, $CD$ and $DA$, each of weight $w$ and length $\ell$. Then, the combined weight $4w$ of the four rods will act at O, the point of intersection of the diagonals $AC$ and $BD$. A weight $w'$ acts at $C$. $P$ and $Q$ are the given two smooth pegs at the same level such that $PQ = 2a$.

Let $M$ be the mid-point of $PQ$. Then, $PM = MQ = a$. The upper sides $AB$ and $AD$ of the rhombus $ABCD$ are in contact with pegs $P$ and $Q$ respectively. Since line $PQ$ in fixed, therefore, the distances will be measured from $PQ$.

$\angle BAO = \angle DAO = \theta$ |Given

Now, depth of O below $PQ = OM = OA - AM$

$= \ell \cos\theta - a \cot\theta$ ...(1)

depth of C below $PQ = CM = AC - AM = 2OA - AM$

$= 2\ell \cos\theta - a \cot\theta$ ...(2)

Let the system be given a small virtual displacement such that $\theta$ becomes $\theta + \delta\theta$.

Then, the equation of virtual work is

$$4w\,\delta(OM) + w'\,\delta(CM) = 0$$

The reactions at $P$ and $Q$ will do no work, since they are perpendicular to the rods while the displacements are along the rods.

The directions of $MO$ and $MC$ from the fixed line $PQ$ to the points of application O and C are the same as the directions of the lines of action $4w$ and $w'$, so that the works done by $4w$ and $w'$ will be positive.

$\Rightarrow \quad 4w\,\delta(\ell\cos\theta - a\cot\theta) + w'\,\delta(2\ell\cos\theta - a\cot\theta) = 0$

$\Rightarrow \quad 4w(-\ell\sin\theta + a\,\text{cosec}^2\theta)\,\delta\theta + w'\,\delta(-2\ell\sin\theta + a\,\text{cosec}^2\theta)\,\delta\theta = 0$

$\Rightarrow \quad \delta\theta\,[4w(-\ell\sin\theta + a\,\text{cosec}^2\theta) + w'\,\delta(-2\ell\sin\theta + a\,\text{cosec}^2\theta) = 0$

$\Rightarrow \quad 4w(-\ell\sin\theta + a\,\text{cosec}^2\theta) + w'(-2\ell\sin\theta + a\,\text{cosec}^2\theta) = 0$ $\quad|\because \delta\theta \neq 0$

$\Rightarrow \quad (4w + 2w')\,\ell\sin\theta = a(4w + w')\,\text{cosec}^2\theta$

$$\Rightarrow \quad \sin^3\theta = \frac{(4w + w')a}{(4w + 2w')\ell}$$

**Example 3:** $ABCD$ is a rhombus formed with four light rods each of length $\ell$ jointed by smooth hinges. A weight $w$ is attached to the lowest hinge $C$ and the frame rest on two smooth pegs is a horizontal line in contact with $AB$ and $AD$. $B$ and $D$ are in a horizontal line and are joined by a string. If the distance of the pegs apart is $2c$ and the angle at $A$ is $2\alpha$, show that the tension in the string is

$$w\tan\alpha\left(\frac{c}{2\ell}\cos ec^3\alpha - 1\right)$$

**Sol.**

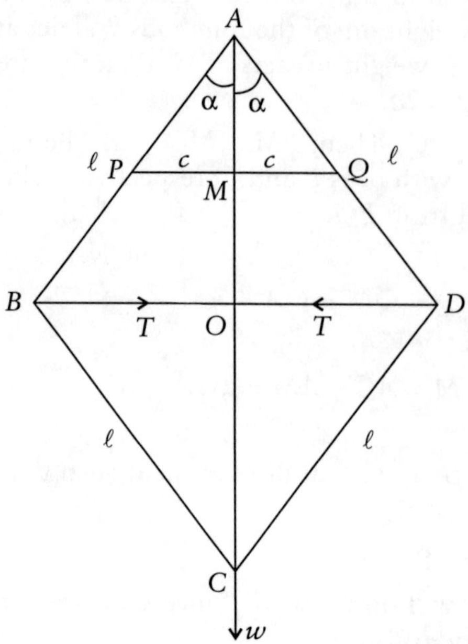


$ABCD$ is a rhombus formed with four light rods $AB$, $BC$, $CD$ and $DA$, each of length $\ell$. A weight $w$ acts at the lowest point $C$ of the framework. $P$ and $Q$ are two smooth pegs in a horizontal line in contact with $AB$ and $AD$ respectively such that $PQ = 2c$. If $M$ is the middle point of $PQ$, then $PM = MQ = c$. Let $O$ be the point of intersection of the diagonals $AC$ and $BD$ of the rhombus $ABCD$.

$B$ and $D$ are joined by a string $BD$. Let $T$ be the tension in the string $BD$. Replace the string $BD$ by two inward force $T$, $T$ at $B$ and $D$ acting along $BD$ and $DB$ respectively.

$\angle BAD = 2\alpha$ |Given

$\therefore\ BAO = \angle DAO = \alpha$ |by geometry

Since $PQ$ is fixed, therefore, the distances will be measured from $PQ$.

Now, $BD = 2\ BO = 2\ AB \sin\alpha$

$= 2\ \ell \sin\alpha = \lambda$ (say) ...(1)

$MC = AC - AM = 2AO - AM = 2\ AB \cos\alpha - PM \cot\alpha$

$= 2\ \ell \cos\alpha - c \cot\alpha$ ...(2)

Let the system be given a small virtual displacement such that $\alpha$ changes to $\alpha + \delta\alpha$ and $\lambda$ (length of the string) changes to $\lambda + \delta\lambda$.

Then, the equation of virtual work is $w\ \delta\ (MC)\ T\delta\ (BD) = 0$

Reactions at the pegs $P$ and $Q$ will do no work. Since the weight $w$ is acting at $C$, a point below $PQ$, therefore, the virtual work done by $w$ will be positive.

$\Rightarrow\quad w\ \delta(2\ell \cos\alpha - c \cot\alpha) - T\ \delta(2\ell \sin\alpha) = 0$

$\Rightarrow\quad w\ (-2\ell \sin\alpha - c\ \text{cosec}^2\ \alpha)\ \delta\alpha - T\ (2\ell \cos\alpha)\ \delta\alpha = 0$

$\Rightarrow\quad \delta\alpha\ [w\ (-2\ell \sin\alpha + c\ \text{cosec}^2\ \alpha) - T\ (2\ell \cos\alpha)] = 0$

$\Rightarrow \quad w(-2\ell \sin\alpha + c \operatorname{cosec}^2\alpha) - T(2\ell\cos\alpha) = 0 \qquad |\because \delta\alpha \neq 0$

$\Rightarrow \quad T(2\ell\cos\alpha) = w(c\operatorname{cosec}^2\alpha - 2\ell\sin\alpha)$

$$\Rightarrow \quad T = \frac{w\sin\alpha(c\operatorname{cosec}^3\alpha - 2\ell)}{2\ell\cos\alpha}$$

$$\Rightarrow \quad T = w\tan\alpha\left(\frac{c}{2\ell}\operatorname{cosec}^3\alpha - 1\right)$$

**Example 4:** A uniform beam of length $2a$ rests in equilibrium against a smooth vertical wall and upon a smooth peg at a distance $b$ from the wall. Show, by principle of virtual work, that in the position of equilibrium, the beam is inclined to the wall at an angle $\sin^{-1}(b/a)^{1/3}$.

**Sol.**

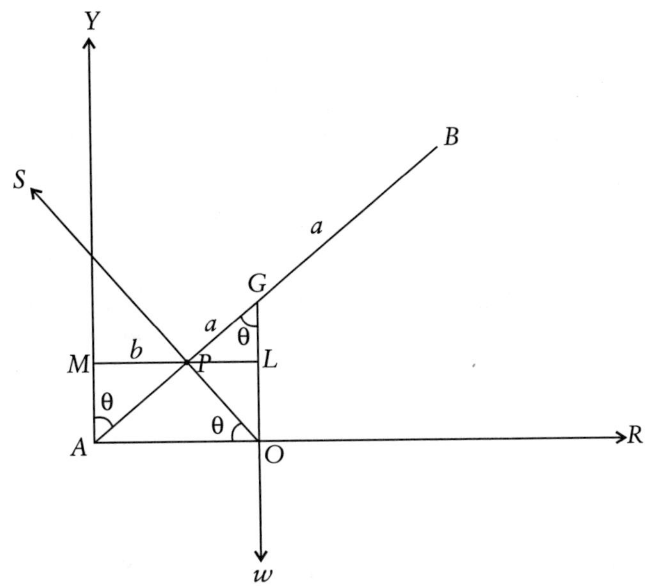


$AB$ is a uniform beam of length $2a$. Let $G$ be the mid-point of $AB$. Then,

$$AG = GB = a \qquad ...(1)$$

Let $w$ be the weight of the beam $AB$. Then, $w$ will act at $G$ vertically downwards.

Let $AM$ be the wall.

Let $P$ be the peg at $a$ distance $b$ from the wall. Then,

$$PM = b \qquad ...(2)$$

Let, in the position of equilibrium, the rod $AB$ is inclined at an angle $\theta$ with the vertical wall $AM$.

The forces acting on the beam $AB$ are:

(i) Its weight $w$ at $G$ acting vertically downwards.

(ii) Reaction $R$ between the wall and the beam at $A$.

(iii) Reaction $S$ between the beam and the peg at $P$.

Since the beam is in equilibrium under the action of above three non-parallel coplanar forces, therefore, all these forces will meet at a point, say $O$.

Produce $MP$ to meet $GO$ at $L$.

Let $\angle BAM = \theta$.

Since $P$ is fixed, therefore, all the distances will be measured from $P$.

Let the system be given a small virtual displacement such that $\theta$ changes to $\theta + \delta\theta$.

Then, the equation of virtual work is

$$-w\,\delta(GL) = 0$$

$$\Rightarrow \quad \delta(GL) = 0 \qquad | \because w \neq 0$$

Note that the reactions $R$ and $S$ do not appear in the equation of virtual work as they do no work.

$$\Rightarrow \quad \delta(GO - LO) = 0 \qquad \Rightarrow \delta(GO - MA) = 0$$

$$\Rightarrow \quad \delta(AG\cos\theta - MP\cot\theta) = 0 \qquad \Rightarrow \delta(a\cos\theta - b\cot\theta) = 0$$

$$\Rightarrow \quad -a\sin\theta\,\delta\theta + b\,\text{cosec}^2\theta\,\delta\theta = 0 \qquad \Rightarrow \delta\theta\,(-a\sin\theta + b\,\text{cosec}^2\theta) = 0$$

$$\Rightarrow \quad -a\sin\theta + b\,\text{cosec}^2\theta = 0 \qquad | \because \delta\theta \neq 0$$

$$\Rightarrow \quad a\sin\theta = b\,\text{cosec}^2\theta \qquad \Rightarrow a\sin\theta = b/\sin^2\theta$$

$$\Rightarrow \quad \sin^3\theta = b/a \qquad \Rightarrow \sin\theta = (b/a)^{1/3} \qquad \Rightarrow \theta = \sin^{-1}(b/a)^{1/3}.$$

**Example 5:** A heavy uniform rod of length 2 $a$ rests with its ends in contact with two smooth inclined planes of inclination $\alpha$ and $BN$ the horizon. Prove by the principle of virtual work, that

$$\tan\theta = 1/2\,(\cot\alpha - \cot\beta)$$

**Sol.**

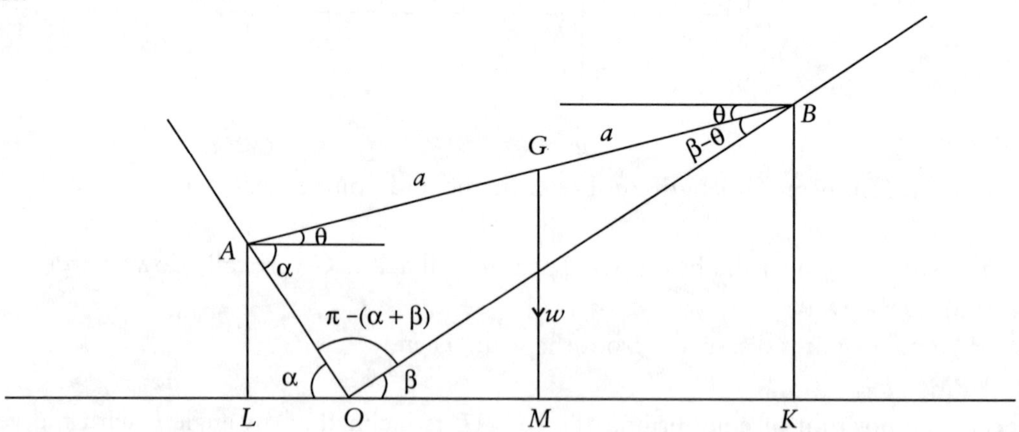


Let $AB$ be the given heavy uniform rod of length $2a$. Let $G$ be the middle point of $AB$. Then,

$$AG = GB = a$$

This rod rests on the planes $OA$ and $OB$ which are inclined at angles $\alpha$ and $\beta$ respectively to the horizon.

From $A$, $G$ and $B$, draw perpendiculars $AL$, $GM$ and $BK$ respectively on the horizontal plane through $O$.

Since the horizontal plane through $O$ is fixed, therefore, we shall measure the distances from this plane in vertically upwards direction.

Let the system be given a small virtual displacement such that $\theta$ changes to $\theta + \delta\theta$ whereas $\alpha$ and $\beta$ remain unaltered.

Then, the equation of virtual work is

$$-w\,\delta(GM) = 0$$

$$\Rightarrow \quad \delta(GM) = 0 \qquad |\because w \neq 0$$

Since the direction of $MG$ from the fixed point $M$ to the point of application $G$ of the weight $w$ is opposite to the direction of $w$, therefore the work done by $w$ will be negative.

Reactions at $A$ and $B$ do not appear in the equation of virtual work, as they do no work.

$$\Rightarrow \quad \delta\{1/2\,(AL + BK)\} = 0 \qquad |\because G \text{ is the mid-point of } AB$$

$$\Rightarrow \quad \delta(AL + BK) = 0$$

From $\Delta OAB$,

$$\frac{OA}{\sin(\beta-\theta)} = \frac{OB}{\sin(\alpha+\theta)} = \frac{AB}{\sin\{\pi-(\alpha+\beta)\}} \qquad | \text{ by sine formula}$$

$$\Rightarrow \quad OA = \frac{2a\sin(\beta-\theta)}{\sin(\alpha+\beta)} \qquad ...(2)$$

$$OB = \frac{2a\sin(\alpha+\theta)}{\sin(\alpha-\beta)} \qquad ...(3)$$

Using (2) and (3), (1) gives

$$\delta\left[\frac{2a\sin(\beta-\theta)\sin\alpha}{\sin(\alpha+\beta)} + \frac{2a\sin(\alpha-\theta)\sin\beta}{\sin(\alpha+\beta)}\right] = 0$$

$$\Rightarrow \quad \delta\left[\frac{a}{\sin(\alpha+\beta)}\{\sin(\beta-\theta)\sin\alpha + \sin(\alpha+\theta)\sin\beta\}\right] = 0$$

$$\Rightarrow \quad \delta\{\sin(\beta-\theta)\sin\alpha + \sin(\alpha+\theta)\sin\beta\} = 0$$

$$\Rightarrow \quad \cos(\beta-\theta)\sin\alpha(-\delta\theta) + \cos(\alpha+\theta)\sin\beta\,\delta\theta = 0$$

$$\Rightarrow \quad \delta\theta\,[-\cos(\beta-\theta)\sin\alpha + \cos(\alpha+\theta)\sin\beta] = 0$$

$$\Rightarrow \quad -\cos(\beta-\theta)\sin\alpha + \cos(\alpha+\theta)\sin\beta = 0 \qquad |\because \delta\theta \neq 0$$

$$\Rightarrow \quad \sin\alpha\,\{-\cos\beta\cos\theta - \sin\beta\sin\theta\} + (\cos\alpha\cos\theta - \sin\alpha\sin\theta)\sin\beta = 0$$

$$\Rightarrow \quad \sin\theta\,(\sin\alpha\sin\beta + \sin\alpha\sin\beta) = \cos\alpha\,[\cos\alpha\sin\beta - \sin\alpha\cos\beta]$$

$$\Rightarrow \quad \tan\theta = \frac{\cos\alpha\sin\beta - \sin\alpha\cos\beta}{2\sin\alpha\sin\beta} \qquad \Rightarrow \tan\theta = 1/2\,(\cot\alpha - \cot\beta)$$

$$\Rightarrow \quad \tan\theta = 1/2\left(\frac{\cos\alpha}{\sin\alpha} - \frac{\cos\beta}{\sin\beta}\right) \quad -\left(\frac{\cos\alpha\sin\beta - \sin\alpha\cos\beta}{\sin\alpha\sin\beta}\right)$$

$$= \frac{\sin(\beta - \alpha)}{2\sin\alpha\sin\beta} \qquad \Rightarrow \theta = \tan^{-1}\left[\frac{\sin(\beta-\alpha)}{2\sin\alpha\sin\beta}\right]$$

This is another form of the expression for θ.

**Example 6:** A square of side $2a$ is placed with its plane vertical between two smooth pegs which are in the same horizontal line at a distance $c$ apart. Show that it will be in equilibrium when the inclination of one of its edges to the horizon is either π/4 or 1/2 $\sin^{-1}(a^2 - c^2/c^2)$.

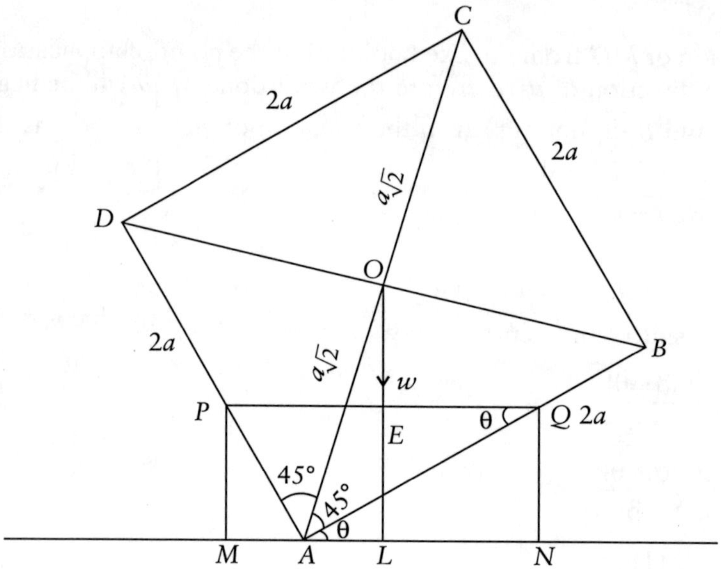


Let $ABCD$ be a square of side $2a$. Let $w$ be the weight of the square. Then, weight $w$ will act at O, the centre of the square. Let $P$ and $Q$ be two pegs in the same horizontal line. Then, $PQ = c$.

Since $PQ$ is a fixed horizontal line, therefore, the distances will be measured vertically upward from $PQ$. Let $AB$ be inclined at an angle θ to the horizon. Join $PQ$ and draw perpendiculars PM, $OL$ and $QN$ from $P$, $O$ and $Q$ respectively upon the horizontal plane through $A$. Let $OL$ meet $PQ$ at $E$.

From Δ $ACD$,

$$AC^2 = AD^2 + CD^2 \qquad \text{|By Pythagoras Theorem}$$

$$= (2a)^2 + (2a)^2 = 8a^2$$

$$\Rightarrow AC = 2\sqrt{2}\, a$$

$$\Rightarrow AO = OC = \sqrt{2}\, a \qquad \text{| by geometry} \qquad ...(1)$$

From Δ $PAQ$, $AQ = PQ \cos\theta = c\cos\theta$

$$\therefore \quad QN = AQ\sin\theta = c\sin\theta\cos\theta = EL \qquad ...(2)$$

From Δ $AOL$,

$$OL = OA\sin(45° + \theta) = a\sqrt{2}\sin(45° + \theta) \qquad ...(3)$$

$$OE = OL - EL$$

$= a\sqrt{2}\ \sin(45° + \theta) - c \sin \theta \cos \theta$ |From (2) and (3)

$= a\sqrt{2}\ (\sin 45° \cos \theta + \cos 45° \sin \theta) - c \sin \theta \cos \theta$

$= a\sqrt{2}\ (\cos \theta + \sin \theta/\sqrt{2}\,) - c \sin \theta \cos \theta$

$= a (\cos \theta + \sin \theta) - c \sin \theta \cos \theta$ ...(4)

Let the system be given a small virtual displacement such that $\theta$ becomes $\theta + \delta\theta$.

Then, the equation of virtual work is $- w\ \delta(EO) = 0$

| Since the direction of $EO$, i.e., the line joining the
| fixed point $E$ on $PQ$ to the point of application $O$
| of $w$, is opposite to the direction of $w$, therefore,
| work done by $w$ will be negative.

The reactions at $P$ and $Q$ do not appear in the equation of virtual work as they do no work.

$\Rightarrow \quad \delta\,(EO) = 0$ $|\because w \neq 0$

$\Rightarrow \quad \delta\,\{a (\cos \theta + \sin \theta) - c \sin \theta \cos \theta\} = 0$

$\Rightarrow \quad a (- \sin \theta + \cos \theta)\ \delta\theta - c (\cos \theta \cos \theta - \sin \theta \sin \theta)\ \delta\theta = 0$

$\Rightarrow \quad \delta\theta\ [a (\cos \theta - \sin \theta) - c (\cos^2 \theta - \sin^2 \theta)] = 0$

$\Rightarrow \quad a (\cos \theta - \sin \theta) - c (\cos^2 \theta - \sin^2 \theta) = 0$ $|\because \delta\theta \neq 0$

$\Rightarrow \quad a (\cos \theta - \sin \theta) - c (\cos \theta - \sin \theta) (\cos \theta + \sin \theta) = 0$

$\Rightarrow \quad (\cos \theta - \sin \theta)\ \{a - c (\cos \theta + \sin \theta)\} = 0$ $\Rightarrow \cos \theta - \sin \theta = 0$

or

$a - \mathrm{c} (\cos \theta + \sin \theta) = 0$ $\Rightarrow \tan \theta = 0$

or

$c (\cos \theta + \sin \theta) = a$ $\Rightarrow \theta = \pi/4$

or

$c^2 (\cos^2 \theta + \sin^2 \theta + 2 \sin \theta + \cos \theta) = a^2$ | squaring both sides

$\Rightarrow \quad \theta = \pi/4$

or

$c^2 (1 + \sin 2\theta) = a^2$ $\Rightarrow \theta = \pi/4$ or $1 + \sin 2\theta = a^2/c^2$

$\Rightarrow \quad \theta = \pi/4$ or $\sin 2\theta = a^2/c^2 - 1$ $\Rightarrow \theta = \pi/4$ or $\sin 2\theta = a^2 - c^2/c^2$

$\Rightarrow \quad \theta = \pi/4$ or $2\theta = \sin^{-1} (a^2 - c^2/c^2)$ $\Rightarrow \theta = \pi/4$ or $\theta = 1/2 \sin^{-1} (a^2 - c^2/c^2)$

**Example 7:** A rectangular lamina *ABCD* rests with its sides *AB*, *AD* on two smooth pegs in a horizontal line. Prove that, if the distance between the pegs is half a diagonal of the rectangle, then, *AB*, *AD* bisect the angle between *AC* and the horizon.

**Sol.** *ABCD* is rectangular lamina which rests with its sides *AB* and *AD* on two smooth pegs *P* and *Q* in a horizontal line *PQ*.

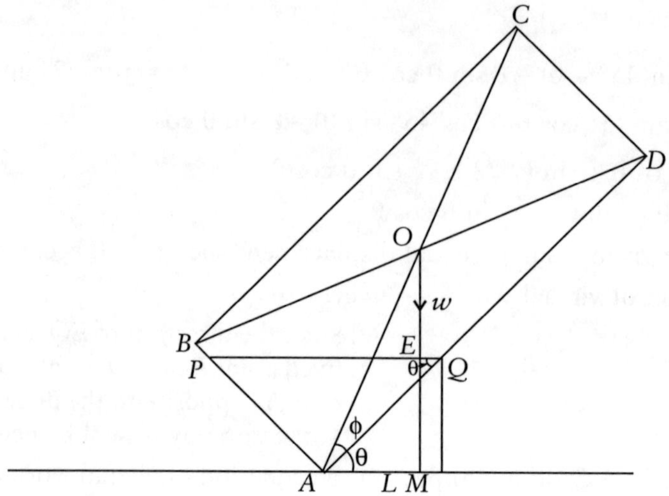


$PQ = 1/2\ AC = AO$ | Given ...(1)

where O is the point of interaction of the diagonals $AC$ and $BD$ of the rectangle $ABCD$.

Let $w$ be the weight of the rectangular lamina. Then, $w$ acts at O vertically downwards.

Since $PQ$ is a fixed horizontal line, the distances will be measured vertically upwards from $PQ$. Let $AD$ be inclined at an angle θ to the horizon.

Let $\angle CAD = \phi$

From O and $Q$ draw perpendiculars $OL$ and $QM$ respectively to the horizontal plane through $A$. Let $OL$ meet $PQ$ at $E$.

Now,

$$OE = OL - EL = OL - QM = OA \sin(\theta + \phi) - AQ \sin\theta$$
$$= OA \sin(\theta + \phi) - PQ \cos\theta \sin\theta$$
$$= OA \sin(\theta + \phi) - AO \cos\theta \sin\theta \qquad |\text{From (1)}$$
$$= OA [\sin(\theta + \phi) - \cos\theta \sin\theta] = y \text{ (say)} \qquad ...(2)$$

Let the system be given a small virtual displacement such that θ becomes θ + δθ whereas φ does not alter.

Then, the equation of virtual work is

$$-w\,\delta(OE) = 0 \qquad |\because O \text{ lies above } E.$$
$$\Rightarrow \quad \delta(OE) = 0 \qquad |\because w \neq 0$$
$$\Rightarrow \quad \delta y = 0 \quad \Rightarrow \delta[OA\{\sin(\theta + \phi) - \cos\theta - \sin\theta\}] = 0$$
$$\Rightarrow \quad OA[\cos(\theta + \phi)\,\delta\theta - (\cos^2\theta - \sin^2\theta)\,\delta\theta] = 0$$
$$\Rightarrow \quad OA\,\delta\theta[\cos(\theta + \phi) - (\cos^2\theta - \sin^2\theta) = 0$$
$$\Rightarrow \quad OA[\cos(\theta + \phi) - (\cos^2\theta - \sin^2\theta)] = 0 \qquad |\because \delta\theta \neq 0$$
$$\Rightarrow \quad \cos(\theta + \phi) - \cos 2\theta = 0 \qquad |\because OA \neq 0$$
$$\Rightarrow \quad \cos(\theta + \phi) = \cos 2\theta \quad \Rightarrow \theta + \phi = 2\theta \Rightarrow \theta = \phi$$

Hence, $AD$ bisects the angle between $AC$ and the horizon.

Again, since $AB \perp AD$, therefore, $AB$ also bisects the angle between $AC$ and the horizon.

**Example 8:** Two equal uniform rods $AB$, $AC$ of length '$a$' are freely jointed at $A$ and placed symmetrically over two smooth pegs on the same horizontal level, distance $c$ apart. A weight, equal to that of one rod, is suspended from the point $A$. Use principle of virtual work to show that in the position of equilibrium, the inclination of either rod with the horizontal is $\theta = \cos^{-1} (3c/2a)^{1/3}$, provided $3c < 2a$.

**Sol.**

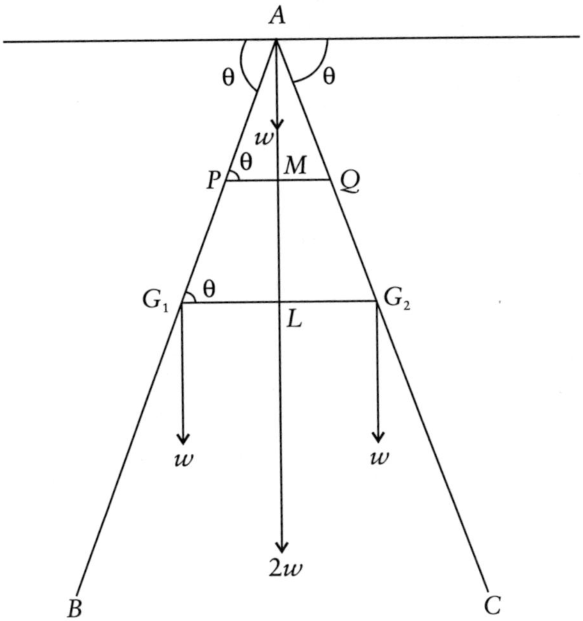


Let $w$ be the weight of each of the two rods $AB$ and $AC$. Let $G_1$ and $G_2$ be the middle points of $AB$ and $AC$. Then, the combined weight $2w$ of the two rods will act at $L$, where $L$ is the middle point of $G_1 G_2$.

A weight $w$ is also suspended from $A$. Let $P$ and $Q$ be two smooth pegs such that $PQ = c$.

Since $PQ$ is a fixed horizontal line, therefore, the distances will be measured from $PQ$.

By geometry, $PM = MQ = 1/2\ PQ = c/2$

From $\Delta\ AMP$, $\tan\theta = AM/PM = AM\ /\ c/2$

$\Rightarrow\quad AM = c/2 \tan\theta$ ...(1)

From $\Delta\ AL/G_1$, $\sin\theta = AL/AG_1$

$\Rightarrow\quad AL = AG_1 \sin\theta = a/2 \sin\theta$ ...(2)

$\therefore\quad ML = AL - AM$

$= a/2 \sin\theta - c/2 \tan\theta$ |From(1) and (2) ...(3)

Let the system be given a small virtual displacement such that $\theta$ becomes $\theta + \delta\theta$.

Then, the equation of virtual work is

$$- w\ \delta\ (AM) + 2w\ \delta\ (ML) = 0$$

$\Rightarrow\quad - w\ \delta\ (c/2 \tan\theta) + 2w\ \delta\ (a/2 \sin\theta - c/2 \tan\theta) = 0$ |From (1) and (2)

$\Rightarrow\quad - w \cdot c/2 \sec^2\theta\ \delta\theta + 2w\ (a/2 \cos\theta - c/2 \sec^2\theta)\ \delta\theta = 0$

$\Rightarrow \quad \delta\theta\,[-w\,c\sec^2\theta + 2w\,(a\cos\theta - c\sec^2\theta)] = 0$

$\Rightarrow \quad -w\,c\sec^2\theta + 2w\,(a\cos\theta - c\sec^2\theta) = 0 \qquad |\because \delta\theta \neq 0$

$\Rightarrow \quad 3w\,c\sec^2\theta = 2w\,a\cos\theta \qquad \Rightarrow \cos^3\theta = 3c/2a$

$\Rightarrow \quad \cos\theta = (3c/2a)^{1/3} \qquad \Rightarrow \theta = \cos^{-1}(3c/2a)^{1/3}$

**Example 9:** A rhombus $ABCD$, formed of four rods, each of length $\ell$ and weight $w$, jointed by smooth hinges, rests in a vertical plane on two smooth pegs in a horizontal line distance $2d$ apart. A weight $W$ is attached to the lowest hinge $C$. $B$ and $D$ are joined by a string. If angle at $A$ is $2\alpha$, show that the tension in the string is

$$\tan\alpha\left\{\frac{d}{2\ell}(W+4w)\operatorname{cosec}^3\alpha-(W+2w)\right\}$$

**Sol.**

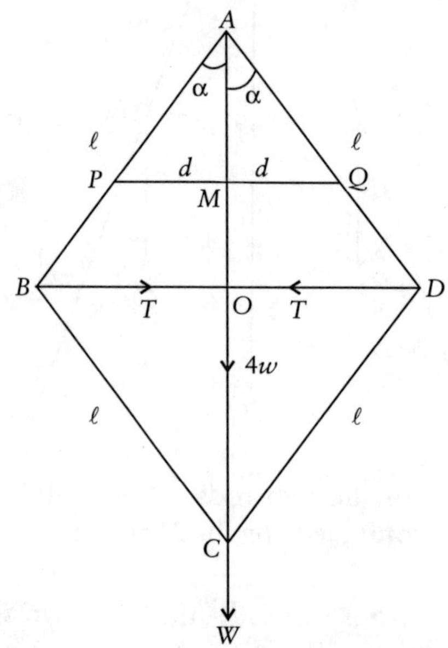


The total weight $4w$ of the four rods acts through $O$, the centre of gravity of the rhombus, in vertically downwards direction. Let $T$ be the tension in the string $BD$. Replace the string by two inward forces $T$, $T$ acting at $B$, $D$ in the directions of $BD$, $DB$ respectively. $P$ and $Q$ are two smooth pegs in a horizontal line distance $2d$ apart. Let $M$ be the mid-point of $PQ$. Then,

$$PM = MQ = d$$

Since the line $PQ$ is fixed, therefore, we shall measure the distances from $PQ$. A weight $W$ is attached to the lowest hinge $C$.

$\angle BAD = 2\alpha \qquad$ |Given

$\therefore \quad \angle BAO = \angle DAO = \alpha \qquad$ |by geometry

Now,

$$BD = 2\,BO = 2\ell\sin\alpha \qquad \ldots(1)$$

$MC = AC - AM = 2\ AO - AM = 2\ell \cos \alpha - d \cot \alpha$ ...(2)

$MO = AO - AM = \ell \cos \alpha - d \cot \alpha$ ...(3)

Let the system be given a small virtual displacement such that $\alpha$ changes to $\alpha + \delta\alpha$.

Then, the equation of virtual work is

$4w\ \delta\ (MO) + W\ \delta\ (MC) - T\ \delta\ (BD) = 0$ |Refer Ex. 3

$\Rightarrow 4w\ \delta\ (\ell \cos \alpha - d \cot \alpha) + W\ \delta\ (2\ell \cos \alpha - d \cot \alpha) - T\ \delta\ (2\ell \sin \alpha) = 0$

$\Rightarrow 4w\ (-\ \ell \sin \alpha + d\ \text{cosec}^2\ \alpha)\ \delta\alpha + W\ (-2\ell \sin \alpha + d\ \text{cosec}^2\ \alpha)\ \delta\alpha - T\ (2\ell \cos \alpha\ \delta\alpha) = 0$

$\Rightarrow \delta\alpha\ [4w\ (-\ell \sin \alpha - d\ \text{cosec}^2\ \alpha) + W\ (-2\ell \sin \alpha + d\ \text{cosec}^2\ \alpha) - T\ (2\ell \cos \alpha) = 0$

$\Rightarrow 4w\ (-\ \ell \sin \alpha + d\ \text{cosec}^2\ \alpha) + W\ (-2\ell \sin \alpha + d\ \text{cosec}^2\ \alpha) + T\ (2\ell \cos \alpha\ ) = 0$ $|\because \delta\alpha \neq 0$

$\Rightarrow T\ (2\ell \cos \alpha) = d\ (4w + W)\ \text{cosec}^2\ \alpha - 2\ell\ (2w + W) \sin \alpha$

$\Rightarrow T = d/2\ell\ (4w + W)\ \text{cosec}^2\ \alpha/\cos \alpha - (2w + W) \sin \alpha/\cos \alpha$

$\Rightarrow T = d/2\ell\ (4w + W)\ \text{cosec}^2/\sin \alpha\ \sin \alpha/\cos \alpha - (2w + W) \tan \alpha$

$\Rightarrow T \tan \alpha\ \{d/2\ell\ (4w + W)\ \text{cosec}^3\ \alpha - (2w + W)\}$

**Example 10:** A rhombus $ABCD$, formed of four light rods each of length '$a$' smoothly jointed together, rests in a vertical plane with $AC$ vertical and $BC$, $CD$ in contact with smooth pegs in the same horizontal line distance '$c$' apart; $B$, $D$ being kept apart by alight rod of length $b$. Show that a weight $w$ placed at the highest point $A$ will produce in $BD$ a thrust.

$$w\frac{2a^2c - b^3}{b^2\sqrt{4a^2 - b^2}}$$

**Sol.** Let $P$, $Q$ be two smooth pegs in the same horizontal line $PQ$ distance $c$ apart. Let $M$ be mid-point of $PQ$.

Then,

$PM = MQ = c/2$

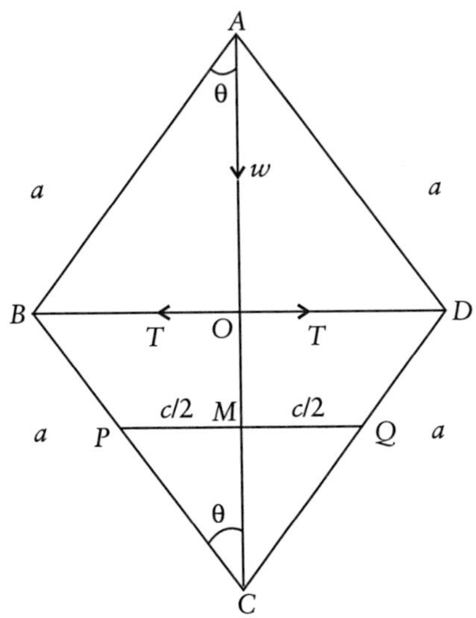

Let each light rod make an angle θ with the vertical. Let O be the C.G. of the rhombus. Let T be the thrust in the rod *BD*.

Replace the rod *BD* by introducing two outward forces, *T*, *T* at *B*, *D* in the directions *DB*, *BD* respectively. Since *PQ* is a fixed horizontal line, therefore, the distances will be measured from *PQ*.

Now,

$$AM = AC - MC = 2\,AO - MC$$

$$= 2a\cos\theta - c/2\cot\theta \qquad \text{...(1)}$$

$$BD = 2\,BO = 2\,AB\sin\theta = 2a\sin\theta = \ell \text{ (say)} \qquad \text{...(2)}$$

Let the system be given a small virtual displacement such that θ changes to θ + δθ and ℓ changes to ℓ + θℓ.

Then, the equation of virtual work is

$$-w\,\delta(AM) + T\,\delta(BD) = 0 \qquad |\because A \text{ lies above } M.$$

$$\Rightarrow -w\,\delta(2a\cos\theta - c/2\cot\theta) + T\,\delta(2a\sin\theta) = 0$$

$$\Rightarrow -w(-2a\sin\theta + c/2\operatorname{cosec}^2\theta)\,\delta\theta + T(2a\cos\theta)\,\delta\theta = 0$$

$$\Rightarrow \delta\theta\,[-w(-2a\sin\theta + c/2\operatorname{cosec}^2\theta) + T(2a\cos\theta)] = 0$$

$$\Rightarrow -w(-2a\sin\theta + c/2\operatorname{cosec}^2\theta) + T(2a\cos\theta) = 0 \qquad |\because \delta\theta \neq 0$$

$$\Rightarrow T(2a\cos\theta) = w(c/2\operatorname{cosec}^2\theta - 2a\sin\theta) \qquad \text{...(3)}$$

In the position of equilibrium,

$$BD = b \qquad |\text{Given}$$

$$\therefore \text{ From (2), } b = 2a\sin\theta$$

$$\Rightarrow \sin\theta = b/2a \qquad \text{...(4)}$$

$$\therefore \cos\theta = \sqrt{1-\sin^2\theta} = \sqrt{1-\frac{b^2}{4a^2}}$$

$$= \frac{\sqrt{4a^2-b^2}}{2a} \qquad \text{...(5)}$$

Substituting these values in (3), we get

$$T\sqrt{4a^2-b^2} = w\left\{\frac{c}{2}\frac{4a^2}{b^2} - b\right\} = w\left(\frac{2a^2c-b^3}{b^2}\right) \quad T = \frac{w(2a^2c-b^3)}{b^2\sqrt{4a^2-b^2}}$$

**Example 11:** Three rigid rods *AB*, *BC*, *CD*, each of length 2*a*, are smoothly jointed at *B* and C. The system is placed in a vertical plane so that the rods *AB*, *CD* are in contact with two smooth pegs distance 2*c* apart in the same horizontal line, the rods *AB*, *CD* make equal angles α with the horizon. Prove that the tension in the string *AD* which will maintain this configuration is $w/4 \operatorname{cosec}\alpha \sec^2\alpha\,[3c/a - (3 + 2\cos^3\alpha)]$

**Sol.**

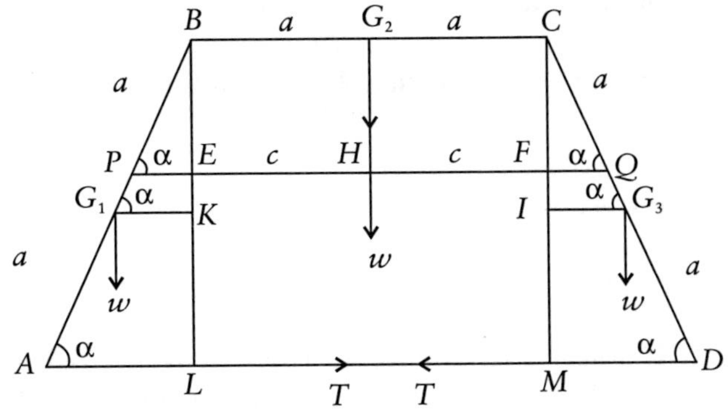


$P$ and $Q$ are two smooth pegs distance $2c$ apart. Let $N$ be the middle point of $PQ$.

Then, $PN = NQ = c$.

Let $G_1$, $G_2$, $G_3$ be the mid-points of the rods $AB$, $BC$, $CD$ respectively. Then, the weight $w$ of each rod $AB$, $BC$, $CD$ will act at $G_1$, $G_2$, $G_3$ respectively.

Draw perpendiculars $BL$, $CM$ to $AD$, $G_1K \perp BL$, $G_2H \perp PQ$ and $G_3I \perp CM$.

Since $PQ$ is a fixed horizontal line, therefore, the distances will be measured from $PQ$.

Let $T$ be the tension in the string $AD$. Replace the string $AD$ by introducing two inward forces $T$, $T$ acting at $A$, $D$ along $AD$ and $DA$ respectively.

Now,

$PE = PH - EH = c - a$ ...(1)

$G_2H = BE = PE \tan \alpha = (c - a) \tan \alpha$ |From (1) ...(2)

$KE = BK - BE = BG_1 \sin \alpha - (c - a) \tan \alpha$ |From (2)

$= a \sin \alpha - (c - a) \tan \alpha = FI$ ...(3)

$AD = AL + LM + MD = AB \cos \alpha + 2\,a + CD \cos \alpha = 2\,a \cos \alpha + 2a + 2a \cos \alpha$

$= 2\,a \cos + 2a \cos \alpha = \ell$ (say) ...(4)

Let the system be given a small virtual displacement such that $\alpha$ changes to $\alpha + \delta\alpha$ and $\ell$ changes to $\ell + \delta\ell$.

Then, equation of the virtual work is

$- w\, \delta\, (G_2H) + w\, \delta\, (KE) + w\, \delta\, (IF) - \alpha\, \delta\, (AD) = 0$ | $\because$ $G_1$, $G_3$ lie below $PQ$ and $G_2$ lies above $PQ$

$\Rightarrow\ - w\, \delta\, \{(c - a) \tan \alpha\} + w\, \delta\, \{a \sin \alpha - (c - a) \tan \alpha\} + w\, \delta\, \{a \sin \alpha - (c - a) \tan \alpha\} - T\delta\, (2a + 4a \cos \alpha) = 0$

$\Rightarrow\ - w\, (c - a) \sec^2 \alpha\, \delta\alpha + 2w\, \{a \cos \alpha - (c - a) \sec^2 \alpha\} - T\, (- 4a \sin \alpha)\, \delta\alpha = 0$

$\Rightarrow\ \delta\alpha\, [-w\, (c - a) \sec^2 \alpha + 2w\, \{a \cos \alpha - (c - a) \sec^2 \alpha\} + T\, 4a \sin \alpha] = 0$

$\Rightarrow\ -w\, (c - a) \sec^2 \alpha + 2w\, \{a \cos \alpha - (c - a) \sec^2 \alpha\} + T\, 4a \sin \alpha = 0$ | $\because$ $\delta\alpha \neq 0$

$\Rightarrow\ T\, (a \sin \alpha) = 3w\, (c - a) \sec^2 \alpha\} - 2aw \cos \alpha = w\, [3c \sec^2 \alpha - a\, (3 \sec^2 \alpha + 2 \cos \alpha)]$

$= w\, [3c \sec^2 \alpha\, [- a \sec^2 \alpha\, (3 + 2 \cos^3 \alpha)]$

$\Rightarrow\ T = w/4 \operatorname{cosec} \alpha \sec^2 \alpha - [3c/a - (3 + 2 \cos^3 \alpha)]$

## EXERCISE 3(B)

1. A square lamina of side $2a$ rests in a vertical plane on two fixed smooth pegs in a horizontal line. Show, by principle of virtual work, that if the sum of the distances of the pegs from the lowest corner is equal to a, then the square lamina is in the position of equilibrium.

   [**Hint.** Refer Ex. 6 solved

   $AP + AQ = c \sin \theta + c \cos \theta = c (\sin \theta + \cos \theta)$

   $$c\sqrt{(\sin\theta + \cos\theta)^2} = c\sqrt{1+\sin 2\theta} = c\sqrt{1+\frac{a^2-c^2}{c^2}} = a \text{ ]}$$

2. A framework $ABC$ consists of three light rods, of which $AB$, $AC$ are each of length $a$, $BC$ is of length $3a/2$, freely jointed together. It rests with $BC$ horizontal, $A$ below $BC$ and the rods $AB$, $AC$ over two smooth pegs $E$ and $F$ in the same horizontal line distant $2b$ apart. A weight $w$ is suspended from $A$. Show that the thrust in the rod $BC$ is $32bw/9\sqrt{7}\,a$.

3. A rhombus $ABCD$ is formed of four light (weightless) rods, each of length $a$, smoothly jointed at their extremities (ends) and rests in a vertical plane on two smooth pegs which are in a horizontal line, distance $2c$ apart and in contact with $AB$ and $AD$. Weights each equal to $w$ are hung from the lowest corner C and from the middle points of the two lower sides(rods), while $B$ and $D$ are connected by a light inextensible string. If $2\alpha$ is the angle of the rhombus at $A$, prove that the tension of the string is

   $$w\left(\frac{3c\operatorname{cosec}^2\alpha - 5a\sin\alpha}{2a\cos\alpha}\right) \text{ Or } \frac{w}{2}\left[\left(\frac{3c}{a}\right)\operatorname{cosec}^3\alpha - 5\right]\tan\alpha$$

4. A uniform rectangular board rests vertically in equilibrium with its sides $a$ and $b$ on two smooth pegs in the same horizontal line at a distance $c$ apart. Prove that the side of length a makes with the vertical an angle $\theta$ given by

   $2c \cos 2\theta = b \cos \theta - a \sin \theta$

## 15. Hooke's Law

According to Hooke's Law, in case of an elastic string, the tension $T$ is given by

$$T = \ell\left(\frac{\ell - a}{a}\right)$$

where

$\lambda$ = modulus of elasticity

$\ell$ = extended length of the string

$a$ = natural length of the string.

Thus,

$$T = \lambda\frac{\text{Final length} - \text{Initial length}}{\text{Initial length}} \quad \Rightarrow T = \lambda\frac{\text{Extension}}{\text{Natural length}}$$

**Note:** $\lambda$ depends upon the material of which the string is made of.

## 16. Work Done in Extending an Elastic String

We know that

$$T = \lambda \frac{x}{\ell} \quad \text{|By Hooke's Law} \quad ...(1)$$

Let the string be further extended so that $x$ becomes $x + \delta x$. Then, further displacement $= \delta x$

$\therefore$ Work done for this displacement $= - T\,\delta x$

Hence, the total work done for the extension $b$

$$= -\int_0^b T\,dx \;= -\int_0^b \frac{\lambda x}{\ell} dx$$

$$= -\frac{\lambda}{\ell}\left(\frac{x^2}{2}\right)_0^b = -\frac{\lambda b^2}{2\ell} \quad ...(2)$$

Again, work done in extending the string from extension $b$ to extension $a$

$$= -\int_b^a \frac{\lambda x}{\ell} dx = -\frac{\lambda}{2\ell}(a^2 - b^2) \;= -\frac{\lambda(a-b)(a+b)}{2\ell} \;= -\left(\frac{\lambda a}{\ell} + \frac{\lambda b}{\ell}\right)(a-b)$$

$$= -(T_1 + T_2) \times \text{Extension}$$

where $T_1$, $T_2$ are the tensions when the extensions are $b$ and $a$.

### Problems on Elastic Strings and Endless Strings

### ILLUSTRATIVE EXAMPLES

**Example 1:** Four equal jointed rods, each of length $a$ and weight $w$, are hung from an angular point, which is connected by an elastic string with the opposite point. If the rods hang in the form of a square and if the modulus of elasticity of the string be equal to the weight of a rod, prove that the unstretched length is $\frac{a\sqrt{2}}{3}$.

**Sol.**

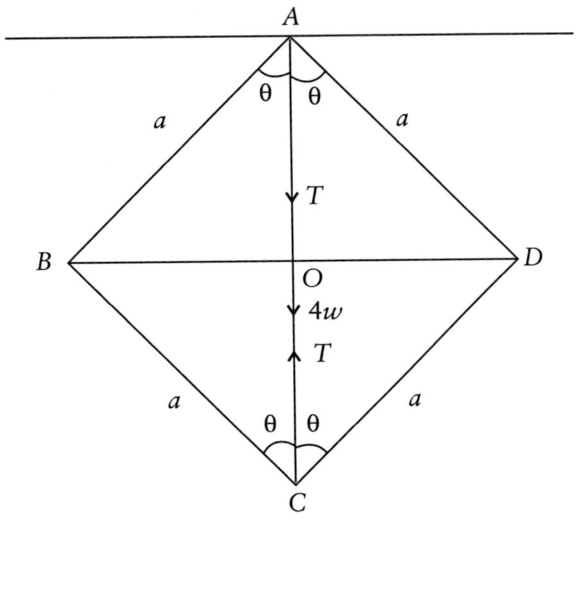

Let $AB$, $BC$, $CD$ and $DA$ be four equal jointed rods, each of length $a$ and weight $w$. Let the rods hang from an angular point $A$ in the form of a square $ABCD$. Since $A$ is a fixed point, therefore, the distances will be measured from $A$.

Let $w$ be the weight of each rod. Then, the combined weight $4w$ of the four rods will act at $O$ vertically downwards, where $O$ is the C.G. of the square $ABCD$. $AC$ is the elastic string connecting $A$ to its opposite end $C$. Let $T$ be the tension in the string $AC$. Replace the string by a force $T$ at $A$ along $AC$ and a force $T$ at $C$ along $CA$.

Let each rod make an angle $\alpha$ with the vertical.

Now,

$$AO = AB \cos\theta = a\cos\theta \qquad \text{...(1)}$$

$$AC = 2\,AO = 2a\cos\theta \qquad \text{...(2)}$$

Let the system be given a small virtual displacement such that $\theta$ changes to $\theta + \delta\theta$.

Then, the equation of virtual work is

$$4w\,\delta(AO) - T\,\delta(AC) = 0 \qquad |\because O \text{ lies below } A.$$

$$\Rightarrow 4w\,\delta(a\cos\theta) - T\,\delta(2a\cos\theta) = 0 \qquad |\text{ From (1) and (2)}$$

$$\Rightarrow 4w(-a\sin\theta\,\delta\theta) - T(-2a\sin\theta\,\delta\theta) = 0$$

$$\Rightarrow \delta\theta\,[-4w\,a\sin\theta + T\,2a\sin\theta] = 0$$

$$\Rightarrow -4w\,a\sin\theta + T\,2a\sin\theta = 0 \qquad |\because \delta\theta \neq 0$$

$$\Rightarrow T = 2w \qquad \text{...(3)}$$

Since the string is elastic, therefore, by Hooke's Law,

$$T = \lambda\frac{\text{extension}}{\text{natural length}} \qquad \Rightarrow = \lambda\frac{AC-\ell}{\ell}$$

where $\ell$ is the natural length of the string.

$$= \lambda\frac{2a\cos\theta-\ell}{\ell} \qquad |\because \text{ Tension acts only when the string is stretched}$$

$$= w\frac{2a\cos\theta-\ell}{\ell} \qquad |\because \lambda = w \qquad \text{...(4)}$$

From (3) and (4), we have

$$2w = w\left(\frac{2a\cos\theta-\ell}{\ell}\right)$$

$$\Rightarrow 3\ell = 2a\cos\theta \qquad \Rightarrow \ell = \frac{2a}{3}\cos\theta$$

In the position of equilibrium,

$$\theta = 45^\circ$$

$$\therefore \quad \ell = \frac{2a}{3}45^\circ = \frac{2a}{3}\frac{1}{\sqrt{2}} = \frac{a\sqrt{2}}{3}$$

**Example 2:** One end of a uniform rod *AB* of length $2a$ and weight $w$ is attached by a frictionless joint to a smooth vertical wall and the other end *B* is smoothly jointed to an equal rod *BC*. The middle points of the rods are jointed by an elastic string of natural length a and modulus of elasticity $4w$. Prove that the system can rest in equilibrium in a vertical plane with *C* in contact with the wall below *A* and the angle between the rods is $2\sin^{-1}\left(\frac{3}{4}\right)$.

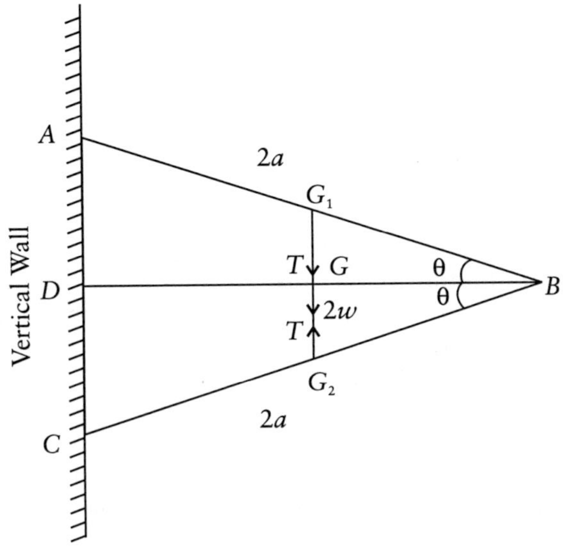


Let $G_1$ and $G_2$ be the mid-joints of the rods *AB* and *BC* respectively. $G_1$ and $G_2$ are joined by an elastic string $G_1G_2$. Let *T* be the tension in the string $G_1G_2$. Replace the string $G_1G_2$ by a force *T* at $G_1$ along $G_1G_2$ and a force *T* at $G_2$ along $G_2G_1$.

The combined weight $2w$ of the two rods acts at *G*, the mid-point of $G_1G_2$. Let each rod be inclined at an angle θ to the horizontal.

Since the point *A* is fixed, therefore, the distances will be measured from *A*.

Now,

$$G_1G_2 = 2\ G_1G = 2\ G_1B \sin\theta = 2a \sin\theta \qquad \text{...(1)}$$

Depth of *G* below $A = AD = 2a \sin\theta$ ...(2)

Let the system be given a small virtual displacement such that θ changes to θ + δθ. Then, the equation of virtual work is

$$2w\ \delta(AD) - T\ \delta(G_1G_2) = 0 \qquad |\because G \text{ lies below } A.$$

$$\Rightarrow\ 2w\ \delta\ (2a \sin\theta) - T\ \delta\ (2a \sin\theta) = 0$$

$$\Rightarrow\ 2w\ (2a \cos\theta\ \delta\theta) - T\ (2a \cos\theta\ \delta\theta) = 0$$

$$\Rightarrow\ \delta\theta\ [4w\ a \cos\theta - 2a\ T \cos\theta] = 0$$

$$\Rightarrow\ 4w\ a \cos\theta - 2a\ T \cos\theta = 0 \qquad |\because \delta\theta \neq 0$$

$$\Rightarrow\ T = 2w \qquad \text{...(3)}$$

Also, by Hooke's Law, we have

$$T = \lambda \frac{G_1G_2 - a}{a}$$

where $a$ is natural length of the string.

$$= 4w\left(\frac{2a\sin\theta - a}{a}\right) \qquad |\because \lambda = 4w$$

$$= 4w\ (2 \sin \theta - 1) \qquad ...(4)$$

From (3) and (4), we have,

$$2w = 4w\ (2 \sin \theta - 1) \Rightarrow 4 \sin \theta - 2 = 1 \qquad \Rightarrow 4 \sin \theta = 3$$

$$\Rightarrow \sin \theta = 3/4 \qquad \Rightarrow \theta = \sin^{-1} (3/4)$$

$\therefore$ Angle between the rods $AB$ and $BC = 2\theta = 2 \sin^{-1} (3/4)$

**Example 3:** A heavy elastic string, whose natural length is $2\ \pi a$, is placed normal a smooth cone whose axis is vertical and semi-vertical angle is $\alpha$. If $w$ be the weight and $\lambda$ the modulus of elasticity of the string, prove that it will be in equilibrium when in the form of a circle whose radius is

$$a\left(1 + \frac{w}{2\pi\lambda}\cot\alpha\right)$$

**Sol.** $O$ is the vertex of the cone which is fixed. Therefore, the distances will be measured from $O$ vertically downwards. $C$ is the centre of the base of the cone.

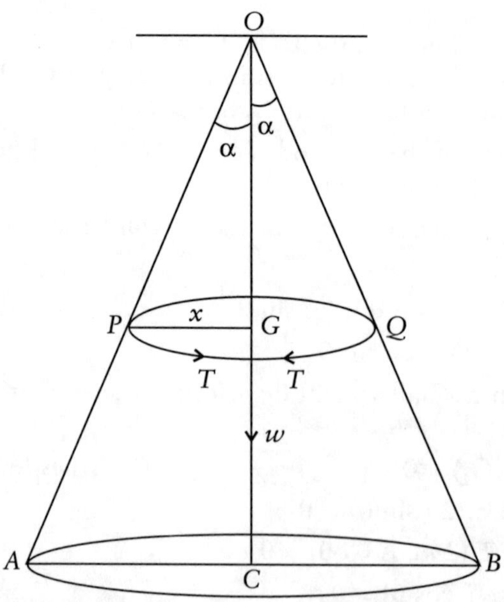


Let $x$ be the radius of the endless chain $PQ$ of weight $w$ resting in the form of a circular band round the cone. The weight $w$ of the string acts at $G$, the centre of the string. Let $\lambda$ be the tension in the string. Replace the string by two inwards forces $T$, $T$ opposite to each other. Then, by Hooke's Law,

$$T = \lambda \left( \frac{2\pi x - 2\pi a}{2\pi a} \right) \text{ where}$$

$2 \pi a$ = natural length of the string (Given)

and, $2 \pi x$ = extended length of the string, where $x$ is the required radius of the string

$\Rightarrow T = \lambda \, (x - a/a)$ ...(1)

Let the system be given a small virtual displacement such that $x$ changes to $x + \delta x$.

Then, the equation of virtual work is

$w \, \delta(OG) - T \, \delta \, (2 \pi x) = 0$ | $\because$ $G$ lies below $O$

$\Rightarrow w \, \delta(x \cot \alpha) - T \, \delta \, (2 \pi x) = 0$ $\Rightarrow w \cot \alpha \, \delta x - 2 \pi T \, \delta x = 0$

$\Rightarrow \delta x \, (w \cot \alpha - 2 \pi T) = 0$

$\Rightarrow w \cot \alpha - 2 \pi T = 0$ | $\because \delta x \neq 0$

$$\therefore \quad T = \frac{w \cot \alpha}{2\pi} \qquad ...(2)$$

From (1) and (2), we have

$$\lambda \left( \frac{x - a}{a} \right) = \frac{w \cot \alpha}{2\pi} \quad \Rightarrow \frac{x}{a} - 1 = \frac{w \cot \alpha}{2\pi\lambda} \quad \Rightarrow \quad x = a \left\{ 1 + \frac{w \cot \alpha}{2\pi\lambda} \right\}$$

**Example 4:** Two particles are connected by two given weightless strings which are placed like a necklace on a smooth cone whose axis is vertical and vertex uppermost. Show that the tension of each string is $w/\pi \cot \alpha$, where $w$ is the weight of each particle and $2\alpha$, the vertical angle of the cone.

**Sol.**

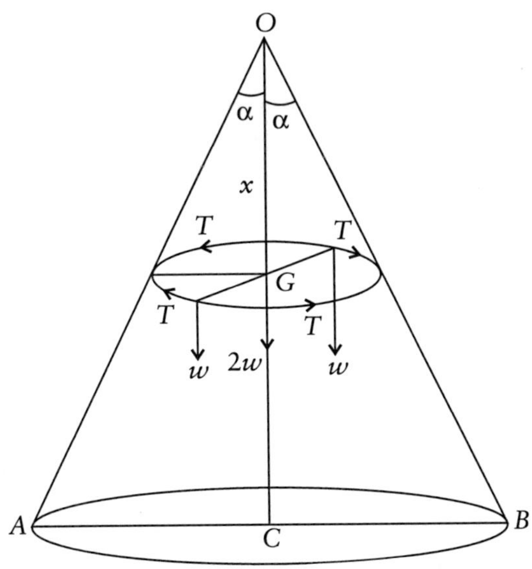


$O$ is the vertex of the cone which is fixed. Therefore, the distances will be measured from $O$ vertically downwards. $C$ is the centre of the base of the cone.

Let $x$ be the depth of each weight $w$ from O. Then, the length of each string is $\pi\ (x \tan\alpha)$. Let $T$ be the tension in each strong.

Replace each string by two inward force $T$, $T$ opposite to each other.

The combined weight $2w$ of the two particles will act at G, at a depth $x$ below O.

Let the system be given a small virtual displacement such that $x$ changes to $x + \delta x$.

Then, the equation of virtual work is

$2w\,\delta(x) - T\,\delta\,(\pi\, x \tan\alpha) - T\delta\,(\pi\, x \tan\alpha) = 0$ $\quad |\because$ G lies below O.

$\Rightarrow 2w\,\delta(x) - 2T\,\delta\,(\pi\, x\ \tan\alpha) = 0$ $\quad \Rightarrow 2w\,\delta x - 2T\,\pi \tan\alpha\,\delta x = 0$

$\Rightarrow \delta x\ \{2w - 2\,T\,\pi \tan\alpha\} = 0$ $\quad \Rightarrow 2w - 2\,T\,\pi\tan\alpha = 0$ $\quad |\because \delta x \neq 0$

$\Rightarrow T = w/\pi \tan\alpha = w/\pi \cot\alpha$

**Example 5:** A conical tent resting on a smooth floor is made up of an indefinitely great number of equal isosceles triangular elements, hinged at the vertex and kept in shape by a heavy circular ring placed on it like necklace. Show that in equilibrium, the semi-vertical angle of the cone is

$$\sin^{-1}\left(\frac{r}{h}\cdot\frac{3w'}{w+3w'}\right)^{\frac{1}{3}}$$

where $w$, $w'$ are the weight of the cone and the ring and $r$, $h$ are the radius of the ring and the slant side of the cone.

**Sol.**

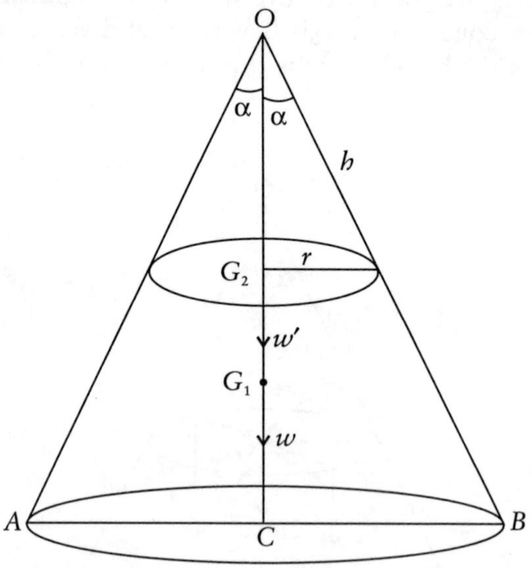


$C$ is the centre of the conical tent $OAB$. Since $C$ is fixed, therefore, the displacements (distances) will be measured from $C$ vertically upwards.

Let $G_1$ be the C.G. of the cone.

Then,

$OG_1 : G_1\,C = 2 : 1$ $\quad \Rightarrow G_1C = 1/3\ OC$

The weight $w$ of the cone will act vertically downwards at $G_1$. The weight $w'$ of the heavy circular ring will act vertically downwards at $G_2$, the centre of the ring.

Let $\alpha$ be the semi-vertical angle of the cone. Then,

$$CG_1 = 1/3\ OC = 1/3\ OA \cos\alpha = 1/3\ h \cos\alpha \quad ...(1)$$

$$CG_2 = OC - OG_2 = h\cos\alpha - r\cot\alpha \quad ...(2)$$

Let the system be given a small virtual displacement such that $\alpha$ changes to $\alpha + \delta\alpha$.

Then, the equation of virtual work is

$w\ \delta(CG_1) - w'\ \delta\ (CG_2) = 0$ |∵ $G_1$ and $G_2$ lie above C

$\Rightarrow\ w\ \delta(CG_1) + w'\ \delta\ (CG_2) = 0$

$\Rightarrow\ w\ \delta(1/3\ h\cos\alpha) + w'\ \delta\ (h\cos\alpha - r\cot\alpha) = 0$ |From (1) and (2)

$\Rightarrow\ w\ (-1/3\ h\sin\alpha\ \delta\alpha) + w'\ \delta\ (-\ h\sin\alpha + r\operatorname{cosec}^2\alpha)\ \delta\alpha = 0$

$\Rightarrow\ \delta\alpha\ [-\ w/3\ h\sin\alpha + w'\ (-\ h\sin\alpha + r\operatorname{cosec}^2\alpha)] = 0$

$\Rightarrow\ -\ w/3\ h\sin\alpha + w'\ (-\ h\sin\alpha + r\operatorname{cosec}^2\alpha) = 0$ |∵ $\delta\alpha \neq 0$

$\Rightarrow\ (w/3 + w')\ h\sin\alpha = w'\ r\operatorname{cosec}^2\alpha$ $\Rightarrow (w + 3w'/3)\ h\sin\alpha = w'\ r\operatorname{cosec}^2\alpha$

$\Rightarrow\ (w + 3w')\ h\sin^3\alpha = 3w'r$ $\Rightarrow \sin^3\alpha = r/h\ \{3w'/(w + 3w')\}$

$$\Rightarrow\ \sin\alpha = \left(\frac{r}{h}\cdot\frac{3w'}{w+3w'}\right)^{\frac{1}{3}} \qquad \Rightarrow\ \alpha = \sin^{-1}\left\{\frac{r}{h}\ \frac{3w'}{w+3w'}\right\}^{\frac{1}{3}}$$

**Example 6:** A smooth sphere of radius $r$ and weight $w$ rests in a horizontal circular hole of radius $a$. A string is wrapped once round the sphere just above the hole and then pulled tight. What must be the tension in the string so that it will just raise the sphere?

**Sol.** Let O be the centre of the sphere and $r$ be the radius of the sphere. The weight of the sphere is $w$ acting through O vertically downwards. Let C be the centre and $AB$ be the diameter of the hole in which the sphere is placed.

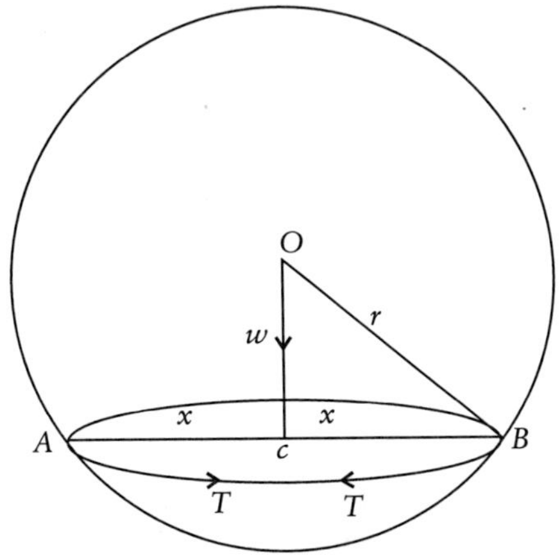


Let $x$ be the radius of the circular band (loop) of the string when it is wrapped once round the sphere just above the hole. Then, the length of the string = $2\ \pi x$.

Since the hole is fixed, therefore, the distances will be measured from the level $AB$ upwards.

Let $T$ be the tension in the string.

Replace the string by two inward opposite force, $T$, $T$.

Let the system be given a small virtual displacement such that $x$ becomes $x + \delta x$. Then, the equation of virtual work is

$$-w\,\delta(CO) - T\,\delta\,(2\,\pi x) = 0 \qquad |\because \text{ O lies above C}$$

$$\Rightarrow\ w\,\delta(CO) + T\,\delta\,(2\,\pi x) = 0$$

$$\Rightarrow\ w\delta\left(\sqrt{r^2 - x^2}\right) + T\,\delta(2\pi x) = 0 \qquad \Rightarrow\ w\frac{-2x\,\delta x}{2\sqrt{r^2 - x^2}} + T\cdot 2\pi\,\delta x = 0$$

$$\Rightarrow\ \delta x\left[\frac{-wx}{\sqrt{r^2 - x^2}} + 2\pi T\right] = 0 \qquad \Rightarrow\ -\frac{wx}{\sqrt{r^2 - x^2}} + 2\pi\,T = 0 \qquad |\because \delta x \neq 0$$

$$\Rightarrow\ T = \frac{wx}{2\pi\sqrt{r^2 - x^2}} \qquad ...(1)$$

In the position of equilibrium,

$$x = a \qquad |\text{Given}$$

$$\therefore\ T = \frac{wx}{2\pi\sqrt{r^2 - x^2}} \qquad |\text{From (1)}$$

**Example 7:** A smooth cone of weight $w$ stands inverted in a circular hole with its axis vertical. A string is wrapped twice round the cone just above the hole and pulled tight. What must be the tension in the string so that it will just raise the cone?

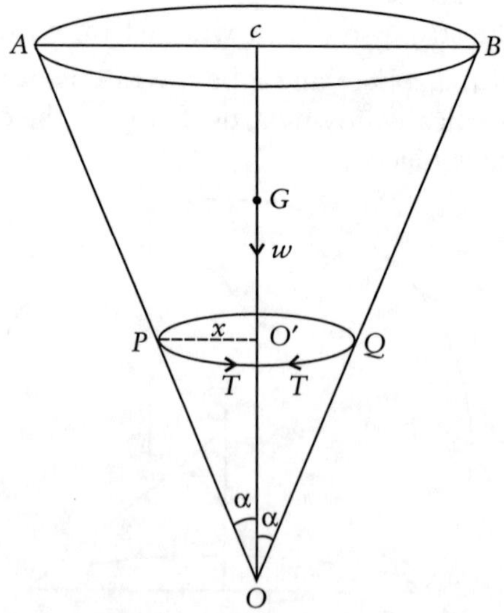


**Sol.** Let $O$ be the vertex and $C$ be the centre of the base of the cone. $PQ$ is the horizontal circular hole whose centre is $O'$. The weight $w$ of the cone will act at $G$, the C.G. of the cone such that

$$OG : GC = 3 : 1 \qquad \therefore\ OG = 3/4\ OC \qquad ...(1)$$

Since the hole is fixed, therefore, the distances will be measured from the fixed horizontal line $PO'Q$ vertically upwards.

A string is wrapped twice round the cone just above the hole. Let $x$ be the radius of the loop of the string. Then, the length of the string wrapped twice round the cone

$= 2\ (2\ \pi x) = 4\ \pi\ x = \ell$ (say)

Let $h$ be the height and $\alpha$ be the semi-vertical angle of the cone

Now, $O'G = OG - OO' = 3/4\ OC - x \cot \alpha = 3h/4 - x \cot \alpha$ ...(2)

Let the system be given a small virtual displacement such that $\ell$ becomes $\ell + \delta\ell$, whose $\ell$ is the length of the string.

Then, the equation of virtual work is

$- w\ \delta(O'G) = T\ \delta(4\ \pi\ x) = 0$ |∵ $G$ lies above $O'$

$\Rightarrow\ w\ \delta(O'G) + T\ \delta(4\ \pi\ x) = 0$

$\Rightarrow\ w\ \delta(3/4\ h - x \cot \alpha) + T\ \delta(4\ \pi\ x) = 0$ |From (2)

$\Rightarrow\ w\ (- \cot \alpha\ \delta x) + T\ (4\ \pi\ \delta x) = 0$

$\Rightarrow\ \delta x\ [- w \cot \alpha + 4\ \pi\ T] = 0$

$\Rightarrow\ - w \cot \alpha + 4\ \pi\ T] = 0$ |∵ $\delta\alpha \neq 0$

$\Rightarrow\ T = w \cot \alpha\ /\ 4\ \pi$

## EXERCISE 3(C)

1. An endless chain of weight $w$ rests in the form of a circular band round a smooth vertical cone which has its vertex upwards. Find the tension in the chain due to its weight, assuming the vertical angle of the cone to be $2\alpha$.

   [**Ans.** $\dfrac{w \cot \alpha}{2\pi}$]

2. A heavy elastic circular cord of natural length $2\ \pi a$ and weight $w$ is placed round a smooth circular cone in a symmetrical position, whose axis in vertical and semi-vertical angle is 45°. Prove that in the position of equilibrium, the tension of the cord is $w/2\pi$ and the vertical depth of the plane of the cord from the vertex of the cone is $a[1 + w/2\pi\lambda]$, where $\lambda$ is the modulus of elasticity of the cord.

### Problems Involving Curves

## ILLUSTRATIVE EXAMPLES

**Example 1:** A heavy rod of length $2\ell$ rests upon a fixed smooth peg at $C$ and its end $B$ upon a smooth curve. If it rests in all positions, show that the curve is a conicoid whole polar equation, with $C$ as origin, is

$$r = \ell + \frac{a}{\sin \theta}$$

**Sol.**

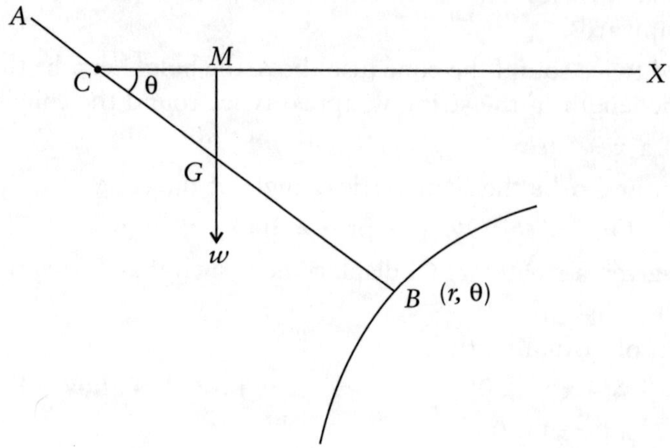


Take fixed smooth peg $C$ as pole and the horizontal line $CX$ through at as the initial line. Let the polar coordinates of $B$ be $(r, \theta)$. Then,

$$CB = r \qquad ...(1)$$

$$\angle BCX = \theta \qquad ...(2)$$

Let $w$ be the weight of the rod $AB$ of length $2\ell$, which acts at its mid-point (C.G.) $G$ vertically downwards. Draw $GM \perp CX$ from $G$.

Now,

$$AG = GB = 1/2\ AB = 1/2\ (2\ell) = \ell \qquad ...(3)$$

$$CG = CB - GB = r - = \ell \qquad |\text{From (1)} \qquad ...(4)$$

$$GM = CG \sin\theta$$

$$= (r - \ell) \sin\theta \qquad |\text{From (4)} \qquad ...(5)$$

Since $CX$ is a fixed level, therefore, the distances will be measured from this level.

Let the system be given an arbitrary small displacement, consistent with the geometrical conditions, such that $\theta$ changes to $\theta + \delta\theta$ and $r$ changes to $r + \delta r$. Then, the equation of virtual work is

$$w\ \delta(GM) = 0 \qquad |\because G \text{ lies below } M$$

$$\Rightarrow w\ \delta\{(r - \ell) \sin\theta\} = 0 \qquad |\text{From (5)}$$

$$\Rightarrow \delta\{(r - \ell) \sin\theta\} = 0 \qquad |\because w \neq 0$$

Integration yields,

$$(r - \ell)\ \sin\theta = \text{constant} = a \text{ (say)}$$

$$r = \ell\ + a/\sin\theta \qquad ...(6)$$

which gives the locus of $B$.

Hence, (6) gives the required equation of the curve which is clearly a conicoid.

**Example 2:** A uniform beam rests tangentially upon a smooth curve in a vertical plane and one end of the beam rests against a smooth vertical wall. If the beam is in equilibrium in any position, find the equation to the curve.

**Sol.**

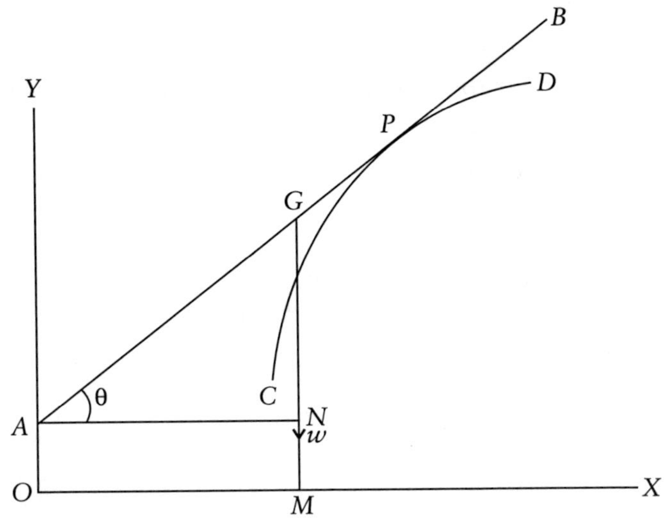


Let $AB$ be the uniform beam resting upon a smooth curve $CPD$ in a vertical plane with one end $A$ resting against a smooth vertical wall $OY$.

Through $O$, draw the fixed horizontal line $OX$. Let $2a$ be the length of the beam and $G$ be the mid-point of $AB$. Then,

$$AG = GB = 1/2\ (AB) = 1/2\ (2a) = a \qquad \text{...(1)}$$

Let $h$ be the height of $G$ above $OX$ and $Q$ be the angle which the rod makes with $OX$. Then, the coordinates of $G$ referred to $OX$ and $OY$ as the coordinate axes are $(a \cos \theta, h)$.

Since the horizontal line $OX$ is fixed, therefore, the distances will be measured from $OX$.

Let the system be given a small virtual displacement such that $\theta$ changes to $\theta + \delta\theta$ and $h$ changes to $h + \delta h$. Then, the equation of virtual work is

$$-w\ \delta(h) = 0$$

$$\Rightarrow\ \delta(h) = 0 \qquad |\because w \neq 0$$

Integration yields $\quad h = \text{constant}$

Hence, the C.G. moves in a horizontal straight line.

Now, equation of line $AB$ is

$$y - h = \tan\theta\ (x - a\cos\theta)$$

$$\Rightarrow\ y - h = x\tan\theta - a\sin\theta \qquad \text{...(1)}$$

The required curve is the envelope of the line $APB$, where $\theta$ is the parameter.

Let us find the envelope.

Differentiating (1) partially with respect to $\theta$, we have

$$0 = x\sec^2\theta - a\cos\theta \qquad \Rightarrow x\sec^2\theta = a\cos\theta$$

$$\Rightarrow\ x = a\cos^3\theta \qquad \text{...(2)}$$

Substituting this value of $x$ in (1), we get

$y - h = a \cos^3 \theta \tan \theta - a \sin \theta = a \sin \theta \cos^2 \theta - a \sin \theta$

$= a \sin \theta (\cos^2 \theta - 1) = -a \sin^3 \theta$ ...(3)

From (2) and (3), we get

$x^{2/3} + (y - h)^{2/3} = (a \cos^3 \theta)^{2/3} + (-a \sin^3 \theta)^{2/3} = a^{2/3} \cos^2 \theta + a^{2/3} \sin^2 \theta$

$= a^{2/3} (\cos^2 \theta + \sin^2 \theta) = a^{2/3}$ ...(4)

Equation (4) gives the required equation of the curve.

**Example 3:** A smooth parabolic wire is fixed with its axis vertical and vertex downwards and in it is placed a uniform rod of length $2\ell$ with its ends resting on the wire. Show that, for equilibrium, the rod is either horizontal, or makes with the horizontal an angle $\theta$ given by $\cos^2 \theta = 2a/\ell$, $4a$ being the latus rectum of the parabola.

**Sol.** Let $AB$ be the given rod of length $2\ell$ with it ends $A$ and $B$ resting on the wire.

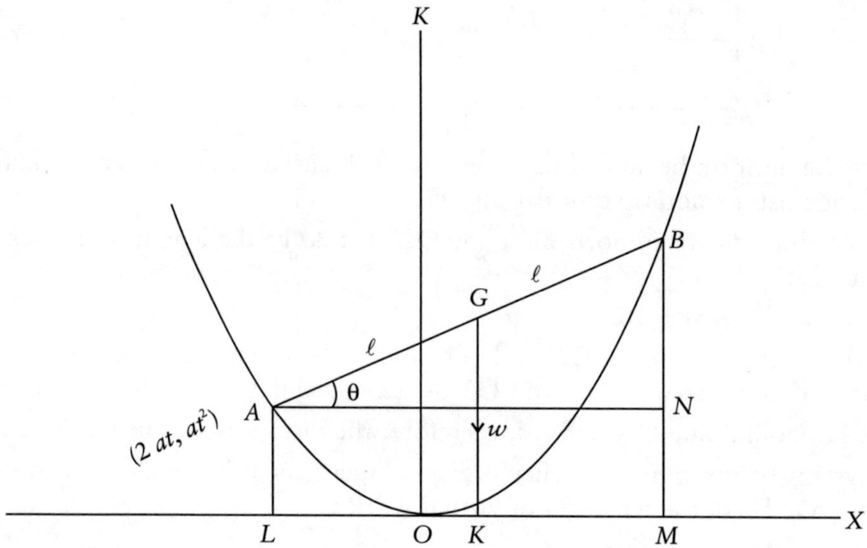


Take the axis $OY$ of the parabola as the $Y$-axis and a line $OX$ passing through $O$ and perpendicular to $OY$ as the $X$-axis.

Then, the equation of the given parabolic arc is

$x^2 = 4\,ay$ ...(1)

Draw $AL \perp LM$, $BM \perp LM$ and $AN \perp BM$.

Let the coordinates of $A$ be $(2\,at, at^2)$.

Let the rod $AB$ make an angle $\theta$ with the $X$-axis. Then,

$AN = 2\ell \cos \theta \qquad \Rightarrow BN = 2\ell \sin \theta$

Therefore, the coordinates of $B$ are

$(2at + 2\ell \cos \theta, at^2 + 2\ell \sin \theta)$

$\because$ $B$ lies on the parabola ...(1)

$\therefore \quad (2at + 2\ell \cos\theta)^2 = 4a\,(at^2 + 2\ell \cos\theta)$

$\Rightarrow \; 4\ell^2 \cos^2\theta + 8\,at\,\ell \cos\theta = 8\,a\ell \sin\theta \quad \Rightarrow 2at\,\ell \cos\theta = 2\,a\ell \sin\theta - \ell^2 \cos^2\theta$

$\Rightarrow \; t = \tan\theta - \ell/2a \cos\theta$ ...(2)

Since $LM$ is fixed, therefore, the distances will be measured from $LM$ vertically upwards.

Let $w$ be the weight of the rod acting at its middle point $G$. Draw $GK \perp LM$.

Let the rod be given a small virtual displacement such that $\theta$ changes into $\theta + \delta\theta$. Then the equation of virtual work is

$-\,w\,\delta\,(GK) = 0$ $\quad |\because G$ lies above $LM$. ...(3)

Now,

$GK = 1/2\,(AL + BM)$ $\quad$ |by geometry

$= 1/2$ (ordinate of $A$ + ordinate of $B$)

$= 1/2\,[at^2 + (at^2 + 2\ell \sin\theta)] = 1/2\,(2at^2 + 2\ell \sin\theta) = at^2 + \ell \sin\theta$

$= a\,(\tan\theta - \ell/2a \cos\theta)^2 + \ell \sin\theta = a \tan^2\theta + \ell^2/4a \cos^2\theta$ ...(4)

Putting the value of $GK$ from (4) in (3), we get

$-\,w\,\delta\,(a \tan^2\theta + \ell^2/4a \cos^2\theta) = 0$

$\Rightarrow \quad \delta\,(a \tan^2\theta + \ell^2/4a \cos^2\theta) = 0$ $\quad |\because w \neq 0$

$\Rightarrow \quad 2a \tan\theta \sec^2\theta\,\delta\theta + \ell^2/4a\,(-2\cos\theta \sin\theta\,\delta\theta) = 0$

$\Rightarrow \quad \delta\theta\,[2a \tan\theta \sec^2\theta - \ell^2/2a \cos\theta \sin\theta] = 0$

$\Rightarrow \quad 2a \tan\theta \sec^2\theta - \ell^2/2a \cos\theta \sin\theta = 0$ $\quad |\because \delta\theta \neq 0$

$\Rightarrow \quad 2a\dfrac{\sin\theta}{\cos^3\theta} - \dfrac{\ell^2}{2a}\cos\theta \sin\theta = 0 \quad \Rightarrow \sin\theta\left(\dfrac{2a}{\cos^3\theta} - \dfrac{\ell^2 \cos\theta}{2a}\right) = 0$

$\Rightarrow$ Either $\sin\theta = 0$ which gives $\theta = 0$, i.e., in the position of equilibrium, the rod is horizontal

Or $\quad \dfrac{2a}{\cos^3\theta} - \dfrac{\ell^2 \cos\theta}{2a} = 0$

$\Rightarrow \quad \dfrac{4a^2 - \ell^2 \cos^4\theta}{2a\cos^3\theta} = 0$

$\Rightarrow \quad 4a^2 - \ell^2 \cos^4\theta = 0$

$\Rightarrow \quad \cos^4\theta = 4a^2/\ell^2 \quad \Rightarrow \cos^2\theta = 2a/\ell$

which gives the inclined position of the rod in the position of equilibrium.

**Example 4:** On a fixed circular wire with centre $O$ and radius $r$ in a vertical plane slide two small smooth rings $A$ and $B$, each of weight $w$. The rings are jointed by a light inextensible string of length $2a$ ($< 2r$) on which slides a small smooth ring $C$ of weight $P$.

Prove that for equilibrium both parts of the string are vertical or else $P$ is at a distance from the centre of the wire equal to $\left\{\dfrac{w}{w+P}(r^2 - a^2)\right\}^{1/2}$.

**Sol.**

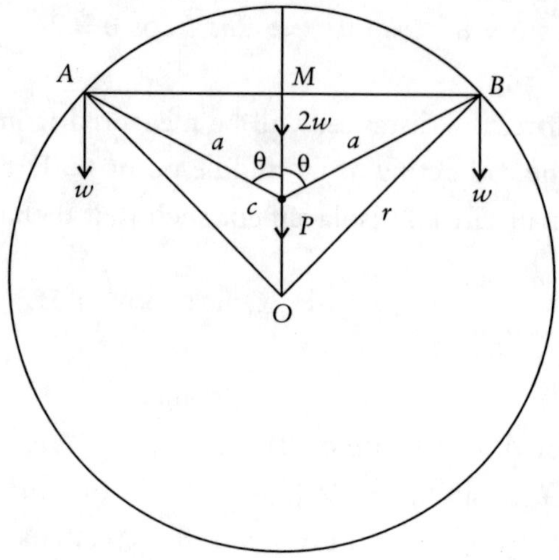


In the position of equilibrium, the ring $C$ will rest symmetrically with respect to the rings $A$ and $B$.

Since the length of the string in $2a$, therefore,

$$AC = BC = a$$

Join $AB$. Draw vertical line $OC$ and produce it to meet $AB$ at $M$.

Let the portion $CA$ and $CB$ of the string be inclined at an angle $\theta$ to the vertical. Let $OC = z$. Then, from $\Delta OBC$.

$$\cos(\angle OCB) = \frac{OC^2 + CB^2 + OB^2}{2OC \cdot CB}$$

$$\Rightarrow \quad \cos(\pi - \theta) = \frac{z^2 + a^2 + r^2}{2za}$$

$$\Rightarrow \quad \cos\theta = \frac{r^2 - a^2 - z^2}{2az} \qquad ...(1)$$

Also,

$$OM = OC + CM = z + BC\cos\theta$$

$$= z + a\left(\frac{r^2 - a^2 - z^2}{2az}\right) \qquad |\text{From (1)}$$

$$= \frac{z^2 + r^2 - a^2}{2z} \qquad ...(2)$$

Since O is fixed, therefore, the distances will be measured from O vertically upwards.

Let the system be given a small virtual displacement such that $z$ alters to $z + \delta z$. Then, the equation of virtual work is

$$-2w\,\delta(OM) - P\,\delta\,(OC) = 0$$

| ∵ $M$ and $P$ are above O; the combined weight $2w$ of the two rings acts at $M$, the mid-point of $AB$ vertically downwards.

$$\Rightarrow \quad 2w\,\delta\,(OM) + P\,\delta\,(OC) = 0 \quad \Rightarrow 2w\delta\left(\frac{z^2+r^2-a^2}{2z}\right) + P\delta(z) = 0$$

$$\Rightarrow \quad w\delta\left(z+\frac{r^2-a^2}{z}\right) + P\delta(z) = 0 \quad \Rightarrow w\left(\delta z - \frac{r^2-a^2}{z^2}\delta z\right) + P\delta z = 0$$

$$\Rightarrow \quad \delta z\left[w\left\{1-\frac{r^2-a^2}{z^2}\right\}+P\right] = 0 \quad \Rightarrow w\left\{1-\frac{r^2-a^2}{z^2}\right\}+P = 0 \qquad | \because \delta z \neq 0$$

$$\Rightarrow \quad P+w = w\left(\frac{r^2-a^2}{z^2}\right) \qquad \Rightarrow z^2 = \frac{w(r^2-a^2)}{P+w} \qquad \Rightarrow z = OC = \left\{\frac{w(r^2-a^2)}{P+w}\right\}^{1/2}$$

## EXERCISE 3(D)

1. One end of a beam rests against a smooth vertical wall and the other end on a smooth curve in a vertical plane perpendicular to the wall. If the beam rests in all positions, show that the curve is an ellipse whose major axis lies along the horizontal line described by the centre of gravity of the beam.
2. A small heavy ring $P$ slides on a smooth wire whose plane is vertical and is connected by a string passing over a small pulley O in the plane of the curve with weight $w$ which hangs freely. If the ring is in equilibrium in any position on the wire, show that the form of the latter must be that of a conic section whose focus is at the pulley.
3. Two small rings of equal weight slide on a fixed elliptical wire whose major axis is vertical. They are connected by a string which passes over a small smooth peg at the upper focus. Show that the weights will be in equilibrium wherever they are placed.
4. Two heavy rings slide on a smooth parabolic wire whose axis is horizontal and plane vertical and are connected by a string passing round a smooth peg at the focus. Prove that in the position of equilibrium, their weights are proportional to the vertical depths, below the axis.
5. Two uniform straight rods $PQ$, $P'Q$ in all respects alike are smoothly jointed at $Q$, and $P$, $P'$ carry small rings which slide on a smooth fixed parabolic wire whose axis is vertical and vertex upwards. Prove that in the symmetrical position of equilibrium, the angle either rod makes with the horizontal is $\sin^{-1}\left\{\frac{aW}{\ell(W+w)}\right\}$, where $W$ is the weight of either rod, $w$ the weight of either ring, $\ell$ the length of either rod and $4a$ the latus rectum of the parabola.
6. Two small rings of equal weights slide on a smooth wire in the shape of a parabola whose axis is vertical and vertex upwards, and attract one another with a force which varies as the distance. If they can rest in any symmetrical position on the curve, show that they will rest in all symmetrical positions.

## MISCELLANEOUS ILLUSTRATING EXAMPLES

**Example 1:** A uniform triangular lamina $ABC$ has a right angle at $C$ and rests in a vertical plane with its sides in contact with two smooth pegs $D$, $E$ in the same horizontal plane, the vertex $C$ being downwards. Prove that, in equilibrium, $AC$ makes an angle $\theta$ with the horizontal, where

$$AC \cos \theta - BC \sin \theta = 3\, DE \cos 2\theta$$

**Sol.** $AMC$ is the given uniform triangular lamina, with right angle at $C$, resting in a vertical plane with its sides $BC$ and $AC$ in contact with two smooth pegs $D$ and $E$ in the same horizontal plane.

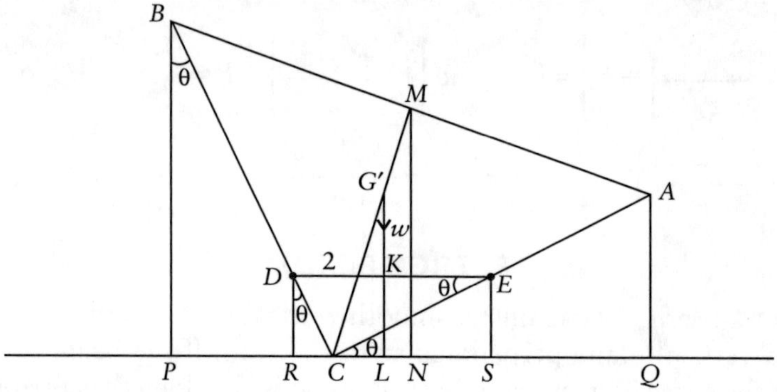


Let $M$ be the mid-point of $AB$.

Join $CM$. Then, clearly, $CM$ is a median of the triangle $ABC$.

Let $G$ be the centre of gravity of the triangle $ABC$. Then, $G$ will lie on $CM$ such that $CG : GM = 2 : 1$.

Draw perpendiculars $BP$, $DR$, $GL$, $MN$, $ES$ and $AQ$ from $B$, $D$, $G$, $M$, $E$ and $A$ respectively to $PQ$, the horizontal through $C$.

Let $\angle ACQ = \theta$

Then, $\angle CBP = \theta$

Since $DE$ is a fixed horizontal line, therefore, the distances will be measured from $DE$ vertically upwards.

Since $M$ is the mid-point of $AB$, therefore,

$MN = 1/2\,(AQ + BP)$ |by geometry

$= 1/2\,(AC \sin \theta + BC \cos \theta)$ ...(1)

$\therefore$ $G$ divides $CM$ in the ration $2 : 1$ $\therefore$ $GL = 2/3$ MN

$= 2/3 \cdot 1/2\,(AC \sin \theta + BC \cos \theta)$ |From (1)

$= 1/3\,(AC \sin \theta + BC \cos \theta)$ ...(2)

From $\Delta\, CED$,

$CE = DE \cos \theta$ ...(3)

From $\Delta\, CES$,

$ES = CE \sin \theta$

$= DE \cos \theta \sin \theta$ |From (2) ...(4)

$\therefore \quad GK = GL - KL = GL - ES$

$= 1/3\ (AC \sin\theta + BC \cos\theta) - DE \cos\theta \sin\theta$ ...(5)

Let the system be given a small virtual displacement such that $\theta$ changes to $\theta + \delta\theta$. Then, the equation of virtual work is

$-\ \delta(GK) = 0$ where $w$ is the weight of the triangular lamina $ABC$. $|\because G$ lies above $K$

$\delta(GK) = 0$ $\quad |\because w \neq 0$

$\Rightarrow \delta[1/3\ (AC \sin\theta + BC \cos\theta) - DE \cos\theta \sin\theta] = 0$ |From (5)

$\Rightarrow 1/3\ (AC \cos\theta - BC \sin\theta)\ \delta\theta - DE\ (\cos^2\theta - \sin^2\theta)\ \delta\theta = 0$

$\Rightarrow 1/3\ (AC \cos\theta - BC \sin\theta) - DE \cos 2\theta = 0$ $\quad |\because \delta\theta \neq 0$

$\Rightarrow AC \cos\theta - MC \sin\theta = 3DE \cos 2\theta$

**Example 2:** An isosceles triangular lamina with its plane vertical rests with its vertex downwards between two smooth pegs in the same horizontal line. Show that there will be equilibrium if the base makes an angle $\sin^{-1}(\cos^2\alpha)$ with the vertical, $2\alpha$ being the vertical angle of the lamina and the length of the base being three times the distance between the pegs.

**Sol.**

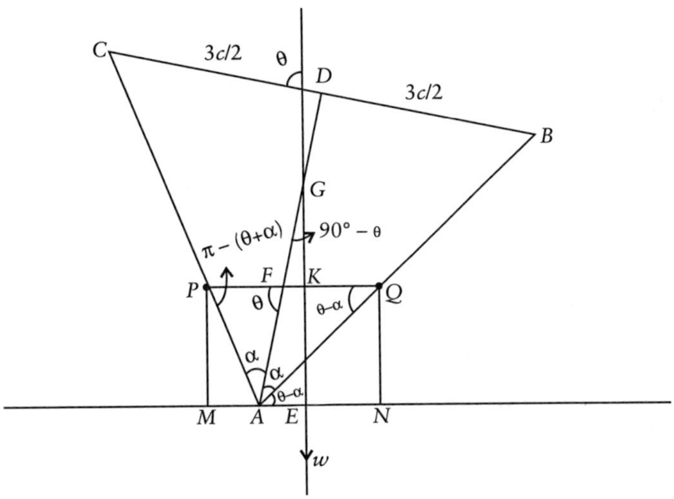


$ABC$ is the given isosceles triangular lamina whose plane is vertical and it rests with its vertex $A$ downwards between two smooth pegs $P$ and $Q$ in the same horizontal line $PQ$. Let $PQ = c$.

Then, $BC = 3c$.

Let $D$ be the mid-point of $BC$. Then, $BD = DC = 3c/2$

Let the base $BC$ make an angle $\theta$ with the vertical. Let $w$ be the weight of the triangular lamina. Then,

$w$ acts at $G$, the C.G. of $\Delta\ ABC$ vertically downwards.

By geometry, $G$ will lie on the median $AD$ such that

$AG : GD = 2 : 1 \quad \therefore \quad AG = 2/3\ AD$

Since $PQ$ is a fixed horizontal line, therefore, the distances will be measured from this line vertically upwards.

Let the system be given a small virtual displacement such that $\theta$ becomes $\theta + \delta\theta$. Then, the equation of virtual work is

$- w\,\delta(GK) = 0$ |$\because$ $G$ is above $PQ$.

$\Rightarrow \delta(GK) = 0$ |$\because$ $w \neq 0$ ...(1)

Now, from $\Delta\, ABD$,

$AD = BD \cot\alpha = 3c/2 \cot\alpha$ ...(2)

$\therefore\quad AG = 2/3\, AD = c\cot\alpha$ |From (2) ...(3)

$GE = AD \sin\angle GAE = c\cot\alpha \sin(\alpha + \theta - \alpha)$

$= c\cot\alpha\sin\theta$ ...(4)

From $\Delta\, APQ$,

$$\frac{AQ}{\sin\{\pi - (\theta+\alpha)\}} = \frac{PQ}{\sin 2\alpha}$$ |by sine formula

$$\Rightarrow \frac{AQ}{\sin(\theta+\alpha)} = \frac{PQ}{\sin 2\alpha}$$

$$\Rightarrow AQ = \frac{c\sin(\theta+\alpha)}{\sin 2\alpha}$$ |$\because$ $PQ = c$ ...(5)

$KE = QN = AQ\sin(\theta - \alpha)$

$$= \frac{c\sin(\theta+\alpha)\sin(\theta-\alpha)}{\sin 2\alpha}$$ |From (5) ...(6)

$GK = GE - KE$

$$= c\cot\alpha\sin\theta - \frac{c\sin(\theta+\alpha)\sin(\theta-\alpha)}{\sin 2\alpha}$$ |From (4) and (6)

$$= c\left\{\cot\alpha\sin\theta - \frac{\sin^2\theta - \sin^2\alpha}{\sin 2\alpha}\right\}$$ ...(7)

|$\because$ $\sin(A+B)\sin(A-B) = \sin^2 A - \sin^2 B$

From (1) and (7), we get

$$\delta\left\{c\left(\cot\alpha\sin\theta - \frac{\sin^2\theta - \sin^2\alpha}{\sin 2\alpha}\right)\right\} = 0$$

$$\Rightarrow \delta\left(\cot\alpha\sin\theta - \frac{\sin^2\theta - \sin^2\alpha}{\sin 2\alpha}\right) = 0$$ |$\because$ $c \neq 0$

$$\Rightarrow \cot\alpha\cos\theta\,\delta\theta - \frac{2\sin\theta\cos\theta\,\delta\theta}{\sin 2\alpha} = 0$$

$$\Rightarrow \cot\alpha\cos\theta - \frac{2\sin\theta\cos\theta}{\sin 2\alpha} = 0$$ |$\because$ $\delta\theta \neq 0$

$$\Rightarrow \quad \cos\theta\left\{\cot\alpha - \frac{2\sin\theta}{\sin 2\alpha}\right\} = 0$$

$\Rightarrow$ Either $\cos\theta = 0 \Rightarrow \theta = \pi/2$ which gives the symmetrical position of equilibrium.

Or $$\cot\alpha - \frac{2\sin\theta}{\sin 2\alpha} = 0$$

$\Rightarrow$ $2\sin\theta = \sin 2\alpha \cot\alpha = 2\sin\alpha\cot\alpha\cos\alpha/\sin\alpha = 2\cos^2\alpha$

$\Rightarrow$ $\sin\theta = \cos^2\alpha \qquad \Rightarrow \theta = \sin^{-1}(\cos^2\alpha)$

**Example 3:** The middle points of the opposite sides of a jointed quadrilateral are connected by light rods of length $\ell$ and $\ell'$. If $T$ and $T'$ be the tensions in these rods, prove that

$$\frac{T}{\ell} + \frac{T'}{\ell'} = 0$$

**Sol.** Let $ABCD$ be the quadrilateral. Let $P$, $Q$, $R$, $S$ be the middle points of $AB$, $CD$, $AD$ and $BC$ respectively. $PQ$ and $RS$ are the light rods.

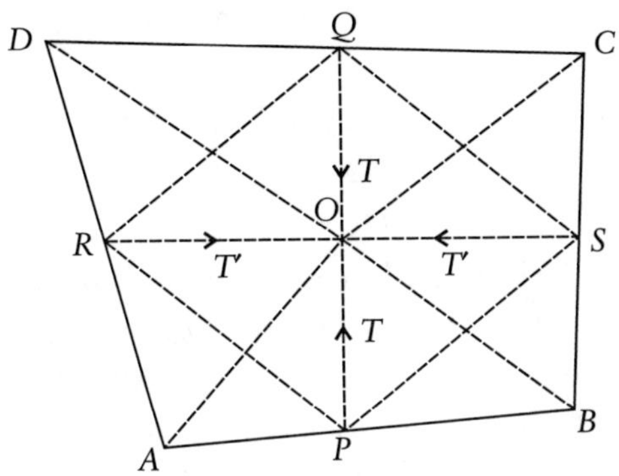


$PQ = \ell \qquad \Rightarrow RS = \ell'$

Join $PS$, $SQ$, $QR$ and $RP$. Then, $PSQR$ is a parallelogram. |by geometry

Let $O$ be the point of intersection of $PQ$ and $RS$.

Join $OA$, $OB$, $OC$ and $OD$.

Let $AB = a$, $BC = b$, $CD = c$ and $DA = d$.

In $\Delta\, OAB$,

$\because$ $OP$ is a median

$\therefore$ $OA^2 + OB^2 = 2(OP^2 + AP^2)$ |by geometry

$= 2\{(1/2\, PQ)^2 + (1/2\, AB)^2\} = 1/2\,(PQ^2 + AB^2)$

$= 1/2\,(\ell^2 + a^2)$ ...(1)

In $\Delta\, OBC$,

$\therefore$ $OS$ is a median

$\therefore$ $OB^2 + OC^2 = 2(OS^2 + BS^2) = 2\{(1/2\, RS)^2 + (1/2\, BC)^2\} = 1/2\,(RS^2 + BC^2)$

$= 1/2\,(\ell'^2 + b^2)$ ...(2)

Subtracting (2) from (1), we get

$$OA^2 - OC^2 = 1/2\ (\ell^2 - \ell'^2 + a^2 - b^2) \quad ...(3)$$

Similarly, from $\Delta\ OAD$,

$$OA^2 + OD^2 = 1/2\ (\ell'^2 + d^2) \quad ...(4)$$

From $\Delta\ OCD$,

$$OD^2 + OC^2 = 1/2\ (\ell^2 + c^2) \quad ...(5)$$

Subtracting (5) from (4), we get

$$OA^2 - OC^2 = 1/2\ (\ell'^2 - \ell^2 + d^2 - c^2) \quad ...(6)$$

From (3) from (6), we have $\Rightarrow \ell^2 - \ell'^2 + a^2 - b^2 = \ell'^2 - \ell^2 + d^2 - c^2$

$$\ell^2 - \ell'^2 = 1/2(b^2 + d^2 - a^2 - c^2) \quad ...(7)$$

Let the system be given a small virtual displacement such that $\ell$ becomes $\ell + \delta\ell$ and $\ell'$ becomes $\ell' + \delta\ell'$ whereas $a, b, c, d$ remain fixed, being the lengths of the rods $AB, BC, CD, DA$ respectively.

Then, the equation of virtual work is

$$-T\,\delta\ell - T'\,\delta\,\ell' = 0 \qquad \Rightarrow T\,\delta\ell + T'\,\delta\,\ell' = 0$$

$$\Rightarrow \quad T\,\delta\ell = -T'\,\delta\,\ell' \quad ...(8)$$

Differentiating (7), we get $\quad -2\ell\,\delta\ell - 2\,\ell'\,\delta\,\ell' = 0$

$$\Rightarrow \quad \ell\,\delta\ell = \ell'\,\delta\,\ell' \quad ...(9)$$

Dividing (8) by (9), we get $\quad \Rightarrow T/\ell = -T'/\ell' \qquad \Rightarrow T/\ell + T'/\ell' = 0$

**Example 4:** Six equal heavy rods, freely hinged at the ends, form a regular hexagon $ABCDEF$, which when hung up by the corner $A$ is kept from altering its shape by two light rods BF and $CE$. Prove that the thrusts in these rods are $5\sqrt{3}/2w$ and $\sqrt{3}/2\,w$, where $w$ is the weight of each rod.

**Sol.** The combined weight $bw$ of the six rods will act at O, the C.G. of the regular hexagon. $BF$ and $CE$ are the two light rods. Let the upper and lower slant rods make an angle $\theta$ with the vertical. Let the thrusts in the rods $BF$ and $CE$ be $T_1$ and $T_2$ respectively.

Replace the rod $BF$ by two outward force, $T_1$, $T_1$ along $FB$ and $BF$ respectively.

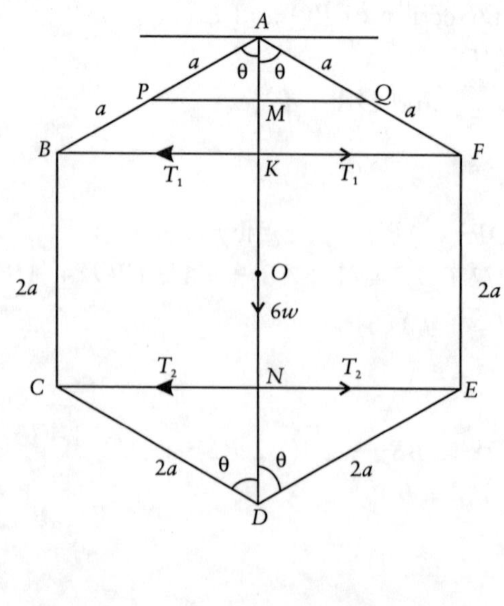

Replace the rod $CE$ by two outward forces $T_2$, $T_2$ along $EC$ and $CE$ respectively.

Since $A$ is fixed, therefore, the distances (displacements) will be measured from $A$ vertically downwards. Let $2a$ be the length of each rod of the regular hexagon $ABCDEF$.

Now,

$$BF = 2\ BK$$

$$= 2 \cdot (2a \sin \theta) = 4a \sin \theta = CE \quad ...(1)$$

$$AO = AK + KO = AB \cos \theta + 1/2\ (BC) = 2a \cos \theta + 1/2\ (2a)$$

$$= 2a \cos \theta + a \quad ...(2)$$

Let the system be given a small virtual displacement such that $\theta$ changes to $\theta + \delta\theta$. Then, the equation of virtual work is

$$6\ w\ \delta\ (AO) + T_1\ \delta\ (BF) + T_2\ \delta\ (CE) = 0 \qquad |\because O \text{ lies below } A$$

$$\Rightarrow \quad 6\ w\ \delta\ (2a \cos \theta + a) + (T_1 + T_2)\ \delta\ (4a \sin \theta) = 0 \qquad |\text{From (1) and (2)}$$

$$\Rightarrow \quad 6\ w\ (-2a \sin \theta\ \delta\theta) + (T_1 + T_2)\ (4a \cos \theta\ \delta\theta) = 0$$

$$\Rightarrow \quad 6\ w\ (-2a \sin \theta) + (T_1 + T_2)\ 4a \cos \theta = 0 \qquad |\because \delta\theta \neq 0$$

$$\Rightarrow \quad T_1 + T_2 = 3\ w \tan \theta \quad ...(3)$$

In the position of equilibrium, $\theta = 60°$

$$\therefore \quad T_1 + T_2 = 3\ \sqrt{3}\ w \qquad |\text{From (3)} \quad ...(4)$$

Now, in the second case, let us consider the equilibrium of the part $ABF$ of the figure. The forces acting on this part are as follows:

(i) Thrust $T_1$ in rod $BF$.

(ii) Resultant weight $2w$ of the two rods $AB$ and $AF$ acting through $M$ vertically downwards.

(iii) Reactions at the points $P$ and $Q$.

Let this part be given a small virtual displacement such that $\theta$ changes to $\theta + \delta\theta$.

Then, the equation of virtual work is

$$2\ w\ \delta\ (AM) + T_1\ \delta\ (BF) = 0 \qquad |\because \text{Reactions do no work}$$

$$\Rightarrow \quad 2\ w\ \delta\ (a \cos \theta) + T_1\ \delta\ (4a \sin \theta) = 0$$

$$\Rightarrow \quad 2\ w\ (-a \sin \theta\ \delta\theta) + T_1\ (4a \cos \theta\ \delta\theta) = 0$$

$$\Rightarrow \quad 2\ w\ (-a \sin \theta) + T_1\ 4a \cos \theta = 0 \qquad |\because \delta\theta \neq 0$$

$$\Rightarrow \quad T_1 = w/2 \tan \theta \quad ...(5)$$

In the position of equilibrium, $\theta = 60°$

$$\therefore \quad T_1 = w\ \sqrt{3}/2 \qquad |\text{From (5)} \quad ...(6)$$

From (4) and (6), we get

$$T_2 = 5\ \sqrt{3}/2\ w \quad ...(7)$$

**Example 5:** A frame consists of five bars forming the sides of a rhombus $ABCD$ with the diagonal $AC$. If four equal forces $P$ act inwards at the middle points of the sides, and at right angles to the respective sides, prove that the tension in $AC$ is $P \cos 2\theta/\sin \theta$ where $\theta$ denotes the angle $BAC$.

**Sol.** Let $T$ be the tension in the rod $AC$. Replace the rod $AC$ by two inward forces $T$ at $A$ along $AC$ and $T$ at $C$ along $CA$.

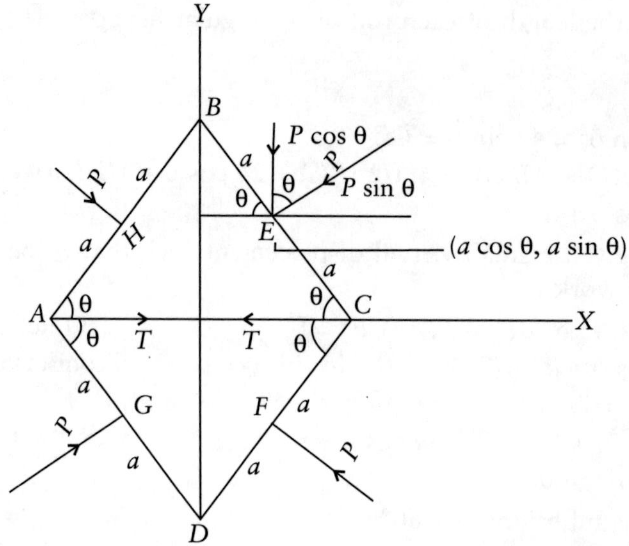


Let the system be given a small virtual displacement such that $\theta$ changes to $\theta + \delta\theta$.

Work done by $P$ at $E$ $(a \cos \theta, a \sin \theta)$

= Algebraic sum of the works done by the resolved parts of $P$, which are $X = -P \sin \theta$, $Y = -P \cos \theta$

$= X\, \delta x + Y\, \delta y$

$= (-P \sin \theta)\, \delta\, (a \cos \theta) + (-P \cos \theta)\, \delta\, (a \sin \theta)$

$= (-P \sin \theta)\, (-a \sin \theta\, \delta\theta) + (-P \cos \theta)\, (a \cos \theta\, \delta\theta)$

$= Pa\, (\sin^2 \theta - \cos^2 \theta)\, \delta\theta$ ...(1)

Similarly, the virtual work done by the force $P$ each at $F$, $G$ and $H$ is

$Pa\, (\sin^2 \theta - \cos^2 \theta)\, \delta\theta$

Total virtual work done by these forces $= 4\, Pa\, (\sin^2 \theta - \cos^2 \theta)\, \delta\theta$ ...(2)

Now, the equation of virtual work is

$-T\, \delta\, (4a \cos \theta) + 4\, Pa\, (\sin^2 \theta - \cos^2 \theta)\, \delta\theta = 0$

$\Rightarrow -T\, (-4a \sin \theta\, \delta\theta) + 4\, Pa\, (\sin^2 \theta - \cos^2 \theta)\, \delta\theta = 0$

$\Rightarrow T\, (4a \sin \theta) + 4\, Pa\, (\sin^2 \theta - \cos^2 \theta) = 0$ $\quad | \because \delta\theta \neq 0$

$\Rightarrow T \sin \theta - P \cos 2\theta = 0$

$\Rightarrow T = P \cos 2\theta / \sin \theta$

**Example 6:** A solid hemisphere is suspended by a string fixed to a point on its rim and to a point on a smooth vertical wall with which the surface of the hemisphere is in contact. If $\theta$, $\phi$ are the inclinations of the hemisphere to the vertical, prove that

$$\tan \phi = 3/8 + \tan \theta$$

**Sol.**

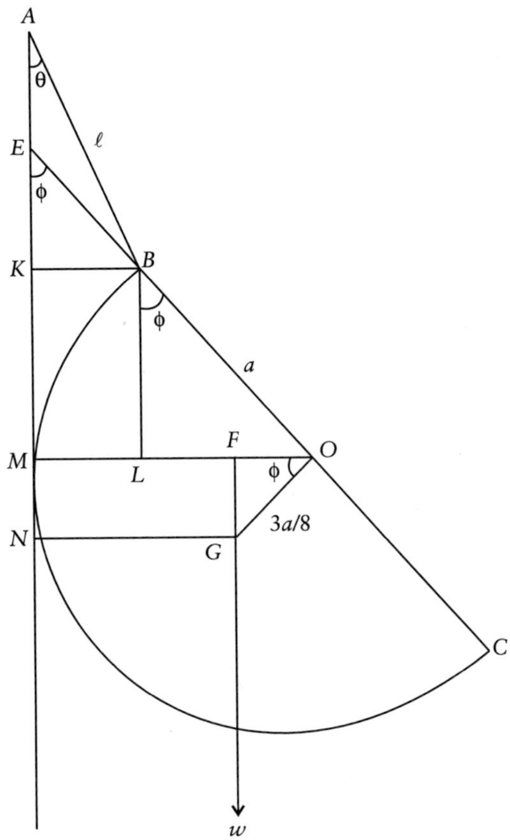


Let $AB = l$, $OB = a$

Then, $OG = 3a/8$

$$AN = AK + KM + MN = AB \cos\theta + OB \cos\phi + OG \sin\phi$$

$$= \ell \cos\theta + a \cos\phi + 3a/8 \text{ sing } \phi$$

Since the point $A$ is fixed, therefore, the distances will be measured from $A$ vertically downwards.

Let the system be given a small virtual displacement such that $\theta$ changes to $\theta + \delta\theta$ and $\phi$ changes to $\phi + \delta\phi$. Then, the equation of virtual work is

$w \, \delta (AN) = 0$ | $\because$ $G$ lies below $A$

$\Rightarrow$ $\delta (AN) = 0$ | $\because w \neq 0$

$\Rightarrow$ $\delta (\ell \cos\theta + a \cos\phi + 3a/8 \sin\phi) = 0$

$\Rightarrow$ $-\ell \sin\theta \, \delta\theta - a \sin\phi \, \delta\phi + 3a/8 \cos\phi \, \delta\phi = 0$

$\Rightarrow$ $\ell \sin\theta \, \delta\theta = a (3/8 \cos\phi - \sin\phi) \, \delta\phi$ ...(1)

Again, $a = OM = OL + CM = a \sin\phi + \ell \sin\theta$

Differentiating this, we have

$$0 = a \cos \phi \, \delta\phi - \ell \cos \theta \, \delta\theta$$

$\Rightarrow \quad \ell \cos \theta \, \delta\theta = -\, a \cos \phi \, \delta\phi$ ...(2)

To eliminate $\delta\theta$ and $\delta\phi$, dividing (1) by (2), we get

$$\tan\theta = -\left\{\frac{\frac{3}{8}\cos\phi - \sin\phi}{\cos\phi}\right\} = -\,3/8 + \tan\phi \qquad \Rightarrow \tan\phi = 3/8 + \tan\theta$$

**Example 7:** A rod $AB$ is movable about a point at $A$ and to $B$ is attached a string whose other end is tied to a ring. The ring slides along a smooth horizontal wire passing through $A$. Prove by the principle of virtual work that the horizontal force necessary to keep the ring at rest is $\dfrac{w\cos\alpha\cos\beta}{2\sin(\alpha+\beta)}$.

where $w$ is the weight of the rod and $\alpha$, $\beta$ are the inclinations of the rod and the string to the horizontal.

**Sol.**

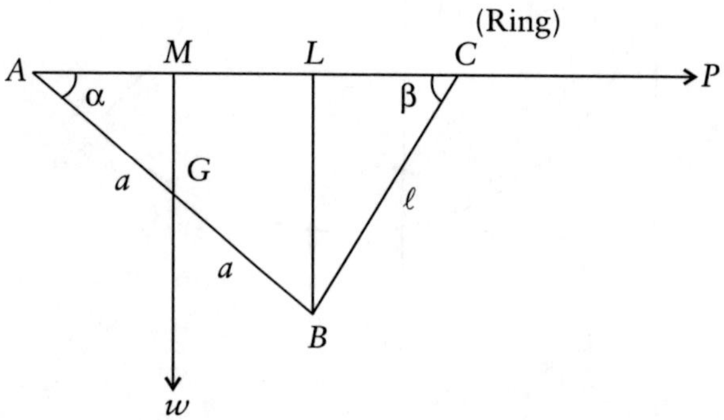


Let $P$ be the required horizontal force.

Since $A$ is fixed, therefore, the distances will be measured from $A$.

Let the system be given a small virtual displacement such that $\alpha$ changes to $\alpha + \delta\alpha$ and $\beta$ changes to $\beta + \delta\beta$.

Then, the equation of virtual work is

$$w\,\delta\,(MG) + P\,\delta\,(AC) = 0$$

$\Rightarrow \quad w\,\delta\,(AG \sin\alpha) + P\,\delta\,(AB\cos\alpha - BC\cos\beta) = 0$

$\Rightarrow \quad w\,\delta\,(a\sin\alpha) + P\,\delta\,(2a\cos\alpha + \ell\cos\beta) = 0$

$\Rightarrow \quad w\,\delta\cos\alpha\,\delta\alpha + P\,(-2a\sin\alpha\,\delta\alpha - \ell\sin\beta\,\delta\beta) = 0 \Rightarrow a\,(w\cos\alpha - 2P\sin\alpha)\,\delta\alpha$
$= \ell\,(P\sin\beta)\,\delta\beta$ ...(1)

Again,

$$BL = 2a\sin\alpha = \ell\sin\beta$$

Differentiating, we get

$2a\cos\alpha\,\delta\alpha = \ell\cos\beta\,\delta\beta$ ...(2)

To eliminate $\delta\alpha$ and $\delta\beta$, dividing (1) by (2), we get

$$\frac{w\cos\alpha - 2P\sin\alpha}{2\cos\alpha} = \frac{P\sin\beta}{\cos\beta}$$

$\Rightarrow$ $2\,P\sin\beta\cos\alpha = w\cos\alpha\cos\beta - 2P\sin\alpha\cos\beta$

$\Rightarrow$ $2\,P(\sin\alpha\cos\beta + \cos\alpha\cos\beta) = w\cos\alpha\cos\beta \Rightarrow$ $2\,P\sin(\alpha+\beta) = w\cos\alpha\cos\beta$

$\Rightarrow$ $P = \dfrac{w\cos\alpha\cos\beta}{2\sin(\alpha+\beta)}$

**Example 8:** A frame formed of four light rods, each of length $a$, freely jointed at $A$, $B$, $C$, $D$ is suspended from $A$. A mass $m$ is suspended from $B$ and $D$ by two strings each of length $\ell$ ($\ell > a/\sqrt{2}$).

The frame is kept in the form of a square by a string $AC$. Find the tension $T$ in $AC$ and show that when.

$\ell = a\sqrt{5}$, $T = 2/3\,mg$.

**Sol.**

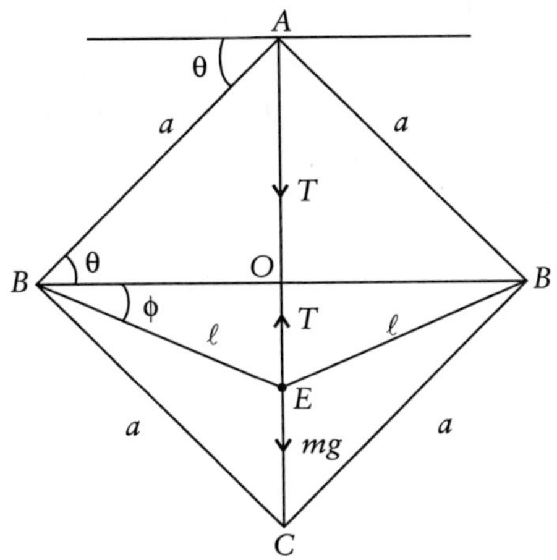


$$\ell > \frac{a}{\sqrt{2}}$$

$\Rightarrow$ $BE = > BO$ which is true.

Since $A$ is a fixed point, therefore, distances will be measured from $A$.

Let $T$ be the tension in the string.

Let the system be given a small virtual displacement such that $\theta$ changes to $\theta + \delta\theta$ and $\phi$ changes to $\phi + \delta\phi$.

Then, the equation of virtual work is

$mg\,\delta(AE) - T\,\delta(AC) = 0$ $\quad|\because E$ lies below $A$

$\Rightarrow mg\,\delta(a\sin\theta + \ell\sin\phi) - T\,\delta(2a\sin\theta) = 0$

$\Rightarrow mg\,\delta(a\cos\theta\,\delta\theta + \ell\cos\phi\,\delta\phi) - T\,\delta(2a\cos\theta\,\delta\theta) = 0$

$\Rightarrow a\cos\theta\,(2T - mg)\,\delta\theta = \ell\cos\phi\,mg\,\delta\phi$ ...(1)

From $\Delta\ AOB$,

$$OB = a \cos \theta \quad ...(2)$$

From $\Delta\ EOB$,

$$OB = \ell \cos \phi \quad ...(3)$$

Equating the two values of $OB$ from (2) and (3), we get

$$a \cos \theta = \ell \cos \phi$$

Differentiating, we get

$$-a \sin \theta\ \delta\theta = -1\ \ell \sin \phi\ \delta\theta$$

$$\Rightarrow \quad a \sin \theta\ \delta\theta = \ell \sin \phi\ \delta\phi \quad ...(4)$$

To eliminate $\delta\theta$ and $\delta\phi$, dividing (1) by (4), we get

$$\frac{\cos\theta(2T - mg)}{\sin\theta} = \frac{\cos\phi mg}{\sin\phi}$$

$\Rightarrow$ $\cot \theta\ (2T - mg) = \cot T\ mg$ $\quad\Rightarrow$ mg $(\cot \theta + \cot \phi) = 2\ T \cot \theta$

$$\Rightarrow \quad T = 1/2\ mg\ (1 + \cot \phi/\cot \theta) \quad ...(5)$$

In the position of equilibrium,

$\theta = 45°$ |As the framework is a square

$\therefore$ $a \cos \theta = \ell \cos \phi$ $\quad\Rightarrow a \cos 45° = \ell \cos \phi$ $\quad\Rightarrow \cos \phi = a/\ell\sqrt{2}$

$$\therefore \quad \cot\phi = \frac{\cos\phi}{\sin\phi} = \frac{\cos\phi}{\sqrt{1-\cos^2\phi}}$$

$$= \frac{\frac{a}{\ell\sqrt{2}}}{\sqrt{1-\left(\frac{a}{\ell\sqrt{2}}\right)^2}} = \frac{a}{\sqrt{2\ell^2 - a^2}}$$

$\therefore$ From (5), we get

$$T = \frac{1}{2}mg\left\{1+\frac{a}{\sqrt{2\ell^2 - a^2}\cot 45°}\right\} = \frac{mg}{2}\left\{1+\frac{a}{\sqrt{2\ell^2 - a^2}}\right\}$$

When $\ell = a\sqrt{5}$, then

$$T = \frac{mg}{2}\left\{1+\frac{a}{\sqrt{10a^2 - a^2}}\right\} = 2/3\ mg$$

**Example 9:** Weights $w_1$, $w_2$ are fastened to a light inextensible string $ABC$ at the points $B$, $C$, the end $A$ being fixed. Prove that, if a horizontal force $P$ is applied at $C$ and in equilibrium $AB$, $BC$ are inclined at angles $\theta$, $\phi$ to the vertical, then

$$P = (w_1 + w_2) \tan \theta = w_2 \tan \phi$$

**Sol.**

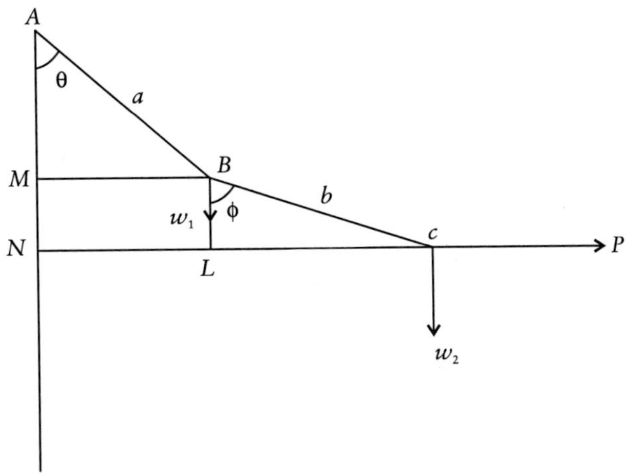


Since the point $A$ is fixed, therefore, the distances (displacements) will be measured from $A$.

$$CN = a \sin\theta + b \sin\phi$$
$$AM = a \cos\theta$$
$$AN = a \cos\theta + b \cos\phi$$

The equation of virtual work is

$$P\,\delta(CN) + w_1\,\delta(AM) + w_2\,\delta(AN) = 0 \qquad |\because B \text{ and } C \text{ lie below } A$$

$\Rightarrow \quad P\,\delta(a\sin\theta + b\sin\phi) + w_1\,\delta(a\cos\theta) + w_2\,\delta(a\cos\theta + b\cos\phi) = 0$

$\Rightarrow \quad P(a\cos\theta\,\delta\theta + b\cos\delta\phi) + w_1(-a\sin\theta\,\delta\theta) + w_2(-a\sin\theta\,\delta\theta - b\sin\phi\,\delta\phi) = 0$

$\Rightarrow \quad (P\,a\cos\theta - w_1\,a\sin\theta - w_2\,a\sin\theta)\,\delta\theta + (P\,b\cos\phi - w_2\,b\sin\phi)\,\delta\phi = 0$

Since $\theta$ and $\phi$ are independent, therefore, $\delta\theta$ and $\delta\phi$ are also independent. Therefore,

$$P\,a\cos\theta = (w_1 + w_2)\,a\sin\theta = 0$$

$\Rightarrow \quad P = (w_1 + w_2)\tan\theta$

and, $P\,b\cos\phi - w_2\,b\sin\phi = 0$

$\Rightarrow \quad P = w_2\tan\phi$

Thus,

$$P = (w_1 + w_2)\tan\theta = w_2\tan\phi$$

**Example 10:** A smooth rod passes through a smooth ring at the focus of an ellipse whose major axis is horizontal and rests with its lowest end on the quadrant of the curve which is farthest removed from the focus. Find the position of equilibrium and show that its length must be at least

$$\frac{3}{4}a + \frac{1}{4}a\sqrt{1+8e^2}$$

where $2a$ is the major axis and $e$ the eccentricity.

**Sol.**

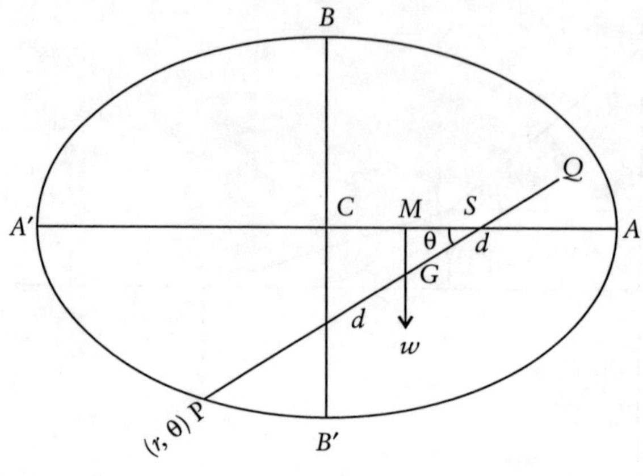


$PQ$ is the rod of length $2d$ passing through the smooth ring at the focus $S$. The weight $w$ of this rod will act through $G$, the mid-point of $PQ$.

Take $S$ as pole and $SA'$ as the initial line. Then, the equation of the ellipse is

$$- = 1 + \ \cos\theta \qquad ...(1)$$

where $\ell$ is the semi-latus rectum of the ellipse.

Let the polar coordinates of $P$ be $(r, \theta)$.

Then, $SP = r$ and $\angle A'\ SP = \theta$ $\quad\Rightarrow SG = SP - PG = r - d \quad\Rightarrow GM = (r - d)\sin\theta$

$$= \frac{\ell\sin\theta}{1+e\cos\theta} - d\sin\theta \qquad |\text{From (1)}$$

Since $AA'$ is fixed, therefore, the distances will be measured from $AA'$ downwards.

Let the rod be given a small virtual displacement such that $\theta$ changes into $\theta + \delta\theta$. Then the equation of virtual work is

$$w\,\delta\,(GM) = 0 \qquad |\because G \text{ lies below } AA'$$

$$\Rightarrow \quad \delta\,(GM) = 0 \qquad |\because w \neq 0$$

$$\Rightarrow \quad \delta\left\{\frac{\ell\sin\theta}{1+e\cos\theta} - d\sin\theta\right\} = 0$$

$$\Rightarrow \quad \ell\left[\frac{(1+\ell\cos\theta)\cos\theta - \sin\theta(-e\sin\theta)}{(1+e\cos\theta)^2}\right]\delta\theta - d\cos\theta\,\delta\theta = 0$$

$$\Rightarrow \quad \ell\frac{\cos\theta - e}{(1+e\cos\theta)^2} - d\cos\theta = 0 \qquad |\because \delta\theta \neq 0$$

$$\Rightarrow \quad d = \frac{\ell(\cos\theta + e)}{\cos\theta(1+e\cos\theta)^2} \qquad ...(2)$$

This gives the position of equilibrium of the rod.

Now, the length of the rod will be least, if $Q$ coincides with $S$, i.e., $r = 2d$.

$$\Rightarrow \quad \frac{\ell}{1+e\cos\theta} = \frac{2\ell(\cos\theta+e)}{\cos\theta(1+e\cos\theta)^2} \quad \Rightarrow \quad \cos\theta(1+e\cos\theta) = 2(\cos\theta+e)$$

$$\Rightarrow \quad \ell\cos^2\theta - \cos\theta - 2e) = 0$$

$$\Rightarrow \quad \cos\theta = \frac{1\pm\sqrt{1+8e^2}}{2e} \qquad \text{...(3)}$$

For +ve sign, $\cos\theta > 1$ which is impossible.

$$\therefore \quad \cos\theta = \frac{1-\sqrt{1+8e^2}}{2e} \qquad \text{...(4)}$$

$$\therefore \quad 2d = \frac{\ell}{1+e\cos\theta} \qquad \Big|\because r = 2d$$

$$= \frac{\ell}{1+\frac{1-\sqrt{1+8e^2}}{2}} = \frac{2\ell}{3-\sqrt{1+8e^2}} = \frac{2\ell\left(3+\sqrt{1+8e^2}\right)}{9-(1+8e^2)}$$

$$= \frac{2\ell\left(3+\sqrt{1+8e^2}\right)}{8(1+e^2)} = \frac{\ell}{4}\frac{3+\sqrt{1+8e^2}}{1-e^2}$$

$$= \frac{a(1-e^2)}{4}\frac{3+\sqrt{1+8e^2}}{1-e^2} \qquad \Big|\because \ell = \frac{b^2}{a} = \frac{a^2(1-e^2)}{a} = a(1-e^2)$$

$$= \frac{a}{4}\left(3+\sqrt{1+8e^2}\right)$$

Hence, the length of the rod must be

$$\frac{3}{4}a + \frac{1}{4}a\sqrt{1+8e^2}$$

**Example 11:** Three equal and similar uniform rods $AB$, $BC$, $CD$, freely jointed at $B$ and $C$, have small smooth weightless strings attached to them at $A$ and $D$. The rings slide on a smooth parabolic wire, whose axis is vertical and vertex upwards and whose latus rectum is half the sum of the lengths of the three rods. Prove that in the position of equilibrium, the inclination $\theta$ of $AB$ or $CD$ to the vertical is given by

$$\cos\theta - \sin\theta + \sin 2\theta = 0$$

**Sol.**

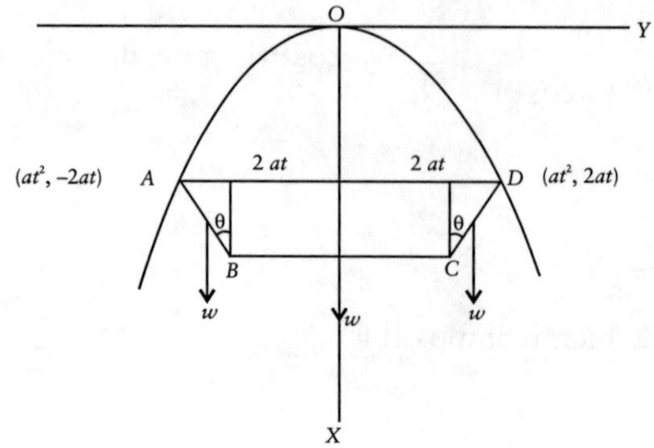


Let the equation of the parabola be

$$y^2 = 4\,ax \quad \text{...(1)}$$

$$AB = BC = CD = 2\ell$$

Latus Rectum = 1/2 $(AB + BC + CD)$ = 1/2 $(6\ell) = 3\ell = 4a$

Let $D \to (at^2, 2at)$

Then, $A \to (at^2, -2at)$

Since the line $OY$ is fixed, therefore, the displacements will be measured from $OY$.

Let the system be given a small virtual displacement such that θ changes to θ + δθ then, the equation of virtual work is

$$2\,w\,\delta(at^2 + \ell\cos\theta) + w\,\delta\,(at^2 + 2\ell\cos\theta) = 0$$

$$\Rightarrow \quad 2\,w\,(2\,at\,\delta t - \ell\sin\theta\,\delta\theta) + w\,\delta(2\,at\,\delta t - 2\ell\sin\theta\,\delta\theta) = 0$$

$$\Rightarrow \quad 6\,at\,\delta t - 4\,\ell\sin\theta\,\delta\theta = 0$$

$$\Rightarrow \quad 3\,at\,\delta t = 2\,\ell\sin\theta\,\delta\theta \quad \text{...(2)}$$

Now, $AD = 4\,at = 2\,\ell + 4\,\ell\sin\theta$ ...(3)

$$\therefore \quad 4\,a\,\delta t = 4\,\ell\cos\theta\,\delta\theta$$

$$\Rightarrow \quad a\,\delta t = \ell\cos\theta\,\delta\theta \quad \text{...(4)}$$

Dividing (2) by (3), we get

$$3t = \frac{2\sin\theta}{\cos\theta} \quad \text{...(5)}$$

From (3), $3\,\ell t = 2\ell + 4\,\ell\sin\theta$ $\quad |\because 4a = 3\ell$

$$\Rightarrow 3t = 2 + 4\sin\theta \quad \text{...(6)}$$

From (4) and (6), $2 + 4\sin\theta = 2\sin\theta/\cos\theta$

$$\Rightarrow \cos\theta - \sin\theta + \sin 2\,\theta = 0$$

## EXERCISE 3(E)

1. A smooth paraboloid of revolution is fixed with its axis vertical and vertex upwards. On it is placed a heavy elastic string of unstretched length $2\,\pi\,c$. When the string is in

equilibrium, show that it rests in the form of a circle of radius $\dfrac{4\pi ac\lambda}{4a\pi\lambda - cw}$, where $w$ is the weight of the string, $\lambda$ the modulus of elasticity and $4a$ the latus rectum of the generating parabola.

2. A prism, whose cross-section is an equilateral triangle, rests with two edges on smooth plane inclined at $\alpha$ and $\beta$ to the horizon. If $\theta$ be the angle which the plane containing these edges makes with the vertical, show that

$$\tan\theta = \frac{2\sqrt{3}\sin\alpha\sin\beta + \sin(\alpha+\beta)}{\sqrt{3}\sin(\alpha \sim \beta)}$$

3. $AB$ is a heavy beam which can turn about a horizontal axis at $A$, a cord fastened to $B$ passes over a small pulley $C$, vertically above $A$, and is tied at the other end to a weight P which moves on a given smooth curve. Show that the curve is of the form.

$4\ c\ P\ r \cos\theta + w\ \{(\ell - r)^2 - c^2 - 4a^2\} = \text{constant},$

where $AB = 2a$, $AC = c$, $\ell$ = length of the string.

4. A smoothly jointed framework of light rods forms a quadrilateral $ABCD$. The middle points $P$, $Q$ of an opposite pair of rods are convected by a string in a state of tension $T$ and the middle points $R$, $S$ of the other pair by a light rod in a state of thrust $X$. Show by the method of virtual work that

$$\frac{T}{PQ} = \frac{X}{RS}.$$

5. Four rods are jointed together to form a parallelogram, the opposite joints are jointed by strings forming the diagonals and the whole system is placed on a smooth horizontal table. Show that their tensions are in the same ratio as their lengths.

[**Hint:**

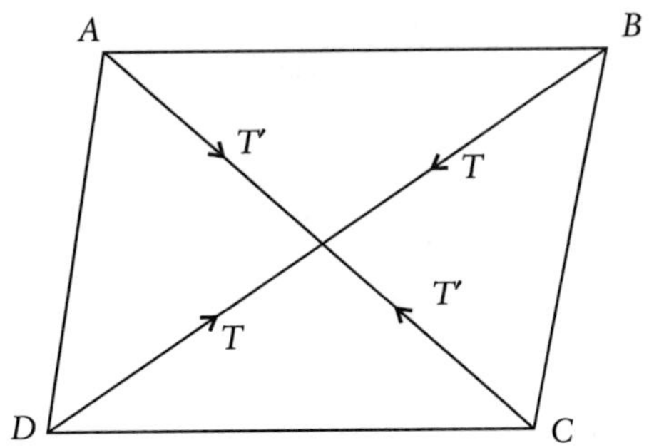


Equation of virtual work is

$$- T\,\delta(BD) - T'\,\delta(AC) = 0$$

$\Rightarrow \quad T\,\delta(BD) = - T'\,\delta(AC)$ ...(1)

Again, $BD^2 + AC^2 = 2\,(AB^2 + AD^2)$ |by geometry

$\Rightarrow \quad 2\,BD\,\delta(BD) + 2\,AC\,\delta(AC) = 0$

$\Rightarrow \quad BD\,\delta(BD) = - AC\,\delta(AC)$ ...(2)

(1) and (2) give

$$\frac{T}{BD} = \frac{T'}{AC}\;]$$

6. A parallelogram $ABCD$ is formed of four rods jointed together. Equal and opposite forces $P$ are applied inwards at $C$ and $A$ and a string connects $B$ and $D$. Prove that the tension in the string is equal to

$P \cdot BD/AC$.

[**Hint:**

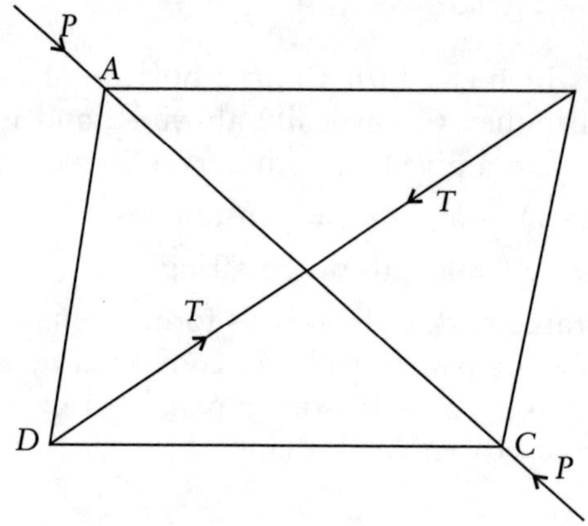


Equation of virtual work is

$$-T\,\delta\,(\text{BD}) - P\,\delta\,(AC) = 0$$

$$\Rightarrow \quad T\,\delta\,(BD) = -P\,\delta\,(AC) \qquad ...(1)$$

$$BD\,\delta\,(BD) = -AC\,\delta\,(AC) \qquad \text{|Refer Hint Q. 5} \qquad ...(2)$$

Dividing (1) by (2), we have,

$$\frac{T}{BD} = \frac{P}{AC}$$

$$\Rightarrow \quad T = P\frac{BD}{AC}\;]$$

7. A flat semi-circular board with its plane vertical and curved edge upwards rests on a smooth horizontal plane and is pressed at two given points of its circumference by two beams which slide in smooth vertical tubes. If the board is in equilibrium, prove that $w \cot \phi = w' \cot \phi'$, where $w, w'$ are the weights of the beams and $\phi, \phi'$ the angles the radii joining the centre to the points of contact of the beams make with the board.

8. $ABCDEF$ is a regular hexagon formed of light rods smoothly jointed at their ends with a diagonal rod $AD$. Four equal forces $P$ act inwards at the middle points of $AB$, $CD$, $DE$, $FA$ and at right angles to them. Find the stress in $AD$ and state whether it is a tension on a thrust.

[**Ans.** $a = P/\sqrt{3}$ ; thrust]

9. Two smooth uniform cylinders, each of radius a and weight $w$, lie on a horizontal plane with their axes parallel and at a distance $4a \sin\theta$ apart. A third equal cylinder is placed in contact with the first two, touching each along a generator and the system is held in equilibrium by an endless string which passes round the three cylinders. Prove that the tension in the string is $1/2\ w \tan\theta$.

10. An endless string of length $2\pi a + \ell$ $(6a < \ell < 8a)$, passes round three equal smooth cylinders of weight $w$ and radius $a$, having their axes horizontal and parallel, and two of these rest on a horizontal plane, and the third lying between them. Prove that the tension in the string is

$$\frac{1}{2}w\frac{\ell - 4a}{\sqrt{(8a-\ell)\ell}}$$

11. A heavy particle $P$ is placed on the concave side of smooth vertical circle whose lowest point is $A$ and highest point $B$. If the particle is acted upon by two forces, in the directions $AP$ and $BP$, equal to $\mu\ BP$ and $\mu\ AP$ respectively, prove that in the position of equilibrium.

$$\tan\theta = \frac{2\mu a}{w}$$

where $\theta$ is the angle made with the vertical to the radius to $P$, $w$ the weight of the particle and $a$ the radius of the circle.

12. A quadrilateral $ABCD$ formed of four uniform rods freely jointed to each other at their ends, the rods $AB$, $AD$ being equal and also the rods $BC$, $CD$ are freely suspended from the point $A$. A string joins $A$ to $C$ and is such that $ABC$ is a right angle. Apply the principle of virtual work to show that the tension of the string is

$$(w + w')\sin^2\theta + w',$$

where $w$ is the weight of an upper rod and $w'$ of a lower rod and $2\theta$ is equal to the angle $BAD$.

13. $ABCD$ is a quadrilateral formed of four uniform freely jointed rods, of which $AB = AD$ and each of weight $w$; and $BC = CD$ and each of weight $w'$. A string joins $A$ to $C$. It is freely suspended from $A$. If $\angle BAD = 2\theta$ and $\angle BCD = 2\phi$, show that the tension in the string is

$$\frac{w\tan\theta + w'(2\tan\theta + \tan\phi)}{\tan\theta + \tan\phi}$$

or $\quad (w + w')(OC/AC) + w'$

14. A quadrilateral in which $AB = BC$ and $CD = DA$ is formed of four uniform rods each of weight $w$, jointed together, it is hung up from $B$, and $A$, $C$ are kept apart by a weightless rod. Show that the thrust in the rod is $1/2\ w\ (3\tan\alpha + \tan\beta)$, where $\alpha$, $\beta$ are the angles the upper and lower rods make with the vertical.

15. Two equal light rods $AOB$, $COD$, freely jointed at O, their middle point, are at rest in a vertical plane with their ends $B$, $C$ on a smooth horizontal table. A string, to the ends of which equal weights are attached, passes over $A$ and $D$. Show that in the position of equilibrium, the angle between the rods in $\tan^{-1}(4/3)$.

16. A regular pentagon *ABCDE*, formed of equal heavy uniform bars, jointed together, is suspended from the joint *A*, and is maintained in the form by a weightless bar *BE*. Prove that the thrust in *BE* is $w \cot(\pi/10)$, where $w$ is the weight of each rod.
17. A regular pentagon ABCDE formed of five equal heavy uniform bars jointed together, is suspended from *A* and kept in shape by a light rod joining the middle points of *BC* and *DE*. Prove that the stress in this rod is $2w \cot 18°$, where $w$ is the weight of each rod.
18. A pentagon *ABCDE* is formed of five equal heavy uniform rods with their extremities freely jointed together. It is suspended from the angular point *A* and is maintained in the form by a light rod joining the angular points *B* and *E*. If the rods *AB* and *AE* make angle $\theta$, and the rods *BC* and *ED* make angle $\phi$ with the vertical, prove that the thrust in *BE* is $w(2 \tan \theta + \tan \phi)$, where $w$ is the weight of each rod.
19. Four light rods are jointed together to form a quadrilateral *OABC*. The lengths are such that $OA = OC = a$, $AB = CD = b$. The framework hangs in a vertical plane with *OA* and *OC* resting in contact with two smooth pegs distance $\ell$ apart and on the same horizontal level. A weight hangs at *B*. If $\theta$ and $\phi$ are the inclinations of *OA* and *AB* respectively to the horizontal, then prove that

$$a \cos \theta = b \cos \phi$$

and $1/2\, \ell \sec^2 \theta \sin \phi = a \sin(\theta + \phi)$
20. A pentagon is formed of five equal rods each of weight $w$ and is suspended from one corner which is joined to the middle point of the opposite side by a string. If two upper and two lower rods make angles $\theta$ and $\phi$ with the vertical, prove that the tension of the string is

$$w\left(\frac{4\tan\theta + 2\tan\phi)}{\tan\theta + \tan\phi}\right)$$

21. Two uniform rods *AB*, *BC* are freely jointed at *B* and hang freely from *A* vertically. If a horizontal force *P* is applied at *C*, the inclinations $\theta$, $\phi$ of *AB* and *AC* to the vertical are given by

$$\tan\theta = \frac{2P}{w_1} + 2w_2$$

$$\tan\phi = \frac{2P}{w_2}$$

where $w_1$, $w_2$ are the weights of the two rods.
22. Two masses rest on the convex side a parabola whose axis is vertical and are connected by a string which passes over a smooth peg at the focus. Show that equilibrium is impossible unless the weights are equal.

[**Hint:**

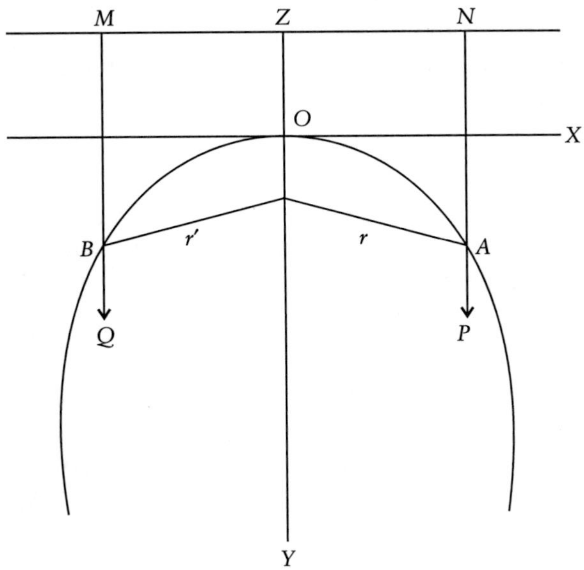


Let the length of the string be $\ell$.

Then, $r + r_1 = \ell$

$\Rightarrow \quad \delta r + \delta r' = 0$ ...(1)

For a parabola,

$r = AM$

$r' = BM$

Equation of virtual work when the distances are being measured from the directrix $MN$ is

$P\delta\,(AM) + Q\,\delta\,(BN) = 0$

$\Rightarrow \quad P\delta\,(r) + Q\,\delta\,(r') = 0$ ...(2)

(1) and (2) give

$P = Q$]

23. A particle $P$ is placed inside a smooth circular tube and acted upon by forces towards the extremities $A$ and $B$ of a fixed diameter $AB$; the forces are respectively proportional to $PA$ and $PB$. Prove that the particle will be at rest in all positions.
24. A particle is attracted by two fixed points by two constant forces. Prove that the curve on which it will rest in all positions is a cartesian oval.
25. A particle $P$ is acted upon by two forces towards two fixed points $S$ and $H$, forces being $\mu/SP$ and $\mu/HP$. Prove that $P$ will rest at all points inside a smooth tube in the form of a curve whose equation is $SP \cdot PH$ = constant.
26. A particle is only free to move on a smooth curve and is acted upon by repulsions $\mu_1 r_{-1}$, $\mu_2 r_{-2}$ from two fixed points where $r_1$ and $r_2$ are the distances from those points.

If the particle can rest at any point of the curve, prove that the curve must be a circle with centre at the point where the two repulsions neutralize each other.

27. Two light rods *AOC* and *BOD*, smoothly hinged, are connected by a string of length $2c \sin \alpha$. The rods rest in a vertical plane, with ends *A* and *B* on a smooth horizontal table. A smooth circular disc of radius a and weight $w$ is placed on the rods above O with its plane vertical so that the rods are tangents to the disc. Prove that the tension of the string in $w/2 \{(a/c) \operatorname{cosec}^2 \alpha + \tan \alpha\}$.

28. Two uniform rods *AB* and *AC* each of length a and weight $w$ are freely jointed at *A* and placed in a vertical plane across a smooth horizontal cylinder of radius $c$. The ends *B* and *C* are connected together by a taut string of length $\ell$ which is horizontal and not in contact with the cylinder. Show that the tension in the string is $w\left[\frac{4ac}{\ell^2} - \frac{\ell}{2\sqrt{4a^2 - \ell^2}}\right]$.

29. Two heavy rings of weights *P* and *Q* slide on a smooth parabolic wire whose axis is horizontal and plane vertical, and are connected by a string passing round a smooth small peg at the focus *S*. Prove that, in the position of equilibrium, their weights are proportional to their vertical depths below the axis, and if *SP* makes an angle θ with the axis, then

$\cot\frac{\theta}{2} = \frac{P}{\sqrt{P^2 + Q^2}}\sqrt{\frac{\ell - 2a}{a}}$, where $\ell$ is the length of the string and $4a$ the latus vectrum of the parabola.

30. A tripod consists of three equal uniform bars, each of length $a$ and weight $w$, which are freely jointed at one extremity, their middle points being jointed by strings, each of length $b$. The tripod is placed with its free ends in contact with a smooth horizontal plane and a weight *W* is attached to the common point. Show that the tension of each string is

$$\frac{2}{3}(2W + 3w)\frac{b}{\sqrt{9a^2 - 12b^2}}.$$

# Index

## T



## U



## V



## W



## Z